Living and Working
in
France

A Survival Handbook

by
David Hampshire

SURVIVAL BOOKS • LONDON • ENGLAND

First Edition 1993
Second Edition 1996
Third Edition 1999
Fourth Edition 2002
Fifth Edition 2003
Sixth Edition 2004
Seventh Edition 2006
Eighth Edition 2006

Copyright © Survival Books 1993, 1996, 1999, 2002, 2003, 2004, 2006
Map and illustrations © Jim Watson
Cover photograph © R Bouwman (🖳 http://www.bigstockphoto.com)

Survival Books Limited
26 York Street Street, London W1U 6PZ, United Kingdom
☎ +44 (0)20-7788 7644, 🖷 +44 (0)870-762 3212
✉ info@survivalbooks.net
🖳 http://www.survivalbooks.net
To order books, please refer to page 587.

British Library Cataloguing in Publication Data.
A CIP record for this book is available
from the British Library.
ISBN-10: 1-905303-01-7
ISBN-13: 978-1-905303-01-4

Printed and bound in Finland by WS Bookwell.

Acknowledgements

My sincere thanks to all those who contributed to the successful publication of this book, in particular Joe Laredo for his meticulous updating of the information in this and previous editions, Séverine Collemare for checking every telephone number, address and website and sundry other information, Andy Bathgate for the latest details of satellite television, Marie Christine Becquet for new insurance information and Kevin Raymond for step-by-step guides to vehicle import and registration. I would also like to thank Kerry Laredo for the page design, layout and indexing. I'm also indebted to John Adams, John Beaumont, Vincent Graf, Beverly Laflamme, Joanna Styles and the many other people who contributed to previous editions. Special thanks go to Jim Watson for the superb cartoons, illustrations, map and cover design.

Titles by Survival Books

Alien's Guides
Britain; France

The Best Places To Buy A Home
France; Spain

Buying a Home
Abroad; Australia & New Zealand;
Bulgaria, Cyprus; Florida; France;
Greece; Ireland; Italy; Portugal;
South Africa; Spain;
Buying, Selling & Letting Property (UK)

Buying and Renting a Home
London; New York

**Foreigners Abroad: Triumphs
& Disasters**
France; Spain

Lifeline Regional Guides
Brittany; Costa Blanca;
Costa del Sol; Dordogne/Lot;
Normandy; Poitou-Charentes;
Provence/Côte d'Azur

Living and Working
Abroad; America;
Australia; Britain; Canada;
The European Union;
The Far East; France; Germany;
The Gulf States & Saudi Arabia; Holland,
Belgium & Luxembourg; Ireland;
Italy; London; New Zealand;
Spain; Switzerland

Earning Money from Your Home
France; Spain

Making a Living
France; Spain

Other Titles
Renovating & Maintaining
Your French Home; Retiring Abroad;
Retiring in France; Retiring in Spain;
Rural Living in France;
Shooting Caterpillars in Spain;
Surprised by France

Order forms are on page 587.

WHAT READERS & REVIEWERS

When you buy a model plane for your child, a video recorder, or some new computer gizmo, you get with it a leaflet or booklet pleading 'Read Me First', or bearing large friendly letters or bold type saying 'IMPORTANT – follow the instructions carefully'. This book should be similarly supplied to all those entering France with anything more durable than a 5-day return ticket. It is worth reading even if you are just visiting briefly, or if you have lived here for years and feel totally knowledgeable and secure. But if you need to find out how France works then it is indispensable. Native French people probably have a less thorough understanding of how their country functions. – Where it is most essential, the book is most up to the minute.

LIVING FRANCE

Rarely has a 'survival guide' contained such useful advice. This book dispels doubts for first-time travellers, yet is also useful for seasoned globetrotters – In a word, if you're planning to move to the USA or go there for a long-term stay, then buy this book both for general reading and as a ready-reference.

AMERICAN CITIZENS ABROAD

It is everything you always wanted to ask but didn't for fear of the contemptuous put down – The best English-language guide – Its pages are stuffed with practical information on everyday subjects and are designed to complement the traditional guidebook.

SWISS NEWS

A complete revelation to me – I found it both enlightening and interesting, not to mention amusing.

CAROLE CLARK

Let's say it at once. David Hampshire's *Living and Working in France* is the best handbook ever produced for visitors and foreign residents in this country; indeed, my discussion with locals showed that it has much to teach even those born and bred in l'Hexagone. – It is Hampshire's meticulous detail which lifts his work way beyond the range of other books with similar titles. Often you think of a supplementary question and search for the answer in vain. With Hampshire this is rarely the case. – He writes with great clarity (and gives French equivalents of all key terms), a touch of humour and a ready eye for the odd (and often illuminating) fact. – This book is absolutely indispensable.

THE RIVIERA REPORTER

A mine of information – I may have avoided some embarrassments and frights if I had read it prior to my first Swiss encounters – Deserves an honoured place on any newcomer's bookshelf.

ENGLISH TEACHERS ASSOCIATION, SWITZERLAND

Have Said About Survival Books

What a great work, wealth of useful information, well-balanced wording and accuracy in details. My compliments!

THOMAS MÜLLER

This handbook has all the practical information one needs to set up home in the UK – The sheer volume of information is almost daunting – Highly recommended for anyone moving to the UK.

AMERICAN CITIZENS ABROAD

A very good book which has answered so many questions and even some I hadn't thought of – I would certainly recommend it.

BRIAN FAIRMAN

We would like to congratulate you on this work: it is really super! We hand it out to our expatriates and they read it with great interest and pleasure.

ICI (SWITZERLAND) AG

Covers just about all the things you want to know on the subject – In answer to the desert island question about the one how-to book on France, this book would be it – Almost 500 pages of solid accurate reading – This book is about enjoyment as much as survival.

THE RECORDER

It's so funny – I love it and definitely need a copy of my own – Thanks very much for having written such a humorous and helpful book.

HEIDI GUILIANI

A must for all foreigners coming to Switzerland.

ANTOINETTE O'DONOGHUE

A comprehensive guide to all things French, written in a highly readable and amusing style, for anyone planning to live, work or retire in France.

THE TIMES

A concise, thorough account of the DOs and DON'Ts for a foreigner in Switzerland – Crammed with useful information and lightened with humorous quips which make the facts more readable.

AMERICAN CITIZENS ABROAD

Covers every conceivable question that may be asked concerning everyday life – I know of no other book that could take the place of this one.

FRANCE IN PRINT

Hats off to *Living and Working in Switzerland*!

RONNIE ALMEIDA

THE AUTHOR

David Hampshire was born in the United Kingdom, where after serving in the Royal Air Force he was employed for many years in the computer industry. He has lived and worked in many countries, including Australia, France, Germany, Malaysia, the Netherlands, Singapore, Switzerland and Spain, where he now resides most of the year. It was while working in Switzerland that he wrote his first book, *Living and Working in Switzerland*, in 1987. David is the author of around 15 books, including *Buying a Home in France*, *Buying a Home in Italy*, *Buying a Home in Spain*, *Buying, Selling & Letting Property*, *Living and Working in France*, *Living and Working in Spain* and *Retiring Abroad*.

CONTENTS

1. FINDING A JOB   19

Economy	21
Workforce	21
Work Attitudes	22
Working Women	22
Salary	23
Industrial Relations	25
Unemployment	25
Employment Prospects	26
Qualifications	28
Medical Examination	29
Language	29
Job Hunting	30
Temporary & Casual Work	37
Seasonal Jobs	38
Language Teachers	41
Au Pairs	42
Voluntary Work	43
Self-employment	44
Starting a Business	46
Illegal Working	51

2. EMPLOYMENT CONDITIONS   53

Employment Contracts	54
Salary & Benefits	57
Working Hours	60
Holidays & Leave	62
Insurance	66
Retirement & Pensions	67
Education & Training	68
Union Membership	69
Other Conditions	70

3. PERMITS & VISAS   75

Visitors	76
Visas	77
Work Permits	82
Residence Permits	84

4. ARRIVAL 91

Immigration 92
Customs 92
Registration 94
Finding Help 95
Checklists 98

5. ACCOMMODATION 101

French Homes 102
Relocation Consultants 104
Temporary Accommodation 104
Buying Property 104
Rented Accommodation 108
Security 113
Moving House 114
Utilities 116
Waste Disposal 124

6. POSTAL SERVICES 127

Business Hours 128
Letters 129
Parcels 134
Registered & Recorded Post 136

7. TELEPHONE SERVICES 139

Emergency & Service Numbers 140
Installation & Registration 142
Directories 145
Using the Telephone 147
Charges 149
Custom & Optional Services 152
Bills 153
Mobile Telephones 155
Public Telephones 157
Fax 159
Internet 159

8. TELEVISION & RADIO 163

Television   164
Radio   173

9. EDUCATION 177

Insurance   179
Adapting to the System   180
Language   181
Home Education   182
Information   182
State or Private School?   183
State Schools   184
Private Schools   198
Apprenticeships   202
Higher Education   203
Further Education   208
Learning French   209

10. PUBLIC TRANSPORT 213

Airline Services   214
Trains   217
Underground Railways   229
Buses & Trams   233
Ferries   235
Eurotunnel   237
Taxis   238

11. MOTORING 241

Importing a Vehicle   243
Buying a Car   245
Selling a Car   249
Vehicle Registration   249
Technical Inspection   251
Road Tax   252
Driving Licence   252
Car Insurance   255

Rules of the Road   260
Road Signs   264
Speed Limits   266
Traffic Police   267
French Roads   270
French Drivers   275
Motorcycles   276
Accidents   277
Drinking & Driving   278
Car Theft   279
Parking   280
Fuel   282
Garages & Servicing   284
Road Maps   284
Car Rental   286
Motoring Organisations   287
Pedestrian Road Rules   287

12. HEALTH   289

Health Risks   291
Emergencies   292
National Health System   293
Doctors   296
Medicines   299
Hospitals & Clinics   301
Contraception & Abortion   305
Childbirth   306
Children's Health   309
Dentists   310
Opticians   312
Counselling   313
Smoking   315
Giving Blood   315
Death   316

13. INSURANCE   319

Insurance Companies & Agents   320
Insurance Contracts   322
Social Security   323

Pensions   336
Private Health Insurance   339
Household Insurance   343
Third-party Liability Insurance   346
Holiday & Travel Insurance   346
Life Insurance   348

14. FINANCE   351

French Currency   352
Importing & Exporting Money   353
Banks   356
Cash & Debit Cards   366
Credit & Charge Cards   367
Loans & Overdrafts   369
Mortgages   369
Value Added Tax   372
Income Tax   373
Property Taxes   384
Wealth Tax   387
Capital Gains Tax   388
Inheritance & Gift Tax   390
Wills   394
Cost of Living   396

15. LEISURE   399

Hotels   403
Bed & Breakfast   408
Self-catering   409
Hostels   412
Camping & Caravanning   414
Naturism   416
Theme Parks   417
Museums & Galleries   420
Cinema   422
Theatre, Opera & Ballet   423
Music   425
Social Clubs   427
Nightlife   428
Gambling   429

Bars & Cafes 429
Restaurants 433
Libraries 443
Day & Evening Classes 444

16. SPORTS 447

Aerial Sports 449
Boules 449
Climbing & Caving 451
Cycling 452
Fishing 454
Football 456
Golf 457
Hiking & Running 458
Hunting 461
Racket Sports 463
Rugby 464
Skiing 465
Swimming 469
Watersports 470
Foreign Sports 472
Other Sports 472

17. SHOPPING 477

Prices 478
Shopping Hours 479
Specialist Food Shops 480
Markets 486
Department & Chain Stores 487
Supermarkets & Hypermarkets 487
Drink 490
Tobacconists' 497
Clothing 497
Newspapers, Magazines & Books 498
Furniture & Furnishings 500
Household Goods 501
Laundry & Dry Cleaning 502
Mail-order Shopping 503
Shopping Abroad 504
Deposits, Receipts & Consumer Rights 506

18. ODDS & ENDS 509

Citizenship	510
Climate	511
Crime	513
Disabled People	515
Geography	515
Government	516
Legal System	520
Marriage & Divorce	522
Military Service	525
Pets	526
Police	531
Population	533
Religion	534
Social Customs	535
Time Difference	539
Tipping	539
Toilets	540

19. THE FRENCH 543

20. MOVING OR LEAVING FRANCE 551

Moving House	552
Leaving France	553

APPENDICES 557

Appendix A: Useful Addresses	558
Appendix B: Further Reading	561
Appendix C: Useful Websites	563
Appendix D: Weights & Measures	566
Appendix E: Map	570

INDEX 573

ORDER FORMS 587

IMPORTANT NOTE

France is a large country with myriad faces and many ethnic groups, religions and customs. Although ostensibly the same throughout the country, rules and regulations tend to be open to local interpretation (Paris is a law unto itself!), and are sometimes even formulated on the spot. **I cannot recommend too strongly that you check with an official and reliable source (not always the same) before making major decisions or undertaking an irreversible course of action.** However, don't believe everything you're told or read, even, dare I say it, herein!

To help you obtain further information and verify data with official sources, useful addresses and references have been included in most chapters and **Appendices A** to **C**. Important points have been emphasised throughout the book **in bold print**, some of which it would be expensive or even dangerous to disregard. **Ignore them at your cost or peril.** Unless specifically stated, the reference to any company, organisation, product or publication in this book doesn't constitute an endorsement or recommendation.

AUTHOR'S NOTES

- Times are shown using the 24-hour clock, e.g. 10am is shown as 10.00 and 10pm as 22.00, which is the usual way of expressing the time in France (see page 539).

- Prices quoted should be taken only as estimates, although they were mostly correct when going to print and fortunately don't usually change greatly overnight. Although prices are sometimes quoted exclusive of value added tax (*hors taxes/HT*) in France, most prices are quoted inclusive of tax (*toutes taxes comprises/TTC*), which is the method used when quoting prices in this book.

- His/he/him/man/men (etc.) also mean her/she/her/woman/women (no offence ladies!). This is done simply to make life easier for both the reader and, in particular, the author, and **isn't** intended to be sexist.

- British English is used throughout, but American English equivalents are given where appropriate.

- The French translation of key words and phrases is shown in brackets in *italics*. Note that the French is given in the singular irrespective of the English, except when the plural is the standard word or phrase. Not also that French acronyms are printed in capital letters (e.g. ASSEDIC), although the French often use only an initial capital (e.g. Assedic).

- Warnings and important points are shown in **bold** type.

- Frequent references are made in this book to the European Union (EU), which comprises Austria, Belgium, Cyprus, the Czech Republic, Denmark, Estonia, Finland, France, Germany, Greece, Hungary, Ireland, Italy, Latvia, Lithuania, Luxembourg, Malta, the Netherlands, Poland, Portugal, Slovakia, Slovenia, Spain, Sweden and the United Kingdom, and the European Economic Area (EEA), which includes the EU countries plus Iceland, Liechtenstein and Norway.

- The following symbols are used in this book: ☎ (telephone), ▤ (fax), ▦ (internet) and ✉ (e-mail).

- Lists of useful addresses, further reading and useful websites are contained in **Appendices A, B** and **C** respectively.

- For those unfamiliar with the metric system of weights and measures, conversion tables are included in **Appendix D**.

- A map of France showing the regions and departments is included in **Appendix E**.

INTRODUCTION

Whether you're already living or working in France or just thinking about it – this is **THE BOOK** you've been looking for. Forget about those glossy guide books, excellent though they are for tourists; this amazing book was written especially with you in mind and is worth its weight in truffles! *Living and Working in France* is designed to meet the needs of anyone wishing to know the essentials of French life, including immigrants, temporary foreign workers, businessmen, students, retirees, long-stay visitors and holiday-homeowners. However long your intended stay in France, you will find the information contained in this book invaluable.

Since it was first published, in 1993, *Living and Working in France* has been the most comprehensive and up-to-date book available to people wishing to live and work in France (or already doing so). To make the information more accessible and helpful, we completely redesigned and enlarged it in 2003, snce when it has been the only publication of its kind updated annually, thus ensuring that you always have the most up-to-date information at your fingertips.

This eighth edition contains added or revised information on topics as diverse as the new directory enquiries numbers and air fare surcharges; 'internet radio' and using a foreign mobile phone in France; rules regarding immigration, naturalisation and the disposal of old cars; prepaid currency cards, text messaging charges and obtaining ADSL2; French wine classification, new car labelling and medicine packaging; 'hand-holding' services and 'agritourism'; giving blood and cremating a pet; finding grape-picking jobs, claiming family allowances and obtaining a Job Seeker's Allowance; lists of France's 'best' markets, golf courses and spa towns; previously unavailable crime statistics; new 'equity release' mortgages and 'living wills'; writing a CV and job application letter in French; new museums, galleries and theme parks; surcharges on high-emission vehicles; changes to inheritance tax regulations, digital and satellite TV, and health insurance and pension arrangements for the self-employed.

For foreigners in France – particularly those who don't speak fluent French – finding out how to overcome the everyday challenges of French life has previously been a case of pot luck. But no more! With a copy of *Living and Working in France* to hand you will have a wealth of information at your fingertips – information is derived from a variety of sources, both official and unofficial, not least the hard won personal experiences of the author, his friends, colleagues and acquaintances. *Living and Working in France* is the most comprehensive and up-to-date source of general information available to foreigners in France. It isn't, however, simply a monologue of dry facts and figures but an entertaining, practical and occasionally humorous look at life in France.

You may have visited France as a tourist, but living and working there is a different matter altogether. Adjusting to a different environment and culture and making a home in any foreign country can be a traumatic and stressful experience, and France is certainly no exception. You need to adapt to new customs and traditions and discover the French way of doing things, which is invariably different from what you're used to. Although this book doesn't contain all the answers, it will usually point you in the right direction and save you both time and money.

Although you may find some of the information a bit daunting, don't be discouraged. Most problems occur once only and fade into insignificance after a short time (as you face the next half dozen!). The majority of foreigners in France would agree that, all things considered, they relish living there. A period spent in France is a wonderful way to enrich your life, broaden your horizons and hopefully also improve your bank balance. I trust that this book will help smooth your way to a happy and rewarding future in your new home.

Bon courage!

David Hampshire
September 2006

1.

FINDING A JOB

Finding work in France isn't always as difficult as the unemployment figures (see page 25) may suggest, particularly in Paris and other large cities, depending of course on your line of business, qualifications and French language ability. Nationals of European Union (EU) and European Economic Area (EEA) countries have the right to work in France or any other member state without a work permit, provided they have a valid passport or national identity card and comply with the member state's laws and regulations on employment. EU nationals are entitled to the same treatment as French citizens in matters of pay, working conditions, access to housing, vocational training, social security entitlements and trade union rights, and their families and immediate dependants are entitled to join them and enjoy the same rights. Nevertheless, there are still barriers to full freedom of movement and the right to work within the EU: for example, many jobs require applicants to have specific skills or vocational qualifications, and qualifications obtained in some member states aren't recognised in others (see **Qualifications** on page 28), although cross-border restrictions are gradually being outlawed by the European Commission (EC). There are also restrictions on employment in the civil service.

With the growth of the internet and the spread of broadband it's possible to carry out many types of business 'remotely' and even from the comfort of your own home, but unless you have a company registered abroad you must still join the French system, which means not only paying French taxes and social security contributions but also having your business 'approved' by the relevant authorities. For example, if you want to conduct two lines of business considered as different occupations (and the French have strictly defined 'job descriptions'), you will have to pay two lots of taxes and contributions!

If you don't qualify to live and work in France by birthright or as an EU national, you must obtain a long-stay visa (see page 78), which is dependent upon obtaining employment. However, France has had a virtual freeze on the employment of non-EU nationals for many years, which has been strengthened recently due to the high unemployment rate. The employment of non-EU nationals must be approved by the Agence Nationale Pour l'Emploi (ANPE – see page 31), which can propose the employment of a French national instead (although this is rare). For a permanent position, the prospective employer must have advertised the post with ANPE for at least five weeks and must also obtain authorisation to employ a non-EU national from the French Ministry of Labour (Ministère de l'Emploi, du Travail et de la Cohésion Sociale, 🖳 http://www.travail.gouv.fr) or the Direction Départementale du Travail, de l'Emploi et de la Formation Professionnelle (DDTEFP) where the business is registered. The authorisation, which is a prerequisite to obtaining a long-stay visa (see page 78), is sent to the Office des Migrations Internationales (OMI, 44 rue Bargue, 75732 Paris Cedex 15, 🖳 http://www.diplomatie.gouv.fr) for transmission to the appropriate French consulate abroad. The consulate notifies the applicant, who can then proceed with the application. When the proposed monthly salary is above that for senior managers (around €3,500 per month), the application is usually approved; it's difficult for non-EU nationals to obtain permission for a lower-paid job unless they have unusual qualifications.

There's an 'accelerated' programme designed to recruit foreign workers in fields where there has been a shortage of available employees (e.g. certain high-tech computer-related fields). This doesn't mean that anyone who can set up a website is guaranteed a long-stay visa (there's normally a minimum salary level, e.g. €27,000 per year), but it does make it easier for non-EU specialists with the requisite qualifications to find employment.

ECONOMY

France is one of the wealthiest countries in the world, with one of the highest per capita gross domestic products in the EU (currently around US$32,825); GDP grew by 2.3 per cent in 2004 and, after falling back to around 1.5 per cent in 2005, is expected to reach 2.5 per cent in 2006 – the highest for two decades. Generally, the French economy appears to be holding its own with those of other major European countries – but this isn't saying much. In fact, in common with them, France is in debt: to the tune of almost 57 per cent of national income (compared with Germany at 63 per cent, the US at 46 per cent and the UK at 38 per cent). Since the start of the new millennium, inflation has been at just under 2 per cent but France failed to reduce its national debt in order to meet an EU ruling that all member states must have 'balanced books' by 2004 (the rules were 'bent' as a result!).

The country has experienced an economic transformation in the last few decades, during which its traditional industries have been thoroughly modernised and a wealth of new high-tech industries have been created, although increasing competition, particularly from Far Eastern countries (known collectively as *le low-cost!*), has meant that traditional industries such as steel, clothing and textile production have become less competitive. Nevertheless, the manufacture of ships, cars, aeroplanes and defence equipment remains significant. The Saint-Nazaire shipyards near Nantes completed the largest ever cruise liner, the Queen Mary 2 in 2004, and the industrial park at Blagnac near Toulouse, where the new 550-seat Airbus A380s are being built, employs around 9,000 people.

Less labour and capital intensive industries such as electronics, pharmaceuticals and communications have flourished since the '80s, although the largest growth in recent years has been in service industries, e.g. banking, insurance and advertising, which now account for over 70 per cent of GDP compared with industry at around 26 per cent and agriculture at a mere 3 per cent. (Despite the continuing decline in the number of farms, France is still Europe's largest agricultural producer with 23 per cent of total EU production.) French industry has increasingly looked beyond its own borders in the last few decades, during which it has been one of the world's leading investors in foreign companies. Conversely, France is the third most popular among Organisation for Economic Co-operation and Development (OECD) countries for foreign investment; France's answer to California's Silicon Valley, Sophia Antipolis on the Côte d'Azur, is the largest technology park in Europe with some 1,200 companies employing 23,000 people, and a second park is under development nearby.

WORKFORCE

French workers enjoy an affluent lifestyle in comparison with those in many other western countries, with high salaries (especially executives and senior managers) and excellent employment conditions (see **Chapter 2**). Much of the French 'working class' (France is supposedly a classless society) consists of skilled (*qualifié*) workers and technicians. French engineers are part of the elite (as in Germany) and highly respected. France has a well educated and trained workforce, and a strong emphasis is placed on training by employers. Even employees doing what many would consider menial jobs, such as shop assistants and waiters, are highly trained (although seldom in politeness!) and aren't looked down on (the really menial tasks are generally undertaken by immigrants). Most French people don't dream of becoming entrepreneurs or businessmen but of working in the public sector, which constitutes some 25 per cent of the workforce compared with around 15 per cent in most other EU countries, and where benefits are second-to-none (e.g. three months' annual holiday and retirement at 55 or even 50!).

WORK ATTITUDES

French firms have traditionally been expected to care for their employees and most have a paternalistic attitude. Experience, maturity and loyalty are highly valued (although qualifications are even more valuable) and newcomers generally find it difficult to secure a senior position with a French company. The traditional hierarchical structure of French businesses, with little contact between management and workers, both of whom are reluctant to take on responsibilities outside their immediate duties, has given way to a more 'modern' reward-for-achievement attitude and relations between management and staff have generally improved, although the French 'old boy' network is still alive and well and can militate against foreigners achieving the promotion they deserve (see **Industrial Relations** on page 25). 'Job hopping' as a way of increasing your salary or promotion prospects is rare.

As in the US, French employers tend to expect high standards and are intolerant of mistakes or inefficiency. However, it's difficult and expensive to fire employees. When it comes to hiring new employees (particularly managers and executives) and making important business decisions, the process is slower in France than in many other western countries.

Business relations tend to be formal: colleagues usually address each other as *vous* rather than *tu* and often use surnames instead of first names, and social relationships with work colleagues are rare. Attire is generally formal, although in some companies Fridays are 'casual dress' days.

Many foreigners, particularly Americans, find that they need to adjust to a slower pace of working life. Most French managers and executives rarely take work home and they **never** work at weekends, which are sacrosanct. However, don't be misled by French people's apparent lack of urgency and casual approach to business – they can be just as hard-headed as any other people.

WORKING WOMEN

The number of working women has increased dramatically in recent years, and some 45 per cent of French women (the vast majority under 40), including 80 per cent of women with one child, now work, representing almost half the workforce. However, around 30 per cent of women work part-time, compared with only 5 per cent of men. Three-quarters of women are employed in distribution and transport, nursing and health care, education, secretarial professions, and service industries such as retailing.

Male chauvinism is alive and well in France and most French women are more concerned with equal rights in the workplace and benefits (such as paid maternity leave and state-run nurseries) than the opportunity to reach the top. The fact that 'the best man for the job is often a woman' is rarely acknowledged by French employers, who are often reluctant to hire women if they think they're planning a family, not least because they must provide generous paid maternity leave, and women must generally be twice as qualified as a man to compete on equal terms. The 1983 law on professional equality (*loi Roudy sur l'égalité professionnelle*) made it easier for women to break into male-dominated trades and professions. However, women still find it difficult to attain management positions, particularly in technical and industrial fields, where there has long been a tradition of prejudice against them. Women have had some success in reaching the top in the professions and in finance, insurance, the media, personnel, advertising and retailing. Career women are generally more accepted and taken more seriously in Paris, which has a more progressive outlook than the provinces (particularly the south, where opinions and attitudes lag behind the north). Nevertheless, over a quarter of France's 2.5m businesses are run by women, by far the highest proportion in Europe. Since 1997, women have had the right to earn 90 per cent of a full-time salary if they work a four-day week (e.g. taking Wednesday off to look after their children).

A woman doing the same or broadly similar work to a man and employed by the same employer is legally entitled to the same salary and other terms of employment. However, despite the Equal Pay Act of 1972, women's salaries are an average of 13 per cent lower than men's. Some 15 per cent of women earn the minimum wage (see page 24). This largely reflects the fact that most women work in lower paid industries and hold lower paid positions than men (including more part-time jobs), rather than discrimination. (Employers of more than 50 staff must publish a breakdown of pay and conditions for their male and female employees.) However, the situation has improved considerably in recent years, and women are much less exploited in France than in many other western European countries.

Women face the additional hazard of sexual harassment, as 'flirting' is an accepted part of French life. If it's any consolation, refusing a sexual advance from your boss rarely results in your losing your job, as it's difficult to fire employees.

SALARY

The Federation of European Employers' *Pay in Europe 2006* report, published in March 2006, ranked France 13th out of 48 in the European salary league table, just below the UK but well below Denmark and Luxembourg. French executive salaries were lower than the international average in the '70s and early '80s but rose much faster than the rate of inflation in the '80s and were augmented by lucrative bonuses and profit-sharing schemes, so that they've now caught up and even surpassed those in other Western countries, although in recent years university graduates and school-leavers have been willing to accept almost any wage in order to get on the career ladder. The average gross annual salary in 2005 was around €17,000. The average manager earned around €40,000 and the average self-employed person around €30,000. Note, however, that social security contributions are higher in France than in most other western countries (see page 328).

It's often difficult to determine the salary you should command, as salaries aren't usually quoted in job advertisements, except in the public sector where employees are paid according to fixed grades, and salaries are public knowledge. Salaries may vary considerably for the same job in different parts of France. Those working in Paris and its environs are generally the highest paid, primarily because of the high cost of living, particularly accommodation. If you have friends or acquaintances working in France or who have worked there, ask them what an average or good salary is for your particular trade or profession. When comparing salaries you must take into account compulsory deductions such as tax and social security (see **Chapters 13** and **14**), and also compare the cost of living (see page 396).

For many employees, particularly executives and senior managers, their remuneration is much more than what they receive in their monthly pay packets. Many companies offer a range of benefits for executives and managers that may include a company car, private health insurance and health screening, expenses-paid holidays, private school fees, inexpensive or interest-free home and other loans, rent-free accommodation, free or subsidised public transport tickets, free or subsidised company restaurant, sports or country club membership, non-contributory company pension, stock options, bonuses and profit-sharing schemes, tickets for sports events and shows, and 'business' conferences in exotic locations (see also **Chapter 2**). Most employees in France also receive an extra month's salary at Christmas, known as the 13th month's salary, and some companies also pay a 14th month's salary before the summer holiday period.

Salaries in many industries are decided by collective bargaining between employers and unions, either regionally or nationally. When there's a collective agreement, employers must offer at least the minimum wage agreed, although this is exceeded by most major companies. Agreements specify minimum wage levels for each position within main employment categories in a particular industry or company and often require bonus payments related to the age or qualifications of the employee or the length of time he has been with the company (*prime d'ancienneté*). This means that wage levels are effectively fixed. Cost of living increases for salaries above the *SMIC* aren't regulated by the government, although the collective agreement may provide for annual increases based on cost of living figures.

The introduction of the 35-hour week (see **Working Hours** on page 60) included guarantees that salaries could not be reduced from the levels paid on a 39-hour week basis. Government incentives available to employers for hiring additional workers did little to mitigate the cost of reducing the working week, and it's likely most salaries will remain static and pay rises will be few and far between for the next several years.

Minimum Wage

At the lower end of the wage scale, there has been a statutory minimum wage (*salaire minimum de croissance/SMIC*) since 1950. When the cost of living index rises by 2 per cent or more in a year, the minimum wage is increased. (In practice, the minimum wage rises every year, usually in July and especially when elections are coming up!) The minimum wage is currently €8.27 per hour, equal to gross pay of €1,254.28 per month for 151.67 hours (the new standard under the terms of the 35-hour working week).

There's a lower *SMIC* for juveniles, those on special job-creation schemes and disabled employees. Unskilled workers (particularly women) are usually employed at or near the minimum wage, semi-skilled workers are usually paid 10 to 20 per cent more, and skilled workers 30 to 40 per cent more (often shown in job advertisements as '*SMIC + 10, 20, 30, 40%*'). Note, however, that many employees, particularly seasonal workers in the farming and tourist industries, are traditionally paid below the minimum wage (although the French government is increasingly clamping down and forcing employers to comply with the law).

Another type of minimum wage is the *revenue minimum d'insertion* (*RMI*), introduced in 1989 as a temporary wage for job seekers but now drawn by a staggering 4m people between the ages of 25 and 60 who don't qualify for unemployment benefit. Rates vary according to circumstances but are at least €400 per month. Foreigners resident in France for at least two years are eligible.

INDUSTRIAL RELATIONS

The French are notorious for their strikes (*grèves*, euphemistically known as *mouvements sociaux*), which are a common feature of French 'working' life – particularly in the public sector, where employees have long been known for their propensity to stop work at the drop of a beret. Recent years have seen strikes among public transport employees and among self-employed groups such as farmers, fishermen, truck drivers, doctors and other medical professionals, and strikes become increasingly common in the run-up to elections and in response to announcements of plant closures or sales to foreign investors.

For a time, strikes in private companies were almost unheard-of in France, but they've recently started to become a more popular means of protesting against increasing threats to job security. In both the public and private sectors, strikes are often seen as the only effective means of communicating with the government and elected officials, as it's the government rather than employers who are expected to resolve most work-related issues. Despite negligible union membership (less than 9 per cent and falling), most workers in France are automatically covered by industry-wide and legally recognised collective agreements (*conventions collectives*).

Nevertheless, there has been a large reduction in strikes in the last decade or so, a less confrontational relationship between employers and employees being due both to high unemployment and new legislation, requiring both sides to discuss their differences and imposing a 'cooling-off' period before a strike can be called.

UNEMPLOYMENT

In an attempt to reduce high unemployment, recent governments have lowered some taxes and introduced a host of job creation schemes offering temporary (i.e. five-year) jobs in the public sector to young people just out of school or training, conveniently taking them off the unemployment lists until after the next round of elections! In 2002, the 35-hour work week, designed to share the available pool of workers and stimulate new employment, generated a mere 1.3 per cent increase in employment (far less than expected – by the government). In an attempt to avert further lay-offs, the government then increased minimum redundancy payments and officially defined 'economic redundancies' (*licenciements économiques*), which can be made only after an employer has undertaken certain procedures (see page 72). As a result of these measures, combined with a general improvement in the economy, unemployment figures have come down in recent years. Currently, around 9 per cent of the workforce (just over 2m people) is officially unemployed, which is the lowest figure for ten years.

Nevertheless, unemployment is still a major problem for those aged under 25, among whom it's nearly three times the national average. France spends more on job creation schemes than any other EU country, yet has the worst job creation record in the OECD, and the government's recent attempt to introduce a 'youth employment contract' was a disaster (see **Indefinite Term Contracts** on page 56).

Other groups badly affected by unemployment are older people, women and blue collar workers, the last currently suffering unemployment rates five times as high as executives and managers. Although unemployment has hit manufacturing industries the hardest, no sector has survived unscathed, including the flourishing service industries in the Paris region. Some of the worst-hit industries have been construction, electronics, communications, the media and banking.

The situation has been worsened, at least in the public mind, by a string of large business failures or reorganisations which have involved hundreds or thousands of redundancies and the closing of entire branches or divisions, e.g. Air Liberté, Danone, Marks & Spencer and Moulinex. Many companies have put a total ban on recruitment and have expected executives to accept fixed- or short-term contracts, rather than life-long security. More than a quarter of France's working population has a short-term contract (*contrat à durée déterminée/CDD*), commonly known as 'precarious' employment (*emploi précaire*). This has prompted the government to introduce a new two-year trial period (see **Employment Contracts** on page 54).

Although only half as many people as in the UK and Germany become unemployed each year (a quarter as many as in the US), only 3 per cent find a new job within the year, compared with the European average of around 9 per cent (35 per cent in the US). Long-term unemployment is a huge problem, where the average period of unemployment is a year (the longest in Europe) and over a million people have been unemployed for more than two years. Anyone aged over 50 who loses his job is unlikely to work again unless he's highly qualified and in demand.

UK citizens receiving unemployment benefit can continue to do so while job hunting in France, provided they register with ANPE (see page 31), and can obtain a Job Seeker's Allowance while in France: obtain leaflets UBL22 and E303 from a Job Centre at least three months before you go.

EMPLOYMENT PROSPECTS

Being attracted to France by its weather, cuisine, wine and lifestyle is understandable but doesn't rate highly as an employment qualification. You should have a positive reason for living and working in France; simply being fed up with your job or the weather isn't the best motive for moving to France. It's extremely difficult to find work in rural areas and isn't easy in cities and large towns (even Paris), especially if your French isn't fluent. You shouldn't plan on finding employment in France unless you have special qualifications or experience for which there's a strong demand. If you want a good job, you must usually be extremely well qualified and speak fluent French. If you intend to come to France without a job, you should have a plan for finding employment on arrival and try to make some contacts before you arrive. If you have a job offer, you should ensure that it's in writing (preferably in French) and check that it isn't likely to be revoked soon after you arrive.

France has a reasonably self-sufficient labour market and doesn't require a large number of skilled or unskilled foreign workers. However, in recent years, French companies have been keen to expand into international markets, which has created opportunities for foreign workers, particularly bilingual and tri-lingual employees. Recent years have seen a marked increase in French investment abroad, and France is experiencing a 'brain drain' as executives and entrepreneurs (and football players!) leave the country, creating something of a vacuum – particularly in high-tech industries (e.g. information technology).

Areas where there's currently a shortage of staff include banking, insurance and renewable energy industries (estimated to need over 100,000 extra employees in the next few years). Generally, there's a shortfall of around 10,000 to 15,000 graduates each year, and by 2010 it's estimated that there will be a shortage of over 400,000 managers. There's also a shortage of butchers, computer technicians, hairdressers, hotel staff, lorry drivers, salespeople and stonemasons.

Casual work can be found in tourism (e.g. at Disneyland Paris and other major theme parks – see page 417), campsites, holiday centres and children's summer camps (*colonie de vacances*) and, of course, hotels and restaurants. For details of employment prospects in various regions of France, refer to *The Best Places to Buy a Home in France* (Survival Books – see page 587).

An increasing number of people in France turn to self-employment or starting a business to make a living (see page 44), although this path is strewn with pitfalls for the newcomer. Bear in mind that only just over 6 per cent of France's workforce is self-employed!

Before moving to France to work, you should dispassionately examine your motives and credentials, and ask yourself the following questions:

- What kind of work can I realistically expect to do?
- What are my qualifications and experience? Are they recognised in France?
- How old am I? (Although discrimination on the basis of age, physical appearance, name and sexual preference is illegal, age discrimination is rife, where only 38 per cent of men aged 55 to 64 work – the lowest percentage in Europe.)
- How good is my French? Unless your French is fluent, you won't be competing on equal terms with the French (you won't anyway, but that's a different matter!). Most French employers aren't interested in employing anyone without, at the very least, an adequate working knowledge of French.
- Are there any jobs in my profession or trade in the area where I wish to live?
- Could I be self-employed or start my own business (see page 44)?

The answers to these questions can be disheartening, but it's better to ask them before moving to France than afterwards.

QUALIFICATIONS

The most important qualification for working (and living) in France is the ability to speak French fluently (see **Language** below). Once you've overcome this hurdle, you should establish whether your trade or professional qualifications and experience are recognised in France. If you aren't experienced, French employers expect studies to be in a relevant discipline and to have included work experience (*un stage*). Professional or trade qualifications are required to work in most fields in France, where qualifications are also often necessary to be self-employed or start a business. It isn't just a matter of hanging up a sign and waiting for the stampede of customers to your door. Many foreigners are required to undergo a 'business' course before they can start work in France (see **Self-employment** on page 44).

Theoretically, qualifications recognised by professional and trade bodies in one EU country should be recognised in France. However, recognition varies from country to country and in some cases foreign qualifications aren't recognised by French employers or professional and trade associations. All academic qualifications should also be recognised, although they may be given less prominence than equivalent French qualifications, depending on the country and the educational establishment. A ruling by the European Court in 1992 declared that where EU examinations are of a similar standard with just certain areas of difference, individuals should be required to take exams only in those areas, and a further directive agreed in June 2006 'entitled' qualified workers such as architects, estate agents, hairdressers and plumbers to set up shop in France. **Nevertheless, it can takes months and even years to obtain permission to work or start a business in France.**

To obtain a certificate of equivalence (*une attestation*) you must send a certified translation of your qualifications. The address to write to varies according to the type of qualification concerned; details (in French) can be found on the website of the French Ministry of Education (🖳 http://www.education.gouv.fr/int/refran.htm).

For certain jobs, you must show your police record (*casier judiciaire*) to a prospective employer. This shows convictions for 'serious' crimes (e.g. not parking tickets). You're the only person entitled to obtain a copy of your police record, from Le Centre du Casier Judiciaire National, 107 rue Landreau, 44076 Nantes Cedex.

A list of professions and trades in France can be found on the website of the Office National d'Information sur l'Enseignement et les Professions (🖳 http://www.onisep.fr). All EU member states issue occupation information sheets containing a common job description with a table of qualifications. These cover a large number of trades and are intended to help someone with the relevant qualifications look for a job in another EU country. For information about equivalent qualifications you can contact the Centre d'Études et de Recherche sur les Qualifications (CEREQ, ☎ 01 44 08 69 10, 🖳 http://www.cereq.fr) or ENIC-NARIC, run by the European Network of Information Centres (🖳 http://www.enic-naric.net). A useful booklet, *Europe Open for Professionals*, is available from the UK Department for Education and Skills (☎ 0870-000 2288). Further information can be obtained from the Bureau de l'Information sur les Systèmes Educatifs et de la Reconnaissance de Diplômes of the Ministère de la Jeunesse, de l'Education Nationale et de la Recherche (☎ 01 55 55 10 10) and from the Département des Affaires Internationales de l'Enseignement Supérieure (☎ 01 40 03 15 03).

If you're contemplating working as a civil servant (*fonctionnaire*) in France, you can obtain details of the requirements, which include competitive exams, on 🖳 http:// www.service-public.fr (on the English version, click on 'Working in the civil service').

MEDICAL EXAMINATION

Most French employers require prospective employees to have a pre-employment medical examination performed by the employer's doctor (*médecin du travail*), who is certified to evaluate your fitness for the job for which you're about to be hired. An offer of employment is usually subject to a prospective employee being given a clean bill of health. However, this may be required only for employees over a certain age (e.g. 40) or for employees in certain jobs, e.g. where good health is of paramount importance for safety reasons.

LANGUAGE

Although English is the *lingua franca* of international commerce and may help you to secure a job in France, the most important qualification for anyone seeking employment is the ability to speak fluent French. Although most French children learn English at school and the majority of educated French people can speak some English, many of them are reluctant to do so, as they have an ingrained fear of making mistakes and 'losing face'. (In a recent survey, 66 per cent of French people claimed to speak only French and a mere 22 per cent admitted to speaking English 'well'.) The French are also extremely proud of their language (to the point of hubris) and – quite rightly – expect everyone living or working in France to speak it.

If necessary you should have French lessons before arriving in France. A sound knowledge of French won't just help you find a job or perform your job better but will also make everyday life much simpler and more enjoyable. If you come to France without being able to speak French you will be excluded from everyday life and will feel uncomfortable until you can understand what's going on around you. You **must** learn French if you wish to have French friends. **The most common reason for negative experiences among foreigners in France, both visitors and residents alike, is that they cannot (or won't) speak French.**

However bad your grammar, poor your vocabulary and terrible your accent, an attempt to speak French will be much better appreciated than your fluent English. Don't, however, be surprised when the French wince at your torture of their beloved tongue, pretend not to understand you even though you've said something 'correctly', or correct minor grammatical or pronunciation errors! The French honestly believe they're doing you a favour by pointing out your mistakes to you while they're fresh in your mind. (This also explains much of their hesitance to use English in public, for fear of being corrected themselves.)

If you don't already speak good French, don't expect to learn it quickly, even if you already have a basic knowledge and take intensive lessons (see **Language Schools** on page 209). It's common for foreigners not to be fluent after a year or more of intensive lessons in France. If your expectations are unrealistic, you will become frustrated, which can affect your confidence. **It takes a long time to reach the level of fluency needed to be able to work in French.** If you don't speak French fluently, you should begin French lessons on arrival and consider taking a menial or even an unpaid voluntary job, as this is one of the quickest ways of improving your French.

Your ability in French and other languages must be listed on your curriculum vitae (CV/résumé) and the level of proficiency stated as follows: some knowledge (*notions*); good (*bien*); very good (*très bien* or *parle, lis, écris*); fluent (*courant*); and mother tongue (*langue maternelle*). When stating your French language ability, it's important not to exaggerate. If you state that your French is very good or fluent, you will almost certainly be interviewed in French (which is also possible even if you have only a little knowledge).

When doing business in France or writing letters to French businesses, communications should always be in French. Most business letters must be written in a very precise style with proper opening and closing greetings. See also **Unsolicited Job Applications** on page 35.

France itself also has over 70 regional languages, the most widely spoken including Alsatian (spoken in Alsace), Basque (Pyrenees), Breton (Brittany), Catalan (Roussillon), Corsican (Corsica), Gascon (south-west) and Occitan (Languedoc). In some areas, schools teach in the regional language as well as in French. However fluent your French, you may still have problems understanding these, as well as some accents – particularly those of the south – and local dialects (*patois*).

JOB HUNTING

As many as 60 per cent of job vacancies in France are never advertised but are filled by 'word of mouth'. When looking for a job, it's therefore best not to put all your eggs in one basket – the more job applications you make, the better your chance of finding the right (or any) job. Contact as many prospective employers as possible, by writing to them, telephoning them or calling on them in person. Whatever job you're looking for, it's important to market yourself appropriately. For example, the recruitment of executives and senior managers is handled almost exclusively by recruitment consultants (see page 32). At the other end of the scale, manual jobs requiring no previous experience may be advertised at ANPE offices (see below), in local newspapers and on notice boards, and the first suitable applicant may be offered the job on the spot. Job hunting resources are listed below.

EU citizens who are receiving unemployment benefit in their own country can continue to receive it while job hunting in any other EU country (see **Unemployment Benefit** on page 334).

Once you've found or been offered a job, you must apply for a residence permit within a week (see page 84). If you're unable to obtain an employment contract, you should produce a letter of employment (*déclaration d'engagement*).

Employment Agencies

Government Employment Service

The French national employment service, the Agence Nationale Pour l'Emploi (ANPE, ☎ 01 46 45 64 85, 💻 http://www.anpe.fr), operates some 600 offices throughout France, providing both local and national job listings, although jobs on offer are mainly non-professional skilled, semi-skilled and unskilled jobs, particularly in industry, retailing and catering, and around 75 per cent of them are temporary (*intérimaire*) or short-term (*CDD*), although higher-level jobs are offered by specialist offices (see below). Offices are listed under *Administration du Travail et de l'Emploi* in the yellow pages or ANPE in the white pages; a list can be obtained from the Issy-les-Moulineaux office (see above).

Local jobs are advertised in ANPE offices and national listings can be found via a free weekly ANPE bulletin. ANPE offices provide free telephones for calling prospective employers (not your mum!). The ANPE website provides many of its services, including a searchable database of job vacancies. To apply for most of the jobs listed online, you must contact an ANPE office, but a few of the listings give you the name and address of the company so that you can apply directly. The website also contains general information about job hunting in France (in French).

The ANPE provides a comprehensive career resource library, including company listings, trade publications and a wide range of reference books, plus an individual career counselling service and advice on job opportunities and prospects in certain fields. Counsellors can review and translate your *résumé*, provide information about the job market, and assist you in evaluating your options and drawing up a job hunting strategy. The ANPE publishes a free booklet, *Guide de la Recherche d'Emploi*, available from any office.

If you're registered as unemployed and have a residence permit, without which you may receive no help, a personal counsellor is assigned to your case. Other services available to residents include intensive career workshops, mock interviews (on videotape), psychological testing and French language tuition (*perfectionnement de la langue française*), although complete beginners don't qualify. For those wishing to start a business, special classes are provided that include writing a business plan, obtaining finance, grants, paperwork and legal requirements. All services are provided free of charge, although they must be approved by your counsellor.

ANPE services are available to all EU nationals and foreign residents in France. However (there's usually a 'however'), offices have a reputation for being unhelpful to foreign job-seekers unless they've previously been employed in France or are unemployed and receiving unemployment benefit. Being a government department, the ANPE isn't service-oriented and the quality of service varies with the region, the office and the person handling your case. If you'd like the ANPE to (try to) find you a job before leaving your home country, you should complete an application at your local job centre, which will forward it to the ANPE.

Some ANPE offices specialise in certain fields and industries. In Paris there are offices dealing exclusively with hotel and restaurant services, tourism, journalism, public works, civil aviation, the entertainment industry, and jobs for disabled people. Around 20 ANPE offices are called *Points Cadres* and deal with executive jobs. The ANPE also operates *Jeunes Diplômés*, a service for young graduates (🖳 http://www. jd.apec.fr); the Association Pour l'Emploi des Cadres (APEC, ☎ 08 10 80 58 05, 🖳 http://www.cadres.apec.fr) for managers and engineers; and the Association Pour l'Emploi des Cadres, Ingénieurs, Techniciens de l'Agriculture (APECITA, ☎ 01 44 53 20 20, 🖳 http://www.apecita.com) for professionals in the agriculture industry.

British Jobcentres can provide free leaflets entitled *Working in France* and *Working Abroad*.

La Cité des Métiers

La Cité des Métiers is a careers resource centre at the Cité de Sciences et de l'Industrie (known as 'La Villette', ☎ 01 40 05 80 00), where you will find information on over 2,500 jobs, magazines and periodicals, mini-computers and staff to help with job applications. Its website (🖳 http://www.cite-sciences.fr – follow the links to Cité des Métiers) provides information about the various services and resources available, opening hours and job fairs and other exhibitions sponsored by La Villette.

EURES

The European Employment Service (EURES) network covers all EU countries plus Iceland and Norway. Members exchange information on job vacancies on a regular basis and you can have your personal details circulated to the employment service in selected countries, e.g. to the ANPE in France. Details are available in local employment service offices in each member country, where advice on how to apply for jobs is provided. In the UK, you can contact your local Employment Service, which publishes information about working in France (ask for the Jobcentre Plus service). EURES also has a website (🖳 http://europa.eu.int/jobs/eures) where you can find contact information for job counsellors in the UK and other EU countries specialising in public sector jobs in France.

Recruitment Consultants

International recruitment consultants or executive search companies (*cabinet de recrutement*) or 'head hunters' (*chasseur de têtes*) acting for French companies and recruitment consultants in France (which are mainly to be found in cities and large towns) are suitable for executive and management positions, although many French agencies will find positions only for French and EU nationals or foreigners with a residence permit. However, recruitment consultants were hard hit by the recession in the '90s, particularly those dealing with executives and senior managers, and many French companies now do their own recruiting or promote in-house.

Consultants place advertisements in daily and weekly newspapers and trade magazines but don't usually mention the client's name, not least to prevent applicants from approaching a company directly. Unless you're a particularly outstanding candidate with half a dozen degrees, are multilingual and have valuable experience, sending an unsolicited CV to a consultant is usually a waste of time.

British people seeking work in France can obtain an *Overseas Placement List*, listing agencies that specialise in finding overseas positions, from the Recruitment and Employment Confederation in London (☎ 020-7009 2100, 🖳 http://www.rec.uk. com – click on 'Looking for Work?' and then on 'Find a Consultancy').

Many foreign (i.e. non-French) recruitment consultancies post job vacancies on the main internet job sites with links to their own recruitment websites. See **Internet** on page 34 for website addresses of the most popular online job hunting sites.

Temporary Agencies

Most employment agencies (*agence de travail temporaire/agence d'intérim*) are allowed to offer only temporary positions, although with an agency you can often secure a temporary job which will lead to a permanent position. Due to the long annual holidays in France and generous maternity leave, companies often require temporary staff (France has the world's second-largest market for temps). Adecco, Manpower (between them the biggest employers in the country with over 400,000 employees), Adia, SOS Intérim and Vediorbis are common in cities and large towns and generally hire office staff and unskilled or semi-skilled labour. Look in the yellow pages under *Intérim (agences)*.

In addition to general temporary agencies dealing with a range of industries and professions, there are agencies specialising in particular fields such as accounting, banking, computers, construction, engineering and technical, hotel and catering, industrial, insurance, nursing and nannying, sales, secretarial and clerical. Most secretarial jobs are for bilinguals or tri-linguals with word processing experience (an agency will usually test your written language and word-processing skills).

To be employed by a temporary agency, you must be eligible to work in France and have a social security number (see page 327). You usually need to register with an agency, which entails completing a form and providing a CV and references (you can register with any number of agencies). Most temporary agencies have websites, and it's often possible to review their vacancies and/or register online.

When registering with a temporary agency, always ensure that you know exactly how much, when and how you will be paid. Your salary should include a payment in lieu of holidays and be net of social security contributions.

Newspapers & Other Publications

Most Parisian and regional newspapers have job sections (*offres d'emploi*) on certain days. Most newspapers also post job advertisements on their websites. The most popular Parisian newspapers for job advertisements are *Le Monde, Le Figaro, France-Soir, Libération, Le Parisien* and *Les Echos* (the daily financial and stock exchange journal). The best newspapers depend on the sort of job you're seeking. If you're looking for a management or professional position, you should obtain copies of *Le Monde, Le Figaro, Libération* and *Les Echos*. *Le Figaro* provides a separate publication, *Carrières et Emplois*, on Wednesdays, which accumulates employment adverts from a variety of sources, and a job supplement, *Figaro Entreprises*, on Mondays. Those seeking employment as technicians, artisans, secretaries, sales clerks, factory workers and manual labourers should try *France-Soir* and *Le Parisien*. *Libération* has adverts for all job categories.

In addition to the above, there are many important regional newspapers in France, e.g. *Sud-Ouest* and *Ouest-France*. There are also a number of newspapers and magazines devoted to careers and jobs, such as *Carrières et Emplois* (which publishes regional issues), *Carrières Publiques et Privées, Emploi, Entreprise et Carrières, Job Pratique, Le Mardi du Travail* and *Rebondir*. Specialist publications include *Courrier Cadres* for management-level jobs (published by APEC – see page 32), the *Journal de l'Hôtellerie* (🖥 http://www.lhotellerie.fr) for hotel and catering jobs, *L'Usine Nouvelle* for factory jobs and *L'Etudiant* for student summer jobs.

Most professions and trade associations publish journals containing job offers (see *Benn's Media Directory Europe*). Jobs are also advertised in various English-language publications, including the *International Herald Tribune, Wall Street Journal Europe, Paris Free Voice*, and *France-USA Contacts* (fortnightly) – see **Appendix B**. You can also place an advertisement in employment wanted (*demandes d'emplois*) columns in most publications. It's best to place an advert in the middle of the week and to avoid the summer and other holiday periods.

Americans should obtain a copy of the *Directory of American Firms Operating in Foreign Countries*, and Britons should look for *Finding Work in France* (Careers Europe), available from Jobcentres.

Internet

The internet has hundreds of sites for job-seekers, including business, recruitment company and newspaper sites. Most of the main international job-finding sites have sections devoted to vacancies in France. Some of the best known are listed below (unless otherwise stated, sites cover all types of job in all parts of France).

- About Guides (🖥 http://f.about.com).
- Bale.fr (🖥 http://www.bale.fr) for IT and communications jobs.
- Cadremploi (🖥 http://www.cadremploi.com) for management jobs.
- Career Builder (🖥 http://www.careerbuilder.com).
- Career Guide (🖥 http://www.career-guide.com).
- Les Echos (🖥 http://lesechos.fr).
- Emailjob.com (🖥 http://www.emailjob.fr).
- Emploi.com (🖥 http://www.emploi.com).

- Emploi Regions (🖥 http://www.emploiregions.com) for jobs in a particular region).
- Employment Guide (🖥 http://www.employmentguide.org.uk).
- Job Pilot (🖥 http://www.jobpilot.fr).
- Jobware International (🖥 http://www.jobware.net).
- Keljob (🖥 http://www.keljob.com).
- Monster (🖥 http://www.monster.fr).
- Offre-emploi.com (🖥 http://www.offre-emploi.com).
- Overseas Jobs (🖥 http://www.overseasjobs.com).
- Regions Job (🖥 http://www.regionsjob.com) for jobs in a particular region.
- Stepstone (🖥 http://www.stepstone.com and follow the links for France).
- Talents.fr (🖥 http://www.talents.fr) for media and culture jobs.
- ANPE and newspaper sites (see above).

Most of these include articles about job hunting in France and information about work permits and qualifications. Don't forget to check the websites of large companies and international organisations (see below).

International Organisations

International organisations with offices in France usually post job vacancies on their websites before taking out expensive advertisements or placing vacancies with recruitment consultants, and some even accept applications online. The largest organisations in France include the OECD, the United Nations Education, Science and Cultural Organisation (UNESCO), the World Bank, the IMF and the International Labour Office – all located in Paris. The ability to speak French may not be of paramount importance to work for an international organisation and, in the case of the OECD and UNESCO, you may not even need a work permit if you're a citizen of a member country. Note, however, that competition for jobs with international organisations is fierce, and the better qualified you are the better your chances.

If you're an EU national, there are a variety of jobs connected with EU bodies, including the Council of Europe, the European Court of Human Rights and the European Parliament (all located in Strasbourg). If you're looking for employment with a foreign (e.g. British) company in France or a French company that does business with your home country, you should contact the relevant Chamber of Commerce, e.g. the Franco-British Chamber of Commerce (☎ 01 53 30 81 30, 🖥 http://www.francobritishchambers.com), which publishes a monthly review where you can advertise your job requirement.

Unsolicited Job Applications

Making unsolicited job applications (*candidature spontanée*) to targeted companies is naturally a hit and miss affair. It can, however, be more successful than responding to advertisements, as you aren't usually competing with other applicants. Some companies recruit a large percentage of employees through unsolicited *résumés*. When writing from abroad, enclosing an international reply coupon may help to elicit a response.

You can apply directly to multinational companies with offices or subsidiaries in France, and to French companies. Useful addresses can usually be obtained from local Chambers of Commerce as well as from the websites of multinational companies. Lists of foreign companies in France can be obtained from relevant consulates and embassies (e.g. there are around 2,000 British companies in France). Details of French companies can be obtained from the Chambre de Commerce et d'Industrie de Paris (☎ 01 53 40 46 00, 🖥 http://www.ccip.fr), which will provide lists of companies in particular fields or industries. French companies are listed by products, services and *départements* in *Kompass France*, available at libraries in France and main libraries and French Chambers of Commerce abroad as well as via the internet (🖥 http://www.kompass.fr).

When writing for jobs, address your letter (*lettre de motivation*) to the personnel director or manager (*Chef du Personnel*) or the relevant head of department (*Chef de Service*) and include your CV (*CV* or *résumé*) and copies of references and qualifications. Try to find out the person's name by phoning the company. If possible, offer to attend an interview and say when you will be available.

Letters should be tailored to individual employers and professionally translated even if you think your French is perfect. Details of translators can be obtained from organisations such as the Institute of Translation and Interpreting in the UK (☎ 01908-325250, 🖥 http://www.iti.org.uk). Note that some 90 per cent of French companies require hand-written letters from job applicants and submit them to graphologists (employers also use astrology, numerology and even more abstruse methods of selecting staff!). You should write on plain paper (but making sure you write straight) and make no mistakes (if you do, start again rather than make corrections). Model letters (*lettre type*) can be obtained from ANPE offices and on its website (see page 31). There are many books available offering model business (and personal) letters, including the *Handbook of Commercial French* (Routledge) and *How to Address Overseas Business Letters* (Foulsham).

Your CV should be no more than two pages long and needn't include a complete career history; better to highlight relevant experience. It shouldn't contain foreign (i.e. non-French) abbreviations. Attach a passport-size photograph of yourself looking businesslike (not a grinning holiday snap!). Include character references, translated from English if necessary. Always follow up an application with a phone call a week or so after sending it.

Keep copies of all applications; this allows UK citizens to have their Job Seeker's Allowance extended for three months.

Networking

Networking (*faire du network*) is simply making business and professional contacts. It's particularly useful in France, where the majority of job vacancies are never advertised. The national employment agency, ANPE, recognises this and runs courses in networking. The keys to success are to look smart, smile, tell (almost) everyone you meet that you're looking for work, make a note of names and telephone numbers and follow them up, ask people for references – in short, not to be backward in coming forward.

It's difficult for most foreigners to make contacts among the French and many turn to the expatriate community, particularly in Paris. If you're already in France, contact or join expatriate social clubs, churches, societies and professional organisations. A useful resource for English-speakers seeking contacts in Paris is *Paris Anglophone* (Frank Books), containing over 2,000 listings. Much of this information is available online at the Paris Anglo website (🖳 http://www.paris-anglo.com), and there are a number of online forums dedicated to living in France, which offer you a chance to network with those who are already there. Links to online forums and chat rooms about France can be found on the Paris Anglo site or at Expatica (🖳 http://www.expatica.com), which has an active French section. Finally don't forget to ask friends and acquaintances working in France if they know of an employer seeking someone with your experience and qualifications.

TEMPORARY & CASUAL WORK

Temporary and casual work (*travail temporaire/intérimaire* and *emploi de proximité*) is usually for a fixed period, ranging from a few hours to a few months (or work may be intermittent). Casual workers are often employed on a daily, first-come-first-served basis. Anyone looking for casual unskilled work in France must usually compete with North Africans, who are usually prepared to work for less money than anyone else, although nobody **should** be paid less than the minimum wage (see page 24). Many employers illegally pay temporary staff in cash without making deductions for social security (see **Illegal Working** on page 51). However, legally, pay must be aligned with that of permanen workers, and most temporary workers found by agencies must have renewable contracts for 18 months or, in exceptional circumstances, 24 months. Temporary and casual work usually includes the following:

- Office work, which is well paid if you're qualified and the easiest work to find due to the large number of temporary secretarial and office staff agencies.

- Work in the building trade, which can be found by applying at building sites and through industrial recruitment agencies (such as Manpower).

- Jobs in shops and stores, which are often available over Christmas and during sales periods.

- Gardening jobs in private gardens (possibly working for a landscape gardener), public parks and garden centres, particularly in spring and summer.

- Peddling ice cream, cold drinks and fast food in summer, e.g. on beaches.

- Working as a deck-hand on a yacht on the French Riviera.

- Market research, which entails asking people personal questions, either in the street or house to house (an ideal job for nosy parkers with fluent French).

- Modelling at art colleges (both sexes are usually required and you don't need to have a 'perfect' body).

- Work as a security guard (long hours for low pay).

- Nursing and auxiliary nursing in hospitals, clinics and nursing homes (temps are often employed through agencies to replace permanent staff at short notice).

- Newspaper, magazine and leaflet distribution.

- Courier work (own transport required – motorcycle, car or van).

- Driving jobs, including coach and truck drivers, and ferrying cars for manufacturers and car hire companies.

- Office cleaning.

- Baby-sitting.

A good source of information about temporary and casual work in France, particularly for students, is the Centre d'Information et de Documentation Jeunesse (CIDJ, ☎ 01 44 49 12 00 or ☎ 08 25 09 06 30, 💻 http://www.cidj.com). The website includes a listing of all the regional offices of the CIDJ in France. The Union Nationale Des Etudiants De France (UNEF, 💻 http://www.unef.fr) publishes *Le Guide Des Étudiants Salariés*, a guide for students seeking part-time jobs in order to finance their studies, available by post (price €2) or downloadable from the website. American students can apply to the Council on International Educational Exchange (CIEE, ☎ 1-800-407-8839 or ☎ 1-207 553 7600, 💻 http://www.ciee.org). Temporary jobs are available from agencies (see page 32) and are advertised in ANPE offices (see page 31) and on notice boards in expatriate clubs, churches and organisations, as well as in expatriate newsletters and newspapers. See also **Seasonal Jobs** below.

SEASONAL JOBS

Seasonal jobs are available throughout the year, the vast majority in the tourist industry. Many seasonal jobs last for the duration of the summer or winter tourist seasons, May to September and December to April respectively, although some are simply casual or temporary jobs for a number of weeks. French fluency is required for all but the most menial and worst paid jobs, and is equally or more important than experience and qualifications (although fluent French alone won't guarantee you a well paid job). Seasonal jobs include most trades in hotels and restaurants, couriers and representatives, a variety of jobs in ski resorts, sports instructors, jobs in bars and clubs, fruit and grape picking and other agricultural jobs, and various jobs in the construction industry. Seasonal employees in the tourist industry have traditionally been paid below the minimum wage, although the authorities have clamped down on employers in recent years.

If you aren't an EU national, it's essential to check whether you will be eligible to work in France, before your arrival. You may also be required to obtain a visa (see page 77). Check with a French embassy or consulate in your home country well in advance of your visit. Foreign students in France can obtain a temporary work permit (*autorisation provisoire de travail*) for part-time work during the summer holiday period and school terms (see page 187).

Note that seasonal workers have few rights and little legal job protection in France, unless they're hired under standard employment contracts (usually *CDD*s – see page 55), and they can generally be fired without compensation at any time.

Lists of summer jobs can be found via the internet (e.g. ⌨ http://www.anpe.fr, ⌨ http://www.cidj.com and ⌨ http://www.jobs-ete-europe.com). There are many books for those seeking holiday jobs, including *Summer Jobs Abroad* and *Work Your Way Around the World* (Vacation Work). If you speak French, you may be interested in *Emplois d'Été en France* (Vac Editions, ☎ 01 42 94 01 01), which carries advertisements from farmers, co-operatives and others, and *1,000 Pistes de Jobs* (available from L'Etudiant, ⌨ http://www.letudiant.fr). See also **Employment Agencies** on page 31 and **Temporary & Casual Work** on page 37.

Hotels & Catering

Hotels and restaurants are the largest employers of seasonal workers, and jobs are available year round, from hotel managers to kitchen hands. Experience, qualifications and fluent French are required for all the best and highest paid positions, although a variety of jobs are available for the untrained, inexperienced and linguistically challenged. If accommodation with cooking facilities or full board isn't provided with a job, it can be expensive and difficult to find. Ensure that your salary is sufficient at least to pay for accommodation, food and other living expenses (see **Cost of Living** on page 396).

The weekly trade magazine *L'Hôtellerie* (☎ 01 45 48 64 64, ⌨ http://www. lhotellerie.fr) is a good source of hotel and catering vacancies, as is *L'Echo Touristique* (☎ 01 56 79 43 00, ⌨ http://www.echotouristique.com). Both publications include job advertisements on their websites.

Holiday Villages

Some companies, such as Club Méditerranée (Club Med), operate both summer and winter holiday 'villages' throughout France for periods of around five months. Applicants should be aged between 20 and 30, fluent in French and at least one other language, and be 'personable'. Club Med recruitment offices are located in Lyon (☎ 08 25 35 25 25, ⌨ http://www.clubmed-jobs.com – available in English). Residents of North America can apply online through Club Med's English-language recruitment website (⌨ http://www. clubmedjobs.com).

Summer Jobs

One of the most popular summer jobs in France – particularly among young people – is grape picking (*vendange*). Goodness knows why, as it's boring, hard work and badly paid. Over 100,000 foreigners are employed on French farms each summer, most of whom are 'professionals' from Morocco, Portugal and Spain who return to the same region each year. Occupational hazards include sunburn, mosquito and other insect bites, cuts from secateurs, rashes on your arms and legs from chemical sprays, and incessant back pain from bending all day long. Accommodation and cooking facilities can be primitive, and the cost of food and accommodation is usually deducted from your pay.

The grape harvest begins in the south in mid-September and moves up towards Alsace by the middle of October. It's possible to move from area to area, particularly as growers recommend workers to each other. The best (often only) way to find work in a vineyard is to turn up and ask for a job (it's almost impossible to arrange work from outside France). Grape pickers can now obtain a *contrat vendange* valid for one month and renewable for a further month, which exempts them from paying social security charges. Note that grape-picking machines are reducing the number of people required each year.

Useful websites for finding grape-picking jobs include 🖳 http://www.grape picking.co.uk, 🖳 http://www.vinomedia.fr, 🖳 http://www.viti-vini.com and the French government employment site, 🖳 http://www.anpe.fr.

Other fruit-picking jobs include strawberries (May to mid-June), peaches (June to September), cherries (mid-May to early June), pears (mid-July to mid-November) and apples (mid-August to mid-October). The harvest begins early in the south, so it's possible to start in May and work through until October (or even mid-November if you pick frozen grapes on Mont Ventoux), following the sun as it ripens the fruit.

Note that fruit picking is usually paid at below the national minimum wage (see page 24), so you shouldn't expect to get rich. It isn't essential to speak French, but it certainly helps. Camping equipment comes in handy if you're fruit picking (other than grapes), as farmers often don't provide accommodation. Information about farm work can be obtained from the Service des Echanges et des Stages Agricoles dans le Monde (SESAME, ☎ 01 40 54 07 08, 🖳 http://www.agriplanete.com).

Holiday Camps

There are many children's and youth holiday 'camps' (*colonie de vacances*) in France, where French (and many foreign) parents sensibly off-load their offspring during the long summer break from June to September. These offer many job opportunities. Information about children's holiday centres is available from local Directions Départementales de la Jeunesse et des Sports, the addresses of which can be obtained from French embassies or from the yellow pages. You may also be able to obtain a job at a theme park, such as Disneyland Paris (see page 417).

One of the largest British recruiters of summer seasonal workers is PGL Young Adventure (☎ 0870-401 4411, 🖳 http://www.pgl.co.uk), which operates around ten activity centres in France and recruit some 1,000 staff for work from May to September. PGL offers a variety of jobs, including couriers, group and entertainment organisers, chalet staff, sports instructors (particularly watersports), teachers, caterers and cooks, and various support staff. Applications should be made by March for the following summer season, and you can download information about employment as well as submit an application online at the website.

Winter Jobs

Ski resorts require an army of temporary workers to cater for the annual invasion of winter sports enthusiasts. Such jobs can be a lot of fun. You will get fit, improve your French and make friends, and may even be able to save some money. Note, however, that although a winter job may be a working holiday to you (with lots of skiing and little work), to your employer it means exactly the opposite! Besides jobs in the hotel and restaurant trades already mentioned on page 39, a variety of other jobs are available, including couriers, resort representatives, chalet staff, ski technicians, and (for the suitably qualified) ski instructors and guides.

As a general rule, the better paid the job, the longer the working hours and the less time off there is for skiing and other pleasurable activities. Employment in a winter resort usually entitles employees to a discounted lift pass. An invaluable book for anyone looking for a job in a ski resort is *Working in Ski Resorts: Europe & North America* (Vacation Work).

LANGUAGE TEACHERS

Language teaching (particularly English) is a good source of permanent, temporary or part-time work (many language schools need extra teachers in summer). This may entail teaching a foreign language at a language school or privately, or even teaching French to expatriates if your French is up to the task. Language schools don't always require a teaching qualification. A university degree and a respectable appearance may suffice (although you should take as many educational certificates with you as possible). For English teaching, the three most widely recognised qualifications are the Certificate in English Language Teaching to Adults (CELTA), the Trinity Teaching English as a Second Language (TESOL) Certificates and the School for International Training (SIT) TESOL Certificate; note, however, that an approved course costs around €1,400. Information about courses in the UK can be found in the *Times Educational Supplement* and in France from the University of London Institute in Paris (formerly the British Institute in Paris, ☎ 01 44 11 73 73, 💻 http://www.bip.lon. ac.uk). Further information about teaching English in France is available from TESOL France (☎ 01 45 81 75 91, 💻 http://www.tesol-france.org).

The British Council in Paris (☎ 01 49 55 73 00) keeps a list of language schools for students, although they won't help you find work. The larger language schools, such as Berlitz, usually pay the lowest wages but are the most flexible on qualifications. More information about teaching English as a second language can be found in *Making a Living in France* (Survival Books – see page 587) and *Teaching English Abroad* (Vacation Work). You could also try placing advertisements in French newspapers and magazines offering private lessons.

You can also apply directly to state schools for a position as a language *assistant(e)*. The recent introduction of informal English classes into the early elementary school curriculum has created a shortage of teachers for this programme, and many schools are looking for part-time native English-speakers to teach games and songs to young children. **Full-time teachers in French state secondary**

schools and universities must be French citizens and possess French teaching qualifications. Part-time language assistants are normally paid only a nominal salary – much less than that offered to a qualified French native teacher. Further information about teaching in France can be obtained from the Ministry of Education (☎ 01 55 55 10 10, 🖳 http://www.education.gouv.fr). The Central Bureau for International Education & Training (☎ 0161-957 7755, 🖳 http://www.british council.org) publishes *A Year Between* and several other titles relating to teaching exchanges. You can order publications on the website, where you can also find links to several European teaching exchange programmes.

AU PAIRS

The au pair system provides an excellent opportunity to travel, improve your French, and generally broaden your education by living and working in France. Single males and females aged between 18 and 27 from most countries are eligible for a position as an au pair. (Although au pair is French, the French commonly refer to a *fille au-pair*, and the official French term is a *stagiaire aide-familiale*.) Au pairs must usually have had a high school education or the equivalent and have a good knowledge of French, and they **must** attend French classes (see page 209) organised for foreign students. If you're an EU national, you need only a valid passport and aren't required to arrange a position before arriving in France, although it's usually wise. Applicants from non-EU countries need a long-stay visa (see page 77) and require an 'engagement agreement' (*déclaration d'engagement*) with a French family and a certificate of registration for French classes at a language school. These must be presented to your local French embassy or consulate with your passport when applying for a visa (see **Long-stay Visa** on page 78).

Au pairs are usually contracted to work for a minimum of six and a maximum of 18 months. Most families require an au pair for at least the whole school year, from September to June. The best time to look for an au pair position is therefore before the beginning of the school year. You should apply as early as possible and not later than a month prior to your preferred start date or at least two months if you need a visa. There are also summer au pair programmes of one to three months between 15th June and 15th September. Enrolment must usually be made before 31st March. Au pairs employed for the summer only aren't required to attend French lessons.

Au pairs are usually placed in French-speaking families with children, although non French-speaking families and families without children can also engage an au pair. Working hours are officially limited to 30 per week, five hours per day (morning or afternoon), six days per week, plus a maximum of three evenings' baby-sitting. You should be given time off to attend French classes and religious services. Au pairs sometimes holiday with the family, or they may be free to take Christmas or Easter holidays at home. Choose a wealthy family and you may be taken on exotic foreign holidays (although they may be less likely to treat you as a family member)!

For your labours you're fed and lodged and paid 'pocket money' of around €320 per month. You're required to pay your own fare from your country to Paris (and back). If you're employed in the provinces, your family will pay the rail fare from Paris to their home and back to Paris at the end of your stay. In Paris, a family may provide a *carte orange*, a monthly public transport pass.

An au pair position can be arranged privately with a family or through an agency. There are au pair agencies in France (a number are listed in Vacation Work's *Live & Work in France*) and many other countries (British agencies are listed in Vacation Work's *Au Pair and Nanny's Guide to Working Abroad*). Agency lists can also be found via the internet (e.g. ⌨ http://www.europa-pages.com/au_pair). Positions can be found via magazines (such as *The Lady* in the UK) and newspapers, although you're usually better off going through an agency. The better agencies vet families, make periodic checks on your welfare, help you overcome problems (whether personal or with your family) and may organise cultural activities (particularly in Paris).

An agency will send you an application form (questionnaire) and usually ask you to provide character (moral) and child-care references, a medical certificate and school references. Some agencies allow you to meet families in France before making a final decision, which is highly desirable, as you can interrogate the family, inspect their home and your accommodation, and meet the children who will make your life heaven or hell! Agency registration fees vary, although there are maximum fees in some countries, e.g. around £50 in the UK. You should contact a number of agencies and compare registration fees and pocket money, both of which may vary considerably (although the terms of employment should be similar). Pocket money is usually higher in Paris than in the provinces.

Many au pairs grow to love their children and families and form lifelong friendships. On the other hand, abuses of the au pair system are common in all countries, and you may be treated as a servant rather than a member of the family and be expected to work long hours and spend most evenings baby-sitting. Many families engage an au pair simply because it costs far less than employing a nanny. If you have any complaints about your duties, you should refer them to the agency that found you your position (if applicable). You're usually required to give notice if you wish to go home before the end of your agreement, although this won't apply if the family has broken the contract.

It's possible for responsible English- and French-speaking young women to obtain employment as a nanny (*nurse*, *nanny* or *nounou*, sometimes called *garde d'enfants*). Duties are basically the same as for an au pair job (see above), although a position as a nanny is a proper job with full employee rights and a real salary! Further information about working as a nanny can be found in *Making a Living in France* (Survival Books – see page 587).

VOLUNTARY WORK

Voluntary work is an excellent way to improve your French and gain valuable work experience, and may even be an *entrée* to a permanent salaried job. Spouses of non-EU citizens who are in France for a job exchange or temporary secondment) may want to consider volunteer work as a way to avoid gaps in their CV or work history when they return home. Whatever your motive, voluntary work can be rewarding.

Much voluntary work in France takes place in international workcamps (*chantiers de jeunes volontaires bénévoles*), where projects may be agricultural, archaeological or environmental or related to gardening, handicrafts, restoring buildings and monuments, social welfare or community services. Camps usually run for two to four weeks between April and October, although some operate year round. The minimum age for volunteers is 16 to 18, and you must usually be under 30, although some camps have no upper age limit. Disabled volunteers are welcomed by many camps. No special qualifications are required; work is unskilled or semi-skilled and is for around five to eight hours a day, five or six days a week. The work is usually physically quite demanding. Voluntary work is (naturally) unpaid; in fact, you must usually pay a registration fee that includes liability and health insurance and your travel costs to and from the workcamp. Although meals and (basic, shared) accommodation are normally provided, you may also be expected to contribute towards the cost of these. The usual visa regulations apply to voluntary workers (see **Chapter 3**), and you will be informed when applying whether you need one. A work or residence permit isn't necessary. Most workcamps consist of volunteers from several countries, and English may be the common language.

There are 12 associations in France sponsoring voluntary work programmes under the auspices of Coordination pour le Travail Volontaire des Jeunes (COTRAVAUX, ☎ 01 48 74 79 20; details can be found on the website of the Fédération Unie des Auberges de Jeunesse/FUAJ, (🖳 http://www.fuaj.org).

There's a variety of unpaid voluntary jobs other than on camps, particularly in Paris and other cities. Contact WICE (☎ 01 45 66 75 50, 🖳 http://www.wice-paris.org) for information about their volunteer opportunities or about other expatriate organisations in the Paris area.

SELF-EMPLOYMENT

Being self-employed in France, as in most other countries, is no simple matter and requires planning, preparation (**most foreigners don't do sufficient homework before moving to France**), determination and a good deal of luck. While hoping for the best, you should anticipate the worst and have a contingency plan and sufficient funds to last until you're established (this also applies to employees). If you're planning to start a business, you must also do battle with the notoriously obstructive French bureaucracy (*bonne chance!*).

If you're an EU-national, you can work as a self-employed individual (*travailleur indépendant*) or as a sole trader (*entreprise individuelle*). A non-EU national with a long-term residence permit (*carte de résident* – see page 86) can be self-employed or a sole trader. However, it's difficult for non-EU nationals to obtain a residence permit to be self-employed.

There are three main categories of self-employed people in France: *profession libérale* (e.g. accountants, doctors, lawyers, writers), *commerçant* (traders and shopkeepers) and *artisan* (craftsmen and tradesmen). To be self-employed in certain trades and professions, you must have an official status (*statut* or *régime*) and it's illegal simply to hang up a sign and start business. For foreigners, self-employment options include foreign language teaching, translating, tour guiding, and representing a foreign company.

To work as a self-employed person, you must usually have the following:

- Qualifications and diplomas that are recognised in France for professions and trades requiring certification (see page 28).
- A residence permit (see page 84).
- A tax registration certificate (*avis d'imposition*).
- A business permit (*carte de commerçant*) – see below.
- Contracts or letters of intent from prospective clients (for those in service industries only).
- To register with your local social security (URSSAF) office and obtain a social security number (see page 327).
- To register with the relevant organisations (*caisses*) for health insurance and pension contributions; until recently, these depended on your activity, but the system is now being consolidated and by 2007 a single organisation, the *Régime Social des Indépendants* (*RSI*, ☐ http://www.le-rsi.fr), will handle all self-employed workers.
- To register for value added tax (*TVA*) at the office nearest to your business location if your turnover is over a certain limit (see page 381).
- To register with the appropriate organisation for your profession or trade within two weeks of starting a business, e.g. the Chambre de Métiers, the Chambre d'Agriculture or the Chambre de Commerce. You can obtain the address of the relevant body from your local town hall; for information about French Chambers of Commerce contact the Assemblée des Chambres Françaises de Commerce et d'Industrie/ACFCI (☎ 01 53 57 17 00, ☐ http://www.acfci.cci.fr – English option).
- To register at your local *tribunal de commerce* (for a commercial business).

Before being permitted to register as self-employed, you may be required to attend a business course (*cours/stage de gestion*) run by the relevant local organisation for your trade or profession, covering all aspects of business administration. Courses last from four to six days and cost around €125. At the end of the course you're issued with a certificate (whether you understood anything or not!), which is a prerequisite for starting certain kinds of business. Most courses are held only in French, and in certain cases you may also need to pass an exam (also in French) to obtain a trading licence. The various organisations issue a certificate that must be presented to your local Chamber of Commerce when registering your business.

Don't be in too much of a hurry to register as self-employed, as from the date of registration you must pay hefty social security, pension and health insurance payments, and are also liable for income tax and VAT (*TVA* – see **Chapter 14**). **However, you should *never* be tempted to start work before you're registered, as there are harsh penalties that may include a large fine (e.g. €15,000), confiscation of machinery or tools, and even deportation and a three-year ban from entering France.**

In financial terms, there are a usually few advantages to self-employment over salaried employment. Social security contributions for the self-employed are much higher than for salaried employees. During your first years in business, your social security contributions may be based on a flat minimum charge of several hundred euros per month, irrespective of your turnover or business results. As a self-employed person in France you aren't entitled to unemployment benefit should your business fail and there are no benefits for accidents at work (except for artisans), although you're insured against invalidity. There's no sick pay for those in *professions libérales*, although *artisans* and *commerçants* are covered provided they've been paying their social security charges for at least a year. As a self-employed person you risk bankruptcy and ruin if your business fails, and it may be advantageous to operate as a limited company, although the government has recently changed the law to offer better protection for those in a *profession libérale*. **Always obtain professional advice before deciding whether to operate as a sole trader or form a company, as it has far-reaching social security, tax and other consequences.** See also **Self-employed** on page 380.

On the other hand, there's one major advantage to being self-employed over that of creating a company. If your activity doesn't involve dealing directly with the public (i.e. face to face), you may use your home as your business premises – provided your lease allows you to in the case of rented accommodation or a communal property, such as an apartment.

It's also wise to join a professional association, as they provide valuable information and assistance and may also offer insurance discounts. Most professional associations are organised locally. Check with your departmental Chambre de Commerce or with the local town hall for information about groups active in your area and profession. For information about the appropriate guild (*chambre de métiers*) for your profession, contact the Assemblée Permanente des Chambres de Métiers (☎ 01 44 43 10 00, ☒ http://www.apcm.com). Further information about being self-employed can be found in *Making a Living in France* (Survival Books – see page 587).

STARTING A BUSINESS

An increasing number of people are starting businesses (*démarrer une entreprise*) in France, although the bureaucracy associated with it is among the most pernicious in the world. France is a red tape jungle and civil servants (*fonctionnaires*) can be inordinately obstructive (endlessly recycling bits of paper to create 'employment' for themselves). If you don't speak French, the red tape can be almost impenetrable. If you need a licence or a loan to start a business, for example, don't plan on getting it in a few weeks or even months – it can take up to a year!

Nevertheless, France is traditionally a country of small companies and individual traders, where the economic philosophy encourages and even nurtures the creation of small businesses. Many of these, however, exist on a shoe string and certainly aren't what would be considered thriving enterprises. As in most countries, people are usually self-employed for the lifestyle and freedom it affords (no clocks or bosses!), rather than the financial rewards. It's important to keep your plans small and manageable and work well within your budget, rather than undertaking some grandiose scheme. As any expert can tell you, France isn't a country for amateur entrepreneurs, particularly amateurs who don't speak fluent French!

Before undertaking any business transactions, it's important to obtain legal advice to ensure that you're operating within the law. There are severe penalties for anyone who ignores the regulations and legal requirements. It's also important to obtain legal advice before establishing a limited business. Non-EU nationals require a special licence (*carte commerçante étranger*) to start a business in France, and no commitments should be made until permission has been granted. In fact, it's best not to start a business until you have the infrastructure established, including an accountant, lawyer and banking facilities. It's important to employ an accountant (*expert comptable*) to do your books, although you shouldn't expect him to be interested in reducing your social security charges and you should question costs that appear too high.

Generally speaking, you shouldn't consider running a business in France in a field where you don't have previous experience. It's often wise to work for someone else in the same line of business in order to gain experience, rather than jump in at the deep end. Always thoroughly investigate an existing or proposed business before investing any money. The majority of businesses established by foreigners are linked to the leisure and catering industries, followed by property investment and development. Types of business include holiday accommodation, e.g. bed and breakfast (*chambres d'hôtes*) and *gîtes* (chalets, apartments and cottages to let), caravan and camping sites, building and allied trades, farming (e.g. dairy, vineyards, fruit, fish and fowl), catering (e.g. bars, cafés and restaurants), hotels, shops, franchises, estate agencies, translation services, language schools, landscape gardening, and holiday and sports centres (e.g. tennis, golf, squash, shooting and horse-riding schools). Nevertheless, you should try to find a niche and not simply set up the same kind of business as other expatriates. Details about running a business and running holiday accommodation in France can be found, respectively, in *Making a Living in France* and *Earning Money From Your French Home* (Survival Books – see page 587).

Finance

A recent survey by accountancy firm KPMG of business start-up costs in nine countries found France to be cheaper than the UK, Germany, the Netherlands and Italy. Nevertheless, most people are far too optimistic about the prospects for a new business in France and over-estimate income levels (it often takes years to make a profit). When estimating your turnover, overestimate the costs (especially start-up costs) and underestimate the revenue (then reduce it by 50 per cent!). While hoping for the best, you should plan for the worst and have sufficient funds to last until you're established (**under-funding is the major cause of business failures, of which there are tens of thousands every year**). French banks are extremely wary of lending to new businesses, especially businesses run by foreigners. If you wish to borrow money to buy property or for a business venture in France, you should carefully consider where and in what currency to raise finance.

Grants, Subsidies & Competitions

There are over 250 different grants and incentives available for new businesses in France, particularly in rural areas. These include EU subsidies, central government grants, regional development grants, redeployment grants, and grants from departments and communities. Grants may take the form of assistance to buy buildings and equipment (or the provision of low-cost business premises), subsidies for job creation, or tax incentives. A government business start-up loan (*prêt à la création d'entreprise/PCE*) of between €3,000 and €8,000 over five years is available under certain conditions; for details contact the Agence pour la Création d'Entreprise (APCE, ☎ 01 42 18 58 58, 🖳 http://www.apce.com).

Female entrepreneurs can benefit from the state *Fonds de Garantie pour la Création, la Reprise ou le Développement d'Entreprises à l'Initiative des Femmes* (*FGIF*); details can be obtained from the *Droits des Femmes* service at your local *préfecture* or via the internet (🖳 http://www.esfin-ides.com).

Most government subsidies are intended to provide support for small businesses already up and running, but there are occasionally specific subsidies available for new businesses, particularly for individuals who have been unemployed for a long period. Some regional governments offer subsidies to new businesses, particularly if local jobs are assured or local skills put to good use. Most grants apply only to the creation of a first business. **Even if you're eligible for a grant and it has been approved, you shouldn't bank on receiving it, as it can take months or even years to materialise.**

There are also many competitions (*concours* or *prix*), at national, regional and departmental level, which can take the form of financial assistance or other benefits. To find out about possible grants, incentives and competitions, start by contacting your local town hall or *mairie*, the relevant *centre de formalités des entreprises* and the departmental chamber of commerce. For further information about grants and incentives, contact Invest in France (AFII), which has offices in Belgium, Germany, Italy, the Netherlands, Spain, Switzerland, the UK, the US (four offices) and in various Asian countries. Its head office is AFII (☎ 01 44 87 17 17, 🖳 http://www.afii.fr). Refer also to *Making a Living in France* (Survival Books – see page 587).

Location

The location for a business is even more important than the location for a home. Local plans regarding communications, industry and major building developments, e.g. housing complexes and new shopping centres, may also be important but may be difficult to find out about. Plans for new motorways and rail links are normally available from local town halls. It's possible to rent business premises, although you may not have the same legal protection as a private lessor and you should seek expert advice.

Employees

Hiring employees shouldn't be taken lightly in France and must be taken into account **before** starting a business. You must enter into a contract under French labour law (see page 54) and employees enjoy extensive rights. It's also **very** expensive to hire employees: in addition to salaries, you must pay 40 to 60 per cent in social security contributions (there are reductions for hiring certain categories of unemployed people), a 13th month's salary and five weeks' paid annual holiday (see **Social Security** on page 323 and **Chapter 2**). According to the Federation of European Employers, labour costs are a higher percentage of gross domestic product in France (119) than in all other European countries except Belgium and Luxembourg. However, there are tax holidays for limited periods for newly formed companies, particularly regarding the first employee: during their first two years' trading, most new businesses are required to pay only around 10 per cent of their first employee's wages in social security contributions.

Business Entity

There are around 13 different types of business entity in France; the most common type created by foreigners is a *Société à Responsabilité Limitée* (*SARL*), a private limited company with a minimum share capital of around €7,600 (part of which can be fixed assets) and at least two shareholders with a maximum of 50. Another common type of company is a *Société Civile Immobilière* (*SCI*), which is a property-holding company. Other types include a *Bureau de Liaison/Représentation* (essentially a 'shop window' for a foreign company), *Succursale* (branch office of a larger company), *Société en Nom Collectif/SNC* (a general partnership), *Société en Commandité Simple/SCS* (a limited partnership), *Société par Actions Simplifiées* (a simplified form of *SARL*), *Entreprise Unipersonelle à Responsabilité Limitée* (a type of *SARL* formed by a sole trader), *Société Anonyme/SA* (similar to a plc in the UK).

It's also possible to set up a franchise (*franchise*), of which there are several thousand in France, or to act as a distributor, agent or representative, for which you may not need to set up a formal company. **It's essential to obtain professional advice regarding the best method of establishing and registering a business, which can dramatically affect your tax position, and you must *never* use a non-trading company (*société civile*) to trade**.

Companies cannot be purchased 'off the shelf', and it usually takes a number of months to establish a company. Incorporating a company takes longer and is more expensive and more complicated than in most other European countries. Note also that, if you form a French company (e.g. a *SARL*) and pay yourself as an employee, you must pay an additional 40 to 60 per cent in social security contributions.

Buying a Business

It's much easier to buy an existing business in France than start a new one and it's also less of a risk. The paperwork for taking over an existing business is simpler (relatively speaking), although it can be expensive in taxes. Note, however, that buying a business that's a going concern is difficult, as the French aren't in a habit of selling businesses, which are usually passed down from generation to generation. If you want to run a licensed business (e.g. butcher's, hairdresser's or chemist's), you must hold a qualification in the profession.

There are often separate prices for the business itself (*fonds* or *fonds de commerce*) and the property or 'walls' (*murs*), e.g. the building housing a hotel or restaurant. The authorities can reassess the value of the *fonds de commerce* if they consider that they've been undervalued and also impose fines. Stock is subject to 19.6 per cent VAT. If you don't buy the building, a separate rental contract (lease/*bail*) must be negotiated. If possible, it's best to purchase a business with the building, particularly if you need to raise a loan.

You can obtain a mortgage of up to 80 per cent on the property, but you must fund the business yourself. The notary's fees when buying a business property are usually around 20 per cent of the purchase price. Note that the protection afforded to domestic tenants doesn't extend to business tenants. Therefore, if you rent business premises, it's essential to take legal advice regarding a lease, which **must** contain a right to rent clause to ensure the future value of the business.

If you plan to buy a business, obtain an independent valuation (or two). Never sign anything you don't understand and, even if you think you understand it, obtain unbiased professional advice, e.g. from local bankers and accountants.

When taking over an existing and operating company, you're obliged by French labour law to respect existing employment contracts (which isn't a bad thing if you require help, as experienced staff are priceless). However, you aren't compelled to renew their contracts if you cannot afford it. (That decision may be subject to review by the authorities, especially if unemployment in the immediate area is a problem.)

You can contact local estate agents and *notaires* for details of businesses for sale in a particular area. The Agence pour la Création d'Entreprise (APCE, ☎ 01 42 18 58 58, 🖳 http://www.apce.com) publishes a bi-monthly bulletin, listing business opportunities. Local and regional Chambers of Commerce are excellent sources of information and operate a regional network called *Bureaux de Rapprochement d'Entreprise* (*BRE*) to bring together sellers and prospective buyers. You can find the address and contact numbers for your local Chamber by contacting the Assemblée des Chambres Françaises de Commerce et d'Industrie (ACFCI, ☎ 01 40 69 37 00) or by looking under *Annuaire* on the ACFCI website (🖳 http://www.acfci.fr). The ACFCI publishes newsletters listing the various opportunities. Businesses are also advertised for sale in many French newspapers and magazines, as well as in *French Property News* and *Living France* (see **Appendix B**).

Information

A useful guide for anyone starting a business in France is *Setting up a Small Business in France* published by the French Chamber of Commerce (☎ 020-7304 4040). Many countries maintain chambers of commerce in France, which are an invaluable source of information and assistance, and international accountants such as Pricewaterhouse Coopers that have offices throughout France can provide additional information (in English) on subjects such as forming a company, company law, taxation and social security.

Among the best sources of local help and information are your Chamber of Commerce, of which there are over 160 and at least one in each department, and your town hall. You can also enlist the services of a *centre de gestion*, a group of accountants, bookkeepers and administrative staff who specialise in assisting entrepreneurs. In fact membership of a *centre de gestion* entitles you to a 20 per cent reduction in income tax (see page 377)!

The Délégation à l'Aménagement du Territoire et de l'Action Régional (DATAR) is the major French government organisation concerned with attracting overseas investment and business ventures. DATAR provides comprehensive information about all aspects of doing business in France. It also implements the French government's policy of providing grants and investment incentives for certain businesses, particularly those located in depressed and under-developed areas. DATAR operates abroad as Invest in France (AFII) and has offices in Belgium, Germany, Italy, the Netherlands, Spain, Switzerland, the UK and the US (four offices) and in various Asian countries. Its head office is AFII (☎ 01 40 74 74 40, 🖳 http://www.afii.fr).

ILLEGAL WORKING

Illegal working (*travail au noir/au black* or *travail clandestin*) thrives in France, particularly among the expatriate community and immigrants from North Africa. (It's illegal for non-EU nationals to work in France without a work permit.) It has been conservatively estimated that some 30 per cent of all work in France isn't declared to the tax authorities, with up to a million people regularly doing 'odd jobs' (*petit boulot*), i.e. working illegally. Many unscrupulous employers use illegal labour in order to pay low wages (below the minimum wage) for long hours and poor working conditions. Abuse is common in industries that traditionally employ casual labour, such as building, farming, services and textiles.

In recent years there has been a clamp-down on illegal working with greater powers given to the police, *gendarmerie*, courts and work inspectors (*inspecteurs de travail*), and increased penalties. Illegal working is punishable by up to two years in prison and fines of between €300 and €30,000 (which are doubled for a second offence). Moreover, if you work illegally, you have no entitlement to social security benefits such as insurance against work injuries, public health care, unemployment pay and a state pension.

If you use illegal labour, you will have no official redress if goods or services are substandard. If you employ someone who's an illegal immigrant, you can be fined €500 to €5,000 and can be imprisoned for up to three years.

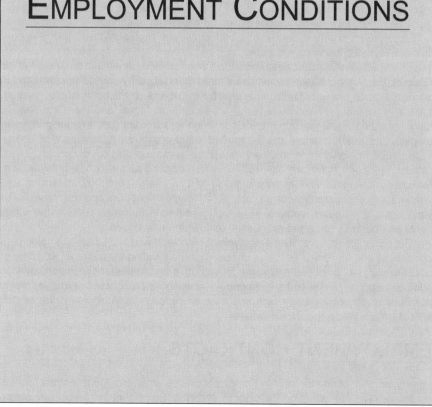

2.

EMPLOYMENT CONDITIONS

French employees, particularly state employees, enjoy excellent employment conditions, which are largely dependent on the French Labour Code (*Code du Travail*), collective agreements (*conventions collectives de travail*), an individual employment contract (*contrat de travail*), and the employer's in-house rules and regulations (*règlements intérieurs/règlements de travail*).

Employees have extensive rights under the French Labour Code. The Code details the minimum conditions of employment, including working hours, overtime payments, holidays, trial and notice periods, dismissal conditions, health and safety regulations, and trade union rights. The Code is described in detail in a number of books, including the *Code du Travail* (VO Editions), and is available in its entirety from the Legifrance website (🖥 http://www.legifrance.gouv.fr), some of which is in English.

Collective agreements (*conventions collectives*) are negotiated between industry associations (*syndicats*) and employers' associations in many industries. These specify the rights and obligations of both employees and employers in a particular industry or occupation and cover around 75 per cent of the workforce. Agreements specify minimum wage levels for each employment category in a particular industry or company. If an employer doesn't abide by the laws or the regulations, employees can report him to the works council or work syndicates (see page 69). Where there's no works council or employee delegation, the case is heard before an industrial tribunal (*conseil de prud'hommes*) comprising employer and syndicate representatives (elected by the workforce). When an employee is wrongfully dismissed, he's awarded damages based on his length of service.

Employment courts, trade unions and employee representatives jointly ensure that employment laws are respected, and regulations are supervised by local work inspectors (*inspecteur du travail*) and the Direction Départmentale du Travail et de l'Emploi. Employment laws cannot be altered or nullified by private agreements. In general, French law forbids discrimination by employers on the basis of sex, religion, race, age, sexual preference, physical appearance or name, and there are specific rules regarding equal job opportunities for men and women (see **Working Women** on page 22). In 2002, a law was introduced forbidding 'moral harassment'.

Salaried foreigners are employed under the same working conditions as French citizens, although there are different rules for certain categories of employee, e.g. directors, managers and factory workers. As in many countries, seasonal and temporary workers aren't always protected by employment laws and may have fewer legal rights than other workers. However, part-time employees receive the same rights and benefits (on a pro rata basis) as full-time employees.

This chapter covers the employment contract and the basic employment conditions, and highlights points to check when negotiating terms for a job, some of which apply to all positions and some to executive and managerial positions only. In addition to these points, you should enquire about your prospective employer and in particular whether he has a good reputation and prospects. A high turnover of staff should be a warning to look elsewhere!

EMPLOYMENT CONTRACTS

Legally, an offer of employment in France constitutes an employment contract (*contrat de travail/d'emploi*), although it's safer to obtain a formal contract (especially before handing in your notice to a previous employer!). Employees usually have a formal contract stating such details as job title, position, salary, working hours, benefits, duties and responsibilities, and the place and duration of employment. Contracts usually contain a paragraph stating the date from which they take effect and to whom they apply. Unless your contract specifies that you will work only in the place of work listed, your employer is entitled to ask you to work elsewhere from time to time.

All employment contracts are subject to French labour law, and references may be made to other regulations such as collective agreements. Anything in contracts contrary to statutory provisions and unfavourable to an employee may be deemed invalid. There are usually no hidden surprises or traps for the unwary in a French employment contract. Nevertheless, as with any contract, you should know exactly what it contains before signing it. If your French isn't fluent, you should try to obtain a translation, although according to French law any exclusion clauses must be 'clear and comprehensible'. If you cannot obtain a written translation (which is likely), you should at least have it translated verbally so that you don't receive any nasty surprises later.

There are two main types of employment contract in France: an indefinite term contract and a term contract.

Temporary Contracts

A temporary contract (*contrat de travail temporaire* or *intérim*) has no minimum or maximum duration and can be issued only in the following circumstances:

● For someone who's replacing a staff member who's temporarily absent (except if striking) and whose function is essential to the running of the business.

● For someone who's filling a post on an interim basis until a permanent staff member takes over.

● In the case of a temporary, unforeseen and otherwise unmanageable increase in the workload of existing staff.

● If the business is seasonal and requires additional workers at specific times of year (e.g. in agriculture for harvesting or in catering for peak periods).

● For workers in specific sectors (e.g. the theatre), where the use of temporary contracts is habitual.

Any other type of short-term contract is regarded as a fixed term contract (see below). A worker engaged on a temporary contract is known as a *salarié intérimaire* or simply *intérimaire*. Details of the obligations of employer and employee can be found on the website of the Monster Company (🖳 http://www.jobpilot.fr/content/service/channel/interim/pratique/contrat.html).

Fixed Term Contracts

A fixed term contract (*contrat à durée déterminée/CDD*) is, as the name suggests, a contract for a limited term. This is normally a maximum of 18 months, although it's limited to nine months if a post is due to be filled permanently and can be extended to two years if the post is due to be suppressed (there's no minimum term). A contract for longer than two years comes under the rules for indefinite term contracts, particularly regarding the dismissal of employees. A term contract must be in writing and for a fixed term or, in the case of temporary employment, for a specific purpose that must be stated in the contract. A term contract ends on the date specified, although it can be renewed twice for a term no longer than the original contract, provided it doesn't exceed two years in total.

A *CDD* can also be for replacement of a specific employee (usually someone on maternity leave) or a general replacement over the summer (to pick up the slack while various employees are off on holiday). *CDD*s are strictly regulated, mainly because they're considered a contributing factor to the ever-increasing 'precariousness' of employment (*précarité d'emploi*). For example, the salary of an employee hired on a fixed term contract mustn't be less than that paid to a similarly qualified person employed in a permanent job. The employee has the right to an end of contract bonus (*indemnité de fin de contrat*) equal to 10 per cent of his salary, in addition to other agreed bonuses, although this doesn't always apply to seasonal employees. Nevertheless, as a result of abuses of the *CDD*, the government has recently allowed companies with fewer than 20 staff to give employees a two-year trial period, during which their contract can be terminated without the complications involved in terminating an indefinite term contract (see below).

Contracts for seasonal and temporary workers fall under the same rules as for a *CDD* contract. A *CDD* can be issued when a permanent employee is on leave (including maternity or sick leave), if there's a temporary increase in business, or at any time in the construction industry or for youth employment schemes.

Indefinite Term Contracts

An indefinite term contract (*contrat à durée indéterminée/CDI*) is the standard employment contract for permanent employees. Surprisingly, it isn't necessary for it to be in writing (unlike a term contract), although you should insist on this; in fact, a standard contract form (*modèle de contrat de travail à durée indéterminée*) can be obtained from URSSAF offices. It often includes a trial period of one to three months (three months is usual), depending on collective agreements, before it becomes legal and binding on both parties.

In an attempt to reduce unemployment by making it simpler for employers to hire (and, especially, fire) workers, the government introduced the *contrat nouvelles embauches* (*CNE*) in August 2005. Although technically a *CDI*, this new contract, which applied only to people over 26, could be revoked for almost any reason within the first two years. Encouraged by the success of this initiative (over 400,000 workers were signed up in the first eight months), the government introduced the *contrat première embauche* in April 2006. Essentially the same type of contract but limited to those under 26, the *CPE* aroused storms of protest, not only from the young it was supposed to help find jobs (who demonstrated violents and destroyed university buildings) but also from unions and anyone opposed to the current government. The ensuing political crisis saw the President instructing the Prime Minister to repeal the

CPE, leaving the government with a copious amount of egg on its face and France's youth facing the prospect of continued unemployment.

SALARY & BENEFITS

Your salary (*salaire*) is stated in your employment contract; salary reviews, planned increases, cost of living rises, etc. may also be included. Salaries may be stated in gross (*brut*) or net (*net*) terms and are usually paid monthly, although they may be quoted in contracts as hourly, monthly or annually. If a bonus is paid, such as a 13th or 14th month's salary (see below), this is stated in your contract. General points such as the payment of your salary into a bank or post office account and the date of salary payments are usually included in employment conditions. Salaries above €3,000 per month must be paid by cheque or direct transfer (not cash), although it's never wise to receive salary in cash, as it makes you subject to scrutiny by the tax authorities! You receive a pay slip (*bulletin de paie*) itemising your salary and deductions and you must keep your pay slips indefinitely, as they can be required as proof of earnings or payment of social security or other insurances, even after your death!

Salaries must be reviewed once a year (usually at the end of the year), although employers aren't required by law to increase salaries which are above the minimum wage, even when the cost of living has increased. Salary increases usually take effect on 1st January. See also **Salary** on page 23.

13th Month's Salary & Bonuses

Most employers in France pay their employees a bonus in December, known as the 13th month's salary (*13ème mois*). A 13th month's salary isn't mandatory unless part of a collective agreement or when it's granted regularly, and it should be stated in your employment contract. In practice its payment is almost universal and it's often taken for granted. In your first and last years of employment, your 13th month's salary and other bonuses should be paid pro rata if you don't work a full calendar year. Some companies also pay a 14th month's salary, usually in July before the summer holiday period. A few companies, e.g. banks and other financial institutions, may pay as many as 15 or 16 months' salary. Where applicable, extra months' salary are guaranteed bonuses and aren't pegged to the company's performance (as with profit-sharing). In some cases, they're paid monthly rather than in a lump sum at the end or in the middle of the year. Senior and middle managers often receive extra bonuses, perhaps linked to profits, equal to around 10 to 20 per cent of their annual salary.

Employees of many French companies are also entitled to participate in bonus schemes (some tied to productivity) and profit-sharing schemes (*participation des salariés aux résultats de l'entreprise/système d'intéressement aux bénéfices*), which must be provided by any company with over 100 employees. Companies are obliged to contribute a minimum amount of their total payroll (this may be up to 20 per cent) to a special fund. Some employers also operate optional investment plans (*plan d'épargne d'entreprise*), where the company holds a portfolio of securities on behalf of its employees, and share option schemes (*options sur actions*). If you're employed on a term contract for a fixed period, you're paid an end-of-contract bonus (*indemnité de fin de contrat*) equal to 10 per cent of your salary, in addition to other bonuses.

Companies with 50 or more employees must have an enterprise committee (*comité d'entreprise*) comprising elected employees. The company pays an amount equal to 1 per cent of its payroll into the committee's fund, to be used at the discretion of the employees to provide benefits such as private day-care, holidays, theatre discounts, holiday gifts and a staff Christmas party. As with training (see page 68), some companies allocate extra funds to their *comité d'entreprise* as a means of attracting employees.

Expenses

Expenses (*frais*) paid by your employer are usually listed in your employment conditions. These may include travel costs from your home to your place of work, usually consisting of a second-class rail season ticket or the equivalent amount in cash (paid monthly with your salary). In the Paris area, most employers pay 50 per cent of the cost of an employee's *carte orange*, a monthly public transport pass. Travelling expenses to and from your place of work are tax deductible.

Companies without a restaurant or canteen may pay a lunch allowance or provide luncheon vouchers (*chèques* or *tickets restaurant*) that can be purchased for half their face value and may be used in local restaurants and some food shops. Expenses paid for travel on company business or for training and education may be detailed in your employment conditions or listed in a separate document.

Relocation Expenses

The payment of relocation expenses (*frais de voyage*) depends on your agreement with your employer and should be included in your employment contract or conditions. Most employers pay travel and relocation costs to France up to a specified amount, although you may be required to sign a special contract stipulating that if you leave the employer before a certain period (e.g. five years), you must repay a percentage of the costs.

If you're hired from outside France, your air ticket and other travel to France are usually booked and paid for by your employer or his local representative. In addition, you can usually claim any onward travel costs, e.g. the cost of transport to and from airports. If you travel by car, you can usually claim a mileage rate or the equivalent air fare.

If you're relocating, an employer may pay a fixed relocation allowance based on your salary, position and size of family, or he may pay the total cost of removal. The allowance should be sufficient to move the contents of an average house, and you must normally pay any excess costs yourself. If you don't want to bring your furniture to France or have only a few belongings to ship, it may be possible to purchase furniture locally up to the limit of your allowance. Check with your employer. When your employer is liable for the total cost, he may ask you to obtain two or three removal estimates.

Generally, you're required to organise and pay for the removal in advance. Your employer will usually reimburse the equivalent amount in euros **after** you've paid the bill, although it may be possible to get him to pay the bill directly or give you a cash advance. If you change jobs within France, your new employer may pay your relocation expenses when it's necessary for you to move house. Don't forget to ask, as he may not offer to pay.

Checklist

- Is the salary adequate, taking into account the cost of living (see page 396)? Is it index-linked and protected against devaluation? This is particularly important if you're paid in a foreign currency that fluctuates wildly or could be devalued.

- Is the total salary (including expenses) paid in euros or will the salary be paid in another country in a different currency, with expenses for living in France?

- Are you paid an overseas allowance for working in France?

- When and how often is the salary reviewed?

- Does the salary include a 13th (or 14th) month's salary and annual or end-of-contract bonuses (see page 57)?

- Is overtime paid or time off given in lieu of extra hours worked?

- Is a free or subsidised company restaurant provided? If not, is an allowance paid or are luncheon vouchers provided? (Some companies provide excellent staff restaurants which save employees both money and time.)

- Is there a clothing allowance? For example, if you arrive in the winter from the tropics, you will probably need to buy new winter clothes.

- Are free work clothes or overalls provided? Does the employer pay for the cleaning of work clothes?

- Does the employer provide any fringe benefits, such as subsidised banking services, low interest loans, cheaper petrol, employees' shop or product discounts, sports and social facilities, and subsidised tickets?

- Will your employer pay for a hotel or pay a lodging allowance until you find permanent accommodation?

- Is subsidised or free, temporary or permanent accommodation provided? If so, is it furnished or unfurnished?

- Must you pay for utilities such as electricity, gas and water?

- If accommodation isn't provided by the employer, is assistance provided to find suitable accommodation? If so, what sort of assistance?

- What will accommodation cost? (See **Chapter 5**.)

- Are your expenses paid while looking for accommodation?

- Is private schooling for your children financed or subsidised? Will the employer pay for a boarding school in France or abroad?

- Will the employer pay for domestic help or towards the cost of a servant or cook?

- Is a car provided? With a chauffeur?

- Is free or subsidised parking provided at your place of work?

- Are you entitled to any miscellaneous benefits, such as membership of a social or sports club or free credit cards?

- Is there an entertainment allowance?

- Are the costs incurred by a move to France (including the cost of selling your home, employing an agent to let it for you or storing household effects) reimbursed?

- Are removal expenses or a relocation allowance paid?

- Does the allowance include travelling expenses for all family members? Is there a limit and is it adequate?

- Are you required to repay relocation expenses (or a percentage) if you resign before a certain period has elapsed?

- Are you required to pay for your relocation in advance? This can run into thousands of euros for normal house contents.

- If employment is for a limited period, will your relocation costs be paid by the employer when you leave France?

- If you aren't shipping household goods and furniture to France, is there an allowance for buying furnishings locally?

- Do relocation expenses include the legal and agent's fees incurred when moving home?

- Does the employer use the services of a relocation consultant (see page 104)?

- Is a travelling allowance (or public transportation) paid from your French residence to your place of work?

WORKING HOURS

Traditionally, the French have had a flexible attitude to working hours, and the idea of fixed office hours is particularly alien to executives and managers. For example, taking a long lunch break, perhaps for a game of tennis or a swim, isn't frowned upon, provided you put in the required hours and don't neglect your work. It isn't unusual for a parent to leave work early to collect children from a nursery, and some employees work only a half-day on Wednesdays when children aren't attending school. These are statutory rights granted to both parents.

In 2000, France introduced a mandatory 35-hour working week for all large employers, and on 1st January 2002 this became effective for all employers. The objective of the 35-hour week scheme, referred to as the 'working hours reduction' programme (*réduction du temps de travail* or *RTT*), is to dramatically reduce unemployment by spreading the existing amount of work across more workers. Companies were encouraged to negotiate with their employees to find flexible ways to distribute the reduced working hours – including a seven-hour day, a four-and-a-half day week or even varying weeks within the same month. Some industries were allowed to recognise seasonal workload variations by granting extra time off during the off-season to compensate employees for longer hours necessary during peak times of year.

These plans were considered radical disruptions of hard-won job security rights and privileges, and there were numerous one-day strikes and several large public demonstrations in protest against them. In fact, (mostly government) predictions that the scheme would create a million new jobs proved wildly optimistic and many of the original provisions have been amended and restrictions relaxed, so that the 35-hour week has generally become the 39-hour week and working practices have largely reverted to tradition, although some have changed irrevocably.

For many years, it wasn't usual practice to have scheduled coffee or tea breaks in France, but with the advent of the 35-hour week and its new 'flexibility' in scheduling, employers can (and do) establish mandatory break periods (*heures de repos*) to adapt working schedules to the new *RTT* rules. However, drinks or cigarettes can usually be taken at an employee's workplace at any time. Many workers traditionally have a two-hour lunch break, particularly in the provinces, although this is no longer standard practice in most companies. Lunch may be anything from a marathon to a quick bite at a café. Eating at your desk is generally frowned upon unless you have urgent work to complete. In Paris, lunch breaks commonly start at 13.00, while in the provinces it's usually 12.00 or 12.30.

Since the introduction of the 35-hour week, time-keeping requirements have become much more complex and nearly all employees must be tracked to ensure that weekly, monthly and annual hours and days worked don't exceed the legal limits. It may come as a nasty surprise to some foreigners to discover that many French employers (including most large companies) require employees to clock in and out of work. If you're caught cheating the clock, you can be dismissed. The working week for round-the-clock shift workers is limited to 25 hours, and night work and shift working is usually paid at higher rates as specified in collective agreements.

The good news is that weekends are sacrosanct and almost no office employees work at weekends. Even most shops are closed on Sundays.

Flexi-time

Many companies operate flexible working hours (*horaire mobile/horaire flexible*). A flexi-time system requires employees to be present between certain hours, known as the block time (*temps bloqué/heures de présence obligatoire*), e.g. from 08.30 to 11.30 and from 13.30 to 16.00. Employees may make up their required working hours by starting earlier than the required block time, reducing their lunch break or working later. Most business premises are open between around 06.30 and 19.00, and smaller companies may allow employees to work as late as they like, provided they don't exceed the maximum permitted daily working hours. Flexi-time rules are often complicated, so they may be contained in a separate set of regulations.

Overtime

In principle, if you work more than 35 hours per week, you must be paid overtime or be given time off in lieu. Employees can be asked to do overtime but cannot be compelled to do more than 130 hours per year, although this can be altered by collective agreements. The total hours worked per week mustn't exceed an average of 44 over 12 consecutive weeks or an absolute maximum of 48 hours per week.

The minimum legal pay for overtime is the normal rate plus 25 per cent for the first eight hours above the standard 35-hour week (i.e. up to 43) and plus 50 per cent for additional hours (i.e. above 43). Employees can be granted time off in lieu at overtime rates (i.e. 1.25 hours for each hour of overtime worked) instead of being paid. Employees cannot be obliged to work on Sundays unless collective agreements state otherwise. If an employee agrees to work on a Sunday, normal overtime rates apply. Official authorisation is usually required for employees to work on Sundays, and time off in lieu must be granted during the normal working week.

Salaried employees, particularly directors (*dirigeants*) and managers/executives (*cadres*), aren't generally paid overtime, although this depends on their contracts. Most categories of manager are subject to both *RTT* and maximum work time regulations, even though their work time may not be tracked on an hourly basis but measured in days per year. Directors, managers and executives generally work long hours, even allowing for their occasionally long lunch breaks, but are accorded additional holiday time to meet *RTT* requirements. For example, in Paris executives often work from 08.30 or 09.00 to 19.00 or 20.00. Senior staff in the south generally work shorter hours than those in Paris and the north, particularly on hot summer days.

Checklist

- What are the weekly working hours?

- Are you required to clock in and out of work?

- Does the employer operate a flexi-time system (see page 61)? If so, what are the fixed working hours? How early can you start? Can you carry forward extra hours worked and take time off at a later date, or carry forward a deficit and make it up later?

- Can you choose whether to take time off in lieu of overtime or be paid?

HOLIDAYS & LEAVE

Annual Holidays

French workers enjoy longer holidays than those in any other country in the world: an average of 39 days each per year compared with 24 in the UK, 17 in Australia and just 14 in the US. Under labour law, an employee is entitled to 2.5 days' paid annual holiday (congé/vacances) for each full month he works. After working for a full year, you're therefore entitled to 30 days off, which equals five weeks (including Saturdays, which are 'traditionally' counted as work days).

Legally, you earn your holiday entitlement over the course of a year that runs from 1st May to 30th April. So, if you start work in January, by 1st May you will have earned ten days of holiday, which you can take during the subsequent year (i.e. starting 1st May). By the next 1st May, you should have accrued a full five weeks of holiday, which is available to you over the next 12 months. Before starting a new job, check that any planned holidays will be honoured by your new employer. This is particularly important if they fall within your trial period (usually the first three months) or before 1st May of your first year in the job, when holidays may not be permitted.

Employers cannot include official French public holidays (see below) as annual holidays. Some collective agreements grant extra days off (usually from one to three) for long service, and many grant additional days off in lieu of overtime or to meet RTT regulations.

Employees are legally entitled to take up to four weeks' paid holiday in a single block between 1st May and 31st October, unless business needs dictate otherwise (although other agreements are possible). Most employees take a three or four-week summer holiday between July and August and one or two weeks in winter (often around the Christmas and New Year holiday period).

Traditionally, August was the sole month for summer holidays, with many businesses closing for the whole month. However, the government has been trying to encourage companies to stagger their employees' holidays throughout the summer, and it's becoming more common for employees to take their main summer holiday in July. Almost half of companies, particularly small businesses and local shops, close for the entire month of July or August, which naturally has adverse effects on the economy. When a company closes during summer, employees are obliged to take their holiday at that time. Many large manufacturers are forced to close because their component suppliers shut during this period and they don't carry large enough stocks to keep them going. Even in those companies that remain open throughout the summer, roughly half of employees are on holiday during July and August.

There are various schemes designed to assist large and low-income families to go away on holiday, including holiday vouchers (bon-vacances) and holiday savings (chèque-vacances), to which certain employers contribute. Further information is available from the Agence Nationale pour les Chèques-Vacances (ANCV, ☎ 08 25 84 43 44, 🖳 http://www.ancv.com).

Public Holidays

The only public holiday (jour férié) that an employer in France is legally obliged to grant with pay is 1st May (irrespective of which day of the week it falls on). However, most collective agreements (see page 54) allow paid holidays on some or all of the following 10 public holidays:

Date	Holiday
1st January	New Year's Day (*Nouvel An/Jour de l'An*)
March or April	Easter Monday (*Lundi de Pâques*)
1st May	Labour Day (*Fête du Travail*)
8th May	VE Day (*Fête de la Libération/Victoire 1945/Anniversaire 1945*)
May	Ascension Day (*Ascension*) – the sixth Thursday after Easter
14th July	Bastille Day (*Fête Nationale*)
15th August	Assumption (*Fête de l'Assomption*)
1st November	All Saints' Day (*Toussaint*)
11th November	Armistice Day (*Fête de l'Armistice*)
25th December	Christmas Day (*Noël*)

The Pentecost/Whit Monday holiday was officially abolished in 2004 but is still widely observed: around half of businesses closed for the day in 2005. When a holiday falls on a Saturday or Sunday, another day (e.g. the previous Friday or following Monday) isn't usually granted as a holiday instead. However, when a public holiday falls on a Tuesday or Thursday, the day before or the day after (i.e. Monday or Friday respectively) may be declared a holiday, depending on the employer. This practice is called 'making a bridge' (*faire le pont*). If a holiday falls on a Wednesday, it's common for employees to take the two preceding or succeeding days off. In May there are usually three or four public holidays and it's possible to have a two-week break while only using a few days of your annual holiday. (In some years, France virtually grinds to a halt due to the *ponts de mai*.)

All public offices, banks, post offices, etc. are closed on public holidays, when only essential work is carried out. Note that foreign embassies and consulates usually observe French public holidays **plus** their own country's national holidays.

Maternity & Paternity Leave

The family is of fundamental importance in France, and female employees are entitled to extensive employment benefits with regard to pregnancy (*grossesse*) and confinement (*couches*). Social security benefits are also generous and are designed to encourage large families (see page 333). Maternity leave (*congé maternité*) is guaranteed for all women irrespective of their length of employment. The permitted leave period is 16 weeks, six weeks prior to birth (*congé prénatal*) and ten weeks after (*congé postnatal*); leave is extended for the third and subsequent children as well as for multiple births or caesareans or other complications. A doctor may authorise additional time off, either before or after the birth, in which case a company must continue to pay your salary.

Women aren't obliged to inform their employers that they're pregnant, although if they don't they won't be entitled to benefits. It's normally to your advantage to do so in any case, as most employers are flexible regarding time off work in connection with childbirth and child care. For example, you will normally be allowed to arrive late (especially if your journey to work involves travelling on public transport) and to have more work breaks. You may also be entitled to a new chair and be exonerated from certain tasks. Employers are obliged to allow you paid time off for routine antenatal examinations. If you're breastfeeding, they must also reduce your daily work time by one hour for your child's first year, but aren't obliged to pay you for this hour.

New fathers are entitled to paternity leave (*congé paternité*) in addition to the three days off normally granted on the birth of a child (*congé de naissance* – see **Compassionate & Special Leave** below), provided they've been making health insurance contributions for at least ten months. The permitted leave period is 11 days for a single birth and 18 days for a multiple birth, which must be taken in a continuous period during the four months following the birth. You must notify your employer at least a month in advance of the days you wish to take. Employees and the self-employed can claim a daily allowance of €67,36. Fathers are entitled to a further three months' unpaid paternity leave. For more information on paternity leave, employees should contact their local CPAM or the self-employed the *caisse* to which they belong.

Parents also have the right to an additional year of unpaid parental leave (*congé parental*), which applies equally to parents of adopted children. Employees also have the right to take paid time off work to care for a sick child. The regulations allow 12 days a year for each child, although a doctor's certificate (*fiche médicale pour enfant*) must be provided.

Provided you don't extend your leave beyond the permitted period, your employer **must** allow you to return to the same job at the same or a higher salary, taking into account general increases in wages and the cost of living. See also **Sickness & Maternity Benefits** on page 332 and **Childbirth** on page 306.

Compassionate & Special Leave

Most companies provide days off for moving house, your own or a family marriage, the birth of a child, the death of a close relative, and other such events. Grounds for compassionate leave (*congé pour convenance personnelle*) are usually defined in collective agreements and may include leave to care for a seriously ill or disabled child (*congé de présence parentale*). The number of days' leave granted varies according to the event, e.g. four days off for your own wedding (but not if you get married during your regular annual holidays!) and one day off to attend a child's wedding or the funeral of a grandparent. Employees who have worked for a company for at least three years are entitled to take a year's sabbatical – naturally **without** pay!

Sick Leave

Employees in France don't receive a quota of sick days as in some countries (e.g. the US), and there's no limit to the amount of time you may take off work due to sickness or accidents. You're normally required to notify your employer immediately of sickness or an accident that prevents you from working. You must also obtain a doctor's certificate (*arrêt de travail*) on the first day of your sickness; otherwise it will count as a day's holiday. If you're off sick, you may leave home only between 10.00 and 12.00 and between 16.00 and 18.00 (these restrictions are apparently to prevent you from moonlighting). For information about sickness benefits see **Sickness & Maternity Benefits** on page 332.

Checklist

● What is the annual holiday entitlement? Does it increase with length of service?

● What are the paid public holidays? Is Monday or Friday a day off when a public holiday falls on a Tuesday or Thursday respectively?

● Will you be allowed to take any holidays already planned when you took up employment?

● Is free air travel to your home country or elsewhere provided for you and your family and, if so, how often?

INSURANCE

All employers in France are required to publish a document listing the dangers and risks to the health and safety of their employees and to provide a minimum level of health and safety insurance.

All French employees, foreign employees working for French companies and the self-employed must contribute to the French social security (*sécurité sociale*) system. Social security includes healthcare (plus sickness and maternity), treatment for injuries at work, family allowances, unemployment insurance and old age (pensions), invalidity and death benefits. Contributions are calculated as a percentage of your gross income and are deducted at source by your employer. Social security contributions are high and total an average of around 60 per cent of gross pay, some 20 per cent of which is paid by employees (the balance by employers). For details, see **Social Security** on page 323.

Health Insurance

Comprehensive health insurance is provided by the French social security system (see page 323), but many industries and professions have their own supplementary health insurance schemes (*mutuelle*) that pay the portion of medical bills not covered by social security – usually 20 or 30 per cent (see page 294). Membership may be obligatory and contributions may be paid wholly by your employer or split between you and your employer. Some employers, particularly foreign companies, provide free comprehensive private health insurance for executives, senior managers and their families. For further information about health insurance see page 339.

In addition to undergoing a medical examination before taking up employment (see page 29), you may also be examined by the company's *médecin du travail* on an annual basis, attesting to your continued fitness for your job, or may be requested to do so at any time by your employer if there's a doubt about your physical condition. A medical examination may also be necessary as a condition of membership of a company health, pension or life insurance scheme.

Salary Insurance

Salary insurance (*assurance salaire*) pays employees' salaries during periods of sickness (*congé maladie*) or after accidents and is provided under social security. After a certain number of consecutive sick days (the number varies with your employer), your salary is no longer paid by your employer but by social security, which is one reason why contributions are so high. Some employers opt to pay their employees' full salaries for a limited period in cases of extended disability or illness, in which case state benefits are paid directly to the employer rather than to the employee.

Unemployment Insurance

Unemployment insurance (*allocation d'assurance chômage*) is compulsory for employees and is covered by social security contributions. In the last few years, the government has legalised a form of private unemployment insurance for some categories of self-employed people and owner-managers of small companies who aren't eligible for state unemployment insurance. For details see **Unemployment Benefit** on page 334.

Checklist

● Is extra insurance cover provided besides obligatory insurance (see **Chapter 13**)?

● Is free life insurance provided (see page 348)?

● Is free private health insurance provided for you **and** your family (see page 339)?

● For how long will your salary be paid if you're sick or have an accident?

RETIREMENT & PENSIONS

Your employment conditions may be valid only until the official French retirement age (*retraite*), which is 60 for both men and women in most trades and professions and 65 for civil servants (although some state employees can retire on a full pension at 55 or even 50). If you wish to continue working after you've reached retirement age, you may be required to negotiate a new employment contract, although you're normally permitted to do certain types of work after retirement (e.g. of an artistic or scientific nature) provided you were practising them alongside your main job before retiring.

In addition to contributing to social security, which provides a state pension (see page 336), most employees contribute to a supplementary company pension fund (*caisse complémentaire de retraite*). Almost every trade or occupation has its own scheme and in many companies it's obligatory for employees to contribute. The rates and details vary slightly, depending on whether you contribute to the fund for managers (*cadres*) or for non-managerial workers (*non-cadres*). For further information see **Supplementary Pensions** on page 337.

Checklist

● What percentage of your salary must you pay into a pension fund (see page 336)?

● Are you required or able to pay a lump sum into the fund in order to receive a full or higher pension?

● Is the pension transferable to another employer?

● Is there a non-contributory pension fund besides the supplementary company scheme? Is it transferable and, if so, what are the conditions?

EDUCATION & TRAINING

Employee training (*formation professionnelle*) is taken seriously, whether it's conducted in your workplace or elsewhere, and employers with ten or more employees must allocate a percentage of their gross payroll to employee education and training. Employers who are keen to attract the best employees, particularly those engaged in high-tech fields, usually allocate extra funds and provide superior training schemes (large companies often spend an amount equal to around 10 per cent of their payroll on training). You're normally entitled to paid vocational training after two years with a company employing over ten people or three years with a company with fewer than ten staff and should apply at least two months in advance (four months if the training is to last more than six months). You're also entitled to unpaid time off for training (*congé individual de formation*), although your employer may postpone this for up to nine months.

Training may include management seminars, technical courses, language lessons or any other form of continuing education. If you need to learn or improve your French or another language in order to perform your job, the cost of language study is usually paid by your employer. However, not all employees benefit equally from training, which is decided by the employer. It's in your interest to investigate courses of study, seminars and lectures that you feel will be of benefit to you (and consequently to your employer). Most employers give reasonable consideration to a request to attend a course during working hours, provided you don't make it a full-time occupation. (Time spent on training must be counted as working hours for purposes of the 35-hour working week rules.) Further information about training can be found via the internet portal set up by the Centres d'Animation et de Ressources de l'Information sur la Formation (🖳 http://www.intercarif.org).

Checklist

● Will the employer provide or pay for professional training or education, if necessary abroad?

● Are free or subsidised French lessons provided for you and your spouse?

UNION MEMBERSHIP

There are numerous trade unions, many grouped into confederations, although French unions aren't as highly organised as those in many other western countries and their power and influence has been reduced considerably since the late '70s, when labour disputes and strikes (*grèves*) were common. Since then, union membership has declined dramatically, membership of the Confédération Générale du Travail (CGT) dropping from over 2.5m to around 1m today. (Other major unions are the Confédération Française des Travailleurs Chrétiens, the Confédération Française de l'Encadrement/Confédération Générale des Cadres, the Confédération Française Démocratique du Travail and the Force Ouvrière.)

Union membership includes only around a fifth of the total workforce and less than 9 per cent of the private sector workforce – the lowest proportion in the EU. Unions are strongest in traditional industries such as mining, railways and automobile manufacturing and have had little success in new high-tech industries. However, they're still capable of causing widespread disruption, as has been demonstrated in recent years.

Under French law, unions are allowed to organise on any company's premises, but 'closed shops' are banned. With the exception of some public sector employees, e.g. the police, employees have the right to strike and cannot be dismissed for striking. Even where workers don't belong to a union, their rights are protected by labour laws. All businesses with more than 11 employees must have a workers' council or a labour management committee comprising employee delegates (*délégués du personnel*) elected by and from the employees. The number of delegates increases in proportion to the number of employees, up to a maximum of 50. Delegates represent employees when they have questions or complaints for management concerning, for example, working conditions, job classification, wages, and the application of labour laws and regulations.

In companies with more than 50 employees, employee delegates must be elected to the board of directors and a labour management committee (*comité d'entreprise*) must be formed. Companies with separate locations (e.g. factories or offices) employing over 50 employees must have a local labour management committee (*comité d'établissement*), with representatives of this committee sitting on a central labour management committee (*comité central d'entreprise*).

In addition to matters relating to terms and conditions of employment, any major changes to the operation, organisation and management of a company must be discussed with the committee before they can be implemented. However, a company isn't usually required to act on the opinion of the labour management committee.

Checklist

● Is there a relevant union which you may join and, if so, what are the conditions and benefits?

● Is there a workers' council and how effective is it?

OTHER CONDITIONS

Trial & Notice Periods

For most jobs in France there's a trial period (*période d'essai*) of one to three months, depending on the type of work and the employer (three months is usual), although as a result of abuses of fixed term contracts, the government has recently allowed companies with fewer than 20 staff to give employees a two-year trial period, during which their contract can be terminated without the complications involved in terminating an indefinite term contract (see **Employment Contracts** on page 54). The trial period isn't required by law, although there's no law forbidding it. The length of a trial period is usually stated in collective agreements. During the trial period, either party may terminate the employment contract without notice or any financial penalty, unless otherwise stated in a collective agreement. If at the end of the trial period an employer hasn't decided whether he wishes to employ you permanently, he may have the right to repeat the trial period, but only once and only to the maximum period allowed by the collective agreement for the industry. After this period, if you haven't been officially dismissed, you're deemed to be hired permanently, irrespective of whether an employment contract exists.

Notice periods are governed by law and collective agreements and usually vary with length of service. The minimum notice period is usually a month for clerical and manual workers, two months for foremen and supervisors, and three months for managerial and senior technical staff. The minimum notice period for employees with over two years' service is two months.

Although many employers prefer employees to leave immediately after giving notice, employees have the right to work their notice period. However, both parties can agree that the employee receives payment in lieu (*indemnité compensatrice de préavis*) of notice. Compensation must also be made for any outstanding paid annual holidays (*indemnité compensatrice de congés payés*) up to the end of the notice period, and all terminated employees receive a redundancy payment (*indemnité de licenciement*) of some sort (see **Dismissal & Redundancy** on page 71).

A term contract (see **Employment Contracts** on page 54) can be terminated before the end of its period only in specific circumstances, i.e. when either the employer or employee has committed a serious offence (*faute grave*), due to an event beyond the control of both parties (*force majeure*), or with the agreement of both parties. Under recently passed regulations designed to modernise labour law, an employee may terminate a *CDD* without penalty if he accepts a job with an indefinite contract (i.e. a *CDI*). If an employer commits a serious offence or illegally dismisses an employee before the end of his contract, the employee is entitled to be paid in full for the remaining period of the contract, plus 10 per cent of his salary and bonuses. If an employee commits a serious offence or unilaterally breaks the contract other than to accept a *CDI* job, he may need to pay damages and loses his right to any bonuses. No compensation is payable if termination is due to *force majeure*.

Part-time Job Restrictions

Restrictions regarding part-time employment (*travail à mi-temps*) may be detailed in your employment conditions. Most companies don't allow full-time employees to work part-time (i.e. moonlight) for another employer, particularly one in the same line of business. You may, however, be permitted to take a part-time teaching job or something similar. (You could always write a book!)

Changing Jobs & Confidentiality

Companies in a high-tech or highly confidential business may have restrictions on employees moving to a competitor (*clause de non-concurrence*), although strictly these aren't legal unless the employer offers employees a financial incentive **not** to change jobs. This is a complicated subject and disputes often need to be resolved by a court of law. French laws regarding industrial secrets and general employer confidentiality are strict. If you breach this confidentiality, you may be dismissed and could be unable to find further employment in France.

Acceptance of Gifts

Employees are normally forbidden to accept gifts (*accepter des dons*) of more than a certain value from customers or suppliers. Many suppliers give bottles of wine or small gifts at Christmas that can usually be accepted without breaching this rule.

Dismissal & Redundancy

The rules governing dismissal (*licenciement*) and severance pay (*indemnité de licenciement*) depend on the size of a company, the employee's length of service, the reason for dismissal (e.g. misconduct or redundancy), and whether the employee has a protected status, such as that enjoyed by union and employee representatives, who can be dismissed only for 'gross misconduct'.

The two main reasons for dismissal are personal (*motif personnel*) and economic (*motif économique*), i.e. when a company is experiencing serious financial problems. An employee can be dismissed at any time during his trial period, usually the first one to three months, without notice or compensation (see page 70). Thereafter, you can be dismissed for personal reasons only in the case of a 'valid and serious offence' (*cause réelle et sérieuse*), e.g. stealing from an employer. It's difficult for an employer to dismiss an employee unless he has blatantly proved his total incompetence or is guilty of some form of gross misconduct.

If an employee is accused of misconduct, a strict procedure must be followed before he can be disciplined or dismissed. He must be summoned by registered letter to attend a formal preliminary hearing with the employer, during which the alleged misconduct is discussed. He has the right to bring another person to the interview, either a colleague or an employee representative (whose name must appear on an official list). If dismissal could result, the employer must mention this as a possibility during the hearing. If the employer decides that the offence warrants dismissal, there's usually a cooling-off period before he can effect the dismissal. The grounds for dismissal must be stated in the dismissal letter, which must also be sent by registered post to the employee's home address.

A dismissed employee is entitled to accrued holiday pay, severance pay if he has at least two years' service, and compensation in lieu of notice when a notice period cannot be observed. Payment must also be made in lieu of any outstanding paid holiday (*indemnité compensatrice de congés payés*) up to the end of the notice period (i.e. for earned holiday not yet used in the current year). Severance pay must equal at least 20 per cent of his average monthly salary for each year of service (i.e. 100 per cent if you've been employed for five years). Collective agreements may provide for increased severance pay. Severance pay may not be payable when an employee is dismissed for a serious breach of conduct – usually a criminal act.

If you're dismissed, you're also entitled to 'back to work assistance' (*plan d'aide au retour à l'emploi/PARE*) from your local ANPE office and, in certain cases, to a relocation grant (*aide à la mobilité géographique*). While out of work, you may claim unemployment benefit at up to 75 per cent of your previous salary for a period depending on the length of time you've contributed to unemployment insurance.

An employee dismissed for misconduct can appeal against the decision to a union or labour court. If the employer didn't abide by the law or the regulations in a particular industry, the employee can have his case heard by his union or syndicate. If there's no union, the case is heard before an industrial tribunal (*conseil des prud'hommes*) comprising both employer and employee representatives (elected by the workforce). If the employee wins the case, he is entitled to severance pay and compensation (e.g. six months' salary or more) for breach of his labour contract, but he may not be reinstated. In order to avoid the expense and publicity of legal proceedings, most employers come to an out-of-court settlement.

When an employee is dismissed for economic reasons, i.e. made redundant, the procedures are strictly regulated. As a result of several high-profile mass redundancies in recent years (notably Marks & Spencer, Danone and Moulinex) which prompted a number of demonstrations and strikes, legislation has been passed to tighten up legal requirements in an attempt to discourage further plant closures and redundancies. (Unfortunately, these measures also tend to discourage businesses from taking on new employees.) Companies intending to fire at least ten workers within a 30-day period or at least 18 workers in a year must consult the relevant administrative authorities as well as the works council or employee delegates before any steps are taken.

This also applies in the case of any planned reorganisation or the sale or transfer of ownership of any portion of the company. A company considering redundancies is obliged to table an 'employment protection plan' (*plan de sauvegarde de l'emploi*) disclosing its reorganisation and restructuring plans and their expected impact on employees. Employers must propose specific action to try to prevent redundancies, including reducing working hours, retraining and redistributing workers within the company, and offering training programmes to permit workers to find new jobs outside the company. There must also be an explicit plan for calling back workers laid off if and when the economic situation improves or new jobs are created within the restructured organisation.

If you're thinking of employing a full-time, part-time or temporary employee, take care that you don't get embroiled in French employee legislation, particularly if you wish to terminate the employment. You should get an employee to sign a written statement agreeing to the terms of the termination of employment, or you could be sued for unfair dismissal. At termination, it's customary to ask an employee to sign a receipt for amounts due (*reçu de solde de tous comptes*), although it has recently been ruled that this document doesn't limit the ex-employee's rights to claim further payments from his former employer.

Checklist

● If a dispute arises over your salary or working conditions, under the law of which country will your employment contract be interpreted?

● Is extra compensation paid if you're made redundant or fired (executives often receive a generous 'golden handshake' if they're made redundant)?

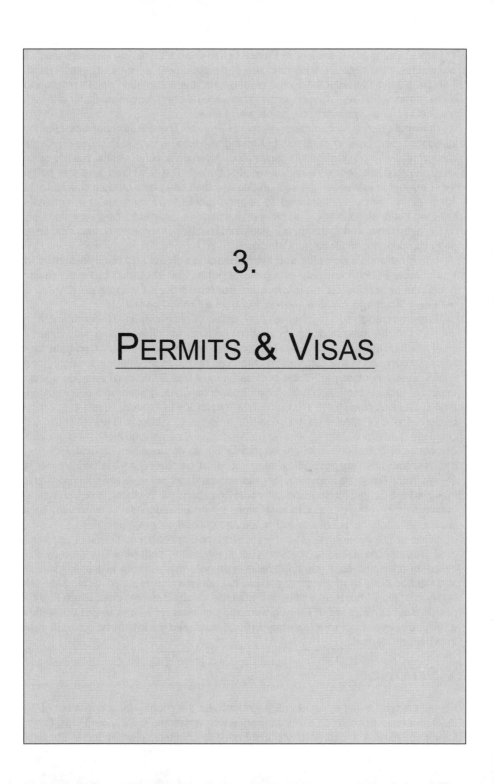

3.

PERMITS & VISAS

Before making any plans to visit France or live or work there, you must ensure that you have the necessary identity card or passport (with a visa if necessary) and, if you're planning to work there or stay long term, the appropriate documentation to obtain a residence and/or work permit. There are different requirements for different nationalities and circumstances, as detailed below.

Immigration is an inflammatory issue in France. The government has recently introduced new laws to curb non-EU immigration and is cracking down on illegal immigrants, who can be forcibly repatriated, although a controversial plan to send immigrant children 'home' was quickly abandoned. The new laws give the police wider powers to prevent illegal immigration and they can make random checks up to 40km (25mi) inside frontiers and at airports, docks, and road and rail terminals handling international traffic. Permit and visa infringements are taken very seriously by the authorities, and there are penalties for breaches of regulations, including fines and even deportation for flagrant abuses.

Immigration is a complex and ever-changing subject and the information in this chapter is intended only as a general guide. You shouldn't base any major decisions or actions on the information contained herein without confirming it with an official and reliable source, such as a French consulate.

French bureaucracy (euphemistically called *l'administration*) is legendary, and you should be prepared for frustration caused by time-wasting and blatant obstruction on the part of officials. (This isn't necessarily xenophobia – they treat their fellow countrymen in the same way!) Often you may wonder whether the right hand knows what any other part of the body is up to (it usually doesn't) and you should expect to receive conflicting information from consulates, government departments, *préfectures* and town halls. Red tape is a way of life in France, where every third person is a civil servant (*fonctionnaire*). In order to obtain a permit, you must complete numerous forms, answer dozens of irrelevant questions and provide mountains of documents with official translations to produce an impressive-looking *dossier*. When dealing with officialdom, you must persevere, as the first answer is always '*Non!*' Never take anything for granted where civil servants are concerned and make sure that you understand all communications. If in doubt, have someone translate them for you. You can sometimes speed up proceedings by employing a lawyer, although this is unusual in France and may be counterproductive.

While in France, you should carry your passport or residence permit (if you have one). You can be asked to produce your identification papers at any time by the police or other officials; if you don't have them, you can be taken to a police station and interrogated. You may carry copies, but you may be required to produce the originals within 24 hours. A residence permit serves as an identity card, which French people must carry by law. **If French bureaucracy ever threatens to get the better of you, treat yourself to a leisurely French meal and your tribulations will pale into insignificance!**

VISITORS

Foreigners who aren't resident in France can visit the country for a maximum of 90 days at a time. EU citizens can visit France with a national identity card only. Other foreigners require a passport. Visitors from EU countries plus Andorra, Canada,

Iceland, Japan, Monaco, New Zealand, Norway, Singapore, South Korea, Switzerland and the US don't require a visa, although French immigration authorities may require non-EU visitors to produce a return ticket and proof of accommodation, health insurance and financial resources. All other nationalities need a visa to visit France (see **Visas** below).

EU nationals who visit France to seek employment or start a business therefore have only 90 days in which to find a job or establish a business. If you haven't found employment and don't have sufficient funds to support yourself, your application will be refused.

If you're a non-EU national, it isn't normally possible to enter France as a visitor and change your status to that of an employee, student or resident. You must return to your country of residence and apply for a long-stay visa (see below).

Non-EU citizens (except citizens of Andorra, Monaco and Switzerland and spouses of French residents – see page 79) who are staying with friends or family must obtain a 'certificate of accommodation' (*attestation d'accueil* – formerly *certificat d'hébergement* and sometimes referred to as *attestation d'hébergement*), valid for 90 days, before departure and present it on arrival in France. Your hosts must apply for the *attestation* at their local town hall, police station or gendarmerie up to six months in advance of your arrival and post it to you.

Note that you must spend at least 90 days outside France before you're eligible for another 90-day period in the country. If you're likely to want to return and require proof that you've spent the required period abroad, you should have your passport stamped at a police station, customs office or an office of the national police (*gendarmerie*) near your point of entry into France. You should ask to make a declaration of your entry (*déclaration d'entrée sur la territoire française*). Note also that visitors may not remain in France for more than 180 days in a year.

VISAS

Visitors from EU countries plus Andorra, Canada, Iceland, Japan, Monaco, New Zealand, Norway, Singapore, South Korea, Switzerland and the US don't require a visa to enter France, either as visitors or for any other purpose. All other nationalities require a visa. Note that some countries (e.g. Ireland and Italy) allow foreigners with close ancestors (e.g. a grandfather) who were born there to apply for a passport of that country, which can allow non-EU citizens to become 'members' of the EU.

A visa is stamped in your passport, which must be valid for at least 90 days **after** the date you intend to leave France. Visas may be valid for a single entry only or for multiple entries within a limited period. There are three main types of visa, as described below.

Short-stay Visas

A short-stay visa (*visa de court séjour*, sometimes referred to as a 'Schengen Visa') is valid for 90 days and is usually valid for multiple entries as well as for free circulation within the group of EU nations that are signatories to the Schengen agreement (i.e. Austria, Belgium, Denmark, Finland, France, Germany, Greece, Italy, Luxembourg, the Netherlands, Portugal, Spain and Sweden). Another type of short-stay visa, often issued to businessmen, is a *visa de circulation*. It allows multiple stays of up to 90 days over a period of three years, with a maximum of 180 days in any calendar year. A short-stay visa costs from €25 to €50, depending on the type. Transit visas valid for three days are issued to rail and some airline passengers travelling through France.

Long-stay Visa

A non-EU national intending to remain in France for more than 90 days, whether to work, study or merely holiday, must obtain a long-stay visa (*visa de long séjour*) **before** arriving and must apply for a residence permit within a week of arrival. If you arrive without a long-stay visa, it's almost impossible to change your status after arrival and, if you wish to remain for longer than 90 days, you must return to your country of residence and apply for a long-stay visa. Non-EU parents with children aged under 18 must also obtain long-stay visas for their children. A long-stay visa isn't necessary for EU nationals planning to stay longer than 90 days in France, although they should apply for a residence permit (see page 84).

Au Pairs

To obtain a long-stay visa for an au pair position, you must usually have an agreement (*déclaration d'engagement*) with a family and a certificate of registration for French-language classes. The family or au pair agency must complete the application forms (*accord de placement au pair d'un stagiaire aide-familiale*) available from the office of the Direction Départementale du Travail et de la Main d'Oeuvre in the department where you will be resident. Two copies of the form are returned to the family or agency, one of which is forwarded to you so that you can apply for a visa. An au pair's residence permit (*permis de stagiaire aide-familiale*) is valid for six months and renewable for up to 18 months. For further information about working as an au pair, see **Au Pairs** on page 42.

Retirees

Non-EU retirees require a long-stay visa to live in France longer than 90 days and should make a visa application to their local French consulate at least four months before their planned departure date. Non-EU retirees are issued with temporary residence permits, which must be renewed each year. All non-employed residents must provide proof that they have an adequate income or financial resources (including health insurance for non-EU nationals) to live in France without working or becoming a burden on the state (see page 81).

Student Visas

There are three types of visa for non-EU nationals planning to study in France, according to the intended length of their stay:

- **Schengen Visa** – A Schengen visa allows multiple entries but is valid for three months only. Applications are made using a short-stay visa form (see **Applications** below) and the fee is the same. However, the requirements for a Schengen visa are the same as for a long-stay visa (see above).

- **Temporary Long-stay Visa** (*visa d'étudiant pour six mois avec plusieurs entrées*) – This allows multiple entries and is valid for three to six months. With this visa it's usually unnecessary to obtain a residence permit. The visa must, however, state that a residence permit is unnecessary, i.e. *le titulaire de ce visa est dispensé de solliciter une carte de séjour* or *le présent visa vaut autorisation de séjour*. Requirements are the same as for an ordinary long-stay visa (see above).

- **One-year Visa** – This visa is valid for between six months and a year but allows only a single entry. Applications are made using a temporary long-stay visa form (see above) and the fee is the same. On arrival in France, you must have a medical examination by a French doctor who is approved by the Office des Migrations Internationales (OMI) and apply for a residence permit (*carte de séjour d'étudiant*) – see **Residence Permits** on page 84.

Fiancé(e)s & Spouses

The status of the fiancé(e) or spouse of a French resident depends on the nationality of the resident, as detailed below.

Fiancé(e)s

Non-EU nationals coming to France to marry a French citizen may need to apply for a long-stay visa. France does not issue a 'fiancé visa'. If you plan to arrive in France less than three months before your marriage, it may be possible to enter France on a short-stay visa and then regularise your situation immediately after your marriage, claiming full benefit of your status as the spouse of a French national. Be sure, however, to declare your entry into France (by requesting a declaration of entry or having your passport stamped with the date you arrived).

Spouse

Non-EU nationals married to a French resident (whether of French or foreign nationality) for between 90 days and a year require a long-stay visa to enter France;

they cannot obtain an extension (beyond 90 days) if they enter France as a visitor. It's normally fairly simple for someone married to a French national to obtain a long-stay visa, simply by presenting their marriage certificate and proof of the French partner's citizenship to the appropriate consulate.

Non-EU nationals who have been married to a French resident for more than a year may be permitted to enter France as visitors and then apply for a residence permit, although a long-stay visa is recommended (check with a French consulate abroad). The foreign spouse of a French citizen is automatically granted a permanent residence permit (*carte de résident* – see page 84) provided the couple has been married for at least a year. The non-EU spouse of an EU national resident in France is granted a temporary five-year residence permit (*carte de séjour*) permitting him or her to live and work in France.

The spouse and children under 18 of a non-EU national with a visa to work in France (*visa de séjour salarié*) may usually accompany him to France, although a visa is required for each family member. Applications for visas for family members must be made at the same time as the main applicant's visa application. Family members don't have the right to work in France unless they have their own *visa de séjour salarié*.

Applications

Applications for visas must be made to the French embassy or consulate in your country of residence. (Applicants for long-stay visas living in a country other than their country of nationality must apply in their country of nationality unless they've been resident abroad for at least a year.) You can usually apply for a visa in person or by post. If you apply in person, you should bear in mind that there are long queues at consulates in major cities (take a big book to read and get there early!).

The documentation required for a visa application depends on the purpose of your visit to France. All applicants require the following:

- A passport valid for at least three months (90 days) beyond the last day of your intended stay in France.

- A ticket (or evidence of having booked a ticket) for your outward and return journey.

- The official visa application form(s), obtainable from a French consulate or via the internet (💻 http://www.service-public.fr and follow the links to '*Étrangers en France*' and then '*Entrée en France*'; the forms are listed under '*Formulaires*' – bizarrely, the forms cannot be found via the English-language version of the site!).

- A number of passport-size photographs on a white background (usually one for each application form, of which there may be up to eight!).

- A stamped, self-addressed envelope.

Depending on the purpose of the visa, some or all of the following documents are also required:

- A 'validated' copy or official translation of your birth certificate or an extract from your civil status record dated within the last three months, as well as those of your spouse and other members of your family.

- An affidavit stating that you've never been convicted of a criminal offence or declared bankrupt.

- Evidence of accommodation: e.g. the title deeds to a property, a rental agreement or a 'certificate of accommodation' (*attestation d'accueil*) from a French family or friends with whom you will be staying (see page 77).

- Evidence of financial independence, which may take the form of bank statements, letters from banks confirming arrangements for regular transfers of funds from abroad, letters from family or friends guaranteeing regular support. Letters should be notarised (witnessed by a public notary). Students should have evidence of funds of at least €600 per month or €400 per month if their accommodation is free, in which case they should submit a letter from an organisation or institution guaranteeing accommodation or evidence of a scholarship or grant. Evidence of financial independence isn't required by someone coming to France to take up paid employment, who must of course be able to supply an employment contract or equivalent (see below). Retirees must provide a copy of a pension book or other proof of regular income or confirmation from a French bank that their monthly income is no less than €500 per head.

- If you're a non-EU national taking up employment in France, a work contract (*certificat d'emploi*) approved by the French Ministry of Labour or the District Labour Department where the business is registered. This must be obtained by the prospective employer in France and sent to the Agence Nationale d'Accueil des Etrangers et des Migrations (ANAEM, ☎ 01 53 69 53 70, 🖳 http://www.anaem. social.fr – a fusion of the Office des Migrations Internationales and the Service Social d'Aide aux Emigrants) for transmission to the appropriate French consulate abroad.

- An undertaking not to engage in any occupation without authorisation (on plain, unheaded paper and signed by you).

- A medical certificate by an OMI-approved doctor, which is necessary for most long-term visa applicants, including employees and their family members, students and au pairs. The examination must be carried out within three months of your taking up residence in France. Applicants must pay a fixed fee.

- A health insurance certificate if you aren't eligible for health treatment under French social security (see page 323) and your stay is for less than six months. **Note that some foreign insurance companies don't provide sufficient cover to satisfy French regulations, and you should check the minimum cover necessary with a French consulate in your country of residence and obtain a letter from your insurance company confirming that your policy is valid in France.** (If you intend to stay longer than six months and you're under 28, you must join the French social security system, which must be done when applying for your residence permit – see page 84.)

- If you're a student, proof of admission from an approved educational establishment, stating that you will be studying for at least 20 hours per week. This is usually a letter of admission (*attestation de pré-inscription*), when registering for the first time, or other evidence of registration (e.g. *certificat/autorisation d'inscription*), depending on the level and type of studies.

- An agreement (*déclaration d'engagement*) with a French family and a certificate of registration for French-language classes if you're an au pair (see page 42).

- A marriage certificate if you're a non-EU national married to a French resident (see page 524).

- Written authorisation from a parent or guardian if you're under 18. (Additional documents are also required by non-EU students under 18.)

Documents should be translated into French, and translations must be made by a translator approved by your local consulate, a list of whom (*liste de traducteurs*) is provided on request by French consulates.

Students on a scholarship from the French government or a foreign government, or on an EU study programme or one arranged by a recognised international organisation require only a valid passport, completed visa application forms, photographs and a letter confirming the value of the grant and the duration of their intended stay. There's no charge for a visa for students on a scholarship.

If you require a visa to enter France and attempt to enter without one, you will be refused entry. If you're in doubt as to whether you require a visa, enquire at a French consulate before making travel plans or go to the website of the Ministère des Affaires Etrangères (🖳 http://www.diplomatie.gouv.fr), where you can enter information about your situation to find the visa you require (on the English-language version of the site, click on 'Entering France'). Other useful sites include that of Invest in France (🖳 http://www.afii.fr – in English), which has general information on settling in France as well as details about visas; and 🖳 http://www.edufrance.fr, which contains general information about studying in France, including visa requirements for students.

Visa applications usually take six to eight weeks to be approved, although they can take much longer and you should allow at least three months.

WORK PERMITS

The following information is of a general nature. For further details, contact your country's embassy in France or the commercial attaché at a French consulate. See also **Starting a Business** on page 46 and **Information** on page 50.

EU Nationals

EU nationals don't require a work permit; a residence permit (see page 84) gives them the right to live and work in France, although even this may not be necessary. Restrictions to the rights to work of nationals of the eight countries that joined the EU in May 2004 were lifted on 1st May 2006, but it's expected that nationals of Bulgaria and Romania, which are due to join the EU in January 2007, will initially have restricted access to the French job market.

Non-EU Nationals

A combined residence and work permit (*carte unique de séjour et de travail* or *carte de séjour salarié*) is issued to non-EU nationals coming to France to take up permanent employment. When you arrive, you have two months in which to apply for a temporary residence permit (*carte de séjour temporaire salarié* – see **Temporary Residence Permit** below) while your application for a *carte unique de séjour et de travail* or *carte de séjour salarié* is being processed (French bureaucracy at its inimitable best). To obtain this, you must present the following:

- A completed long-stay visa (*visa de long séjour*) application form (see page 78).

- An 'introductory' employment contract (a contract submitted by the employer stating that the position has been registered with the national employment agency and other relevant authorities).

- A medical certificate (from an examination carried out by an OMI-approved doctor).

Non-EU nationals wishing to start or manage a business or undertake any commercial activity in France must obtain a business permit (*carte de commerçant*). Business permits aren't required by holders of permanent residence permits (*carte de résident*), owners and investors in companies (not managers), and self-employed workers performing a service (rather than a commercial activity). An application for a business permit should be made abroad at a French consulate when applying for a visa. Your residence permit is stamped *non-salarié, profession libérale* and you aren't permitted to work as a salaried employee in France. If you're already resident in France, you can apply for a business permit at your local town hall or *préfecture*. You must provide details relating to the incorporation of the prospective business, a detailed description of the proposed business activity, proof of financial resources, and an affidavit stating that you've never been convicted of a criminal offence or declared bankrupt. It can take up to six months to obtain a business permit, although a temporary permit can be issued within a shorter period.

Students

After completing their first year of study, students can obtain a temporary work permit (*autorisation provisoire de travail*) for part-time (*mi-temps*) work, provided they have a residence permit (see page 84) and are attending an educational institution that provides students with French social security health cover or a scholarship (*bourse*). They may work for a maximum total of 884 hours per year, which averages 19.5 hours per week for 52 weeks.

To apply for a work permit, you must submit your student card (*carte d'étudiant*) and residence permit, and a letter from the prospective employer (stating his name and address, the job title and description, salary, working hours, place of work and length of employment) to your local Direction Départementale du Travail et de l'Emploi. Secondary and technical school students under the age of 18 also need a letter of authorisation from their parents and a *certificat de scolarité*. (Written parental consent is required for anyone under 18 wishing to work in France.)

RESIDENCE PERMITS

In general, all foreigners remaining in France for longer than 90 days in succession (for any reason) require a residence permit (*titre de séjour*). Where applicable, a residence permit holder's dependants are also granted a permit. Children can be listed on a parent's permit until the age of 18, although they require their own residence permit at the age of 16 if they're working. Different types of residence permit are issued according to your status, including permits for long-stay visitors (*visiteur*), salaried employees (*salarié*), transferees (*détaché*), family members (*membre de famille*), students (*étudiant*) and traders (*commerçant*). A combined residence and work permit (*carte unique de séjour et de travail* or *carte de séjour salarié*) is issued to non-EU nationals taking up permanent employment in France (see page 83).

There are two main categories of residence permit in France: a *carte de séjour* and a *carte de résident*. The *carte de séjour* is referred to below as a temporary residence permit and the *carte de résident* as a permanent residence permit.

Temporary Residence Permits

Until November 2003, a temporary residence permit (*carte de séjour*) was required by all foreigners aged 18 and above, both EU and non-EU nationals, who were to remain in France for more than 90 days (around 120,000 are issued each year). A new law (called the *loi Sarkozy*) is generally believed to have waived the requirement for EU citizens to obtain a *carte de séjour*, although the actual wording of the law is ambiguous. EU citizens are therefore advised to contact their departmental *préfecture* in order to check whether a *carte de séjour* is required – particularly as you can be fined up to €1,500 for failing to apply for one! The information below is provided on the assumption that a *carte de séjour* is required. **In any case, whether or not you require a *carte de séjour*, you must meet the criteria for residence, i.e. adequate financial means of support and, unless you qualify for state health benefits, private health insurance.**

The period of validity of a temporary residence permit varies according to your circumstances, as described below. Note, however, that a temporary residence permit automatically becomes invalid if you spend over six months outside France and it can be revoked at any time if you no longer meet the conditions for which it was issued (or if you obtained a permit fraudulently). After three years of continuous residence in France, the holder of a temporary residence permit can obtain a permanent residence permit (see below).

EU Nationals

Unless advised otherwise (see above), EU nationals who are or will be working in France are issued with residence permits (*carte de séjour de ressortissant d'un état membre de l'UE*) valid for ten years and automatically renewable for further ten-year periods.

EU nationals who are unemployed and have no proof of income are issued with a one-year temporary residence permit, provided they have the means to support themselves during this period.

Pensioners and other EU nationals who wish to live in France without working receive residence permits valid for five years, provided they can provide proof that they have sufficient income or financial resources not to be a burden on the state. Retirees have their permit stamped 'retired' (*retraité*), allowing for automatic social security cover.

Non-EU Nationals

Non-EU employees must apply for a temporary residence permit (*carte de séjour temporaire salarié*) within two months of arrival. This is valid for a maximum of a year and can be renewed two months before its expiry date, upon application and presentation of a new employment contract or verification of your continued employment. If you're taking up long-term employment, you must apply for a *carte unique de séjour et de travail* or a *carte de séjour salarié* (see page 83).

Employees transferred to a French company for a limited period (*statut détaché*) may not stay longer than 18 months initially, with a possible extension to 27 months. If you're taking up employment for less than a year, your permit is valid only for the period of employment. The permit has the annotation *salarié* or the professional activity for which the contract was approved and lists the department(s) where the holder can be employed.

Non-EU spouses of EU nationals or French residents are granted a five-year residence permit (*carte de séjour*) permitting them to live and work in France. Dependants of non-EU nationals are entitled to a temporary residence permit marked '*vie privée et familiale*', prohibiting them from working in France.

Students

Students on a one-year visa (see page 79) should apply for a student's residence permit (*carte de séjour d'étudiant*), which is valid for a further year and can be renewed annually for the duration of the course. Students who have studied in France for the preceding two years and have a parent who has lived in France for at least four years don't require a permit.

Permanent Residence Permit

A permanent residence permit (*carte de résident*) is usually issued to foreigners who have lived in France for three consecutive years (the exception is the foreign spouse of a French resident, who's automatically granted a permanent residence permit after one year of marriage – see page 79) and speak fluent French. It's valid for ten years and renewable provided the holder can furnish proof that he's practising a profession in France or has sufficient financial resources to maintain himself and his dependants. A permanent residence permit authorises the holder to undertake any professional activity (subject to qualifications and registration) in any French department, even if employment was previously forbidden. See also **Citizenship** on page 510.

Applications

An application for a residence permit must be made to the *préfecture de police* in towns that have them and otherwise to your local town hall (*mairie*) in small towns or the police (*gendarmerie/commissariat de police*) in large towns and cities. If permits aren't issued locally, you will be referred to the Direction de la Réglementation of your department's *préfecture* or the nearest *sous-préfecture*. In large towns and cities, many police stations have a foreigners' office (*bureau des étrangers*). In Paris, applications must be made to the appropriate police centre (*centre d'accueil des étrangers*) for the area (*arrondissement*) where you live. Centres are open from 08.45 to 16.30 Mondays to Fridays.

Students should apply to their local town hall or *préfecture*. (There's a special counter at the *préfecture* in Paris.) It's also worthwhile obtaining a student card (*carte d'étudiant*), which entitles you to certain privileges. Contact your school or university for details of how to apply.

If you arrive in France with a long-stay visa, you must apply for a residence permit within a week. EU nationals who visit France with the intention of finding employment or starting a business have 90 days in which to find a job and apply for a residence permit, if applicable. If you don't have a regular income or adequate financial resources, the application will be refused. **Failure to apply for a residence permit within the specified period is a serious offence and can result in a fine.** Note also that it isn't possible to obtain a residence permit while living in temporary accommodation such as a hotel or caravan site.

Documents

You will be notified of the documentation required to apply for a residence permit, which depends on your situation and nationality (and on the issuing office!). The following documents are usually required by all applicants, including those from EU countries (if applicable):

● A valid passport, with a long-stay visa if necessary, or a national identity card (EU countries only)*.

- A 'validated' copy or official translation of your birth certificate or an extract from your civil status record dated within the last three months*.

- A number (usually three) of black and white (white background) or colour passport-size photographs*.

- Proof of residence, which may consist of a copy of a lease or purchase contract or a utility bill. If you're a lodger, the owner must provide an *attestation d'accueil* confirming that you're resident in his home (see page 77).

- Two stamped, self-addressed envelopes.

- Evidence of financial independence (see page 81).

- Details of your French bank account.

- Evidence of health insurance or a medical certificate from an OMI-approved doctor if you aren't covered by French social security. British retirees must produce a form E121 available from the DSS Overseas Branch. If you're covered by French social security, you must produce your social security number.

* If you're accompanied by any dependants, they also require a passport, birth certificate and photographs. (Note that British dependants must have their own passport irrespective of their age.)

In addition to the above, you will be required to produce the following, as appropriate:

- A marriage or divorce certificate or other papers relating to your marital status (this isn't usually required by EU nationals, but British applicants require a copy of their marriage certificate because the maiden name of a married woman isn't included in a British passport). The spouse of a French citizen or of a foreigner resident in France must produce his or her marriage certificate and proof of nationality or legal residence of the spouse when applying for a residence permit.

- An employment contract or letter of employment if you're taking up employment in France (see page 54).

- A pre-registration or admission letter to an educational institution and/or a student's card if you're a student.

- An au pair contract (see page 42) and a certificate of registration for French-language classes if you're an au pair.

- Evidence of adequate financial resources (e.g. a copy of a pension book or other proof of regular income or confirmation from a French bank that your monthly income is no less than €500 per head) and private health insurance if you're a retiree or not working.

If you don't have the required documents, you will be sent away to obtain them. Certain documents must be translated by a notarised translator (listed under *Traducteurs – Traductions Officielles Certifiées* in the yellow pages), but you shouldn't have documents translated in advance, as the requirements often vary with the area or office and your nationality and you might be wasting your time and money.

You will be given a date (usually from 2 to 12 weeks after your application) when you can collect your permit (usually from the *préfecture de police*). In the meantime, or if it isn't possible to issue a residence permit immediately, you're given a temporary authorisation (*récipissé de demande de carte de séjour* or an *attestation d'application de résidence*) valid for up to three months and renewable. You should keep this as evidence that you've applied for your residence permit.

An initial *carte de séjour* costs €220 (€55 for students), a renewal or change (see below) €55. Certain categories of person are exempt from these charges, including those on temporary work contracts and those who have stayed regularly in France for at least five years.

Renewals

An application for renewal of a residence permit should be made one or two months before its expiry date. When you renew your residence permit, you must reconfirm your status and provide documentary evidence, as for the original application (see above). For renewal of a *carte unique de séjour et de travail* or a *carte de séjour salarié*, you may be asked to provide proof that you've declared your income and paid your taxes for the previous year. If you're applying for a renewal of your residence permit and don't have all the necessary documents, you can apply for an extension (*prolongation*).

If you're a student wishing to renew a residence permit, you require a certificate stating that you've attended classes during the past year and passed your exams (*certificat d'assiduité*).

Retirees and other non-employed people can renew their permits for additional five-year periods provided they can prove that they still have adequate financial resources and private health insurance.

There's a fee for the renewal of a residence permit (which varies according to the type of permit), paid in the form of tax stamps (*timbres fiscaux*), which you purchase at a tobacconist's (*tabac*).

If a renewal is refused, you must leave France when your permit expires.

Changes

If your circumstances change, you must inform the authorities so that your residence permit can be updated. If you move house, you must inform the town hall with jurisdiction over your new place of residence and produce proof of your new address. This is particularly important if you're in the process of renewing your residence permit, as the change of address must be recorded before a new permit can be issued.

If you're a non-EU national and want the status of your residence permit changed to allow you to work in France, you must undergo a process called *régularisation*. An application must be made to the *préfecture* with proof of residence, a written job offer, and a letter explaining why a French or EU national cannot do the job. The application is sent to the Direction Départementale du Travail for approval, which can take up to six months to obtain.

There's a fee for having a residence permit changed (which varies according to the type of permit), paid in the form of tax stamps (*timbres fiscaux*), which you purchase at a tobacconist's (*tabac*).

4.

ARRIVAL

On arrival in France, your first task is to negotiate immigration and customs. In order to do so, you must have obtained in advance any necessary visas and permits (see **Chapter 3**). Once you've been allowed to enter the country, you may need to register with your embassy or consulate and may want to find local sources of information, advice and help. This chapter contains information on all these topics, as well as handy checklists of tasks that must be completed before your arrival in France, or soon after.

IMMIGRATION

France is a signatory to the Schengen agreement (named after a Luxembourg village on the Moselle River where the agreement was signed), which came into effect on 1st January 1995 and introduced an open-border policy between certain EU member countries. These are Austria, Belgium, France, Germany, Greece, Iceland, Italy, Luxembourg, the Netherlands, Portugal, Spain and Sweden. Under the agreement, immigration checks and passport controls take place when you first arrive in a Schengen country, after which you can travel freely between them. This means that, when you arrive in France from another Schengen country, there are usually no immigration checks or passport controls. (Note that this doesn't apply if you're arriving from the UK.)

Nnon-EU nationals arriving by air or sea from outside the EU must go through immigration (*police des frontières*) for non-EU citizens. **If you require a visa to enter France and attempt to enter without one, you will be refused entry** (see page 77). If you have a single-entry visa, it will be cancelled by the immigration official. If you think you will need to prove your date of entry, you should obtain a declaration of entry (*déclaration d'entrée sur le territoire*); it's wise to obtain one in any case.

Immigration officials may ask non-EU visitors to produce a return ticket, proof of accommodation, health insurance and financial resources (e.g. cash, travellers' cheques and credit cards). If you're a non-EU national coming to France to work, study or live, you may be asked to show documentary evidence (see page 80). The onus is on visitors to show that they won't violate French law. Immigration officials aren't required to prove that you will breach the law and can refuse you entry on the grounds of suspicion only. Young people may be more susceptible to interrogation, especially ones with 'strange' attire, and should therefore carry international credit or charge cards, a return or onward travel ticket, a student identity card, and a letter from an employer or college stating the purpose of their visit.

French immigration officials are usually polite and efficient, although they're occasionally a little over-zealous in their attempts to exclude illegal immigrants.

CUSTOMS

Those arriving from outside the EU (including EU citizens) are subject to customs checks and limitations on what may be imported duty-free. The shipment of personal (household) effects to France from another EU country isn't subject to customs formalities, although an inventory must be provided. There are no restrictions on the import or export of French or foreign banknotes or securities, although if you enter or leave France with €10,000 or more in cash or negotiable instruments (see page 353), you must make a declaration to French customs.

Information about duty-free allowances can be found on page 505, the import of pets on page 526 and that of vehicles on page 93. If you require general information about customs regulations or have specific questions, contact the Centre Renseignement des Douanes (☎ 08 25 30 82 63, 💻 http://www.douanes.gouv.fr) or your nearest customs office. The website lists local and regional customs office addresses.

Visitors

If you're visiting France (i.e. for less than 90 days), your belongings aren't subject to duty or VAT and may be imported without formality, provided their nature and quantity doesn't imply any commercial aim. This applies to the import of private cars, camping vehicles (including trailers and caravans), motorcycles, aircraft, boats (see below) and personal effects. All means of transport and personal effects imported duty-free mustn't be sold, loaned or given away in France and must be re-exported before the end of the 90-day period.

If you enter France from another Schengen country (see above), you may drive (at a walking pace) through the border without stopping. However, any goods and pets that you're carrying mustn't be the subject of any prohibition or restriction (see page 92). Customs officials may stop anyone for a spot check, e.g. for drugs or illegal immigrants. If you enter France from Spain – particularly if you're a single male in an old car – your vehicle is likely to be searched and 'inspected' by a sniffer dog. Occasionally you will come across an obstructive customs officer who will insist on inspecting everything in your car, and unfortunately there's nothing you can do to prevent him.

If you arrive at a seaport by private boat, there are no particular customs formalities, although you must show the boat's registration papers if asked. If you arrive at a river port or land border with a boat, you may be asked to produce registration papers for the boat and its outboard motor(s). A foreign-registered boat may remain in France for a maximum of six months in a calendar year, after which it must be re-exported or permanently imported (and duty and tax paid).

Non-EU Nationals

If you're a non-EU national planning to take up permanent or temporary residence, you're permitted to import your furniture and personal effects free of duty. These include vehicles, mobile homes, pleasure boats and aircraft. However, to qualify for duty-free importation, articles must have been owned and used for at least six months. Value added tax must be paid on items owned for less than six months that weren't purchased within the EU. If goods were purchased within the EU, a VAT receipt must be produced.

To import personal effects, an application must be made to the Direction Régionale des Douanes in the area where you will be resident. Customs clearance can be carried out by a customs office in an internal town in France, rather than at the border, in which case you should obtain a certificate (*carte de libre circulation*) proving that you've declared your belongings on entry into France and are entitled to travel with them.

All items should be imported within a year of the date of your change of residence – in one or a number of consignments, although it's best to have one consignment only. After a year's residence in France, you must pay French VAT (*TVA*) on further imports from outside the EU, except in certain circumstances, such as property resulting from an inheritance. A complete inventory of items to be imported (even if they're imported in a number of consignments) must be provided for customs officials, together with proof of residence in your former country and proof of settlement in France. If there's more than one consignment, subsequent consignments should be cleared through the same customs office.

If you use a removal company to transport your belongings, it will usually provide the necessary forms and take care of the paperwork. Many of the forms are now available online, either through the Customs website (🖳 http://www.douane. gouv.fr) or by following the links on the Service Public site (🖳 http://www.service-public.fr). If the removal company packs your belongings, ask for the containers to be marked 'Mover Packed'; this will speed the customs clearance process.

Always keep a copy of forms and communications with customs officials – both in France and in your previous or permanent country of residence. An official record of the export of valuables from any country will allow you to re-import them later.

Prohibited & Restricted Goods

Certain goods are subject to special regulations, and in some cases their import (and export) is prohibited or restricted. This applies in particular to animal products, plants (see below), wild fauna and flora and products derived from them, live animals, medicines and medical products (except for prescribed medicines), guns and ammunition, certain goods and technologies with a dual civil/military purpose, and works of art and collectors' items. If you're unsure whether any goods you're importing fall into the above categories, you should check with French customs.

To import certain types of plant, you must obtain a phytosanitary health certificate (*certificat sanitaire*). Details of the types of plant for which a certificate is required and how to obtain one can be obtained from a regional Service de la Protection des Végétaux or your country's customs department.

If you make it through customs unscathed with your car loaded to the gunwales with illicit goods, don't be too quick to break out the champagne in celebration: France has 'flying' customs officials (*douane volante*) with the power to stop and search vehicles at random anywhere within its borders (they often stop vehicles at motorway toll stations and roundabouts on trunk roads).

REGISTRATION

All foreigners intending to remain in France for longer than 90 days must register with the local authorities within a week of arrival and obtain a residence permit, although this may not be necessary for EU nationals. **Failure to apply for a residence**

permit, if required, within 90 days is a serious offence and may result in a fine.
For further information see **Residence Permits** on page 84.

Nationals of some countries must register with their local embassy or consulate after taking up residence. Even if registration isn't mandatory, most embassies like to keep a record of their country's citizens resident in France (it helps them to justify their existence) and it can be to your benefit (e.g. in a national or international crisis).

FINDING HELP

One of the biggest difficulties facing new arrivals in France is how and where to find help with day-to-day problems, particularly as many administrative matters are handled at a regional, departmental or even local level rather than nationally. The availability of local information varies according to your employer, the town or area where you live (e.g. residents of Paris are better served than those living in rural areas), your nationality, your French proficiency (there's an abundance of information available in French, but little in English and other foreign languages) and to some extent your sex (women are better served than men through numerous women's clubs). You should exploit the following sources of local information as well as social clubs (see page 427).

Company

Some companies, particularly international companies, employ staff to help new arrivals or contract this job out to a relocation consultant (see page 104). However, most French employers are totally unaware of (or uninterested in) the problems and difficulties faced by foreign employees and their families.

Colleagues & Friends

In France it isn't what you know, but who you know that can make all the difference between success and failure. String-pulling (i.e. the use of contacts) is widespread, and when it comes to breaking through the numerous layers of bureaucracy, a telephone call on your behalf from a French neighbour or colleague can work wonders. Any contact can be of help, even professionals such as a bank manager or insurance agent (in many cases, such people will become friends). **But take care!** Although colleagues and friends can often offer advice and invariably mean well, you're likely to receive much irrelevant and even inaccurate information, and you should check everything you're told for yourself.

Local Community

Your local community is usually an excellent source of reliable information, but you usually need to speak French to benefit from it. Your town hall (*mairie*), which is often the local registry of births, deaths and marriages, passport office, land registry, council office, citizens' advice bureau and tourist office, should be your first port of call for most kinds of local information, although even there you may not be given accurate or relevant information.

Embassy or Consulate

Most embassies and consulates provide their nationals with local information including details of lawyers, interpreters, doctors, dentists, schools, and social and expatriate organisations, although some are more helpful than others (the British Embassy in Paris is particularly unapproachable). The American Embassy has a particularly good website (🖳 http://www.amb-usa.fr – click on 'Guide for American Citizens Residing in France'), which includes a good deal of information (in English) about living and working in France, including lists of English-speaking professionals, from doctors to private investigators. Much of the information comes from their popular *Blue Book*, which can be downloaded from the site or obtained from the US Embassy (☎ 08 10 26 46 26).

Hand-holding Services

A number of English-speaking expatriates offer 'hand-holding' services to new arrivals. As with any service provider, some are worth their weight in gold while others are a complete waste of time and money, so it's essential to ask for and follow up references before paying a joining or annual membership fee (typically around €100 each). Services may range from help with house hunting and buying to finding tradesmen and completing tax returns. An extensive and well established network of hand-holding services is the Granny Network (☎ 02 51 98 23 96, 🖳 http://www. grannynetwork.com), which operates in 13 areas of France.

Expatriate Organisations

There's usually at least one English-language expatriate organisation in major French cities; in Paris foreigners are well served by English-speaking clubs and organisations (see below) and there are several Anglophone organisations in the Bordeaux area. Contacts can be found through many expatriate magazines and newspapers (see page 498). An English-speaking counsellor in certain parts of France can be found via 🖳 http://www.counsellinginfrance.com.

In Paris, the American Church (☎ 01 40 62 05 00, 🖳 http://www.acparis.org), runs an annual newcomer's orientation series in October called 'Bloom Where You Are Planted'. The programme is designed to help foreigners adjust to life in France and consists of seminars on topics such as overcoming culture shock, survival skills, personal and professional opportunities, networking, enjoying France and its food, fashion, travel and wine. The capital also houses The Association of American Wives of Europeans (☎ 01 40 70 11 80, ✉ aawe@aaweparis.org), which is a member of the Federation of American Women's Clubs Overseas (FAWCO), the Association France Grande-Bretagne (☎ 01 55 78 71 71), whose aim is to foster links between the two nations, The British & Commonwealth Women's Association (☎ 01 47 20 50 91, 🖥 http://www.bcwa.org), and WICE (☎ 01 45 66 75 50, 🖥 http://www.wice-paris.org), an anglophone expatriate organisation which operates a 'Living in France' programme for newcomers.

Associations outside the capital include Anglophones Pau-Pyrénées (🖥 http://pau.anglophones.com), the Association France Grande-Bretagne Cannes (☎ 04 93 99 04 28) and the Mulhouse English Speaking Society (☎ 03 89 66 56 80). There are French 'versions' of the Round Table and 41 Club associations – La Table Ronde Française (🖥 http://www.trfr.asso.fr) and Le Club 41 Français (🖥 http://www.club41 francais.asso.fr) – which may have English-speaking members.

The British Community Committee publishes a free *Digest of British and Franco-British Clubs, Societies and Institutions,* available from British consulates in France (see **Appendix A**). An organisation offering bespoke directories of local information is Purple Pages (France ☎ 05 45 29 59 74 or UK ☎ 0871-900 8305, 🖥 http://www.purplepages.info). Directories covering the Brittany, Normandy, Provence-Alpes-Côte d'Azur and Poitou-Charentes regions and the departments of Dordogne, Lot and Lot-et-Garonne are available in book form under the series title *Lifeline* (Survival Books – see page 587). Other local and regional organisations are listed in *The Best Places to Buy a Home in France* (Survival Books – see page 587).

AVF

An organisation of particular interest to foreigners moving to France is the Union Nationale des Accueils des Villes Françaises (AVF). The AVF is a national organisation comprising over 600 local volunteer associations, which provide a welcome for individuals and families and help them to settle into their new environment. Each association operates a centre where information and advice is available free of charge. The address of local associations can be found on the AVF website (🖥 http://www.avf-accueil.com), where some information is available in English and there's a list of groups in each department as well as details such as whether information and services are available in English. Groups often contain at least one fluent English-speaker. Foreigners planning to move to France can obtain information about particular areas from the Union Nationale des AVF, Relations Internationales (☎ 01 47 70 45 85, 🖥 http://www.avf.asso.fr).

CIRA

If you don't know which administrative department to contact for particular information (which is often the case in France), you can ask your local Centre Interministériel de Renseignements Administratifs (CIRA). As its name suggests, CIRA is a 'pan-governmental' organisation, which can answer questions on a range of subjects, including employment, finance, accommodation, health, consumer affairs, the environment and education. There are nine information centres (in Bordeaux, Lille, Limoges, Lyon, Marseille, Metz, Paris, Rennes and Toulouse) but one central telephone number (☎ 08 21 08 09 10 or simply ☎ 3939).

Publications

A useful reference book is the *Guide des Sources d'Information*, published by the Centre de Formation et de Perfectionnement des Journalistes (CFPJ), which will direct you to a variety of information sources. Lists of useful publications are included in **Appendix A**.

The Disabled

Disabled people can obtain advice and help from the Association des Paralysés de France (☎ 01 40 78 69 00, 🖥 http://www.apf.asso.fr), which isn't only for those who are paralysed, the Association pour Adultes et Jeunes Handicappés (APAJH, ☎ 01 48 74 91 59, 🖥 http://www.apajh.org) and the Fédération Nationale des Accidentés de Travail et des Handicappés (☎ 04 77 49 42 42, 🖥 http://www.fnath.org). See also **Disabled People** on page 515.

Disabled people looking for work or employment-related information should contact the Association Gestion du Fonds d'Insertion Personnes Handicappées (AGEFIPH, 🖥 http://www.agefiph.asso.fr, which provides contact details for the 18 regional associations).

If you're seriously and permanently disabled, you should apply to the Commission Technique d'Orientation et de Reclassement Professionel (COTOREP) for an invalidity card (*carte d'invalidité civile*), which entitles you to a number of benefits.

CHECKLISTS

Before Arrival

The following checklist contains a summary of the tasks that should be completed (if possible) before your arrival in France:

- Obtain a visa, if necessary, for you and your family members (see **Chapter 3**). Obviously this **must** be done before arrival.

- Visit France before your move to compare communities and schools and to arrange schooling for your children (see **Chapter 9**).

- Find temporary or permanent accommodation.

- Arrange for shipment of your personal effects (see page 114).

- Arrange health insurance for yourself and your family (see page 339). This is essential if you don't have a private insurance policy and won't be covered by French social security.

- Obtain an International Driving Permit (IDP), if necessary (see page 253).

- Open a bank account and transfer funds (you can open an account with many French banks while abroad). It's wise to obtain some euros before arriving, as this will save you having to queue to change money on arrival.

- If you don't already have one, obtain an international credit or charge card, which may be useful during your first few months, particularly until you've opened a bank account. Note, however, that credit cards aren't universally accepted in France, particularly those without a microchip.

- Don't forget to bring all your family's official documents, including birth certificates, driving licences, marriage certificate, divorce papers or death certificate (if a widow or widower), educational diplomas, professional certificates and job references, school records and student identity cards, employment references, copies of medical and dental records, bank account and credit card details, insurance policies and receipts for any valuables. You will also need the documents necessary to obtain a residence permit (see page 84).

- If you don't already speak it fluently, learn as much French as possible (see **Language Courses** on page 209).

After Arrival

The following checklist contains a summary of tasks to be completed after arrival in France (if not done before):

- On arrival at a French airport or port, have your visa cancelled and your passport stamped, as applicable.

- If you aren't taking a car with you, you may wish to rent one for a week or two until buying one locally (see page 286). Note that it's practically impossible to get around in rural areas without a car.

- Apply for a residence permit at your local town hall or *préfecture* within a week of your arrival (see page 84).

- Register with your local embassy or consulate (see page 95).

- Make sure that your employer has applied for a social security card as soon as you start working (see page 323).

- Give the details of your bank account to your employer and anyone else who may be paying you.

- Arrange schooling for your children (see **Chapter 9**).

- Find a local doctor and dentist (see **Chapter 12**).

- Arrange necessary insurance (see **Chapter 13** and **Car Insurance** on page 255).

- Introduce yourself to your local mayor and invite your neighbours for an *apéritif* within a few weeks of your arrival. This is particularly important in villages and rural areas if you want to be accepted and become part of the community.

5.

ACCOMMODATION

In most areas of France, accommodation (to buy or rent) isn't difficult to find, although there are a few exceptions. For example, in Paris, rental accommodation is in high demand and short supply and rents can be astronomical. Property prices and rents vary considerably with the region and city. For example, €100,000 will buy you a small detached modern house or a large property in need of renovation in Normandy or Brittany, Limousin or Poitou-Charentes but only a tiny studio flat in Paris or a one-bedroom apartment on the Côte d'Azur; a 50m² (500ft²) two-bedroom apartment in a reasonable area of Paris will cost you between €1,000 and €2,000 per month to rent but around 50 per cent less in a provincial city such as Bordeaux. In fact, property in Paris and on the French Riviera is among the most expensive in the world, although prices are reasonable in most other regions. In cities and large towns, apartments are much more common than houses, particularly in Paris, where houses are rare and prohibitively expensive.

In rural areas there's a depopulation crisis due to the mass exodus of people from the land to the cities and factories in the last 30 years. Provincial France is losing its population to the cities at the rate of around 100,000 people a year. It's estimated that one in every 12 properties is vacant and the number is even higher in some areas. Some communities offer inexpensive or even free housing to families with school-age children in an attempt to preserve local schools and keep communities alive.

Accommodation accounts for around 20 to 25 per cent of the average family's budget and can be much higher in expensive areas. In cities and many towns, property isn't regarded as a good investment, and many prefer to rent. (Tenants in France have security of tenure and rents are strictly controlled). Many Parisians rent their principal home but own up to three holiday homes, e.g. one in the country near Paris for weekends, one on the Mediterranean coast for summer holidays and another in the Alps for skiing. The French aren't particularly mobile and tend to move home much less frequently than people in some other countries, e.g. the UK and the US; homes are often kept in a family and passed down the generations.

FRENCH HOMES

Most families live in detached homes and apartments, and semi-detached and terraced properties are relatively rare. Some 45 per cent of the population live in apartments (although less than 10 per cent in tower blocks, which tend to be in less desirable neighbourhoods), which are more common in France than in most other European countries. In cities and suburbs, most people have little choice, as houses are in short supply and prohibitively expensive. In the major cities, there are many *bourgeois* apartments built in the 19th or early 20th century, with large rooms, high ceilings and huge windows. Unless modernised, they have old-fashioned bathrooms and kitchens and may have primitive electrical and heating systems. Many apartments don't have their own source of hot water and heating, which is shared with other apartments in the same building.

French homes are usually built to high structural standards and, whether you buy a new or an old home, it will usually be sturdy, and older homes often have metre-thick walls. Many have a wealth of interesting period features, including vast fireplaces, wooden staircases, attics, cellars (*caves*) and a profusion of alcoves and annexes. Many houses have a basement (*sous-sol*), used as a garage and cellar. In most old houses and many new ones, fireplaces remain even when central heating is installed. In warmer regions, floors are often tiled and walls are painted rather than papered, while in cooler regions, floors may be of bare wood or carpeted (although ground floor rooms are often tiled) and walls are more likely to be papered. When wallpaper is used, it's often garish and may cover everything, including doors and even ceilings! Properties throughout France are usually built in a distinct local (often unique) style using local materials. There are stringent regulations in most areas relating to the style and design of new homes and the restoration of old buildings.

In older rural properties, the kitchen (*cuisine*) is the most important room in the house. It's usually huge with a large wood-burning stove for cooking and providing hot water, a huge solid wood dining table and possibly a bread oven. Country kitchens are worlds apart from modern open-plan fitted kitchens (called *cuisines américaines*) and are devoid of shiny formica, plastic laminates and pristine order. They're often stark in comparison with modern kitchens, with stone or tiled floors, a predominance of wood, tiles and marble and no window.

Refrigerators (*frigos*) and stoves (*cuisinières*) are often quite small in Frqnce. Stoves in rural homes usually run on bottled gas or a combination of bottled gas and electricity. Many homes have a gas water heater (*chaudière*) which heats the water for the bathroom and kitchen. Most homes don't have a separate utility room, and the washing machine and dryer are usually housed in the kitchen or the basement. Homes often have a separate toilet (*toilette* or *WC/waters*) and the bathroom (*salle de bains*) often has a *bidet* as well as a bath (*baignoire*) and/or a shower (*douche*). Baths, some of which may be shorter than baths in some other countries, are more common than showers in older homes, while showers are found in most modern homes. Many old, unmodernised homes don't have a bath, shower room or inside toilet.

Although new properties are often lacking in character, they're usually spacious and well endowed with modern conveniences and services, which certainly cannot be taken for granted in older rural properties. The standard fixtures and fittings in modern houses are more comprehensive and of better quality than those found in old houses. The French generally prefer modern homes to older houses with 'charm and character' (i.e. expensive to maintain and sometimes in danger of falling down). You do, however, often find pseudo-period features such as beams and fireplaces in new homes. Central heating, double-glazing and insulation are common in new houses. Central heating may be electric, gas, oil-fired or (sometimes) wood-burning. Air-conditioning used to be rare, even in the south, but it's now becoming more popular and often features the latest dual-purpose heating and ventilation systems (which are the most expensive to have installed). For details of heating and air-conditioning, see *Buying a Home in France* (Survival Books – see page 587).

Many properties have shutters, both for security and as a means of insulation. Often external shutters are supplemented by internal shutters, which are fixed directly to the window frames. Windows open inwards, rather than outwards as in most other countries. In the south and south-west (and even in parts of the north), many homes have swimming pools, and homes throughout France have a paved patio or terrace that's often covered to provide shade.

RELOCATION CONSULTANTS

If you're fortunate enough to have your move paid for by your employer, it's likely that he will arrange for a relocation consultant to handle the details. There are fewer relocation consultants in France (most are based in Paris) than in many other European countries and they usually deal only with corporate clients with lots of money to pay their fees. Fees depend on the services required, packages usually ranging from around €1,250 to €3,000.

The main service provided by relocation consultants is finding accommodation (for rent or purchase) and arranging viewing. Other services include conducting negotiations, drawing up contracts, arranging mortgages, organising surveys and insurance, and handling the move. Consultants may also provide reports on local amenities and services, such as schools, health services, public transport, and sports and social facilities. Some companies provide daily advice and assistance and help in dealing with officials. Finding rental accommodation for single people or couples without children can usually be done in a week or two, while locating family homes may take up to four weeks, depending on the location and requirements. You should usually allow two to three months between your initial visit and moving into a purchased or rented property.

TEMPORARY ACCOMMODATION

On arrival, you may find it necessary to stay in temporary accommodation for a few weeks or months before moving into permanent accommodation or while waiting for your furniture to arrive. Some employers provide rooms, self-contained apartments or hostels for employees and their families, although this is rare and usually for short periods only.

Many hotels and bed and breakfast establishments cater for long-term guests and offer reduced weekly or monthly rates. In most areas, particularly in Paris and other main cities, serviced and holiday apartments are available. These are fully self-contained furnished apartments with their own bathrooms and kitchens, which are cheaper and more convenient than a hotel, particularly for families. Self-catering holiday accommodation is prohibitively expensive during the main holiday season (June to August) but may be affordable at other times. One of the easiest ways to find temporary accommodation in Paris is through an agent such as Allô Logement Temporaire (☎ 01 42 72 00 06, 🖳 http://www.allo-logement-temporaire.asso.fr).

For information about French hotels, bed and breakfast and self-catering accommodation, and hostels, see **Chapter 15**.

BUYING PROPERTY

Property is considerably cheaper than in many other western countries, and many foreign buyers find that they can buy a size or style of home that they couldn't afford in their home countries (e.g. prices are as little as a third of those in the UK), although prices have been increasing by an average of around 10 per cent for a number of years. While it's still possible to find a rural ruin for restoration for €25,000, there's little that's habitable, other than a tiny apartment, in any part of the country for under €100,000 and even a studio flat in Paris can cost up to €300,000.

Before buying a property, you should be clear about your long-term plans and goals. If you're staying for only a short period, e.g. less than three years, you're usually better off renting. If you don't know how long you will be staying in France, it's **definitely** better to rent first (see page 108). Buying a house or an apartment is usually a good long-term investment and preferable to renting over a period of five or more years. Nevertheless, the French don't often buy domestic property as an investment but as a home for life and you shouldn't expect to make a quick profit when buying property. Generally property values increase in line with inflation, meaning you must usually own a home for around three years simply to recover the high costs associated with buying, although prices rise much faster than average (up to 30 per cent) in some fashionable areas (e.g. the Mediterranean coast and parts of the west coast). The professional fees and taxes associated with the purchase of properties older than five years are the highest in Europe and add an average of around 15 per cent to the cost. Note also that capital gains tax (see page 388) can wipe out a third of any profit made on the sale of a second home.

One of the most common mistakes when buying a rural property is to buy a house that's much larger than you need, simply because it seems to offer such good value. Don't, on the other hand, buy a property that's too small! Bear in mind that extra space can easily be swallowed up, particularly as you will inevitably discover that you have many more relatives and 'friends' than you realised!

Another common mistake is buying a property with too large a plot. Although it's tempting to buy lots of land, you should think carefully about what you're going to do with it. After you've installed a swimming pool, tennis court and croquet lawn, you will still have a lot of change left out of even two or three acres. Do you like gardening or are you prepared to live in a jungle? A large garden needs a lot of upkeep (i.e. work!). A big house with acres of land may also seem like a good investment, but bear in mind that, should you need to sell, buyers may be thin on the ground, particularly when the price has doubled or trebled after the cost of renovation. In most areas there's a small market for renovated rural property. Although there are usually plenty of buyers in the €50,000 to €100,000 price range, they become much scarcer at €150,000 or more unless a property is exceptional, i.e. outstandingly attractive, in a popular area and with a superb location. It's common for homes to take six months to sell, and in some areas even attractive properties remain on the market for a number of years.

There has been resistance to foreigners buying property in some areas, although few towns have actually blocked sales to foreigners to deter speculators. Understandably, the locals don't want property prices driven up by foreigners (many of whom are prepared to pay well above a property's true market value) to levels they can no longer afford. However, foreigners are generally welcomed by the local populace, as they boost the economy and in rural areas often buy derelict properties that the French won't touch (although the French themselves are increasingly turning to property restoration – once the preserve of the 'mad' British). And residents in rural areas who take the time to integrate into the local community are invariably warmly welcomed.

If you're looking for a holiday home (*résidence secondaire*), you may wish to investigate mobile homes (*mobil-home*) or a scheme that restricts your occupancy of a property to a number of weeks a year. These include leaseback (*propriété allégée* or *leaseback*), part-ownership (*bi-propriété*) – which could be through a company, e.g. an *SCI* – and timesharing (*multipropriété* or a number of other euphemisms). **Don't rush into any of these schemes without fully researching the market, and before you're absolutely clear about what you want and what you can realistically expect to get for your money.** For information about such ownership schemes, see *Buying a Home in France* (Survival Books – see page 587).

Another factor to beware of when buying property in France, or anywhere abroad, is the possibility of an adverse exchange rate swing between the time you sign a contract and the time you transfer money to pay for the property. It's possible to 'insure' against such an eventuality by fixing the exchange rate, although you may regret doing so if there's a swing in your favour!

As when buying property anywhere, it's never advisable to be in too much of a hurry. It's a lucky person who finds absolutely the right property first time. Have a good look around in the area you've chosen and make sure you have a clear picture of the relative prices and the types of property available. There's a huge range of property (and prices) available, from derelict farmhouses and crumbling *châteaux* requiring complete restoration to modern townhouses, chalets and apartments with all modern conveniences. There's no shortage of properties for sale, whatever kind of property you're looking for (despite what estate agents might tell you), although bargain properties in need of restoration are becoming hard to come by, especially in popular areas. Wait until you find something you fall head over heels in love with and then think about it for another week or two before rushing headlong to the altar! One of the best things about buying property in France is that there's always another 'dream' home around the next corner – and the second or third is often even better than the others. If you don't find what you're looking for, you can always buy a plot and have a house built to your own specifications.

The most important point to bear in mind when buying property is to obtain expert professional advice from someone who's familiar with French law. It isn't wise to rely solely on advice given by those with a financial interest in selling you a property, although it may be excellent and entirely unbiased. You will find that the relatively small cost (in comparison with the cost of a property) of obtaining expert advice is money well spent, if only for the peace of mind it affords. Many people have had their fingers burnt by rushing into deals without proper care and consideration. It isn't that France is full of crooks out to rob unsuspecting foreigners (although like most countries, it has its fair share); in fact, buyers in France have a much higher degree of legal protection than in many other European countries. However, it's too easy to fall in love with the beauty and ambience of France and sign a contract without giving it sufficient thought. **If you don't know the country well and don't speak French fluently, obtain legal advice before signing a contract!**

You can find professionals who speak English and other languages in most areas of France, and many expatriate professionals (e.g. architects, builders, surveyors) also practise there. **However, don't assume when dealing with a fellow countryman that he'll offer you a better deal or do a better job than a French**

person (the opposite may be true). It's also wise to check the credentials of professionals you employ, whether French or foreign.

The more homework you do before buying a property the better, including obtaining advice from existing expatriate homeowners. Buying a property is a complex and vast subject and to cover it in depth is beyond the scope of this book. Fortunately there's a wealth of information available for French property buyers, including *Buying a Home in France, The Best Places to Buy a Home in France* and *Renovating & Maintaining Your French Home* (Survival Books – see page 587) and a number of specialist English-language French property magazines and newspapers (see **Appendix B**).

RENTED ACCOMMODATION

If you're staying in France for only a few years (say, less than three), renting is usually the best solution. It's also the answer for those who don't want the trouble, expense and restrictions associated with buying a property. Even if you're planning to buy, it's often prudent to rent for 6 to 12 months, taking in the worst part of the year (weather-wise) in order to reduce your chance of making an expensive error. This allows you to become familiar with the region and the climate and gives you plenty of time to look around for a permanent home at your leisure.

Renting is common in France, where some 45 per cent of the population live in rented accommodation (many French families prefer to rent and don't see property as a good investment). Tenants have security of tenure, and rentals are strictly controlled under French law. France has a strong rental market and it's possible to rent every kind of property, from a tiny studio apartment (bedsitter) to a huge rambling *château*. In large cities, most rental properties are apartments, which are generally preferred to houses. Large apartments and houses are more difficult to find than small one- or two-room apartments, particularly in Paris and other cities.

Most rental properties are let unfurnished (*non-meublé* or *nu*), particularly for lets longer than a year, and long-term furnished (*meublé*) properties are difficult to find. On the other hand, if you're looking for a home for less than a year, you're better off looking for a furnished apartment or house. You don't have the same legal protection in a furnished property, although for short-term renters this isn't usually so important.

In France, 'unfurnished' doesn't just mean without furniture. An unfurnished property usually has no light fixtures, curtain rods or even an outdoor TV aerial. There's also no cooker, refrigerator or dishwasher and there may even be no kitchen units, carpets or kitchen sink! Always ask before viewing, as you may save yourself a wasted trip. If the previous tenant has fitted items such as carpets and kitchen cupboards, he may ask you for a rebate (*reprise*) to leave them behind. You should negotiate the rebate and ensure that you receive value for money. A *reprise* isn't enforceable, although if the tenant has the approval of the landlord it's difficult to avoid paying it, even though it may amount to little more than a bribe.

Many apartment blocks have a caretaker or janitor (*gardien(ne)* – the word *concierge* is seldom used nowadays). She (it's usually a woman, perhaps assisted by her husband) usually lives in a tiny flat at the entrance to grand apartment blocks, particularly in Paris, and her job includes cleaning the entrance hall and stair wells, brass polishing, receiving goods and packages, distributing mail, carrying out minor repairs, tending the gardens and surrounding areas, and ensuring that the rubbish is collected. She will also keep a spare set of keys to your apartment, which is handy if you lose yours. The *gardienne* is an important person in the daily life of an apartment block and it's wise to establish and maintain a good relationship with her, tipping her generously for extra services. Although a few are 'dragons', most are worth their weight in gold. Sadly, the number of *gardiennes* is on the decline. Although paid meagre salaries, they're increasingly being replaced by the ubiquitous 'digi-code' (*digi-code*), a pad on which you enter a number to obtain entry to an apartment block. Apart from the loss of extra services provided by the *gardienne*, the digi-code 'security' system is extremely insecure. The code number is invariably given to all and sundry and crime has risen as a result.

Finding a Rental Property

Your success or failure in finding a suitable rental property depends on many factors, not least the type of rental you're seeking (a one-bedroom apartment is easier to find than a four-bedroom detached house), how much you want to pay and the area where you wish to live. There are a number of ways of finding a property to rent, including the following:

● Ask friends, relatives and acquaintances to help spread the word, particularly if you're looking in the area where you already live. A lot of rental properties are found by word of mouth, particularly in Paris, where it's almost impossible to find somewhere with a reasonable rent unless you have connections.

● Check the advertisements in local newspapers and magazines.

● Visit accommodation and letting agents. Most cities and large towns have estate agents (*agences immobilières*) who also act as letting agents. Look under *Agences de Location et de Propriétés* in the yellow pages. It's often better to deal with an agent than directly with owners, particularly with regard to contracts and legal matters.

● Look for advertisements in shop windows and on notice boards in shopping centres, supermarkets, universities and colleges, and company offices.

● Check newsletters published by churches, clubs and expatriate organisations, and their notice boards.

Among the best newspapers for rental property in Paris are the daily *Le Figaro* and weekly newspapers such as *De Particulier à Particulier* (Thursdays) and *J'annonce* (Wednesdays). Other sources for accommodation in Paris for English-speaking foreigners are *France-USA Contacts* and *Paris Free Voice*, both available free at English-language bookshops, restaurants and public offices in Paris (see **Newspapers, Magazines & Books** on page 498 and **Appendix B**).

To find accommodation through advertisements (*offres de locations/ location offres*) in local newspapers you must usually be quick off the mark. Buy newspapers as soon as they're published and start phoning straight away. You must be available to inspect properties immediately or at any time. Even if you start phoning at the crack of dawn, you're still likely to find a queue when you arrive to view a property in Paris. Advertisers may be private owners, property managers or letting agencies (particularly in major cities). You can insert a 'rental wanted' (*demandes de locations/location demandes*) advertisement in many newspapers and on notice boards, but don't count on success using this method.

When looking for rental accommodation, try to avoid the months of September and October, when French people return from their summer holidays and (in university towns and cities) students are looking for accommodation.

In Paris and Marseille, rental accommodation is listed according to area (*arrondissement* or *banlieue*). Street numbers in cities and towns may have a suffix such as *bis* or *ter* – equivalent to B and C in UK addresses. If you're given directions, obtain information such as the stairway (*escalier*), floor (*étage*) and whether it's on the left or right (*à gauche/à droite*). If a building has a door code (*digi-code*), make sure you obtain the code in advance!

Note that the size of properties is usually expressed as a digit indicating the number of main rooms (i.e. living and bedrooms and not the kitchen, bathrooms, etc.) preceded by a letter: usually T (for *type*) for houses and F (which stands for . . . no one seems to know!) for apartments. A one-room apartment therefore has a combined living and sleeping room (it may have a separate kitchen and bathroom) and is called a *studio*. A two-room (*deux-pièces*) apartment usually has one bedroom, a living room, kitchen and bathroom. A three-room (*trois-pièces* or T3 or F3) apartment has two bedrooms, a four-room (*quatre-pièces*) apartment three bedrooms and so on. The average size of a two-room apartment is around 50m^2 (500ft^2). The following is a guide to the meaning of other abbreviations commonly used in advertisements for rented accommodation:

Abbreviation	Term	Meaning
appt	appartement	apartment
bur	bureau	office
chbr	chambre	bedroom
cuis	cuisine	kitchen
ét	étage	floor
imm	immeuble	building
ling	lingerie	linen room
p	pièce	room
rés	résidence	residence
s. d'eau	salle d'eau	shower room
sdb	salle de bain	bathroom
séj	séjour	living room

Rental Costs

Rental costs vary considerably according to the size (number of bedrooms) and quality of a property, its age and the facilities provided. Prices are calculated according to the number of main rooms (*pièces*) and the floor area (in square metres). However, the most significant factor affecting rental prices is the region, the city and the neighbourhood. Like everywhere, rental prices in France are dictated by supply and demand and are higher in Cannes, Grenoble, Lyon and Nice than in Bordeaux, Marseille, Strasbourg and Toulouse. Rental accommodation in Paris is in high demand and short supply, and the prices are among the highest in Europe and often double those in other French cities.

The lowest prices are found in small towns and rural areas, although good rental accommodation is often difficult to find. As a general rule, the further a property is from a large city or town (or town centre), public transport or other facilities, the cheaper it is. Rental prices for short-term lets, e.g. less than a year, are higher than for longer lets, particularly in popular holiday areas, where many properties are let furnished as self-catering holiday accommodation.

In Paris, you should expect to pay at least €30 per m^2; a tiny studio apartment of around 20m^2 (215ft^2) in a reasonable area costs around €500 per month, while a two or three-bedroom apartment (125m^2/1,345ft^2) in a fashionable *arrondissement* can cost up to €5,000 per month. In the provinces, you can rent a two-bedroom apartment for as little as €250 per month, although in most areas you should expect to pay around twice as much. Anything with a terrace or balcony is usually more expensive. Generally, the higher the floor the more expensive an apartment will be (you pay for the view, the extra light and the absence of street noise). However, if a block doesn't have a lift, apartments on lower floors are the most expensive. Houses can be rented in most rural areas and on the outskirts of some towns; for a three-bedroom house, you can expect to pay at least €500 per month – double that in parts of the Ile-de-France and the south-east, including the Alps. Rental prices are often open to negotiation and you may be able to secure a 5 to 10 per cent reduction if there isn't a queue of customers behind you, but many types of rental accommodation are subject to fixed rates, which increase annually in line with an 'index' published in the magazine *Le Particulier*. For details of prices and availability of rental accommodation in different areas, consult *The Best Places to Buy a Home in France* (Survival Books – see page 587).

If you rent a property through an agent, you must pay the agent's commission, typically 10 to 15 per cent of a year's rent or 10 per cent of the first year's rent plus 1 per cent for subsequent years. Provided rent isn't paid in advance at more than two-monthly intervals, the landlord can ask for a deposit (*caution*) equal to two months' rent. The deposit must be returned within two months of the termination of the lease, less any amount due to the landlord (for damages, redecoration, etc.). Although it's illegal, many tenants don't pay their last two months' rent and forfeit their deposit. Rent is normally paid a month in advance and you cannot be required to pay your rent by direct debit.

Note that tenants must have insurance (see page 344) and pay charges for services such as heating, hot water, rubbish removal, upkeep of grounds and gardens, use of a lift, communal lighting, swimming pool maintenance, and possibly a caretaker's services. Always check whether rent is inclusive or exclusive of charges, which is usually stated in advertisements. Service charges are calculated monthly (payable with the rent) and are usually higher in a new building than an old one. Other utilities, such as gas and electricity, are usually paid separately by tenants. You may also need to pay the *taxe d'habitation* (see page 384), although this is usually included in your rent.

The landlord may want proof that you're able to pay the rent, such as a bank statement or your last three pay slips, or an employer's confirmation of employment stating your salary. If your salary isn't three (or sometimes four) times the amount of the rental, the owner may insist that your employer signs the lease or provides a guarantee. If you're unemployed (e.g. renting while looking for work), you may need to provide a bank deposit (*caution bancaire*), i.e. up to 18 months' advance rent in a blocked account. Students may require a letter from a parent or sponsor stating their financial support and must be 18 or over to sign a lease in France. Your landlord may also require bank references, income tax receipts, references from previous landlords and a photocopy of your passport showing your name, date and place of birth, the date of issue and the expiry date.

Rental Contracts

A rental contract (*contrat de location*) or lease (*bail*) is usually a standard document. The rental period must be at least three years if it's for a named individual (*bail en nom propre*) and cannot be for an unspecified period. Company leases are usually for a minimum of six years.

Make sure that your contract is as complete as possible and includes an exact description of what you're renting and for what use, plus the exact dates and length of the lease. Two originals should be provided (one for the tenant and the other for the landlord), and the cost of drawing up the contract should be met equally. It's common for a tenant to be asked to sign an inventory, particularly for a furnished property (see page 113), which should be annexed to the lease. A tenant is responsible for any damage caused and must take out insurance against damage to a property (see page 344). Rents may be increased only once per year and only by a statutory amount (linked to increases in the cost of construction). Rental laws and protection don't extend to holiday lettings, furnished lettings or sub-lettings.

A tenant may terminate the lease at any time provided he gives three months' notice by registered letter (*lettre recommandée avec accusé de réception*). He must pay rent for the full three-month notice period, even if he moves out early. All important communications to your landlord **must** be sent by registered post and you must also keep a copy. The notice period can be shortened to a month under certain circumstances, e.g. when you're transferred by your employer at short notice, become unemployed or fall ill (and are over 60 years old).

A lease (*bail*) is deemed to have been renewed automatically for a further three years if the landlord doesn't give notice. If the landlord wishes to renew the lease but change the terms, he must give notice (which is normally done by registered letter to avoid any misunderstanding) and provide the new terms at least six months before the lease is due to expire. The tenant must accept the new lease at least three months before the lease expires; otherwise, he's deemed to have accepted notice to leave. He can, however, challenge the new rent or terms. If neither the landlord nor the tenant gives notice to alter the existing lease during the time limits imposed, it's automatically renewed for a further three years with the same rent and terms.

At the end of an agreement a landlord can ask you to vacate a property only when he wishes to sell it or use it for himself or his family, or if you havenn't fulfilled your obligations, e.g. regularly paid the rent. In order to evict you the landlord must obtain a court order and give you six months' notice to quit. Should he do so, you can move out before the six months notice has expired and aren't required to pay the rent after moving out. Note that you cannot be evicted during the winter months, usually between mid-November and mid-March. If the owner decides to sell the property at the end of or during a rental contract, you have first option to purchase. If you decline to buy and the landlord sells the property, you cannot be evicted if your agreement is for a fixed term.

Inventory

One of the most important jobs when moving into rented accommodation is to complete an inventory (*état des lieux*) of the contents and a report on its condition. This includes the condition of fixtures and fittings, the state of furniture and carpets (if furnished), the cleanliness and state of the decoration, and anything missing or in need of repair. An inventory is normally provided by your landlord or letting agent. If an inventory isn't provided, you should insist on one being prepared and annexed to the lease. This can be done (for around €150) by a *huissier*, who's an official authorised to prepare factual legal documents, or it can be drawn up by the landlord and tenant. If you have one drawn up by a *huissier*, his fee must be split equally between the landlord and yourself and you have a better chance of getting your deposit back, as in the event of a dispute his evidence overrides that of all other parties.

Don't sign the inventory until you've moved in. If you find a serious fault after signing the inventory, send a registered letter to your landlord asking for it to be attached to the inventory. You normally have a month in which to do this after moving in. Central heating is exempt from the one month limit until used (*sous réserve de bon fonctionnement en période de froid*).

An inventory should be drawn up when moving in (*état des lieux d'entrée*) and when moving out (*état des lieux de sortie*). If the two inventories don't correspond, the tenant must make good any damage or deficiency or the landlord can do so and deduct the cost from your deposit. Although French landlords are generally no better or worse than landlords in most other countries, some will do almost anything to avoid repaying a deposit.

SECURITY

When moving into a new home, it's wise to replace the locks (or lock barrels) as soon as possible and fit high security locks, as you have no idea how many keys are in circulation for the existing ones. Some apartments and houses may be fitted with high security door locks that are individually numbered. Extra keys for these locks cannot be cut at an ordinary *serrurerie*, and you must obtain details from the previous owner or the landlord to have additional keys cut or to change the lock barrels. At the same time as changing locks, you may wish to have an alarm system fitted, which is the best way to deter intruders and may also reduce your home contents insurance (see page 343).

If you're likely to be leaving your home unoccupied for long periods, your insurance company may insist on extra security measures such as two, or even three, locks on external doors (one of a deadlock mortise type) and internally-lockable shutters (or grilles) on windows, which must be locked when the property is vacant. In high risk areas, you may be required to fit extra locks and shutters, security blinds or gratings on windows. However, no matter how secure your home, a thief can usually break in if he's determined enough, e.g. through the roof or by knocking a hole in a wall! In isolated areas, thieves can strip a house bare at their leisure and an alarm won't be much of a deterrent if there's nobody around to hear it. If you have a holiday home, it isn't wise to leave anything of great value (monetary or sentimental) there. If you vacate a rented house or apartment for an extended period, it may be obligatory to notify your caretaker, landlord or insurance company, and leave a key with the caretaker or landlord in case of emergencies.

If you have a break-in, you should report it immediately to your local *gendarmerie*, where you must make a statement (*plainte*), of which you receive a copy. This is required by your insurance company if you make a claim. Note that a generous donation to the local police at Christmas may 'encourage' them to keep a watchful eye on your home when you're away.

Another important aspect of home security is ensuring that you have early warning of a fire, which is easily accomplished by installing smoke detectors. Battery-operated smoke detectors can be purchased for around €8, although they aren't as easy to find in France as in some countries so you may be better off importing them, and should be tested weekly to ensure that the batteries aren't exhausted. You can also fit an electric-powered gas detector that activates an alarm when a gas leak is detected.

MOVING HOUSE

After you've found a home in France, it usually takes just a few weeks to have your belongings shipped from within continental Europe. From anywhere else the time varies considerably, e.g. four weeks from the east coast of America, six weeks from the west coast and the Far East, and around eight weeks from Australasia. Customs clearance isn't necessary when shipping your household effects within the EU. However, when shipping your effects from a non-EU country to France, you should enquire about customs formalities in advance; if you fail to follow the correct procedure, you can encounter numerous problems and delays and may be charged duty or even fined. The relevant forms to be completed by non-EU citizens depend on whether your French home will be your main residence or a holiday home.

Removal companies usually take care of the administration and ensure that the right documents are provided and correctly completed (see also **Customs** on page 92).

For international removals, you should use a company that's a member of the International Federation of Furniture Removers (FIDI, 💻 http://fidi.com) or the Overseas Moving Network International (OMNI, 💻 http://www.omnimoving.com), with experience in France. Members of FIDI and OMNI usually subscribe to an advance payment scheme that provides a guarantee. If a member company fails to fulfil its commitments to a customer, the removal is completed at the agreed cost by another company or your money is refunded. Some removal companies have subsidiaries or affiliates in France, which may be more convenient if you encounter problems or need to make an insurance claim.

Obtain at least three written quotations before choosing a company. Costs vary considerably, although you should expect to pay at least €5,000 to move the contents of a three to four-bedroom house. Note that prices may be higher in the summer and immediately after Christmas. If you need to store your belongings between moving out of your old home and moving into your new one, most companies will do this for a minimal charge (e.g. €15 per week); some provide free storage for up to four weeks. If you're flexible about the delivery date, most removal companies will quote a lower fee based on a 'part load', where the cost is shared with other deliveries. This can result in savings of 50 per cent or more compared with an 'individual' delivery, but make sure you don't leave essential items to be delivered in a part load – you may have to wait two or three weeks for them to arrive.

Make a list of everything to be moved and give a copy to the removal company. Don't include anything illegal (e.g. guns, bombs, drugs and pornographic videos) with your belongings, as customs checks can be rigorous and penalties severe. Some companies won't take alcohol and some may be reluctant to take plants, although there are no restrictions on the import of most plants (see page 94). Give the shipping company **detailed** instructions how to find your French address from the nearest motorway (or main road) and a telephone number on which you can be contacted. Note also that if your new home has restricted access (or is surrounded by soft ground), you may incur additional costs (make sure you inform the shipping company in advance!).

Be sure to fully insure your belongings during removal with a well established insurance company. Insurance premiums are usually 1 to 2 per cent of the declared value of your goods, depending on the type of cover chosen. It's prudent to make a photographic or video record of valuables for insurance purposes. Most insurance policies cover for 'all risks' on a replacement value basis. Note that china, glass and other breakables can usually be included in an all-risks policy only when they're packed by the removal company. If you need to make a claim, be sure to read the small print, as some companies require you to make a claim within a few days, although seven is usual. Send a claim by registered post. Some insurance companies apply an 'excess' of around 1 per cent of the total shipment value when assessing claims. This means that if your shipment is valued at €30,000 and you make a claim for less than €300, you won't receive anything.

If you plan to transport your belongings to France personally, check the customs requirements of the countries you must pass through, in advance. If you're importing household goods from another European country, it's possible to hire a self-drive van in France. Hiring a van outside France isn't recommended, as you must usually return it to the country where it was hired. Generally, it isn't wise to do your own move unless it's a simple job. It's certainly no fun heaving beds and wardrobes up stairs and squeezing them into impossible spaces. If you're taking pets with you, you may need to tranquillise them, as most pets are frightened (even more than people) by the chaos and stress of moving house. See also **Pets** on page 526.

Bear in mind when moving home that everything that can go wrong often does, so allow plenty of time and try not to arrange your move from your old home on the same day as the new owner/tenant is moving in. That's just asking for fate to intervene! See also the checklists in **Chapter 20**.

UTILITIES

As well as electricity and gas, French homes use oil (*fioul* or *fuel*) and wood (*bois*) for heating and hot water, and the government offers tax credits for the installation of energy systems running on renewable fuel (e.g. wood and solar energy). According to the Ministry for Industry, 100KWh of heating costs around €12 using electricity, €5 using natural gas, €9 with bottled gas and €8 with oil. Electricity and gas are supplied by the state-owned Electricité de France/Gaz de France (EDF/GDF, 🖳 http://www. edf.fr and http://www.gdf.fr), although there are local electricity companies in some areas, and commercial users now have a choice of private suppliers (domestic users, as usual, must wait longer). For information about making the most efficient use of electricity and gas, contact the Agence de l'Environnement et de la Maîtrise de l'Energie (ADEME, ☎ 08 00 31 03 11, 🖳 http://www.ademe.fr), which will advise you where to find your nearest *Point Info Energie* (*PIE*).

Many utility bills can now be paid online. Telefact is one company offering such a service for France Télécom, EDF, GDF and certain water company bills (🖳 http:// www.telefact.fr – in French only).

Electricity

Unlike other western countries, France generates some 80 per cent of its electricity from nuclear power, the balance coming mostly from various hydro-electric power stations, although there are plans to build a power station near Nevers (Nièvre) to burn coal discovered nearby – two years after France's last coal mine was closed. Despite objections to plans to build 'third-generation' reactors (and to nuclear power in general), the government is committed to pursuing a largely nuclear power-generation policy.

There are currently 19 nuclear reactors in France (a map showing their location can be found on 🖳 http://www.edf.fr (click on '*Plan rapproché*). France's nuclear policy means that its electricity is among the cheapest in Europe (it supplies electricity to its neighbours for less than they can produce it themselves and owns nine other European electricity companies, including Seeboard in the UK), although prices were raised by 1.7 per cent in August 2006 – the first increase for three years.

Due to the moderate cost of electricity and the high degree of insulation in new homes, electric heating is more common in France than in other European countries.

Connection

The first thing to check before moving into a home is whether there are any light fittings. When moving house, most French people remove not only bulbs, but also bulb-holders, ceiling roses and sometimes even the flex, leaving you with bare (and live) wires protruding from the ceiling! This isn't merely parsimony but because in France lampshades are normally sold complete with bulb-holder, flex and ceiling rose, although these can be bought separately. One thing to note is that, although bulbs are similar to those sold in the UK, for example, bulb-holders (*douille*) have a larger diameter and won't fit British lampshades, so if you plan to bring lampshades from the UK, make sure you bring a good supply of bulb-holders as well. (In any case, these are generally of poor quality in France.) It's worthwhile also bringing ceiling roses, as these are expensive in France and there's limited choice.

You must usually apply to your local EDF office for an electricity connection (*branchement*) and a contract specifying the power supply installed (see below) and the tariff required (see page 119). To have your electricity connected, you must prove that you're the owner by producing an *attestation* or a lease (*bail*) if you're renting. You must also show your passport or residence permit (*carte de séjour*). If you wish to pay your bill by direct debit from a bank or post office account, don't forget to take along your account details (*relevé d'identité bancaire*).

When moving house, most people tell EDF a few days before they leave (EDF requests at least two days' notice) and the EDF assumes that someone else is taking over the property. To ensure that your electricity supply is connected and that you don't pay for someone else's electricity, you should contact your local EDF office and ask them to read the meter (*relevé spécial*) before taking over a property. If the property has an existing electricity supply, you must pay an 'access' fee (*frais d'accès*) of €14. Non-residents may be required to pay a deposit, which is refundable against future bills.

When buying electrical appliances, the label PROMETELEC (Association pour le Développement et l'Amélioration des Installations Intérieures) indicates that they're safe. The safety of electrical materials is usually indicated by the French safety standards association's initials 'NF' (*Normes Françaises*). The EDF & GDF publish a number of leaflets detailing their services and tariffs, including one in French and English, *Le Service du Gaz et de l'Électricité*. The EDF publishes a useful free booklet (in French), *EDF répond à vos questions*, available from any EDF office. Your local electricity board may also have a booklet (*livret de l'usager de l'électricité*) explaining the electricity supply and apparatus. If you have any questions regarding the electricity supply, contact your local EDF office (listed in the yellow pages and searchable on 🖳 http://particuliers.edf.fr – enter the name of your commune in the box top right). Information can also be obtained via a local rate telephone line (☎ 08 10 12 61 26).

Power Supply

The electricity supply in France is delivered to homes at 380/440 volts through three separate phases (not one as in some countries) and is then shared across the three phases at 220/240 volts with a frequency of 50 Hertz (cycles). Some appliances, such as large immersion heaters and cookers, draw power from all three phases. Older buildings may still have 110/120 volt supplies, although these have been converted to 220/240 in most areas.

If you're moving from a country with a 110V supply (e.g. the US), your electrical equipment will require a converter or a transformer (*transformateur*) to convert it to 240V, although some electrical appliances (e.g. electric razors and hair dryers) are fitted with a 110/240 volt switch. Check for the switch, which may be inside the casing, and make sure that it's switched to 240V **before** connecting it to the power supply. Converters are suitable only for appliances without circuit boards or microchips that don't need to be plugged in for long periods (e.g. heaters, hair dryers, vacuum cleaners and coffee machines). Electronic appliances such as computers, fax machines, TVs and video/DVD players must be connected to the supply via a step-down transformer. Add the wattage of the devices you intend to connect to a transformer and make sure that its power rating exceeds this sum. Converters and transformers can be bought in most DIY shops, although in most cases it's simpler to buy new appliances in France (see **Household Goods** on page 501).

An additional problem with some electrical equipment is the frequency rating, which in some countries, e.g. the US, is designed to run at 60 Hertz (Hz) and not France's 50Hz. Electrical equipment without a motor is generally unaffected by the drop in frequency to 50Hz (except TVs, see page 164). Equipment with a motor may run with a 20 per cent drop in speed; however, automatic washing machines, cookers, electric clocks and hi-fi equipment are unusable in France if not designed for 50Hz operation. To find out, look at the label on the back of the equipment. If it says 50/60Hz, it should work. If it says 60Hz, you might try it anyway, but first ensure that the voltage is correct as outlined above. Bear in mind that the transformers and motors of electrical devices designed to run at 60Hz will run hotter at 50Hz, so you should ensure that equipment has sufficient space around it for cooling.

In many rural areas the lights often flicker and occasionally go off and come back on almost immediately (just long enough to crash your computer!). Power cuts of several minutes or hours are fairly frequent in some areas, particularly during thunderstorms, and in some departments (e.g. Gers) there's a high risk of lightning strikes. If you live in an area with an unstable electricity supply, it's prudent to obtain a power stabiliser for a computer or other vital equipment to prevent it being switched off when the power drops. If you use a computer, it's also wise to fit an uninterruptable power supply (UPS) with a battery back-up, which allows you time (around five minutes) to save your work and shut down your computer after a power failure. If you're worried about lightning strikes, you can install an 'anti-lightning' device (*parafoudre*) in your fuse box. (You should also keep torches, candles and preferably a gas lamp handy!)

If the power keeps tripping off when you attempt to use a number of high-powered appliances simultaneously, it probably means that the rating (*puissance*) of your power supply is too low. This is a common problem in France. If this is the case, you must ask the EDF to uprate the power supply to your property, although this can increase your standing charge (see below) by up to 40 per cent. The power setting is usually shown on your meter (*compteur*). The possible ratings are 3, 6, 9, 12, 15, 18, 24, 30 and 36 kilowatts (KW or Kva). To calculate the power supply required, list all the electrical appliances you have (plus any you intend installing, such as an electric shower or dishwasher) and the power consumption of each. Add the power consumption of the appliances you're likely to operate simultaneously to obtain the total number of kilowatts required. The three lower rates (3, 6 and 9KW) don't cater for electric heating, which needs a power supply of 12KW to 18KW. If you have an integrated electrical heating system, however, you can have a gadget called a *délesteur* installed, which momentarily cuts off convectors, under-floor heating and water-heater, etc. when other high-consumption appliances are in use but without noticeable temperature fluctuations; it may therefore be possible to avoid a higher supply rating. If you have appliances such as a washing machine, dishwasher, water heater and electric heating in an average-size house (e.g. two to three bedrooms), you will probably need an 18KW supply. If you have numerous high-wattage electrical appliances and electric heating, you may need the maximum 36KW supply.

The French use both unearthed two-pin and earthed three-pin plugs and sockets; although two-pin sockets are now illegal, many older homes still have them. Three-pin plugs and sockets should be used for all high-power appliances (e.g. heaters, irons and drills). Adapter plugs are available in DIY shops, although it's cheaper (and safer) to replace foreign plugs with the appropriate French plugs.

Your standing charge (*abonnement*) depends on the rating of your supply and the tariff you choose, which also affects the amount you pay for electricity consumed, as explained below.

Tariffs

The EDF offers three domestic tariff options (*tarif bleu*), described below.

● **Basic Tariff** (*option base*) – With this tariff, there's no difference between day and night rates and the meter has just one dial. This system isn't recommended unless you use little or no electricity! The standing charge per year is from around €24 (3KW power supply) to around €835 (36KW power supply); charges can be paid in monthly instalments. The price per KWh is €0.1290 for a 3KW supply and €0.1057 for all other supplies.

● **Peak/Off-peak Tariff** (*option heures pleines/heures creuses*) – With this tariff, you can select your own reduced rate period or periods up to a maxiumum of eight hours daily, e.g. from 22.30 to 06.30, or 02.30 to 07.30 and 13.30 to 16.30. The low rate is generally used to heat hot water and charge night storage heaters. You can have relays installed by EDF to switch on your immersion water heater, tumble dryer or dishwasher during the cheap period. The meter has two dials, one for peak hours marked *heures pleines* (or *HP*) with an image of the sun on it, and one for the off-peak hours marked *heures creuses* (or *HC*) with an image of the moon on it. Your bill will show your peak and off-peak consumption separately.

The standing charge per year is from €105 (6KW power supply) to around €1,335 (36KW power supply). Note that this tariff doesn't apply to a 3KW supply. The price per KWh is €0.0644 during the *heures creuses* and €0.1057 at *heures pleines*.

You can have a special light and/or buzzer installed by an electrician giving you a 30-minute warning of the start of the higher rate. You can also have your heavy consumption appliances connected to a remote control switch (*télécommande*) so that they switch off automatically during the high rate period and switch on again when the period ends.

● **'Tempo' Tariff** (*option Tempo*) – With this tariff, which is available only for supplies of 9KW or more, the year is divided into 'blue', 'white' and 'red' days (*jours bleus/blancs/rouges*), each with different charges for peak and off-peak use (see **Peak/Off-peak Tariff** above). There are 300 blue days, including all Sundays and most Saturdays; 43 white days, spread through the year; and 22 red days, on selected weekdays between 1st November and 31st March (guaranteed to be the coldest days of the year!). The standing charge ranges from around €163 (9KW) to €553 (36KW) and the peak/off-peak rates for each colour day are as follows: blue €0.0452/0.0561; white €0.0922/0.1092; red €0.17092/€0.4781. You can have a complicated management system installed, at a cost of between €300 and €800, to ensure that you minimise use on red days – or you can switch everything off and go skiing or simply freeze!

Since January 2003, a tax called the *contribution au service public* has been applied to all electricity bills at the rate of €0.33 per KWh.

Meters

Meters are usually installed in a box on an outside wall of a property. However, if your meter isn't accessible or a house isn't permanently occupied, make sure you leave the keys with a neighbour or make special arrangements to have your meter read. (You can have your meter connected to an exterior box for around €75). If your meter cannot be read, you will receive an estimate based on your previous bills, although it **must** be read at least once a year.

Billing

You're normally billed for your electricity every two months but may receive monthly bills if your consumption is above a certain level. A number of bills (*facture*) received throughout the year, e.g. alternate bills, are estimated. Bills include a standing charge (*abonnement*), VAT (*TVA*) and local taxes (*taxes locales*). VAT is levied at 5.5 per cent on the standing charge and 19.6 per cent on the total power consumption. Local taxes (*taxe commune/département*) are around 12 per cent and where applicable are levied on around 80 per cent of the consumption and standing charge total before VAT is added. VAT at 19.6 per cent is also levied on the local taxes.

Bills can be paid by direct debit (*prélèvement automatique*). It's also possible to pay a fixed amount each month by standing order based on your estimated usage;

at the end of the year you receive a bill for the amount owing or a rebate of the amount overpaid. These methods of payment are preferable, particularly if you spend a lot of time away from home or you're non-resident. If you're non-resident, you can have your bills sent to an address outside France. If you don't pay a bill on time, interest (*majoration*) can be charged at 1.5 times the current interest rate. If your bills still aren't paid after a certain period, your electricity company can cut your service.

Gas

Mains Gas

Mains gas (*gaz de ville*) is available only in around 80 towns and cities. Domestic supplies are currently provided only by the state-owned Gaz de France (GDF), part of the same company as Electricité de France. (Commercial supplies were privatised in 2004 but domestic users must wait until July 2007.) If you buy a property without a mains gas supply, you can obtain a new connection (*raccordement*), provided of course mains gas is available in the area. If the property is within 35m (115ft) of a supply, connection costs €321; if not, you must obtain a quotation for connection, which can be **very** expensive. When moving into a property already connected to mains gas, you must contact GDF to have the gas switched on and/or have the meter read and to have the account switched to your name. This can usually be done at the same time as you arrange for your electricity supply (see page 117). There's a connection (*mise en service*) fee of around €14.

Billing: As with electricity, you're normally billed every three months. If your electricity is supplied by EDF, your gas is included on the same bill as your electricity. As with other utility bills, gas bills can be paid by direct debit (*prélèvement automatique*), or a fixed amount can be paid each month. Meters are read every four or six months.

Tariffs: Gas charges are determined by the amount of gas you use. There are four tariffs: *base* (less than 1,000KWh per year, i.e. cooking only), *B0* (between 1,000 and 6,000KWh, i.e. cooking and water heating), *B1* (between 6,000 and 30,000KWh, i.e. for homes with gas central heating) and *B2I* (above 30,000KWh, i.e. if you live in a centrally heated chateau!). Current standing and consumption charges are shown below.

	Base	B0	B1	B2I
Annual Standing Charge	€24	€34	€119	€187
Consumption Per KWh	€0.0602	€0.0501	€0.036–40*	€0.0345–425*

* Charges for options B1 and B2I vary slightly from town to town; you can find out the exact tariff for a particular town on the GDF website (🖳 http://dolcevita.gazde france.fr – click on '*Les tarifs de Gaz de France*' and then enter a postcode).

In apartment buildings where a shared gas supply is used only for cooking, a standard fee for gas may be included in your service charge. As with heating and hot water charges, this isn't particularly desirable if you own a holiday home in France.

Note that VAT at 5.5 per cent is levied on standing charges and at 19.6 per cent on consumption. Further information is available from your local EDF/GDF office, who will also be able to provide you with a free assessment of your requirements and advise the best tariff for your consumption (☎ 08 10 16 30 00).

Bottled Gas

Most rural homes have cookers and some also water heaters that use bottled gas. Cookers often have a combination of electric and (bottled) gas rings. Check when moving in that the gas bottle isn't empty. Keep a spare bottle or two handy and make sure you ask how to change them, as this can be quite a complicated procedure, involving safety switches, etc.. Bottled gas is more expensive than mains gas. Bottles come in 35kg, 13kg and 5/6kg sizes. A small one used just for cooking will last an average family around six weeks. Bottles can be bought at most petrol stations and super/hypermarkets, but you should trade in an empty bottle for a new one; otherwise it's much more expensive. An exchange bottle costs around €20. If you need to buy a gas bottle, you will be asked to register and pay a deposit (e.g. €40). Some village shops also sell bottled gas. There are several different types of bottle (e.g. Antargaz, Butagaz, Primagaz and Totalgaz, each a different colour) the supplier of one type won't accept a bottle of another type. (Check **before** you unload your 35kg bottles!) Note also that the connectors usually turn in the opposite direction to most threaded devices.

Some houses keep their gas bottles outside, often under a lean-to. If you do this you must buy propane gas, as it can withstand a greater range of temperatures than butane, which is for internal use only (in fact, propane gas bottles **must** be kept outside a house). Ignore those who say this doesn't matter on the Côte d'Azur, as even there temperature variations can be huge. Note also that butane requires a different demand valve (détendeur), i.e. 28M.bar 1300g/h instead of 37M/bar 1500g/h for propane.

Gas Tanks

Gas central heating is common in France, although in rural areas the gas supply comes from a gas tank (citerne) installed on the property, rather than a mains supply or bottles. Tanks can be hired, from suppliers such as Total and Antargaz, for around €300 per year, or you can pay a deposit of around €1,500, which is refunded if you take out a contract for the supply of gas for a fixed period. **If you take over a property with a gas tank, you must not only pay the deposit but also have it filled and pay for a full tank of gas (which can cost around €1,000), irrespective of how much was left in it!**

Oil, Wood, Wind & Solar Power

Around 27 per cent of French homes use an oil-fired heating system (chauffage au fioul). The price of heating oil has increased dramatically since mid-2004 and is now around €0.65 per litre. You may be offered a choice between ordinaire and supérieur, the latter obviously costing more; in fact, it isn't 'superior' but merely freezes at a lower temperature (-25°C instead of -15°C) and so is unnecessary unless you live at the top of a mountain and have an external tank. Oil is usually available from a number of local suppliers and it may pay you to shop around. Savings can also be made if you combine a delivery with neighbours. As oil causes a rapid build-up of deposits, it's essential to have your system cleaned and checked annually (costing around €120) and to replace the jet regularly. It's recommended to have the tank (*cuve*) cleaned every ten years or so, which costs around €300. Note also that you should wait at least two hours after an oil delivery before restarting your boiler, in order to allow any foreign bodies in the tank to settle to the bottom. For information about the use of fuel for heating, contact Chauffage Fioul, an association of petroleum manufacturers, distributors and retailers (☎ 08 10 34 34 34, 💻 http://www. chaleurfioul.com).

The French consume more wood for heating than the inhabitants of any other European country. Around 7m homes use wood for heating (*chauffage au bois*) and millions more have wood fires for effect. Wood for fuel is measured in cubic metres of stacked wood (called *stères*), but this includes the spaces in between and is therefore equivalent to between 0.6m^3 and 0.8m^3 of actual wood, depending on how it's cut and stacked. In terms of calorific value, one *stère* is roughly equivalent to 150 litres of oil. Check whether your commune supplies wood from local forests (*affouage*); otherwise you will need to find a supplier (often a local farmer), who will charge around €35 per *stère*. It's possible to obtain tax relief on the installation of wood-burning stoves. Chimney sweeping (*ramonage*) costs around €35 to €50 and should be done at least once a year; although you can no longer be fined for failing to have your chimney swept regularly, your house insurance may be invalidated in the event of a fire if you haven't done so.

France currently generates a mere 1 per cent of European wind power but has recently committed resources to an increase in wind power generation, using state-of-the art 'windmills' (*éoliens*), although – like every other innovation in France – plans have aroused controversy and opposition.

Solar panels can be installed for between around €2,000 and €5,500, although a government grant is available under the *Plan Soleil* scheme. For details contact ADEME (see page 116).

Water

Mains water in France is supplied by a number of private companies, the largest of which are Vivendi, Lyonnaise des Eaux, Cise (part of the Saint-Gobaun group) and Saur (Bouygues group), who between them supply three-quarters of the water in France. Most properties are metered, so that you pay only for the water you use. If you need to have a water meter installed, there's a small non-refundable charge. When moving into a new house, ask the local water company to read your meter. Owners of a community property can have individual meters installed.

If you own a property in or near a village, you can usually be connected to a mains water system. However, connection can be expensive, as you must pay for digging the channels required for pipes. Obtain a quotation (*devis*) from the local water company for the connection of the supply and the installation of a water meter. Expect the connection to cost at least €800, depending on the type of terrain and soil (or rock!) which must be dug to lay pipes. If you're thinking of buying a property and installing a mains water supply, obtain an estimate **before** signing the purchase contract.

Water shortages are rare in towns but fairly common in some rural areas during long hot summers, when the water may periodically be switched off. It's possible to have a storage tank installed for emergencies and you should also have a rainwater or household waste water tank for watering the garden and washing cars.

If you rely on a well (*puits*) or spring (*source*) for your water, bear in mind that these can dry up, particularly in parts of central and southern France, which continue to experience droughts. **Always confirm that a rural property has a reliable water source.** If the source is on a neighbour's land, make sure that there's no dispute about the ownership of the water and your rights to use it, e.g. that it cannot be stopped or drained away by your neighbours. You don't pay water charges for well water or water from a stream or river running through your property. If a supply is marked *eau non potable*, the water should not be drunk.

Although French homes have no holding tanks and hot water is heated directly from the mains, you shouldn't use hot water for making drinks but should heat cold water (e.g. in a kettle).

Further information about water supplies can be found in *Renovating & Maintaining Your French Home* (Survival Books – see page 587).

Cost

It's usual to have a contract for a certain amount of water and if you exceed this amount you incur a higher charge. There's no flat fee (*forfait*), which has been abolished, although 'special charges' may be levied. French water varies by up to 100 per cent in price from region to region, depending on its availability or scarcity, and is among the most expensive in the world. It can cost as much as €3.60 per cubic metre or as little as €1.75; the national average is around €2.75 (or 0.275 centimes per litre). Note that, if you have a septic tank (*fosse septique*) as opposed to mains drainage (*tout à l'égout*), your water bill will be much lower, e.g. €0.75 per cubic metre (see page 124). You're billed by your local water company annually or every six months and can pay by direct debit. In community properties, the water bill for the whole building is usually divided among the apartments according to their size, although they may be individually metered.

If you need to install a hot water boiler and immersion heater, ensure it's large enough for the size of the property, e.g. 100 litres for a studio, 150 litres for a two-room apartment, 200 litres for a three- or four-room flat or house, and 300 litres for five to seven rooms.

WASTE DISPOSAL

Properties in urban areas are normally connected to mains drainage (*tout à l'égout*), whereas those in rural parts usually have individual sewage systems – most commonly septic tanks (*fosse septique*). Note, however, that a law which came into force in December 2005 requires the installation of mains drainage wherever it's considered cost-effective, which generally means in the centre of all French villages. The necessary work is likely to take a few years, and you should check whether your village is to be 'connected'. Where mains drainage is installed, there will be a one-off charge for connection made to all properties within the area of the system, which must be connected within two years of the installation, plus an annual service charge. Charges for mains drainage are normally included in property taxes (see page 384).

There are various septic tank systems, the most usual being a *fosse toutes eaux*, which takes all waste water except rainwater. Some older *fosses toutes eaux* have an aerator (*brouilleur* or *batteur*) to help break down the solid matter and allow it to settle while clear water overflows into an underground drainage system. Note, that these are now more or less obsolete, so it may be difficult to obtain spare parts if required. Note also, that individual sewage systems are subject to strict regulations, which are currently in the process of being updated to meet EU standards, and inspections will become routine. **Before buying a property with its own sewage system, you should have it checked by an expert. Before buying a property or plot without a system, you should obtain expert advice as to whether such a system can be installed and what the cost will be.**

A *fosse toutes eaux* must be emptied at least once a year, depending on whether a property is permanently inhabited or not, a *fosse septique* every three to five years; the cost of emptying is around €200. Note that you mustn't use certain cleaning agents, such as ammonia, in a septic tank, as they will destroy it, and you may need to put specially formulated products into the tank to keep it working properly.

Household rubbish is collected once or twice a week in most urban and rural areas, although in some remote parts you must take your rubbish to a waste disposal site (see below). Many areas also have voluntary recycling systems, whereby certain materials (e.g. paper, cardboard and rigid plastic but not plastic bags) can be put in special (usually coloured) bags for separate collection (sometimes on different days). Glass isn't usually collected but must be taken to a bottle bank, of which there's one in most villages and all towns. (You shouldn't put bottles that have contained oil nor light bulbs in a bottle bank.) A pilot scheme in the Territoire de Belfort, whereby householders are charged for rubbish collection according to the weight of non-recycled waste, has decreased the latter from around the French average of 420kg per house per year to around 80kg and may be introduced in other departments. All recyclable materials and garden waste can be taken to a waste disposal site (*déchetterie*), which are normally open only on two or three days per week. You can find out where your nearest disposal site is and you may be issued with a pass, which you must present on arrival to confirm that you live locally.

Bonfires are usually permitted as long as they don't cause a nuisance but may be forbidden at certain times of year (e.g. from March to September); check with your town hall.

Charges for rubbish collection are usually included in property taxes (see page 384), although some communes make a charge (e.g. €75 per year) for the emptying of 'wheelie' bins; there's no charge for the use of a *déchetterie*.

6.

POSTAL SERVICES

The French Post Office (La Poste) is a state-owned company, and post offices (*bureau de poste* or simply *poste*) in France are always staffed by post office employees, who are French civil servants (*fonctionnaires*); there are no post offices run by private businesses as in the UK, for example. However, privatisation of the postal service began in 2003, La Poste's monopoly of the handling of letters between 50 and 100g is due to end in 2006 (although in September 2006 no alternative services were available) and the service will be completely liberalised by 2009. There are around 17,000 post offices, 60 per cent of them in communes of fewer than 2,000 inhabitants but, as in other countries, those in the least populated areas are gradually being closed.

The identifying colour used by La Poste is yellow, which is the colour of French post office signs, post vans and post boxes, which can be found in virtually all villages, as well as towns and cities. The post office logo looks like a blue paper aeroplane on a yellow background. Signs for post offices in towns vary widely and include *PTT* (the old name for the post office), *PT, P et T, Bureau de Poste* or simply *Poste*. Post offices are listed in the yellow pages under *Poste: Services*.

In addition to the usual post office services, a range of other services are provided. These include telephone calls, telegram and fax transmissions (see page 159), domestic and international cash transfers, payment of telephone and utility bills, and the distribution of mail-order catalogues. La Poste also started offers email services (see page 159), including free and permanent email addresses as well as e-commerce services for small businesses, and banking services, including cheque and savings accounts, mortgage and retirement plans (see page 356), money changing and transfer services (see page 353). Post offices usually have photocopy and franking machines. You can even write to Father Christmas!

Main post offices usually have different counters (*guichets*) for different services, e.g. post office cheques (*CCP*), postal orders (*mandat*), *poste restante* and bulk stamps (*timbres en gros*), although some counters provide all services (*tous services/toutes opérations*). Before joining a queue, make sure it's the correct one; if you join the wrong queue you'll need to start again (there are often long queues). If you need different services, you must queue a number of times if there's no window for all services. Stamps are sold at most windows and most handle letters and packages (*envoi de lettres et paquets*), except perhaps very large parcels.

The Post Office produces numerous leaflets and brochures, including *Tarifs Courrier – Colis*, or you can call ☎ 08 20 80 80 00 for general information or ☎ 08 10 82 18 21 for information regarding international post. La Poste's website (🖳 http://www.laposte.fr) contains information on all its services, including a searchable database of post offices (the listings don't include opening hours or the times of the last collection each day), although only limited information is available in English.

Note that French companies are usually slow to reply to letters and it's often necessary to follow up a letter with a telephone call.

BUSINESS HOURS

Business hours for main post offices in towns and cities in France are usually from 08.00 or 09.00 to 19.00, Mondays to Fridays and from 08.00 or 09.00 to noon on Saturdays. Main post offices in major towns don't close for lunch and may also provide limited services outside normal business hours. In small towns and villages post offices close for lunch, e.g. from 12.00 to 13.30 or 14.30. Opening hours in rural areas vary considerably. Some village post offices are open just three hours a day from 09.00 to 12.00 Mondays to Saturdays, while others are open from 08.00 to 12.00 and 13.30 or 14.30 to 16.30 Mondays to Fridays and from 08.00 to 11.30 on Saturdays. In some villages opening hours are irregular, e.g. 07.00 to 10.30, 13.45 to 15.30 and 16.30 to 18.00 Mondays to Fridays, and 07.00 to 11.00 on Saturdays.

In Paris, a post office is open in each *arrondissement* from 08.00 to 11.00 and sometimes 13.00 on Saturdays. The central post office at 52 rue du Louvre, 1er is open 24 hours a day, every day (although after 19.00 only letters are dealt with), but it's best to avoid Saturday afternoons and Sundays unless you're desperate. The post office at 71 avenue des Champs-Elysées, 8e is open from 08.00 to 22.00 Mondays to Saturdays, and from 10.00 to 12.00 and 14.00 to 20.00 on Sundays. In other major cities and large towns, main post offices are also open for a few hours on Sundays.

LETTERS

The French letter post (*courrier*) delivery service used to have a reputation for being among the slowest in Europe and, although services have improved markedly in recent years, it's still far from reliable in many areas. 'Economy' class letters can take eons, and although a 'priority' letter posted within France can generally be expected to arrive the next day (barring strikes or mishaps), four or five days isn't unusual!

Delivery times in Europe vary considerably according to the countries concerned, e.g. two days for a letter from France to the Netherlands or Germany and around six days to Italy. Air mail (*par avion/poste aérienne*) from major French cities to the US takes five to ten days. Letters may arrive quicker when sent from main post offices. Strictly speaking, there's no longer a distinction between air mail and surface mail, as most international post is sent by air.

In addition to slow deliveries, post sometimes arrives in tatters. If you're sending anything remotely fragile, make sure that you pack it **very** carefully. Naturally, the post office takes no responsibility for late delivery or damaged post. Nevertheless, service is usually efficient – if not always friendly!

Letter post rates apply only to letters and documents; other items may not be sent using this service, however small, but must be sent as 'parcels' (see page 134).

Tariffs

There are two categories of domestic letter post (there are supplements for post to French overseas territories – see page 516): 'priority' (*service prioritaire*), which is supposed to ensure delivery the next working day, although this is by no means guaranteed, and 'non-priority' (*service non prioritaire*) for letters up to 250g, which can take much longer. Post office staff will assume you want to use the rapid service unless you state otherwise. Charges for letters up to 250g (the limit for *service prioritaire* is 3kg) due to come into effect in October 2006 are shown below.

Weight (g)	Cost (€)	
	Prioritaire	Non prioritaire
Up to 20	0.54	0.49
20 – 50	0.86	0.70
50 – 100	1.30	0.84
100 – 250	2.11	1.57

For foreign destinations, which are grouped into two zones (*zone* – see below), there's a choice between 'priority' (*prioritaire*) and 'economy' (*séconomique*). Zones and prices for letters up to 200g are shown below. Note that, as there's a single economy tariff for all letters up to 100g, it's often cheaper to use the priority service. Note also that there's a limit of 3kg on letters to certain countries, mostly in Africa. Details of postal tariffs can be found on La Poste's website (🖥 http://www.laposte.fr).

Weight (g)	Cost (€) – *prioritaire/économique*	
	Zone 1	Zone 2
Up to 20	0.60/1.35	0.85/1.70
20 – 50	1.15/1.35	1.70/1.70
50 – 100	1.40/1.35	2.30/1.70
100 – 250	4.00/2.80	5.50/3.00

Zone 1 includes EU countries and Switzerland.

Zone 2 rest of world.

Stamps

Stamps can be purchased at tobacconist's shops (*bureau de tabac* – see page 497) or from coin-operated machines outside main post offices, which is often more convenient than buying them from a post office. Post offices also have machines that print postage labels for the amount required (*vignettes d'affranchisement* or *etiquettes*). Note, however, that these are printed individually and, if you have a large number of letters to post, it can take a long time for all the labels to be printed. Self-adhesive (*auto-collant*) stamps for domestic letters up to 20g are sold in sheets of ten (*carnet*).

La Poste's latest promotional campaign is to persuade customers to use pre-stamped envelopes (*enveloppes pré-timbrées*) – a service known as *le prêt-à-poster*. Not surprisingly, these are rather expensive when purchased individually, although savings can be made by buying in bulk. Stamped window envelopes (*avec fenêtre*) are also available, as are stamped envelopes with decorative designs (usually of local sights), stamped domestic postcards (*carte postale préaffranchise*) and international stamped envelopes (*enveloppe internationale*) for letters up to 20g. There are also postage-paid envelopes for letters up to 500g to Denmark, Finland, Germany, Ireland, the Netherlands, Portugal, Spain, Sweden, Switzerland and the UK with a guaranteed maximum delivery time of three days (called *'Postexport Premier'*), costing around €6 (up to 100g) and €10 (over 100g).

Stamps can be purchased online, using a credit card for payment, but there's a handling charge of €4.57 for all orders (including pre-stamped envelopes and other products) totalling less than €38.

It's no longer necessary to affix an air mail (*par avion*) label or use air mail envelopes for international post, as all post is automatically sent by air to distant locations. Aerogrammes (*aérogramme*) are available from post offices and cost €0.76 for anywhere in the world.

Some post offices have a dedicated window (marked *Timbres de Collection*) for commemorative stamps and first-day covers. Brochures describing special stamps and first day covers are available from main post offices. For further information, contact the Service Philatélique de la Poste (☎ 01 41 87 42 00) or go to the stamp buying section (*'Achetez vos timbres'*) on the La Poste website (🖳 http://www. laposte.fr), where you can also see and purchase a range of stamp-collecting accessories and publications. Note that some stamps, usually collectors' stamps, have a surtax (*avec surtaxe*) which goes to the Red Cross or another charity.

Freepost (*libre réponse*), where the addressee pays the cost of postage, is available in France, but isn't widely used.

Note that road tax discs (see page 252) and official fiscal stamps (*timbre fiscal*), used to legalise documents, pay government taxes and motoring fines, must be purchased from a tobacconist's or a tax office and cannot be bought at a post office.

Addresses

The international identification letter for French addresses is 'F', which precedes the post (zip) code (*code postal*), although its use isn't obligatory. France uses five-digit postcodes, where the first two digits indicate the *département* and the last three the town or commune or, in the case of Paris, Lyon and Marseille, a district (*arrondissement*); for example, 75005 indicates the fifth *arrondissement* of Paris. Paris addresses are often given with the *arrondissement* written, for example, 6ème/6e. To translate this into the postcode, simply add 7500 to make 75006. All postcodes are listed by *commune* in alphabetical order in a yellow *Code Postal* booklet, available at any post office or on the post office website; they're also shown after each commune name in telephone books.

Small villages (*lieu-dit*) often use the postcode of a nearby village or town, and the affiliated village/town name should be also given in the address. Traditionally, the street address is written with a comma after the house number (i.e. 69, rue du Vin), but the post office advises that no punctuation should appear in the street and city lines of a 'properly' addressed letter (i.e. one that can be read by a machine!). Similarly, the addressee's surname, the street name, the *lieu-dit* (if applicable) and the post town should all be written or typed in capital letters. A properly written French address is shown below:

> Monsieur ROUGENEZ Jean
> 69 RUE DU VIN
> ESCARGEAUX
> F-12345 GRENOUILLEVILLE
> France

Many people include the department (or even region) name after the postcode, although this isn't necessary (and the post office discourages it). CEDEX (*Courrier d'Entreprise à Distribution Exceptionnelle*) is a special delivery service for business post and where applicable is included in addresses after the town, sometimes followed by a number, e.g. 75006 PARIS CEDEX 09. Post boxes (*boîte postale/BP*) are shown in addresses as *BP 01*, for example. It's customary for the sender (*expéditeur*) to write his own address on the back of an envelope.

Envelopes with printed boxes (*enveloppe précasée*) for addresses and postcodes are available from post offices and stationers. Note that French window envelopes have the window to the right of centre and not to the left as in the UK, for example.

Post & Letter Boxes

Post boxes (*boîte aux lettres*) are yellow and are usually on a pillar or set into (or attached to) a wall. They can sometimes be difficult to locate, although there's always one outside post offices and railway stations and usually one outside tobacconists'. It's best to post urgent letters at a main post office or railway station, as collections are more frequent and delivery is expedited. In cities and at main post offices, there's often a choice of boxes: for example, one box for local post (within the town, *commune* or *département*), another for other destinations (*autres destinations* or *départements étrangers*). There may be other boxes for economy post (*tarif réduit*) or packets/periodicals (*paquets – journaux périodiques*). In Paris, there are often separate boxes for the city (i.e. postcodes beginning 75) and the suburbs (*banlieue*). There are also special post boxes labelled *pneumatique*, where post for addresses within the city and to some suburbs is delivered within three hours (post is sent by compressed air under the streets of Paris).

French postmen (*facteur*) aren't obliged to deliver post to your front door unless it's on the street. If it isn't, you must install a letter box at the boundary of your property on the street. **Home letter boxes must meet specific requirements as to size, accessibility and how and where they're mounted.** For example, the opening must be at least 23cm (9in) wide and 2.4cm (1in) high and the box must be at least 40cm (1ft 6in) but not more than 1.8m (6ft) above the ground. 'Approved' boxes can be bought for around €10 in most DIY stores (in fact, smaller ones are usually more expensive). See the La Poste website for details or ask at your local post office if you plan to install your own letter box. (You may wish to give your postman a key to your letter box so that he can deliver items which won't fit through the slot.)

If you live in an apartment block with a caretaker (*gardienne*), she may receive and distribute letters (and parcels) to tenants. Otherwise letters are put in your letter box in the foyer (make sure that it has a lock). Often letter boxes aren't large enough for magazines and packets, which are left in a common storage space. In some apartment blocks in main cities it isn't unusual for post to be stolen, so if possible you should install a letter box large enough to hold all your post or rent a post box at a main post office (see **Collection** below).

Deliveries

In rural areas there's one post delivery a day, and you may be able to have your outgoing post collected by your postman. If the postman calls with post requiring a signature or payment when nobody is at home, he will leave a collection form (*avis de passage*). Post is kept at the post office for 15 days, after which it's returned to the sender, so if you're going to be away from home for longer than 15 days, you should ask the post office to hold your post (see **Collection** below). If a letter cannot be delivered, e.g. because it's wrongly addressed or because the addressee has moved, it will be returned with a note stating, e.g. '*n'habite pas à l'adresse indiquée – renvoyer à l'expéditeur*'. This is sometimes abbreviated to '*NPAI*'.

If you want your post to be redirected, you must complete an *ordre de réexpédition temporaire* at least a week in advance. Identification is required. Post can be redirected indefinitely and the service costs around €20 for up to six months and around €3 per month thereafter. If you're moving house, you should complete a permanent change of address card (*ordre de réexpédition définitif*); this service also costs around €20 for six months and is renewable for a further six months.

You will receive copious junk mail (*courrier indésirable* or *publicité*), e.g. unsolicited letters, retail brochures and free newspapers – estimated to amount to some 40kg per household. However, you should be sure to look between the pages of junk for 'real' post. It isn't unknown for foreigners to throw away important bills and correspondence during their first few weeks! The French tax authority is notorious for sending important forms and information in plastic wrappers that resemble those used for advertisements and junk magazines. You may be able to lessen the amount of junk mail you receive by putting up a '*Pas de pub*' sign or writing to the Syndicat des Entreprises de Vente par Correspondance, 60 rue de la Boétie, 75008 Paris.

Your postman may present you with a calendar each year around Christmas, designed to encourage you to tip him for thoughtfully delivering your post (albeit often late and mangled).

Collection

If you've received an *avis de passage* (see above), you must take it to your local post office, the address of which is written on the form. In large post offices there may be a window marked *retrait des lettres et paquets*. You usually need some form of identification (*pièce d'identité*), e.g. your passport, *carte de séjour* or French driving licence, although this may not be asked for. A post office may refuse to give letters to a spouse if they're addressed to his or her partner, or to a house owner if they're addressed to his tenants or guests, although this often isn't a problem. You can give someone authorisation to collect a letter or parcel on your behalf by entering the details on the back of the collection form in the box marked '*vous ne pouvez pas vous déplacer*', for which both your identification and that of the collector is required. It's possible to set up a permanent authorisation (*procuration*) with the local post office granting permission for a spouse or other adult member of your household to collect registered or other post in your name using their own identity documents.

If you're going to be away from your home for up to a month, you can have your post retained by the local post office (*garde du courrier*) for around €12. Alternatively, you can have post redirected (see page 133).

You can receive post at any post office in France via the international *poste restante* service. If there's more than one post office in the town, include its name in the address to avoid confusion. Letters should be addressed as follows:

> Marmaduke BLENKINSOP
> Poste Restante
> POSTE CENTRALE
> Postcode CITY NAME [e.g. 75001 PARIS]
> France

Post sent to a *poste restante* address is returned to the sender if it's unclaimed after 30 days. Identification (e.g. a passport) is necessary for collection. There's a fee of €0.54 (i.e. the standard letter rate) for each letter received. If you have an American Express card or use American Express travellers' cheques, you can have post sent to an American Express office in France. Standard letters are held free of charge; registered letters and packages aren't accepted. Post, which should be marked 'Client Mail Service', is kept for 30 days before being returned to the sender. Post can be held for up to two months for €18 or forwarded to another office or address, for which there's a charge of €20 for up to two weeks, €22 for six months or €40 for a year within France (a 'change of address pack' is available from La Poste for €32) and €55/€100 to another country. Other companies provide similar post-holding services for customers, e.g. Thomas Cook and Western Union.

You can rent a post office box (*boîte postale/BP*) at most post offices for an annual fee. All your post will be stored there and the postman will no longer deliver to your home. You can arrange to be informed when registered or express post arrives.

PARCELS

The Post Office provides a (confusing and ever-changing) range of parcel (*colis*) services, both domestic and international, now collectively called *ColiPoste*. International parcels are usually limited to 30kg, although there are lower limits, e.g. 20kg, for some countries. Parcels heavier than 5kg must be taken to a main post office. Parcels to addresses outside the EU must have an international green customs label (*déclaration de douane*) affixed to them. **Security regulations require you to present identification when sending parcels over 250g.**

Parcels posted in France must be securely packaged, and it's wise to buy padded envelopes (à bulles) or cardboard boxes sold at post offices. Padded envelopes come in four sizes and are also sold from self-service machines at main post offices; the boxes also come in various sizes. The post office also sells a wide range of pre-paid packaging for specific contents (emballages Colissimo and emballages Colissimo internationaux), such as reinforced boxes for bottles and packaging for CDs, DVDs and video tapes (costing between around €8 and €12 within France and between around €18 and €36 outside France). Boxes, padded bags and large envelopes are also sold in stationery shops.

When sending small parcels from a post office, use the window marked Paquets (if there is one). In larger branches, there's usually an automatic coin-operated weighing machine that issues the correct postage for packages.

Standard

The standard (économique) domestic parcel service is called 'Colissimo' (the name has changed four times in as many years!), which is supposed to take three to five days. Sample rates are: €5.10 (up to 500g), €6.20 (500g–1kg), €7 (1–2kg), €8 (2–3kg) and €10 (3–5kg). The standard international parcel service is called 'Colis Economique International', supposedly taking 9 to 15 days; the 'rapid' service 'Colissimo International' and taking four to eight days, depending on the destination. There are four zones (different from those for letter post – just to confuse you) but the 'economic' service isn't available to Zone A (EU countries plus Norway and Switzerland) – to confuse you further. Minimum costs are are €15 for a parcel up to 1kg sent to an EU country, Norway or Switzerland and €14.50 for a parcel up to 1kg sent to non-EU European countries. To send a 1kg parcel to the US will cost you €16 ('economic') or €21 ('rapid'). For other destinations and weights ask at a post office or consult the La Poste website (🖥 http://www.laposte.fr). All services include minimal insurance against loss or damage in transit.

Express

The fastest way to send letters or parcels is via the Chronopost International service (called EMS in most other European countries), which serves around 220 countries. There are two principal services: 'comfort', 'classic' and 'premium' (yes, these are the 'French' names!). Within France, the first of these services guarantees delivery by 18.00 the following day, the second by 13.00 and the last by 10.00. Minimum rates, for a parcel up to 2kg, are around €15 (comfort), €25 (classic) and €32 (premium). For international deliveries, there are different tariffs for documents and goods and no fewer than nine zones, two of which cover countries both in and outside the EU (confused yet?). Minimum rates – in this case for parcels up to 500g – start at around €35 (comfort), €37 (classic) or €57 (premium) for Zone 1 (within the EU). Promised delivery times are one to two days to major cities or one to three days for other destinations (classic), and the next day before 10.30 (premium). Details can be found on 🖥 http://www.fr.chronopost.com.

An alternative service for international parcels is *'Postexport'*, which is a postage-paid envelope designed for documents weighing between 20g and 2kg. This is much cheaper (and simpler to understand) than *Chronopost* or a courier service and takes on average only a day or two longer. Costs range from around €2 to €20 depending on destination and irrespective of weight. For example, sending a 2kg package to western Europe (including the padded envelope) costs just €13.75 compared with around €85 (excluding packaging) by *Chronopost*. You can buy envelopes in advance and simply hand them in at any post office when you want to use them.

French railways (SNCF) also operate an express package and parcel service (*Service National des Messageries/SERNAM*) within France and to most European countries. The 'special express' service operates from door-to-door and the 'direct express' service from station-to-station. Charges vary according to the speed of delivery, the distance, and whether the package is to be collected or delivered at either end. DHL and UPS also provide a domestic freight service, which guarantees airport-to-airport delivery within four hours, plus optional delivery at the receiving end.

REGISTERED & RECORDED POST

Registered post is commonly used in France when sending official documents and communications, when proof of despatch and/or receipt is required. You can send a registered letter (*lettre recommandée*) with (*avec*) or without (*sans*) proof of delivery (*avis de réception*). There are three levels of compensation (*indemnité forfaitaire*) for domestic registered letters and parcels:

- **Letters** – €2.50 for compensation of €16, €3.10 for €153 compensation, and €4 for €458 compensation.

- **Parcels** – €2.50 for compensation of €31, €3.10 for €153 compensation, and €4.30 for €458 compensation.

For international post, registration costs €4 for compensation of €45.73. All these costs are in addition to postage. The sender's address must be written on the back of registered letters. You receive a receipt for a registered letter or parcel. Proof of delivery costs an additional €1.30 for both domestic and international post. Items worth over €458 can be insured for a fee of €0.38 per €76.22 of the declared value (*valeur déclarée*) up to a maximum of €5,000, subject to a minimum charge of €2.29.

A domestic recorded or 'tracked' service (*courier suivi*) enables you to check the progress of your post and find out when it arrives (via the internet). The normal service, *La Lettre Suivie*, costs €0.91 **in addition to** the normal price of rapid post; pre-stamped envelopes – a service called *Distingo Suivi* – cost €1.53 for up to 20g, €2.05 for 20–50g and €2.56 for 50–100g (there are also envelopes for up to 1kg), which means that you're paying €0.12, €0.39 and €0.54 respectively for the envelopes. Pre-stamped envelopes are also available for international post (see **Stamps** on page 130). It's possible to combine the recorded service with registered post (*le prêt-à-recommander suivi*) if you need a signed receipt and also want to be able to track your letter. Bar-coded envelopes for trackable registered letters start at €7.62. It's even possible to send an electronic registered letter (see 💻 http://www.laposte.fr for details).

Registered letters require a signature and proof of identity on delivery – normally of the person to whom they're addressed. If the addressee is absent when delivery is made, a notice is left and the letter must be collected from the local post office (see **Collection** on page 133). When proof of delivery (*avis de réception*) is requested, a receipt is returned to the sender.

7.

TELEPHONE SERVICES

France has the third-largest telephone network in the world, and over 90 per cent of French households have a telephone. The French aren't, however, such habitual telephone users as some people, particularly North Americans, and they don't usually spend hours on the telephone; business people in particular prefer to meet or exchange letters than to conduct business over the telephone. France has one of the most modern telephone systems in the world, although numbers outside France are often difficult (sometimes impossible) to obtain. Tariffs are reasonable by European standards (see page 149) and there's a range of service providers to choose from. France also has an efficient mobile telephone service, encompassing virtually the whole country (see page 155).

The telephone network is operated by France Télécom (FT), which is 55 per cent state-owned (and one of the most indebted companies in the world!), but since 2002 call services have been open to competition, which has resulted in an intense price war; considerable savings can be made on domestic and international calls by shopping around for the lowest rates.

EMERGENCY & SERVICE NUMBERS

The national emergency numbers (*services d'urgence et d'assistance*) in France are:

Number	Service
15	Ambulance (*Service d'Aide Médicale d'Urgence/SAMU*) or to contact a duty doctor out of hours
17	Police (*police-secours*)
18	Fire (*sapeurs-pompiers/feu centrale d'alarme*)

If you aren't sure which emergency service you need (or cannot remember which number is for which service), it's best to call the Fire number (18), as the *pompiers* handle the widest range of emergency situations, including road accidents and natural disasters, and will notify an ambulance or police if they believe the situation warrants it. Calls to emergency numbers are free from public and private telephones.

There's a move to make the standard emergency phone number 112 in all EU member countries. This number will work in France, usually connecting you to the emergency services switchboard for your department, which will dispatch the appropriate service (ambulance, police or fire) to assist you. In some areas, the 112 service may have personnel who speak English or other foreign languages, but you cannot rely on this, particularly outside the Paris area, and should ensure that you and all family members know how to place an emergency call, giving your name, street address or location and requesting the appropriate service in reasonably clear French.

In addition to the national emergency numbers shown above, you should make a note of the number of your local ambulance service (*ambulance*), police station (*gendarmerie*) and fire service (*pompiers*), for which a space is usually provided in telephone books. Gas and electricity emergency numbers are listed in telephone directories under *EDF/GDF*. Other numbers to note are the poison emergency service (*centre anti-poisons*), Samaritans (*SOS Amitié*) and various other help organisations listed at the front of telephone directories. There's a 24-hour information/assistance telephone number (113) for problems associated with drugs, alcohol and smoking (*Drogue/Alcool/Tabac Info-Service*). There's also an internet helpline for women (*SOS Femmes*, 🖳 http://www.sosfemmes.com) and *Suicide Ecoute* for those contemplating suicide (☎ 01 45 39 40 00). In Paris, there's *SOS Médecins* (☎ 08 20 33 24 24 or ☎ 01 47 07 77 77) and *SOS Dentaire* (☎ 01 43 37 51 00). Contact numbers for *SOS Médecins* in other parts of France can be found on 🖳 http://www.sosmedecins-france.fr. In Paris and other main cities, there are emergency telephone boxes at major junctions marked *Services Médicaux* with direct lines to emergency services, and throughout France, there are free SOS call boxes on motorways and some other roads. See also **Emergencies** on page 292.

Information and help is available in English on ☎ 08 00 36 47 75 (or ☎ +33 1 55 78 60 56 from abroad) during normal office hours Mondays to Saturdays. Other useful telephone service numbers (in French) include those listed below (calls are free unless otherwise stated).

Number (s)	Service
1013	After-sales service and to report telephone breakdowns or line problems
1014	Private customer services
1016	Business customer services (or ☎ 08 25 33 11 22)
12	Directory enquiries (see page 146)
3000	For details of your current phone bill and 24-hour recorded information about FT's offers and call plans, which you can also book
3103/3125	To pick up messages, if you subscribe to FT's *Top Message* service (see page 153)
3131	To find out the number of your last caller (see **Caller Identification** on page 153)
3201/3250	Weather forecast (€0.34 per minute)
3212	International directory enquiries (see page 146)
3651	To prevent your number appearing on the telephone of the person you're calling (see **Caller Identification** on page 153)
3699	Speaking clock (*horloge parlante*).

France Télécom publishes a bi-monthly magazine, *Le Mag'Agence*, giving details of all its services, charges and special offers.

INSTALLATION & REGISTRATION

If you're planning to move into a property without an existing telephone line, you will need to have one installed. In this case, you must normally visit your local France Télécom office, which you will find in the yellow pages under *Télécommunications: service*, although it may be possible to obtain a telephone number before moving to France. In either case, you will need to prove that you're the owner or tenant of the property in question, e.g. with an electricity bill, confirmation of purchase (*attestation d'acquisition*) or a lease (*bail*). You will also require your passport or residence permit (*carte de séjour*). France Télécom publishes a *Set Up Guide* in English. If there's already a telephone line near the property, the charge is €109. **If you buy a property in a remote area without a telephone line, it may be expensive to have a telephone installed, as you must pay for the line to your property.** Contact FT for an estimate. If you're restoring a derelict building or building a new house, you should have trenches dug for the telephone cable if you want a below ground connection (you may be able to have an above ground connection via a wire from the nearest pylon). This work can be carried out by FT, but their charges are high and it's possible to do it yourself, although you must observe certain standards. Details of the required depth of trenches and the type of conduit (*gaine*) to use, etc., can be obtained from FT.

When you go to the FT agency, you will need to know what kind of telephone sockets are already installed in the property, how many telephones you want, where you want them installed and what kind of telephone you want (if you're buying from FT). If you want a number of telephone points installed, you should arrange this in advance. You may also want to upgrade a line (e.g. to ADSL – see **Broadband** below).

You will also be asked whether you want a listed or unlisted number (see **Directories** on page 145) and must inform FT where you want your bill sent and how you wish to pay it (see page 153). If you wish to pay your bill by direct debit, you must provide your account details (*relevé d'identité bancaire*). You can also request an itemised bill at the same time.

You may be given a telephone number on the spot, although you should wait until you receive written confirmation before giving it to anyone. Note that it isn't possible simply to take over the telephone number of the previous occupant. You will receive a letter stating that you have a mixed line (*ligne mixte*), which is simply a line allowing both incoming and outgoing calls. If you own a property and are letting it for holidays, you can arrange to have outgoing calls limited to the local area, or to regional or national calls only, but you cannot limit the service just to incoming calls.

To have a line installed takes from a few days in a city to weeks or possibly a month or more in remote rural areas, although 90 per cent of new customers have a line installed within two weeks. In certain areas there's a waiting list and you can have a line installed quickly only if you need a telephone for your safety or security, e.g. if you're an invalid, in which case a medical certificate is required. Business lines may be installed quicker than domestic lines.

When moving into a home with a telephone line, you must have the account transferred to your name and a telephone number issued to you. This can usually be done within 48 hours. Note that FT always changes the telephone number when the ownership or tenancy of a property changes. To do this, you can simply dial 1014 or go to the FT website (🖳 http://www.francetelecom.com and follow the links to *l'@gence sur le net*). Some information is available on the English-language section of the website, but it's limited to business services and investment details. English-language assistance can be obtained via email (✉ engft.paris@francetelecom.fr) and phone (☎ 08 00 36 47 75 or ☎ +33 1 55 78 60 56 from abroad) during normal office hours Mondays to Saturdays. The charge for taking over an existing line is €55.

If you're taking over a property from the previous occupants, you should arrange for the telephone account to be transferred to your name from the day you take possession. **Always check that the previous occupant has closed his account before you take over the line.** If you move into a property where the telephone hasn't been disconnected or transferred to your name, you should ask FT for a special reading (*relevé spécial*).

Broadband

There are two types of 'broadband' connection: asymmetric digital subscriber lines (ADSL) and integrated services digital network (ISDN) lines. France Télécom is committed to extending the availability of ADSL, but it isn't available in all areas and may even be available in one part of a village but not another! To find out if ADSL is available in your area, go to 🖳 http://www.francetelecom.fr, click on '*internet et multimédia*' (on the left) and '*abonnement express*' on the right, then enter your current telephone number (or a neighbour's) or the number of the department in which you live or intend to live. If broadband is available, it's possible to upgrade an existing line to an ADSL (known as le *haut-débit* or *ADSL*) at no extra charge. Installation of ADSL costs the same as a standard line (see above). France Télécom offers various combined phone and internet access packages for compulsive internet surfers (see **Internet** on page 159). France Télécom expects broadband to be available throughout France by 2007.

Yet another technological 'advance' is ADSL2, which offers even faster download and upload speeds (up to 20Mbits per second), but is currently available only within 1.5km of an 'exchange' and requires an upgrade to your ADSL box (supplied by most ISPs). To find out whether ADSL2 is available to you, go to one of the following websites and enter your phone number or post code as required: 🖳 http://www.degrouptest.com, 🖳 http://www.dslvalley.com, 🖳 http://www.zoneadsl.com. An even faster connection (up to 100Mb/s), known as le *très haut débit*, is available to businesses in certain parts of the country and is expected to spread to the private sector in the coming years as part of France Télécom's 'Fiber to the Home' (FTTH) initiative.

Another alternative is a connection via a mobile phone with 3G ('third generation') technology, which uses high-speed mobile phone access to internet protocol (IP) services and allows you to see the person you're speaking to, set up 'video conferences' and watch films. Advantages include high-speed connection (often faster than conventional broadband) and availability anywhere with mobile phone reception, making 3G technology ideal for homeowners in rural areas where telephone lines aren't available. On the other hand, 3G technology is still in its infancy (although 4g is already in gestation!) and monthly costs are similar to conventional broadband. To access high-speed internet using 3G technology you need a 3G mobile phone or a mobile phone and a 3G card, and a laptop computer or PDA to connect to your phone. 3G internet access software is available from most mobile phone companies (some offer free downloads from their website). Monthly costs vary greatly according to the amount of connection time and whether your mobile phone has a pre-paid or contract arrangement; packages start at €15 a month. Internet connection with a contract is invariably cheaper than with a pre-paid arrangement, and some of the best deals are for companies and the self-employed. It's expected that prices will fall over the next few years as competition increases and technology improves.

For those whose French (let alone their 'techno-speak') isn't up to the complexities of all this, French telecomms company Téléconnect offers an 'AngloPak' consisting of an English-language helpline (☎ 08 05 02 40 40) and English translations of all documentation and contracts. The service costs €29.95 per month, including two hours of 'free' calls; for details go to 🖳 http://www.tele connectfrance.com. See also **Mobile Telephones** on page 155 and **Internet Telephony** on page 161.

Alternative Providers

There are currently around 20 alternative telephone service providers in France, some of which advertise in the English-language press (see **Appendix B**). To help find your way through the maze of alternative telephone providers, you may want to consult a service such as BudgeTelecom (🖳 http://www.budgetelecom.com) where you can compare the available tariffs based on your own calling pattern and review customer evaluations of the services available from each provider. If you wish to use another provider (or several different providers, for different types of call), you will need to open a separate account with each. Note, however, that you must still have an account with FT for line rental. See also **Alternative Providers** on page 147.

Telephones

You can buy a telephone (*téléphone*) from FT or any retailer. Cordless (*sans fil*) telephones are widely available. The standard French telephone connector is a large block with a single blade-like plug. Adapter plugs allowing you to connect a standard RJ11 phone plug to a French phone point aren't easy to find in France, although they're available in some airport shops and larger computer shops, and it's preferable to buy them before you move to France (e.g. from Maplin, 🖳 http://www.maplin.co.uk, Radio Shack/Tandy or RSComponents, 🖳 http://www.rs-components.com, or TeleAdapt,

🖳 http://www.teleadapt.com). Note, however, that they cost around €40, so it may be cheaper to buy a new telephone! See also **Modems** on page 160.

DIRECTORIES

When you have a telephone installed, your name and number is usually automatically included in the next issue of your local telephone directory (*annuaire*) as well as the internet telephone directory. Like most telephone companies, FT sells its list of subscribers to businesses, but you can choose to have an unlisted number, which saves you from the affliction of telephone marketing, which is increasingly prevalent in France. There are three options (known as *Services Vie privée*), all of which are free:

- **Orange List (*liste orange*)** – Your details aren't made available to businesses.

- **Chamois List (*liste chamois*)** – In addition to the above, your details aren't included in printed or electronic (e.g. online) directories.

- **Red List (*liste rouge*)** – In addition to the above, your number isn't given out by directory enquiries.

The chamois and red options are particularly useful if you have a phone line reserved for a fax machine and don't want to be inundated with fax advertisements. From 2006, directories will include mobile telephone numbers: if you have a mobile contract, your number will automatically be listed unless you tell FT you don't want it listed; if you don't have a contract, you must ask for your number to be listed. You can also ask for your email address, postal address and profession to be included.

Telephone directories are published by department (*département*). Not all directories are published at the same time (the issue date for new directories is listed at the front). Some departments have more than one volume (*tome*), e.g. the Paris white pages (*pages blanches*) are in five volumes and the yellow pages (*pages jaunes*) two volumes. Yellow pages, which contain only business and official (e.g. government) telephone numbers, are included with the white pages in one volume for departments with few subscribers or published in a separate volume or volumes. When there's more than one volume, the index is included at the front of the first volume. You can obtain a copy of white or yellow pages for other departments for a fee of around €7.50 per volume (☎ 08 00 30 23 02) or refer to them in libraries or at main post offices. There are also local yellow pages (*Les Pages Jaunes Locales*) in some areas (e.g. Paris), and business to business directories (*Professionnels à Professionnels/PAP*) are published in national and regional editions as well as in a CD-ROM version available to businesses. The yellow pages for the whole of France can also be accessed on line at 🖳 http://www.pagesjaunes.fr.

Telephone directories (both white and yellow pages) contain a wealth of information, including emergency information and numbers, useful local numbers, FT numbers and services, tariffs, international codes and costs, how to use the telephone (in English, French, German, Italian and Spanish), public telephone information, information about bills, directories and Télécom products, administration numbers, and maps of the department(s) covered by the telephone book.

Subscribers are listed in the white pages under their town or *commune* (or *arrondissement* in Paris, Lyon and Marseille) and not alphabetically for the whole of a department or city. It isn't enough to know that someone lives, for example, in the department of Dordogne; you must know the town. You will receive little or no help from directory enquiries (who aren't always helpful at the best of times) unless you know the town or village where the subscriber is located – in which case, you might as well look up the number yourself! The advantage of the listing system is that you can easily find the numbers of people in your town or village if you know their address but not their name. (Another potential disadvantage is that people can easily find your number.)

When your application for a telephone line has been accepted, you're given a voucher (*bon*) for a copy of your local telephone directory; the issuing office is usually housed in the same building as the Télécom agency. Annual directories are supposed to be delivered to your door or building when they're available, but in some outlying areas delivery is haphazard at best. If you cannot obtain a directory, call ☎ 1014.

Directory Enquiries

For domestic directory enquiries, you can no longer simply dial 12, but must instead choose between umpteen services and endure a barrage of advertising (without being told how much you're being charged for the privilege!) before being given the number you want. All directory enquiries numbers begin 118; companies purporting to offer a free service (from a fixed line telephone) are listed below, along with their websites for further information. Details of all directory enquries services can be found on a dedicated website, 🖥 http://www.appel118.fr.

Number	Company	Website
118000	Le 118 000 SAS	http://www.le118000.fr
118075	Le Numéro	http://www.leparisien.com
118218	Le Numéro	http://www.118218.fr
118247	Telegate France	http://www.le118247.fr
118318	Le Numéro	http://www.lenumero.fr
118444	PCCI	-
118713	Le Numéro	http://www.lenumero.fr

Some of the above services also provide numbers outside France, although there may be a charge. For both domestic and international numbers, however, it's easier and cheaper to use an online telephone directory, e.g. 🖥 http://www.pagesjaunes.fr for France.

USING THE TELEPHONE

Using the telephone in France is simplicity itself. All French telephone numbers have ten digits, beginning with a two-digit regional code (01 for the Ile-de-France, 02 for the north-west, 03 north-east, 04 south-east and 05 south-west) and followed by another two-digit area code. If you're calling within France, you must **always** dial all ten digits, even if you're phoning your next-door neighbour.

Codes for the overseas departments (*DOM*), which have six-figure numbers, are as follows: French Guyana (05 94), Guadeloupe (05 90), Martinique (05 96), Mayotte (02 69), Réunion (02 62), Saint-Pierre-et-Miquelon (05 08). (Monaco isn't part of France and has its own country code of 377.)

Numbers beginning 06 are mobile telephone numbers (see page 155), and those beginning 08 are special rate numbers (see page 151).

International Calls

It's possible to make international direct dialling (IDD) calls to most countries from both private and public telephones. A full list of country codes, plus area codes for main cities and time differences, is shown in the information pages (*les info téléphoniques*) of your yellow pages. To make an international call you must first dial 00, then the country code, the area code (**without** the first zero) and the subscriber's number.

France subscribes to a Home Direct service (called *France Direct*) that allows you to call a number giving you direct and free access to an operator in the country that you're calling, e.g. for British Telecom in the UK dial ☎ 08 00 99 00 44. The operator will connect you to the number required. Note, however, that this service can be used only for reverse charge (collect) calls. For any other country, dial 12 and ask for the relevant *France Direct* number; there's no longer a list of Home Direct codes in French telephone directories. You can also use the *France Direct* service from some 50 countries to make calls to France via an FT operator.

To obtain an operator from one of the four major US telephone companies dial ☎ 08 00 99 00 11 (AT&T), ☎ 08 00 99 00 19 (MCI), ☎ 08 00 99 00 87 (Sprint) or ☎ 08 00 99 00 13 (IDB Worldcom). (Note that these are French 08 00 numbers, not American 0800 numbers and that the latter aren't toll-free when dialled from abroad.) These companies also offer long-distance calling cards that provide access to English-speaking operators, and AT&T offers a US Direct service, whereby you can call an operator in any state (except Alaska).

France Télécom publishes a useful free booklet, *Guide du Téléphone International*, containing information in both French and English. See also **Internet Telephony** on page 161.

Alternative Providers

If you're using an alternative telephone provider (i.e. not France Télécom) for local or long-distance calls (see page 144), you must normally dial a code to route your call to the appropriate telephone company. For example, to use Cégétel for long-distance domestic calls, you replace the first zero of the area code with a 7 (e.g. ☎ 01 40 20

70 00 becomes ☎ 71 40 20 70 00) and dial 70 instead of 00 for international calls. To route local calls through Cégétel, you must dial ☎ 3695 and then the entire ten-digit phone number. Each provider has its own code or procedure for accessing its network. It's possible to have subscriptions with several different telephone providers, and each one will indicate to you what numbers you need to dial to route your calls correctly. Alternatively, you can notify FT of your default provider and they will set up your phone line to automatically route calls to whichever of the alternative telephone providers you prefer without having to use the extra numbers. This facility costs around €11 and takes a week or two to set up (during which time you can use a prefix).

If you have all your calls automatically routed via another provider, it's possible to revert to the FT system by dialling 8 before the number. This service, which is useful if there's a problem with your alternative provider, must be ordered in advance from FT and it's free.

An increasing number of expatriates (and French people) make use of a 'callback' service, such as those provided by Eurotelsat (🖥 http://www.eurotelsat.com) and Kallback (🖥 http://www.kallback.com). It's no longer necessary to wait to be called back and, as with an alternative provider, you simply dial a local freephone number or a code before the number you want. Calls are routed via the cheapest provider, and companies claim that you can save up to 70 per cent (compared with FT rates) on international calls.

Reverse Charge Calls

It's possible to make a reverse charge (collect) call (*communication en PCV/payable chez vous*) to another French number, but only if that number is set up to receive reverse charge calls (*service imprévisto*). To make a reverse charge call, you must dial ☎ 3006 followed by the telephone number. If the number you're calling isn't set up to receive reverse charge calls, you won't be connected. To set up a phone to receive reverse charge calls, dial ☎ 1014. Set-up is free but there's a charge of €0.40 per call received in addition to the call charge. Reverse charge calls cannot be made to numbers outside France.

Person-to-Person Calls

Person-to-person (*avec préavis*) calls can also be made via the operator. These calls can also be made to certain countries via the Home Direct service (see page 147). As with anything requiring interaction with the operator, this can be a slow (and expensive) process and it may be easier, cheaper and less stressful to make a short call and ask someone to call you back.

Recorded Messages

After dialling, you may hear the following recorded message: '*Le numéro que vous demandez n'est pas attribué; veuillez consulter le service des renseignements*' ('The number you've dialled is not recognised; please use Directory Enquiries'). Note that there's a charge of €0.80 for using Directory Enquiries (see page 146).

If the number you're calling is engaged, you may hear an engaged tone (i.e. a series of short beeps) or you may hear a series of 'musical' tones followed by a recorded message: *'La ligne de votre correspondent est occupé; pour le rappeler automatiquement, appuyez sur la touche cinq'* ('The line you've dialled is engaged; for 'ring-back', press 5'). If you dial 5 before replacing the receiver, your telephone will automatically be called back by the telephone you're trying to reach as soon as it's free. There's no charge for this service. If the person you're calling is using *Signal d'Appel* (see page 152), you will hear the following message: *'Veuillez patienter. Votre correspondant est en ligne. Nous lui indiquons votre appel par un signal sonore'* ('Please wait. The person you're calling is on the line and knows you're waiting'). If he doesn't clear the line within a few seconds, the message will give way to a normal engaged tone and you must redial. Sometimes when lines are busy, you won't be put on hold but will be instructed to ring back later, e.g. *Toutes nos lignes sont indisponibles. Veuillez nous rappeler ultérieurement.*

Greetings

The usual French 'greeting' on the telephone is simply *allô* inflected as a question (*'Allô?'*). If you're using the operator, he may say, *'Ne quittez pas'* ('Hold the line'). 'I'm trying to connect you' is *'J'essaie de vous mettre en relation'*, and 'Go ahead' may be simply *'Parlez'* ('Speak') or *'Je vous écoute'* ('I'm listening').

Numbers

One of the hardest things to do in any foreign language is to understand telephone numbers given to you orally. This is particularly difficult in French, as telephone numbers are dictated in the same way as they're written, i.e. normally two digits at a time. For example 04 15 48 17 33 is *zéro quatre, quinze, quarante-huit, dix-sept, trente-trois*. It's therefore wise to practise your French numbers (particularly those from 70 to 100). Note that the French don't say 'double' when two digits are the same: for example, 22 is *vingt-deux*. Note also that some numbers aren't written in pairs, e.g. 0800 300 400; these are also spoken as written – in this case *zéro huit cents, trois cents, quatre cents.*

CHARGES

Deregulation of the telecommunications market has resulted in an intense price war, and considerable savings can be made on national as well as international calls by shopping around for the lowest rates. However, as there are around 20 alternative providers in France, it's impossible to list all their tariffs here, and only FT's are given in detail. Comparisons between the rates offered by different service providers can be found via the internet (e.g. 🖥 http://www.comparatel.fr and http://www.budge telecom.com) or you can contact the Association Française des Utilisateurs de Télécommunications (AFUTT, ☎ 01 47 41 09 11, 🖥 http://www.afutt.org) on Mondays to Thursdays between 10.30 and 12.30. Line rental and call charges are explained below; for information about installation and registration charges, see page 142.

Line Rental

The monthly line rental or service charge (*abonnement*) is €14 for a standard line or ADSL. If you use an alternative provider (see page 147), there may be a separate monthly fee in addition to your call charges, although most providers have dropped these.

Calls

Domestic Calls

France Télécom's tariffs depend on the destination and time of calls. Calls at peak times (*heures pleines*), which are Mondays to Fridays from 08.00 to 19.00 and Saturdays from 08.00 to 12.00, are charged at the 'normal' rate (*tarif normal*); calls at all other times (*heures creuses*), including all day on public holidays, are charged at a reduced rate (*tarif réduit*).

Call charges are based on an initial 'connection' charge (*mise en relation* or *crédit-temps*), which pays for a minute or 39 seconds depending on whether the call is local (i.e. calls to numbers starting with the same four digits as your own) or not, plus a per-minute rate after that time. The term 'unit' (*unité*) is sometimes used for the initial charge, although you may receive different definitions of the term, even from FT staff! France Télécom's current standard charges for calls from and to fixed lines are shown below.

	Initial Charge	Peak Minute	Off-peak Minute
Local Calls	€0.09 (60 seconds)	€0.033	€0.018
Other Calls	€0.11 (39 seconds)	€0.090	€0.063

France Télécom no longer publicises these rates, however, but offers instead an array of 'all-inclusive' packages (*forfait*), of which there are currently 20. Packages require a fixed monthly payment (e.g. between €1.50 and €10) in return for reduced price or, in some cases, 'free' calls, which makes it all but impossible to calculate what you're paying for each call or to compare rates with those of other providers. A recent comparison between rates charged by the five major providers showed a price variation between €0.13 and €0.16 for a three-minute, off-peak local call, and between €0.27 and €0.40 for a ten-minute, peak rate local call, with FT's charges – not surprisingly – generally the highest, although if you're a telephone-addict you may find their 'unlimited use' (*illimité*) packages good value.

Alternative telephone service providers (see page 147) also offer a variety of call packages, consisting of a combination of varying initial charges and lengths followed by different per-minute charges and, in some cases, a single rate for all times of day and all destinations. Cégétel, for example, charges a connection fee of €0.118 followed by a standard per-minute charge of €0.013 to all fixed lines in France, irrespective of the distance or time of the call.

Calls from fixed telephones to mobile phones are more expensive. FT, for example, currently makes an initial charge of €0.21 for 30 seconds followed by €0.21 per minute during peak times and €0.10 per minute during off-peak hours for calls to SFR or its own Orange mobile phones. Calls to a Bouygues mobile phone cost €0.25 at peak times or €0.13 during off-peak hours after a connection charge of €0.24. For details of charges for calls from mobile phones, see page 155.

International Calls

France Télécom has eight tariff levels for international calls, listed on its website. All international calls are subject to an initial charge of €0.12 (unless you're using the *Option Plus* or *Les Heures* package, in which case it's €0.11) for a period varying from 5 to 27 seconds, depending on the tariff. Calls to western Europe and North America (except Hawaii and Alaska) are charged at the cheapest tariff and cost €0.22 per minute during peak periods (see above) and €0.12 per minute off-peak. Calls to Australia and New Zealand cost €0.49/0.34 per minute.

Other telephone providers have different tariff structures for international calls. Most alternative providers also offer a variety of discount plans, such as half price on all calls to a designated 'favourite country' or to specific overseas phone numbers frequently called.

Special Rate Numbers

Special rate numbers, all of which begin 08, include the following (all charges apply from a fixed-line telephone; calls from a mobile cost more):

Prefix	Charge
08 00/05/09 (*Numéro Vert*)	Free
08 10/11/19/60 (*Numéro Azur*)	Local call charge (see page 149)
08 20/21/70/71 (*Numéro Indigo*)	€0.12 per minute
08 25/26/84/90	€0.15 per minute
08 91	€0.30 per minute
08 92	€0.45 per minute
08 93	€0.75 per minute
08 97	€0.60 per call
08 98	€1.20 per call
08 99	Over €1.20 per call

Other Charges

Charges for equipment rental, credit card calls and (if you use the same provider) internet connection will be included on your bill (see page 153), as will any charges for custom and optional services (see below).

CUSTOM & OPTIONAL SERVICES

France Télécom provides a range of custom and optional telephone services, described as 'comfort services' (*service confort*). Almost all services can be ordered online at the FT website (🖥 http://www.francetelecom.com – click on '*l'@gence en ligne'*), where you can also find a detailed description of the services available and their prices. *Services confort* can be ordered individually or as part of a package and include those detailed below. Some services involve an annual subscription charge, others a fixed charge each time the service is used. Due to increased competition, some services that were previously charged are now free. It pays to check with FT or read the advertising material that comes with your telephone bill to find out about the latest special offers. For details of all custom and optional services, call ☎ 1014.

- **Call Barring (*Blocage d'Appels*)** – Allows you to block all incoming calls. €3.80 per month.

- **Call Transfer (*Transfert d'Appel*)** – Allows you to divert calls to another telephone number automatically, e.g. from home to office (or vice versa) or to a mobile telephone. Dial *21* followed by the number to which you wish your calls to be transferred, followed by a hash (#) sign (*dièse*). €1.50 per month plus €0.11 per call.

- **Call Waiting (*Signal d'Appel*)** – Lets you know when another caller is trying to contact you when you're already making a call and allows you to speak to him without terminating your call. To activate press the 'R' button (for *raccrocher*: to hang up) followed by 2. If your phone doesn't have an 'R' button, just hang up briefly to change connections. Free.

- **Call Waiting while Online ('*@llo'*)** – If you have a shared line for telephone and internet access (see page 150), this service allows you to 'see' an incoming call while you're online. The caller's number is displayed on your computer screen and you can take the call via the computer or the telephone or transfer it to an answering service. €1.50 per month.

- **Three-way Conversation (*Conversation à Trois*)** – Allows you to hold a three-way conversation, either within France or overseas. Free.

- **Reminder Call (*Mémo Appel*)** – Allows you to programme your telephone to ring at a set time, e.g. to wake you or to remind you of an appointment or to make an important call. To make a reminder call, dial *55* followed by the time you wish to be called, using the 24-hour clock. For example, if you wish to be woken at 07.30, you dial *55*0730 followed by hash (*dièse*). To have a reminder call at 15.30 dial *55*1530#. €0.565 per call.

- **Answering Service (*Top Message*)** – Allows you to receive messages while you're on the telephone as well as when you're unable (or don't want) to answer the phone. If you've received a message, you will hear an interrupted dial tone the next time you pick up the receiver. Sometimes, the message service will automatically call you to tell you that you have a new message. Sometimes it won't. Free.

- **Ring Back (*AutoRappel*)** – Allows you to obtain an automatic call back by dialling 5 if the number you dial is engaged (see **Recorded Messages** on page 149). Free.

- **Caller Identification (*Présentation du Numéro/Nom*)** – This is available on telephones with a built-in display (or you can plug a display unit in to your phone) and allows you to see either a caller's telephone number or both his number and his name and business name as listed in the telephone directory. The service costs €1.50 per month for the number only and €2.30 for both name and number. If you don't wish your details to appear on the telephones of people you're calling, you can dial ☎ 3651 before the number or opt for *secret permanent* (both free services). If your telephone doesn't have a display, you can find out the the number of your last caller by dialling ☎ 3131 (free).

- **New Number (*Annonce du Nouveau Numéro*)** – When moving out of a property, it's possible to have callers advised of your new number for up to 12 months. €6 per month.

- **Call Monitoring (*Allofact*)** – Monitor your calling habits over any period. Free but you must register by calling FT's order line (☎ 3000).

BILLS

France Télécom bills its customers every two months and allows you two weeks to pay your bill (*facture*). Bills include VAT (*TVA*) at 19.6 per cent, although an ex-VAT figure (*HT*) is shown as well as the total including VAT (*TTC*). You can request an itemised bill (*facturation détaillée*) which lists all calls with the date and time, the number called, the duration and the charge, and is particularly useful if you let a second home in France or lend it to friends. This service is free but must be requested a month in advance. You can monitor your calling habits over any period by using Allofact (see above) or via the FT website (🖳 http://www.francetelecom.com and then following '*lEspace Client*').

Bills can be paid by post by sending a cheque to France Télécom, at a post office or at your local FT office. Simply detach the tear-off part of your bill and send or present it with payment. You can pay your telephone bill by *titre interbancaire de paiement* (*TIP*), whereby your bank account details are pre-printed on the tear-off part of the bill, which you simply date and sign and return, or by direct debit (*prélèvement automatique*), which is recommended if you spend a lot of time away from home or are non-resident, as they will ensure that you won't be disconnected for non-payment. If you're non-resident, you can have bills sent to an address outside France. If you pay your bills by direct debit, your invoice will specify the date of the debit from your account, usually around 20 days after receipt of the invoice. Contact your local FT agent for information.

If you don't pay your bill by the date due, you will receive a reminder (a letter or a telephone call) about a week after the due date. Late payment of a bill incurs a penalty of 10 per cent of the sum due. If payment still hasn't been made two weeks after the due date, FT may progressively reduce your telephone service (*service restreint*), depending on your payment record. If a reduced service is implemented, first the international service will be terminated, followed by a restriction to local calls and finally to emergency calls only. You will receive a letter before your service is totally disconnected and the bill must be paid immediately to prevent your being cut off. If you're cut off, you must pay the outstanding bill, a reconnection fee of €46.12 (as for a new connection) and you may also need to pay a deposit.

France Télécom bills include the following details:

Item	Meaning
Numéro de client	Your account number
Numéro de facture	Invoice number
Date de la facture	Date of invoice
Somme à payer avant le ...	Amount due by ...
Prochaine facture vers le ...	Next bill due on ...
Montant	Amount
HT	Excluding VAT
TTC	Including VAT
Abonnements, forfaits et options	Line rentals, call plans and optional services
Communications	Calls
Total facture	Total amount due
TVA payée sur les débits (19,60%)	VAT payable (at 19.6%)
Somme à payer	Amount due
Dernier montant dû à France Télécom	Amount due on last invoice
Règlements comptabilisés au ...	Payments received by ...
Solde reporté	Amount brought forward
Prix unitaire mensuel	Monthly charge

If you receive a bill with which you don't agree, you should pay your usual charge and contest the bill with your telephone company. They will investigate it and won't disconnect you while it's in dispute, provided you pay something. Check also for

© Joe Laredo

▲ Champagne, Ardennes
© Joe Laredo

◄ Les Mazuts, Lot
© Survival Books

▼ Mont St. Michel, Manche
© outdoorimages
(www.bigstockphoto.com)

◄ Eiffel Tower, Paris
© ErikN (www.bigstockphoto.com)

Sacre Coeur, Paris
© Xavier Pironet (www.bigstockphoto.com)

Montreuil-sur-Mer,
Pas-de-Calais
© Survival Books

Mountain village, Corsica
© circlesquare (www.bigstockphoto.com)

Carcassonne old city, Aude
© Survival Books

© leadinglights
(www.istockphoto.com)

Bayeux cathedral,
Calvados

▶

▶

St Vallier du Thiey,
Alpes-Maritimes

▲ American war graves
St. Laurent-sur-Mer, Calvados
© Survival Books

▲ Gerberoy, Oise
© Joe Laredo

▶
Pavement artists, Paris
© Joe Laredo

▼ Etretat, Seine-Maritime
© Survival Books

▲ Château de Fougères, Ille-et-Vilaine
© Survival Books

counterfeit bills produced by foreign companies. The give-away is the address to which to send the money, which is usually abroad.

MOBILE TELEPHONES

After a relatively slow start in introducing mobile telephones (*portable* or, increasingly, *mobile*), France has one of Europe's fastest growing cellular populations. Mobile phones are now so widespread that some businesses (e.g. restaurants, cinemas, theatres, concert halls, etc.) ban them and some even use mobile phone jammers that can detect and jam every handset within 100m.

There are currently three mobile phone service providers: Bouygues (☎ 08 25 82 56 14 or ☎ +33 6 60 61 46 14 from abroad, ▢ http://www.bouyguestelecom.fr), France Télécom, operating under the Orange trademark (☎ 08 00 10 07 40 or ☎ +33 6 07 62 64 64 from abroad, ▢ http://www.orange.fr), and SFR (☎ 08 00 10 60 00, ▢ http://www.sfr.fr). Buying a mobile phone is an absolute minefield, there are not only three networks to choose from but also a wide range of tariffs covering connection fees, monthly subscriptions, insurance and call charges. To further complicate matters, all three providers have business ties to one or more of the fixed telephone services (SFR with Cégétel, for example) and offer various deals combining mobile and fixed line services.

The major decision when buying a mobile phone is whether to take out a contract, whereby you pay a fixed monthly charge and obtain a certain amount of call time 'free', or to use a 'pay-as-you talk' system, whereby you pay only for calls using a phone card. If you take out a contract, the cost of the telephone itself is usually lower than if you use pay-as-you-talk; it may even be free. Before deciding, shop around and compare phone prices and features, set-up and connection charges and most importantly call rates. Note also that, if you opt for pay-as-you-talk, there's usually a time limit of one or two months on the use of each card; if you don't make many calls, you may be wasting money on cards you don't use.

The most popular contracts usually give you a set number of hours of outgoing calls (e.g. two, three or five) for a flat monthly fee. Hours included in the fee may be limited to evenings and weekends or split between peak and off-peak calling times. Fees are normally reduced if you agree to a contract of 12 months or more or order certain add-on features or services. All mobile telephone bills must now include a complete list of calls made, including the exact duration and the time charged for. If you have a problem with a mobile phone service provider, you can call the Direction Générale de la Concurrence, de la Consommation et de la Répressions des Fraudes (DGCCRF, ☎ 01 40 27 16 00 or ☎ 3939).

If you want to use a foreign mobile in France, it's usually possible to buy a SIM card, which will give you a French mobile number and allow you to make and receive calls in France. You pay around €20 or €30 for connection to one of the French networks and can choose between a monthly contract and a 'pay-as-you-talk' card, which can be topped up (in values of €10, €20 and €35) as required. Note, however, that you **must** top it up at least twice a year, or you will lose your number and have to be reconnected. An alternative is to set up a SIM 'contract' in your home country, e.g. with 0044.co.uk in the UK. However, from mid-2007 mobile 'roaming' charges are expected to fall by up to 70 per cent thanks to a proposed EC law.

Text messaging (*envoyer des SMS/textos*) is as much an addiction in France as anywhere else (over 12m messages were sent in 2005), and France is set to become the first European country to regulate mobile phone operators' charges, which are due to be limited to 3.5 cents per message.

All mobile phone numbers have the prefix 06 and there's a special (i.e. expensive) charge rate applied when you call an 06 number from a fixed phone in France (see page 151). Calls between mobile phones of the same company are generally discounted and most companies offer similar 'frequent caller' plans to those available for fixed phone services (see page 150).

There has been a rash of mobile phone thefts, particularly in Paris, where thieves (sometimes travelling on skateboards or rollerskates) pluck the phone from the hand of its owner in mid-conversation. It's possible to insure not only the phone itself and the value of the SIM card, but also against the cost of calls made by anyone who finds or steals it, as well as against damage to the phone if you drop it or step on it and even, in some cases, against the phone breaking down. Insurance is offered by the three service providers – Bouygues, Orange and SFR – as well as by Darty, FNAC and The Phone House, among others. Insurance is usually for a minimum of a year and premiums vary from around €35 to over €100, so you should check exactly what is and isn't covered. Most insurers offer two levels of insurance, the higher level including the cost of calls made by the thief. When choosing whether to include this, bear in mind that the average cost of calls made by thieves before the line is blocked (see below) is around €250. Check also whether you can claim more than once a year, whether you're covered if your phone is stolen from your car and whether there's an excess (*franchise*). If you're buying a phone, don't allow yourself to be pressurised into buying the insurance offered by the retailer; check the other options first. (If your phone is more than two years old, it may not be worth insuring, as thieves tend to target newer phones.)

If you lose your phone, whether or not it's insured, you should phone your service provider immediately to report the loss and give the identification number of your phone (which, of course, you've written down somewhere you can find it quickly!). All new phones have an IMEI code, which appears beside the battery; if you can't find it, dial *#06# on your phone and it will appear on the display. The contact numbers are: Bouygues 08 25 82 56 14 or ☎ +33 6 60 61 46 14 from abroad; Orange ☎ 08 00 10 07 40 or ☎ +33 6 07 62 64 64 from abroad; SFR ☎ 06 10 00 19 00 or ☎ +33 6 10 00 19 00 from abroad. You should also report the loss to your local police and, if the phone is insured, your insurer.

In recent years there has been widespread publicity regarding a possible health risk to users from the microwave radiation emitted by mobile phones. New mobile phones must now state the amount of energy absorbed by the user (known as the *débit d'absorption spécifique* or *DAS*). This is measured in watts per kilo (W/kg), and the maximum permitted *DAS* is 2W/kg for the head and body. The French government has published a free leaflet, *Le Téléphone Mobile Santé et Sécurité*, containing guidelines for the 'safe' use of mobiles (including keeping them away from 'sensitive' body areas and not using them in poor reception areas, where they use maximum power), which are available from the Ministry of Health (☎ 01 40

56 60 00, ⌨ http://www.sante.gouv.fr). A mobile phone should be kept at least 15cm from a pacemaker, insulin pump or other electronic implant.

PUBLIC TELEPHONES

Despite the increasing use of mobile telephones (see page 155), public telephone boxes (*cabine téléphonique*) can be found in all towns and villages: in post offices, bus and railway stations, airports, bars, cafés, restaurants and other businesses, and of course, in the streets. Most telephone boxes are Perspex kiosks, and most public telephones (*téléphone publique*) accept telephone cards (see below), *Carte France Télécom* (see below) and bank (i.e. debit) cards, although many won't accept credit cards, particularly those without a microchip.

Public telephones are also available at some post offices, where you're allocated a booth and you pay for your calls at the counter afterwards. To make a call from a hotel room, you may be able to dial direct (after dialling 0 or 1, for example) or you may need to make calls via the hotel receptionist. Note that hotels impose a surcharge (which can be 100 or 200 per cent!) on the cost of calls; cafés and restaurants also set their own charges. Most hotels have public telephones in the foyer.

Public telephones are provided on high-speed trains (*TGV*) and allow both domestic and international calls. They can be operated with a *télécarte* or a *Carte France Télécom* (see below). There are usually three telephones on each *TGV*, one in first class, one in second class and one in the bar. On some trains you will see 'no telephone' signs, indicating that you aren't supposed to use your mobile phone.

Calls to emergency services can be made free from any telephone box, and all public telephones allow international direct dialling (IDD); international calls can also be made via the operator. There are free SOS (e.g. breakdown) telephones on motorways and at main junctions in Paris and other large cities (marked *Services Médicaux*), for use in the event of accidents or medical emergencies.

Telephone Cards

Télécarte

Telephone cards (*télécarte*) are available from post offices, railway stations, tobacconists', cafés, news kiosks, banks and various shops where the sign *TELECARTE EN VENTE ICI* is displayed. Telephone cards are available in two values: €5 (for 50 units – see page 150) and €15 (for 120 units).

A new type of phone card is a scratch card, which gives you a code allowing you to make calls from a public or private telephone. France Télécom offers four such cards, which it calls *Le Ticket de Téléphone*, allowing either national or international calls up to a value of €7.50 or €15. You scratch the back of the card to reveal the code, which must be dialled after the *Ticket* access code, 3089, before you can dial the number you want. Other telephone companies (e.g. France Monde and Kertel) offer scratch cards, which may provide better value than FT's. La Poste also offers cards, called *Kertel*, which are 'rechargeable' at post offices.

Carte France Télécom

You can obtain a free telephone 'credit' card from FT, called a *Carte France Télécom* (*CFT*), which can be used both domestically and in over 40 other countries, calls being charged to your French telephone account. With a *CFT* you can make international calls to and from France, but not from a foreign country to a country other than France. Cards can be used with any public or private telephone; you simply dial an access code. You receive a detailed invoice for calls made with a *CFT* with your telephone bill every two months or you can have your calls charged directly to a major credit card.

Credit Cards

At major French airports, such as Charles de Gaulle (Paris), Lyon and Nice, as well as in most railway stations, there are public telephones that accept international credit cards, e.g. American Express, Diners Club, Eurocard, MasterCard and Visa. The cost of calls is automatically debited to your credit card account. Note that, although using credit cards is convenient, it can be **very** expensive. On some credit card phones there's a charge of 12 units (around €2) each time a card is used, although telephones have a button allowing you to make multiple 'follow on' calls without paying this charge each time.

Procedure

The procedure when using a phone card or credit card in most public telephones is as follows:

1. Lift the receiver (*Décrochez* is displayed).
2. Insert your card in the slot or dial a free number (*Introduire carte ou faire numéro libre*). In some telephone boxes you must close the compartment where the card is inserted; the message *Fermez le volet SVP* is displayed.
3. Wait (*Patientez SVP*) while your card is checked. Your card's remaining credit will be displayed, e.g. *crédit: 0040 unité(s)*.
4. Dial (*Numérotez*). When using a scratch card or *CFT*, you must enter a personal identification number followed by the code on the card before the number you wish to call.
5. Hang up when you've finished (*Raccrochez SVP*) or use the 'follow on' button to make another call.
6. If you don't retrieve your card immediately, you will hear a beep and the message *Retirez votre carte* will be displayed. If the message *Carte épuisée* appears, your card has run out of credit.

FAX

Fax machines can be purchased (but not rented) from FT and purchased or rented from private companies and shops. Shop around for the best price. Before bringing a fax machine to France, check that it will work there (i.e. is compatible or *agréé*) or that it can be modified. For example, some British fax machines won't work in France, although it's possible to buy adapters for UK phones and fax machines (see **Telephones** on page 144). Note, however, that getting a fax machine repaired in France may be impossible unless the same machine is sold there. If you have a personal computer, you can usually send and receive faxes using your modem. Public fax machines (*Postéclair*) can be found in central post offices in most towns, although you can only send faxes and cannot receive them. The cost is €1.22 for the first page and €0.91 for subsequent pages within France, €4.57 and €2.74 to Europe, North America and North Africa, and €6.86 and €3.81 to all other destinations.

Beware of bogus fax bills (usually for hundreds of euros) purporting to be from FT. This is a Europe-wide scam and often includes 'the right to inclusion in an annual directory of fax owners'. The give-away is usually the address, which is often abroad! To prevent people sending you junk faxes, ring the national 'eradication' line (☎ 08 26 10 00 09).

INTERNET

There has recently been a proliferation of internet service providers (*fournisseur d'accès/FAI* or *serveur*), over 200 currently offering a variety of products and prices. France Télécom offers Orange (formerly Wanadoo), a package that includes email (see below) and on-line shopping. AOL Compuserve France is the other major internet contender. Between them, Orange and AOL have some two-thirds of the market. Contact details of some of the major French internet service providers (ISPs) are as follows:

● **Alice France** (formerly Tiscali) – ☎ 1033, 🖳 http://www.aliceadsl.fr.

● **AOL** – ☎ 08 92 02 03 04, 🖳 http://www.aol.fr.

● **Club Internet** – ☎ 3204, 🖳 http://www.club-internet.fr.

● **Free** – ☎ 3244, 🖳 http://www.free.fr.

● **FreeSurf** – ☎ 08 26 00 76 50, 🖳 http://www.freesurf.fr.

● **Orange** – ☎ 3900 or 08 92 69 91 14, 🖳 http://www.orange.fr.

For details of all the French ISPs, go to 🖳 http://www.lesproviders.com; for a comparison of ISP services and charges, consult one of the dedicated internet magazines, such as *Internet Pratique* and *Net@scope*, or visit the Budgetelecom website (🖳 http://www.budgetelecom.com), which provides information on current offers, customer evaluations and direct links to provider websites.

There are many online shopping facilities, including railway and airline tickets, and you can even file many tax forms and official documents online as well as make tax payments. One advantage of French internet services is that junk mail is strictly controlled and therefore less of a nuisance than in many other countries. The French search engine (*moteur de recherche*) is called Voilà (⌨ http://www.voila.fr).

Internet 'cafés' (*webcafé*) are becoming increasingly popular in France, where almost 850 communes have been awarded the appelation '*Villes Internet*' for introducing public internet centres; the complete list of *villes internet* can be found on ⌨ http://www.villes-internet.net.

Charges

France has a number of 'free' internet access services, where you pay only for your telephone connection time, not for access to the ISP. Alternatively, most service providers (including the free ones) offer various monthly plans which include all connection charges, usually at a rate that's lower than the standard telephone charges. For as little as €6 to €10 per month, you can usually have five or ten hours online, although most ISPs now offer packages including broadband internet connection (see page 143) and telephone for around €30 per month. In Paris and other urban centres with cable television, it's often possible to have a combined TV and broadband internet access package.

If you already have an AOL account with a fixed monthly fee for unlimited access, you may (or may not!) have to pay for connection time in France and you will be unable simply to reregister your account in France; you must cancel your email address(es) and hope they're still available when you re-register!

Modems

Foreign modems (*modem*) will usually work in France, although they may not receive faxes (Big Dish Satellite, ⌨ http://www.bigdishsat.com, sell converters for this purpose); French modems generally work better.

Email

Email is variously called *email, mail, courier électronique, courriel* and *mél* (the 'official' word and an abbreviation of *message électronique*) – other useful vocabulary is @ (*arobase*), dot (*point*), hyphen (*tiret* or *trait d'union*) and slash (*slash*). If you don't have access to the internet, La Poste also offers the facility to send and receive emails via around 1,000 post offices as well as via its website (⌨ http://www. laposte.fr or ⌨ http://www.laposte.net), where information about the service can be found. Messages can even be picked up via telephone (☎ 08 92 68 13 50). Note that, if you don't have a La Poste or Hotmail account, you can pick up your emails from another computer by going to ⌨ http://www.mailstart.com and entering your email address and password, although you're unable to download attachments. This service is free once per week; if you need to use it more often, you can pay a small subscription (around €15 per year) for your own 'WebBox'. AOL users cannot use this service.

If you want a French domain name or URL (i.e. one ending .fr), you must have a company registered in France, your site must be in French (other languages are optional) and you must pay around €300 for the name. For a list of approved domain name registrars (in France and other countries), go to ▣ http://www.icann.org/registrars/accredited-list.html.

Internet Telephony

If you have a broadband internet connection, you can make long-distance and international phone 'calls' free (or almost free) to anyone with a broadband connection. 'Voice over internet protocol' (VOIP) is a new technology that's revolutionising the telecommunications market and will eventually (some say within five years) make today's telephone technology (both land lines and mobile networks) obsolete. A leading company in this field is Skype (▣ http://www.skype.com), recently purchased by Ebay, which has over 50m users worldwide. Microsoft also has a popular system, MSN Messenger (▣ http://messenger.msn.co.uk), and there are numerous other companies in the market – a web search on 'internet phone' will throw up many other internet phone providers. All you need is access to a local broadband provider and a headset (costing as little as $10) or a special phone, and you're in business. Calls to other computers anywhere in the world are free, while calls to landlines are charged at a few cents per minute.

8.

TELEVISION & RADIO

French television (TV) and radio broadcasting is partly state-owned and partly in private hands; two TV and five radio stations are under government control. Cable TV is available in the main cities and towns, although it's less common than in many other western European countries. Satellite TV was largely ignored by the French and was watched mainly by expatriates until the advent of digital satellite with its enhanced features and relatively easy installation and use. The leading service provider is CanalSatellite (with 30 per cent of the market), followed by France Télécom SA, Suez, Canal+ and TF1. All broadcasting is overseen by the Conseil Supérieur de l'Audiovisuel (CSA).

TV and radio programmes are listed in daily newspapers, some of which (e.g. the Saturday edition of *Le Figaro* and the Sunday edition of *Le Monde*) provide free weekly programme guides with reviews and comments, and there's a plethora of weekly TV magazines, including pocket (A5) size publications, e.g. *Télé Poche* and *Télé Z*, as well as A4 magazines. Guides are normally published two weeks in advance. The annual *World Radio TV Handbook* by David G. Bobbett (Watson-Guptil Publications) contains over 600 pages of information and the frequencies of radio and TV stations worldwide.

TELEVISION

French TV is generally no worse than that in most other European countries, i.e. largely a succession of news, sport, talk and game shows and dubbed American films and sitcoms (French TV rarely shows foreign material in its original language), although there are occasional interesting documentaries and French series and films.

Standards

The standards for TV reception in France aren't the same as in some other countries, and TV sets and video recorders (see below) operating on the PAL system or the North American NTSC system won't function properly (or at all) in France. Most European countries use the PAL-B/G standard, except for the UK, which uses a modified PAL-I system that's incompatible with other European countries. Naturally, France has its own standard, called SECAM-L, which is different from the SECAM standard used elsewhere in the world, e.g. SECAM-B/G in the Middle East and North African countries, and SECAM-D/K in eastern European and many African countries.

If you want to import a TV set, it must be a multi-standard TV; otherwise you must buy one in France. Most new television sets available in France contain automatic circuitry that can switch between SECAM-L, PAL-I and PAL-B/G. If you have a PAL TV, it's also possible to buy a SECAM to PAL transcoder that converts SECAM signals to PAL. If you decide to buy a TV in France, you will also find it advantageous to buy one with teletext, which, apart from allowing you to display programme schedules, also provides a wealth of useful and interesting information. Note, that a SECAM-standard TV isn't required to receive most satellite broadcasts, which are different from terrestrial broadcasts (see page 168).

A portable colour TV can be purchased from around €150 for a 36cm (14in) with remote control. A 55cm (21in) TV costs between €200 and €1,500 depending on the make and features, and a 82cm (32in) model from €750. Special offers can be up to 50 per cent cheaper than the prices quoted, particularly at hypermarkets such as Cora and Auchan or at appliance discount chains such as But, Darty and Boulanger.

Video & DVD Players

A British or US video cassette recorder (VCR) won't work properly with a French TV unless it's dual-standard (with SECAM). Although you can play back a SECAM video on a PAL VCR, the picture will be in black and white. Most video machines (*magnétoscope*) sold in France are multi-standard PAL and SECAM and many contain an NTSC playback feature, allowing Americans to play video tapes via a PAL or SECAM television. Some multi-standard TVs also have an 'NTSC-in' jack plug connection allowing you to play US videos. If you have a PAL TV, it's also possible to buy a SECAM to PAL transcoder that converts SECAM signals to PAL. Video recordings can be converted from PAL or SECAM to NTSC or vice versa, although the cost is prohibitive. Some people opt for two TVs, one to receive French TV programmes and another (i.e. PAL or NTSC) to play their favourite videos. DVDs will play properly on any TV set and usually have the added advantage of offering a choice of languages.

Terrestrial

France has six terrestrial stations broadcasting throughout the country: France 2 and France 3 (both state-owned and operated by France Télévision), TF1, Canal Plus, M6 and Arte/France 5 (see below). Reception is poor in some areas, particularly if you're in a valley or surrounded by tower blocks.

It's possible to receive digital TV (see page 170) in some areas via an aerial, using a system known as *TNT*. You can buy a set-top box to decode the signals or a TV set with a built-in decoder. No English-language channels can be received, however.

There's advertising (*publicité* or *pub*) on all French channels, although France 2 and 3 aren't permitted to raise more than 25 per cent of their revenue from it. These channels, which share 40 per cent of the TV audience, have benefited from a large injection of public funds in recent years in order to carry fewer advertisements and return to 'quality' (open to interpretation) public service programming. They're permitted to show advertisements between programmes only, whereas private channels may have an advertising break during films and other major programmes. On all terrestrial channels, advertising may not average more than six minutes per hour per day, with a maximum of 12 minutes in any single hour. Nevertheless, TV advertising and the endless trailers for forthcoming programmes are highly intrusive; a random hop (the French have coined the word *zapping*!) through the half-dozen terrestrial TV channels usually lands on at least three commercial breaks and/or two trailers.

Main evening news programmes start at around 20.00 and last half an hour. These are usually followed by weather forecasts (*prévision météorologique* or simply *météo*), which often include a traffic forecast for the coming weekend, especially when a school holiday is approaching. The news and weather is usually followed by a film or feature documentary on most channels. Note, however, that French TV channels aren't allowed to show films on Friday or Saturday nights, as this is deemed unfair competition for the cinemas!

Films and some programmes are coded 10, 12, 16 or 18 in order to indicate their suitability (or unsuitability) for childen of those ages; the code is permanently displayed on the screen (except the 10 code, which is visible for only five minutes).

TF1

TF1 (Télévision Française 1, 💻 http://www.tf1.fr) was France's first private channel (privatised in April 1987) and boasts 40 per cent of the viewing audience or double that of its nearest rival, France 2. Its programming is conservative, although usually of good quality, with the notable exception of mindless game shows and soaps. Its news reporting is generally weak, although popular. TF1 is well known for showing Formula One racing.

France 2

Previously called Antenne 2, France 2 (💻 http://www.france2.fr) is France's second-most popular channel and is generally liberal and progressive in its programming. Programmes include special events, interviews and cultural events. News coverage is fairly nondescript and similar to TF1's. It runs several of the better American dramas (*ER*, for example, called *Urgences*) and during the week runs major films.

France 3

France 3 (💻 http://www.france3.fr) shares much of its programming with the other public channel, France 2, augmented by regional news, documentaries and environmental programmes. Each region has its own news department which contributes stories to the national review every evening before summarising the region's news. The quality of programmes has improved in the last few years and they're generally more intellectual than those on TF1 and France 2.

Canal Plus

Canal Plus (or Canal+, 💻 http://www.canalplus.fr) was launched in 1984 and is Europe's biggest pay channel (*chaîne à péage*) with some 50 per cent of the market. Apart from a few unscrambled (*en clair*) programmes, indicated in newspapers and programme guides by a + or * sign, the signal is scrambled. To receive scrambled programmes you must obtain a decoder (*décodeur*), on which there's a returnable deposit (*depôt de garantie*) of around €15, and pay a subscription of around €30 per month, although there are periodical offers to hook you, such as your first year for just €15. Although financed mainly by subscriptions from over 5m subscribers in France (plus a further 1.5m in Belgium, Germany, Poland and Spain), Canal Plus also carries advertisements. It specialises in films and sports programmes, particularly live soccer matches. It shows its share of second-rate films, although in recent years the selection has expanded to include many television premiers of hit films, both French and American. Canal Plus offers four additional channels as part of its cable and digital satellite service (see page 170).

Arte/France 5

Arte (pronounced 'artay', 🖳 http://www.arte-tv.com) and France 5 (also known as *La Cinq*, 🖳 http://www.france5.fr) broadcast on the same frequency for terrestrial TV but on separate channels on satellite and cable. Arte (from 19.00 until around 00.30 on terrestrial TV) started as a Franco-German 'cultural' station funded by the respective governments but has gradually grown into a pan-European enterprise, including the national broadcasters of Belgium, Switzerland, Spain, Poland, Austria, Finland and the Netherlands. Programmes are broadcast in the languages of all the participating countries, although reception in France is usually dubbed or subtitled in French. Arte provides a welcome cultural alternative to commercial broadcasting and its output largely consists of documentaries and cultural transmissions (e.g. classical music, operas, debates, concerts, and ballets), foreign films with subtitles, English comedy and **no game shows**. It's considered by many to be excessively highbrow and attracts only around 2 per cent of viewers. France 5 broadcasts standard and educational programmes from 06.00 to 19.00.

M6

Launched in 1987, M6 (🖳 http://www.m6.fr) broadcasts mostly general entertainment programmes. It screens many American programmes and other mainstream shows plus soft-porn movies. It often has surprisingly good programmes considering its low profile and budget. Note that M6 is difficult to receive in some areas.

Foreign Stations

If you live close to a French border and have the appropriate aerial, you may also be able to receive foreign stations. In the Nord-Pas-de-Calais region it's possible to receive British and Belgian stations, those in northern Lorraine can receive Luxembourg TV, and in Alsace many people watch German and Swiss TV stations and may receive the German-language version of Arte. Those near the Spanish and Italian borders can usually receive programmes broadcast in those countries, and in certain parts of the Côte d'Azur you can receive Télé Monte Carlo (which is also now available on most cable and satellite networks in France).

Cable

Cable TV (*télévision par câble*) is available only in and around 100 or so cities and large towns and, although the number of subscribers increases annually, the percentage of homes with access to cable TV is low compared with many other European countries. Around 1,600 communes have cable service (which sounds impressive unless you know that there are over 36,500 communes in France!). Cables also carry telephone 'lines', and providers usually offer combined TV, telephone and internet services, which can be goood value. To check whether your town or commune is currently wired for cable television, internet or telephone services, check the website of AFORM, a French cable industry association (🖳 http:// www.aform.org and follow the link for '*Les villes câblées*').

The major cable operators are France Télécom Câble, UPC France, Noos and NC Numéricable. Costs range from around €10 per month for a basic package to €30 per month for a 'TV addict' package, including 24-hour, seven-day-a-week internet access. Note that in some apartment blocks with cable service, you can receive only around two-thirds of the programmes available. Basic cable access usually includes a number of foreign channels such as Sky News, CNN, BBC World, Euronews and CNBC, as well as a variety of Spanish, Portuguese, Italian and Arabic-language channels. France has several channels, e.g. Canal Plus and Pink TV (see **Satellite** below), available by cable as well as satellite, and several, such as La Sept, available only to cable TV subscribers. Programme listings for the most popular French cable stations are included in French TV guides.

Satellite

France is well served by satellite TV (*télévision par satellite*), and there are a number of satellites positioned over Europe carrying over 3,000 channels broadcasting in a variety of languages, new channels appearing almost daily. The primary source of English-language programmes is Sky TV (see below), but even if you don't wish to subscribe to Sky, you will have access to around 100 English-language channels, including all the BBC channels (see **BBC** below) and ITV channels 1–4. . However, these won't include ITV1, CH4 or CH5, even though they're free-to-view (FTV, also called free-to-air/FTA); to receive these channels, you must currently subscribe to Sky (their minimum package includes all three channels) or buy an FTV card.

A new 'gay' channel, Pink TV (🖳 http://www.pinktv.fr), part-owned by TF1, was launched at the end of 2004 and is currently available only by satellite and cable (for a €9 subscription).

Astra & Eutelsat

The Astra satellites offer TV addicts a huge choice of English- and foreign-language channels, at least 100 (or over 500 with digital TV) of which can be received throughout France with a 60 or 85cm dish. Among the many English-language channels available on Astra are all the BBC's and channels (see **BBC** below) and ITV channels 1–4, The Discovery Channels, The Disney Channel, Eurosport, Film Four, Plus, Sky Cinema 1 & 2, Sky Movies 1-9, Sky News, Sky One, Sky Sports (three channels), TCM, UK Gold and UKTV Gold. Other channels are broadcast in Dutch, German, Japanese, Swedish and various Indian languages. The signal for many channels is scrambled (the decoder is usually built into the receiver) and viewers must pay a monthly subscription to receive programmes. The best served by unscrambled (clear) channels are German-speakers (many German channels on Astra are clear). A bonus of Astra is the availability of radio stations, including all the national BBC stations (see **Satellite Radio** on page 175).

Eutelsat runs a fleet of communications satellites carrying TV channels to over 50m homes, although its channels are mostly non-English. The English-language channels on Eutelsat include BBC World, CNBC Europe and Eurosport. Other channels are broadcast in Arabic, French, German, Hungarian, Italian, Polish, Portuguese, Spanish and Turkish. Further information can be found on Eutelsat's website (🖳 http://www.eutelsat.org).

Sky Television

In order to receive Sky television you need a Sky digital receiver (digibox) and a dish. There are two ways to obtain the equipment and the necessary Sky 'smart' card. You can subscribe in the UK or Ireland (personally, if you have an address there, or via a friend) and then take the Sky receiver and card to France, although for the first year of your contract the digibox must be connected to a telephone line (so that Sky can sell you interactive services); if you export it during this period and connect it to a foreign telephone line, Sky will terminate your contract (Sky's call centre can tell what country a call/connection is being made from). After the first year, the digibox no longer needs to be connected to a telephone line and so can (although strictly should not) be exported. Similarly, a Sky card shouldn't be used outside the UK.

Alternatively, you can buy a digibox and obtain a Sky card 'privately' in France (a number of satellite companies supply Sky cards); however, you're subject to the same restrictions as noted above. Moreover, Sky receivers and cards are much more expensive in France: a receiver and card cost around €400 plus the monthly subscription, while the card on its own costs around €200 (plus the subscription). To receive Sky TV in France, a dish must be at least 1.2m in diameter (costing from around €200).

You must subscribe to Sky to receive most English-language channels (other than Sky News, which isn't scrambled). If you subscribe to the basic package, costing around GB£15, you will have access to around 100 channels, including all the BBC's channels and ITV channels 1–4. Various other packages are available costing up to around GB£42.50, for which you have access to the Movie and Sports channels, along with many interactive services such as Sky News Active.

Further information about Sky installation (in the UK) and programme packages can be found on Sky's website (🖳 http://www.sky.com).

Digital TV

The benefits of digital TV, which was launched in 1998 by Sky in the UK, include a superior picture, CD quality sound, including Dolby Digital 5.1, widescreen format and access to many more channels. To watch digital satellite TV, you require a Sky digibox (see above), although it's possible to receive some (French) digital channels via an ordinary aerial.

France's Canal Plus (see page 166) offers four digital channels, available separately or in combination to anyone with a standard satellite dish and access to the Astra satellites. The subscription fee is the same as for analogue reception (see page 166), but you must pay an additional €8 for a digital terminal (*terminal numérique*) and €40 for access, plus a €70 deposit. These channels often broadcast in *version multi* (*VM*), allowing the viewer to choose between the original language and French dubbing.

Canal Plus now has competition from Télévision Par Satellite (TPS, via Eutelsat – see above), which offers a slightly different range of channels, although most of the same French-language channels are available on both services, and TV5 Europe.

TNT is a new digital service offering access to Canal Plus and TPS on subscription or to 11 other channels free, although you must buy a decoder (*décodeur*), which costs between €60 and €150.

Digital TV distributors offer a range of interactive services in addition to television programming, including home shopping and banking, games and software downloads. To make use of these services, you will need to be able to connect your decoder box to a nearby telephone point.

BBC

The BBC has recently stopped encrypting (scrambling) its channels coming from the Astra satellite that it shares with Sky, which means that you don't need a Sky Digibox to receive the BBC channels, including BBC interactive services; any digital satellite receiver will work.

The BBC's commercial subsidiary, BBC World Television (formerly called BBC Worldwide Television) broadcasts two 24-hour channels: BBC World (24-hour news and information) and BBC Prime (general entertainment). BBC World is free-to-view, while BBC Prime is encrypted. BBC World is normally included as part of the 'international' packages offered by cable and digital satellite service providers, whereas BBC Prime costs GB£88, and there's a one-time charge of GB£14 for a smart card.

For more information and a programme guide contact BBC World Television (☎ 020-8433 2221). A programme guide is also listed on the internet (🖳 http://www.bbc.co.uk/worldservice/programmes) and both BBC World and BBC Prime have their own websites (🖳 http://www.bbcworld.com and 🖳 http://www.bbcprime.com). When accessing them, you need to enter the name of the country so that schedules appear in local time.

Equipment

A satellite receiver for free-to-view analogue channels doesn't need any kind of built-in decoder; the received signal will be the French standard SECAM, but most modern TVs are SECAM/PAL compatible, even though this may not be stated on the TV or even in the TV's handbook. If you have a PAL-only TV, the picture will be in black and white but, provided the TV is connected to the satellite receiver using a SCART lead, the sound will be good.

A 60cm dish (*antenne parabolique* or simply *parabole*) is adequate for analogue TV. They're sold by most large supermarkets and specialist chains such as Darty and Boulanger and cost from around €70 to €150, plus the cost of installation. Shop around, as prices vary enormously and there are frequent special offers. Darty and other large appliance retailers often run promotions for satellite dishes, decoders and services, some of which can be ordered via their websites for home delivery within two or three days. Below is a list of the popular satellite positions over Europe (the most popular are marked with an asterisk). All these satellites except Atlantic Bird transmit both analogue and digital signals, although the former are being phased out; Atlantic Bird currently transmits only analogue signals.

- **Arabsat fleet** – 26.0° east (Arabic).

- **Astra 1 fleet*** – 19.2° east (European).

- **Astra 2 fleet*** – 28.2° east (Sky digital UK+).

- **Atlantic Bird** – 5.0° west (French).

- **Eutelsat W2** – 16.0° east (European).

- **Hispasat fleet*** – 30.0° west (Spanish).

- **Hotbird fleet*** – 13.0° east (European).

- **Nilesat fleet** – 7.0° west (Arabic).

- **PAS 3R/6/6B** – 43.0° west (American).

- **Sirius/Thor fleet** – 1.0° west (European).

- **Turksat** – 42.0° east (Turkish).

The dish size required to receive the above satellites varies from 35cm to 2m according to location; check with a local installer, as online 'link budgets' aren't always reliable.

You can install a motorised 1.2 or 1.5m dish and receive hundreds of stations in a multitude of languages from around the world. If you wish to receive satellite TV on two or more TVs, you can buy a system with two or more receivers. To receive stations from two or more satellites simultaneously, you need a motorised dish or a dish with a double feed (dual LNBs) antenna. **When buying a system, ensure that it can receive programmes from all existing and planned satellites.**

Location

To receive programmes from any satellite, there must be no obstacles (e.g. trees, buildings or mountains) between the satellite and your dish, so **check before renting or buying if being able to receive satellite broadcasts is important to you.** You should also check whether you need permission from your landlord or the local authorities. There are strict laws regarding the positioning of antennas in urban areas, although in rural areas rules are more relaxed. Dishes can be mounted in a variety of unobtrusive positions and can be painted or patterned to blend with the background.

Programme Guides

Many satellite stations provide teletext information, which includes programme schedules. The main French-language channels are included in most television listings in newspapers and magazines, but these may cover only 'prime time, i.e. the evening. Satellite programme listings are included in a number of British publications such as *What Satellite, Satellite Times* and *Satellite TV,* available on subscription and from some international news kiosks. If you don't have time to sift through all the available satellite channel listings to find programmes you're interested in, the Euro TV website (🖥 http://www.eurotv.com) can do it for you!

TV Licence

A TV licence (*redevance sur les postes de télévision*) is required by most TV owners, costing €116 a year. The licence fee covers any number of TVs (owned or rented), irrespective of where they're located in France, e.g. holiday homes, motor vehicles or boats, although you must pay for a separate licence for TVs in rented accommodation, e.g. *gîtes,* and the government is considering levying the licence on each set. Even if you only have a foreign TV which you use solely for watching videos, you must have a valid licence! If you import a TV capable of receiving French TV programmes, you must report within 30 days of import to your local Centre Régional de la Redevance Audiovisuelle (listed under *Les infos administratives/Impôts et taxes* in the yellow pages – or you can obtain the address from your local post office).

The licence fee subsidises France 2 (40 per cent) and France 3 (80 per cent), and also contributes towards Radio France and Radio France International. The licence fee is now levied in conjunction with the *taxe d'habitation* (see page 386) and is therefore payable in December each year, although it's possible to pay in monthly instalments. If you're over 65 (on 1st January of the relevant year), paid no income tax in the previous year and live alone (or with other people in the same situation), you're exempt (*exonéré*) from paying for a licence. Apply to your regional Centre de la Redevance.

If you buy a TV in France, the retailer must inform the relevant authority and the TV licence fee will be added to your next residential tax bill. You will be fined if you're discovered to have a TV without a licence when an inspector calls. If you don't pay the annual fee on time, you must visit the local *commisariat* to explain why and pay an *agrandissement* of 30 per cent for late payment. If you dispose of your TV and don't replace it, you must notify the authorities, or you remain liable to pay the licence fee. (You may be asked whether you sold your TV so that the new owner can be sent a bill!)

Video & DVD

Films on video cassette and DVD are expensive (video cassettes cost around €20 and DVDs around €25) and there aren't many cassettes available in English, although most DVDs can be watched in English – but not all (check the box before buying or renting). Most shops that rent or sell video tapes also offer DVDs, which are gradually superseding videos. Films can be rented for around €3.50 per day. A new facility is the automated 'kiosk', from which DVDs can be rented at the touch of a few buttons for as little as €1.70 (for six hours). You must pay a small membership fee (e.g. €2) to qualify for a cheaper rate. Most hypermarkets carry a large selection of DVDs.

RADIO

Radio was deregulated in France in the '80s, since when scores of local commercial radio stations have sprung up, representing diverse ethnic groups, lifestyles and communities. Local stations often have small catchment areas and low transmitting power, although many have been grouped into national networks. The largest is operated by NRJ, a popular Paris music station. A radio licence isn't required.

French Radio

French radio is dominated by the five stations run by state-owned Radio France, although there are numerous independent stations.

Radio France

All five stations are available throughout France, although the frequencies vary from region to region. Information on all Radio France channels, including programme schedules, is available on 🖳 http://www.radiofrance.fr.

France-Bleu: Mixes light music and 'easy listening rock' with regional features and interviews.

France-Culture: Much of France-Culture's output is highbrow (some would say pretentious) and includes talks, debates and interviews on the arts and literature.

France-Info: An all-news channel, with detailed news broadcasts every half hour, followed by interviews and discussions of major issues. Individual news stories and some features are repeated several times throughout the day.

France-Inter: The main channel, broadcasting news bulletins, current events, magazine programmes, discussions, light music and plays. During the summer it broadcasts news bulletins in English (at 09.00 and 16.00).

France-Musiques: Broadcasts mostly classical music but also some jazz and 'world' music as well as cultural discussion programmes.

Other Stations

French radio stations are often original and progressive, particularly in Paris, and play a wide variety of music. There's a wealth of excellent FM stations in Paris and other cities, although in some rural areas you may be lucky to receive a few FM stations clearly, e.g. one chat show and one playing nothing but folk music! Among the most popular FM stations are Kiss FM (89.0), France Info (105.5) and Radio Classique (101.1), which is also available throughout France on other wavelengths. Other popular stations include Fun Radio, part of a new wave of youth-oriented radio stations that have saturated airwaves in recent years.

Many French people tune to radio stations such as Radio Luxembourg/RTL (104.3) and Europe 1 (104.7) and 2 (103.9), Radio Monte-Carlo and Radio Sud, all of which originally broadcast from outside French territory to circumvent the earlier French government monopoly on radio stations. Now that private radio has been legalised, most maintain broadcasting facilities within France (usually in or near Paris). Together they have a larger audience than Radio France.

Since 1st January 1996, at least 40 per cent of popular music broadcasts have had to consist of songs sung in French. (Despite their linguistic jingoism, most French people prefer to listen to English-language songs, which is understandable given the generally dire quality of French songs!) Stations that don't comply can be fined or even closed, although enforcement of the language regulations varies according to the political climate. Some radio stations get around the rules by playing all French-language music during the early hours of the morning, but most alternate French and 'foreign' songs.

English-language Radio

Apart from English-language songs, there's little radio in English, although in a few areas there are English-language stations run by expatriates (e.g. Riviera Radio on 106.5FM in the south of France, Sud Radio on 96.1FM in the south-west, Lot radio on 88–89FM and occasional programmes on Radio Périgueux 103 on 102.3FM and Radio Plaisance on 95.9FM). Radio France Internationale (RFI) broadcasts in English for three-and-a-half hours every day in the Paris region on 738MW. Paris Live Radio, a new English-language station broadcast from next door to the Moulin Rouge, plans to broadcast on 963AM in the near future; in the meantime, it can be heard live online at ▢ http://www.parislive.fm. Radio France International (RFI) is France's world service station, broadcasting 24 hours a day in some 15 languages on short wave.

The motorway system has its own radio network, and the Autoroute Info stations play popular music and carry frequent traffic and accident reports, often in English, German and Spanish during summer holiday period. The frequency is indicated on signs along the motorway; 107.7 is often used. If you're interested in receiving radio stations from further afield, you should obtain a copy of the *World Radio TV Handbook* by David G. Bobbett (Watson-Guptil Publications).

If you have an internet connection and the appropriate software (e.g. Real Player, a free download from 🖥 http://www.real.com, or Windows Media Player, a standard feature of the Windows operating system), you can listen to hundreds of radio stations via your computer (sometimes referred to as 'internet radio'). What's more, you have a choice of 'live' or recorded programmes, including classics that are no longer broadcast. The BBC (see below) is one of many organisations offering this service, some of which broadcast only via the internet; search the web for 'internet radio' to find the main stations.

BBC

The BBC World Service is broadcast on short wave on several frequencies (e.g. 12095, 9410, 7325, 6195, 3955, 648 and 198kHz) simultaneously and you can usually receive a good signal on one of them. The signal strength varies according to where you live, the time of day and year, the power and positioning of your receiver, and atmospheric conditions. The World Service is available on medium wave (648MW) in the northern half of France. You can also receive BBC national radio stations (on long wave) in most northern and western areas of France (the Nord-Pas-de-Calais, Normandy, Brittany, Pays-de-la-Loire, Ile-de-France and Centre regions) and parts of Champagne-Ardenne, northern Burgundy. All BBC radio stations, including the World Service, are available via the Astra satellite (see below). BBC radio stations can be heard via your PC using a Radio Player (which can be downloaded free from 🖥 http://www.bbc.co.uk/radio) and, if you're really desperate, you can hear recordings of BBC radio programmes on your computer via 🖥 http://www.bbc.co.uk/worldservice/schedules/frequencies/eurwfreq.shtml.

Cable, Digital & Satellite Radio

If you have satellite TV, you can also receive many radio stations. For example, BBC Radio 1, 2, 3, 4 and 5, BBC World Service, Sky Radio, Virgin 1215 and many foreign-language stations are broadcast via the Astra satellites (see page 168). Paris Live Radio (see above) is available via cable (NC Numéricable channel 150) and the internet (🖥 http://www.parislive.fm) as well as satellite (CanalSatellite channel 118) and digital radio (1463.232Mhz LG). Digital satellite TV subscribers also have a choice of many French and international radio stations. Details are usually available in the monthly satellite subscriber newsletter. Satellite radio stations are listed in British satellite TV magazines such as the *Satellite Times*.

9.

EDUCATION

France spends more per capita on education than many other western countries (e.g. 20 per cent more than the UK) and has traditionally been noted for its high academic standards, although in a comparative survey of the educational attainments of 15 year olds in 32 countries conducted by the OECD in 2001, France was only in mid-league. The state-funded school system is supported by a comprehensive network of private schools, including many distinguished international schools. Around 15 per cent of French children attend private schools, most of which are co-educational day schools (education is almost exclusively co-educational), but a private education has little snob value – and it's considerably cheaper than in the UK, for example. Higher education standards are only average, however, with the notable exception of the elite *grandes écoles*, which are rated among the world's best educational establishments. The French are proud of their schools and resent government interference, although there are almost continual 'reforms' of the educational system. They have a respect, even a love of learning, and reforms are argued at great length and with surprising passion.

Critics of the French education system complain that its teaching methods are too traditional and unimaginative, with most learning by rote. Classrooms are arranged in traditional style, with desks in serried ranks, and children spend much of their time copying information. It's also accused of being inflexible and training only the mind rather than encouraging self-expression and personal development. French schools place a great emphasis on the French language (particularly grammar), arithmetic and the sciences. Schools usually impose more discipline than most foreign children are used to (teachers may use any disciplinary method other than violence), as well as more homework (*devoirs du soir*), which increases with the age of the child (there isn't any at elementary level) and can become onerous, particularly for children used to the British education system.

French teachers generally have high expectations of pupils and the system is hard on slow learners and the not so bright; although most schools have special classes for children with learning difficulties, these are beginning to disappear as education budgets are cut. France has a highly competitive and selective examination system that separates the brighter students from the less academically gifted at around the age of 14. From primary school level, children are subjected to constant testing (at least twice a week in every subject). However, despite the generally high standards, there have been reports of an increasing number of children entering secondary education unable to read or write adequately.

Education in France is compulsory between the ages of 6 and 16, and state schools are entirely free from nursery school through to university (free state schools have existed in France for over a century), but you have the right to educate your children at home (see **Home Education** on page 182). Some 80 per cent of children continue their schooling beyond the age of 16 and there are around 2m students in *lycées*, private institutions, *grandes écoles* and universities. Free education is also provided for the children of foreign residents, although non-resident, non-EU students require a student visa (see **Chapter 3**).

It was Napoleon who decided that children should study the same subjects, at the same level, at the same time in a particular region. Some 200 years later the system is largely unchanged and the syllabus and textbooks are broadly the same in all schools of the same level throughout France. This means that children moving between schools can continue their education with the minimum disruption. Regions do, however, have a certain amount of autonomy in setting school timetables.

Average class sizes have fallen overall in the last few decades, although they're still thought by some to be too large and the number of teachers is gradually being diminished (some 8,000 who left or retired in 2005/06 weren't replaced), and it isn't unusual to find classes of 50 or more pupils. The average number of children per class is currently around 25.5 (nursery school), 22 (primary school), 24 (*collège*) and 27.5 (*lycée*).

Parent-teacher associations are common (if you wish to join, elections are usually in October), and parent-teacher meetings, where parents can discuss a child's progress with teachers, are held regularly (there's normally one shortly after the start of the first term). If you have a problem, you should contact your local education mediator.

Truancy is a rare offence in France, where a child can be expelled for forging a parent's signature to skip classes and parents of children who regularly play truant can be fined up to €2,000. Note, however, that in some areas (e.g. some Parisian suburbs), state schools are plagued by violence, vandalism and drug abuse – to such an extent that the French Education Minister recently proposed a police presence in 'problem' schools. There has also been an increase in bullying and racketeering among pupils, and a dedicated helpline called *Jeunes Violence Ecoute*, operated by the Fédération des Écoles, des Parents et des Educateurs (see **Information** below), is available for pupils, and others, who fear contacting the authorities or parents directly (☎ 08 00 20 22 23). Another helpline, *SOS Violences Scolaires* is on ☎ 08 10 55 55 00. In an attempt to improve school discipline, all pupils and their parents must now sign a 'school life contract' (*contrat de vie scolaire*), confirming their willingness to cooperate with teachers and their commitment to education.

In recent years, there has been disquiet, particularly among *lycée* students, over class overcrowding and a shortage of teachers. Another increasing problem in state schools, particularly *collèges*, is teacher absenteeism and strikes, which are accelerating the drift towards the private sector.

INSURANCE

All schoolchildren in France should be covered by liability insurance for damage and injury to themselves and third parties while at school or travelling to and from school; insurance isn't obligatory except for school trips such as skiing holidays, but it's highly recommended. Cover may be provided by your existing insurance policies (e.g. household), but it's likely to be the bare minimum. Basic school insurance (*assurance scolaire de base*), covering a child for all school-related activitiy, can be taken out for as little as €10 per year, but for a few euros more (between around €12 and €25 per year), you can cover your child for all eventualities, whether school-related or not; this is known as a *contrat scolaire et extrascolaire*.

Policies are often provided by parents' associations as well as by traditional insurance companies. Costs vary according to the type of cover, the level of compensation in the event of an accident or injury, and the size of the excess (deductible) on a claim, which with cheaper policies may be €20 or €30. You may obtain a reduction if you 'remove' risks already covered by other insurance policies.

When comparing insurance policies, check the cover provided (e.g. is your child covered outside term time?). Whatever cover you choose, ask the insurer to provide an *attestation d'assurance scolaire*, which you must present to the school authorities. Some schools provide an insurance proposal form at the beginning of each school year.

ADAPTING TO THE SYSTEM

Generally, the younger your child is when he enters the system, the easier he will cope. Conversely the older he is, the more problems he will have adjusting. Teenagers often have considerable problems learning French and adjusting to French school life. In some schools, foreign children who cannot understand the language may be neglected and just expected to get on with it. In your early days, it's important to check exactly what your children are doing at school and whether they're making progress (not just with the language, but also with their lessons). As a parent, you should be prepared to support your children through this difficult period. If you aren't fluent in French, you will already be aware how frustrating it is being unable to express yourself adequately, which can easily lead to feelings of inferiority or inadequacy. It's also important for parents to ensure that their children maintain their native language, as it can easily be neglected (surveys show that the children of English-speaking residents are losing their ability to read and write English). See also **Language** below.

For many, the experience of schooling and living in a foreign land is a stimulating challenge, providing invaluable cultural and educational experiences. Your child may become bilingual and will certainly become a 'world' citizen, less likely to be prejudiced against foreigners and foreign ideas. This is particularly true if he attends an international school with pupils from different countries (many state schools also have pupils from a number of countries and backgrounds). However, before making major decisions about your child's future education, it's important to consider his ability, character and needs.

It's possible for children over 15 to experience the French school system before moving by participating in an international exchange programme such as that run by AFS International Youth Development (☎ 0113-242 6136, 🖳 http://www.afsuk.org). Parents with young children who are planning to move to France may be interested in En Famille France, an exchange organisation founded in the late '70s by Frenchman Jacques Pinault. It specialises in six-month exchange visits for children aged 9 to 13 between European countries and France. Children stay with a French family and attend a French school. One of the most important aspects of the scheme, however, is that children must be enthusiastic about the exchange. It can take up to a year to match two families, so you should make enquiries as early as possible. For further information contact En Famille France (☎ 05 57 43 52 48, 🖳 http://www.enfamille.com).

LANGUAGE

For most children, particularly those under ten, studying in French isn't such a handicap as it may appear at first. The majority of children adapt quickly and most become reasonably fluent within three to six months (if only it were so easy for adults!). However, all children don't adapt equally well to a change of language and culture, particularly children over ten (at around ten children begin to learn languages more slowly), many of whom encounter difficulties during their first year. On the other hand, foreign children often acquire a sort of celebrity status, particularly in rural schools, which helps their integration.

It should be borne in mind that the state school system generally makes little or no concession to non-French speakers, for example by providing intensive French lessons. Indeed, non-French speaking children may be put in the class below their age group or made to repeat a year until their language skills have reached an adequate level. This can make the first few months quite an ordeal for non French-speaking children. However, some state schools do provide free intensive French lessons (*classes d'initiation/CLIN* or *Français Langue Etrangère/FLE*) for foreign children and some have international sections for foreign pupils. It may be worthwhile inquiring about the availability of extra French classes before choosing where to live. Note that, while attending a *CLIN*, children may fall behind in other subjects.

Foreign children are tested (like French children) and put into a class suitable to their level of French, even if this means being taught with younger children or slow-learners. However, a child of six or seven must be permitted to enter the first year of primary school (*cours préparatoire/CP*), even if he speaks no French. An older child can be refused entry to the *CP* or another class and can be obliged to attend a *CLIN* against his parents' wishes. Once your child has acquired a sufficient knowledge of spoken and written French, he's integrated into a regular class in a local school.

The only schools in France using English as the teaching language are a few foreign and international private schools (see page 199). A number of multilingual French schools teach students in both English and French. If your children attend any other school, they must study all subjects in French (except a few schools where a local language, e.g. Breton, is also used). If your local state school doesn't provide extra French classes, your only choice will be to pay for private lessons or send your child to another (possibly private) school, where extra tuition is provided.

Some parents send a child to an English-speaking school for a year and then move them to a bilingual or French school; others find it better to throw their children in at the deep end. Your choice should depend on the character, ability and wishes of your child. Whatever you decide, it will help if your child has some intensive French lessons before arriving. It may also be possible to organise an educational or cultural exchange with a French school or family before moving, which is a considerable help in integrating a child into the language and culture (see page 180).

Many state schools teach regional languages, including Alsatian, Basque, Breton, Catalan, Corsican and Occitan. Where applicable, these are usually optional and are taught for around three hours a week, generally outside normal school hours. The exception is Breton, which is used exclusively in the early classes in certain schools in Brittany. See also **Language** on page 29 and **Language Schools** on page 209.

English-speaking parents should also bear in mind that young children attending a French school can quickly lose their command of their native language, which may need reinforcing at home (e.g. through reading and writing, games, films and computer-based activities), and, if possible, regular trips to your home country or membership of a foreign-language club or association. Bilingualism is a complex subject; a detailed analysis of the issues involved and ways of dealing with them is contained in *A Parents' and Teachers' Guide to Bilingualism* by Colin Baker (Multilingual Matters).

HOME EDUCATION

Some 10,000 children are estimated to be educated at home in France, including the children of many expatriates. Those taught at home must reach a level of education similar to that attained by schoolchildren, including a reasonable level of maths, history, geography, science, spoken and written French and a foreign language as well as having lessons in art, culture and sport. Home educators must inform the local town hall and education authorities at least a week before the start of each academic year and are subject to inspections at least once a year.

A number of publications provide further information about home education, including *Apprendre Autrement* (send an SAE to Marcel Mahl, 20 avenue de la Gare, 31230 L'Isle-en-Dodon) and *One-to-One: A Practical Guide to Learning at Home, Age 0–11* (order on 🖳 http://www.nezertbooks.net). Other relevant websites include 🖳 http://ecolesdifferentes.free.fr, 🖳 http://www.education-otherwise.org, 🖳 http://www.freedom-in-education.co.uk and 🖳 http://www.lesenfantsdabord.org.

INFORMATION

Information about French schools, both state and private, can be obtained from French embassies and consulates abroad, and from foreign embassies, educational organisations and government departments in France. The Fédération des Écoles, des Parents et des Educateurs (☎ 01 47 53 62 70, 🖳 http://www.ecoledesparents. org) provides free advice for parents on all aspects of education and careers, as does the Office National d'Information sur les Enseignements et les Professions (ONISEP), which has regional offices and publishes regional guides to education and careers.

Useful websites include the Ministry of Education's site (🖳 http://www. education.gouv.fr), Eurydice (🖳 http://www.eurydice.org), where there's information in English about the French education system, and the Service Public site (🖳 http://www.service-public.fr), which has sections on education (*enseignement*) and training (*formation*). The French Ministry of Education provides a nationwide free information service through Centre d'Information et d'Orientation (CIO) offices. For the address of your local CIO office, contact your town hall (*mairie*), which can also provide local information.

STATE OR PRIVATE SCHOOL?

If you're able to choose between state and private education, there are many considerations to be made before choosing the most appropriate school – not least the language of study (see above). State education in France is perceived by many to be of a higher quality than private education (among the most famous schools in Paris are the Henri IV and Louis le Grand *lycées*, both state schools). French parents have traditionally sent their children to a private school only for linguistic or religious reasons or when they needed extra assistance that was unavailable in a state school. In recent years, however, there has been a surge in demand for private school places as an increasing number of parents become disillusioned with the state education system. In 2005, some 50,000 applicants were unable to obtain places as private school attendance reached the 2m mark. The following checklist will help you decide whether state or private education will be better for your child:

● Language and other integration problems mean that enrolling a child in a French state school isn't recommended for less than a year, particularly a teenage child who isn't fluent in French. If you're uncertain how long you will be staying in France, it's probably better to assume a long stay.

● The area where you choose to live will affect your choice of school(s). For example, it's usually necessary to send your child to a state school near your home (see **Enrolment** on page 186). If you choose a private day school, you must take into account the distance from your home to the school.

● Where you're going when you leave France may be an important consideration with regard to your child's language of tuition and system of education in France, as will his age – now and when you plan to leave France. Consider also what plans you have for his future education and in which country this is to take place. The younger a child is, the easier it will be to place him in a suitable school.

● Ask your child how he views the thought of studying in French but consider also what language is best from a long-term point of view and whether schooling is available in his mother tongue.

● Ask yourself whether your child will need help with his studies, and more importantly, whether you will be able to help him, particularly with his French.

● Find out what the school hours and holiday periods are, and consider how these will affect your family's work and leisure activities. Many state schools in France have compulsory Saturday morning classes.

● Ask whether special or extra tutoring is available in French or other subjects, if necessary.

● If religion is an important aspect in your choice of school, your options may be limited. There's no compulsory religious instruction in French state schools. In fact, state schools ban even displays of religious affiliation, even crucifixes (some Moslem children have even been expelled for wearing headscarves). Most international schools are non-denominational.

- French state schools are usually co-educational, so if you want your child to go to a single-sex school you may need to find a private establishment.

- Consider whether you're prepared or wish to send your child to a boarding school and, if so, in which country.

- Consider the secondary and higher education prospects of prospective schools and whether the examinations your child would take are recognised in your home country or the country where you plan to live after leaving France. If applicable, check whether the French *baccalauréat* examination (see page 196) is recognised as a university entrance qualification in the country you plan to move to.

- Check a prospective school's academic record? Most schools provide exam pass rate statistics.

- Find out how large the classes are and what the pupil-teacher ratio is.

Obtain the opinions and advice of others who have been faced with the same decisions and problems as yourself, and collect as much information from as many different sources as possible before making a decision. Speak to teachers and the parents of children attending the schools on your shortlist. Don't forget to discuss the alternatives with your children before making a decision! See also **Choosing a Private School** on page 201.

Don't assume either that all state schools are alike: some are more 'welcoming' of foreigners than others, particularly regarding help with language learning. Even before buying a home in France, it's wise to check with the *mairie* whether there are other foreigners in the area and whether the local schools have staff and facilities to cater for children who speak little or no French or whether they're likely to be sent to a 'special education institution' for children with learning difficulties, as is often the case. (You will also find out whether you and your children are likely to receive a warm welcome into the community.) If not, you should budget for private French lessons or send your child to a private school or even a boarding school abroad until he has mastered the language, which can take as long as two years (see **Learning French** on page 209) – or choose somewhere else to live.

Also check the reputation of the local *collège* (see **State Schools** below) and be wary if it's in a *zone d'éducation prioritaire* (*ZEP*), which is a euphemism for an area where the majority of children have behavioural problems! Note, however, that private schools in such areas can be as bad as state schools.

STATE SCHOOLS

Although French state-funded schools are called 'public schools' (*école publique*), the term 'state' has been used in preference to public in this book in order to prevent confusion, as a 'public school' in the UK is a private, fee-paying school. The state school system in France differs considerably from the school systems in, for example, the UK or the US, particularly regarding secondary education.

The Ministry of National Education, Youth and Sport is responsible for most of France's state education system, which divides the country into 28 regions or districts (*académies*), each of which is a group of several *départements* headed by a superintendent (*recteur*) and attached to at least one university. The *académies* set the curriculum and examinations (all schools in the same *académie* have the same exam questions), and a high degree of consultation ensures that standards vary little from region to region. Although the state provides a large proportion of the funding for the French education system, in recent years some of the responsibility has been transferred to regions (for *lycées*) and departments (for *collèges*).

Pupils usually go to nearby nursery and primary schools, although attending secondary school often entails travelling long distances. One of the consequences of the depopulation of rural areas in recent years has been the closure of many schools, resulting in children having to travel further to school, although in most areas there's an efficient school bus service.

A general criticism of French state schools often made by foreigners is the lack of extra-curricular activities such as sport, music, drama, and arts and crafts. According to a recent Ministry of Education report, 60 per cent of pupils have no access to gymnasia or sports grounds and 20 per cent no access to a swimming pool, and 25 per cent of schools have inadequate sports facilities. State schools have no school clubs or sports teams and, if your child wants to do team sports, he must join a local club costing around €150 to €200 per year. This means parents need to ferry children back and forth for games and social events (Americans will be used to this!). However, although not part of the curriculum, a variety of sports activities are organised through local sports associations (e.g. Écoles Municipales de Sport), which may also organise non-sporting activities such as dance and music. Fees are low (e.g. €75 to €150 per year) and activities usually take place directly after school. Some organisations also sell second-hand sports equipment. French state schools also make limited use of computers; homework is always handwritten (usually, and bizarrely, on squared paper).

On the plus side, children are taught calligraphy (French handwriting may be quite different from the style you're used to), grammar (every French child knows the difference between a direct object and an indirect object!), philosphy and ethics, environmental studies and civics. And, in place of extra-curricular activities are 'discovery classes' at primary school level (see page 193) and – a uniquely French idea – an annual 'taste week' in October, during which schoolchildren are initiated into the finer points of *le bon goût*!

Note that class numbering in French state schools differs considerably from the US and British systems. The French system is almost the exact reverse of the US system. Instead of counting from 1 to 12, the French start with the 11th form (grade) at the age of six and end with the first form, followed by the *classe terminale*, the last year of a secondary high school (*lycée*) at 18 or 19. If pupils fall behind at secondary school, they're often required to repeat a year (*redoubler*), although this is seldom the case in nursery and primary schools thanks to the introduction of a more flexible system of cycles (see page 189).

Having made the decision to send your child to a state school, you should stick to it for at least a year to give it a fair trial. It may take a child this long to fully adapt to a new language, a change of environment and a different curriculum. State schools have special education sections (*sections d'education spéciale/SES*) for children with learning difficulties due to psychological, emotional or behavioural problems and for slow learners. Those who have difficulty with the language can take advantage of an *orthophoniste*, a specialist who deals with all sorts of speech and pronunciation problems. If you need to change your child's school, you must obtain a *certificat de radiation* from his current school.

Enrolment

Children must attend a state school within a certain distance of their home, so if you have a preference for a particular school, it's important to buy or rent a home within that school's catchment area (which may change periodically in accordance with demographic changes). You may make a request (*dérogation*) for your child to attend a different school from the one assigned by your town hall, but you must usually have good reasons for such a request, e.g. another of your children already attends your preferred school, the preferred school is close to your home or place of work, or it teaches a unique course that you wish your child to follow, such as certain foreign languages. The transfer must be approved by the *directeurs* of both schools.

Information about schools in a particular area can be obtained from the schools information service (*service des écoles*) at your local town hall. If you wish to arrange your child's education before arriving in France, you should write to the Inspecteur d'Académie of the *département* where you're going to live, with details of the child's age, previous schooling and knowledge of French.

To enrol your child in a French school you must compile an 'enrolment file' (*dossier d'inscription*) at your town hall (for primary schools) or at the *rectorat* school service (for secondary schools) and must supply the documents listed below. You will then be given a registration form to take to the school.

● Your child's birth certificate or passport, with an official French translation (if necessary). If your child was born in France, you must take along your family record book (*livret de famille*) or birth certificate (*extrait de l'acte de naissance*).

● Proof of immunisation. In France, immunisations are recorded in a child's health book (*carnet de santé*), which is issued to parents when a child is born. When you arrive in France, you're issued with a *carnet de santé* by your *mairie* for all school-age children. For more information, see **Children's Health** on page 309.

● Proof of residence in the form of an electricity or telephone bill in your name. If you don't have any bills (lucky you!), a rent receipt, lease or proof of property ownership (*attestation d'acquisition*) is acceptable.

● If your child is coming from another French school, a *certificat de radiation* issued by his previous school.

● Evidence of insurance (see page 179).

School Hours

Most state schools have adopted the four-day week (*semaine de quatre jours*) with Wednesday remaining free (a tradition dating back to the separation of church and state almost 100 years ago, when parents were expected to arrange religious instruction for their children on Wednesdays) and the lack of Saturday lessons compensated for by reducing holiday periods (the option favoured by most parents in a recent survey), although most *collèges* also have lessons on Wednesday mornings. The changes are now official, although a few *départements* still institute Saturday morning classes for primary school children and in the Paris area schools changed to a five-day Monday to Friday week in September 2002. Contact your local education department or town hall to find out the position regarding school hours in your area.

School hours vary. Nursery school hours are from 08.30 or 09.00 to 11.30 or 12.00 and from 13.30 or 14.00 to around 16.30. There's a 15-minute break in the mornings and afternoons. Primary school consists of 26 hours per week, usually from 08.30 to 11.30 and 13.30 to 16.30. Secondary schools have the longest hours. In a *collège*, students attend school for 27 or 28 hours per week and in a *lycée* for around 30 to 36 hours (depending on the type of *lycée*). The school hours for a *lycée* are usually from 08.00 to 12.00 and 14.00 to 17.00, although some start at 09.00 and finish at 18.00. At both *collège* and *lycée*, children aren't obliged to remain in school if they have no lesson.

Most schools have a (free) bus, which collects children from outlying regions and returns them home at the end of the day. Due to the roundabout journey, this often adds considerably to the school day (although children usually enjoy the journey and it's a good way for them to make friends). Many parents prefer to take children to and from school or take them to school and allow them to get the bus home. State schools and communities usually provide an after-school nursery (*garderie*) for working mothers, although many working mothers arrange to be free on Wednesdays to be with their children.

Holidays

French children have the longest school holidays (*vacances scolaires*) in the world, with 117 days (excluding weekends in term time and some public holidays). They generally attend school for 160 days a year only, from early September until late June, although they compensate with long school hours and abundant homework (from primary school onwards). Winter and spring school holidays vary from town to town according to a system of zones (see below) in order to allow ski resorts to cope with the flood of children during these periods. Term dates may be modified to take account of local circumstances.

Zone	Cities/Towns
A	Caen, Clermont-Ferrand, Grenoble, Montpellier, Nancy-Metz, Nantes, Rennes and Toulouse
B	Aix-Marseille, Amiens, Besançon, Dijon, Lille, Limoges, Lyon, Nice, Orléans-Tours, Poitiers, Reims, Rouen and Strasbourg
C	Bordeaux, Créteil, Paris and Versailles

The year is made up of five terms, each averaging around seven weeks. The table below shows the school calendar (*calendrier scolaire*) for 2005/06 and 2006/07.

Holiday		Dates	
		2006/07	**2007/08**
All Saints (*Toussaint*)		25th Oct – 6th Nov	27th Oct – 8th Nov
New Year (*Noël*)		23rd Dec – 8th Jan	22nd Dec – 7th Jan
Winter (*Hiver*)	Zone A:	10th – 26th Feb	16th – 3rd Mar
	Zone B:	24th Feb – 12th Mar	9th Feb – 25th Mar
	Zone C:	17th Feb – 5th Mar	23rd Feb – 10th Mar
Spring (*Printemps*)	Zone A:	31st Mar – 16th Apr	12th – 28th Apr
	Zone B:	14th Apr – 2nd May	5th – 21st Apr
	Zone C:	7th – 23rd Apr	19th Apr – 5th May
Summer (*Eté/Grandes Vacances*)	3rd Jul – 3rd Sep		3rd Jul – 3rd Sep

Schools are also closed on public holidays (see page 63) when they fall within term time. School holiday dates are published by schools and local communities well in advance, thus allowing parents ample time to schedule family holidays. Normally you aren't permitted to withdraw your children from classes during the school term except for visits to a doctor or dentist, when the teacher should be informed in advance. In primary school a note to the teacher is sufficient, while in secondary school an official absence form must be completed by the teacher concerned and submitted to the school office. For absences of more than two days, a doctor's certificate is required. If your child requires emergency medical care while at school, you will be asked to sign an authorisation, as you will for school trips (see page 193).

The government issues instructions regarding student employment during the last term of the academic year. The rules apply to tertiary level students and students in secondary and technical schools aged 16 or more, although those in secondary education aged 14 or 15 are eligible for a permit for part-time summer employment, provided it's only light work and for not more than half the summer holiday period.

Provisions

Education is free in France, but pens, stationery and sports clothes/equipment must be purchased by parents. Most other provisions are provided in primary schools (ages 6 to 11) and in *collèges* (ages 12 to 15), although parents may need to buy some books, but everything must be purchased by parents for children attending a *lycée*. A number of passport-size photographs are required by secondary school students. The average parent can expect to pay around €400 per year per *lycée* student (more for technical subjects). This can be hard on low-income families, although they may qualify for a 'back to school allowance' (*allocation de rentrée scolaire*) of around €250 for each child between 6 and 15. All grants must be applied for by the end of March for the following school year. It's also possible to buy second-hand books at the start of the term, when schools hold second-hand book sales (*bourse aux livres*).

Primary school children require the following articles:

- School bag or satchel.
- Pencil case, pencils and crayons, stationery, etc..
- Gym shoes, shorts and a towel for games and exercise periods.
- Sports bag for the above if the satchel is too small.

Be warned that children are expected to bring a lot of books home every evening for their homework; these can be heavy and it's widely believed that carrying them can damage children's spines. Schools may provide lockers but seldom enough for all pupils, and lockers are often broken into in some schools.

You may be given a list of items required (*liste des fournitures de rentrée*), which can run to three pages of A4, at the end of the summer term or the beginning of the autumn term (the latter causing parents to flock to the supermarket on the first day of school to buy everything that's required). Note, however, that some items are 'optional'; if in doubt, wait until term begins to see whether these are really required or were simply added to the list willy nilly. Don't forget name tapes (*noms tissés sur ruban*) for coats and sports equipment; you can order them from a *mercerie* or simply write on tape in indelible ink, but it's better to sew them to clothing than to use iron-on tapes that can fall (or be pulled) off.

At nursery school, children usually take snacks for breaks but either go home for lunch or eat at the school canteen (*cantine*), where gourmet-style meals are available for around €1.50 per meal, paid a month in advance. The cost of lunch at a nursery or primary school varies with the area, the parents' income and whether they live within the catchment area. Lunch at a secondary school costs around €100 per term. Children who have school lunches are called *demi-pensionaires*, those who go home for lunch *externes*. Taking a packed lunch isn't usually considered an option and may even be forbidden. Children are normally expected to eat everything when they have school lunch, which may consist of five courses (including wine – for the teachers!) can last up to two hours, and there may be no 'tuck shop' or even vending machines.

With the exception of a few 'exclusive' schools, school uniforms are non-existent, although there may be 'house rules' concerning what may and may not be worn. There has recently been some debate over the introduction of uniforms, as in any case children usually devise their own 'uniforms', which can cost far more than a conventional school uniform. In some areas the theft (e.g. by 'mugging') of designer clothes by 'gangs' is widespread and has resulted in children being discouraged from wearing expensive clothes to school. Controversially, pupils aren't allowed to wear any 'signs of religious affiliation' such as crucifixes or headscarves.

Nursery & Primary School Cycles

Nursery and primary schooling are divided into educational cycles (*cycles pédagogiques*). There are three cycles, each of three years' duration, as follows:

1. *Cycle des Apprentissages Premiers*, comprising the three sections of nursery school from the age of three to six (*les petits*, *les moyens* and *les grands* – see **Nursery School** below).

2. *Cycle des Apprentissages Fondamentaux*, comprising the final year of nursery school and the first two years of primary school (*cours préparatoire/CP* and *cours élémentaire 1/CE1*).

3. *Cycle des Approfondissements*, including the primary school years *cours élémentaire 2/CE2*, *cours moyen 1/CM1* and *cours moyen 2/CM2*.

Although each cycle normally lasts three years, it can be completed in two or four years, depending on a child's progress. The decision whether a child is ready to progress to the next cycle is made jointly by a teachers' council (*conseil des maîtres de cycles*), the school director, the pupil's teachers and a psycho-pedagogical group. It's no longer possible to fail a year and have to repeat it, as the new system allows pupils to progress at their own speed and doesn't require them to repeat the same work as in the previous year. Parents are able to appeal against a school's decision regarding progression to the next cycle. A school record book (*livret scolaire*) is maintained for each child during the three cycles.

Nursery School

France has a long tradition of free, state-funded, nursery schools and has one of the best programmes in the world, although in many areas facilities are in short supply and you may need to enrol your child virtually at conception! (Normal enrolment takes place during the April before the start of the school year.) Around 80 per cent of women with one child and around 50 per cent of those with three children work, and most make use of some form of nursery school. Around 30 per cent of children attend nursery school at the age of two, and virtually all by the time they're four – a level of attendance matched only by Belgium.

Children between two months and three years can be left at a nursery or crèche (*crèche*), normally provided that both parents work. There are four kinds of crèche: 'collective' crèches (*crèche collective*) run by the local community, which are the most popular choice and therefore oversubscribed (only around 9 per cent of parents find places); 'mini-crèches' (*mini-crèche*), which are similar to collective crèches, only smaller; parental crèches (*crèche parentale*), organised by groups of parents and limited to 16 children; and family crèches (*crèche familiale*), where you leave your children at the home of an 'maternal assistant' (*assistante maternelle*). If you leave your child with an *assistante maternelle*, make sure that she's accredited (*agréée*) by the Protection Maternelle et Infantile (PMI). Crèches are usually open between 07.00 and 19.00 on weekdays. The cost of a *crèche collective* varies according to the number of children accommodated, the parents' salaries and the commune; an *assistante maternelle* costs a minimum of €22 per day. To find out about parental crèches, contact the Association des Collectifs Enfants Parents Professionels (ACEPP, ☎ 01 44 73 85 20, 🖳 http://www.acepp.asso.fr).

If you need to leave your children only occasionally (i.e. both parents don't work full time), children between three months and six years old can be left for up to a day at a time at a *halte-garderie* or *jardin d'enfants* or a *multi-accueil* centre (limited to 20 children); prices vary but can be as low as €2 per hour. If your children need looking after for a short time before or after school, they can be accommodated by an *accueil péri-scolaire* or a *centre de loisirs sans hébergement* (minimum age three years), sometimes attached to a nursery school (see below). If you can afford it, you can employ a child-minder (*garde d'enfant à domicile*) or nanny (*nounou*), who must however be declared to the authorities as a salaried employee. A child-minder or nanny must be paid at least the minimum wage (see page 24). Note, however, that you can obtain a tax reduction against crèche or child-minding expenses.

Nursery schooling (*école maternelle*) from the age of two to six years is optional. However, a place is theoretically available in nursery school for every three-year-old whose parents request one. The place must be in a nursery school or an infant class (*classe enfantine*) in a primary school as close as possible to the child's home. Priority is given to children living in underprivileged areas, children with two working parents, children from families with three or more young children, and children who live too far from school to go home for lunch.

Nursery school hours are generally from 08.30 or 09.00 to 11.30 or 12.00 and from 13.30 or 14.00 to 16.00 or 16.30, with the exception of Wednesdays, when there's no school. Young children usually sleep for two hours after lunch. Children can attend for half a day, which many foreign parents prefer, particularly at first when a child doesn't speak French. There's usually a morning session on Saturdays, depending on the *département*, although this is optional. Children may have lunch at school canteen by arrangement (see **Provisions** above). If parents are unable to collect their children when school is over, there's usually a supervised nursery (*garderie*) until around 18.00 for a small fee.

Nursery school has traditionally been divided into three stages, according to age: *les petits* – from two to four years; *les moyens* – from four to five years; *les grands* – from five to six years. The three years of primary school from age three to six are included in the first of the new *cycles pédagogiques* (see above) and the last year is incorporated in the second cycle.

Nursery school is designed to introduce children to the social environment of school and to develop the basic skills of coordination. It encourages the development of self-awareness and provides an introduction to group activities. Exercises include arts and crafts (e.g. drawing, painting and pottery), music, educational games and perceptual activities, e.g. listening skills. During the final years, the rudiments of reading, writing and arithmetic are taught in preparation for primary school.

Primary School

Primary school (*école primaire*) attendance is compulsory between the ages of 6 and 11 for 26 hours per week. Schools are established and maintained by local communities, although overall responsibility lies with the state. Since the '80s, the primary school population has been decreasing, causing a reduction in the number of classes. In many rural areas this has led to the closure of schools and children having to travel to schools in neighbouring towns, or schools having to share teachers and equipment such as computers. There are several schemes in operation around the country to find better ways of organising primary education, particularly staff, half of whom are over 50 and reluctant to change. One scheme makes part-time use of graduates to assist teachers in an attempt to inject new blood into the system.

Each primary school has a director (*directeur/directrice*), who presides over the school council (*conseil d'école*). The council makes decisions regarding school regulations, communication between teachers and parents, school meals, after-school care (*garderie*), extra-curricular activities, security and hygiene. The school council usually meets twice a year and comprises a teachers' committee (*comité des maîtres*), a parents' committee (*comité des parents*), and representatives of the local education authority and municipality. The parents' committee is the equivalent of the parent-teacher association (PTA) in many other countries.

The five years of primary school are structured as follows:

Age	Form/Grade	Course
6 – 7	11e	*cours préparatoire/CP*
7 – 8	10e	*cours élémentaire 1/CE1*
8 – 9	9e	*cours élémentaire 2/CE2*
9 – 10	8e	*cours moyen 1/CM1*
10 – 11	7e	*cours moyen 2/CM2*

The subjects taught at primary school are divided into three main groups: French, history, geography and civic studies; mathematics, science and technology; physical education and sport, arts and crafts, and music. Minimum and maximum numbers of tuition hours are set for each group of subjects, up to a total of 26 hours per week. Teachers are allowed some flexibility in determining the hours so that they can place more emphasis on certain subjects for particular pupils, based on their strengths and weaknesses.

The main objectives of primary school are the learning and consolidation of the basics: reading, writing and mathematics. There are no examinations at the end of primary school, although a child's primary record is forwarded to his secondary school. However, all children are expected to be able to read and write French by the end of their first term in primary school and are tested to see whether they're up to standard. Primary school children have a notebook (*cahier de texte*) that they bring home each day. Parents sign the book to verify that a child has done his homework and teachers use it to convey messages to parents, e.g. special items a child requires for school the next day.

An hour's foreign language tuition per week is included in primary school years *CM1* and *CM2*. Most pupils (over 80 per cent) choose to learn English, although the French government is trying to encourage them to learn other foreign languages, including regional and immigrant languages, e.g. Arabic (all part of the losing battle to counteract the growing influence of the English language in France!). From the 2005/06 school year, it was intended that all *CE1* pupils be taught at least two foreign languages (although it isn't yet clear whether enough teachers will be found to teach them!). Foreign language tuition is necessarily basic, and English-speaking parents shouldn't expect it to improve their children's English; in fact, they would be better off starting to learn a third language.

Homework is required from the start of primary school, and the transition from *CE1* to *CE2* can be a difficult one, children suddenly being subjected to increased pressure of work and having to undergo regular tests in all subjects.

One of the unique aspects of French primary education is the 'discovery class' (*classe de découverte*), when pupils spend one to three weeks in a new environment. It may be held in the country (*classe verte/classe de nature*), mountains (*classe de neige*), by the sea (*classe de mer*) or even abroad. It isn't a holiday camp and pupils follow their normal lessons, augmented by field trips and other special activities. The most popular discovery class is the skiing trip, which usually takes place in January or February. Financial assistance is available for parents who are unable to pay.

Secondary School

Secondary education is compulsory until the age of 16 and includes attendance at a *collège* until the age of 15. At 15, continuing education is decided by examination, students with the greatest academic aptitude going to a *lycée* (high school) until they're 18 (*cycle long*) to study for the *baccalauréat* (see page 196) and others following shortened studies (*cycle court*) in a vocational course. These include the study for a *brevet d'enseignement professionnel* (*BEP*) or *certificat d'aptitude professionnelle* (*CAP*), which can lead to a *baccalauréat professionnel*, in a 'professional' *lycée* (see page 194). At the end of *collège*, a certificate of competence is issued for particular skills, provided a certain level of language ability has also been attained. Students can repeat a year until they pass the final examinations, and few leave without a certificate.

The secondary school(s) your child may attend is primarily determined by where you live. In some rural areas there's little or no choice, while in Paris and other cities there are usually a number of possibilities. As in all countries, the schools with the best reputations and exam results are the most popular and are therefore the most difficult to gain entry to. Parents should plan well ahead, particularly if they want a child to be accepted by a superior *collège* or *lycée*. Some *collèges* are attached to *lycées*, with *collège* students granted preferential entrance to the *lycée*.

Collège

At the age of 11 all children attend a *collège* (formerly known as a *collège d'enseignement secondaire/CES*), headed by a *principal*. Each *collège* has a school council (*conseil d'établissement*) composed of administrative staff and representatives of teachers, parents, students and the local authorities. Its task is to make recommendations regarding teaching and other matters of importance to the school community.

The school year is organised on a trimester basis (a period of three months equating to a term), students being evaluated by teachers (*conseil des professeurs*) at the end of each trimester. This evaluation is particularly important, as it determines the future studies open to a student and the type of *baccalauréat* he may take (see page 196). Parents' organisations (*associations des parents/délégués des parents*) also play an important role in determining a student's future studies. It's common for school class councils (*conseil de classes*) to recommend that a student repeat a year of *collège*, although this can be done only with the parents' permission. If parents don't agree, they can appeal against the decision, although if they lose the appeal they must abide by the appeal commission's decision.

A few *collèges* offer boarding (*internat*), although this isn't as common as it used to be; arrangements are similar to those for an *internat* at a *lycée* (see below).

The four years of *collège* education are numbered from the 6th to the 3rd and are divided into two, two-year cycles:

Cycle d'Observation: The first two years of *collège* (sixth and fifth forms) are called the 'observation' cycle, where all students follow a common curriculum. General lessons total around 24 hours per week and include French, mathematics, a modern foreign language, history, geography, economics, civics, physics and chemistry, biology and geology, technology, artistic subjects, physical education and sport. An extra three hours (*heure de soutien*) of lessons are set each week in subjects selected by the *collège* (usually French, mathematics and a foreign language), depending on individual students' needs. At the end of the fifth form students move to the orientation cycle (fourth form) or repeat the fifth form.

Cycle d'Orientation: The last two years of *collège* (fourth and third forms) are called the 'orientation cycle' because students are allowed some choice of subjects and can thus begin to decide the future direction (*orientation*) of their studies. Students follow a common curriculum of around 25 hours of lessons a week in the same subjects as in the sixth and fifth forms. In addition to the core subjects, there are compulsory lessons in one second foreign language chosen from a list of options (*option obligatoire*), and optional classes (*options facultatives*) in a regional language or a classical language (i.e. Greek or Latin). Decisions regarding future studies are made at the end of the third form (at around the age of 14), when exams are taken to decide whether students go on to a *lycée* and sit the *baccalauréat* (see page 196), attend a vocational *lycée* or take an apprenticeship.

Technology fourth and third forms offer a more practical educational approach for students suited to a less academic form of learning. Students who attain the age of 14 or 15 and haven't reached the necessary level to move on to the fourth form are taught in small pre-vocational classes (*Classes Préprofessionnelles de Niveau/CPPN*). Here they receive extra lessons and special assistance, particularly in French and mathematics, in order to enable them to continue their studies. Others move into preparatory apprenticeship classes (*Classes Préparatoires à l'Apprentissage/CPA*) – see **Vocational Lycée** on page 196.

At the end of their last year at *collège*, students sit a written examination (*brevet des collèges*) in French, mathematics and history/geography. The *brevet* is the entrance examination to a *lycée*, although failure doesn't exclude students from going on to higher education.

Lycée

A *lycée* (headed by a *proviseur*) is roughly equivalent to a sixth form college in the UK and similar in standard to a grammar or high school (but higher than a US high school or two-year college). It provides an excellent education that's equal to that of any school system in the world. It's the aim of all ambitious students to attend a *lycée*, and competition for places is fierce. There are far fewer *lycées* than *collèges* and consequently there's less choice. In rural areas, *lycées* take students from a wide area and, because of the travelling distances involved, many offer boarding from Mondays to Fridays. At a *lycée*, students are treated more like university students and aren't required to remain in school if they don't have a lesson. However, the informal, often casual, air contrasts with the constant pressure of monthly tests (*interrogation*) and the writing of formal dissertations in most subjects. It goes without saying that, unless a student is prepared to work hard, it's a waste of time attending a *lycée*. There are two types of *lycée*, described below.

Some *lycées* offer boarding (*internat*) for four nights per week (Mondays to Thursdays); a few accept boarders (*internes*) on Sunday nights. Sports and social activities, as well as supervised homework periods, are generally organised in the evenings. Most *internats* are single-sex, but it may be possible for children of the other sex to rent a room nearby and dine at the school as well as taking part in evening activities – in which case they're known as *internes externés!* Costs are reasonable: around €2,500 per year for an *interne* and somewhat less for an *interne externé*.

General & Technology Lycée (*Lycée d'Enseignement Général et Technologique*): A general and technology *lycée* prepares students for the general or technology *baccalauréat* (see page 196) or the technical certificate (*brevet de technicien/BT*). There are also professional *lycées* (*Lycées Professionnels/LP*) and *Centres de Formation d'Apprentis* (*CFA*) offering courses leading to vocational certificates (see **Vocational Lycée** below).

The course is divided into second (*seconde*), first (*première*) and final (*terminale*) years. Second form or *classe de seconde de détermination* is so called because it prepares students to choose the type of *baccalauréat* they will take (see page 196). Few second-form students specialise and work for a specific *baccalauréat*; exceptions are music or dance and certain technical certificates. During their second form, students study French, mathematics, a modern foreign language, history, geography, physics, chemistry, biology and geology, and have physical education and sports lessons.

They also choose subjects from one of the following two groups:

- **Academic** – Introduction to economics and social studies and one or two other subjects from: a second modern language, a regional language, a classical language, management, computers, information technology, artistic subjects and specialised sporting activities.

- **Practical** – One or two specialised technology subjects, such as industrial technology, science and laboratory technology, medical and social science, or applied arts. The inclusion of at least one technology subject is compulsory for students planning to progress to the first form and sit the corresponding technology *baccalauréat* (see page 196).

It's possible to transfer from a practical to an academic course or vice versa by way of a transition class (*classe passerelle*).

After the second form, students move on to one of the courses leading to the *baccalauréat* examination (see page 196). General and technology *lycées* also offer post-*baccalauréat* classes to students who have obtained a technology *baccalauréat* or a *BT*. These students can study for a further two years for the *brevet de technicien supérieur* (*BTS*), encompassing some 90 areas of specialisation. Holders of a *BTS* are capable of entering a trade or occupation and assuming a responsible technical or administrative position. The *BTS* programme has developed rapidly since its introduction due to good employment prospects, and it's often chosen in preference to a university course. It may also offer the possibility of a sandwich course giving practical experience in commerce or industry, and *BTS* students can apply for one of over 1,400 grants of around €450 to obtain work experience in another EU country.

Vocational Lycée (*Lycée Professionnel/LP*): Vocational *lycée* courses lead to vocational certificates. These include the *brevet d'études professionnel* (*BEP*) and the *certificat d'aptitude professionnelle* (*CAP*). The *BEP* certificate covers the range of knowledge required in a particular trade, industrial, commercial, administrative or social sector, rather than a specific skill. The *CAP* is more specialised and is awarded for skill in a particular trade, e.g. carpentry, plumbing or dressmaking. In addition to school lessons, the *BEP* and *CAP* programmes include practical periods with companies providing students with an introduction to the workplace.

After passing the *CAP*, students may be permitted to enter the 'special second form' (*seconde spéciale* or *spécifique*), where they undertake three years of technological studies leading to the *BT*. Students with a *BEP* or *CAP* can also take a technology or vocational *baccalauréat*, known as a *baccalauréat professionnel*, after a further two years' study (see below). Almost every occupation in France has some form of recognised apprenticeship or certificate, including filing clerks, shop assistants and waiters, without which it's difficult to get a job in a particular field. See also **Apprenticeships** on page 202.

Baccalauréat

The *baccalauréat* (commonly called the *bac*) is taken at a *lycée* at the age of 18 or 19 and is an automatic entrance qualification to a French university. Those who pass are known as *bacheliers*. There are over 30 *baccalauréats* to choose from, but three main groups, as follows:

● **General *baccalauréat*** – The general *bac* is an academic diploma and prepares students for higher education rather than for a trade or profession. It enables students to continue their studies at university, in preparatory classes for a *grande école* (see below), in a higher technicians' section (*STS*), in a university institute of technology or in specialised schools. There are three main types of general *bac*: literature and classics; science; economic and social sciences.

● **Technology *baccalauréat*** – This is awarded for both general knowledge and training in modern technologies. It's the first stage of higher technical training, usually at a university institute of technology or *STS*, and occasionally at a university or *grande école*. There are eight types of technology *bac*: industrial; science and technology; laboratory science; medical and social science; agriculture; environment; hotel and catering; music and dance.

● **Vocational** *baccalauréat* – Also known as the *baccalauréat professionnel*, this is chosen by an increasing number of students each year and has enjoyed huge success since its introduction. The majority of those who pass the exam go straight into employment, although it also entitles them to enter higher education. A major feature of the vocational *baccalauréat* course is that students spend a quarter of their time training in industry.

Within these basic types, there are four 'series' (*série*) of *bac*: A, B, C and D in ascending order of difficulty and importance. For example, those wishing to study medicine usually take *Bac* D, and *Bacs* C and D are the most common among those wishing to attend a *grande école* (see page 206). Among students planning to go to university, *Bacs* A and B are common. Students can always lower their expectations, but once started on a lower track, it's difficult to change to a higher one.

In the second form, students can choose to follow the vocational system (*système d'orientation*) or selection system (*système de sélection*). Those who choose the vocational system must sit the *baccalauréat* in subjects such as law, science, medicine, dentistry, pharmacy, management and economic sciences, social sciences or fine arts. The selection system is for those who wish to attend superior institutions of higher education. These students must pass the *baccalauréat* and a competitive examination, or pass the *baccalauréat*, provide a school record and attend an interview with an examining board. The selection system applies to institutes of technology (*IUT*), institutes of political studies (*IEP*), and post-*baccalauréat* establishments preparing students for the *BTS* or for entry to a *grande école* preparatory school (see below).

The courses taken during a student's final two years at a *lycée* depend on the type of *baccalauréat* selected. There are seven major subjects in the first form and eight in *terminale*. The *baccalauréat* is taken in two parts, the first of which consists of an examination in French language and literature (*baccalauréat de français*) taken in the first form. This must be passed before any other exams can be taken. The second part of the *bac* is taken in *terminale*. Students who fail the *bac* can retake it the following year.

The French *baccalauréat* examination is marked out of 20, as are all French exams. An average of 10 is a pass, 12/13 is quite good (*mention assez bien*), 14/15 is good (*mention bien*) and 16 and over is very good/excellent (*mention très bien*). Marks of 16 or more are extremely rare, so in reality a mark of 12 to 14 can be considered as good or very good and anything above 14 as excellent. Note, however, that not all subjects are regarded as equal, and some are 'weighted' in accordance with the type of *bac* according to a complex system of 'coefficients' (*coefficient*), although French is usually given high priority; if you fail in French, you generally fail your *bac*.

European universities and most US colleges recognise the French *baccalauréat* as an entrance qualification, although foreign students must provide proof of their English language ability to study in the UK or the US. A US university may grant credits to a *bachelier* allowing him to graduate in three years instead of four. The international baccalaureate option (*option internationale du baccalauréat/OIB*) and international baccalaureate (IB) examinations are offered by some international *lycées* in France (and *lycées* with international sections) – see page 199.

Grandes Écoles Preparatory School

Grandes écoles preparatory schools (classes préparatoires aux grandes écoles/CPGE or prépa for short) are the first step for anyone with ambitions to attend a grande école, France's elite higher education institutions (see page 206). Admission to a prépa is based on a student's grades in his final (terminale) year at lycée and the subjects chosen. For example to attend a science CPGE a student must take a C or D science baccalauréat. Usually students require an average of 14 (mention bien) to be accepted.

Applications must be made by 1st May, i.e. before actually sitting the baccalauréat, with provisional selection based on school reports for the final year of lycée and teachers' reports. Successful students spend two years (one in the case of veterinary students) in a CPGE, which is generally an integral part of a lycée, although it may be housed within a grande école. Entrance to a prépa constitutes a first selection procedure, before the competitive examination (concours) for the grande école, taken at the end of the two-year period. This exam has a failure rate of around 90 per cent!

Students who fail the entrance examination may be permitted to remain at a preparatory school for another year and retake the exam if their grades are high enough. If they fail again they must change track, which for most students means going to a university. However, even partial success in one of the CPGE examinations can bring exemption from all or part of the diplôme d'études universitaires générales (DEUG), the examination taken at the end of the second year of university (see page 204).

PRIVATE SCHOOLS

There's a wide range of private schools (écoles privées) in France, including parochial (mostly Catholic) schools, bilingual schools, international schools and a variety of foreign schools, including US and British schools (see below). Together they educate around 15 per cent of French children. Most private schools are co-educational, non-denominational day schools ('Catholic' private schools usually admit non-Catholics and aren't allowed to promote Catholicism). Most private schools operate a Monday to Friday timetable. There are few private boarding schools (internat) in France, although some schools provide weekly (Monday to Friday) boarding or accommodate children with 'host' families.

The cost of private schooling can be surprisingly low, particularly for those used to UK fees: annual fees of €2,250 are common. Not surprisingly, private education is becoming increasingly popular and many schools are oversubscribed. Enrolment is often carried out on a first-come-first-served basis, and prospective pupils (and their parents) may have to arrive **very** early on enrolment day to be sure of a place – for admission to some schools, overnight camping is recommended!

For a list of French boarding schools in a particular town or region, visit 🖳 http:// www.service-public.fr and search for 'Ecoles privées' or contact your local Centre d'Information et d'Orientation (ask at your mairie for details). The Office de Documentation et d'Information de l'Enseignement Privé (ODIEP, ☎ 01 43 29 90 70) provides information about private schools from nursery to university level. UNAPEL (☎ 01 53 73 73 90, 💻 http://www.apel.assoc.fr) provides information about parochial schools. The Centre National de Documentation sur l'Enseignement Privé (☎ 01 47 05 32 68, 💻 http://www.fabert.com) publishes a list of all French private schools.

Bilingual, International & Foreign Schools

Some schools are classified as bilingual (*avec section bilingue* or *classes bilingues*) or international (e.g. *lycée international* or *avec section internationale*). Certain bilingual schools, such as the Ecole Active Bilingue in Paris, have US, British and French sections. The Ecole Internationale de Paris teaches in both French and English. Note, however, that the curriculum in most bilingual schools is tailored to children whose mother tongue is French. Places in bilingual and international schools are in strong demand and there are usually stiff entrance requirements.

There are international schools in Aix-en-Provence, Bordeaux, Cannes, Grenoble, Lille, Lyon, Nice and nearby Sophia Antipolis, Saint-Etienne, Strasbourg and Toulouse, as well as in Luynes in Alpes-Maritimes and in Monaco. The Lycée International at Saint-Germain-en-Laye (near Paris) has nine national sections (American, British, Danish, Dutch, German, Italian, Portuguese, Spanish and Swedish). Each section aims to teach children about the language, literature and history of the particular language/country selected. All other lessons are taught in French. Where applicable, students who don't speak French are usually given intensive French lessons for three to six months.

Most of the few American and British schools are in the Paris area and on the French Riviera. Most English-language private schools offer a comprehensive English-as-a-Second-Language (ESL) programme and number students from many countries. The only school in France teaching the UK curriculum is the British School of Paris (☎ 01 34 80 45 90, 💻 http://www.britishschool.fr).

A free list of US and British schools teaching entirely in English, international sections in French *lycées*, and bilingual and international schools can be obtained from the British Council (☎ 01 49 55 73 00 and ☎ 08 92 68 44 14).

Most private schools teaching in French provide intensive French tuition for non-French-speakers. Schools specialising in teaching non-French students are listed in our sister-publication, *The Best Places to Buy a Home in France* (see page 587). There are also private colleges for students aged 16 or older who need additional help with their *baccalauréat* studies or who wish to study subjects unavailable at their local *lycée*.

Curriculum

Private schools in France teach a variety of syllabi, including the British GCSE and A Level examinations, American High School Diploma and college entrance examinations (e.g. ACT, SAT, achievement tests and AP exams) and the OIB and IB (see below). However, many schools offer bilingual children the French *baccalauréat* only. Among private schools in France are a number that follow special or unorthodox methods of teaching, such as Montessori nursery schools and Rudolf Steiner schools. There are also private schools in some areas for children with special language requirements.

Some private schools offer an international baccalaureate option (*option internationale du baccalauréat/OIB*) in addition to the French *baccalauréat* examination. The *OIB* is intended for bilingual French students or foreign students with fluent French who are planning to enter a French university. The *OIB* is a French exam and shouldn't be confused with the international baccalaureate (IB), which is classed as a foreign diploma in France. The IB, which originated in Switzerland in 1968 and has its headquarters in Geneva, is an internationally recognised university entrance qualification. As an international examination it's second to none. It's taught in over 500 schools in around 65 countries but in only nine French schools, only three of which provide bilingual education: the Ecoles Actives Bilingues Jeannine Manuel in Paris and Lille and the International School of Sophia Antipolis (ISSA) near Nice. In fact, the ISSA is the only IB school where classes are taught in both French and English.

Private schools have smaller classes and a more relaxed, less rigid regime and curriculum than state schools. They provide a more varied and international approach to sport, culture and art, and a wider choice of academic subjects. Many also provide English-language summer school programmes, combining academic lessons with sports, arts and crafts and other extra-curricular activities. Their aim is the development of the child as an individual and the encouragement of his unique talents, which is made possible by the small classes. The results are self-evident and many private secondary schools have a near 100 per cent university placement rate.

Fees & Enrolment

There are two main types of private school in France: those that have a contract with the French government (*sous contrat d'association*) and those that don't (*hors contrat* or *école libre*). A private school that has a contract with the government must follow the same educational programme as state schools, for which it receives government subsidies, and is therefore less expensive than an *hors contrat* school. A private school without a contract with the government is free to set its own curriculum, receives no state subsidies and is consequently more expensive.

Private school fees also vary considerably according to the quality, reputation and location of a school. Not surprisingly, schools located in the Paris area are the most expensive. Fees at a Catholic private school that's *sous contrat* may be as low as €300 per year, whereas fees at an independent (*hors contrat*) international senior day school can be as high as €12,000 or €15,000 per year. Fees aren't all-inclusive, and there are additional obligatory charges, such as registration fees, and optional charges. For example, lunches may be included in school fees or charged separately, e.g. €100 to €150 per month.

You should make applications to private schools as far in advance as possible. You're usually requested to send previous school reports, exam results and records. Before enrolling your child in a private school, ensure that you understand the withdrawal conditions in the school contract.

Choosing a Private School

The following checklist is designed to help you choose an appropriate private school.

- Does the school have a good reputation? How long has it been established?

- Does the school have a good academic record? For example, what percentage of students obtain good examination passes and go on to top universities? All the best schools provide exam pass-rate statistics.

- What does the curriculum include? What examinations are set? Are examinations recognised both in France and internationally? Do they fit in with your future education plans? Ask to see a typical student timetable to check the ratio of academic to non-academic subjects. Check the number of free study periods and whether they're supervised.

- How large are the classes and what is the student/teacher ratio? Does the stated class size tally with the number of desks in the classrooms?

- What are the qualification requirements for teachers? What nationalities are the majority of teachers? Ask for a list of the teaching staff and their qualifications.

- What are the classrooms like? For example their size, space, cleanliness, lighting, furniture and furnishings. Are there signs of creative teaching, e.g. wall charts, maps, posters and students' work on display?

- What is the teacher turnover? A high teacher turnover is a particularly bad sign and usually suggests badly paid teachers with poor working conditions.

- What extras must you pay? For example, lunches, art supplies, sports equipment, outings, clothing, health and accident insurance (see page 179), textbooks and stationery. Some schools charge parents for absolutely everything.

- Which countries do most students come from?

- Is religion an important consideration in your choice of school?

- Are intensive English or French lessons provided for children who don't meet the required standard?

- What is the quality and variety of food provided? What is the dining room like? Does the school have a dietician?

- What languages does the school teach as obligatory or optional subjects?

- What is the student turnover?

- What are the school terms and holiday periods? Private school holidays are usually longer than state school holidays (e.g. four weeks at Easter and Christmas and ten weeks in the summer) and they often don't coincide with state school holiday periods.

- If you're considering a day school, what are the school hours? Is transport provided to and from school?

- What are the withdrawal conditions, should you need or wish to remove your child? A term's notice is usual.

- What sports instruction and facilities are provided? Where are the sports facilities?

- What are the facilities for arts and science subjects, e.g. arts and crafts, music, computer studies, biology, science, hobbies, drama, cookery and photography? Ask to see the classrooms, facilities, equipment and some student projects.

- What sort of outings are organised?

- What medical facilities does the school provide, e.g. infirmary, resident doctor or nurse?

- What punishments are applied and for what sorts of offence?

- What reports are provided for parents and how often?

- Last but not least – unless someone else is paying – what are the fees?

Before making a final choice, it's important to visit the schools on your shortlist during term time and talk to teachers and students (if possible, also speak to former students and their parents). Where possible, check out the answers to the above questions in person and don't rely on a school's prospectus or director to provide the information. If you're unhappy with the answers, look elsewhere. If necessary take someone with you who speaks fluent French.

Finally, having made your choice, keep a check on your child's progress and listen to his complaints. Compare notes with other parents. If something doesn't seem right, try to establish whether the complaint is founded or not; if it is, take action to have the problem resolved. Never forget that you're paying a lot of money for your child's education and you should ensure that you receive good value. See also **State or Private School?** on page 183.

APPRENTICESHIPS

Many young people in France look forward to starting work and learning a trade, and the vast majority who don't go on to higher education (see page 203) enter an apprenticeship or another form of vocational training. A strong emphasis is placed on training, and few school-leavers go directly into a job without it. It's normal practice for those leaving school at 16 to attend a technical college or train as an apprentice. Most parents and students are acutely aware that academic qualifications and training are of paramount importance in obtaining a good job (or any job), and virtually every child is given the opportunity to study for a trade diploma or degree. A French apprenticeship (*apprentissage*) aims to give people aged between 16 and 26 who have completed compulsory schooling a general, theoretical and practical training, leading to a certificate of vocational or technological education at secondary or a higher level. The French apprenticeship scheme is recognised as one of the best in the world.

An apprenticeship is a combination of on-the-job training and further education, where one or two days per week (a minimum of 400 hours per year) are spent at an apprentice training centre (*centre de formation d'apprentis/CFA*). An apprenticeship lasts from one to three years, depending on the type of profession and the qualification sought. It can be in almost any vocation from carpentry to hairdressing, in the private or public sector. School careers officers are available to advise parents and students on a choice of career. Employers pay a small salary that increases with age and experience, and also pay for apprenticeship schooling and possibly the cost of travel to and from school.

Other types of vocational training aimed principally at jobseekers (*demandeur d'emploi*) include the following:

- **Adaptation Contracts** (*contrat d'adaptation à un emploi*) provide for training during working hours and allow people aged between 16 and 25 to adapt their qualifications to their position in a company. The contract can be for a fixed period of 6 to 12 months or for an indefinite duration. Training lasts for a total of 200 hours and includes practical, on-the-job training and general, vocational and technological education. See also **Vocational Lycée** on page 196.

- **Qualification Contracts** (*contrat de qualification*) are intended to allow people between 16 and 25 without adequate qualifications to obtain a vocational qualification with a company. They last from six months to two years and a minimum of 25 per cent of the contract period is spent on general, technological and vocational training leading to a recognised vocational qualification.

- **Orientation Contracts** (*contrat d'orientation*) are for 16 to 25-year-olds without professional or technological qualifications and last up to nine months.

Further information about apprenticeships and vocational training can be obtained from a regional Direction du Travail, de l'Emploi et de la Formation Professionnelle, from ANPE (see page 31) and from Centre d'Information et d'Orientation (CIO) offices. For the address of your local CIO office, contact your *mairie*.

HIGHER EDUCATION

France has numerous higher education (*enseignement supérieur*) institutions, including over 75 traditional universities (13 in the Paris region) and around 250 *grandes écoles* and *écoles supérieures* (see page 206).

Universities

Universities are the weakest part of the French education system and are obliged to accept anyone who passes the French *baccalauréat* examination – some 30 per cent of secondary students (around 1m) – resulting in overcrowding, under-funding and a general lowering of standards. Lecture halls are packed and students have no tutorial system and little supervision. These problems are exacerbated by the length of time it takes to obtain a degree in France, where the average leaving age is 29. Most courses aren't tailored to specific careers and, not surprisingly, a huge number of students fail to obtain a degree. Despite the high dropout rate, most people are opposed to limiting admissions, which they feel would compromise the principle of equality. However, the upshot is that unemployment among graduates is high and most universities have little prestige.

Although still famous (particularly among foreigners), the Sorbonne is little more than a building housing part of the sprawling Université de Paris, and it has lost much of its eminence within France to the *grandes écoles* (in fact it's so overcrowded that conditions are said to be 'of third world standard'!).

Qualifications

Anyone who passes the French *baccalauréat* examination (see page 196) is guaranteed entry to a university. Schools of medicine, dentistry and pharmacy are attached to certain universities, and entry is restricted to the top 25 per cent of students with a *Baccalauréat* C. Other restricted entry institutions include schools of economics and law. However, one of the most difficult to gain acceptance to is a veterinary school, a popular and lucrative profession in France (where there are over 10m dogs!). There are just four veterinary schools in France, all with a highly competitive entrance examination.

Foreign students number around 130,000 or 10 per cent of university intake. Most are from North Africa, although there's a large number from EU countries, South America and China. There are quotas for foreign students at certain universities and for particular courses. For example, foreign students are limited to 5 per cent of the number of French students in medical and dental studies at universities in and around Paris. Foreign students are admitted to French universities on the basis of equivalent qualifications to the French *baccalauréat*. French universities accept British A Levels as an entrance qualification, but an American high school diploma isn't generally accepted, and American students must usually have spent a year at college or have a BA, BBA or BSc degree. All foreign students require a thorough knowledge of French, which is usually examined if no *baccalauréat* certificate is supplied. French language preparatory courses are provided. There's a special university entrance examination for mature students without a *baccalauréat*, although mature students are rare in France, where the idea of going back to school after working isn't popular.

Curriculum & Exams

During their first two years at university (called Stage I), students study a core curriculum, and in their second year they take the *diplôme d'études universitaires générales* or *DEUG*). There are nine types of *DEUG*, students being able to specialise in economic and social administration, law, literature and language, the arts, economics and management, science and technical studies, physical and sports studies, human and social sciences, and theology. The *DEUG* has a high failure rate, almost half of undergraduates failing to complete their degrees, although a new tutoring system, whereby older students help younger ones, has helped to reduce the number who fail. Those who fail may be given a third year to pass, but no longer.

Those who pass the *DEUG* can take a degree (*licence*) in arts and sciences (equivalent to a BA or BSc) after a further year, or a further two years in the case of economics and law. The *licence* is classified as the first year of Stage II studies. However, a two-year *DEUG* or three-year degree has little value in the French job market, where competition for top jobs is fierce.

A *maîtrise*, roughly equivalent to an MA, is awarded after completion of the second year of Stage II studies, one year after gaining a *licence*. In certain subjects, e.g. science and technology, business studies and computer science, a *licence* isn't awarded, and after obtaining a *DEUG* students study for a further two years for a *maîtrise*. Students can study for a further three or four years after receiving their *maîtrise* for a doctorate (*doctorat*) or Stage III degree.

Another type of degree, called a *magistère*, is awarded in certain subjects for three years' study after obtaining a *DEUG* or *diplôme universitaire de technologie* (*DUT*), the latter awarded on completion of a two-year course of study at a university institute of technology (*Institut Universitaire de Technologie/IUT*). The *magistère* course combines the acquisition of basic knowledge, an introduction to research and its practical application within a professional framework.

Recent reforms aim to 'harmonise' French higher education with that of other European countries by introducing a system known as *licence, master, doctorat* (*LMD*) and awarding students 'credits' (*crédits*) for each course. A *DEUG*, for example, is worth 120 credits and a degree 300.

Like most schools, universities offer few extra-curricular sports and social activities (the most popular extra-curricular activity is the pursuit of love!). There aren't even inexpensive university bars in France!

Enrolment

Overseas students must complete an initial registration form (*dossier de demande de première admission en premier cycle*) and lodge their application by 1st February for entry the following October (the academic year runs from October to June). Application forms are available from the cultural sections of French embassies. Applicants must present a residence permit valid for at least a year or that of their parents if the latter have a three-year residence permit. Applicants apply for three universities, at least two of which must be outside Paris. There's no central clearing system and applicants must apply to each university separately. Most French students normally apply via their school, which submits their applications for them. However, for some arcane reason, a different system applies in Paris, where provisional applications must be made via Minitel (no other form of application is accepted) using a system called *Recensement Automatisé des Voeux des Elèves* (which conveniently, if irrelevantly, abbreviates to *RAVEL*) in early March, followed by a definitive application in July, once they've received their *bac* results.

Fees & Grants

University students don't pay tuition fees, and costs for foreign students are minimal. Between €150 and €300, depending on the options chosen, is sufficient to cover registration fees, including obligatory fees for health insurance and social security. Students over 26 are required to take out health insurance in their country of origin or insurance under the French social security system on arrival in France. Government grants (*bourse*) are awarded to 20 per cent of students. The maximum grant is now around €3,000 per year, although most are less than €1,000. Some 12,000 grants of around €400 per month are available to students wishing to study abroad. Note that students require numerous passport-size photographs (usually on a white background) and photocopies and translations of assorted documents.

To apply for a grant, students must prepare a *dossier social étudiant* by the end of April and submit it to the Centre National des Oeuvres Universitaires et Scolaires (CNOUS – see **Information** below). Banks will make long-term, low-interest loans for quite large amounts if they judge the application to come from a high-calibre student. Scholarships are also provided by international organisations and foreign governments.

Parents are obliged by law to support their children at university until they're 20, after which age they're officially financially self-reliant. One in three students support themselves during their studies by working part-time during terms and over holiday periods (see **Temporary & Casual Work** on page 37).

Accommodation

Foreign students must make their own arrangements for accommodation. Students are eligible for a room in a university hall of residence, although places are limited and accommodation is generally of poor quality. Students should expect to pay around €150 per month for a room in a hall of residence and between €225 and €300 per month for a private room (or more in Paris). Foreign students need around €600 to €1,000 per month to live in Paris (less in the provinces). Many students attend the nearest university to their home and treat university as an extension of school, particularly in Paris and other large cities where accommodation is expensive.

Grandes Ecoles & Ecoles Supérieures

Somewhat surprisingly in a country boasting of its commitment to equality (*égalité*), France has the most elitist higher education system in the world. *Grandes écoles* and *écoles supérieures* are university colleges specialising in professional training, to which entrance is by competitive examination (*concours*). Before being eligible for a *grande école*, students must spend two years at a special preparatory school (*Classes Préparatoires aux Grandes Écoles/CPGE*, see page 198). *Grandes écoles* were founded under Napoleon to provide the engineers and administrators of the Republic, and today they number around 250 and together have some 80,000 students. They're dedicated to training high-level specialists, particularly in engineering, applied science, administration and management studies. *Grandes écoles* are outside the university system and are controlled by the ministry to which their speciality is linked. At each *grande école* all students take the same subjects, with no courses offered outside a school's speciality.

Although they're required to work hard, with little time for play, students at *grandes écoles* enjoy a pampered and privileged existence. Compared with the impoverished and over-crowded universities, *grandes écoles* are lavishly funded and equipped. The state spends around €40,000 educating a student at a *grande école*, compared with just €12,000 at a university. They're castigated for elitism, perpetuating the class system, and comprising a male dominated club for the rich and privileged. Only 1 per cent of *grandes écoles* students come from a working class background compared with around 15 per cent in universities, and only 10 per cent are women. Virtually no foreigners are admitted. Critics of *grandes écoles* also complain that they undermine France's universities, which as a result are the weakest part of the country's educational system.

The most celebrated *grandes écoles* include the Conservatoire National des Arts et Métiers (CNAM), Ecole Centrale, Ecole Polytechnique (usually known simply as *X* from its badge of crossed cannons), Ecole des Ponts et Chaussées (known as Ponts) and Ecole des Mines (all engineering), Ecole des Hautes Etudes Commerciales/HEC, Ecole Supérieure de Commerce/Sup de Co and Ecole Supérieure des Sciences Economiques et Commerciales (business and management), Ecole Normale Supérieure/ENS/Normal Sup (research and teaching), Institut d'Etudes Politiques/IEP/Sciences Po (politics), Ecole Nationale Supérieure des Beaux-Arts (fine arts) and Ecole Nationale d'Agronomie (agriculture). The cream of *grandes écoles* and the most recent is the Ecole Nationale d'Administration/ENA, the post-graduate nursery of France's civil service mandarins and political elite (graduates are called *énarques*).

A magnificent career is virtually guaranteed to graduates of *grandes écoles*, who fill the top positions in government, the civil service and most industries in France. Many companies appoint only *grande école* graduates to management positions, and they're usually preferred to business school graduates with an MBA. It's common practice for newspaper articles to state the *grande école* attended by a prominent academic, executive or politician, and many graduates include it on their business cards.

American Universities & Colleges

There are a number of American colleges and universities in France, including the American University in Paris (AUP), where all classes are taught in English and the 1,000 strong student body comes from over 70 countries. The AUP offers both BA and BSc degrees, and students can study for a BA in seven fields, including international business, art, history and European culture. Fees for a full academic year are around €12,000, excluding health insurance, accommodation and deposits. A popular American college in Paris is the Parsons School of Design (a division of New York's New School for Social Research), where students take a four-year Bachelor of Fine Arts (BFA) degree. The Paris American Academy, which specialises in fine arts, fashion, languages and interior design, also has a good reputation. There are many other American colleges in Paris offering courses in a range of subjects and degrees (from a BA to an MBA).

Information

The Centre Régional des Oeuvres Universitaires et Scolaires (CROUS, ☎ 01 40 51 36 00) is responsible for foreign students in France and provides information about courses, grants and accommodation. CROUS subsidises university accommodation and restaurants, but not all are subsidised so you should contact CROUS before choosing a university. In Paris, students can contact the Centre National des Oeuvres Universitaires et Scolaires (CNOUS, ☎ 01 44 18 53 00, 💻 http://www.cnous.fr). The French Ministry of Education's website (💻 http://www.education.fr) gives information about the organisation of the French university system, and the cultural sections of French embassies provide information about higher education. A complete list of the state and private universities in France, entitled *Le Guide des Études Supérieures*, is published annually by *L'Étudiant* magazine. All state universities are also listed on the Education Ministry's website (see above), and the Ministry has recently set up a new site aimed at making it easier for students who have obtained their *bac* to find a suitable course in France or abroad, obtain a grant and even find accommodation (💻 http://www.etudiant.gouv.fr).

FURTHER EDUCATION

Further education generally embraces everything except first degree courses taken at universities, *grandes écoles* and other institutions of higher education, although the distinction between further and higher education (see page 203) is often blurred. Each year many thousands of students attend further education courses at universities alone, often of short duration and job-related, although courses may be full or part-time and include summer terms. France has many private colleges and other university-level institutions, some affiliated to foreign (usually US) universities. These include business and commercial colleges, hotel and restaurant schools, language schools and finishing schools.

Many educational institutions offer American MBA degree courses, including the European University in Paris and Toulouse. Among the most popular MBA subjects are banking, business administration, communications, economics, European languages, information systems, management, marketing, public relations, and social and political studies. Tuition fees are high and study periods strictly organised. Although most courses are taught in English, some schools require students to be fluent in both English and French, e.g. the European Institute for Business Administration (INSEAD) at Fontainebleau, one of Europe's most prestigious business schools. Many US universities also run summer courses in France; these are advertised in publications such as *FUSAC* and *Paris Voice* (see **Appendix B**). Details of courses available to Americans can be found in *The Grown-Up's Guide to Living in France* (Ten Speed Press).

Many further education courses are of the 'open learning' variety, where students study mostly at home. These include literally hundreds of academic, professional and vocational correspondence courses offered by private colleges. Many universities offer correspondence courses to students who want to study for a degree but are unable to attend a university due to their circumstances, e.g. health, distance, job or family commitments. These courses are particularly targeted at mature students. Over 30,000 students take part in correspondence courses taught through universities with distance learning centres, and through the Centre National d'Enseignement à Distance (🖳 http://www.cned.fr), which prepares students for competitive exams and provides specific training.

The latest development in French education is 'virtual universities', where students can study via the internet (although they must take their exams in the 'real world'!). Universities offering 'virtual' courses include Pierre Mendès-France (in Grenoble), Nancy II, Paris-Dauphine, Paris-Sud, Sophia-Antipolis (near Nice) and the Institut d'Administration des Entreprises de Paris.

Another type of course offered by universities and schools allows those in employment to enrol in evening courses and take advantage of specially planned timetables. The Conservatoire National des Arts et Métiers (CNAM) and its regional centres admit students without any formal qualifications to a wide range of courses, many leading to a degree.

General information about local further education and training is available from town halls and libraries, and the French Ministry of Education provides a free information service through departmental Centre d'Information et d'Orientation (CIO) offices. See also **Day & Evening Classes** on page 444.

LEARNING FRENCH

If you want to make the most of the French way of life and your time in France, it's essential to learn French as soon as possible. For people living in France permanently, learning French isn't an option, but a necessity. **Your business and social enjoyment and success in France will be directly related to the degree to which you master French.** Although it isn't easy, even the most non-linguistic person can acquire a working knowledge of French. All that's required is perseverance and a little help, particularly if you have only English-speaking colleagues and friends.

Most people can teach themselves a great deal through the use of books, tapes, videos/DVDs, computer programmes and online courses (see **Self-help** below). However, even the best students require some help. Teaching French is big business in France, with classes offered by language schools (see below), French and foreign colleges and universities, private and international schools, foreign and international organisations (such as the British Institute in Paris), local associations and clubs, and private teachers. Most universities provide language courses, and many organisations offer holiday courses year-round, particularly for children and young adults (it's best to stay with a local French family). Tuition ranges from courses for complete beginners, through specialised business or cultural courses to university-level courses leading to recognised diplomas. If you already speak French but need conversational practice, you may prefer to enrol in an art or craft course at a local institute or club (see **Day & Evening Classes** on page 444).

In some areas the Centre Culturel provides free French lessons to foreigners. If you're officially registered as unemployed and have a residence permit, you can obtain free lessons (*perfectionnement de la langue française*) from the ANPE (see page 31), although complete beginners don't qualify (contact your local ANPE office for information). For information about exchange programmes for children, see **Adapting to the System** on page 180.

Self-help

There are numerous self-study French courses available, including those offered by the BBC (🖳 http://www.bbc.co.uk/education/languages/french), Eurotalk (🖳 http://www.eurotalk.co.uk) and Linguaphone (🖳 http://www.linguaphone.co.uk). Websites offering free tutorials include 🖳 http://www.france-pub.com/french, 🖳 http://www.frenchassistant.com and 🖳 http://www.frenchtutorial.com. A quarterly publication, *Bien-dire* (sic), is aimed at adult learners (🖳 http://www.learningfrench.com), and the About French language website (🖳 http://www.french.about.com) provides copious information about the language and tips to help you learn.

There are several things you can do to speed up your language learning, including watching television (particularly quiz shows where the words appear on the screen as they're spoken) and DVDs (where you can select French or English subtitles), reading (especially children's books and product catalogues, where the words are accompanied by pictures), joining a club or association, and (most enjoyable) making French friends. Finding a French 'penfriend' while abroad is a good way to improve your language skills, and there are a number of websites aimed at putting people in touch for this purpose, including 🖳 http://www.friendsabroad.com and 🖳 http://www.mylanguageexchange.com.

Language Schools

There are many language schools (*école de langues*) in cities and large towns. One of the most famous French language teaching organisations is the Alliance Française (AF, ☎ 01 42 84 90 00, 🖳 http://www.alliancefr.org), a state-approved, non-profit organisation with over 1,000 centres in 138 countries, including 32 centres in France, mainly in large towns and cities. The AF runs general, special and intensive courses, and can also arrange a homestay in France with a host family.

Another non-profit organisation is Centre d'Echanges Internationaux (☎ 01 43 29 60 20), offering intensive French language courses for juniors (13 to 18 years) and adults throughout France. Courses include accommodation in their own international centres, with a French family, or in a hotel, bed-and-breakfast or self-catering studio. Junior courses can be combined with tuition in a variety of sports and other activities, including horse riding, tennis, windsurfing, canoeing, diving and dancing.

Another well-known school is Berlitz (☎ 01 40 74 00 17, 🖳 http://www.berlitz.com) with around 16 schools in France, including five in Paris. And the British organisation CESA Languages Abroad (UK ☎ 01209-211800, ⌨ http://www.ces alanguages.com) offers advice and arranges language courses.

Most language schools run various classes, and which one you choose will depend on your language ability, how many hours you wish to study a week, how much money you want to spend and how quickly you wish to learn. Language classes generally fall into the following categories: extensive (4 to 10 hours per week); intensive (15 to 20 hours); total immersion (20 to 40 or more). Some offer telephone lessons, which are particularly practical if you're busy or don't live near a language school.

Don't expect to become fluent in a short time unless you have a particular flair for languages or already have a good command of French. Unless you desperately need to learn French quickly, it's better to arrange your lessons over a long period. However, don't commit yourself to a long course of study, particularly an expensive one, before ensuring that it's the right course. The cost of a one-week total immersion course is usually between €2,500 and €3,000! Most schools offer free tests to help you find the appropriate level and a free introductory lesson.

Individual Lessons

You may prefer to have individual lessons, which are a quicker, although more expensive way of learning a language. The main advantage of individual lessons is that you learn at your own speed and aren't held back by slow learners or left floundering in the wake of the class genius. You can advertise for a teacher in your local newspapers, on shopping centre/supermarket bulletin boards and university notice boards, and through your or your spouse's employer. Otherwise, look for advertisements in the English-language press (see **Appendix B**). Don't forget to ask your friends, neighbours and colleagues if they can recommend a teacher.

Individual lessons by the hour cost from around €50 at a school or €15 to €35 with a private tutor, although you may find someone willing to trade French lessons for lessons in your native language, especially if it's English. In some areas (particularly in Paris), there are discussion groups that meet regularly to converse in French and other languages; these are usually advertised in the English-language press (see **Appendix B**).

Information

The Best Places to Buy a Home in France (see page 587) includes lists of language schools in the most popular regions of France. A comprehensive list of schools, institutions and organisations providing French language courses throughout France is contained in a booklet, *Cours de Français Langue Étrangère et Stages Pédagogie de Français Langue Étrangère en France*. It includes information about the type of course, organisation, dates and costs, and other practical information, and is available from French consulates and from the Association pour la Diffusion de la Pensée Française (ADPF, ☎ 01 43 13 11 00, ⌨ http://www.adpf.asso.fr). For further information about the French language, see **Language** on pages 29 and 181.

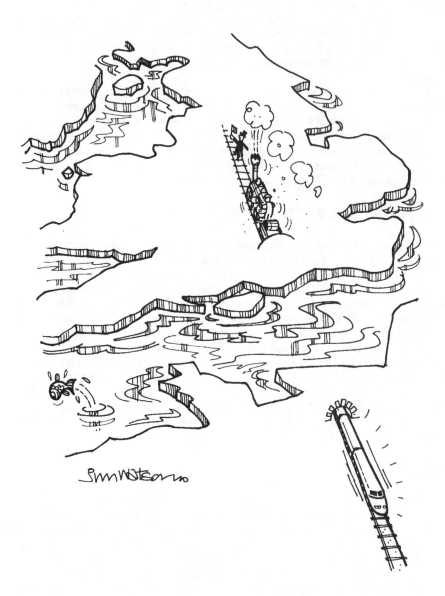

10.

PUBLIC TRANSPORT

Public transport (*transport public*) services in France vary considerably according to where you live. They're generally excellent in cities, most of which have efficient local bus and rail services, many supplemented by underground railway and tram networks. French railways provide an excellent and fast rail service, particularly between cities served by the *TGV* (see page 218). France is also served by excellent international and domestic airline services and extensive international ferry services along its north coast. On the negative side, bus and rail services are poor or non-existent in rural areas (although the provision of public transport has recently been improved by the amalgamation of neighbouring communes into *agglomérations*), and it's generally essential to have your own transport if you live in the country.

Paris has one of the most efficient, best integrated and cheapest public transport systems of any major city in the world. In addition to its world-famous *métro*, public transport services include the *RER* express rail system, an extensive suburban rail network and comprehensive bus services; a tram service, due to open at the end of 2006, will cover 8km (5mi) of southern Paris and have 19 stops (the capital's original tram network, closed in 1937, had over 1,000km of track!). Other cities have similar systems, and several have reintroduced trams in recent years.

Most cities are moving towards more 'ecological' public transport systems, with for example buses running on biofuel or batteries, and encouraging or even obliging people to use them by restricting the circulation of private vehicles. Thanks to government subsidies, however, public transport is generally inexpensive, although this doesn't stop the French from complaining about the cost. Various commuter and visitor discount tickets are also available.

Students visiting or living in France should obtain an International Student Identity Card (ISIC) and non-students an International Youth Card (IYC), which offer young people a range of travel discounts. They're available from most student travel offices and student organisations. The French Government Tourist Office publishes a booklet, *France Youth Travel*, for those aged under 26. A number of local and regional organisations in France offer a *carte jeune*, which entitles the holder to discounts on local transport (and in some cases driving lessons) as well as entertainment. The cost of a *carte jeune* varies between around €10 and €45 according to the number of discounts offered.

AIRLINE SERVICES

The state-owned national airline, Air France, is France's major carrier, flying to over 30 French, 65 European and 120 other destinations in over 70 countries. Air France and its various subsidiaries (known collectively as Groupe Air France) has a fleet of over 200 aircraft and carries 16m passengers annually. It provides a high standard of service and, as you would expect, excellent in-flight cuisine. Smoking is banned on French domestic flights and on Air France international flights of less than two hours.

International Flights

All major international airlines provide scheduled services to Paris, and many also fly to other main French cities such as Bordeaux, Lyon, Marseille, Nice and Toulouse.

Air France shares many international routes with just one foreign carrier and is thus able to charge high fares. The lack of competition means that international and domestic flights are among the world's most expensive. However, some opposition is starting to appear and high fares on some transatlantic flights have been reduced in recent years by travel agents such as Nouvelles Frontières and no-frills airlines such as BMIbaby, EasyJet, Flybe and Ryanair. British visitors are especially well served by cheap flights, particularly from London Stansted airport, to many regional French airports, although routes change with disturbing frequency and advertised prices aren't always obtainable. France's second airline, Air Littoral, was rescued from the receivers and offers flights to European destinations from its hubs in Montpellier and Nice, but a 'low cost' airline, Flyeco, launched in June 2004, has already 'crashed'.

Domestic Flights

Sadly, most of France's regional airlines have been swallowed by Air France (☎ 08 20 82 08 20 for bookings, 🖳 http://www.airfrance.fr), which now dominates the domestic flight market, although there are still a few regional services, e.g. the Compagnie Aérienne Corse Mediterranée and Corsair, which operate flights to Corsica, and Air Outre-Mer, which offers daily flights to Réunion. Air France operates domestic services between major cities such as Paris, Bordeaux, Lyon, Marseille, Mulhouse/Basel, Nice, Strasbourg and Toulouse. Many domestic flights are timed to connect with international arrivals in Paris.

Competition on major domestic routes from *TGVs* (see page 218), e.g. Paris-Lyon and Paris-Marseille (which has attracted twice as many passengers as the corresponding air route), has helped reduce air fares and flying is sometimes cheaper than travelling by train and quicker on most routes. Any destination in mainland France or Corsica can be reached in less than 100 minutes by air, although stricter security now means that check-in times can be up to 45 minutes before departure.

Tickets

Air France offers cut-price tickets (called *Tempo*), which must be booked at least two weeks in advance, for periods including a Saturday (e.g. Paris-Bordeaux for around €100 instead of the full fare of over €350) and *Coups de Coeur* discounts on certain flights, bookable only on Wednesdays via the internet (🖳 http://www.air france.fr). Children between 4 and 12 years old may travel alone provided the airline is informed at the time of booking. Special offers for frequent fliers are provided by most European and international airlines, including Air France, which is nevertheless one of the most expensive airlines for intercontinental flights to France.

All airline passengers buying tickets in France must now pay a surcharge (euphemistically called a *taxe de solidarité*) of between €1 and €40 (depending on the destination and seat class), which is supposed to go to an international fund, Unitaid, designed to combat disease in the developing world – a charge which many believe to be illegal – and there is talk of the possible introduction of 'environmental' surcharges.

After London, Paris is one of the cheapest European destinations from North America. Apart from special offers, the cheapest way to get to Paris from North America is with an apex fare, which must usually be booked 21 days in advance, travelling midweek and staying at least seven days. Thanks to the strong link between France and Quebec, there are frequent air services between France and Canada, mostly from Paris to Toronto or Montreal. From other countries, it's worthwhile comparing the cost of a direct flight to Paris with a flight via another European city. **If you're planning to fly out of France during school holidays, book well in advance, particularly if you're heading for a popular destination such as London or New York.**

Airports

The main French airports handling intercontinental flights are Paris Roissy-Charles de Gaulle (CDG) and Paris Orly (see below), Lyon-Saint-Exupéry (formerly Satolas), Nice-Côte-d'Azur and Marseille-Provence. Many of France's regional airports have flights to a number of European destinations, particularly London Stansted. Flights to North African countries are also common from regional airports, mainly to cater for migrant workers. Nice is France's busiest provincial airport with direct scheduled flights to around 80 cities worldwide, closely followed by Marseille, which serves around 70 international destinations.

Among the many other French airports served by international flights are Beauvais (sometimes called Paris/Beauvais, although it's around 80km/50mi north of the city), Bergerac, Biarritz, Bordeaux, Brest, Brive-la-Gaillarde, Caen, Carcassonne, Chambéry, Cherbourg, Clermont-Ferrand, Dijon, Dinard, Grenoble, Hyères/Toulon, La Rochelle, Le Havre, Lille, Limoges, Lourdes, Montpellier, Mulhouse/Basel, Nancy/Metz, Nantes, Nîmes, Pau, Perpignan, Quimper, Reims, Rennes, Rodez, Strasbourg, Toulouse and Tours/Poitiers. There are also international flights to Ajaccio, Bastia, Calvi and Figari in Corsica. Depending on your destination, it's sometimes cheaper or quicker to fly to an international airport outside France, such as Luxembourg for north-eastern France and Geneva for eastern France.

Long and short-term parking is available at major airports, including reserved parking for the disabled, and car hire is also available at Paris and principal provincial airports. Details of all French airports and their services can be found online (🖥 http://www.aeroport.fr).

Paris

Paris is served by direct flights from almost every major capital city in the world and there are also direct flights from over 30 US and Canadian cities operated by around 12 airlines. Most local taxis outside Paris have special rates for passengers going to either of the two airports, and you can often arrange with your local taxi service to pick you up at the airport on your return. For those who drive to the airport, there are car parks at both CDG and Orly, which charge around €2.75 per hour up to around €22 for 24 hours, although CDG has a long-term car park where you can leave your car for 24 hours for just €12. Even for short periods, this can be cheaper than taking a taxi from your home to the airport and saves you the inconvenience of having to carry heavy luggage on buses or trains. The Aéroports de Paris website (🖳 http://www.adp.fr) has information on both CDG and Orly, including access maps (and even pre-ordering from the airport duty-free shops!).

Roissy-Charles de Gaulle: Charles de Gaulle or Roissy (as it's usually called) is 23km (14mi) north-east of the centre of Paris. There are two terminals (*aérogare*): terminal 2 serves Air France plus Air Inter, Air Bremen, Air Madagascar, Air Seychelles, Alitalia, Austrian Airlines, Brymon Airways, Canadian Airlines, Crossair, CSA, Interflug, LOT, Luxair, MALEV and Tyrolean Airways; terminal 1 serves all other foreign airlines. The terminals are linked by a free bus service, and there's a bus service to Orly, costing €16. For Roissy airport information ☎ 01 48 62 22 80.

A high-speed link from Roissy to the centre of Paris is planned but won't be a reality before 2012; until then, the quickest way to travel between central Paris and Roissy airport is to take the *RER* line B (see page 217), which takes 35 minutes. A free shuttle bus operates from the *RER* station at Châtelet Les Halles and from Roissy railway station to the terminals. There are also a variety of bus services to and from central Paris operated by Air France, RATP (see page 230) and private operators, e.g. hotels. Most services operate from around 05.00 until 23.00 and run every 15 or 30 minutes, taking around 50 minutes. Single fares are around €8.50.

Orly: Orly airport is 14km (9mi) south of central Paris and has two terminals: *Sud* serving mainly international flights and *Ouest* (recently refurbished) serving mainly domestic flights. The quickest way to get to Orly from central Paris is to take *RER* line B in the direction of St. Rémy-les-Chevreuses and change at Antony for the *Orlyval* train. There are also trains every 15 minutes (30 minutes after 20.00) on *RER* line C from the Gare d'Austerlitz to Orly SNCF station. Bus services from central Paris are similar to those for Roissy-Charles de Gaulle (see above), costing around €6 and taking 40 minutes. Orly airport information is available on ☎ 01 49 75 15 15.

TRAINS

The French railway network extends to every corner of France. It's the largest in western Europe, with over 31,000km (19,400mi) of track, serving around 5,000 passenger stations and carrying over 800m passengers per year. The French railway system is operated by the state-owned Société Nationale des Chemins de Fer Français (SNCF) and is one of the most efficient in Europe. French high-speed trains (see **TGV** below) compete successfully with road and air travel over long distances, both in cost and speed. Despite huge government subsidies and recent price increases, however, the SNCF manages to run up an annual deficit. The destination of trains is usually written or displayed on the outside of carriages.

Main Lines

Many things in France emanate from or are routed via Paris and this is true of the railway system. (Paris and the Ile-de-France region provide the SNCF with around two-thirds of its passengers.) There aren't many cross-country train routes in France and it's often necessary to travel via Paris to reach a destination.

There are direct trains from French cities to many major European cities, including Amsterdam, Barcelona, Basle, Berlin, Brussels, Cologne, Florence, Frankfurt, Geneva, Hamburg, London, Madrid, Milan, Munich, Rome, Rotterdam, Venice, Vienna and Zurich. Some of the international services run only at night, and daytime journeys may also involve a change of train.

Paris has six main railway stations, each serving a main line (*grande ligne*), as detailed below:

Station	Regions & Countries Served
Gare d'Austerlitz	Central and south-west France (including Toulouse), except *TGV Atlantique* routes, Spain and Portugal
Gare de l'Est	East (Nancy, Strasbourg), Germany and Eastern Europe
Gare de Lyon	South and south-east (Lyon, Marseille, Côte d'Azur),including *TGV Méditerranée*, *Rhône-Alpes* and *Sud-Est* routes, Switzerland, Italy, the Balkans and Greece
Gare Montparnasse	West (Brittany) plus *TGV Atlantique* routes, including Bordeaux
Gare du Nord	North, *TGV Nord Europe* (Lille and London), and *Thalys* (Belgium, Holland and Scandinavian countries)
Gare Saint-Lazare	North-west (Dieppe, Cherbourg-Octeville, Le Havre, etc.)

If you buy a ticket for a journey starting in Paris, the departure station is indicated on it. All the stations mentioned above are on the *métro* and some are also on the *RER* (see page 231). It's best to allow around a hour to travel between stations, except between Gare Saint-Lazare, Gare du Nord and Gare de l'Est, which are close together (the Gare Saint-Lazare and the Gare du Nord are now linked by underground). The main stations in Paris also provide access to the city's comprehensive suburban rail service (*réseau banlieue*).

TGV

The SNCF operates high-speed trains (*train à grande vitesse*, abbreviated to *TGV*) on most of its main lines (see map in **Appendix E**). Launched in 1981, these are among the world's fastest trains, capable of over 550kph (around 350mph). Double-decker *TGVs* (*Duplex*), which were introduced in 1995, have around 45 per cent more capacity than standard trains (up to 550 passengers) and no reduction in speed.

TGV services operate to over 50 French cities, carrying more than 40,000 passengers a day. The *TGV* has revolutionised domestic travel in France, and air travel on *TGV* routes has fallen significantly, e.g. Paris-Lyon, on which route there are around 35 trains per day in each direction, with over 75 per cent seat occupancy, carrying more than 20,000 passengers daily. It takes just three hours with the *TGV*, at an average speed of 300kph, to travel from Paris to Marseille.

To run at maximum operating speed a *TGV* must run on special lines, which presently extend into Belgium (*TGV Nord Europe* with a service called *Thalys* linking Paris with Brussels and Amsterdam) but only as far as Le Mans and Vendôme to the south-west (*TGV Atlantique*) and Valence to the south-east (*TGV Méditerranée*). Other destinations are reached via a mixture of dedicated *TGV* lines and mixed traffic lines. The *TGV* rail network totals 5,500km (3,400mi) of dedicated and mixed lines, and there are five main lines (see table above). A recent line circumventing Paris means that some services (e.g. Lyon-Nantes and Bordeaux-Lille) are now direct and don't involve changing trains in Paris.

Recent additions to the TGV network include a twice-daily service from Paris to Saint-Malo (in Brittany), which welcomed its first high-speed train in December 2005, and there are (controversial) plans to extend the *TGV* network with Paris-Metz (via Reims, Strasbourg and Nancy, scheduled for 2007) and Paris-Bordeaux (via Tours and Angoulême, due for completion in 2013) routes, and a Montpellier-Perpignan-Barcelona link (2009), and routes between Arles and Nice in the south-east and between Rennes and Le Mans in the north-west, although plans (and estimated completion dates) change every few months. The *TGV* also operates between Paris and Switzerland (Berne, Geneva, Lausanne and Neuchâtel) — Paris to Geneva, for example, takes around 3.5 hours.

The *TGV* is almost totally silent and smooth, even when running at its maximum speed. Trains are often long, with up to 20 carriages and four engines. Trains are air-conditioned and include first- and second-class carriages, a bar/relaxation area, a stationery and tobacco shop, and sometimes a nursery. Carriages and compartments are colour-coded: red for first class, blue-green for second class and yellow for the bar. In second-class carriages, seats are arranged in airline fashion and are comfortable with reasonable space, pull down trays and foot rests. First-class seats are naturally more comfortable and roomy, although much more expensive. Luggage space is provided above seats and at the end of carriages. All seats must be reserved and no standing passengers are permitted. There are 'mobile-free' carriages on certain routes and the number of non-smoking seats was recently increased. Smoking is now forbidden in all first class carriages (numbered 5 and 15) and in all carriages on *Atlantique* routes, and it's likely that all TGV trains will be completely non-smoking before long.

The basic fare on the *TGV* is the same as on ordinary trains (see page 223), except that there's a booking fee that varies according to the day and time of travel and the length of the journey but averages around 10 per cent of the ticket price; the fee is 'included' in the price quoted. Bookings can now be made up to 90 days in advance. Depending on the route and the time of travel, you may need to book weeks, days or just minutes before your departure. A new system allows those who miss their TGV to exchange their ticket for one for the next ordinary train.

A recent initiative is the '*Intéractif Détente Train à Grande Vitesse*' (*iDTGV*), which consists of two 'zones': the '*iDzen*', where electronics (including mobile phones) are banned and you can be supplied with magazines, ear plugs and an eye mask to help you doze off, and the '*iDzap*', where the opposite applies and you can even hire DVD players and games consoles. You're even invited to register your interests so that you can be 'matched' with like-minded travellers and arrange shared onward transport (and, who knows, accommodation?) with them. More attractive perhaps are the fares, which start at just €19 for a single journey and can be booked in English via Rail Europe (UK ☎ 0870-837 1371, 💻 http://www.raileurope.co.uk/idtgv) or in French at 💻 http://www.idtgv.com.

Eurostar

The Channel Tunnel – the world's most expensive hole in the ground – joins France with the UK by rail, surfacing at Sangatte (near Calais) in Pas-de-Calais and Folkestone in Sussex. Since October 2003, when a new high-speed line from Folkestone to London Waterloo was opened, the London to Paris journey time has been reduced to 2h35m. The improvement comes at a price: a 'flexible' return fare costs over €400, although a 'fixed' return trip including a weekend booked at least three weeks in advance can be had for just €70 and return tickets for under €100 can be had from London to other French cities via Paris. A direct London to Avignon route started in summer 2003. Smoking is prohibited on all Eurostar trains. You can obtain train information in English or make a booking by calling a UK number (☎ 01233-617575) or via the Eurostar website (💻 http://www.eurostar.com), where cheap late bookings can be made online – but only on Tuesdays! For car-train services through the Channel Tunnel, see **Eurotunnel** on page 237.

Other Trains

Standard trains have either electric (*Corail*) or gas turbine (*Turbotrain*) locomotives, which, although not in the *TGV* league, are fast and comfortable. Some branch lines operate *express* and *rapide* diesel trains. The slowest trains are the suburban *omnibus* services (some with double-deck carriages), which stop at every station. An *express* or *train express régional* (*TER*) stops only at main stations and is second in speed to the *TGV* (see above). A *rapide* is faster than an *omnibus* but slower than an *express*. The SNCF also operates an extensive Motorail service (see page 228).

Some non-*TGV* international trains, including *Trans-Europ-Express* (*TEE*) and *Trans-Europ-Nuit* (*TEN*), are first class only. Booking is necessary and a supplement is payable in addition to a first-class fare. Booking is recommended on all long-distance trains, particularly during peak periods, e.g. school and public holidays.

Scenic Trains

Despite their love of high-speed trains, the French still have a soft spot for their scenic trains, which they affectionately call *petits trains*. These include the *vapeur du Trieux* running from Paimpol to Portrieux in northern Brittany, the *petit train de Bligny-sur-Ouche* near Beaune in Burgundy, the *chemin de fer du Tarn* in the south, the *chemin de fer du Vivarais* from Tournon to Lamastre north of Lyon, the *Sécheron* vintage electric train south of Grenoble, and the *chemin de fer de Provence* or *train des pignes* running between Digne-les-Bains and Nice in the south-east. Spectacular mountain railways include the *train de la mer de glace*, which wends its way from Chamonix to Montenvers in the Alps, the *petit train jaune* running from Villefranche in the Pyrenees and stopping at the highest SNCF station (1,592m/5,223ft), and the *petit train de la Rhune*, a rack railway which hoists a train to the peak of La Rhune in the Basque country. Corsica's *le Trinighellu* ('Little Train') runs on narrow-gauge track and is a delight for train fans. France's railway preservation society, AJECTA (☎ 01 64 08 60 62, 🖳 http://www.ajecta. org), runs excursions from Paris using restored steam trains, and you can take a day trip on the Orient Express from the Gare du Nord to Calais and back or longer trips to the UK and Eastern Europe (☎ 01 55 62 18 00, 🖳 http://www.orient-express.com).

Facilities

Trains

Luggage: Most trains have sections at the ends of carriages for the storage of large items of luggage as well as overhead racks for smaller items. **Beware of luggage thieves when travelling on trains and try to store your bags in an overhead rack where you can keep an eye on them.**

Restaurants & Bars: All *TGV* and most other fast trains have a bar-buffet and/or a restaurant car (*wagon-restaurant*) with waiter service. All rail catering is expensive and, with the exception of restaurant cars, of poor quality by French standards (it's better to take your own 'picnic'). On *TGV* and *Corail* trains, first-class passengers can order a tray meal at their seat, which should be done when making your booking. Some *Corail* services provide a Grill-Express and/or self-service restaurant and inter-city trains have a mobile drinks and snacks service (*minibar*) at your seat.

Toilets: There are toilets on inter-city trains. If you accidentally drop something down one, be careful how you try to retrieve it. A man who dropped his wallet down a *TGV* toilet got his hand trapped when he tried to recover it!

Telephones: Public telephones are available on *TGV*s and permit both domestic and international calls with a *télécarte* (see page 157). There are three telephones on each *TGV*: one in first class, one in second class and one in the bar. The use of mobile phones isn't allowed on most trains and there are signs indicating this, although many people ignore them.

Smoking: Since the beginning of 2006, smoking has been forbidden on all trains.

Stations

Platforms: Note that station platforms (*quais*) aren't always clearly numbered, so make sure you're waiting at the correct one. Lines (*voies*) often have different numbers from platforms and this can be confusing. *TGV* platforms have a yellow line marked on the surface, outside which passengers must stand for safety. At smaller stations you may need to cross the track to exit the station; if so, you must be very careful! If you're seeing someone off at a main station, you must sometimes purchase a platform ticket, although it's unlikely that anyone will check that you have one.

Restaurants & Bars: Most railway stations have a restaurant in or near them and the main stations in Paris have a choice of restaurants, brasseries and snack bars, most serving good food at a reasonable price. Some, such as the Gare de Lyon restaurant, are famous for their cuisine. Station restaurants in small towns are often well patronised by locals, which is always a good sign. Snacks and drinks at station cafés and bars can be expensive and poor quality. Some main railway stations provide toilets, washing facilities, including hair dryers and showers, and some provide nappy/diaper-changing rooms. There are photocopiers and instant passport photograph machines at most inter-city and international railway stations. At main stations in Lyon, Marseille and Paris (Gare de Lyon) there are kiosks where you can hire portable DVD players and discs (a service known '*Cinétrain*').

Shops: In a drive to increase revenue, the SNCF plans to create shopping centres in its 50 or so main stations; a 3,000m² precinct in Paris' Gare du Nord station was the first to open, in November 2002.

Luggage: Luggage offices (*consigne*) are provided at most stations, where you're charged around €5 per item (inlcuding bicycles and wheelchairs) for 24 hours. There are also luggage lockers (*consigne automatique*) of various sizes, for which you must have the exact change (e.g. €3.40, €5 or €7.50); items may be left for up to 72 hours. Note that luggage lockers may be unavailable if there's a 'security alert'. Luggage trolleys are available free at main stations, although you need a €1 coin, which is refunded when the trolley is returned to a storage location (as in supermarkets). However, some stations have temporarily suspended luggage storage facilities because of stricter security measures. Porters are available at most main stations and charge around €1 per bag. People who are unable to carry their bags may request assistance from the reception desk (*accueil*) at any main station. You will be charged €5 for this service.

The SNCF doesn't accept responsibility for lost luggage or luggage stolen from lockers, unless you can prove that there was negligence on its part or that the locker was faulty; even then the compensation is likely to be derisory. However, you can register (*enregistrer*) your luggage (including skis) for a fee, in which case you're entitled to compensation according to the weight of your luggage. You must inspect your luggage when you collect it and make a claim by registered post within three days. The *Service Bagages à Domicile* leaflet, available at station information desks, gives full information and current charges (☎ 08 25 84 58 45).

Parking & Car Rental: Car parks are often provided close to railway stations, where long-term parking costs around €10 for the first 24 hours, reducing thereafter. Monthly parking tickets cost from around €70. You can rent an Avis car from around 200 main railway stations (see page 286) and leave it at any other station which operates the same service. Cars can be booked at the same time as your train ticket.

Bicycles: Bicycles can be hired from many stations and transported on trains (see **Cycling** on page 452). The SNCF publishes a brochure, *Guide Train + Vélo*.

Tickets

Tickets (*billet*) can be purchased by telephone (☎ 08 92 35 35 35) and internet (🖳 http://www.voyages-sncf.com), at station ticket offices, rail travel centres and appointed travel agents and via ticket machines (*billetterie automatique*). A ticket must be purchased and validated before boarding a train (see **Ticket Validation** on page 226). Single tickets are *aller simple* and return tickets *aller-retour*. All tickets are valid for two months. There are two classes on most trains: first class (*première classe*) and second class (*deuxième classe*), with the exception of *TEE* and *TEN* international trains, which are first class only. At major stations staff may speak English or other languages, e.g. German, Italian or Spanish.

Tariffs

There are two tariffs (*tarif*), depending on the day and the departure time of a journey:

- **Off-peak** (*tarif bleu*) – Usually from 10.00 on Mondays to 15.00 on Fridays, 08.00 on Saturdays to 15.00 on Sundays and 20.00 on Sundays to 06.00 on Mondays.

- **Peak** (*tarif blanc*) – The intervening periods, and on a few special days and public holidays.

The relevant period is indicated on timetables. A daily travel calendar (*Calendrier Voyageurs*) is published by the SNCF and is available free at stations; it's updated every six months. Fares are determined by the tariff applicable at the start of a journey, e.g. a journey that starts in the off-peak period and runs into the peak period is charged at the reduced ('blue') tariff. If you're discovered travelling in a peak ('white') period with a ticket that only entitles you to travel off peak, you must pay the higher fare and a fine. Various discounts are available (see **Season & Special Tickets** below). The above tariff periods don't apply to *TGV*s.

Discounts

Season tickets and special discount tickets are available for various types of traveller, including those listed below. **The SNCF has a complicated fare structure and you should check to ensure that you pay the lowest possible fare.**

Senior Citizens: Those who are over 60 (or as the French delicately put it, those of *le troisième âge*) can buy a *Carte Senior*, which costs €50 and provides a 50 per cent reduction in off-peak periods and a 25 per cent reduction in peak periods (see page 223). There's also a 25 per cent reduction on international journeys to 27 European countries, and the card can be used on the national railway networks of several European countries. The *Carte Senior* is valid on all trains except regional trains in Paris and can be purchased from SNCF offices abroad as well as in France. *Carte Senior* holders are also entitled to discounts of up to 50 per cent on entertainment and museum fees and other travel discounts. Discounts are often listed in entertainment publications such as *Pariscope* (see page 402). Even without a card, those over 60 are entitled to a 25 per cent reduction on all journeys starting in an off-peak period (known as the *tarif découverte senior*).

Children: Children under four who don't require a separate seat travel free and children aged from 4 to 11 travel for half-fare. Children under four who do require a separate seat travel for a standard charge of €8 (known as the *Forfait Bambin*), one way only, which includes any booking fee. The same charge applies to first and second class. Children and youths aged from 12 to 25 can save 20 or 50 per cent (depending on the tariff period) with a card called *La Carte 12-25* (see page 224). Children aged from 4 to 14 can travel in the care of a *Jeune Voyageur Service* (*JVS*) host on selected routes for an additional fee of €39. For further information see the booklet, *Votre Enfant Voyage en Train* or *Guide Service Jeune Voyageur*.

Children under 12 can buy a *Carte Enfant +* (€65), which is valid for a year and entitles the holder and up to three other people (one of whom must be an adult) to travel at a 50 per cent reduction during off-peak periods and at a 25 per cent discount during peak periods. It also permits a family dog or cat to travel free. A *Carte Enfant +* doesn't include travel on Parisian suburban railways.

Students & Apprentices: Students and apprentices aged up to 21 and 23 respectively can purchase weekly or monthly discount cards for all trains except *TGVs* (for which a special monthly pass is available). *La Carte 12–25* provides a 50 per cent reduction in off-peak periods and 25 per cent off peak-time journeys. It's valid for one year and costs €49. There's also *Tarif Découverte 12–25* entitling youths to a 25 per cent reduction on journeys started in an off-peak period.

Families: Parents with three or more children aged under 18 can purchase a family card (*Carte Famille Nombreuse*), which costs €18, is valid for three years and entitles holders to discounts on all rail fares, whether travelling independently or as a family. Discounts start at 30 per cent for a family with three children and rise to 75 per cent for families with six or more children. The *Carte Famille Nombreuse* is available only to French residents, as it's a social service subsidised by the French government. Cards, which take up to ten days to obtain, can be applied for at SNCF stations town halls and family benefit offices, where you must present identification for both parents (including national identity cards if appropriate), birth certificates or copies of your *livret de famille* or equivalent for each child, and a photograph of each family member.

Couples: Any two adults travelling together have two options for reduced-price rail travel. The first, *Découverte à Deux*, provides a 25 per cent reduction on all first or second-class travel on journeys starting in an off-peak period. The second, *Découverte Séjour,* gives a 25 per cent reduction on return journeys of less than 200km (124mi) which include a Saturday night stay.

Groups: Groups of ten or more people of any age travelling together are entitled to discounts of varying amounts. Information is provided at SNCF stations. In all groups, children aged 4 to 11 pay half the reduced fare.

Commuters: Commuters can obtain a season ticket called *Modulopass* valid for 6 or 12 months, allowing a 50 per cent reduction. An annual season ticket can be paid for in monthly instalments. Weekly (*hebdomadaire*) and monthly (*mensuel*) commuter tickets are also available in all regions. The cost varies according to whether you want a ticket between two particular stations (*trajets domicile-travail*) or a 'go-anywhere' card (*carte de libre circulation*). You must provide a passport photograph and present your passport or *carte de séjour*. Those who live more than 75km (47mi) from their place of work may be entitled to an *abonnement de travail*, valid for a week or a month at a time. You will need confirmation from your employer that you travel more than this distance daily.

Disabled: Disabled passengers are entitled to a range of reductions, depending on the extent of their disability. In certain cases, a person accompanying a disabled person is entitled to travel free. Information is provided in the SNCF booklet *Guide Pratique du Voyaguer à Mobilité Réduite.*

Other Discounts: Other reductions available include the following:

● **Holiday Tickets** – You can buy a holiday ticket (*billet séjour*) allowing a 25 per cent reduction on a single, return or circular journey of over 1,000km (620mi) or an annual holiday ticket (*billet de congé annuel*) allowing a one-time 25 per cent reduction on a single or return ticket for a journey over 200km (124mi). Both tickets are valid for two months and journeys must start during an off-peak period and there must be a Sunday between the outward and return journeys. An annual holiday ticket application should be endorsed by your employer.

● **Advance Purchase Tickets** – *Découverte J8* and *Découverte J30* tickets entitle you to fare reductions by paying for your ticket 8 or 30 days in advance. Tickets are available only for the train reserved, and refunds are possible only up to four days before travel. Fares include ordinary seats (*place assise*) and 'beds' (*place couchée*) on overnight trains.

Note that some of the tickets described above are offered by regional transport authorities and may be available in certain areas only. Further details are available from the information or ticket office at any railway station. The SNCF booklet, *Le Guide du Voyageur*, available from main stations, provides invaluable information.

Pets

You must buy a half-fare second-class ticket for a pet if it weighs over 6kg; it's also valid in first class. If a pet is transported in a bag or basket no bigger than 45cm x 30cm x 25cm, the single fare is €5.10, irrespective of distance. Dogs must be muzzled. Holders of a *Carte Enfant +* (see **Children** on page 223) are entitled to take a dog or cat with them free.

Booking

Seats can be reserved on most trains (a nominal booking fee is included in the ticket price) and **must** be reserved on *TGVs*. The fee for a *TGV* booking varies with the time and day of the week. However, you can travel on the *TGV* following or preceding the one you booked without changing your ticket. When reserving a seat you can choose first or second class, smoking (*fumeurs*) or non-smoking (*non-fumeurs*) – in second class only – and a window (*fenêtre*) or corridor (*couloir*) seat. All *TGV* tickets include a seat number. Bookings can be made up to two months before departure. Seats can be reserved via telephone (☎ 08 92 35 35 35) and both reserved and paid for online (🖥 http://www.voyages-sncf.com). Seats can also be reserved via automatic ticket machines (see below). Eurostar bookings can be made by phone in

English (☎ 08 92 35 35 39). At main stations, bookings may need to be made at a particular window (marked '*Locations*') and there may be a separate window for information ('*Renseignements*') . Tickets for seats that aren't paid for in advance must be collected from an SNCF station within 48 hours.

Ticket Machines: Tickets can be purchased from ticket machines (*billetterie automatique*) at SNCF stations (the French love ticket machines and using them is usually preferable to queueing). There are dedicated machines (*billetterie automatique grandes lignes*) for main line tickets, e.g. a *TGV*. Machines have touch-sensitive screens and some can be set to operate in various languages by pressing the appropriate flag symbol, e.g. the Union Jack for English (Americans must defer to the British in this rare instance). Payment can be made in cash, although this is now mainly reserved for local journey ticket machines (*billetterie automatique lignes régionales*), which sometimes accept only coins. Tickets costing up to €760 can be paid for with a credit or debit card, which you insert in the machine when requested. Some *grandes lignes* machines accept only cards.

Ticket Validation: With the exception of tickets purchased outside France and passes already marked with a validity date, all tickets are valid for several days and therefore **must** be date stamped in a special machine (*composteur*) before boarding a train. This includes booked *TGV* tickets (called '*Resa*') and the return ticket of a day return. Stamping machines have a sign '*COMPOSTEZ VOTRE BILLET*' and are mounted on pillars at the entrance to platforms (*accès aux quais*); the SNCF is in the process of replacing existing orange machines, which often don't work, with new blue ones in an effort to reduce ticket fraud. Insert one end of your ticket in the machine face up and a code number is stamped on the reverse (if you don't hear a satisfying 'chonk' or the stamp is illegible, try again).

If you break a journey and continue it the same day, your ticket remains valid. However, if you break a journey overnight (or longer), you must re-stamp your ticket before continuing your journey. If you validate your ticket and then miss your train, and there are no more trains that day or you decide not to travel, you must go to the ticket office and have your ticket 'un-validated'.

There are ticket inspectors (who normally operate in threes) on most French trains, and failure to validate your ticket will result in a fine, calculated as follows:

● If you inform a ticket inspector on the train **before** he approaches you that you were unable to buy or stamp your ticket for reasons beyond your control, e.g. the ticket office was closed or the *composteur* was out of order, you will be charged the normal ticket price plus €3 for a journey up to 75km (47mi) or the normal ticket price plus €9 for a journey over 75km (47mi).

● If a ticket inspector 'catches' you without a validated ticket, the fine is the normal ticket price plus €9 (if you pay on the spot) or €31 (if you wish to pay later) if you bought the ticket that day, or the normal ticket price plus €18 (on the spot) or €40 (later) if you bought the ticket at an earlier date.

● If your ticket is invalid for any other reason, you can be fined €3 on top of the ticket price.

● If you have an invalid ticket in the Ile-de-France region, the penalties are €20 on the spot or €42 later whatever the circumstances.

If you argue with a ticket inspector, he's entitled to increase the penalty to over €120. If you're found guilty of fraud (e.g. you've scratched off the date on your ticket or hide in a toilet), you can be fined €130, and persistent offenders face fines of up to €7,500 and six months in prison. It's illegal to board a train without a ticket, even if you're merely seeing someone off. There are (controversial) plans to replace ticket inspectors on certain trains with a computerised ticket checking system called *Equipment Agent Seul (EAS)*.

Refunds: If you buy a ticket for a specific date and seat and then decide not to use it, you can obtain a 100 per cent refund from any SNCF ticket office before and up to an hour after the scheduled time of departure. Thereafter (up to 60 days) a 10 per cent charge is levied on your ticket price, i.e. you obtain a 90 per cent refund. For all unreserved tickets a 10 per cent refund charge is levied, but you must make your claim within the overall validity period printed on the ticket. No refund is possible for a ticket costing €4.50 or less.

The refund charge isn't levied if the service you planned to use didn't run, although you must have written evidence from a member of the station staff. If a *TGV* is over 30 minutes late, the SNCF will refund 30 per cent of the ticket price (*engagement régularité*). (*TGV* drivers have their bonus reduced if a train is late without good reason.) Other trains must be at least an hour late before 30 per cent of the ticket price is refunded. These refunds apply to journeys of at least 100km (62mi) and don't apply if a delay, due to maintenance or repair work for example, has previously been announced.

Finding Your Seat

To find your carriage, check the number on your ticket against the notice board showing the layout of trains (*Composition des Trains*) or the number on the outside of carriages. *TGV* carriage numbers are marked on the platform surface and displayed next to doors. Seat numbers are marked on tickets (e.g. '*VOIT 18: 32'* = carriage 18, seat number 32) and displayed on the top of seats.

Night Trains

A range of sleeping accommodation is provided on night trains, depending on your budget and the size of your party, as detailed below. **You should beware of thieves and armed robbers on overnight trains, especially those running along the Mediterranean coast and across the Italian border.** After a spate of robberies a number of years ago security locks were fitted to sleeping compartments; however, you should still take care before opening the door, as crooks sometimes pose as attendants. There are dedicated compartments for women travelling alone. Bookings can be made at SNCF offices, travel agencies and motoring organisations abroad, and at railway stations, rail travel centres and SNCF-appointed travel agencies in France.

There are the following types of 'accommodation' on night trains:

● **Reclining Seat** – You can (try to) sleep on a reclining seat (*siège inclinable*); there's no charge, but seats must be reserved.

- **Couchettes** – *Couchettes* (*places couchées*) are provided in four-berth compartments in first class and in six-berth compartments in second class, for which there's a booking fee of between €15 and €17.50 depending on the type of train. Although a sleeping-bag sheet, pillow and blankets are provided, passengers don't usually undress, as compartments aren't segregated according to sex. Washrooms and toilets are provided at the ends of carriages. *Couchettes* are non-smoking, although smoking is permitted in corridors.

- **Sleepers** – Sleepers (*voiture-lits*) provide sleeping accommodation for one to three people with a proper bed and private washing facilities. Single and double sleepers are provided in first class, and double and triple sleepers in second class. Each sleeper carriage has an attendant, who serves snacks and drinks. Trains display the *TEN* (*Trans Euro Nuit*) emblem on carriages when they cross borders. Sleepers cost around €100.

Motorail

Motorail is a European network of special trains (known as *auto-trains*), generally running overnight, carrying passengers and their cars or motorbikes over distances of up to 1,500km (900mi). Caravans cannot be taken on Motorail trains, and you're recommended not to fit roof racks or roof boxes, as they may not be allowed (there's no hard and fast rule!), but SUVs and 'people carriers' are now admitted (for a £50 surcharge). The SNCF provides an extensive motorail network of some 130 routes linking most regions of France. The principal Motorail services from the UK operate from Calais and Dieppe to Avignon, Biarritz, Bordeaux, Brive-la-Gaillarde, Narbonne, Nice and Toulouse. Trains don't run every day and on most routes operate during peak months only (e.g. summer and Christmas holidays).

A wide range of sleeping accommodation (see **Night Trains** above) is available. Breakfast is included in the price and is served in the station buffet on arrival at your destination, although there are interminable queues and it's usually more convenient to buy breakfast at a local café. Check your car carefully for damage before driving off, particularly the exhaust pipe, which can be dented or broken on ramps. Any damage must be reported before leaving the station. Motorail journeys are expensive (e.g. a minimum of GB£230 for a family to travel from London to Brive-la-Gaillarde one way) and it's cheaper for most people to drive, although it's usually slower and not as relaxing (trains are now equipped with a 'bar car'!). The main advantage of Motorail is that you travel overnight and (with luck) arrive feeling refreshed after a good night's sleep. Note that there's a big difference between peak and off-peak fares (see page 223).

A comprehensive timetable (*Guide Trains Autos et Motos Accompagnées*) is published for bookings made through a railway station or travel agent in France, containing routes, tariffs, general information and access maps for motorail stations. Passengers in the UK can obtain a brochure, *Motorail for Motorists – the Expressway into Europe*. Further information can be found on the French Motorail website (🖳 http://www.raileurope.co.uk/frenchmotorail) or by calling UK ☎ 0870-241 5415.

Information & Timetables

All SNCF rail enquiries are now centralised on a premium-rate (€0.34 per minute) telephone number (☎ 3635 – press 1 for details of delays or cancellations, 2 for recorded timetable information or 3 to speak to someone). The SNCF head office is at 10 place Budapest, 75009 Paris (☎ 01 53 25 60 00, 💻 http://www.sncf.com) and it has offices in many countries, including the UK (French Travel, 178 Piccadilly, London W1V 0BA, ☎ 0870-241 4243 or 0870-584 8848 for European tickets, 💻 http://www.raileurope.co.uk). Rail information can also be found on the SNCF website (💻 http://www.voyages-sncf.com).

The SNCF publishes a free quarterly magazine in some countries, e.g. *Top Rail* in the UK, plus a wealth of free brochures and booklets detailing its services, including *Le Guide du Voyageur*, available from French stations. It also organises hotel accommodation, bus and coach services, boat cruises and package holidays. The SNCF has teamed up with Expedia, one of America's largest online travel agencies, to offer flights, car hire, package holidays and other services (💻 http://www.voyages-sncf.com).

At major stations, arrivals (*arrivées*) and departures (*départs*) are shown on large electronic boards. When you buy a rail ticket with a reserved seat, e.g. for a *TGV*, the departure time is printed on your ticket.

French timetables (*horaire*) are usually accurate, particularly rail timetables for *TGV* and other fast trains. Rail timetables are published in national, regional and local versions, and also for individual routes or lines. (Note that some routes have separate timetables for each direction!)

The SNCF also publishes three regional timetables: for the *Nord Est*, *Atlantique* and *Sud Est et Corse*. There are separate timetables and guides (*Horaires et Guide Pratique*) for *TGV* routes. Pocket timetables are published for main lines, and a *Lignes Affaires* timetable is published containing times for a selection of the most popular trains linking major centres from Mondays to Fridays. In most regions, a *Guide Régional des Transports* is available from local railway and bus stations. Rail timetables are updated twice a year: around 1st June and 24th September (exact dates vary annually).

Many rail services operate only from Mondays to Saturdays (*semaine*) and not on Sundays and holidays (*dimanches et fêtes*) and some run at different times on different days of the week. Before planning a trip, check that your planned travel dates aren't 'special days' (*jour particulier*) such as a public holiday, when there are usually restricted services – unless you have no option.

If your train is late and you want to find out what has happened to it, you can call ☎ 08 91 70 50 00.

UNDERGROUND RAILWAYS

A number of French cities have underground railways or subways (*métro*), including Lille (which boasted the world's first driverless system), Lyon, Marseille, Paris, Toulouse and most recently Rennes, whose *Val* system claims to be the world's smallest underground network. (The French will boast about anything!) In most cities, public transport tickets and passes permit travel on all modes of transport, including the underground, buses, trams and suburban trains. No smoking is permitted on underground trains or in stations.

Paris

The Paris *métro* dates from 1898 and is one of the world's oldest and most famous 'underground' railways (some of it runs overground). It has 200km (123mi) of track, 322 stations and 13 main lines plus a number of short supplementary lines. (The network is to be extended north to Aubervilliers by 2007.) In the centre of Paris, you're rarely more than five minutes' walk from a *métro* station. Some 4.5m people use the *métro* daily, and it's one of the most efficient and cheapest urban transport systems in the world.

Trains run from 05.30 until around 01.00 and there's a frequent service during the day with trains running every 40 seconds at peak times and every 90 seconds at other times. The *métro* is operated by the Régie Autonome des Transports Parisiens (RATP), and a single all-purpose ticket is valid for all public transport in the capital (*métro*, *RER*, buses and suburban trains). A flat fare is charged for journeys irrespective of distance, although you aren't permitted to break your journey and cannot make a round trip. Tickets are sold at *métro* stations, bus terminals, tobacconists', RATP offices and ticket machines. A ticket for a single journey costs €1.40 and ten tickets (called a *carnet* although actually issued as ten separate tickets) cost €10.70. Children under four travel free and those under ten for half fare. See also **Season & Visitors' Tickets** on page 223.

Ticket control is automated at all stations and you must insert your ticket in a 'turnstile' date/time stamping machine (*composteur*) to gain access to platforms. Always retain your ticket until you've completed your journey and pass the point marked *Limite de Validité des Billets*. If you travel without a valid ticket and are discovered during a random check by a ticket inspector (*contrôleur*), you must pay a fine of around €15 on the spot (there's a fine of €30 if you're caught jumping over a turnstile at a station). Ticket checks are often made at the beginning of the month when monthly tickets are renewed.

Métro stations are easily recognisable by a huge 'M' sign (some have distinctive art nouveau designs). *Métro* and neighbourhood maps (*plan de quartier*) are displayed outside and inside stations, and there are computerised maps (*système d'information de trajets urbains/SITU*) at many stations: simply enter the name of the street you want and you're given a print-out showing the quickest way to get there, including on foot.

Main lines are numbered from 1 to 13, and the two supplementary lines are numbered 3b and 7b. To make sure you take a train going in the right direction, note the name of the station at the end of the line (or lines) you intend to travel on and follow the signs indicating that direction, e.g. *Direction Porte d'Orléans*. If you need to change trains, look for *Correspondance* signs. Up to six lines may cross at an intersection. When changing lines, there's often a long walk, although some stations have moving walkways.

To open the door on older trains you push the silver handle upwards. New trains have pushbuttons. Doors on trains close automatically and a warning signal is sounded just before they close. **You should be wary of pickpockets when travelling on the *métro*, particularly when boarding trains**, as they tend to 'strike' just as the doors are closing, leaving you bagless or walletless on the train as it pulls away. However, serious crime and violence are rare, although it's wise to avoid empty carriages and some stations (such as Château Rouge, Châtelet-Les-Halles, Gare du Nord, Réaumur, Saint Denis, Sébastopol and Strasbourg) at night. There are alarms (*borne d'alarme*) on stations.

Certain seats are reserved for the disabled, elderly or pregnant, although the French aren't usually eager to give up their seat and you may need to ask (and experience Parisian indifference first-hand!).

RER

The *RER* (*Réseau Express Régional*) is an express underground rail system that's independent of the *métro* and links most suburbs with the centre of Paris. It's much quicker than the *métro*, as there are fewer stops. There are four *RER* sectors (A, B, C and D), each comprising up to eight lines (e.g. A1, B2). Sectors A and B are operated jointly by the SNCF and RATP, and sectors C and D exclusively by the SNCF.

The *RER* generally operates from 05.30 until around 00.30, with trains around every 15 minutes. Line B3 goes to Roissy-Charles de Gaulle airport, line C2 to Orly airport and line C5 to Versailles. Line A runs to a specially built station at Marne-la-Vallée-Chessy for Disneyland Paris. The journey from central Paris to Disneyland takes around 40 minutes and trains run every ten minutes in peak periods and every 20 minutes off peak. The *RER* also links Charles de Gaulle airport with the Gare du Nord, and the Gare du Nord with the Gare de Lyon and is to be extended further east in the next few years.

Within the central area (*Ville de Paris*), a *métro* ticket is valid on *RER* trains. Outside this area the *RER* has a different ticket system from the *métro*, prices increasing according to the distance travelled. *RER* tickets can be purchased only at *RER* station ticket offices. A ticket for the central zone costs €1.40, as for the *métro*. *RER* tickets must be machine-stamped before journeys are commenced and also, unlike *métro* tickets, when exiting an *RER* station. If you've completed your journey, the machine will display *Passez* ('proceed') and retain your ticket. Where you're able to continue your journey, the machine will return your ticket and display *Prenez votre ticket* ('take your ticket').

Disabled Travellers

Disabled people who aren't in wheelchairs can book a free travel companion (*voyage accompagné*) a day in advance for *métro* and *RER* (and many bus) journeys between 08.00 and 20.00, Mondays to Fridays. Contact the RATP – see below. The *métro* isn't suitable for wheelchairs, but *RER* lines A and B allow wheelchair access. An *RER* access guide is published for wheelchair users and is available from RATP head office, 54 quai dea l Rapée, 75012 Paris (☎ 01 58 78 20 20 or ☎ 08 92 68 77

14). There's also information for disabled travellers (and people with push-chairs!) on the RATP website (⌨ http://www.ratp.fr), and general information for disabled people in Paris on the websites of Pauline Hephaistos Survey Projects (PHSP, ⌨ http://www.accessinparis.org), which publishes a useful book, *Access in Paris*, the Association des Paralysés de France (⌨ http://www.apf.asso.fr) and a group called Mobile en Ville (⌨ http://www.mobile-en-ville.asso.fr).

Discounts

The RATP provides weekly, monthly and annual season tickets, plus tickets for visitors, groups of children and certain other categories of passenger, as follows:

Carte Orange: The *Carte Orange* allows unlimited travel within the Ile-de-France. The cost varies according to how many fare zones you wish to include. Central Paris (as far as the *Périphérique*) consists of zones 1 and 2, and zones 3 to 5 encompass the outer suburbs and the airports. A further three zones (6 to 8) extend to outer parts of the Ile-de-France. The SNCF publishes a *Plan des Zones Carte Orange*.

A monthly card (*Carte Orange Mensuelle*) is valid for a calendar month, irrespective of when you buy it. A weekly card (*Carte Orange Hebdomadaire*) is valid for the current week if you buy it before Thursday or for the following week if purchased after Thursday. To buy a weekly or monthly *Carte Orange*, you need an identity card with your photograph, full name, address and signature. There are instant photo booths at many Paris railway and *métro* stations. You must complete a *coupon vert* for a weekly card or a *coupon orange* for a monthly card the first time you buy one. After obtaining your identity card, you can buy a *Carte Orange* from ticket machines.

You should carry your card in the slot in the plastic wallet provided along with your identity card and write the number of your *Carte Orange* on the card. This prevents cards from being used by someone else, as they aren't transferable. Failure to do this can result in a fine if it's discovered during a spot check. Weekly and monthly cards can be used within the applicable zones on all four levels of Paris public transport (*métro*, RER, SNCF and buses, including buses operated by private operators that are affiliated to the two main groups of companies, APTR and ADATRIF). A weekly card costs from €15.70 (for zones 1 and 2) and a monthly card from €51.50.

If you commute to work for a company with more than ten employees, you pay just 40 per cent of the price of your season ticket, 40 per cent being paid by your employer and the remaining 20 per cent by central and local governments.

Carte Imagine-R: In the Ile-de-France region (including Paris), schoolchildren and apprentices under 26 can obtain a *Carte Imagine-R*, which functions like a *Carte Orange* (see above). It's sold at train and underground stations.

Carte Intégrale: The *Carte Intégrale* is an annual ticket costing €520.30 for zones 1 and 2 and €1,413.50 for all eight zones. It's also possible to buy a ticket covering any combination of zones, from two to seven. You can pay monthly by standing order (*prélèvement*) at no extra cost.

Visitors' Tickets: Visitors to Paris can buy a *Paris Visite* ticket for zones 1 to 3, zones 1 to 5 or all eight zones plus Orlybus, Orlyrail, Roissyrail and Marne-la-Vallée-Chessy (for Disneyland Paris). Tickets can be purchased for one day (€8.35

for three zones, €16.75 for five zones or €23.65 for all zones) two days (€13.70 to €34.30), three days (€18.25 – €42.65) or five days (€26.65 – €53.35). A *Paris Visite* ticket allows unlimited travel on all public transport, including the *métro* and *RER*, the SNCF Paris network, the bus network (including *Montmartrobus*, *Noctambus* and *Orlybus* – see **Buses & Trams** below), and the Montmartre funicular. It also entitles holders to discounts (worth around €37) on admission fees to various tourist attractions and a 50 per cent reduction on the cost of bicycle hire.

A one-day *Mobilis* ticket is also available, the price of which depends on the number of zones required (from €5.40 for zones 1 to 2, up to €18.40 for all eight zones). Note that the Orlybus, Orlyrail and Roissyrail services aren't included in the *Mobilis* ticket. Neither are there any reductions on visits to cultural sites.

Visitors' tickets are available from main *métro* and *RER* stations, Paris tourist offices, main SNCF railway stations and Paris airports. Note that, unless you travel extensively on public transport, it's cheaper to buy a *carnet* of ten *métro*/bus tickets than a visitor's ticket. This is particularly true if you will be spending most of your time in central Paris, where walking between areas and attractions is possible.

Information

Prices for all RATP rail and bus tickets are available from *métro* stations and RATP offices. For RATP information telephone ☎ 08 92 68 77 14 (in English) between 06.00 and 21.00 or consult the RATP website (⌨ http://www.ratp.fr).

BUSES & TRAMS

There's a nationwide campaign in France for 'car-free' cities, and there are excellent bus services in Paris and other major cities, and many also have tram or trolley bus systems, including Bordeaux, Caen, Lyon, Le Mans, Montpellier, Nancy, Nantes, Nice, Orléans, Rouen, Strasbourg, Toulon and Valenciennes. The town of Châteauroux (in Indre) recently became the first in France to offer free bus travel in order to persuade citizens to abandon their cars, and in Lille commuters are offered half-price bus travel. However, in rural areas, buses are few and far between, and the scant services that exist are usually designed to meet the needs of schoolchildren, workers, and shoppers on market days. This means that buses usually run early and late in the day with little or nothing in between, and may cease altogether during the long summer school holiday period (July and August). Note that a city bus is generally called an *autobus* and a country bus a *car* or *autocar*. Smoking isn't permitted on buses in France.

The best place to enquire about bus services is at a tourist office or railway station. In large towns and cities, buses run to and from bus stations (*gare d'autobus/routière*), which are usually next to railway stations. In rural areas, bus services are often operated by the SNCF and operate to and from a railway station. An SNCF bus, on which rail tickets and passes are valid, is shown as an *autocar* in rail timetables. The SNCF also provides bus tours throughout France. Private bus services are often confusing and uncoordinated and usually leave from different locations rather than a central bus station. Some towns provide free or discount bus passes to senior citizens (over 60) on production of an identity card, passport, or *carte de séjour* and proof of local residence.

There are no national bus companies in France operating scheduled services, although many long-distance buses are operated by foreign companies such as Euroways/Eurolines, Riviera Express, Europabus, Miracle Bus and Grey-Green Coaches. Eurolines (🖥 http://www.eurolines.com or 🖥 http://www.eurolines.fr) operates regular services from the UK to over 50 French cities, including Bordeaux, Cannes, Lyon, Montpellier, Nice, Orléans, Paris, Perpignan, Reims, Saint-Malo and Strasbourg. Discounts are available to students and young people on some routes.

Bus and coach passengers are required by law to wear seatbelts if they're fitted. Failure to do so renders you liable for a €135 fine.

Paris

Paris has over 112km (70mi) of bus lanes, so buses move at a reasonable speed, although they're inevitably slower during rush hours and always slower than the *métro* (but you see more of the city from a bus). Operating hours vary, although buses are in service on most routes from 07.00 or 07.30 to between 20.30 and 21.00. On main routes, evening buses (*autobus du soir*) run until at least midnight. From Mondays to Saturdays there's a 10- to 15-minute service during peak hours, and a reduced service after 20.30. On Sundays and public holidays, services are severely restricted on most routes. Night buses ('*Noctambus*') provide a one-hour service on ten routes (a night bus map is available from *métro* stations).

As with the *métro*, a ticket for a single journey costs €1.40 and ten tickets, called a *carnet*, cost €10.70. The *métro* and buses use the same ticket. A ticket is valid for two sections or fare stages, marked *fin de section* at stops. Two tickets are needed for trips encompassing three fare stages and up to four tickets for trips to the suburbs (or six or seven if you're going from one side of Paris to the other – in which case you're far better off using the underground).

Paris bus stops (many of which have shelters) are indicated by a post with red and yellow panels marked with the name of the stop (e.g. a street or corner), as shown on route plans. Each stop displays the numbers of the buses stopping there, a map showing all stops along the route(s), and the times of the first and last buses. Most stops display a full timetable. The route number and destination is displayed on the front of buses and the route on the sides. Route maps are also displayed inside buses, and stops may be announced as they're approached. There are numerous private sight-seeing bus tours in Paris, although it's much cheaper to use scheduled RATP buses (the RATP recommends certain routes for sightseers) or an RATP excursion bus.

To stop a bus, you must signal to the driver by waving your arm. On boarding a bus you must stamp (*composter*) your ticket by inserting it in the stamping machine (*composteur*) next to the driver. A ticket inspector (*contrôleur*) may ask to see your ticket and, if it isn't stamped, you will be fined. If you have a *Carte Orange* or other pass valid on Paris buses (see page 232), show it to the driver as you board. When you want a bus to stop, you signal to the driver by pressing a button or pulling a cord. A 'stop requested' (*arrêt demandé*) sign will light up above the driver. Buses usually have separate entrance (*montée*) and exit (*sortie*) doors.

Free bus route maps are available at bus terminals, *métro* stations, tourist offices and RATP offices as well as on the RATP website (🖳 http://www.ratp.fr). Printed maps include the *Petit Plan de Paris*, *Grand Plan de Paris*, *Grand Plan d'Ile-de-France* and area maps. The RATP also publishes *Paris Patchwork*, a pocket-size guide filled with bus route maps and useful information, available free from RATP offices and *métro* stations. Many bus guides are available from bookshops, including *Plan de Paris par Arrondissements*, containing detailed diagrams of all bus routes, and *Guide Paris Autobus* (Ponchet Plan Net).

FERRIES

Cross-Channel Services

Ferry services operate year round between France and the UK/Ireland. There's a wide choice of routes for travellers between France and the UK, depending on where you live and your intended route. These include (from east to west):

● **Dover/Dunkerque** – Norfolk Line (🖳 http://www.norfolkline.com).

● **Dover/Calais** – P&O Ferries (🖳 http://www.poferries.com) and Sea France (🖳 http://www.seafrance.co.uk).

● **Dover/Boulogne** – Speed Ferries (🖳 http://www.speedferries.com).

● **Newhaven/Dieppe** – Transmanche Ferries (🖳 http://www.transmancheferries.com).

● **Portsmouth/Le Havre** – LD Lines (🖳 http://www.ldlines.co.uk).

● **Portsmouth/Caen** – Brittany Ferries.

● **Portsmouth/Saint-Malo** – Brittany Ferries.

● **Poole/Cherbourg** – Brittany Ferries.

● **Poole/Saint-Malo** – Brittany Ferries and Condor Ferries (🖳 http://www.condorferries.co.uk), the latter operating via Guernsey and Jersey.

● **Weymouth/Saint-Malo** via Guernsey and Jersey – Condor Ferries.

● **Plymouth/Roscoff** – Brittany Ferries.

● **Cork/Roscoff** – Brittany Ferries.

Some ferry services operate during the summer months only, e.g. May to September, and the frequency of services varies from dozens a day on the busiest (Calais-Dover) route during the summer peak period, to one a week on longer routes. Services are less frequent during the winter months, when bad weather can also cause cancellations. On the longer routes (i.e. from Portsmouth/Le Havre westward) there are overnight services.

Most ferries also have day cabins with en suite facilities that provide somewhere to leave luggage, shower and change, or just have a nap. Berths, single cabins and pullman seats are usually available, and most ships have a restaurant, self-service cafeteria and a children's play area. Many ships cater for children and mothers and have play areas, baby-feeding and changing rooms. On longer routes, most ships provide hairdressing, fast-photo developing, pools, saunas, live entertainment, cinemas and discos. All major ferry operators offer 'business class' tickets, typically costing an extra €15 to €20 per person, per trip. For this, you may enjoy a quieter lounge, free tea, coffee (sometimes even champagne!) and newspapers, and fax, photocopier and other facilities. Generally the longer the route, the better and wider the range of facilities provided, which often makes it worthwhile considering alternative routes to the Calais-Dover crossing, on which ferries are often crowded.

When travelling, take any items you require during the crossing with you, as you aren't allowed access to the car decks during journeys. **One of the first things you should do after boarding a ferry is to study the safety procedures.** Announcements are usually made in various languages.

Fares

Since Speed Ferries began operating between Dover and Boulogne in 2003, undercutting the Dover/Calais operators, there has been an intense price war (and not a few unsavoury practices, such as preventing boats from docking) and fares have generally come down, although they remain notoriously unpredictable and can vary by hundreds of pounds (according to the operator, time of year, time of day, duration of return ticket and, it would appear, sheer luck), peak rates still being outrageously high, e.g. a standard Calais/Dover return with P&O for a vehicle up to 5m (16ft) in length costs around €540 (€270 single) including only the driver and one passenger, which works out at over €10 per mile! It isn't necessarily an advantage to book early, although P&O recently announced the introduction of an 'airline-style' system, whereby the earlier you book, the cheaper the fare.

It's worth ringing the ferry operators to ask about special offers, but otherwise finding the cheapest fare is best done online, as staff won't be able to tell you the cheapest times to travel but will merely give you a price for each of the criteria you give, exactly as will their websites. An alternative to checking the sites of each operator separately is to use a comparative site, such as Channelcrossings.net (🖳 http://www.channelcrossings.net), Cross-Channel Ferry Tickets (🖳 http://www.cross-channel-ferry-tickets.co.uk), Direct Ferries (🖳 http://www.direct ferries.com), Ferrybooker.com (🖳 http://www.ferrybooker.co.uk), International Life Leisure 2000 (🖳 http://www.ferrysavers.com) and Into Ferries (🖳 http://www.into ferries.co.uk), although finding the best fare is still a laborious matter of inputting endless permutations of dates and times. Brochures rarely include the range of fares and never indicate all the variations. Children under four years old usually travel free and those aged 4 to 14 travel for half fare. Students may be entitled to a small discount during off-peak periods. Bicycles are transported free on most services.

Some operators offer discounts to regular travellers. For example, Brittany Ferries runs a Property Owners' Travel Club (UK ☎ 0870-366 5333 or French ☎ 08 25 82 88 22), offering savings of up to 30 per cent on single and standard return fares, and Sea France a 'Carnet', consisting of five return crossings for a car and passengers for GB£400 (UK ☎ 0870-5 711711, 🖥 www.seafrance.com). P&O offers a 'season ticket' for five or more crossings per year. Most operators offer travel and accommodation packages, and in some cases these work out cheaper than the crossing alone!

Booking

It isn't always necessary to make a booking, although it's wise when travelling during the summer peak period, particularly on a Friday or Saturday (and when you require a berth on an overnight service). Like air travel, ferry services are sometimes subject to delays due to strikes, out-of-service ferries or simply 'volume' (a euphemism for deliberate overbooking!). Check-in times vary from 20 to 60 minutes in advance of sailing for motorists and from 20 to 45 minutes for foot passengers. Comprehensive free timetables and guides are published by shipping companies and are available from travel agents. Bookings can be made by telephone or online.

Domestic Services

There are a number of ferry (*navette* or *ferry*) services operating within France, including daily car ferry services between Marseille, Nice and Toulon and the Corsican ports of Ajaccio, Bastia, Calvi, Ile Rousse, Porto-Vecchio and Propriano (crossing times are from 5 to 12 hours). Car ferry services also operate between Royan and Le Verdon (in the Gironde estuary) and between Blaye and Lamarque (also in Gironde); services operate during daylight hours throughout the year and crossings take around 30 and 25 minutes respectively. A hydrofoil operates in summer from Nice to Cannes and Monaco, and there's a regular ferry service from Cannes to the Ile Sainte-Marguerite, where the 'Man in the Iron Mask' was imprisoned. Several ferries operate in the Golfe du Morbihan in Brittany. In some areas there are river ferry (*bac*) services, such as those across the Seine between Rouen and Le Havre. There are also ferry services between Saint-Malo (and Granville and other small ports on the west coast of Manche) and the Channel Islands of Jersey, Guernsey and Alderney (foot passengers only).

EUROTUNNEL

Eurotunnel (formerly Le Shuttle) operates a shuttle car train service between Coquelles (near Calais) and Folkestone via the Channel Tunnel. Owing billions of euros, it was officially declared bankrupt in August 2006 but maintains that its service will be unaffected (?). There are three trains per hour during peak periods, and the crossing takes just 35 minutes. Each train can carry around 180 cars. Fares are generally higher than those offered by the ferry operators, e.g. a peak (summer) club class return costs around €600 and an off-peak (January to March) return around €280 for a vehicle and all passengers. It's wise to book, and you shouldn't expect to get a place in summer on spec, particularly on Fridays, Saturdays and Sundays.

Trains carry all types of vehicle, including cycles, motorcycles, cars, trucks, buses, caravans and motor-homes, although you pay more for vehicles over 1.85m (6ft 1in) high. Note also that caravans and motorhomes must have their gas supplies disconnected and gas bottles must be shut off (gas bottles are routinely inspected, so make sure they're accessible).

Eurotunnel is constantly changing its incentives for regular users. It currently offers Frequent Traveller Fares, which allows you to book ten single crossings (at certain times) for £39/€55 each over the course of a year. For general information call ☎ 0870-538 8388 or ☎ 0800-096 9992 in the UK or ☎ 03 21 00 61 00 in France or visit the Eurotunnel website (🖳 http://www.eurotunnel.com).

TAXIS

Taxi ranks (station de taxi) are usually to be found outside railway stations, at airports and at main junctions in towns and cities. At some taxi ranks, e.g. at Charles de Gaulle airport, a button is provided to call a taxi when none are waiting. You can hail a taxi in the street, but it must be at least 50m (160ft) from a taxi rank where people are waiting. You can also call a radio taxi by telephone (usually provided at taxi ranks), but you must pay for the taxi's journey to the pick-up point. Some radio taxi companies operate a system where customers pay an annual fee for priority service. You can also hire chauffeur-driven cars (voiture de place) in most towns and cities, either by the hour or for a fixed fee for a particular trip.

Despite their reputation for unscrupulousness and rudeness, French taxi drivers are generally no more (or less!) surly than any other 'public servants'. Nevertheless, taxi drivers must obey strict regulations and can refuse to pick you up if you're obviously drunk or 'if your clothes are dirty or you have BO'! They're entitled to pick up additional passengers along the route, but may not charge them extra (except a fourth passenger). Drivers aren't usually permitted to accept fares outside their normal operating area (shown on the light on top of the vehicle), e.g. the Ile-de-France for Paris taxis. In many cities there are simply too many cabs and the situation is exacerbated by unlicensed operators. Beware of illegal and unmetered cabs operating in main cities and preying on foreign visitors. If you're obliged to take one of these, always agree the fare in advance.

Drivers may ask you not to smoke (many taxis have défense de fumer signs inside) and you can ask them not to, although many drivers expect you to acquiesce if they ask your permission and open their window. Drivers may refuse to carry animals (except guide dogs, which must be allowed), although most have no objection to small dogs; there's a set charge (e.g. €0.60 in Paris). Taxis adapted for use by the disabled are available in major cities but must be booked. Consult the yellow pages.

Outside major towns, taxis can be expensive (e.g. €30 for a 20-minute ride). Note that taxis in rural areas often double as ambulances, so don't think you've gone mad if you see a taxi-driver wearing a white coat! It's possible to book a taxi online (e.g. 🖳 http://infotaxiparis.free.fr or 🖳 http://www.taxis-bleus.com in Paris). Most mobile telephone service providers also allow you to contact a local taxi company in Paris and other main cities by dialling a short code. However, although they may give you priority booking, these calls are usually expensive (e.g. €0.90).

Paris

Parisian taxis are among the cheapest in Europe and are ordinary cars fitted with a meter and a light on top. Although there are around 15,000 taxis in Paris, it's often difficult to find one, particularly during lunch times and rush hours and when it's raining and you don't have an umbrella! Taxi ranks are indicated by blue and white 'taxi' signs. A taxi for hire is indicated by a white light on the roof. A driver must take you if the light on top of his vehicle is lit, unless he's on the last half hour of his shift indicated by a meter inside the taxi on the rear window shelf. An orange light means a taxi is engaged; when no lights are on or the meter is concealed by a black cover, the driver is off duty.

There are three fare rates, and the prevailing rate is indicated by a small light on a taxi's roof beneath the main light. Rate A (around €0.60 per km) operates from 07.00 to 19.00 Mondays to Fridays as far as (and including) the *Boulevard Périphérique*. Rate B (around €1 per km) runs from 19.00 to 07.00 and is also the day rate for journeys to the Hauts-de-Seine, Seine-Saint-Denis and Val-de-Marne departments. Rate C (around €1.20 per km) is the rate for the departments listed above between 19.00 and 07.00, the outer suburbs (*tarif banlieue*) and airports beyond the *Périphérique*. Drivers are supposed to reset the meter tariff when crossing from the suburbs into the central area of Paris (marked by the *Périphérique*).

Rates are displayed on the meter inside the taxi, and extra charges are shown on a notice affixed to the rear left window. These include pick-up charges (*prise en charge*, of around €2), pick-ups at main railway stations and airports (around €0.70), luggage heavier than 5kg (around €0.90 per item), a fourth adult (around €2.60) and pets (around €0.60). Waiting time is charged at over €25 per hour. **Taxi drivers cannot claim a return fare, whatever the destination.** It's customary to round fares up to the nearest euro and add a tip of around 10 to 15 per cent (more at night). Note that very few Paris taxi drivers accept credit cards or cheques.

A useful website for information about taxis in Paris is 🖳 http://infotaxiparis.free.fr (in English and French). For further information (or to make a complaint about a Paris taxi driver), write to the Service des Taxis de la Préfecture de Police, 36 rue des Morillons, 75015 Paris (☎ 08 21 00 25 25). If you intend to make a complaint, obtain a receipt (*bulletin de voiture*) and indicate the taxi number and the date and time of the fare.

11.

<u>MOTORING</u>

France has an extensive motorway network of over 9,500km (6,000mi) supplemented by a comprehensive network (around 30,000km/18,500mi) of trunk roads, which vary from almost motorway standard dual-carriageways to narrow two-lane roads passing through a succession of villages where the speed limit is 50kph (30mph). The motorways, on the other hand, are among Europe's finest roads. However, they're also among the world's most expensive, being mostly toll roads built by private companies. Whereas motorways are often virtually empty, trunk roads are usually jammed by drivers who are reluctant to pay or who cannot afford the high motorways tolls and are particularly over-used by heavy goods vehicles (some 70 per cent of goods transported through France travel by road). If you're travelling long distances, it may be cheaper to fly or take a *TGV* than to use the motorways and will almost certainly be quicker and less stressful. In rural areas, a car is generally a necessity, and driving can be enjoyable in remote areas, particularly outside the tourist season, where it's possible to drive for miles without seeing another motorist (or a caravan).

If you live in a city, particularly Paris, a car is usually a liability. Traffic density and pollution in cities is increasing (it's estimated that around 16,000 people die prematurely each year because of traffic-induced air pollution). Paris is one of Europe's most traffic-polluted cities and it often experiences poor air quality in summer, with consequent restrictions on vehicle movement (see *pastille verte* on page 252); a reduction in road speed limits (*un pic de pollution*) is automatically triggered when ozone levels reach 240 micrograms per cubic metre of air. Parking in cities (especially Paris) can be a nightmare (dealing with parking takes up 60 per cent of the Paris Highway Department's workload). Some cities have drastically cut the number of vehicles entering the central area with dramatic results. For example, Bordeaux has seen a reduction of 80 per cent in road accidents since restricting traffic, instituting a system of buses and taxi-buses, and encouraging people to cycle and walk, and the Mayor of Paris has radical plans to exclude all except residents' and essential service vehicles from the centre of Paris by 2012 (the first phase, due to be implemented by 2007, will see the speed limit reduced to 30kph and Phase 2 the pedestrianisation of the area surrounding Les Halles) and to ban all pre-1993 (the date of the introduction of the catalytic converter) vehicles from the city. Some towns provide free buses (see page 233) and others have annual 'no car' days – though usually on Sundays! France is in the forefront of the development of electric vehicles, which are now commercially available (see **New Cars** on page 246).

Rush hours are from around 06.30 to 08.30 and 16.30 to 18.30, Mondays to Fridays, when town centres are best avoided. A recent phenomenon, known as *l'effet des 35 heures*, is an advanced rush hour on Friday afternoons caused by workers on a 35-hour week knocking off early for the weekend. Paris, where traffic moves at around the same speed as a hundred years ago, is to be avoided by motorists at all times (except perhaps between 02.00 and 04.00). Friday afternoons are particularly busy on holiday weekends and also immediately before and after the lunch period – usually from around 12.00 to 15.00. Traffic jams (*bouchon/embouteillage*) are notorious at the start and end of holiday periods, particularly on roads out of Paris and other northern cities as sunseekers flock southwards. Some areas and roads (particularly the *Autoroute du Soleil* – commonly known as the '*autoroute de la mort*') are to be avoided in July and August, when 6m French people and around over 1m foreigners set off on their annual holidays (*grandes vacances*). The most important days to stay at home are the first Saturday in July, when Parisians escape the city (*la départ*), and the last Sunday in August when they return (*la rentrée*). The 15th July and 15th August are also best avoided.

Anyone who has driven in France won't be surprised to learn that it has a high accident record. There were over 8,000 road deaths in 2002 – almost twice as many as in the UK or Japan (in proportion to the number of vehicles) – averaging a death every two hours and meaning that around one French people in every 100 would on the roads. These alarming statistics prompted the government to launch a major campaign to reduce the number of accident casualties, although it's based on 'cure' rather than 'prevention', with 1,200 extra traffic police, 24-hour radar controls (see page 267), remote-control cameras and heavier punishments for rule-breakers. This has had surprising success, a 'mere' 5,318 people dying within 30 days of a road accident (the new European 'definition' of road death) in 2005, and 108,076 people being injured, both figures having fallen annually for three years. The French are reluctant to use taxis when they go out for a meal or to a party (or even to let a non-drinking spouse take the wheel!), so it isn't surprising that some 40 per cent of accidents involve 'drunken' drivers (see **Drinking & Driving** on page 278); the most dangerous times for driving in France are consequently at night and on Sunday afternoons.

As you may know, the French drive on the right-hand side of the road. It saves confusion if you do likewise! If you aren't used to driving on the right, take it easy until you're accustomed to it. Be particularly alert when leaving lay-bys, T-junctions, one-way streets, petrol stations and car parks, as it's easy to lapse into driving on the left. It's helpful to display a reminder (e.g. 'Think right!') on your car's dashboard.

Always check your rear view and wing mirrors carefully before overtaking, as French motorists seem to appear from nowhere and zoom past at a 'zillion' miles an hour, especially on country roads. If you drive a right-hand drive car, take extra care when overtaking. It's wise to have a special 'overtaking mirror' (e.g. one designed for caravan towing) fitted.

Be particularly wary of moped (*vélomoteur*) riders and cyclists. It isn't always easy to see them, particularly when they're hidden by the blind spots of a car or are riding at night without lights. Many young moped riders seem to have a death wish and hundreds lose their lives each year. They're constantly pulling out into traffic or turning without looking or signalling. **When overtaking mopeds and cyclists, ALWAYS give them a wide . . . . WIDE berth.** If you knock them off their bikes, you may have a difficult time convincing the police that it wasn't your fault; far better to avoid them (and the police).

Information about driving in France (and other European countries) can be found on the Automobile Association's website (🖳 http://www.theaa.com), from which the *European Motoring Advice* guide can be downloaded.

IMPORTING A VEHICLE

A new or used vehicle (including boats and planes) on which VAT (*TVA*) has been paid in another EU country can be imported free of French VAT by a French resident. If you buy a new car abroad on which VAT hasn't been paid (VAT should already have been paid on a second-hand car), VAT is due immediately on its arrival in France. VAT is calculated on the invoice price if the vehicle is less than six months old or has covered less than 6,000km (3,728mi); otherwise a reduction is made according to its age, and VAT is payable on the balance. It's therefore advantageous to buy a tax-free car and use it abroad for six months before importing it. However, if you're resident in France and buy a tax-free car abroad, you have a limited time to export it, e.g. two months when buying a car in the UK. The VAT rate is 19.6 per cent for all cars and caravans, and for motorcycles above 240cc.

In addition to VAT, customs duty must be paid on cars imported from outside the EU; there's no duty on cars imported from another EU country, provided that you produce purchase and registration documents. The rate of duty varies with the country of origin (some countries have reciprocal agreements with the EU resulting in lower duty rates) and, of course, the value of the vehicle in France, calculated using the *Argus* guide to second-hand car prices (see page 247).

Tax and duty must be paid in cash or by banker's draft at the point of importation or at the local tax office (Hôtel/Recette des Impôts) where you live. If you have a choice, it's preferable to pay at your local tax office. After you've paid VAT or confirmed that VAT isn't payable, you receive a customs certificate (*Certificat de Douane* 846A) permitting you to register the vehicle in France (see page 249). Note that you require form 846A even when there's no VAT to pay, e.g. when importing a vehicle from another EU country. An imported vehicle must be registered in France within three months. However, before you can register it, you must contact your local Direction Régionale de l'Industrie, de la Recherche et de l'Environnement (DRIRE), listed in the yellow pages, which will send you a checklist of the documentation required. This may include the following:

● The customs certificate (*Certificat de Douane 846A*) mentioned above.

● A manufacturer's certificate of construction (*certificat/attestation de conformité*).

● Proof of origin of the vehicle (*justification de l'origine du véhicule*) or a certificate of sale (*certificat de vente*).

● Evidence that VAT has been paid in the country of origin (*déclaration d'impôt*).

● A registration request form (*demande de certificat d'immatriculation*) and a *demande d'identification* (confirming the vehicle's details).

● The foreign registration document (*titre de circulation étranger*).

● A test certificate (*rapport de contrôle technique*) not more than six months old if the vehicle is more than four years old.

The recommended procedure for obtaining these documents is as follows:

1. Visit the DRIRE with all your vehicle documents, including the vehicle identification number (VIN) and proof of your identity and address (plus copies just in case) and tell them you want to register a car. They should enter the VIN into their computer. If the number is recognised, which it should be if your car isn't too old and was built

for the European market, they will give you a *certificat/attestation de conformité* and ask you to pay around €30; you may then proceed to Step 2.

If the VIN isn't recognised, you must contact the vehicle manufacturer to obtain a certificate (if your car has a non-European specification or has been modified, buy another car!). This will cost you up to €150, depending on the manufacturer, and you will still have to pay the DRIRE €30 for the French certificate.

2. Go to your local Hôtel des Impôts and ask for a *déclaration d'impôt*. Present your car registration document, the *attestation de conformité* from the DRIRE and your proof of residence and you should be given the appropriate form – free (unless the vehicle is brand new).

3. If the vehicle is more than four years old, take it to a test centre (see page 251). If it fails the test, it must be rectified and documentation provided to prove that this has been done (*justification*).

4. Take all the documents you've now amassed to the local *préfecture* (not a *sous-préfecture*, where you won't be able to get everything done on the spot but must wait while the paperwork is sent to and from the *préfecture*) and ask for a registration application form (*demande de certificat d'immatriculation*) and a *demande d'identification* (confirming the vehicle's details). Fill in the forms, hand in your documents and wait.

   Note that your home vehicle registration document will probably be withheld by the *préfecture* (and you may never see it again), so keep a copy to send to your home registration authority, telling them that the vehicle has been re-registered in France.

4. Take all your documents to an insurance company or broker and to a garage or other outlet to obtain a registration document and registration plates (see **Vehicle Registration** on page 249).

It's possible to do all the above in a day, but you should expect it to take **much** longer. **It's imperative that you have the correct pieces of paper at each stage, or you will be wasting your time.**

If you import a caravan or camper van, even one manufactured in France, the fixtures and fittings are likely to need modifying to conform with French regulations (unless it was equipped in France), so you're advised not to attempt it but to sell your van in your home country and buy a new one in France. Although the British Caravan Council created a 'European' norm (EN1645) with the intention of facilitating the import of caravans to other EU countries, no other EU country has adopted it! If you're planning to import an old car, contact the Fédération Française des Véhicules d'Epoque (FFVE, ☎ 02 23 20 14 14) for information.

BUYING A CAR

Unlike people in most Western countries, the French generally drive cars manufactured in their own country. This isn't simply chauvinism, as French cars are relatively cheap (thanks to government subsidies) and usually very good and, when they need servicing or break down, you can have them repaired at a reasonable cost at a almost any garage in France. Needless to say, however, Japanese cars have become popular in recent years (Toyota have built a manufacturing plant in Valenciennes), while Fiat and Audi/VW are the best-selling foreign makes, and the two main French manufacturers, Renault and Peugeot-Citroën, which once shared three-quarters of the domestic market have suffered declining sales.

The availability of local service facilities is, of course, linked to the number of cars sold in France. Peugeot-Citroën and Renault dealers can be found in every large town and there many Audi-VW, Fiat, Ford, Mercedes and Opel (General Motors/Vauxahll) dealers. Dealers for other makes are few and far between. It's difficult to find garages that can repair US, British and some Japanese cars, and the nearest dealer may be a long way from your home or workplace. If you buy a rare car, it's wise to carry a basic selection of spare parts, as service stations in France may not stock them and you may need to wait several days for them to be sent from abroad. On the other hand, if you're buying a French-made car with the intention of using it abroad (e.g. in the UK), check that you will be able to find spare parts for it. France's most popular car, the Renault Twingo, for example, isn't sold in the UK and so repairs and servicing may be expensive or impossible.

The cost of running a car (e.g. insurance, taxes, petrol, servicing and depreciation) in France is among the highest in the EU. Those contemplating buying a 'sports utility vehicle', known in France as a '*quat-quat*' (short for *quatre-quatre*, meaning four-by-four), should note that the government is planning to impose a purchase tax of up to €3,500 on such vehicles, whereas purchasers of 'green' cars (those that emit less than 140g of carbon monoxide per km) may be entitled to a rebate of up to €700. See also **Registration Document** on page 250.

New Cars

New car prices are higher in France than in most other European countries, although lower than those in the UK, and many French people buy their cars in Belgium or Portugal, where most new cars are up to 20 per cent cheaper than in France. You should make sure, however, that the local French dealer of a car purchased abroad will agree to service it under the terms of the warranty. Since 1st October 2002 dealers have been allowed to operate anywhere in the EU and price differences should largely disappear within a few years. Personally importing a car from the US is usually much cheaper than buying the same car in France or elsewhere in Europe but you must ensure that it's manufactured to French specifications or it may not be approved by the DRIRE (see page 244).

Making comparisons between new car prices in those countries which have adopted the euro currency is easy, but attention should be paid to the different levels of standard equipment and warranty levels. Most dealers will offer one or two extras free of charge, giving up to a 10 per cent discount on the list price, and some offer 'cash back' deals; you should shop around for the best package. The French government occasionally provides a subsidy (e.g. up to €760) for owners of old bangers who buy new cars (designed to help French car manufacturers), and some dealers offer a hire purchase option (*vente à crédit*).

All new cars sold in France must now be labelled with their 'energy efficiency' (i.e. the amount of carbon dioxide their engines emit for every kilometre travelled), with colour codes ranging from dark green for the most environmentally-friendly models (emissions of less than 100g/km) to red for the most polluting (over 250g/km) and there's a surcharge on the cost of a registration document for high-emission cars (see **Registration Document** on page 250).

The environmentally-conscious can do even better than buying a dark-green-label car and invest in a vehicle that runs on a mixture of propane and butane, known as liquid-petroleum gas (LPG – *gaz de pétrole liquéfié*, *GPL* or *Gépel* in French), or convert a conventional car to run on LPG, which produces less harmful emissions than petrol, including around 15 per cent less carbon dioxide as well as less carbon monoxide. There are around 200,000 LPG-powered cars on French roads, and they're manufactured by Daihatsu, Ford, Rover, Opel and others. Although new LPG cars cost around €1,600 more than ordinary cars (and conversion of an ordinary car costs between €2,000 and €3,500), tax credits of between €1,525 and €2,300 are available and fuel costs around half as much as petrol, so that major savings can be made. Engine wear and noise are also reduced. Note, however, that LPG-powered cars aren't permitted to use certain road tunnels and there have been a number of spectacular explosions involving LPG-powered vehicles. The *Guide GPL* is available from petrol stations supplying LPG and from the Comité Français du Butane et du Propane (🖳 http://www.cfbp.fr). See also **Fuel** on page 282. If you live in Paris, you can even buy an electric car (which are tax-free and entitled to free parking) – and hope that the promised 100 charging points are installed before your batteries go flat!

A recent initiative, pioneered by Gaz de France and Citroën in the department of Haute-Garonne in late 2005, allows drivers of a new version of the C3 car to fill it with mains gas (known as *gaz naturel de ville/GNV* to distinguish it from LPG), costing roughly the same as diesel and charged to your home gas bill; like LPG, mains gas generates significantly lower emissions than petrol. *GNV* is used by over 1,000 French buses, two of which caught fire in 2005 as a result of faulty safety valves.

It's possible to buy a car in France for which you don't require a licence. But that's about the only advantage of these vehicles (known officially as *voiturettes* but colloquially as *sans permis* – an allusion to illegal immigrants, who are known as *sans papiers*); the disadvantages are that they're tiny (strictly two-seaters with no boot), have an official top speed of around 60kph/40mph (although downhill with a following wind they can reach a hair-raising 80kph/50mph), aren't allowed on motorways or dual-carriageways and cost an alarming €7,500 for even a basic model. There is, however a lively second-hand market in *sans permis* vehicles, which are often changed every two years.

Used Cars

Used cars (*voiture d'occasion*) in France are expensive in relation to new cars and generally more expensive than in the UK, for example. It's often best to buy a car that's around two years old, as depreciation in the first two years is considerable. If you intend to buy a used car in France, whether privately or from a garage, check the following:

- That it has passed the official technical inspection (see page 251), if applicable.

- That it hasn't been involved in a major accident. A declaration that it's accident free (*sans accident/non-accidenté*) should be obtained in writing.

- That the chassis number tallies with the registration document (see page 249), which should be in the name of the vendor when sold privately.

- That the service coupons have been completed and stamped, and that servicing has been carried out by an authorised dealer.

- That the price roughly corresponds to those in the weekly *Argus* guide (see below).

- That you receive a guarantee, signed by the vendor, that the car isn't under a hire purchase agreement (*certificat de non-gage*).

- That you also receive a *certificat de non-opposition* confirming that the vendor agrees to sell you the car (i.e. you aren't stealing it!).

- Whether a warranty or guarantee is available; if so, obtain the relevant documents.

A *certificat de non-opposition* is valid for two months and a *certificat de non-gage* for one month only **and you must re-register the car within this period** (see **Vehicle Registration** on page 249). A *certificat de non-gage* can be obtained from your *préfecture* or via the internet (🖥 http://www.interieur.gouv.fr). **Never buy a car without a registration document, as it could be stolen.**

Car dealers give warranties of 3 to 12 months on used cars depending on the age of the car and the model. Used car dealers, rather than franchised dealers, have the same dreadful (and well-deserved) reputation as in other countries and caution must be taken when buying from them. If you're buying a used car from a garage, try to negotiate a reduction, particularly when you're paying cash and aren't trading in another vehicle.

All national and local (including free) newspapers carry advertisements for used cars. Specialist journals for used-car buyers include the monthly *Auto Journal* (🖥 http://www.autojournal.fr). *La Centrale des Particuliers* (🖥 http://www.la centrale.fr) and *L'Argus* magazine (🖥 http://www.argusauto.com) are published weekly, and the latter includes a guide to second-hand car prices. *L'Argus* updates its prices every six months and these are used throughout the industry, e.g. by dealers buying or selling cars and by insurance companies when calculating values for insurance premiums and claims. You should pay within around 10 per cent of the *Argus* value, depending on condition and the certified kilometre reading. Second-hand prices vary with the region and are generally higher in remote areas than in Paris and other major cities.

Note that all cars containing parts made from asbestos (*amiante*) are illegal (i.e. no one is allowed to buy or sell them) owing to the health threat posed to mechanics. As most pre-1997 vehicles have brake and clutch pads and gaskets containing asbestos, you should ask the seller for confirmation that asbestos parts have been replaced. If in doubt, have the vehicle checked before buying it.

SELLING A CAR

Before selling a car in France, you must obtain a 'certificate of sale' form (*certificat de vente*) from your town hall, *préfecture* or a garage selling cars. The form must be completed in duplicate; one copy is given to the buyer and the other is sent to the registration office. When selling a car, you must give the buyer the purchase invoice, the technical inspection badge (see page 251), the road tax *vignette* (with the receipt) if applicable (see page 252) and the registration document (see below). Before handing over the registration document, write 'sold to' (*vendue à* – all cars are feminine) and the buyer's name, and sign and date it. Don't forget to remove your insurance tab (see page 257) from the windscreen. You must also provide a signed guarantee (*certificat de non-gage*) that the car isn't under a hire purchase or lease agreement. Other points to note when selling a car are:

- Inform your insurance company.

- When selling privately, insist on payment in cash or with a banker's draft (*chèque de banque*), which is standard practice. If you cannot tell a banker's draft from a personal cheque, insist on cash. **Never accept a personal cheque.**

- With the purchaser, draw up a list of minor damage and faults and ask him to sign that he accepts these (*'lue et approuvée'* or *'Monsieur X accepte l'état du véhicule'* followed by the date). Include in the receipt that you're selling the car without a guarantee (*sans garantie*), the price paid and the car's kilometre reading. The new owner may ask for a declaration in writing that the car is accident-free (*sans accident/non-accidenté*); this refers to major accidents causing structural damage and not slight knocks.

The best places to advertise a car for sale are in local newspapers, on free local notice boards, and in the Friday and Saturday editions of major newspapers. Many people put a for sale (*à vendre*, often reduced to *AV*) notice in their car with a telephone number and park it in a prominent place.

If you're unable to sell an old car and need to dispose of it, new regulations require you to have it destroyed by a registered scrapyard (*casse*), which will usually charge you between €50 and €200. A list of registered yards can be found on the Ministry of Ecology's website (🖳 http://www.ecologie.gouv.fr – click on '*Véhicules hors d'usage*' in the left panel and then '*liste des démolisseurs et des broyeurs agréés*' at the foot of the page).

VEHICLE REGISTRATION

When you import a car into France or buy a new or second-hand car, it must be registered at the *préfecture* or *sous-préfecture* in the department where you're resident within 15 days (although the process is usually carried out by the dealer in the case of a new car purchase). In Paris, the registration is done by the *préfecture de police* or the town hall (*mairie*) of your *arrondissement*. If you import a car, you must obtain customs clearance and have it inspected by the DRIRE before it can be registered (see **Importing a Vehicle** on page 243).

Registration Document

A vehicle registration document is known as a 'grey card' (*carte grise*). *Sans permis* vehicles (see page 247) have a *mini-carte grise*, but the registration procedure is otherwise the same as with ordinary cars. It must be applied for in person at your local *préfecture*. (The government intends to make it possible to obtain a registration document by post or online, thus depriving millions of people of the joy of queuing for hours to get one.) Since June 2004, *cartes grises* have incorporated a tear-off portion, which must be completed by the vendor. You must present this and the sales certificate (*certificat de vente*), *certificat de non-gage* and *certificat de non-opposition* that you received from the vendor (see **Used Cars** on page 247), technical inspection certificate, if applicable (see page 251), and a photocopy of your *carte de séjour* or passport and complete a registration request form (*demande de certificat d'immatriculation*), available in some cases from your *mairie* or *hôtel de ville*.

If you move to a new address in the same department, you must currently inform your *préfecture* of your change of address. However, if you move to a different department, you must re-register your car with the new *préfecture* within three months. **You're recommended to do this as soon as possible, as cars registered in another department are prime targets for thieves and vandals.** You must present the tear-off portion of your registration document, your *carte de séjour* (if applicable) and proof of residence; you may also be asked for a *certificat de résidence* obtainable from your local town hall. The fee for a revised registration document is €33.

EU legislation dictates that this system was due to end in June 2006, when a national or 'personalised' numbering system was to remove this necessity and a car would retain the same registration number for life, but in August 2006 the French were typically still discussing the implementation of this law (i.e. procrastinating). When you receive a registration document with a new registration number, e.g. after importing a car or moving to a new department, you must fit new registration plates within 48 hours.

If a woman marries and changes her name, it's unnecessary for her to change her registration document. If you lose your registration document or have it stolen, you must report it to the police, who will issue you with a certificate allowing you to obtain a replacement from the *préfecture*.

The fee for a registration document varies according to the size of a vehicle's engine, according to a scale of 'fiscal horsepower' (*chevaux fiscaux*), which isn't the same as the actual horsepower (*chevaux DIN*) produced by the engine, and fee scales vary with the region; for example, they're up to 50 per cent higher in Paris than in the provinces. Current fees for a car less than ten years old are between €150 and €250 for a 5hp car (approximately equivalent to a 1,200cc petrol engine or a 1,400cc diesel engine), €180 to €280 for 6hp (1,400/1,600cc) and €210 to €325 for 7hp (1,700/2,000cc), although the government plans to increase fees by as much as 100 per cent for 4x4s and other gas-guzzling vehicles and in January 2006 introduced a surcharge of €2 per gram of carbon dioxide above 200 per kilometre travelled and €4 per gram above 250g. For a car more than ten years old, fees are roughly half the above.

Registration Number

Currently, the last two digits of a car's registration number (*numéro d'immatriculation*) correspond to the number of the department where it's registered, e.g. 62 for Pas-de-Calais. (Personalised numbers don't exist, although it's possible to obtain a sort of personalised number by requesting a number that starts with a particular digit or sequence of digits and waiting until it becomes available.) The other numbers and letters have no significance but give an indication of the age of a vehicle (unless it has been re-registered), as letters and numbers are issued in sequence (e.g. 1234 XH 62 is an older number than 1234 XK 62). However, number plates are set to change in 2006, when the initial department number is to disappear in favour of a two letters/three figures/two letters format. Letters and numbers will be bigger, and plates will have a space on the right for a departmental or other identifying logo. As usual, however, the French are conducting endless discussions as to the best system.

Plates are made on the spot by supermarkets and ironmongers (*quincaillerie*) on production of your registration document (the cost is around €25 per pair). The white plate goes at the front and the yellow one at the rear.

TECHNICAL INSPECTION

All cars over four years old are required to have a technical inspection (*contrôle technique*) every two years, carried out at an authorised test centre (garages don't carry out tests, as in the UK, for example). Tests cover over 50 points, including steering, suspension, fuel tank, bodywork, seats, seatbelts, mirrors, windscreen, windscreen wipers and horn, all of which must be functional and in good condition, and emission levels. Around 20 per cent of vehicles tested are found to be in unsatisfactory condition. Tested items are listed on a report (*certificat d'inspection/autobilan*). Tests take around three-quarters of an hour but a time must usually be booked. There's no fixed charge for a test and each centre can set its own rate, but the average is around €55.

If your car passes the test, you receive a badge (*macaron*) which you must affix to your windscreen next to your insurance tab. You normally have two months' grace at the end of each two-year period in which to submit your car for a test. After this period, you can be fined €90 for not displaying a valid badge; the fine increases to €380 if your badge is more than a month out of date. The test must be re-taken when a car over four years old is sold if it was last tested more than six months previously.

Cars over 25 years old can be classified as 'collectors' vehicles' (*véhicule de collection*), which means that they're exempt from the technical inspection under certain conditions (e.g. they can only be used at weekends and on certain roads in certain parts of the country), although an initial test is required to obtain a registration document. Note that, even if your car passes the technical inspection, you can be fined up to €137 if it isn't roadworthy (e.g. for each tyre without 1.6mm of tread over its entire surface). All new tyres purchased in France have bumps in the grooves to enable you to check tyre wear; once the tread is worn down to the top of the bumps, it's time to buy new tyres.

A green disc (*pastille verte*) is provided by car dealers for new cars and can be obtained for older cars (petrol-driven vehicles manufactured since 1993 and diesel-engine vehicles manufactured since 1997) from a *préfecture*. The disc must be displayed on the windscreen, and cars displaying it are the only vehicles allowed to circulate in cities such as Paris on 'bad air quality days' (level 3), known as *pics de pollution*. Discs should be renewed every two years. There are proposals to introduce a *pastille noire* for environmentally-unfriendly vehicles such as sports utility vehicles in Paris, where they will be banned from certain areas and on bad air days.

ROAD TAX

French-registered private vehicles no longer require a road tax certificate (*vignette automobile*), except certain camper vans. If you use a vehicle over 3.5 tonnes for your business, it must be taxed, and if you run a business that has more than three vehicles, you must pay tax on the fourth, fifth, etc.. If you have vehicles that need taxing, you must declare them to the tax authorities when you acquire them and before 10th December each year. Forms 2856 and 2857 must be completed; these, along with other relevant information, can be found on the Tax Office's website (💻 http://www.impots.gouv.fr). If your vehicle requires a *vignette*, keep the receipt with your other car papers, as this proves that you didn't acquire it illegally and also enables you to obtain a replacement if it's stolen. If you need to replace your *vignette*, visit any tax office (*Centre des Impôts*) and produce your receipt. If you lose the receipt, you can obtain another from the issuing office, which keeps a record of payments.

Since January 2006 a tax has been added to the cost of a registration document for cars that emit more than a certain amount of carbon dioxide (see **Registration Document** on page 250). The use of most motorways (*autoroute*) and certain bridges and tunnels is 'taxed' in the form of tolls (see **French Roads** on page 270).

DRIVING LICENCE

The minimum age for driving a car in France is 18, although *sans permis* vehicles (see page 247) can be driven at 14. (For age restrictions on riding mopeds and motorcycles, see page 276.) Those between 16 and 18 may follow an accompanied or 'anticipated' learning programme (*apprentissage accompagné* or *apprentissage anticipé de la conduite/AAC*, commonly known as *conduite accompagnée*) consisting of at least 20 hours' instruction by a qualified driving instructor, culminating in a written test (*épreuve théorique générale/ETG* or *code*), followed by (provided the test has been passed) 3,000km (1,875mi) of accompanied driving (this is a requirement for all learners, irrespective of age); the practical test cannot be taken until the age of 18. Note that, if you wish to accompany a learner driver, you must obtain your insurance company's permission. The cost of a course of 20 hours' instruction, including the theory and practical tests, is around €675, although 16- to 25-year-olds can now obtain an interest-free bank loan to cover the cost. Almost 200,000 teenagers every year opt for the accompanied apprenticeship and 80 per cent of them pass compared with only 50 per cent of those who start learning as adults.

Irrespective of your age, you now have three years (previously two) to pass the practical test after passing the theory test and may take it up to five times during this period; if you fail it on the fifth attempt, you must retake the theory test (*code*) as well as the practical (or give up). If you fail the practical test, you must wait at least two weeks (or a month if you fail at the second or subsequent attempt) before you may retake it. There are further courses available to those who pass (*stage post-permis*), although uptake is understandably low.

Note that the practical part of the driving test has recently been increased from 20 to 35 minutes and, in accordance with new EU directives, tests will in future include use of a car's instruments and systems, including checking tyre pressures and oil and water levels. New drivers have fewer points on their licences and must observe lower speed limits than other motorists for three years after passing their test (see **Points** on page 254 and **Speed Limits** on page 266). Drivers over 75 years of age must pass a medical examination every two years in order to retain their licence.

A standard car licence (called a *permis B*) also entitles you to ride a motorcycle up to 125cc, provided you've held it for at least two years (although you must retake the theory exam if you've held a licence for more than five years without riding a motorcycle). Note, however, that you must have a licence *E(B)*, for which additional training is required, to tow a caravan or trailer weighing more than 750kg (1,650lb) if it's heavier than your car or if the combined weight of the car and caravan/trailer is more than 3.5 tonnes. If a caravan or trailer exceeds 500kg (1,100lb), it must be insured and have its own registration document (see page 250).

A French driving licence is pink and contains a photograph. It's issued for life, and recent proposals to make licences expire when the holder reaches the age of 70 were dismissed, as were suggestions that French licences should be superseded by European ones. However, if your foreign licence has limited validity (UK licences expire when you reach 70), you may be unable to renew it in the country of issue but must apply for a French licence.

You can drive in France for at least a year on most foreign driving licences or an International Driver's Permit (IDP). An IDP must be obtained from the country where your current licence was issued. (If you hold a French licence and want an IDP for driving in other countries, it can be obtained from your *préfecture* on production of your current licence and two passport-size photographs; it's free and is valid for five years at a time.) The Second EU Driving Licence Directive provides, among other things, for the mutual recognition of driving licences issued by EU member states. If EU citizens move from one member country to another, it's no longer necessary for them to obtain a local driving licence after one year. **However, a resident who commits a motoring offence in France involving a loss of licence points (see below) is obliged to exchange his foreign licence for a French one so that the penalty may be applied (non-residents escape the penalty but must still pay fines).** Note also that most French officials (including *gendarmes*) are unaware of the aforementioned Directive and none too impressed when it's quoted to them.

You can expect the procedure to take at least two months, so you should apply to your local *préfecture* or *sous-préfecture* well in advance (i.e. before your year is up or, if you're an EU citizen, before your home licence expires). You will need a valid, translated driving licence, proof of residence, your *carte de séjour* (if applicable), two passport-size photographs, a self-addressed registered envelope and the fee (currently around €25) in the form of fiscal stamps (*timbre fiscal*), obtainable from tobacconists', as well as a copy of the penalty notice (*PV*) if applicable.

Some non-EU countries and some US states (e.g. Florida, Illinois, Kansas, Kentucky, Michigan, New Hampshire, Pennsylvania and South Carolina) have reciprocal agreements with France to waive the driving test, but applicants must take the written exam concerning rules of the road (including road sign recognition). If you need to take a driving test, it's wise to take a course through a certified driving school, some of which have sections for English-speakers.

The French authorities will confiscate your foreign driving licence and return it to the country of issue or retain it and return it to you when you leave France permanently. However, you should take a copy of your foreign licence before surrendering it, as your French licence will show that you have been driving only since it was issued, which may make life difficult if you want to rent a car and could affect your insurance no-claims bonus.

If you're a UK citizen and become resident in France, you should note that the DVLA won't renew a British driving licence with a foreign address, so when it expires you must either give a fictitious address or exchange it for a French licence. In the former case, to prevent 'misunderstandings' with the police, you should obtain a form F.45 (*enregistrement d'un permis de conduire de l'Union Européenne*), which you should staple to your UK licence; it's free, but (like everything to do with motoring documentation) can take a long time to obtain. If your UK licence is due to expire, you should take the F.45, along with the documentation listed above, to the *préfecture* in order to be issued with a French licence (take a good book!).

If you lose your French driving licence or it's stolen, you must report the matter to the police and obtain an acknowledgement (*récépissé de déclaration de perte ou de vol de pièces d'identité*), which is valid until a replacement licence is issued. Note, however, that a replacement licence may cost twice as much as the original.

Points

Driving penalties in France are based on a points system. Drivers normally start with 12 licence points, and between one and six points are deducted for each offence, depending on its gravity (see **Fines & Penalties** on page 268). However, new drivers are allowed only six points for three years after passing their test (two years if they've followed an accompanied learning programme – see page 252) and, if they lose any points during that period, they must wait three years from the date of the offence to obtain the remaining six points. If they lose all six points during the probationary period, their licence is suspended and they must wait six months before being able to retake their test.

When an offence is registered, you receive a letter of notification from the *préfecture* stating the number of points lost and the number remaining. Points are automatically reinstated after three years but, if you lose all 12 points within this period, you receive a demand to surrender your licence within a week to your local *préfecture* and you're usually banned from driving for a minimum of six months (six years or more if you've been convicted of manslaughter). Depending on your record, you may need to pass a written test, a practical driving test and/or medical and 'psychotechnical' examinations to regain your licence.

You can reinstate four licence points at any time (but not more than once every two years) by undertaking a two-day 'awareness course' (*stage de sensibilisation*) run by Améliorer la Sécurité et le Comportement des Usagers de la Route (ASCUR). All drivers who have had a licence for less than two years and who lose four or more points are obliged to take an awareness course, which costs €230 (but any fine you've had to pay is refunded!). To find your nearest ASCUR centre, contact your *préfecture* or visit ▄ http://www.securite-routiere.equipement.gouv.fr.

Information

For more information about driving licences, contact the Ministère de l'Équipement, des Transports et du Logement, Arche de la Défense, 92055 La Défense (▄ http:// www.equipement.gouv.fr). The points system is explained in a booklet *Permis à Points* available from police stations and on ▄ http://www.permis-a-points.com. See also **Speed Limits** on page 266 and **Traffic Police** on page 267.

CAR INSURANCE

As in most other countries, car insurance is essential in France and driving without it is a serious offence, for which you can be fined up to €7,500 and imprisoned for up to six months. All imported motor vehicles plus trailers and semi-trailers must also be insured. If you arrive in France with a vehicle without valid insurance, you can buy a temporary policy valid for 8, 15 or 30 days from the vehicle insurance department of the French customs office at your point of entry. However, motorists insured in an EU country or Liechtenstein, Norway or Switzerland are automatically covered for third-party liability in France (see **Green Card** below). The following categories of car insurance are available in France:

- **Third Party** (*responsabilité civile, minimale, tiers illimitée* and *au tiers*) – the minimum required by law in France and includes unlimited medical costs and damage to third-party property.

- **Third Party, Fire & Theft** (TPF&T; *tiers personnes/restreinte/intermédiaire/vol et incendie*), known in some countries as part comprehensive – includes cover against fire, natural hazards (e.g. falling rocks), theft and legal expenses (*défense-recours*). TPF&T includes damage to (or theft of) contents and radio.

- **Multi-risk Collision** (*multirisque collision*) – covers all risks listed under TPF&T (see above) plus damage caused to your own vehicle in the event of a collision with a person, vehicle, or animal belonging to an 'identifiable person'.

- **Comprehensive** (*multirisque tous accidents/tous risques*) – covers all the risks listed under TPF&T and multi-risk collision (see above) and includes damage to your vehicle however caused and whether a third party can be identified or not. Note, however, that illegally parked cars automatically lose their comprehensive cover. Comprehensive insurance is usually compulsory for lease and credit-purchase contracts.

Glass breakage (*bris de glace*) is often included in TPF&T comprehensive insurance, but you should check, as there may be an additional premium. Driver protection (*protection du conducteur/assurance conducteur*) is usually optional. It enables the driver of a vehicle involved in an accident to claim for bodily injury to himself, including compensation for his incapacity to work or for his beneficiaries should he be killed. However, if you have an accident while breaking the law, e.g. drunken driving or illegal parking, your comprehensive insurance may be automatically downgraded to third party only – or nullified altogether. This means that you must pay for your own repairs and medical expenses, which can be **very** expensive. Additional insurance can be purchased for contents and accessories such as an expensive car stereo. High-value cars (e.g. worth over €20,000) must usually have an approved alarm installed and/or the registration number engraved on all windows in order to be insured against theft.

Trailer owners should note that these are normally insured only when attached to your car and damaged in an accident; to insure them for theft, whether attached to your car or not, you must register them in their own right as if they were a caravan or another vehicle. You should also check whether your insurance policy covers items stolen from your car. **When motoring in France (or anywhere else), don't assume that your valuables are safe in the boot of your car, particularly if the boot can be opened from the inside.**

If your car is insured in your name, your children may use it 'occasionally', but whether you need to tell your insurer and pay a higher premium depends on two factors. Insurers distinguish between 'habitual' and 'occasional' drivers (*conducteur habituel/occasionel*) – and also, in most cases, between men and women. If your daughter, who is an inexperienced driver, wants to be an occasional driver of your car, most companies will allow this free of charge. For a male driver, however, virtually all companies impose a surcharge, called a 'repurchase of excess' (*un rachat de franchise*) or a 'new driver excess' (*une franchise jeune conducteur*), costing from around €150. If you allow your son to drive your car without informing your insurer and he causes an accident, you could face a penalty of up to €500. If he is found to be the main user of the car, your insurance policy could be rendered invalid. Once your son has been driving for two or three years (depending on the insurer), you may not have to pay a surcharge for occasional use. When he finally takes out his own insurance, however, he will be regarded as a new driver and will normally pay a 'novice surcharge' (*surprime conducteurs novices*) – which also applies to women.

Green Card

Although all motorists insured in an EU country or Liechtenstein, Norway or Switzerland are automatically covered for third-party liability in France, British motorists should note that British insurance companies usually insist on your applying for a certificate of motor insurance (commonly known as a 'green card') if you're driving to France (or any other European country). Most companies will issue a green card for a maximum of 90 days per year. (This is because British insurers know that you're far more likely to have an accident when driving on the right!) Nevertheless, you should shop around, as some companies allow drivers a green card for up to six months a year (e.g. Liverpool Victoria, ☎ 0800-015 4752) or even for an unlimited time (e.g. Saga, ☎ 0800-015 4752 – for the over-50s only). Another way round the restriction is to return to the UK for at least 24 hours after 90 days and obtain another green card! If you're British and have fully comprehensive insurance, a green card is essential, as it extends your comprehensive insurance abroad. There's usually no charge for a green card for a short period abroad (e.g. up to 5 days) but thereafter there may be a small charge (e.g. around £1 per day).

If you drive a British-registered car and spend a period longer than the validity of a green card on the continent, you may need to take out a special (i.e. expensive) European insurance policy or obtain insurance with a European company. If you wish to import a foreign-registered car into France permanently, you may find that your (foreign) insurance company will refuse to insure it or will do so only for a short period, although since 1st January 1993, EU residents can theoretically insure their cars in any EU country, so you may have no option but to buy a new car in France.

All French insurance companies provide an automatic green card (*carte internationale d'assurance automobile/carte verte* – even though it's yellow in France!), extending your normal insurance cover to most other European countries.

Contracts

You will initially be given a provisional insurance contract (*police d'assurance provisoire*) by your insurer or broker and will receive a definitive contract (*police définitive*) a few weeks later. With the contract is a green tear-off tab (*vignette*), which you must display in the windscreen of your vehicle as confirmation of insurance (*attestation d'assurance*). A special holder is usually provided. Each tab is valid for a limited period (e.g. six months) and you will be sent a replacement automatically (provided you've paid your premiums!). Non-display of the tab, even if it has fallen off the windscreen and is in the car, can result in a fine of around €150. See also **Insurance Contracts** on page 322. It's possible to insure a vehicle for less than a year (e.g. three months) and you can also insure a vehicle for a single journey over 1,000km (620mi).

Premiums

Insurance premiums are high in France – a reflection of the high accident rate, the large number of stolen and vandalised cars, and the high taxes (around 35 per cent) levied on car insurance. Premiums vary considerably according to numerous factors, including the type of insurance (see page 255) and car, your age and accident record and where you live. For example, premiums are highest in Paris and other cities and lowest in rural areas; they're lower for cars over three years old; drivers with less than three years' experience usually pay a 'penalty' and drivers under 25 pay higher premiums. However, the maximum penalty for young drivers is 100 per cent or double the normal premium. A surcharge is usually made when a car isn't garaged overnight. Some premiums are based on the number of kilometres (*kilomètrage*) driven each year. Always shop around and obtain a number of quotations but beware of companies making 'special offers' of low premiums, as your policy may be cancelled if you make a claim!

You can reduce your premium by choosing to pay a higher excess (*franchise*), e.g. the first €300 to €750 of a claim instead of the usual €125 to €250. If you're convicted of drunken or dangerous driving, your premium will be increased considerably, e.g. by up to 150 per cent. Value added tax (*TVA*) at 19.6 per cent is payable on insurance premiums.

No-claims Bonus

A foreign no-claims bonus is usually valid in France, but you must provide written evidence from your present or previous insurance company, not just an insurance renewal notice. You may also need an official translation. Always insist on having your no-claims bonus recognised, even if you don't receive the same reduction as you received abroad (shop around!). If you haven't held car insurance for two years, you're usually no longer entitled to a no-claims bonus in France.

A French no-claims bonus isn't as generous as those in some other countries and is usually 5 per cent for each year's accident-free driving up to a maximum of 50 per cent after ten years. If you have an accident for which you're responsible, you're usually required to pay a penalty (*malus*) or your bonus (*bonus*) is reduced. Your premium will be increased by 25 per cent each time you're responsible for an accident or 12.5 per cent if you're partly to blame, up to a maximum premium three-and-a-half times the standard premium. If you're judged to be less than 30 per cent responsible, you won't usually lose your no-claims bonus. However, if you've had the maximum bonus for three years, one accident won't reduce it even if you were at fault. All penalties are cancelled if you have no accidents for two years. There's no premium increase if your car is damaged while legally parked (although you must be able to prove it and identify the party responsible) or as a result of fire or theft, and you should still receive your bonus for the current year. The same normally applies to glass breakage.

Claims

Claims are decided on the information provided in accident report forms (*constat amiable d'accident de voiture/constat européen d'accident*) completed by drivers, as well as in reports by insurance company experts and police reports (see **Accidents** on page 277). You must notify your insurance company of a claim resulting from an accident within a limited period, e.g. two to five days. After reporting your car stolen, 30 days must elapse before an insurance company will consider a claim. **It often takes a long time – even years! – to resolve claims in France.**

If your car is damaged in an accident, you may take it to any reputable repairer (*carrosserie*), where the damage must usually be inspected and the repair sanctioned by your insurance company's assessor (*expert*), although sometimes an independent assessment may be permitted. Assessors normally visit different repairers on different days of the week, so you should arrange to take your car on the relevant day. (Some assessors have a weekly 'clinic' at their office where you can have damage inspected.) You should tell your insurer at least a day in advance so that he can advise the assessor. You may then be able to leave the car with the repairer or you may have to return it another day for the repair to be carried out. For minor repairs, an inspection may be unnecessary.

Cancellation

French insurance companies are forbidden by law to cancel third-party cover after a claim, except in the case of drunken driving or when a driver is subsequently disqualified from driving for longer than a month. A company can, however, refuse to renew your policy at the end of the current contract period, although they must give you two months' notice. If you find it difficult to obtain cover, the Bureau Central de Tarification can demand that the company of your choice provide you with cover, the premium being fixed by the Bureau.

Like other French insurance policies, a car insurance policy is automatically renewed annually unless you cancel it (*résilier*) in writing, and you must do so at least two months before the end of your annual insurance period, although the notice period is sometimes only a month and in a few cases three months, so you should check. You may cancel your insurance without notice if the premium is increased by more than the official index (*indice*), based on the Index of Construction Costs published by INSEE, the terms are altered, or your car has been declared a write-off or stolen. Policies can also be cancelled without notice for certain personal reasons, such as moving house, a change of job, divorce and retirement. Standard cancellation letters (*lettre type de résiliation*) are usually provided by insurance companies and brokers.

Breakdown Insurance

Breakdown insurance (*assurance dépannage*) is provided by car insurance companies and motoring organisations (see page 287). If you're motoring abroad or you live abroad and are motoring in France, it's important to have breakdown insurance (which may include limited holiday and travel insurance – see page 346), including repatriation for your family and your car in the event of an accident or breakdown. Most foreign breakdown companies provide multi-lingual, 24-hour centres where assistance is available for motoring, medical, legal and travel problems. Some organisations also provide economical annual motoring policies for those who frequently travel abroad, e.g. owners of holiday homes in France. **If your car is registered outside France, you may be unable to obtain breakdown insurance from a French insurance company.**

French insurance companies provide an optional accident and breakdown service (*contrat d'assistance*) for policyholders for around €30 per year. This is adopted by some 90 per cent of French motorists. The breakdown service usually covers the policyholder, his spouse, single dependent children, and parents and grandparents living under the same roof. The 24-hour telephone number of the breakdown service's head office is shown on the insurance tab affixed to your windscreen (see page 257). If you break down anywhere in France, you simply call the emergency number and give your location, and a recovery vehicle is sent to your aid.

Although accidents are covered anywhere in France, in the event of a breakdown you need to be at least a certain distance from your home, e.g. 25 or 50km (15 to 30mi). The service provides for towing your vehicle to the nearest garage and contributes towards the expenses incurred as a result of a breakdown or an accident, e.g. alternative transport and hotel bills. If your car is unusable for more than 48 hours in France and over five days abroad, your insurance company will usually pay for alternative transport home, e.g. first-class rail travel or car hire in France or tourist-class air travel abroad. The retrieval of your vehicle is also guaranteed from within France or abroad. Such policies may include cover for personal accident, injury and illness even when you aren't using your car, although they aren't adequate as holiday and travel insurance (see page 346). See also **Breakdown Services** on page 272.

RULES OF THE ROAD

The following guide to road rules may help you to adjust to driving in France. Don't, however, expect other motorists to adhere to them (most French drivers invent their own 'rules'). All motorists in France must be familiar with the highway code (*Code de la Route*), available from bookshops throughout France (around €15), when they take their test, but most promptly ignore it as soon as they've passed. Note that there isn't a single official highway code, but numerous versions of it produced by different publishers (e.g. Ediser and Rousseau)! The Prévention Routière (see page 278) produces a leaflet in English called *Keep Right* highlighting the major rules and conventions, and a similar guide, entitled *Welcome on* [sic] *France's Roads*, including a list of common fines, is downloadable from the Sécurité Routière website (🖥 http://www.securiteroutiere.gouv.fr – click on '*Les dépliants thématiques*' under '*Ressources*'). These are both rather basic, however. For more detailed guidance, you should obtain the *Guide Pratique et Juridique de l'Automobiliste* (Editions Grancher), which explains the rights and obligations of car owners. If your French motoring vocabulary is wanting, *Hadley's French Motoring Phrase Book & Dictionary* (Hadley Pager Info) is a handy reference.

Equipment

All motorists must carry a full set of spare bulbs and fuses. It's recommended also to carry a red breakdown triangle (compulsory if your car doesn't have hazard warning lights), a fire extinguisher and a first-aid kit. An 'F' nationality plate (*plaque de nationalité*) must be affixed to the rear of a French-registered car when motoring abroad. Most French registration plates incorporate the nationality letter. Similarly, drivers of foreign-registered cars in France must have the appropriate nationality plate affixed to the rear of their cars; you can be fined on the spot for not displaying one.

The wearing of seatbelts (*ceinture de sécurité*) is compulsory for both front- and rear-seat passengers (unless belts aren't fitted; front belts are mandatory on cars registered after January 1965 and rear seatbelts on cars registered after October 1978). Even passengers can be fined for not wearing a seatbelt (see **Fines & Penalties** on page 268). **If you have an accident and weren't wearing a seatbelt, your insurance company can refuse to pay a claim for personal injury.**

Studded tyres may be used from 1st November to 31st March (although this can be extended in bad weather) on vehicles weighing under 3.5 tonnes. Vehicles fitted with studded tyres or snow chains are restricted to a maximum speed of 90kph (56mph) and a '90' disc must be affixed to the rear. You can be fined for not having chains in your car in winter in mountain areas, even when there's no snow!

Lights & Horns

A recent government 'directive', which may become EU law, advises motorists to use dipped headlights (low beam) day and night when driving outside built-up areas between the end of October and the end of March (i.e. when the clocks are on winter time). In any case, it's illegal to drive on side (parking) lights (*codes* or *veilleuses*) at any time. It's also illegal to use full beam (*pleins phares*) when you're following a vehicle or when a vehicle is approaching from the opposite direction; failure to dip your lights can cost you a penalty point on your licence. You should also use dipped headlights (*codes*) in tunnels and when driving onto and off cross-Channel ferries. Side lights should be left on when parked at night on an unlit road.

You should flash your headlights only to warn other road users of your presence, although the French usually do so to mean "get out of my way" and occasionally to warn other motorists of police speed checks and road blocks, which is illegal and punishable by a fine. Hazard warning lights (*feux de détresse* or *warnings*) may be used to warn other drivers of an obstruction, e.g. an accident or a traffic jam and **should** be used when being towed.

The use of horns (*Klaxon*) in built-up areas is restricted to situations where it's necessary to avoid an accident; in any case, a horn should be used as a warning signal and not an expression of frustration (Parisian drivers please note!).

Mobile Phones

Mobile (cellular) phones (*portable* or *mobile*) shouldn't be used while driving, even with a 'hands-free' system. As with non-use of seatbelts, you can be fined on the spot (see **Fines & Penalties** on page 268).

Children

The driver is responsible for all passengers under 13, who should travel in the back of a car whenever possible. **It's dangerous to fit a child seat (even a rear-facing seat) in the front of a car fitted with a passenger airbag**; some airbags can be disabled for this purpose. Babies weighing under 9kg (20lb), i.e. aged under around nine months, must ride in a rear-facing baby seat. Infants weighing between 9 and 18kg (20 and 40lb), i.e. aged between around nine months and three or four years, must ride in a front-facing child seat and children over 18kg and up to ten years of age must ride on a raised seat and wear a standard seatbelt.

Priority

The traditional French rule that you should give way to traffic coming from your right (*priorité à droite*) still applies in some cases, and it's important to know what these are. **Failure to observe this rule is the cause of many accidents and punishable by fines and licence penalties (see page 268).** The rules are as follows:

- You must give way to the right:

  - At junctions marked by a triangular sign with a red border showing a black X, including junctions normally traffic-light controlled when the lights are out of order or flashing amber – see below. (Note that any junction can be denoted by this sign and not only a crossroads.)

  - At roundabouts (see below).

  - In car parks.

  - Wherever you see the sign '*Vous n'avez pas la priorité*' ('You don't have priority').

- You don't need to give way to the right (but should still take care):

  - At junctions marked by a triangular sign with a red border showing a black X and the words *Passage protégé* underneath.

  - At junctions marked by a triangular sign with a red border showing a broad vertical arrow with a thinner horizontal line through it.

  - Where the main road is joined by a private road or exit or a dirt track.

- Diamond-shaped yellow signs with a white border, which are posted at regular intervals (e.g. every 5km) on some national roads, indicate that you have priority at all junctions. If this sign has a thick diagonal black line through it, however, it means that you no longer have priority at every junction and must obey individual junction signs (see above).

If you're ever in doubt about who has the right of way, it's wise to give way (particularly to large trucks!), and you should **always** give way to trams and to emergency (ambulance, fire, police) and public utility (electricity, gas, telephone, water) vehicles when their lights are flashing or sirens sounding (or they don't look as if they're going to stop!).

Roundabouts

Vehicles on a roundabout (*sens giratoire* or *rond-point*) usually have priority and not those entering it, who are faced with a 'Give Way' sign ('*Cédez le passage*' or '*Vous n'avez pas la priorité'*). If there are no such signs (as most notably on the *Etoile* in Paris – see page 270), vehicles entering the roundabout have priority. British drivers should note that traffic flows anti-clockwise round roundabouts and not clockwise.

Traffic Lights

The sequence of French traffic lights (*feux*) is red, green, amber (yellow) and back to red. Amber means stop at the stop line; you may proceed only if the amber light appears after you've crossed the stop line or when stopping may cause an accident. Traffic lights are often suspended above the road, although most are on posts at the side, with smaller lights at eye level for motorists who are too close to see the main lights (an excellent idea). In Paris and other cities there's a two-second delay after one set of lights changes to red before the other set changes to green, to allow time for those who don't care to stop at red lights or cannot tell the difference between red and green (a significant proportion of Parisian drivers). You can be fined around €300 and penalised four licence points (see page 252) for driving through a red light.

An amber or green filter light, usually flashing and with a direction arrow, may be shown in addition to the main signal. This means that you may drive in the direction shown by the arrow, but must give priority to pedestrians or other traffic. Flashing amber lights are a warning to proceed with caution and are often used at junctions at night, in which case you should be **very** careful and observe the priority signs (see above). Occasionally you will see a flashing red light, meaning stop or no entry, e.g. at a railway crossing.

Level Crossings

Most level crossings have automatic barriers; red lights start flashing and a bell rings a few seconds before the barriers come down, indicating that you must stop. At crossings without barriers, a similar light system is in operation, and there may be the classic French sign, '*Un train peut en cacher un autre*'.

Road Markings

White lines mark the separation of traffic lanes. A solid single line means no overtaking in either direction. A solid line to the right of the centre line, i.e. on your side of the road, means that overtaking is prohibited in your direction. You may overtake only when there's a single broken line in the middle of the road or double lines with a broken line on your side of the road. Note, however, that if the gaps between the lines are short and the lines long you should overtake only slow-moving vehicles. No overtaking may also be shown by the international sign of two cars side by side (one red and one black). Processions, funeral corteges, horse riders and foot soldiers mustn't be overtaken at more than 30kph (18mph).

Don't drive in bus, taxi or cycle lanes (you can be fined for doing so) unless necessary to avoid a stationary vehicle or another obstruction. Bus lanes are identified by a continuous yellow line parallel to the kerb. Be sure to keep clear of tram lines and outside the restricted area, delineated by a line.

Stopping & Overtaking

If you want or need to stop on a main road, you must drive your car completely off the road, but beware of ditches and soft verges (*accotements non-stabilisés*).

The French are obsessive overtakers and will do so at the most dangerous moments, often cutting in sharply within inches of your front bumper. It's therefore wise to decelerate when being overtaken. You must indicate left before and while overtaking; on single carriageway roads you must indicate right when moving back into your lane, but this isn't necessary on dual-carriageways or motorways.

Many French motorists seem to have an aversion to driving in the right-hand lane on a three-lane road, in effect reducing it to two lanes, but it's an offence not to move over to the right-hand lane if it's safe to do so. It's illegal to overtake on an inside lane unless traffic is being channelled in a different direction, although this is a favourite manoeuvre among impatient French drivers.

Loads & Trailers

Cars mustn't be overloaded (particularly roof-racks), and luggage weight shouldn't exceed that recommended in manufacturers' handbooks. Carrying bicycles on the back of a car is illegal if they obscure the rear lights or the number plate. The police make spot checks and fine offenders around €75.

The maximum dimensions for caravans or trailers are 2.5m (8.2ft) wide and 11m (36ft) long, or a combined length of 18m (59ft) for car and caravan/trailer. No passengers may be carried in a moving caravan. On narrow roads, drivers towing a caravan or trailer are (where possible) required to slow or pull in to the side of the road to allow faster vehicles to overtake (although they rarely do). The speed limits for a towing car depend on the weight of the trailer or caravan (see **Speed Limits** on page 266). A special licence is required for towing heavy trailers or caravans (see **Driving Licence** on page 252).

Goods Vehicles

Goods vehicles over 7.5 tonnes are banned from roads between 10.00 Saturday and 22.00 Sunday, and from 22.00 on the eve of a public holiday to 22.00 on the day of the holiday. In Paris, goods vehicles aren't permitted to travel out of the city between 16.00 and 19.00 on Fridays to allow car drivers to get a head start for the weekend.

ROAD SIGNS

Although France generally adheres to international standard road signs, there are also many unique signs with instructions or information in French. Some of the most common are listed below:

Sign	Meaning
Absence de marquage	No road markings (usually after resurfacing)
Accotements non stabilisés	Soft verge (shoulder)
Allumez vos feux/lanternes/phares	Switch on your lights, e.g. for a tunnel
Attention travaux	Beware roadworks
Autres directions	Other directions or all directions other than those signposted
Bande d'arrêt d'urgence supprimée	No hard shoulder
Cédez le passage	Give way (usually shown underneath the international 'give way' sign)
Chaussée déformée	Uneven road surface
Déviation	Diversion
Eteignez vos feux/lanternes/phares	Switch off your lights, e.g. after leaving a tunnel
Gravillons	Loose chippings (after road resurfacing)
Impasse	No through road, cul-de-sac or dead end
Nids de poules	Potholes
Passage protégé	You have priority
Poids lourds (or *PL*)	Route for heavy traffic (lorries, etc.)
Ralentir	Slow down
Ralentisseur/Dos d'âne	Hump designed to slow motorists, usually with a 20 or 30kph speed restriction sign
Rappel	Reminder (of a speed limit or other restriction)
Risque de verglas	Risk of ice on road
Route barrée	Road closed
Sauf desserte locale	Access only, e.g. below a 'no entry' sign
Sauf riverains	Except residents, e.g. below a 'no entry' sign
Sens interdit	No entry
Sens unique	One-way street
Serrez à droite/gauche	Keep to the right/left
Sortie d'usine	Factory entrance
Stationnement interdit	No parking
Toutes directions	All directions, usually meaning all directions except the town centre (*centre ville*)
Véhicules légers (or *VL*)	Light vehicles (i.e. cars and small vans) as opposed to *poids lourds* (see above)
Véhicules lents	Slow vehicles (which are usually confined to the right-hand lane on a hill)
Vitesse réduite	Reduced speed limit
Vous n'avez pas la priorité	You don't have priority (i.e. 'give way to the right')

Always come to a complete stop when you're faced with a *Stop* sign and a solid white line across the road and ensure that you stop **behind** the line. (Junctions are a favourite spot for police patrols.)

The Autoroutes du Sud de la France publishes a booklet explaining motorway signs and symbols, which is available from motorway toll booths or from the ASF (☎ 08 92 70 70 01, 🖳 http://www.asf.fr). See also **French Roads** on page 270.

SPEED LIMITS

The following speed limits are in force throughout France:

Road	Speed Limits (see notes below)
Motorways	130/110kph (81/69mph)
Dual-carriageways	110/100kph (69/62mph)
Other roads	90/80kph (56/50mph)
Built-up areas/towns	50kph (31mph) or as signposted

- Speed limits are reduced in rain (*par temps de pluie*), when the second limit shown above applies. When visibility is less than 50m (162ft), e.g. in fog or heavy rain, speed limits are automatically reduced to 50kph on **all** roads.

- Speed limits in built-up areas (*agglomération*) such as small towns and villages often aren't posted. Unless a lower speed limit (such as 40 or 45kph) is posted, the limit is 50kph and starts with the town or village's name sign, which usually has black letters on a white background with a red border. The end of the speed limit is indicated by the town's sign with a diagonal red line through it. A village sign with white letters on a dark blue background doesn't indicate a speed restriction unless otherwise indicated.

- Speed limits also apply to cars towing a trailer or caravan, provided the trailer's weight doesn't exceed that of the car. If the trailer's weight exceeds that of the car by less than 30 per cent, you're limited to 65kph (39mph); if the trailer is more than 30 per cent heavier than the car, you mustn't exceed 45kph (28mph). A plate showing the permitted maximum speed must be displayed at the rear of the trailer. Cars towing trailers with restricted speeds aren't permitted to use the left lane on a three-lane motorway.

- Vehicles fitted with studded tyres or snow chains are restricted to 90kph (56mph) and a '90' plate must be displayed at the rear.

- For two years after passing your driving test in France, you're designated a 'young' driver (*jeune conducteur*), irrespective of your age, and must display a *disque réglementaire* consisting of a red capital letter A on a white background on the back of any car being driven. During this period you mustn't exceed 80kph (50mph) on roads where the limit is normally 90kph, 100kph (62mph) on roads with a 110kph limit, or 110kph (69mph) on motorways with a 130kph limit. Visitors who have held a licence for less than two years are also subject to these speed restrictions, but aren't required to display a disc.

- There's a **minimum** speed of 80kph (50mph) on motorways in the outside (overtaking) lane during daylight, in dry weather on level surfaces and in good visibility, i.e. perfect conditions.

- The word *rappel* (reminder) is often displayed beneath speed restriction signs to remind motorists that the limit is still in force.

- Sleeping policemen (*ralentisseur* or *dos d'âne*) are common on many major and minor roads and are often accompanied by a 30kph (18mph) sign; if you don't slow down, you risk damaging your vehicle!

The use of radar speed checks is widespread (including on motorways). Around 1,000 of these are already in place with an additional 1,000 due to be installed in 2006/07 (find out where they are on 🖳 http://www.controleradar.org). Police also use concealed cameras to snap speeding motorists. French drivers often flash their headlights to warn other motorists of speed checks, although this is illegal, as are radar-detection devices (see **Fines & Penalties** below). Speed limits are enforced by motorcycle traffic police operating in pairs.

If your car has a GPS system, you can be 'caught' speeding by a new Big Brother-style satellite surveillance system called '*Lavia*' (short for *Limitation s'adaptant à la vitesse autorisée*). Note also that motorway toll tickets are timed and you can be convicted of speeding if you complete a section of motorway in less than a certain time!

French drivers routinely speed everywhere, generally at least 20kph above the speed limit and often far more: a recent motoring magazine survey (in Var) found that the **average** speed on motorways was 160kph (100mph) and on *routes nationales* 107kph (67mph)! Drivers rarely slow down for villages and are often irritated by motorists who do so. Usually you're 'allowed' to be 10 per cent above the limit, so if you're clocked at 55kph in a 50kph zone, or 99kph in an 90kph zone, you won't normally be penalised – but don't bank on it! See **Fines & Penalties** below.

TRAFFIC POLICE

In France, the *gendarmerie nationale*, which is actually a branch of the army, is responsible for road patrols, and *gendarmes* use both cars and motorcycles. The police can stop motorists (called a *contrôle*) and ask for identification and car papers at any time (and also check your tyres, lights, etc.). These may include your passport or residence permit, driving licence (French if held), vehicle registration document (*carte grise*) and insurance certificate. It's wise to make a copy of all these documents and keep the originals on your person (you should never leave them in the car). Police may accept copies, provided you present the originals at a *gendarmerie* within five days; if you don't have even copies of the required documents, you will be fined (see **Fines & Penalties** below). If a vehicle isn't registered in your name, you will also need a letter of authorisation from the owner. If you're driving a rented foreign-registered vehicle, you should ask the rental company for a 'hired/leased vehicle certificate'. You're entitled to ask the name and particulars of any policeman or *gendarme* who stops you, but it's probably better to do so **after** you've found out what you've been stopped for!

Fines & Penalties

Fines can be imposed for a range of traffic offences. For offences not involving third parties (e.g. exceeding the speed limit or failing to stop at a *Stop* sign), police can demand an on-the-spot fine of up to €135. On-the-spot fines are commonly applied to non-resident foreigners, whose vehicles are usually impounded if they're unable to pay. (French police may take you to a bank to allow you to withdraw cash!) It's well known that French traffic police target foreigners, although it's naturally officially denied. (It certainly looks suspicious when police produce pre-written tickets in English!)

Residents who are unable to pay fines on the spot are given 30 days to pay and fines are automatically increased (significantly) if they aren't paid on time. A 30 per cent reduction is granted to residents who pay a fine on the spot or within 24 hours. You can opt for your case to go to court rather than pay a fixed penalty, in which case you must usually pay a deposit (*amende forfaitaire*). The papers are sent to a police court (*tribunal de police*), where the case is dealt with in your absence. The case can be dismissed (extremely rare), the €135 fine confirmed (actually a €129 fine plus €6 costs) or the fine increased. You receive the verdict in the form of an *ordonnance pénale* and have 30 days to appeal against the judgement, should you wish to do so.

If you receive a fine by post (e.g. having been caught speeding by a camera), you must pay it within seven days or the fine is increased: e.g. a €90 fine becomes a €135 fine after seven days and €345 after a month.

Speeding

Speeding fines vary with the type of road and driving conditions. On a dry country road, for example, the fine for exceeding the limit by less than 40kph is €135 (reduced to €90 if paid within three days) and for exceeding it by between 40 and 50kph, €1,500; if you're more than 50kph over the limit, you must attend a tribunal, which will decide the fine to be imposed. If you fail to pay a fine within 30 days, it's automatically increased (e.g. a €135 fine rises to €375).

Under the licence points system (see page 252), motorists also lose one to four points for speeding, depending on how many kph they were exceeding the limit by: up to 20kph (one point), between 20 and 30kph (two points), between 30 and 40kph (three points). If you're more than 40kph over the limit, your licence is confiscated. If you're apprehended for speeding in your first year or for not displaying the 'A' disc, you will be penalised four points irrespective of your excess speed.

Drunk Driving

If you're found to have between 50 and 80mg of alcohol per 100ml of blood, you're fined between €135 and €750 and lose three points from your licence. Above 80mg, you can be fined up to €4,500 and lose your licence. Drunken drivers can be jailed for up to two years (or have to do four years' community service), without even having caused a serious accident. If you maim or kill someone, you can be faced with a €30,000 fine and four years in prison. See also **Drinking & Driving** on page 278.

Other Offences

Fines and penalties for other offences include the following:

- One point for straddling an unbroken white line.

- Three points for crossing an unbroken white line.

- €11 to €38 for failing to present necessary documents on demand (rising to €135 if you don't present them within five days).

- €35 to €150 and three points for changing direction without warning or driving on the hard shoulder of a motorway.

- €135 for carrying a child under ten in the front seat of a car (other than in an approved child seat) or a child under 13 without a seatbelt or child seat.

- €135 for parking or driving in a bus lane (and cameras have been set up in Paris to catch those who do so).

- €35 to €135 and two points for using a mobile phone while driving (note that these also apply to the use of a 'hands-free' system, although you may get away with a lesser punishment).

- €135 and two points for stopping or driving on the central reservation of a motorway.

- €135 and three penalty points for not wearing a crash helmet or seatbelt (note that passengers can also be fined, although only the driver loses points).

- €135 to €750 and one point for failing to dip your headlights when necessary.

- €135 to €750 and two points for accelerating while being overtaken or failing to move into a lane to the right to allow another vehicle to overtake.

- €135 to €750 and four points for ignoring priority signs or failing to stop at a stop sign or red light.

- €135 to €750 and three points for driving on the wrong side of the road (Britons beware!) and dangerous overtaking (e.g. crossing an unbroken white line), parking or stopping.

- €135 to €750 and three points for failing to leave at least a two-second gap between your car and the one in front (which applies to 90 per cent of motorists). Note that police patrol some motorways from the air to catch tail-gaters.

- €1,500 and the suspension of your licence for using a radar detector.

If you're found responsible for an accident in which someone is injured, you can lose four points and, if someone is killed, six points. For multiple offences (e.g. driving through a red light on the wrong side of the road and killing a pedestrian), you can lose up to eight points. Officially you 'only' lose six points for refusing to take a breathalyser test or being over the limit, although you will usually have your licence withdrawn on the spot and receive a suspension.

Punishment for infringing the rules of the road can be **very** severe. A new category of offence has recently been created, relating to drivers who 'deliberately put the lives of others in danger', for which you can be fined €15,000 and imprisoned for up to three years. If you're found responsible for the death of another road user, you can be fined up to €100,000 and imprisoned for up to seven years.

FRENCH ROADS

France has a good road system that includes everything from motorways (*autoroute*) to forest dirt tracks (*route forestière*). French motorways are excellent and most other main roads are also very good, although roads are generally poorer in areas with low traffic density (i.e. most of rural France). Roads are classified as follows and are identified by their prefix and colour-coded markers:

Prefix	Colour	Classification
A (*autoroute*)	Blue	Motorways – usually toll roads (*autoroute à péage*); usually marked red/yellow on maps
E (*route européenne*)	Green	European motorways or motorway-standard trunk roads traversing a number of countries, e.g. the *Autoroute de l'Est* (A4) is also the E25
N (*route nationale*)	Red	National trunk roads (financed by the central or regional government); usually shown in red
D (*route départementale*)	Yellow	Departmental roads (funded by departments); marked in yellow or white on maps
C (*route communale*)	White	Minor roads (funded by communes); white on most maps
R (*route rurale*)	White	Minor roads in rural areas; white on most maps
RF (*route forestière*)	Green	Forest tracks; shown only on local maps

Motorways

France boasts one of Europe's best motorway (*autoroute*) networks, totalling over 9,500km (some 6,000mi). Because of the continuous expansion of the network (2005 saw the completion of a continuous motorway route from Calais to Spain via Bordeaux and 2006 of the A89 from Bordeaux to Switzerland, barring a short section in Dordogne), you shouldn't use a motoring atlas that's more than a few years out of date. A good guide to French motorways and their services is *Bonne Route!* by Anna Fitter (Anthony Nelson). Because of the toll system (see below), driving on motorways is considered a luxury by many French people; consequently, they have the lowest traffic density of any European motorways and are France's safest roads (although that isn't saying a great deal – see **Accidents** on page 277) and your risk of dying on a motorway – with the notable exception of the *Périphérique* (see below) – is around four times lower than on any other road.

Some motorways have colourful names, such as *Autoroute du Soleil* (A6/A7), *Autoroute l'Océane* (A11), *Autoroute des Deux Mers* (A61). Signs on motorways inform you about interesting local sights and features, and regional motorway maps are distributed free by operators. On motorways there's an excellent system of electronic information boards on overhead gantries, where everything from safety warnings to the time and temperature is displayed.

Tolls

Most motorways are toll roads (*à péage*), which are among the most expensive in Europe, although there are plans to privatise half the motorways in southern France, which could reduce charges by up to 30 per cent. Motorway travel costs an average of €0.07 per kilometre for a car, e.g. €65 from Calais to Montpellier and €75 from Calais to Menton (not a great deal less than it costs to fly with a budget airline from London to Nice – and the petrol in an aeroplane is free!). There are five toll categories on most motorways, e.g. motorhomes and cars towing trailers or caravans are charged more than cars alone. Rates aren't standardised throughout the country and vary with the age of the motorway and the services provided (some are two or three times higher per km than others). A new system of tolls has been introduced in some areas with higher tolls during peak periods. There are no tolls on the sections of motorways around cities. An *Autoroute Tarifs* leaflet and other traffic information is available from the Association des Sociétés Françaises d'Autoroutes (☎ 08 92 68 10 77, ⌨ http://www.autoroutes.fr).

On most motorways, a ticket is issued at or shortly after each joining point. At the toll-booth (*péage*) you may need to press a button to obtain your ticket or it may be ejected automatically. When you reach another toll-booth or exit from the motorway, hand your ticket to the attendant; the toll due is usually shown on a display. Tolls may also be levied at intermediate points. On some stretches, tickets aren't issued and a fixed toll is charged. On these roads there may be unmanned toll-booths for those with the correct change, shown by the sign '*Monnaie exacte*'. Throw the correct amount into the basket and wait for the light to change green. If you don't have the correct change, choose a lane with the sign '*Sans monnaie*' (which means 'No change' and not 'No money'!). There's often a separate lane with a '*CB*' (for *carte bleue*) sign where you can pay by bank or credit card, provided it has a microchip (there's no need to enter your PIN). Insert your ticket first, then your card and press the red button if you want a receipt. There's usually less of a queue in *CB* lanes, which are also handy if you really don't have any money!

If you use motorways regularly, it's worth investing in a remote control 'box' (*télébadge*) to stick inside your windscreen, which enables you to drive through the *Télépéage* lane without even having to wind down your window (and usually without having to queue); the toll is deducted automatically from your bank account. You pay an annual subscription of between €10 and €20 depending on the region (more in the Alps) plus a deposit of around €30, which is refundable when you return the box (both added to your first bill), but if you use the motorway on your way to and from work you can benefit from a reduction of up to 35 per cent in toll charges. *Télébadges* can be obtained from offices of your local motorway company (Société d'Autoroutes – listed under *Autoroutes* in the yellow pages), which are normally situated near toll stations. You need to supply your bank details, proof of address and, to qualify for the work-use discount, confirmation from your employer that you drive to and from work. Some 600,000 people use the system.

Tolls are also levied for the use of major tunnels, e.g. Mont Blanc (Chamonix to Entrèves, Italy, 11.6km/7.2mi), Fréjus (Modane to Bardonecchia, Italy, 12.8km/8mi) and Bielsa (Aragnouet to Bielsa, Spain, 3km/1.86mi), and bridges, e.g. the Tancarville, Saint-Nazaire and Normandie.

Rest Areas & Service Stations

Most motorways (and *routes nationales* – see below) have rest areas (*aire de repos* or simply *aire*) every 10 to 20km (6 to 12mi) with toilets, drinking water and picnic tables. Toilets and telephones are also provided at motorway toll booths. Camping isn't allowed in rest areas, and toll charges are valid for 24 hours only.

Twenty-four hour service areas (*aire de service*) are provided every 30 to 50km (19 to 31mi), offering petrol stations, vending machines, shops (selling newspapers, gifts, food, snacks and hot drinks), a café or self-service restaurant, and possibly an *à la carte* restaurant. Service areas cater for babies, young children, the elderly and the disabled, and some also have motels and provide tourist information services. Service stations often also have facilities for minor car repairs. In the summer, roadside attractions are set up at service areas in an effort to stress and tiredness. These may include bouncy castles and clown shows for children, free nappies and meals for babies, and eye tests and even massages for drivers! Not surprisingly, service stations have better (i.e. cleaner) toilet facilities than rest areas.

Although they're usually of a high standard, motorway restaurants are mainly self-service rather than *haute cuisine* and don't offer the best value. You will save money by leaving the motorway and finding an inexpensive and friendly local establishment. Petrol prices on motorways are the highest in France and it's much cheaper to fill up at supermarkets, although garages within 10km (6mi) of a motorway are allowed to advertise their prices on the motorway, which has helped to bring down motorway prices in some areas.

Breakdown Services

If you break down on a motorway, you must park your car on the hard shoulder (*bande d'arrêt d'urgence*) and place an emergency triangle 30m (100ft) behind it. Free emergency telephones (*poste d'urgence*) are mounted on orange posts every 2km (1.25mi) on motorways and you may walk along the hard shoulder to the nearest phone, indicated by arrows. Each telephone is numbered and directly connected to the motorway security centre (Centre de Sécurité). Say whether you've broken down (*tombé en panne*) or have had an accident (*accidenté*), and give the number of your telephone and the location of your car, i.e. before (*avant*) or after (*après*) the emergency telephone. A breakdown truck (*dépanneur*) or first-aid help (*service de secours*) will be sent, as required. The standard charge for the recovery of a broken-down vehicle from a motorway is around €97 (€119.50 if it weighs over 1.8 tonnes), which applies whether the vehicle can be towed to a rest area for repair or needs to be taken to a garage or any other location designated by you (within reason!). A multi-language service is provided in English, German, Italian and Spanish on some motorways, e.g. the A7 between Lyon and Marseille.

Minor repairs of up to around half an hour are usually done on the spot. For anything more serious you will need to be towed to a garage. There are fixed charges for emergency repairs and towing, e.g. €65 for requesting a breakdown service and around €100 for repairing a vehicle on the spot (up to 30 minutes' work) or towing it up to 5km (3mi) beyond the next motorway exit. Note that charges are increased by 50 per cent for breakdowns between 18.00 and 06.00 on weekdays and throughout the weekend and public holidays. If you're unable to continue your journey, breakdown companies must provide free transport to take you and your passengers off the motorway and provide assistance in finding accommodation and alternative transport. See also **Breakdown Insurance** on page 259.

Other Roads

Unlike French motorways, main trunk roads (*route nationale*) are jammed by drivers (including those of heavy goods vehicles) who are reluctant to pay or cannot afford the high motorway tolls. If you must get from A to B in the shortest possible time, there's no alternative to the motorway (apart from taking a plane or train). However, if you aren't in too much of a hurry, want to save money **and** wish to see something of France, you should avoid motorways. The money saved on tolls can pay for a good meal or an (inexpensive) hotel room. *Routes nationales* and other secondary roads are often straight and many are dual carriageways, on which you can usually make good time at (legal) speeds of between 90 and 110kph (56 to 68mph). On the other hand, many trunk roads pass through towns and villages, where the limit is reduced to 50kph (30mph), which can make for slow progress.

All 'N' and 'D' class roads (see page 270) have white kilometre stones on the right and some have smaller stones every 100m (325ft). On 'N' class roads the tops of kilometre stones are painted red and have the road number painted on the side. Kilometre stones on 'D' class roads have yellow tops. In general, signposting is good, even in the most remote rural areas, thanks largely to the vast numbers of tourists who invade France each year. However, in some areas you will find that signs disappear or everywhere is signposted except where you want to go, and signs out of towns may be non-existent. Usually only large towns or cities are signposted as you approach a ring road system, so you should plan your journey accordingly and make a note of the major destinations on your route. Road signs in towns and cities are often mind-boggling in their number and variety. **Note that signposts indicating straight ahead usually point at or across the intended road, i.e. to the left or right, rather than vertically as in most other countries.** In towns, only the town centre (*centre ville*) and 'all directions' (*toutes directions*) may be signposted. If you don't want the town centre, simply follow the *toutes directions* or 'other directions' (*autres directions*) signs until you (hopefully) see a sign for where you want to go.

On mountain roads, driving conditions can be treacherous or even prohibitive, and studded tyres or chains may be obligatory (see **Equipment** on page 260). Many mountain passes are closed in winter (check with a French motoring organisation).

Paris

Paris is a beautiful city but should be avoided at all cost when driving, especially if you need to park there, which is usually almost impossible. If you cannot avoid driving in Paris, at least give the *Place Charles de Gaulle/Étoile* (at the top of the *Champs-Elysées*) a wide berth. One of the worst free-for-alls in the whole of Europe, it's a vast roundabout where 12 roads converge, all with (theoretical) *priorité à droite*. Because of the impossibility of apportioning blame in this circus, if you have an accident, responsibility is automatically shared equally between the drivers concerned, irrespective of who had right of way. The *Place de la Concorde* is, if anything, even worse, and a road to avoid unless you have a death-wish is the *Boulevard périphérique* (usually referred to simply as the *Périphérique*), an eight-lane race track around the city centre on which there's an average of one fatal accident a day! (There's an inner ring road, which is slower but safer.)

Information

In June each year, the French Ministry of Transport issues a 'wily bison' map (*Carte de Bison Futé*) showing areas of congestion and providing information about alternative routes (*itinéraire bis*), indicated by yellow or green signs with the word *Bis*. The map is available free from petrol stations and tourist offices in France and from French Government Tourist Offices abroad as well as via the internet (🖳 http://www.bison-fute.equipement.gouv.fr). Information about long-term roadworks can be found on 🖳 http://www.trafic.asf.fr. There are around 90 information rest areas throughout France, indicated by a black 'i' and an *Information Bison Futé* sign. Green-arrowed holiday routes (*flèches vertes*) avoiding large towns and cities are also recommended. Colour-coded traffic days and traffic jams (*orange* for bad, *rouge* for very bad and *noir* for 'stay at home') are announced on the radio and television.

Up-to-date information about roads can be obtained by phoning the Centre Régional d'Information et de Coordination Routières (☎ 08 06 02 20 22), by tuning in to *Autoroute Info* on 107.7FM or via the internet (e.g. 🖳 http://www.cofiroute.fr, 🖳 http://www.info-autoroute.com or 🖳 http://www.trafic.asf.fr). General information about motorways, tolls and driving in France can be obtained from French Government Tourist Offices abroad (see page 402). Disabled travellers can contact the Ministère de l'Equipement, des Transports et du Logement, Direction des Routes, Service du Contrôle des Autoroutes (☎ 01 40 81 21 22). Details of planned new roads are provided in *The Best Places to Buy a Home in France* (Survival Books).

FRENCH DRIVERS

France has some of the most dangerous drivers (*chauffard*) in Europe, who seem to use their brakes only when their horn or headlights don't work. Foreigners (particularly *les rosbifs*) should be aware that many French drivers become apoplectic when overtaken by them. Most French people's personalities (yes, women's too!) change the moment they get behind the wheel of a car, when even the gentlest person can become an impatient, intolerant and even aggressive maniac with an unshakeable conviction in his own immortality. The French themselves have a quite different opinion of their driving: according to a survey by the Association Française de Prévention des Comportements au Volant, no fewer than 98 per cent consider themselves to be 'courteous' and 'responsible' – a sad case of self-delusion.

The French revere racing drivers (Alain Prost et al) and the majority of drivers are assailed by an uncontrollable urge to drive everywhere at maximum speed (women – young and old – often drive faster than men). To a French person, the racing line on a bend (which usually means driving on the wrong side of the road!) is *de rigueur* and overtaking is an obligation; me first (*moi d'abord*) is the French driver's motto.

Even when not overtaking or cutting corners, the French have an unnerving tendency to wander across the centre line, threatening a head-on collision with anything coming in the opposite direction. When following another vehicle (and even when they have no intention of overtaking it), French drivers sit a few metres (or even centimetres) from its rear bumper trying to push it along irrespective of traffic density, road and weather conditions or the prevailing speed limit. They're among Europe's worst tail-gaters, despite a recent (and ludicrously unenforceable) law forbidding driving within two seconds of the car in front (referred to as the *distance de sécurité* and sometimes shown on motorways by arrows marked on the road surface). Always try to leave a large gap between your car and the one in front in order to give yourself time to stop should the vehicles in front decide to get together, without the inevitable tail-gater behind you ploughing into your boot. Observe the simple rule: the closer the car is behind you, the further you should be from the vehicle in front.

Beware of lorries and buses on narrow roads, as lorry drivers believe they have a divine right to three-quarters of the road and expect you to pull over. Don't, however, pull over too far, as many rural roads have soft verges and ditches.

What makes driving in France even more hazardous is that for many months of the year French roads are jammed with assorted foreigners, including many (such as the British) who don't even know which side of the road to drive on and whose driving habits vary from exemplary to suicidal.

Most French drivers have little respect for traffic rules, particularly anything to do with parking (in Paris, a car is a device used to create parking spaces). French drivers wear their dents with pride and there are many (many) dented cars in France – particularly in Paris (a '75' registration number acts as a warning to other motorists to keep well clear).

But don't be too discouraged by the road hogs and tail-gaters. Driving in France can be a pleasant experience (Paris excepted), particularly when using country roads that are almost traffic-free most of the time. If you come from a country where traffic drives on the left, rest assured that most people quickly get used to driving on the 'wrong' side of the road. Just take it easy at first, particularly at junctions, and bear in mind that there are other foreigners around just as confused as you are!

MOTORCYCLES

The French are keen motorcyclists and there are more bikers per head of population in France than in any other European country, although there's only one French motorbike manufacturer: Voxan, whose factory is at Issoire in Puy-de-Dôme (🖳 http://www.voxan.com). Perhaps for this reason, the French aren't generally prejudiced against bikers, as motorists are in many other countries. Nevertheless, motorcycling is a dangerous pursuit: over 20 per cent of road casualties are motorcyclists and, over the same distance, a motorcyclist is 14 times as likely to have an accident than a car driver (although one has to wonder whether this is due to intrinsic dangers of motorcycle riding or to the way most motorcyclists flout the rules of the road ...)

Some rules apply to all motorcycles (collectively known as *deux-roues*); others apply to certain types of motorcycle only. Speed limits for all motorcycles are the same as for cars (see page 266) – although you wouldn't think so. Third party insurance is always necessary, as well as passenger insurance. All bikes must also be registered (see page 249), have registration plates and carry a nationality sticker (*plaque de nationalité*). Approved crash helmets must be worn by all motorcycle riders and passengers. Motorcycles above 50cc are permitted to use motorways (tolls are lower than for cars, although the cost of a long journey can still be considerable). Dipped headlamps must be used at all times by riders of motorcycles over 125cc (see also below).

When parking a bike in a city, lock it securely and if possible chain it to an immovable object. Take extra care when parking in a public place overnight, particularly in Paris, where bike theft is rife.

Mopeds

From the age of 14, children can ride a moped (variously known as a *cyclomoteur*, *scooter*, *vélomoteur* or *Mobylette*, the last being a trade name) with an engine capacity below 50cc capable of a maximum speed of 45kph (28mph) – despite the contorsions of riders attempting to eke an extra kph or two from their machines. Mopeds must be registered (see page 249) and riders without a full licence must take a test (*brevet de sécurité routière/BSR*) consisting of a theory paper (*attestation scolaire de sécurité routière/ASSR1*), taken at school, and five hours of practical training, four and a half of which must be on public roads, with a driving school (at a cost of around €75). Third-party insurance is necessary, and a metal tab with the owner's name (*plaque de nom*) must be attached to the handlebars.

Mopeds aren't permitted on motorways, and riders must use cycle paths where provided. Two-stroke petrol (*mélange deux-temps*) is available at most petrol stations, although an electric version of the classic Solex (last manufactured in the

1980s, although imitations are still built), known as the *E-solex*, may be available in the near future.

Mopeds can be lethal in the wrong hands (most teenagers have as much road sense as hedgehogs and rabbits) and hundreds are killed each year. If you have a child with a moped, it's important to impress upon him the need to take care (particularly in winter) and not take unnecessary risks, e.g. always observe traffic signs and signal before making manoeuvres.

Other Motorbikes

Sixteen-year-olds can ride a motorcycle of up to 125cc (officially known as a *moto légère*), for which they require a licence *A1*. The requisite theory test, the *ASSR2*, can be taken at school. Eighteen-year-olds can begin 'progessive training' (*formation progressive*) for a full motorcycle (*motocyclette* or *moto*) licence (*A*), although they're limited to bikes below 34 horsepower until the age of 21. If you aren't at school, you can take an *attestation de sécurité routière* (*ASR*), which takes the place of the *ASSR1* and *2*, through an adult education provider such as GRETA. A car licence (*B*) entitles you to ride a motorcycle of up to 125cc, provided you've been driving for at least two years (although you must retake the theory exam if you've held a licence for more than five years without riding a motorcycle). However, it's recommended that you take a course of riding lessons with a *moto-école*, which costs around €300.

ACCIDENTS

If you're unfortunate enough to be involved in a car accident (*accident d'auto*), you must do the following **in addition to** the standard procedures that apply in all countries:

1. Stop immediately. Switch on your hazard warning lights and place a warning triangle at the edge of the road 30m (100ft) behind your car, ensuring that it can be seen from at least 100m (325ft).

2. If anyone is injured, immediately call the fire service (*sapeurs-pompiers*) by dialling 18. Emergency phones (orange pillars with SOS written on them) are positioned at 2km (1.2mi) intervals on motorways and every 4km (2.5mi) on other roads. To use them press and release the button marked *pour demander au secours* ('to summon help') and speak into the metal grille. Give the number of the telephone and as many other details as possible. The mobile (cellular) phone emergency number is 112. **If you take an injured person to hospital yourself and he dies in your car, you could be sued for a great deal of money!** If there are no injuries and if damage to vehicles or property isn't serious, it's unnecessary to call the police, unless another driver has obviously been drinking or appears incapable of driving. **You must never leave the scene of an accident, however minor, before completing this procedure, as this is a serious offence.**

3. If either you or the other driver(s) involved decides to call the police, don't move your vehicle or allow other vehicles to be moved unless this is necessary to unblock the road.

4. In the case of an accident involving two or more vehicles, it's standard practice for drivers to complete an accident report form (*constat amiable*) provided by insurance companies (keep one in your car). As the name implies, this is an 'amicable statement', where drivers agree (more or less) on what happened. It isn't obligatory to complete a *constat*, although an insurance claim made out in any other form can take longer to process. If your French isn't good, you may complete a *constat* in another language. At the bottom of the form there are a number of statements describing the circumstances of the accident. You should tick the boxes that apply, add up the number of ticks and enter the number in the box at the bottom. This prevents the form from being altered later.

    It's important to check the details included on forms completed by other drivers against official documents, particularly those relating to a driver's identity, driving licence, car registration and insurance details. Drivers must sign each other's forms. Always check exactly what the other driver has written before signing. **Don't sign a statement, particularly one written in French, unless you're certain you understand and agree with every word.** In the event of a dispute, a local bailiff (*huissier de justice*) should be called to prepare an independent report (*constat d'huissier*). If the police attend the scene of an accident, they will also make their own report.

If you witness an accident or its aftermath, it's a criminal offence not to try to assist anyone in danger, at least by calling for help, and you can be fined up to €75,000 and imprisoned for up to five years for failing to do so.

France has a national fund, the Fonds de Garantie Automobile (FGA, 🖳 http://www. fga.fr) that pays compensation to people injured and vehicles damaged by hit-and-run drivers. However, you can claim for damage to your vehicle only if the person responsible can be identified and is uninsured or insolvent. To make a claim, those in the south-east of France should contact the Marseille office at 39 boulevard Vincent Delpuech, 13255 Marseille Cedex 06 (☎ 04 91 83 27 27); those in all other parts of France should contact the Paris office at 64 rue de France, 94682 Vincennes Cedex (☎ 01 43 98 77 00). Accident prevention is promoted by Prévention Routière (☎ 01 44 15 27 00, 🖳 http://www.preventionroutiere.fr). Other useful contacts are the Fondation Anne-Cellier Contre l'Insécurité Routière (☎ 01 45 00 95 35) and the Ligue Contre la Violence Routière (☎ 01 45 32 91 00).

DRINKING & DRIVING

Alcohol is reckoned to be a major factor in some 40 per cent of France's road accidents, i.e. over 2,000 deaths per year. The permitted blood alcohol concentration is 50mg of alcohol per 100ml of blood, but the amount you can drink and remain below the limit depends on whether you regularly imbibe, and your sex and weight. An 'average' man can generally drink a maximum of two (12cl) glasses of wine, two small glasses of beer or two 4cl measures of spirits; for most women the limits are even lower. Note that your alcohol level rises considerably when you drink on an empty stomach (which is why the French eat lots of bread!). **The safest thing to do is not to drink at all when driving.**

Random breath tests (*Alcooltest*) can be (and are) carried out by the police, and motorists who are involved in accidents or who infringe motoring regulations are routinely tested for alcohol and drugs. If you're found to have more than 25mg of alcohol per 100ml of air in your lungs, you're obliged to take a blood test.

Penalties usually depend on the level of alcohol in your blood and whether you're involved in an accident (see **Fines & Penalties** on page 268). **If you have an accident while under the influence of alcohol, your car and health insurance could be nullified. This means that you must pay your own and any third party's car repairs, medical expenses and other damages.** Your car insurance premium will also be increased by up to 150 per cent.

CAR THEFT

Car theft is rampant in France, which has one of the highest rates of vehicle theft – and car burning! – in Europe (the theft of contents or accessories from motor vehicles is even more commonplace). If you drive anything other than a worthless heap, you should have theft insurance that includes personal effects (see **Car Insurance** on page 255). It's particularly important to protect your car if you own a model that's desirable to car thieves, e.g. most new sports and executive cars, which are often stolen to order by professional crooks. In Provence and on the Côte d'Azur stolen cars often find their way to Africa and may already be on a ferry by the time the owners report them stolen.

It's wise to have your car fitted with an alarm, an ignition disabling system or other anti-theft device, plus a visible deterrent, such as a steering or gear lock. Even a good security system won't stop someone breaking into your car (which usually takes most thieves a matter of seconds) and may not prevent your car being stolen, but it will at least make it more difficult and may persuade a thief to look for an easier target.

When leaving your car unattended, store any valuables (including clothes) in the boot or out of sight. **Never** leave the key in your car, even when you're paying for petrol, and never leave your original car papers in your car, even if you have copies. If possible avoid parking in long-term car parks, as these are favourite hunting grounds for car thieves. Foreign-registered cars, particularly camper vans and motorhomes, are popular targets, particularly when parked in ports. When parking overnight or when it's dark, parking in a well-lit area may deter thieves. If your car is stolen or anything is stolen from it, report this immediately to the police in the area where it was stolen. You can report by telephone but must go to the station to complete a statement. Don't, however, expect the police to find anything or even take any interest in your loss; of the 250,000 vehicles stolen each year, only around two-thirds are recovered. Report a theft to your insurance company as soon as possible.

Highway Piracy

Highway piracy (*les pirates de la route*) is an increasing problem in some areas, where foreign drivers are often targets. Gangs deliberately bump or ram cars to make drivers stop, usually late at night when there's little traffic about. A driver may also pose as a plain clothes policeman and try to get you to stop by flashing a fake badge or setting up a bogus road block. In the worst cases, thieves take not just the car and its contents, but even the clothes the victims are wearing. Travelling at night is becoming increasingly hazardous and should be avoided if possible. See also **Crime** on page 513.

PARKING

Parking in most towns and cities (Paris excepted) isn't such a problem or as expensive as in many other European countries. However, parking is usually restricted in cities and towns and prohibited altogether in certain areas. Parking regulations may vary with the area of a city, the time of day, the day of the week, and whether the date is odd or even (seriously!). In many towns, parking is permitted on one side of the street (the side with odd-numbered houses) for the first half of the month and on the 'even' side for the second half of the month. This is called *stationnement alterné semi-mensuel* and is shown by a sign. (Note that the French for 'parking' is *stationnement*; *parking* means 'car park'.) Parking may also alternate weekly or daily; parking on alternate days is indicated by a sign stating '*Côté du Stationnement – Jours Pairs*' (even) or '*Jours Impairs*' (odd). In Paris, signs may indicate that parking is forbidden on one side of the street at certain times (e.g. for street cleaning).

On-street parking is forbidden in many streets in the centre of Paris and other cities. Parking is forbidden in Paris on main access routes, designated as red routes (*axe rouge*). '*Stationnement interdit*' means parking is forbidden and may be accompanied by the sign of a 'P' with a line through it. No parking may be indicated by a '*Stationnement gênant*' sign with a picture of a lorry towing away a vehicle (if you park in a taxi rank or in front of a private garage, you're likely to find your car towed away or your tyres slashed!) or by yellow kerb markings. It's forbidden to park in front of a fire hydrant. In Paris, it's illegal to leave a car in the same spot on a public road for more than 24 hours. Parking a caravan on roads is forbidden at any time in Paris and some other towns and cities, and overnight parking in a lay-by isn't permitted anywhere in France, although you can stop for a rest if you're falling asleep at the wheel. On roads outside town limits, you **must** pull off the road to stop.

Blue Zones

In many cities and towns there are 'blue zones' (*zone bleue*), indicated by blue street markings. Here you can park free for one hour between 09.00 and 12.00 and from 14.00 or 14.30 until 19.00 from Mondays to Saturdays, with no limit outside these hours or on Sundays and public holidays. Parking isn't restricted between 12.00 and 14.00, meaning you can park free from 11.00 until 14.00 or from 12.00 until 15.00. You must display a parking disc (*disque de contrôle/stationnement*) in your windscreen. These are available free or for a small fee from garages, travel agencies, motoring organisations, tourist offices, police stations, tobacconists' and some shops. Set your time of arrival in the left box, and the time you should leave by is displayed in the right box, e.g. if you set 10.00 in the left box, 11.00 is displayed in the right box. If you overstay your free time, you can be fined.

Ticket Machines

In most French cities, parking meters have been replaced by ticket machines (*horodateurs*). If a parking sign has the word '*Horodateur*' beneath it or there's a '*Stationnement payant*' sign, perhaps with '*Payant*' also marked on the road, it means that you must obtain a ticket from a nearby machine. Parking must usually be paid for between 09.00 and 19.00, although it's free from 12.00 to 14.00 (even traffic wardens stop for lunch). The cost is around €0.65 to €1 per hour (more at railway stations) and machines usually accept 5 cent, 10 cent, 20 cent, 50 cent, €1 and €2 coins. In some towns the first 30 minutes is free, one hour costs €0.30, 90 minutes €0.65 and two hours (often the maximum period) €1.55. Buy a ticket for the period required and place it behind your windscreen where it can be seen by a warden.

Car Parks

There are car parks (*parking*) in cities and towns, where parking rates vary from €0.30 to €2 per hour or €2.50 to €15 for 24 hours. Car parks in central Paris charge €1.50 to €3 per hour and €12 to €20 for 24 hours. Long-term parking, e.g. at railway stations, is available in most towns for up to €10 for the first 24 hours with a reducing scale thereafter. Monthly tickets can be purchased, reducing your parking expenses if you park frequently. On entering most car parks, you take a ticket from machine (usually you must press a button). You must pay **before** collecting your car, either at a cash desk (*caisse*) or in a machine and **cannot** pay at the exit. Machines may accept coins and banknotes, e.g. €5, €10 and €20, and debit and credit cards. After paying, you usually have around 15 minutes to find the exit, where you insert your ticket in a machine and hope the barrier rises.

Discounts

In most cities, local residents can pay reduced parking fees by obtaining a permit from the local town hall. This must be affixed to the right-hand side of your windscreen. Subscription cards for ticket machines are also available for residents and commuters in most cities. Disabled motorists are provided with free or reserved parking in most towns, shopping centres and at airports, but they must display an official disabled motorist's badge (*macaron*) inside their windscreen. These are free but can take two months to obtain. Apply with your *carte d'invalidité* to the Commission d'Education Spécialisée (CDES) if you're under 20 or the Commission Technique d'Orientation et de Reclassement Professionnel (COTOREP) if you're over 20. Disabled drivers can also obtain a European parking card (*carte européenne de stationnement*) entitling them to disabled parking privileges throughout Europe.

Fines

Fines for illegal parking are based on the severity of the offence. Throughout France you're fined around €11 for not paying or for overstaying your time in a legal parking spot, which increases to €33 if the fine isn't paid within three months. Fines for illegal parking are €35, €68 or €135, which increase to €75, €180 and €375 respectively if they aren't paid within three months. Parking fines can often be paid by buying a fiscal stamp (*timbre fiscal*) from a tobacconist's and affixing it to the notice that's sent to the relevant authority. Since January 2006, it has been possible to pay them online – a scheme set to be extended to the whole country by the end of 2007. You can usually agree a payment schedule for a large fine, rather than pay it in a lump sum. If your car is given a ticket (*papillon*) and isn't moved within an hour, it will be given a second ticket and after two hours a wheel clamp may be fitted or it may be towed way.

Paris has six car pounds (*fourrière*) and in addition to a parking fine of between €35 and €135 you must also pay a fee to release your car from a pound (or to have a clamp removed), plus a daily storage charge. However, if you don't collect your car within 10 to 45 days it may be sold (so don't park illegally before taking a long trip abroad!). Most pounds are open from around 08.00 to 20.00 Mondays to Saturdays.

Paris

Parking in Paris is usually nothing less than a nightmare. Parisians are parking anarchists and are world champions at the art of creative parking (you will often see cars parked millimetres apart and even a number of cars squeezed into a single space!). Parking on street corners and even on pavements is a favourite sport. Note, however, that if you park illegally, you aren't covered by comprehensive insurance should your car be damaged (which is highly likely). Needless to say, car parks are expensive. They're also often full. When visiting Paris, use public transport, which is cheap and efficient (see **Chapter 10**).

FUEL

Leaded petrol is no longer available and has been replaced by *super* (4-star/98 octane), which has a potassium content, although this is also being phased out and is no longer available at most petrol stations. Unleaded petrol (*sans plomb*) is usually available in two grades, 95 octane and 98 octane. Diesel fuel is called *diesel* (pronounced 'dee-ezel') or *gazole* or *gasoil* (both pronounced 'gazwal') and is available at all service stations. To help prevent errors, petrol pumps and pipes are colour coded green for unleaded, red for 4-star and black for diesel. The nozzles of 4-star petrol pumps are also usually larger than those of unleaded pumps and won't fit the petrol filler hole of a car fitted with a catalyser. Nevertheless, pay attention, particularly when a garage attendant is filling your car. Liquid petroleum gas (LPG) is also available and there are around 1,800 petrol stations offering LPG (*GPL* or *Gépel*), particularly on motorways (a free map is available from petrol stations). See also page 247. Note that the general word for fuel is *carburant* and petrol is *essence*; *fuel* (or *fioul*) is heating oil, and *pétrole* is paraffin or oil (the black stuff that comes out of the ground).

The cost of fuel has risen dramatically in recent years, although prices vary considerably (by up to €0.15 per litre) with the area, town and the petrol station. The cheapest source is usually hyper/supermarkets, while rural petrol stations are the most expensive. The costs per litre in September 2006 were around €1.10 (diesel), €1.25 (ordinary unleaded) and €1.30 (premium unleaded). LPG costs around €0.85 per litre. To help tourists and travellers on motorways locate inexpensive petrol, petrol stations within 10km (6mi) of a motorway are allowed to advertise their prices on the motorway, and a leaflet called *La Carte de l'Essence Moins Chère*, showing supermarkets a short detour from main routes, is available from French Government Tourist Offices.

Self-service petrol stations (*libre service*) are common and include most motorway and supermarket stations. Manned petrol stations are more usual in small towns and villages. To ask for a fill-up, say *'le plein s'il vous plaît'*. Service may include cleaning your windscreen and checking oil and tyre pressures; tips aren't expected, although they won't be refused! When paying at self-service petrol stations, simply tell the cashier your pump number. Debit cards and major credit cards are accepted by most petrol stations.

There are 24-hour petrol stations on motorways, and some other stations have automatic pumps accepting debit or credit cards, which can be used when the station is open (to save queuing) or closed. Insert your card (you may need to lift a flap – *Soulevez le volet*) and you will receive the following instructions, sometimes on an LCD display, sometimes by recorded message. (Some automatic pumps have instructions in English as well as French.)

- *Sélectionnez votre carburant*: 'Choose your fuel.' Press the button corresponding to the type of fuel you require.

- *Validez ou choix autre carburant*: 'Confirm or choose other fuel.' Press the button marked *'Val'* or change your choice of fuel.

- *Composez votre code confidentiel et validez*: 'Enter your PIN and confirm.' Enter the four-digit PIN for your card and press *'Val'*.

- *Impression ticket?*: 'Do you want a receipt?' Press *'Oui'* or *'Non'*.

- *Servez-vous jusqu'à €...*: 'Serve yourself to a maximum value of €...' Remove the nozzle and fill up without exceeding the value indicated. Replace the nozzle and your card will be returned to you. If you've requested a receipt, this will be printed automatically; you don't need to reinsert your card.

You may see *Veuillez patienter* between instructions, which means 'Please wait'. You may also be asked *Avez-vous une carte client?*, which means 'Do you have a customer loyalty card?'.

Most petrol stations have toilets, sometimes located outside the main building, when it may be necessary to ask an attendant for the key. Many petrol stations provide services such as a car wash, vacuum cleaners and air and often have a shop selling confectionery, canned and bottled drinks and snacks, which are usually expensive, newspapers and magazines, motoring accessories and sundry other items. Routine servicing and repairs are also carried out at some petrol stations.

GARAGES & SERVICING

Garages are required to display a list of their charges for routine repairs and servicing, and many also display their hourly rate for different types of work, e.g. mechanical, electrical or bodywork. The quality of work is usually of a high standard and charges compare favourably with those in other European countries (they're usually much lower than in the UK). It's generally cheaper to have your car serviced at a village garage than at a main dealer, although the quality of work may vary considerably from garage to garage. Note that when a car is under warranty it must usually be serviced by an approved dealer in order not to invalidate the warranty, although since October 2002 dealers no longer have exclusive rights to servicing and the supply of spare parts, which were previously marked up by up to 400 per cent. (On the other hand, new car dealers are no longer obliged to offer after-sales service.) If you need urgent assistance, particularly with an exotic foreign car, you're more likely to receive sympathetic help from a small general garage than a large specialist dealer. If you drive a rare car, it's wise to carry a basic selection of spare parts, as service stations in France may not stock them and you may need to wait several days for them to be sent from abroad.

Garages are generally open from 08.00 to 19.00 and close for lunch between 12.00 and 13.30. Many garages close for the whole month of August. Some garages provide 24-hour breakdown assistance (at a price – e.g. €150 for 15km/10mi).

Garages don't usually provide a free 'loan car' (*véhicule de remplacement*) while yours is being serviced or repaired, although your insurance company may do so; otherwise, you can usually hire a car from a garage at a reasonable rate. Some garages will collect your car from your home or office and deliver it after a service, or will drop you off at a railway or bus station or in a local town and pick you up when your car is ready for collection.

ROAD MAPS

A variety of road maps (*carte routière*) is available in France, although the most widely distributed are those of Michelin and IGN. Michelin red maps of the whole of France (scale: 1cm = 10km) can be purchased as a single sheet (721), in booklet form (723), as a reversible sheet (722), or in two halves: north (724) and south (725).

Michelin also publishes a route planning map (726), called *Grands Itinéraires*, showing motorways and alternative routes, distances and journey times, 24-hour service stations and peak periods to avoid. For minor country roads, Michelin yellow maps (scale: 1cm = 2km) are indispensable, and there are also regional and departmental maps (1cm = 1.75km). Towns and places mentioned in the Michelin red guide (see page 401) are underlined in red on Michelin yellow maps, and the names of towns with a plan in the red guide are enclosed in a rectangle. Conversely, the Michelin red guide directs you to the appropriate yellow map. The Michelin red guide is much more than a 'tourist' guide and includes numerous detailed town plans and references to main routes. Michelin green guides (see page 401) contain more detailed town plans than those in the red guide. Michelin maps and guides are inexpensive (particularly yellow maps) and available throughout France. The Michelin *Motoring Atlas of France* and *Road Atlas of France* (Hamlyn) contain the complete Michelin yellow maps (see above) plus town plans, and are much cheaper than buying all the yellow maps. The spiral bound version is best.

Excellent regional road maps are also published by the Institut Géographique National (IGN). These include town plans, tourist information and an index of places of interest. The brown series of 18 regional road maps, with a scale of 1cm = 2.5km, contain town plans and an index. Larger scale IGN maps include the green series of 74 maps with a scale of 1cm = 1km, *cartes de promenade* (1cm = 1km) and town and local maps (various scales), both of which series are blue. These maps have the advantage of showing every building, track and waterway as well as contour lines. IGN also produces a single road map of France (scale: 1cm = 10km).

Every June the French Ministry of Transport issues a free map (*Carte de Bison Futé*) showing areas of congestion and indicating alternative routes (see page 274). Motorway maps are distributed free by motorway operators. *Bonne Route: Discovering French Motorways* by Anne Fitter (Anthony Nelson) is also useful.

Free local town maps are available from tourist offices. More detailed town maps are available from book shops, newsagents and kiosks. Among the indispensable Paris maps are the Editions Leconte *Plan de Paris* and *Paris par Arrondissements* (Editions L'Indispensable) containing detailed street maps for each district plus *métro* and bus route maps. Village maps can usually be obtained from town halls.

Unfortunately, France has no large-scale rural maps with comprehensive street indexes. If it's any consolation, a map may not be much help in rural areas, as streets often have no names and houses have no numbers. In any case, the more willing you are to risk getting lost, the more likely you are to see the real France! A map showing the regions and departments of France is shown on page 570.

An alternative to poring over maps is to use Michelin's website (🖥 http://www. viamichelin.com), where you can obtain a recommended route between any two towns or communes in France (and some routes through other countries) and even make hotel and restaurant bookings along the way. The IGN website (🖥 http:// www.IGN.fr) doesn't include maps, but it's possible to order maps online and other services, such as route planning and hotel and restaurant information, are due to be available soon. Those with money to burn may like to splash €500 or more on a global positioning system (GPS) navigation device, complete with reassuringly calm oral instructions, such as that offered by TomTom (🖥 http://www.tomtom.com).

CAR RENTAL

Car rental companies such as Avis, Eurodollar, Europcar, Hertz, National Citer and Thrifty have offices in most cities and large towns and at major airports. Look under *Location de voitures* in the yellow pages. If you're a visitor, it's wise to book a rental car before arriving in France. Fly-drive deals are available through most airlines and travel agencies. French railways (SNCF) offer inclusive train and car rental deals, and their *France Vacances Pass* includes car rental. You can rent an Avis car from 196 SNCF stations and leave it at any station operating the *Train + auto* scheme (leaflets are available at SNCF stations and include a map of participating stations).

Car rental in France is expensive, particularly for short periods, although rates have fallen in recent years. Prices, which include VAT (*TVA*) at 19.6 per cent, can vary widely from one company to another (e.g. €35 to €75 for a one-day rental of a small car such as a Peugeot 106 or Renault Twingo), so it pays to shop around, although rates also vary according to your age and the number of years you've been driving. Rates normally include 100km 'free' (above 100km you pay around €0.50 per km). Reduced rates are available for weekends, usually from 12.00 on Friday to 09.00 on Monday, and rates fall considerably over longer periods, e.g. €200 to €250 per week. There may, however, be a large excess (*franchise*), e.g. €2,500, and you may be charged extra (as much as €20 per day!) for collision damage waiver (CDW), which reduces or cancels the excess. (It's possible to take out an annual insurance policy against having to pay an excess on rental cars for as little as €60, e.g. via Insurance 4 Car Hire, UK ☎ 020-7012 6300, 🖳 http://www. insurance4carhire.com).

Local rental companies are usually cheaper than the nationals, although cars must be returned to the pick-up point. Older cars can be hired from many garages at low rates. If required, check in advance that you're permitted to take a car out of France (usually prohibited).

To hire a car you must be a minimum of 18 years old, although most companies have increased this to 21 or even 25, and most companies have an upper age limit of 60 or 65. Drivers must have held a full licence for at least a year. International companies require payment by credit card, although local firms may allow you to pay a cash deposit of €150 to €300 (or the whole rental period may need to be paid in advance). You may also need to produce a residence permit and other identification. If you're driving a rented foreign-registered vehicle, you should ask the rental company for a 'hired/leased vehicle certificate'.

Optional extras include a portable telephone, luggage rack, snow chains and child seats. Instead of a standard car, you can hire a 4-wheel drive car, estate car, minibus, luxury car or convertible, possibly with a choice of manual or automatic gearbox. Minibuses accessible to wheelchairs can also be hired, e.g. from Hertz. Vans and pick-ups are available by the hour, half-day or day.

Cars can be rented in France through major international rental companies such as Alamo (🖳 http://www.alamo.com), Avis (🖳 http://www.avis.com), Budget (🖳 http://www.budget.com) and Hertz (🖳 http://www.hertz.com) by booking through their US offices and paying by credit card. This is a legitimate practice and can save 50 per cent or more on local hire rates. Telephone numbers of other US-based rental companies can be obtained from international directory enquiries, although you may not be able to access toll-free (800) numbers.

MOTORING ORGANISATIONS

There are a number of motoring organisations in France, although membership isn't as large as in many other European countries. Breakdown insurance is also provided by insurance companies and most motorists take advantage of their low rates (see page 259). Motoring organisations offer membership for individuals, couples and families and many also offer 'premium' levels of membership that include additional services. For example, Europ Assistance (☎ 01 41 85 85 85, ⌨ http://www.europ-assistance.com) offers three annual membership levels: individual, couple and family, which include breakdown and travel assistance in around 45 European countries. It also offers seasonal membership. You can register online.

Other services provided by motoring organisations include vehicle serviceability checks, health and legal assistance, insurance and financial services, tourist services (e.g. a camping carnet and petrol coupons) and expert advice. Motoring organisations, like insurance companies, don't usually operate their own breakdown rescue vehicles but appoint approved garages to assist members.

Other motoring organisations include the Automobile Club de l'Ile de France (☎ 01 40 55 43 00, ⌨ http://www.automobileclub.org), Automobile Club de France (☎ 01 43 12 43 12), and Touring Club de France (TCF, ☎ 01 42 65 90 70).

PEDESTRIAN ROAD RULES

As in other countries, being a pedestrian is almost as dangerous as being a motorist; over 10 per cent of people killed on French roads are pedestrians. Pedestrian crossings (*passage à piétons*) are distinguished by black and white or red and white stripes on the road, but aren't normally illuminated, e.g. by flashing or static lights. Many also have humps to encourage motorists to slow down. In towns, pedestrian crossings are incorporated with traffic lights. Motorists are required by law to stop for a pedestrian waiting at a pedestrian crossing **only** if he signals his intention to cross, e.g. by giving a clear hand signal or placing one foot on the crossing. Take extreme care when using pedestrian crossings, particularly in Paris, as motorists are reluctant to stop and may even try to drive around you while you're on a crossing (it's said that French pedestrian crossings function as a form of population control). However, you will be pleased to hear that running over pedestrians on pedestrian crossings (or anywhere else for that matter) is a serious offence.

At a crossing with lights, pedestrians must wait for a green light (or green man) before crossing the road, irrespective of whether there's any traffic. You can be fined for crossing the road at the wrong place or ignoring pedestrian lights and crossings. Pedestrians in France are generally better disciplined than those in many other countries and they usually wait for the green light, although where there's no crossing they're prone to wandering across the road without even looking. Pedestrians must use footpaths where provided or may use a bicycle path when there's no footpath. Where there's no footpath or bicycle path, you should walk on the left side of the road (facing the oncoming traffic). An increasing number of towns and cities have central pedestrian areas (*secteur piétonnier* or *zone piétonne*) barred to traffic, while other roads are often barred to pedestrians (indicated by an '*Interdit aux Piétons*' sign).

12.

HEALTH

Averege life expectancy at birth in France has risen almost five years in the last two decades and is now the highest in the world after Japan: around 83 for women (compared with the EU average of 81.4) and 75.3 for men (the EU average). Almost half of male deaths between 15 and 45 are due to road accidents and suicide (France has Europe's highest suicide rate by over 65s – over 3,000 per year). The infant mortality rate is around 4.4 deaths before the age of one year per 1,000 live births (around the European average), and a child born in France in 2006 has an even chance of living to be 100. In fact, people are now living so long that a new 'category' of person has been created, *le quatrième âge*, which refers to those over 75 (those in *le troisième âge* are now positively wet behind the ears).

France has long been a nation of hypochondriacs (famously satirised by Molière in *Le Malade Imaginaire*) and the French visit their doctors more often than most other Europeans and buy large quantities of medicines, health foods and vitamin pills – in fact they're the European champions of pill-taking, spending an average of €285 per head on medicines compared with the Germans at €245 and the British at €200.

The quality of French healthcare and healthcare facilities is among the best in the world. The standard of hospital treatment is second to none, and there are virtually no waiting lists for operations or hospital beds. (Many British people obtain treatment in France at the expense of the British National Health Service to avoid long waiting lists!) Public and private medicine operate alongside one another and there's no difference in the quality of treatment provided by public hospitals and private establishments, although the former may have more medical equipment. However, local hospital services, particularly hospitals with casualty departments, are limited in rural areas. Nevertheless, private treatment costs around half or even a third as much as similar treatment in the UK (e.g. around GB£900 for a cataract operation, compared with GB£3,000 in the UK).

France devotes a greater proportion of its GDP to healthcare than to defence or education, around half of it being spent on hospitals, a quarter on doctors' salaries and a fifth on medicines. Yet the system is in dire financial straits. As a result of the cost of the public health service spiralling out of control (the annual overspend has reached several billion euros!), doctors are now subject to periodic checks on the necessity of their prescriptions and in 2003 over 80 medicines were removed from the list of (4,500!) treatments reimbursed by the state; a further 835 are to be struck off by 2006. A wide-ranging reform of the health service, aimed at 'treating you better while spending less', was approved by parliament in July 2004 and has already seen the introduction (in January 2005) of the 'regular doctor' system (see **Doctors** on page 296) and of a compulsory €1 levy on all consultations (see **National Health System** on page 293). Other impending reforms include the creation of a computerised health record for every resident (from 2007). However, while most people recognise the need for reform, they're reluctant to lose hospitals and the right to unlimited second opinions and an endless supply of free pills.

In general, French healthcare places the emphasis on preventive medicine rather than treating sickness. Alternative medicine (*médecine douce*) is popular, particularly acupuncture and homeopathy. These treatments are recognised by France's medical council (Ordre des Médecins) and reimbursed by the national health service when prescribed by a doctor. France is the world leader in homeopathy, and some 15 per cent of the population regularly consults homeopathic doctors; chemists often have free leaflets explaining homeopathic treatments. Other types of treatment (e.g. osteopathy and chiropractic) are available but may not be reimbursed (see page 295). There are over 3,000 health associations in France – one for every conceivable ailment. A complete list, *L'Annuaire des Associations de Santé*, can be found on 🖳 http://www.annuaire-assoc-sante.com. A useful booklet, called *Health Care Resources in Paris* (€9), is published by WICE (☎ 01 45 66 75 50, 🖳 http://www.wice-paris.org).

HEALTH RISKS

Despite the common stereotype of the French as wine-swilling gourmets stuffing themselves with rich foods, many have become health freaks in recent years. Fitness and health centres flourish in most towns, and jogging (*footing*) has become fashionable. Smoking has declined considerably and is now a minority habit, although it's still more prevalent than in many other European countries and is estimated to kill 30,000 people per year (see page 315). Air pollution (caused by vehicles not smokers!) is an increasing problem in Paris and other French cities (particularly Grenoble, Lyon and Strasbourg), where it's blamed for a sharp rise in asthma cases. It's estimated that around 16,000 people die prematurely each year as a result of air pollution. There's also a high and increasing rate of stress in cities.

The incidence of heart disease is among the lowest in the world, a fact that has recently been officially contributed in part to the largely Mediterranean diet. However, the French have a high incidence of cirrhosis of the liver and other problems associated with excessive alcohol consumption, and there has recently been an increase in the number of sufferers from Alzheimer's disease to over half a million (it affects around 10 per cent of those over 65 and 50 per cent of those over 85). Among expatriates, sunstroke, change of diet, too much rich food and (surprise, surprise) too much alcohol are the most common causes of health problems. Nevertheless, when you've had too much of *la bonne vie*, you can take yourself off to a spa for a few weeks to rejuvenate your system (in preparation for another bout of over-indulgence). France's spa towns, which are concentrated in the mountainous regions, include Dax, the country's first, and Salies-de-Béarn (in Aquitaine), Aix-les-Bains, Evian and Thonon-les-Bains (Rhône-Alpes), Alet-les-Bains, Amelie-les-Bains and Avène-les-Bains (Languedoc-Roussillon), Chaudes-Aigues, Mont-Dore and Vichy (Auvergne), Dignes-les-Bains and Gréoux-les-Bains (Provence), Vittel (Alsace-Lorraine) and Lourdes (Midi-Pyrénées), where drinkers can expect miracles! Among the most popular treatments offered is thalassotherapy (*thalassothérapie*), a sea water 'cure' recommended for arthritis, circulation problems, depression and fatigue; it's even available on the national health service!

The claim that drinking red wine helps to reduce heart and other diseases – e.g. in *Your Good Health: The Medicinal Benefits of Wine Drinking* by Dr E. Maury (Souvenir Press) – has recently been challenged by other medical experts. However, it's generally agreed that drinking excessive amounts of red wine (or any alcohol) can destroy your brain and cause liver failure! As French producers sometimes warn buyers: *l'abus d'alcool est dangereux pour la santé, consommez avec modération* (alcohol abuse is dangerous for your health, consume in moderation).

Essential vaccinations, renewable every ten years, are polio and tetanus, which are 65 per cent reimbursed or 100 per cent if part of a free health check-up (*bilan de santé*), available to those on *CMU* (see page 324). Free flu jabs are available in October for over 65s and those with certain complaints.

You can safely drink mains water unless it's labelled as non-drinking (*eau non-potable*), although the wine (especially a Château Mouton Rothschild) is more enjoyable. Those who enjoy swimming in lakes and rivers, on the other hand, should be aware of the potentially fatal Weil's disease (*leptospirose*), transmitted through the urine of rats and other rodents, which is on the increase, particularly in Aquitaine.

EMERGENCIES

France's emergency medical services are among the best in the world but may operate in a slightly different way from those you're used to. The action to take in a medical emergency depends on the degree of urgency. In a life-threatening emergency such as a heart attack, poisoning or serious accident, dial 15 for your nearest *Service d'Aide Médicale d'Urgence* (*SAMU*) unit. *SAMU* is a special emergency service that works closely with local public hospital emergency and intensive care units. Its ambulances are manned by medical personnel and equipped with resuscitation equipment. *SAMU* has a central telephone number for each region and the duty doctor decides whether to send a *SAMU* mobile unit, refer the call to another ambulance service, or call a doctor for a home visit. In the most critical situations, *SAMU* can arrange transport to hospital by aeroplane, helicopter or, if appropriate, boat. If you call the fire brigade or police services, they will request a *SAMU* unit if they consider it necessary.

You can also call the local fire brigade (*sapeurs-pompiers* or *pompiers*) in an emergency by dialling 18. The fire brigade and public ambulance services are combined, and the fire brigade is equipped to deal with accidents and emergency medical cases. It operates its own ambulances, which are equipped with resuscitation equipment, and the *pompiers* will arrive with a doctor.

If you need an ambulance but the emergency isn't life-threatening, call the local public assistance (*assistance publique*) or municipal ambulance (*ambulance municipale*) service. There are also private ambulances in most towns providing a 24-hour service, listed by town under *Ambulances* in yellow pages. Ambulance staff are trained to provide first-aid and oxygen. In an emergency an ambulance will take a patient to the nearest hospital equipped to deal with that type of emergency. In small towns the local taxi service also provides an 'ambulance' service.

You will be billed for the services of *SAMU*, the fire service or the public ambulance service, although the cost will be reimbursed by social security and your complementary insurance policy (see page 321), if you have one, in the same way as other medical costs (see **National Health System** below). In an emergency, any hospital must treat you, irrespective of your ability to pay.

There are 24-hour medical and dental services in major cities and large towns (numbers are listed in telephone directories). For example, in Paris, you can call *SOS Médecins* (☎ 01 47 07 77 77) for medical emergencies, and *SOS Dentaire* (☎ 01 43

37 51 00) for dental emergencies. Contact numbers for *SOS Médecins* in other parts of France can be found on 🖥 http://www.sosmedecins-france.fr. *SOS* doctors and dentists are equipped with radio cars and respond quickly to calls. A home visit in Paris costs from around €32 before 19.00 and €48 after 19.00, plus the cost of any treatment. In Paris and other main cities, there are emergency medical telephone boxes at major junctions marked '*Services Médicaux*', with direct lines to emergency services. See also **Emergency & Service Numbers** on page 140 and **Counselling** on page 313.

If someone has swallowed poison, call your local 'anti-poison centre' (*centre anti-poison*), listed at the front of telephone directories. The morning-after pill (*contraception d'urgence*) can be purchased without a prescription from chemists'.

If you're unsure who to call, telephone your local police, who will tell you who to contact or call the appropriate service for you. Whoever you call, give the age of the patient and if possible, specify the type of emergency. **Keep a record of the telephone numbers of your doctor, local hospitals and clinics, ambulance service, poison control, dentist and other emergency services (e.g. fire, police) next to your telephone.**

If you're able, you can go to a hospital emergency or casualty department (*urgences*). Note that not all hospitals have paediatric units, particularly private hospitals and, if your child needs emergency treatment, you should take him to a hospital catering for paediatric emergencies. **Check in advance which local hospitals are equipped to deal with emergencies and the quickest route from your home. This information may be of vital importance in the event of an emergency, when a delay could mean the difference between life and death.**

NATIONAL HEALTH SYSTEM

France has an excellent, although expensive, national health system. If you qualify for healthcare under the national health system, you and your family are entitled to subsidised or (in certain cases) free medical and dental treatment. Benefits include general and specialist care, hospitalisation, laboratory services, medicines, dental care, maternity care, appliances and transportation. Those who don't automatically qualify can contribute voluntarily or take out private health insurance (see page 339). For details of eligibility for visitors and foreign residents, see **Eligibility & Exemptions** on page 324.

Under the national health system, health treatment is assigned a basic monetary value (*tarif de convention*), of which social security pays a proportion, as follows:

Practitioner/Treatment	Reimbursement
Maternity-related care	100 per cent
Hospitalisation	80 per cent
Doctor, dentist and midwife services; consultations as an out-patient; basic dental care; miscellaneous items, e.g. laboratory work, apparatus, ambulance services	70 per cent
Spectacles	65 per cent

| Services of medical auxiliaries, e.g. nurses and therapists | 60 per cent |
| Medicines (see page 299 for details) | 0 to 100 per cent |

The above figures are intended only as a guide and should be confirmed with social security and practitioners, as they can vary with your circumstances and social security 'status'. For example, certain patients classified as needing serious long-term treatment, e.g. diabetic, cancer and cardiac patients, receive 100 per cent reimbursement for all treatment. The cost of buying or hiring medical instruments such as walking sticks, wheelchairs and special pillows and mattresses is reimbursed up to specified limits.

The reimbursement you receive from social security applies to the *tarif de convention*, which is not necessarily the same as the amount you pay. For example, if a blood test costs €75 and the *tarif de convention* is €60, you would be reimbursed 70 per cent of €60 (€42) leaving you with a bill of €33. The balance of medical bills, called the *ticket modérateur*, can be paid by a complementary health insurance scheme, to which many people subscribe (see **Private Health Insurance** on page 339).

Since 1st January 2005, €1 has been deducted from all reimbursements except those relating to treatment for children, women over six months pregnant and those on *CMU* (see page 324), in order to reduce the social security debt.

When choosing a medical practitioner, e.g. a doctor or dentist, it's important to verify whether he has an agreement (*convention*) with social security. If he has an agreement, he's known as *conventionné* and will charge a fixed amount for treatment as specified under the *tarif de convention*. If he has no agreement, he's termed *non-conventionné* and the bill may be two to five times that set by the *tarif de convention*; some *non-conventionné* practitioners are approved (*agréé*) by social security, but only a small proportion of their fees are reimbursed. A few medical professionals are classified as *conventionné honoraires libres*; although they're *conventionné*, they're permitted to charge higher fees than the standard rates. These include practitioners who perform specialist treatment (*dépassement exceptionnel*) and those with a particular qualification or expertise (*dépassement permanent*). If you're in any doubt, you should ask what the fee is for a consultation or treatment and what percentage will be reimbursed by social security.

If you're non-resident you may be asked to pay in cash, although cheques drawn on a French bank are acceptable. If you're unable to pay your portion of the bill (the *ticket modérateur*), you can apply to your social security payment centre (Caisse Primaire d'Assurance Maladie/CPAM) for a waiver (*prise en charge*). In the case of urgent or necessary treatment, approval is a formality.

If you're entitled to national health cover, you will be issued with an electronic credit-card-style card (*carte à puce*), called the *Carte Vitale*, which contains your social security number and covers all members of your family. (Children under 16 are included on only one parent's card.) A *Carte Vitale* is valid for three years and can be re-validated by machine in the town halls of most towns and cities. At the end of 2006, the *Carte Vitale* will be replaced by the *Carte Vitale 2*, which will carry a photograph of the holder and will be linked to a computerised system known as a *dossier médical personnel* (*DMP*), containing all your medical records and vital information such as your blood group and allergies. The idea behind the new system (like most health service innovations) is to save the government money by reducing a phenomenon known as *nomadisme*, whereby patients seek opinions on the same ailment from several doctors, which is estimated to cost €3 billion per year.

Reimbursement Procedure

When you visit a medical practitioner whose fees are wholly or partly refundable by social security, simply present your *Carte Vitale* and reimbursement will be automatically 'triggered', although you must still pay the doctor and wait for your bank account to be reimbursed, which should be done withing five days. (For some reason best known to French social security, doctors aren't paid by the system.) Since 1st January 2005, a charge of €1 has been added to all consultation fees as part of the government's effort to reduce the social security debt and this isn't reimbursed except in the case of treatment for children, women over six months pregnant and those on *CMU* (see page 324).

If a medical practitioner isn't linked to the *Carte Vitale* system (of if he treats you at home or his computer is out of order), he will complete a treatment form (*feuille de soins*). This may be one of several colours: for example, doctors use a brown and white form and dentists a green and white form. The treatment provided and the cost of the consultation are listed on the form, which must be sent to your local CPAM for reimbursement. **Don't forget to sign and date the *feuille de soins* at the bottom right before sending it**. If forms aren't correctly completed, they will be returned.

If medicines are prescribed, your doctor will also give you a prescription (*ordonnance*) for you to take to a chemist. An increasing number of chemists (pharmacists) have computer systems enabling them to deduct the appropriate percentage of the bill reimbursed by social security, leaving you to pay only the unreimbursed portion. Some are also 'linked' to certain complementary insurance schemes, so that once you've registered with the chemist, you won't have to pay anything. Simply present your *ordonnance* to the chemist and the reimbursement procedure is taken care of for you. If your chemist isn't computerised or doesn't recognise your complementary insurer, you must pay for your medicines and make a claim for reimbursement to social security and/or your complementary insurance policy later. In this case, the chemist will give you a copy of the *feuille de soins*, with confirmation that the medicines have been issued to you, for you to send to your CPAM or insurer (the CPAM may forward the details direct to your insurer).

If you're requesting a reimbursement for auxiliary services prescribed by a doctor, you must accompany the *feuille de soins* with a copy of the doctor's original prescription. You can save a number of *feuilles de soins* and send them together.

The refund will be paid directly into the bank or post office account that was designated when you registered with social security. It's possible to receive payment in cash, although this isn't encouraged. You will receive your reimbursement any time from a few days to a few weeks after application, depending on the office and the amount involved. You will receive a statement from the office, confirming the amounts reimbursed to your account. Normally, you will automatically receive reimbursement of the 'complementary' sum (*ticket modérateur*) from your complementary insurance policy (sometimes before the social security refund). If you don't, you must send the social security statement to your complementary insurer. Always keep a copy of your *feuilles de soins* and check that reimbursements are received and correct.

To be reimbursed by social security for certain medical treatment, you must obtain prior approval from your CPAM. This may include physical examinations, non-routine dental care, contact lenses and non-standard lenses for glasses, certain laboratory and radiology tests, physiotherapy and speech therapy, and thermal and therapeutic treatments. Your medical practitioner will give you a proposal form (*demande d'entente préalable*) and, unless treatment is urgently required, you should apply at least 21 days before the proposed treatment and obtain a receipt for your application (if made in person) or send it by registered post. If you don't receive a reply from your CPAM within ten working days, it's deemed to have agreed to the request. See also **Social Security** on page 323.

Treatment Abroad

If you're entitled to social security health benefits in France (see page 324), you can take advantage of reciprocal healthcare agreements in other EU countries (as well as certain other countries, e.g. Algeria and Morocco). In some cases you must obtain a form (e.g. E101 and E106 for temporary workers) or a European Health Insurance Card (*Carte Européenne d'Assurance Maladie/CEAM*) from your CPAM before leaving France. Note that a *CEAM* is valid only for a year at a time. Within the EU, the cost of treatment will normally be covered by the national health service of the country you're in. Outside the EU, full payment (possibly in cash) must usually be made in advance, although you may be reimbursed on your return to France (you must obtain detailed receipts). Note that reimbursement is based on the cost of comparable treatment in France, which may be far below what you're charged abroad. In certain countries, e.g. Canada, Japan, Switzerland and the US, medical treatment is **very** expensive and you're advised to take out travel or holiday insurance (see page 346) when visiting these countries. This is wise wherever you're travelling, as it provides considerably better medical cover than reciprocal healthcare agreements and includes many other benefits such as repatriation. If you travel abroad frequently, it's worthwhile having an international health insurance policy (see page 340). Check also what cover is provided by your French bank's international credit card and your car insurance policy.

DOCTORS

There are around three doctors (*médecins*) per 1,000 population in France (compared with 1.7 in the UK, 4.4 in Spain and 5.9 in Italy), around 45 per cent of them women, and there are excellent doctors throughout the country, although finding a doctor who speaks good (or any) English can be a problem, particularly in rural areas. Many embassies and consulates maintain a list of doctors and specialists in their area who speak English (and other foreign languages), and your employer, colleagues or neighbours may be able to recommend someone. Town halls and chemists keep a list of local practitioners. You can obtain a list of doctors registered with social security from your local social security office. General practitioners or family doctors (*médecin généraliste*) are listed in the yellow pages under *Médecins Généralistes* and specialists under *Médecins Qualifiés* followed by their speciality, e.g. *Gynécologie Médicale*. (There are as many specialists as general practitioners.) All French doctors and specialists are registered with the Ordre des Médecins.

Until recently, you could choose to see any doctor or specialist at any time and weren't required to register with a particular doctor, which made it easy to obtain a second opinion, should you wish to do so. You're now required to appoint an 'acting doctor' (*médecin traitant*) and to obtain a referral from him before seeing another doctor or specialist, including a medical auxiliary such as a nurse, physiotherapist or chiropodist, or a gynaecologist, ophthalmologist or paediatrician.

Many French doctors are specialists in acupuncture and homeopathy, both of which are reimbursed by social security when performed or prescribed by a doctor or practitioner who is *conventionné* (see page 293). It's normal practice to pay a doctor or other medical practitioner after each visit, whether you're a private or social security patient (see **Reimbursement Procedure** on page 295). A routine visit to the doctor costs €21 (€26 for treatment to a child), of which €1 isn't reimbursed by social security but is by some *mutuelles*; home visits cost more (e.g. €40).

A consultation with a specialist costs at least €24, but a visit to a psychiatrist, neuro-psychiatrist or neurologist will cost you €41, and specialists who are *non-conventionné* can charge €45 or more.

Many doctors are in single practices but an increasing number work in group practices, and there are also healthcare centres (*centre médical et social*), which may offer services that are usually unavailable at doctors' surgeries, e.g. health screening, vaccinations, dental care (*soins dentaires*) and nursing care (*soins infirmiers*). Some centres specialise in a particular field of medicine, such as cancer or heart treatment. For example, as part of a Health Department initiative to fight breast cancer, women aged between 50 and 74 can obtain free screening (*dépistage*) at centres listed on 🖳 http://www.rendezvoussanteplus.net. Although it isn't always necessary to make an appointment, it's preferable (unless you like waiting for hours). As when visiting a doctor, check whether the centre is *conventionné* (see page 293). In some areas, there are outpatient services (*centre de soins*) run by private organisations such as the Red Cross. You can obtain a list of local healthcare centres from your town hall.

Hours

Doctors' surgery hours may vary from day to day, e.g. morning surgery from 09.00 to 11.30 or 12.00 Tuesdays to Saturdays and afternoons from 14.00 to 16.30 Mondays to Fridays. Certain periods may be set aside for appointments (*rendezvous*) and others for 'open consultation' (*consultation libre*), when no appointment is necessary; patients are seen in the order they arrive. Lists of doctors receiving patients on Sundays and public holidays are displayed on chemists' doors and can be obtained from police stations. Local newspapers also usually contain lists of doctors (and vets) who are on call over the weekend (under the heading *Urgences*). If your doctor is unavailable, his surgery will give you the name of a standby doctor. If you need a doctor or medicines in a non-urgent situation and are unable to contact your doctor, your local police station (*commissariat de police*) will give you the telephone number of a duty doctor or the address of a chemist's that's open. If this isn't possible, dial ☎ 15 and ask for the number of your nearest duty doctor. If you're unable to attend a surgery, your doctor may make a house call, although many won't.

Treatment

When you visit a doctor, you're invariably prescribed a number of medicines, which are liberally dispensed in France. (The standing of a doctor with his patients often depends on the number of medicines prescribed!) For some ailments you will be prescribed a rectal suppository (*suppositoire*), which are the fastest way of getting drugs into the bloodstream (via the bowel or lower intestine), although this practice is dying out. Never take a suppository orally – they're usually difficult to confuse with oral pills, on account of their size and shape.

It's also common practice to have your temperature taken rectally, so if you're bashful you may prefer to choose a doctor of a particular sex. You can request that your temperature be taken orally, although you may need to provide your own oral thermometer. If medicine needs to be administered by a nurse, e.g. by injection, or other nursing services are necessary, your doctor or chemist will give you the name of a local nurse. Treatment can be administered at your home or at a nurse's office and is paid for by social security.

Medical Examinations

Employees in France must (by law) have a medical examination when they're hired and annually thereafter. If you contribute to social security, you will be issued with a medical certificate (*certificat de santé*), which must be obtained privately if you aren't covered by social security. A more thorough medical check (*bilan de santé*) is available free on demand every five years (a total of nine during a person's adult life) under social security. Technically it's mandatory for everyone to have a physical examination between the ages of 25 and 35 and between the ages of 45 and 55. A couple must undergo a physical examination no more than two months prior to marriage, which includes a blood test and chest X-ray. You may also require a medical examination (and certificate) before being allowed to participate in certain sports (e.g. when joining a club).

In France, the results of medical tests (e.g. blood, urine, heart and smear) and X-rays are the property of the patient, who receives a copy, and doctors must provide medical records within a week of a request. You should keep these in a safe place, as you will be asked to produce them if you require further treatment (in some cases even for treatment for a different condition). And after any operation or other medical 'act' you're entitled to access to your *dossier* (ask your doctor). If you're denied access to records, contact the Commission d'Accès au Documents Administratifs (CADA, ☎ 01 42 75 79 99, 🖳 http://www.cada.fr.). See also **Children's Health** on page 309.

MEDICINES

The French take a lot of medicines (*médicaments – drogues* are narcotics!) and are Europe's largest consumers of sleeping pills, tranquillisers and anti-depressants such as Prozac and Valium. Medicines prescribed by doctors represent over 80 per cent of sales, and doctors habitually prescribe three or four different remedies for each ailment. The French have traditionally been prescribed more antibiotics than any other Europeans, a third of which are reckoned to be unnecessary or ineffective, and have the highest incidence of anti-biotic-resistant bacteria in Europe, with the result that the government is now campaigning (among both doctors and patients) for a reduction in antibiotics prescription. The cost of prescription medicines is controlled by the government (prices are reviewed twice a year), although there are no price controls on non-prescription medicines.

Social security pays the whole cost of essential medication for certain illnesses or conditions, e.g. insulin and heart pills, (labelled '100 per cent'), 65 per cent of medicines designated as important (with white labels), and 35 per cent for *médicaments de confort* (with blue labels) – see **Reimbursement Procedure** on page 295. A few medicines aren't reimbursed at all, including most contraceptive pills (see **Contraceptives & Abortion** on page 305). Note that medicines deemed to be 'ineffective' won't be reimbursed at all. (Of the 100 most prescribed medicines in France, 23 fall into this category!) The complete list of 'ineffective' medicines can be found on 🖳 http://agmed.sante.gouv.fr. **If you must pay for your own medicines, it can be expensive, e.g. €100 or more for a course of antibiotics.**

The brand names for medicines often vary from country to country, so if you regularly take a particular medicine you should ask your doctor for the generic name. If you wish to match a medicine prescribed abroad, you need a current prescription with the medicine's trade name, the manufacturer's name, the chemical composition and the dosage. Although you aren't obliged to accept it, a chemist may propose a generic product which is cheaper than the brand on your prescription (as part of the government's scheme to reduce health spending). Despite an almost 100 per cent increase in the use of generic medicines between 2002 and 2005, the French are second only to the Spanish in the European league of preferring branded products, only 6.4 per cent of them accepting generic alternatives compared with 20.6 per cent of Britons and 22.7 per cent of Germans. **Note, however, that under legislation which became effective in July 2003 social security reimbursement (see page 293) is based on the generic equivalent of branded medicines (if one exists).** Generic products, which are up to a third cheaper than branded products, are usually identified by the prefix '*Gé*'. Most foreign medicines have an equivalent in France, although particular brands may be difficult or impossible to obtain. It's possible to have medicines sent from abroad and no import duty or value added tax (*TVA*) is payable. If you're visiting France for a short period, you should take sufficient medicines to cover the length of your stay. In an emergency, a local doctor will write a prescription (*ordonnance*) that can be filled by a local chemist, or a hospital may refill a prescription from its own pharmacy.

A triangular 'traffic' sign with a red border and a black car symbol on a medicine packet indicates that it can cause drowsiness and that you shouldn't drive or operate machinery when taking it, but colour-coded packaging is being introduced to indicate the level of drowsiness caused by each medicine: yellow means 'drive with care', orange 'drive only with your doctor's permission' and red 'don't drive'. **Pregnant women should check with their doctor before taking any medication, including pain-killers.**

Chemists'

Prescription and non-prescription medicines are obtained from chemists' (*pharmacie*), denoted by a sign consisting of a green cross on a white background (which is usually illuminated and flashing when the shop is open). A chemist must own and run his own shop (chain chemists are illegal) and their numbers are strictly controlled, although there's at least one chemist in every town and many villages. Most chemists' are open from 09.00 to 19.00 or 19.30 from Mondays to Saturdays, although many close for lunch from 12.00 or 12.30 to 14.00. Some are closed on Mondays and others may be closed on Saturday afternoons since the introduction of the 35-hour week. Outside normal opening hours, a notice giving the address of the nearest duty chemist (*pharmacie de garde*) is displayed in the windows of chemists' (the telephone numbers of local doctors on call may also be shown). This information is also published in local newspapers and listed in monthly bulletins issued by town halls. In most cities, several chemists' are open until late evening or early morning and in Paris a 24-hour service is provided by the Pharmacie Les Champs, 84 avenue des Champs-Elysées, 75008 Paris (☎ 01 45 62 02 41). There are also American and British chemists in the capital, stocking familiar American and British medicines.

Chemists are trained and obliged to give first aid and they can also perform tests such as blood pressure. They can supply a wider range of medicines over the counter without a prescription than is available in Britain and the US, although some medicines sold freely in other countries require a doctor's prescription in France. A chemist will recommend non-prescription medicines for minor ailments and may also recommend a local doctor, specialist, nurse or dentist. (Some chemists regard this type of recommendation as unethical and will prefer to give you a list of practitioners). Chemists are trained to distinguish between around 50 species of edible and poisonous fungi (*champignon*) and will tell you whether those you've picked are delicious or deadly. They're also trained to identify local snakes to enable them to prescribe the correct antidote for bites. Crutches (*béquilles*) can be hired from chemists for around €3 per week, plus a deposit of around €15.

French chemists aren't cluttered with the non-medical wares found in American and British chemists, although many sell cosmetics and toiletries (these are called *parapharmacies*) and most stock animal medicines and baby products (e.g. feeding bottles). Chemists are cheaper than a *parfumerie* for cosmetics but more expensive than a supermarket or hypermarket. Only a limited range of non-prescription medicines can be purchased in supermarkets and hypermarkets. A *droguerie*, which is a sort of hardware store selling toiletries, cleaning supplies, a wide range of general household goods, paint, garden supplies, tools and DIY supplies, shouldn't be confused with an American drug store. See also **Health Food** on page 485.

Prescriptions

Prescriptions may be printed or handwritten; in the latter case, as in most countries, they're invariably illegible but a chemist will (usually!) be able to decipher them and will explain to you (and write on the medicine boxes) what you need to take when. Whereas you must pay the full cost of non-prescription medicines, prescription medicines may be partly or wholly reimbursed by social security and/or your complementary insurance policy (see **Medicines** on page 299). You don't have to wait for a prescription to be 'made up' (as, for example, in the UK); medicines are pre-packaged and all a chemist has to do is find them, although some may be out of stock and need ordering. Many French doctors prescribe homeopathic medicines, stocked by all chemists, many of which specialise in homeopathy.

HOSPITALS & CLINICS

France boasts a higher number of hospital beds in proportion to its population than most other European countries (8.7 per 1,000 compared with 7.6 in Spain and Italy and 6.9 in the UK), although the introduction of the 35-hour week and a recent shortage of doctors and nurses, particularly in the provinces, have led to the closure of many wards, and in the summer months, when staff are on holiday, some hospitals are forced virtually to close. There's also a shortage of certain specialists, e.g. anaesthetists, gynaecologists and ophthalmologists, partly due to a recent increase in malpractice lawsuits.

All cities and large towns have at least one hospital (*hôpital*) or clinic (*clinique*), indicated by the international hospital sign of a red 'H' on a white background. Hospitals are listed in the yellow pages under *Hôpitaux et Hospices*. There are many types of hospital, both public and private (see below). Like doctors and other medical practitioners, hospitals are either *conventionné* or *non-conventionné* (see page 293). Every large town has at least one *hôpital conventionné*, which may be public or private, usually with a direct payment agreement with social security. Private hospitals and clinics that are *non-conventionné* may also have an agreement (*agréé*) with social security, whereby around 30 per cent of the fees are usually paid by social security. For non-urgent hospital treatment, check in advance the reimbursement made by social security and, if applicable, the amount your complementary insurance policy or other private health insurance will pay. If you're admitted to a hospital or other medical institution, you should be given a document outlining your rights (*charte des droits et libertés*).

Public Hospitals

There are generally three categories of public hospital: hospital centres or short-stay hospitals (*hôpital de court séjour*), medium-stay centres (*centre de moyen séjour*) and long-term treatment centres (*centre et unité de long séjour*). Hospital centres include general hospitals, *assistance publique* (*AP*) hospitals in Paris, specialist hospitals and regional centres (*centre hospitalier régional/CHR* or *centre hospitalier universitaire/CHU* when associated with a university). Public hospitals must accept all patients in an emergency irrespective of their ability to pay.

Medium-stay hospitals are usually for patients who have previously been treated in a short-stay hospital centre. They contain facilities for convalescence, occupational and physical therapy, and recuperative treatment for drug and alcohol abuse and mental illness. Long-term treatment centres are for those who are unable to care for themselves without assistance and include psychiatric hospitals and nursing homes for the aged (*maisons de retraite*).

There are over 35 *CHU*s in France (12 in Paris), where medical students do their training. *CHU*s are rated among the best hospitals in France (indeed in the world), and professors and senior staff must undergo intensive training to secure their appointments. Rural community hospitals are also classified as hospital centres, although they're usually less well equipped than other short-stay hospitals and you should go to a large hospital if possible.

Not all hospitals have accident and emergency (*urgences*) departments, and you should check where your nearest A&E centre is to be found (see Emergencies on page 292).

Private Hospitals & Clinics

Most private hospitals (*hôpital privé*) and clinics (*clinique*) specialise in inpatient care in particular fields of medicine, such as obstetrics and surgery, rather than being full-service hospitals (the American Hospital in Paris is a rare exception). You should check in advance. The cost of treatment in a private hospital or clinic is generally much higher than in a public hospital, where a large proportion of costs are reimbursed by social security. However, some private hospitals participate in the French social security system and operate in the same way as public hospitals. These include the Hertford British and International hospitals in Paris (see below).

If your French is poor, you may prefer to be treated at a private hospital or clinic with English-speaking staff, as most public hospitals make little or no allowance for foreigners who don't speak French. There are a number of expatriate hospitals in the Paris area, including the American Hospital in Paris (☎ 01 46 41 25 25 or ☎ 01 47 47 70 15 for emergencies, 🖳 http://www.american-hospital.org) and the Hertford British Hospital, also known as the Hôpital Franco-Britannique (☎ 01 46 39 22 22), which specialises in maternity care. Most staff at all levels in these hospitals speak English. Fees at the American hospital are much higher than at French hospitals, although they can usually be reclaimed through the French social security system and most *mutuelles* (see page 321) and are accepted by most American medical insurance companies.

Long-term Care

The elderly are better catered for in France than in many other countries, although the great majority of old people are looked after at home by relatives (adult children are obliged by law to support ageing parents according to their means) and the cost of retirement homes and other accommodation can be prohibitive. Nevertheless, there are some 5,000 retirement homes in France, including public and private establishments.

There are several types of retirement home (*maison de retraite*), which can be with or without medical support (*avec ou sans cure médicale*): a *foyer-logement* for people on low incomes; a *foyer-soleil*, where accommodation for old and younger people is mixed; a *village-retraite*, where accommodation is in detached bungalows (*pavillon*), usually in a rural area (e.g. the Village Seniors du Grand Logis near Saintes in Charente-Maritime) and there are holiday-camp-style facilities and entertainment; and a *résidence avec services* or *résidence services*, consisting of apartments (normally two-room), some of which are offered unfurnished. Some communes run their own retirement homes (ask at your town hall), and some establishments offer temporary accommodation.

A traditional retirement home can cost up to €2,000 per month and a long-stay hospital over €1,000 per month (more in Paris). *Village-retraite* accommodation costs between €1,000 and €1,500 per month (or from €75,000 to buy) and apartments €600 to €1,200 per month. On the other hand, for those who qualify, *foyer-logements* can cost as little as €300 per month.

There are various state benefits for old people, and a new social security allowance, *allocation personnalisée à l'autonomie* (*APA*), was introduced in 2001 to help those requiring long-term care, who can also insure against becoming a burden on their children (see page 335).

Details of facilities for the elderly are contained in *Le Guide des Maisons de Retraite* (Pétrarque) and *Le Guide du Logement Senior* (Balland) and can be found online, e.g. 🖳 http://www.maisons-de-retraite.net, a directory of homes, and 🖳 http://www.plan-retraite.fr, the site of the Association Française de Protection et d'Assistance aux Personnes Agées, which contains general information and a list of homes in Ile-de-France.

Accommodation

The basic hospital accommodation that is reimbursed at 80 per cent by social security is a two- or three-bed room (*régime commun*). A supplement must be paid for a private room (if available), although it may be paid in part or in full by your complementary or other private health insurance. You can usually rent a radio, TV or telephone for a small daily fee if they aren't included in the room fee. A bed is also usually provided for relatives if required. You must normally provide your own pyjamas, robes, towels and toiletries. The best hospital accommodation is similar to five-star hotels with food and wine (and prices!) to match. Catering in basic accommodation varies from good to adequate.

Children

Children aged 15 and under are usually treated in a paediatric unit well stocked with games, toys, books and other children. However, not all hospitals have paediatric units, particularly private hospitals. Children who require long-term hospitalisation may, depending on their health, be given school lessons in hospital. Many hospitals permit a parent to stay with a child and some allow children, depending on their health, to attend during the day and return home at night. A free booklet, *L'Hôpital et l'Enfant* (in French), contains information and advice for parents with children in hospital.

Procedure

Except for emergency treatment (see page 292), you're admitted or referred to a hospital or clinic for treatment only after a recommendation (*attestation*) from a doctor or a specialist. Normally you're admitted to a hospital in your own *département*, unless specialist surgery or treatment is necessary which is unavailable there. If you wish to be treated in hospital by your own doctor, you must check that he's able to do so. Except in the case of emergencies, you must provide the following documents on admission to a public hospital in order to receive reimbursement from social security:

● Your social security registration card (*carte d'immatriculation*) or *Carte Vitale*.

● A doctor's certificate (*attestation*) stating the reason for hospitalisation.

● Documents provided by your social security office (*caisse*) stating the conditions under which you're insured, e.g. if you're unemployed you need a document stating that you're entitled to unemployment benefits.

An employer must provide an *accident de travail* form when an employee is hospitalised as a result of an accident at work. If a woman is hospitalised to give birth or in connection with a pregnancy, she must have a *carnet de maternité* (see **Childbirth** below). If you aren't covered by social security, you must provide evidence of your health insurance (e.g. a European Health Insurance Card), salary or ability to pay. If you're unable to pay, you may be refused treatment at a private hospital or clinic, except in the case of an emergency.

Upon admission to a hospital you should receive an information booklet (*livret d'accueil*) containing meal schedules, visiting hours, floor plan, doctors' names, hospital rules, and a description of the uniforms and name tags worn by hospital staff. (If you don't, ask for one.) Visiting hours are usually from 13.30 or 14.00 to 20.30 or 21.00 daily but tend to be flexible for immediate family members; visits can be made outside these hours in exceptional circumstances. In a private clinic there may be no restrictions on visiting hours.

Hospital stays are kept to a minimum, and much treatment is performed on an outpatient basis (*hôpital de jour*) and your convalescence takes place at home (*hospitalisation à domicile/HAD*), supervised by visiting doctors and nurses. The main exception to this rule is postnatal care (see **Childbirth** below). You can usually leave hospital at any time without a doctor's consent by signing a release form (*décharge de responsabilité*).

Costs

Hospital bills can be **very** high, e.g. €150 to €250 per day for medicine, accommodation and meals plus €250 to €300 for surgery, or much more for a major operation. If you're paying a bill yourself for elective surgery, you should shop around, not just in France but in other countries, as the price can vary considerably. Note, however, that some operations are performed in France for half or a third of the price in some other European countries. If you're covered by French social security, 80 per cent of your hospital bill will normally be paid by the state. (Some types of plastic surgery are also paid for, e.g. breast reduction in certain circumstances and some ear and nose operations.)

Patients covered by social security are charged a fixed daily fee (*forfait journalier/indemnité journalière*) for meals of €15 (to increase to €16 in January 2007), unless hospitalisation was due to an accident at work or you're exempt on the grounds of low income, although some hospitals waive the charge on the day of admission. This fee is usually reimbursed by complementary health insurance.

If a medical bill is expected to be above a certain amount (which is increased annually in line with inflation), you can apply to social security for a *prise en charge*, which means that the full bill will be sent directly to social security. Otherwise, you must pay the bill when you leave hospital, unless you've made prior arrangements for it to be paid by your insurance company. You must pay for hospital outpatient treatment in the same way as a visit to a doctor or specialist (see **Reimbursement Procedure** on page 295).

Certain patients, classified as needing serious long-term treatment, receive 100 per cent reimbursement, e.g. cardiac, diabetes and cancer patients. Pensioners receive free hospital treatment under social security, although up to 90 per cent of their pension may be deducted to compensate for the cost of treatment (while in hospital). A stay at a spa is usually reimbursed at 70 per cent or higher when recommended by a doctor and approved by social security. Convalescence after a serious illness is often paid 100 per cent by social security.

CONTRACEPTION & ABORTION

Contraceptives are freely available in France and there are no age restrictions. A doctor's prescription is necessary for birth control pills (*pilule*) and certain contraceptive devices. Most birth control pills aren't reimbursed at all by social security, including all the latest pills; only some older pills are reimbursed. Condoms (*préservatif* – a preservative is a *conservateur* and Condom is a town in southern France) are widely available, e.g. in underground stations and high schools, and can be bought cheaply in chemists', supermarkets and other shops. The 'morning-after pill' (*contraception d'urgence*) can be purchased without a prescription from chemists' and is reimbursed (it's issued free to minors in an effort to reduce unwanted teenage pregnancies).

Abortion (*interruption volontaire de grossesse/IVG*) has been legal in France since 1974 and in 1982 became subject to reimbursement through social security, although it's still a controversion subject. There has recently been a public outcry against the right of mothers to choose abortion if a problem is detected by an antenatal scan (some doctors refuse to perform scans as a protest against the 'legalisation of eugenics'), and the government may introduce legislation to restrict entitlement to abortion.

Abortions must normally be performed in a hospital before the tenth week of pregnancy. There are no abortion clinics in France. Therapeutic abortions are allowed at any time during a pregnancy if the life of the mother is at risk or there's a high probability that a child will be born with a serious or incurable disorder. A doctor may refuse to perform an abortion, but in general abortion is available on demand for all except girls under the age of 18, who require the consent of a parent or guardian or a children's judge. A woman doesn't need the consent of the father to have an abortion, irrespective of her marital status.

Information

Further information about family planning can be obtained from the Mouvement Français du Planning Familial (☎ 01 42 60 93 20, 🖳 http://www.planning-familial.org). There are also information centres (*établissement d'information*) and family planning centres (*centre de planification familiale*), staffed by specialised counsellors and medical professionals, throughout France. These provide information and counselling (usually free) about contraception, abortion, and sexual and marital problems. Family planning centres also prescribe contraceptives, diagnose pregnancies, and provide gynaecological examinations and treatment.

CHILDBIRTH

Childbirth invariably takes place in a hospital, where a stay of at least five days and as many as 12 is normal, depending on factors such as the number of beds available and the mother's and baby's health. Most hospital maternity units are equipped with single and double rooms. You can choose to have a baby at home, but it's unlikely you will receive support from doctors or other medical staff or from social security.

Procedure

As soon as your pregnancy is confirmed (by a blood test), your doctor will give you some general information about the progress of your pregnancy and a form to be completed and sent to the local Caisse d'Allocations Familiales (CAF), who will issue you with a reference number (and a card confirming it) relating to claims for family allowances. The CAF will also send you information about your entitlement to these and how to claim them (see **Family Allowances** on page 333). You may be 'allocated' to a maternity hospital or clinic or, if you live equidistant from two or more, you may be given a choice, in which case you should visit the establishments (but ring first, as they aren't used to such visits) and talk to people who have given birth there before making your decision.

You must have blood and urine tests and should continue to see your doctor or a midwife at your chosen hospital every month. At the end of your 11th, 22nd and 33rd weeks of pregnancy, you will be given an ultrasound scan (*échographie*) to check on the progress of the foetus. **If you don't wish to know the sex of your child, you should say so before each scan is made.** After the first scan, you will be asked to take an additional blood test to check for the likelihood of Down's syndrome (*syndrome de Down* or *Trisomie 21*).

Expectant mothers are normally supervised by a midwife; it's possible to consult an obstetrician, but he will usually become closely involved in a birth only if complications are expected or when it's classified as 'high-risk'. You can, of course, engage a private obstetrician to attend you before, during and after giving birth; this won't be paid for by social security but may be covered by private health insurance.

In any case, you should register at the hospital, when a bed will be provisionally reserved for you at the appropriate time and, in theory, guaranteed for you whenever your baby decides to pop out. Before booking a bed in a hospital or clinic, you should ask if it's *conventionné* (see page 293). Other things you may wish to investigate are whether your husband is allowed to attend the delivery, whether 'alternative' birthing positions (e.g. crouching or on your side) are permitted, which is less common in France than in many other Western countries, and what clothes and other articles you need to provide; at some hospitals, you need to provide only clothes. If you wish to join antenatal classes at the hospital (or elsewhere), you may need to sign up for these well in advance, although usually around the sixth month is sufficient; if your French isn't good and you don't wish to join a class, it may be possible to arrange individual lessons.

One of the main topics of discussion at antenatal classes (and the subject of a special lesson) is the epidural (*péridurale*), which is usually the only form of pain relief offered during labour, and you should make it clear if you don't want an epidural (although you would be wise to keep your options open until labour begins!).

The French aren't great proponents of 'natural' birthing methods, and you will normally be required to have a drip connected to your arm or hand and heart-beat and breathing (the baby's, not yours) monitors strapped to your belly throughout labour. Almost nothing is left to 'chance', and if a baby is reluctant to make its appearance in the world, you will be wheeled into the operating theatre for a caesarian section. In contrast, you will be encouraged to breast feed (*allaiter*) rather than bottle feed (*donner le biberon*), although you're free to bottle feed if you prefer.

Births must be registered within three working days at the town hall of the district where they take place. In fact, this will be done automatically if you don't do it yourself, but your signature won't appear on the birth certificate. Registration applies to everyone irrespective of their nationality and whether they're resident in France or just visiting. When registering a birth, you must produce a certificate signed by a doctor or midwife and the parents' passports or identity cards. You should receive copies of the complete birth certificate (*acte de naissance – copie intgérale*) as well as 'summaries' (*extrait de l'acte de naissance*), which are required by various bodies, e.g. the tax office (see below). The hospital will issue you with a health record book (*carnet de santé*) for your child, which details all the treatment (e.g. vaccinations) he will need until he's 18. Children born to foreign nationals should be registered at the local consulate or embassy in order to obtain a national birth certificate and passport for a child, which may take several weeks and cost €100 or more.

Note than whenever someone born in France is required to produce his birth certificate, what is actually required is an extract (*extrait*) from the local record book, which contains details not only of his birth but also of his current status (*état civil*). Any such extract must be no more than three months old.

If you have private health insurance, don't forget to notify your health insurance company about the birth of a child. Also notify the tax office and make sure that your income tax payments are adjusted accordingly (see page 381).

France used to have a list of names taken from the Christian calendar, to which parents were limited when naming a child. However, the law has now changed and you may name your child anything that isn't 'prejudicial' to the child. Children may now be given as a surname either their father's or their mother's (maiden) name or both their parents' family names (hyphenated, in either order), and parents are asked to complete a *déclaration conjointe de choix de nom* at the time of registering a birth; if you fail to complete a declaration, the child will be given the father's name only.

Costs

The cost of a midwife (see **Information & Support** below) is €15.30 for a consultation and €152.45 for a birth (extra for twins!). Social security pays 100 per cent of most medical expenses relating to a pregnancy, including medical examinations and tests, antenatal care and the delivery. It even pays for a physical examination for the father – to check whether he's likely to survive the ordeal! However, it's expensive to have a child in a hospital if you aren't covered by social security or don't have private medical insurance, in which case it may be cheaper to have your child abroad (or at home).

To qualify for social security maternity benefit (*allocation pour jeune enfant* – see page 332), mothers-to-be must undergo at least four antenatal examinations during their third, sixth, eighth and ninth months of pregnancy. Scans (*échographies*), using sound waves, are used to check foetal growth and to detect abnormalities (usually after 11, 22 and 33 weeks). After your first examination you receive a certificate (*attestation de premier examen prénatal obligatoire*) that must be sent to your CAF to ensure that you receive your social security benefits.

Information & Support

Midwives (*sages-femmes*), who are qualified nurses with special training, handle most routine pregnancies and play an important part in childbirth. They're responsible for educating and supporting pregnant women and their families. Midwives can advise women before they become pregnant, in addition to providing moral, physical and emotional support, both during pregnancy and after a birth. All public hospitals and many private clinics offer childbirth classes, although these may take the form or discussions rather than instruction. French social security also pays for physiotherapy (*kinésithérapie*) after childbirth.

Chemists can provide advice for pregnant women and new mothers concerning nutrition and supplements, and the care and feeding of babies. In some areas there are mother and child protection centres (Centre de Protection Maternelle et Infantile/PMI) providing free services to pregnant women and children under six, covered by social security. A list of local PMI centres is available from your town hall. Your family doctor or obstetrician will advise you about postnatal examinations and check-ups.

Many organisations provide counselling services for pregnant women, including SOS Bébé (☎ 01 42 47 08 67, 🖳 http://www.sosbebe.org), the Association Française des Femmes Enceintes (AFFE, ☎ 08 92 69 10 09, 🖳 http://www.affe. asso.fr) and the English-speaking International Counselling Service (contact via the American Church – see below). A book of interest to mothers-to-be is *ABCs of Motherhood in Paris* published by Message, a Paris-based English-language mothers' support group; it's available from most Paris expatriate groups, including WICE (see page 291) and the American Church (65 quai d'Orsay, 75007 Paris (☎ 01 40 62 05 00, 🖳 http://www.acparis.org), and via the Message website (🖳 http://www.messageparis.org). Information and help for mothers of premature babies are available from the Fondation de France in association with Sparadrap (🖳 http://www.sparadrap.org), which publishes a 16-page booklet (€3.50).

CHILDREN'S HEALTH

France provides excellent healthcare for children, including a comprehensive programme of preventive treatment and a variety of dedicated medical facilities, and all children are required to have monthly check-ups during infancy and three check-ups during their school years.

As in many other Western countries, there's a growing obesity problem in France, where over 15 per cent of children aged seven to nine are classified as obese and the obesity rate among teenagers has doubled in the last decade. Recent government measures aim to tackle the problem, as well as that of teenage smoking. Children can obtain a 'health kit' (*kit de santé*) from any of the 1,675 Centres d'Information et de Documentation Jeunesse (🖳 http://www.cidj.com). Booklets providing information for children about safe sex are available free from Crips d'Ile-de-France (☎ 01 56 80 33 60). For information about hospitalisation for children, see page 304.

Carnet de Santé

Children born in France are issued with a *carnet de santé* (health record book), in which is recorded every medical occurrence in their lives, including vaccinations, childhood illnesses, general medical care and surgery. It should always be taken with you on a medical visit with your child and must be produced when a child starts school. You can obtain a *carnet de santé* for children who weren't born in France from your local town hall on production of their passport. If you're covered by social security, it's provided free; otherwise there's a small fee. Examinations, vaccinations (see below) and check-ups required during a child's first six years are listed in the *carnet de santé*. The *carnet de santé* may be replaced by the *Carte Vitale 2* (see page 294) in the near future.

Vaccinations

Vaccinations against diphtheria (*diphtérie*), polio (*polio*) and tetanus (*tétanos*), collectively called *DPT*, and whooping cough (*coqueluche*) are given between the third and fifth months after birth (via three, monthly injections – usually in both thighs). *DPT* boosters are administered at 12 to 15 months and again at five to six years and are repeated thereafter at five- to six-year intervals. All children must be vaccinated again tuberculosis (*tuberculose*) by means of a BCG (*BCG*) before the age of six years but the vaccination isn't recommended before the age of two and there is controversy over the effectiveness of the vaccination, which can have adverse effects, such as causing an abscess or, in rare cases, paralysis. **Without these compulsory vaccinations, your child may not be admitted to school.**

Although it isn't compulsory, a multiple vaccination called ROR (or *rudirouvax*) against measles (*rougeole*), mumps (*oreillons*) and German measles (*rubéole*) is recommended between the age of 12 and 15 months. Vaccinations are provided free. When you arrive in France, you should bring proof of your child's immunisations with you. Children under three are also required to have a daily dose of vitamin D and fluoride.

DENTISTS

There are excellent dentists (*dentiste*) throughout France, where there are around 330 dentists per 100,000 inhabitants – similar to Germany, Switzerland and the US, but fewer than Italy (550 per 100,000) and more than the UK (around 300). Few French dentists speak fluent English ('Aaargh!' is the same in any language). Many embassies keep a list of dentists speaking their national language, and your employer, colleagues or neighbours may be able to recommend someone. Town halls maintain lists of local dentists, and local chemists may recommend someone or narrow the choice for you. You can obtain a list of dentists registered with social security from your local social security office. Dentists are listed in the yellow pages under *Dentistes*. Usually only names, addresses and telephone numbers are listed, and information such as specialities, surgery hours and whether they treat children (some don't) isn't provided. Many 'ordinary' dentists are qualified to perform non-routine treatment, e.g. endodontics (*endodontie*) or periodontics (*paradontie*), carried out by specialists in many other countries, but some treatment is available only from a 'surgeon dentist' (*chirurgien dentiste*). Dentists also usually carry out routine teeth cleaning themselves, and hygienists are rare.

Hours

Dentists' surgery hours vary considerably but are typically 09.00 to 12.00 and 14.00 to 19.00. Some dentists have Saturday morning surgeries, e.g. 09.00 to 12.00. You must make an appointment. (You shouldn't expect to receive a reminder from a dentist that you're due for a regular check-up.) Many dentists provide an emergency service, and there are emergency services in most major cities. In Paris, there's a 24-hour home emergency dental service called *SOS Dentaire* (☎ 01 43 37 51 00).

Costs

Dental treatment can be expensive, e.g. €1,500 for a crown fitted by a 'specialist', although the normal charge is between €300 and €600. A standard check-up costs €20, fillings (*reconstitution coronaire*) start at €17 and tooth extraction €34, while even plaque removal (*détartrage*) can set you back around €30. There's no additional €1 charge as for doctor's consultations. As with doctors, however, you should check whether a dentist is *conventionné* if you want costs to be reimbursed (see **National Health System** on page 293). Social security pays 70 per cent of the cost of dental care and prosthetic treatment, e.g. crowns and bridges. For orthodontic work, which is generally restricted to children under 12, you must obtain in advance a written description of the treatment required and an estimate of the cost for social security; you should be reimbursed 100 per cent of the cost.

However, these percentages apply to the theoretical cost of treatment as established by social security, which is often far lower than the actual cost. For example, the official cost of a crown is €107.50, so that the state will reimburse you only €75.25, whereas the cheapest crown usually costs around €350, and a ceramic crown can set you back up to €1,000 (dentists may charge what they like). You must pay the full cost of false teeth. Sometimes it pays to have private treatment, as social security pays dentists only a small amount for some jobs (such as cleaning teeth) and they're therefore less likely to do a thorough job.

Always obtain a written estimate before committing yourself to a large bill. If you or your family require expensive cosmetic dental treatment, e.g. crowns, bridges, braces or false teeth, it may be cheaper to have treatment abroad (e.g. in the UK). Alternatively, ask your dentist if he can reduce the cost by reducing the work involved. See also **Dental Insurance** on page 342.

Like doctors, dentists may give you a treatment form (*feuille de soins*), on which is listed the treatment provided and the cost. It's normal practice to pay a dentist after a course of treatment is completed, although if you're having expensive treatment such as a crown or bridge, your dentist may ask for a deposit (see **Reimbursement Procedure** on page 295).

OPTICIANS

There are no free eye tests for children or elderly people in France, where to obtain reimbursement (at 70 per cent) from social security it's necessary to have your eyes examined by an ophthalmologist (*ophtalmologue*), although you may have to wait weeks or even months for an appointment (the number of registered ophthalmologists is dwindling). An ophthalmologist is a specialist medical doctor trained in diagnosing and treating disorders of the eye, performing sight tests, and prescribing spectacles and contact lenses. As with doctors, some ophthalmologists are *conventionné*, meaning that they charge the basic rate of €27 for a consultation, whereas others (roughly half) aren't, which means that they may (and do) charge more but you will be reimbursed only at the basic rate. Treatment, including surgery, is reimbursed at only 65 per cent.

If glasses are necessary, the ophthalmologist will write a prescription which you then take to an optician, who is trained to test eyesight and to manufacture spectacles. To be reimbursed, you must choose an optician who's approved (*agréé*) by social security. Social security pays for 65 per cent of the cost of lenses and a 'basic' frame, provided your vision has changed or your spectacles are broken beyond repair. Note, however, that the approved cost of a basic frame is a mere €2.84 and of standard lenses €7.32, so your social security refund may be as little as €6.60 (hardly worth the paperwork!). The balance may be picked up by a *mutuelle* if you have one. Larger refunds are available for contact lenses, bifocals or tinted lenses, but you may need prior approval from your *caisse*; if applicable, your optician will complete the necessary documents for social security.

Children under six are entitled to an unlimited number of pairs of glasses, reimbursed at 65 per cent of €33 to €55, depending on the correction required; children over six are reimbursed for only one pair per year. Laser treatment for short-sightedness isn't reimbursed and costs between €250 and €400 per eye for the latest 'Lasik' treatment.

Some opticians test eyes as well as supplying glasses but these aren't reimbursed by social security, although some *mutuelles* cover the cost of optician-prescribed glasses. In Paris and other cities, there are large optical chains where spectacles can be made within an hour. Prices for spectacles and contact lenses aren't controlled and are generally higher than in some other European countries (for example, soft contact lenses are cheaper in the UK and Germany), so it's wise to shop around and compare costs. The French generally prefer spectacles to contact lenses, as the former are often a fashion accessory (or even a fashion 'statement'), but both are widely available. Always obtain an estimate for lenses and ask about charges for eye tests, fittings, adjustments, lens-care kits and follow-up visits. Non-standard lenses can increase the cost of spectacles considerably. Ask the cost of replacement lenses; if they're expensive, it may be worthwhile taking out insurance. Many opticians and retailers offer insurance against accidental damage for a nominal fee.

It isn't necessary to register with an optician or optometrist (*opticien*). You simply make an appointment with the optician of your choice. Ask your colleagues, friends or neighbours if they can recommend someone. Opticians are listed in the yellow pages under *Opticiens* and ophthalmologists under *Ophtalmologues*.

It's wise to have your eyes tested before you arrive in France and to bring a spare pair of spectacles and/or contact lenses with you. You should also bring a copy of your prescription in case you need to obtain replacement spectacles or contact lenses urgently.

COUNSELLING

Counselling and help are available throughout France for various health and social problems, including drug and nicotine addiction, alcoholism, compulsive gambling, obesity, teenage pregnancy, rape, AIDS, attempted suicide and psychiatric disorders, as well as problems related to homosexuality, adolescence, marriage and relationships, child abuse and family violence.

There's a 24-hour information/assistance telephone number (☎ 113) for problems associated with drugs, alcohol and smoking (*Drogue/Alcool/Tabac Info-Service*). There are also self-help groups in all areas for problems such as alcoholism, gambling and weight control (e.g. Weight Watchers). There are psychologists (*psychologue*), psychiatrists (*psychiatre*) and psychoanalysts (*psychanalyste*) in public as well as private practice, and consultations with those in public practice may be reimbursed by social security.

The telephone numbers of various local counselling and help services (*Services d'Assistance*) are listed at the front of telephone books and include numbers for *SOS Amitié*, the French equivalent of the Samaritans, which provides a free counselling service in times of personal crisis. (To find the number of your nearest *SOS Amitié* centre if you don't have a directory, call ☎ 01 40 09 15 22.) SOS Help is an English-speaking Paris-based telephone crisis line in operation from 15.00 to 23.00 daily (☎ 01 46 21 46 46), and there's an English-language Centre for International Psychological Help (CAPI) in Aquitaine (☎ 05 56 72 31 22, 🖳 http://www. capi.mailbox.as.com). For counselling services for pregnant women and mothers, see **Information & Support** on page 308.

Alcoholism

One of France's major health problems is alcoholism, which is directly responsible for the loss of 17,000 lives a year, mostly in poor urban and rural areas (usually as a result of drinking cheap red wine rather than spirits). The legal age for drinking alcohol is 16, although there's virtually no enforcement and children are readily served and sold alcohol everywhere. There are a number of English-speaking Alcoholics Anonymous (*Alcooliques Anonymes*) groups in Paris (☎ 01 48 06 43 68 for information) and other areas, and French-speaking groups throughout France.

Drugs

Although it's a serious health and social problem, the use of illegal drugs is less widespread in France than in North America and some other European countries such as the UK, Germany and the Netherlands, although it's reckoned that France has Europe's highest number of adolescent cannabis users. In total, it's estimated that there are over 150,000 heroin addicts and 7m cannabis smokers, but the law is seldom enforced and few drug users questioned are convicted.

For nationwide free information about drug-related problems contact *Drug Info Services* (☎ 08 00 23 13 13). A list of regional organisations providing information and treatment for drug abuse can be obtained from the Mission Interministérielle de Lutte contre la Toxicomanie (☎ 01 44 63 20 50). The government maintains a website (💻 http://www.drogues.gouv.fr) on which you can find a list of local help organisations.

AIDS & Other STDs

As in most Western countries, the spread of Acquired Immune Deficiency Syndrome (AIDS, known in French as *Syndrome Immuno-Déficitaire Acquis* or *SIDA*) continues to cause anxiety. France has the highest incidence of AIDS in the EU, largely as a result of its large African population. There are around 100,000 HIV-positive people in France, and there were around 7,000 new cases of HIV in 2004, over half of them male homosexuals (mostly in their thirties) and a third people of sub-Saharan African origin (two-thirds of these women); although the annual number of deaths has decreased since 1995, on average a person contracts HIV in France every 90 minutes.

There has also recently been an increase in cases of syphilis in Paris, and genital herpes is spreading among 15 to 25 year olds. In an attempt to combat sexually-transmitted diseases (STDs), the use of condoms (*préservatif*) has been widely encouraged through a comprehensive (if obscure) advertising campaign, although it has taken a long time to get the 'safe sex' message across. Condom machines have been installed in various public places, including *métro* stations and high schools. Condoms can also be bought cheaply in chemists', supermarkets and other shops.

Public health centres provide free information and confidential tests (*dépistage*) for AIDS and other STDs (*maladie sexuellement transmissible/MST*), and treatment is provided free or at a nominal cost.

General information about STDs can be obtained from the Ligue Nationale Contre les Maladies Vénériennes (☎ 01 40 78 26 00). Telephone information is available 24 hours a day on ☎ 08 00 84 08 00 and you can obtain free and anonymous AIDS testing at 1 place Fontenoy, 75350 Paris Cedex 07 (even the organisation offering the service is anonymous!). FACTS, the Association for Anglophones touched by HIV, is an English-language support group which can be contacted on ☎ 01 44 93 16 69 on Mondays and Wednesdays from 18.00 to 22.00; the FACTS office is open on Mondays to Fridays from 09.00 to 16.00 (☎ 01 44 93 16 32). Information and advice about AIDS is available from the Centres Régionaux d'Information et de Prevention du SIDA (CRIPS, 💻 http://www.lecrips.net), which has offices in Aquitaine, Auvergne, Ile-de-France, Nord-Pas-de-Calais, Pays-de-la-Loire, Provence-Alpes-Côtes-d'Azur and Rhône-Alpes. The Association Herpès has set up an information line (☎ 08 25 80 08 08). Booklets providing information for children about safe sex are available free from Crips d'Ile-de-France (☎ 01 56 80 33 33).

SMOKING

France has 12m smokers and, although overall numbers are falling, almost one in four children between 11 and 17 smoke, despite a law forbidding anyone under 16 from buying cigarettes. The incidence of smoking remains higher in France than in most other European countries, and it's estimated that over 50,000 deaths a year are directly attributable to smoking and that it adds some €8 billion to the state healthcare bill.

The sale of cigarettes is strictly controlled by the state, which owns the French cigarette manufacturers and collects nearly €10 billion in taxes annually from the sale of cigarettes and cigars; taxes have been dramatically increased in the last few years to encourage people to stop smoking – and to compensate the treasury for any decline in the number of smokers (the average packet of 20 costs around €5) and loss of revenue from tobacco advertising, which is banned! Cigarettes can be purchased only at a licensed tobaconnist's (*bureau de tabac* or simply *tabac*), although smuggling is rife, particularly along France's eastern frontiers. They're no longer sold in packs of ten (another attempt to discourage young smokers).

France has traditionally been extremely tolerant of smokers, and most people are indifferent or oblivious to the wishes or rights of non-smokers. Passive smoking is much less of an issue in France than in many other countries, although smoking is prohibited in certain public buildings, including schools, shops and offices open to the public and there are calls for a complete ban in public places (said to be favoured by over three-quarters of the population). Restaurants and cafes must provide an area for non-smokers. If they cannot do this, they're considered by the law to be entirely non-smoking. However, many establishments either ignore the law or create a remote non-smoking section or floor where most customers wouldn't wish to be seen dead. Since the beginning of 2006, smoking has been banned on all buses and trains in France and the SNCF is 'encouraging' smokers to extinguish cigarettes on entering stations. Smoking is forbidden on French domestic flights, and Air France international flights of less than two hours. Individuals who break the no-smoking laws can be fined between €75 and €200, and employers who fail to enforce them can be fined between €450 and €1,000. However, only the police and SNCF inspectors on French trains have the authority to impose a penalty, and complaints are rarely followed up.

Information and advice on smoking prevention and 'quit smoking' programmes (many run by hospitals) can be obtained via the internet (🖳 http://www.stop-tabac.ch).

GIVING BLOOD

As in the UK, the collection of blood is organised on a rather ad hoc basis and if you wish to give blood you should look out for signs advertising a local collection session or contact the Etablissement Français du Sang (☎ 01 55 93 95 00, 🖳 http://www.dondusang.net) to find out about sessions near you. You must be aged between 18 and 65 (60 for first-time donors) but you cannot give blood if you've had a blood transfusion at any time in your life, nor for four months after being tattooed or pierced.

If you've spent more than 12 months in the UK between 1980 and 1996, you may give blood only for non-therapeutic use, e.g. doctor training (owing to the perceived risk of passing on CJD).

DEATH

Procedure

When someone dies in France, the attending doctor completes a death certificate (*constatation de décès*), but the medical cause of death is treated as confidential and doesn't appear on death certificates. This can lead to problems if the body is to be sent abroad for burial, when a foreign coroner may require a post mortem examination. If a death takes place at home in Paris, a coroner (*médecin de l'état civil/médecin légiste*) must be called, although in the provinces a family doctor can complete the death certificate. An inquest (*enquête judiciaire*) must be held when a death occurs in a public place or when it could have been caused by a criminal act. In the case of the death of a French resident, you should make several copies of a death certificate.

A death must be registered within 24 hours at the town hall in the district where it took place. Anyone can register a death, but you must present your own identification and that of the deceased. If the deceased was a foreigner, the town hall will require his passport or *carte de séjour*. The family record book (*livret de famille*) is required for a French citizen (see page 524). Deaths of foreign nationals in France should also be registered at your local consulate or embassy.

Within a week of a death, you should inform banks, employer, retirement fund, insurers and *notaire*, as appropriate, as well as next of kin; within a month, a surviving spouse should apply for any pension refund (*réversion* – see page 349); and within six months you should provide a *déclaration des revenues* (on form 2042N) to the tax office showing all the income of the deceased's household between 1st January last and the date of death. See also **Wills** on page 394.

Euthanasia is illegal in France, although the current Health Minister has vowed to press for its legalisation.

Burial & Cremation

Cemeteries (*cimetière*) are secular and are usually owned by local authorities, who license a local undertaker (*pompes funèbres*) to perform burials. Before a burial can take place, the town hall must issue an 'act of death' (*acte de décès*) and a burial or cremation permit (*permis d'inhumer/de crémation*), as well as a permit to transport the body if it's to be buried outside the commune. You also need the mayor's permission to be buried in the commune where you have a second home. You should obtain at least six copies of the *acte de décès*. Bodies are normally buried or cremated within six days of death.

It's possible to reserve a burial plot (*concession*) for 15, 30 or 50 years or indefinitely. (You can even dig your own grave if you wish!) If a plot hasn't been reserved, the body will be buried in communal ground (*terrain communal*), where graves are maintained free of charge by the local authority for five years. After this period, the remains are disinterred and buried in a common grave. You're allowed to erect any monument but are responsible for the upkeep of a grave.

It's common for a coffin to be left uncovered while friends and relatives pay their last respects, and you should inform the undertakers if you want the coffin closed.

Until recently there weren't many crematoria (*crématoire*), although they can now be found in most large cities. You're entitled to scatter ashes anywhere except on a public right of way.

Costs

Dying in France is expensive and is best avoided if at all possible. However, the cost has recently been reduced, at least in the Paris area, with the opening of 'supermarkets for the dead' by the Roc-Eclerc chain (💻 http://www.roceclerc.com) – not without considerable opposition from undertakers. Always obtain a quotation (*devis*) for a funeral in advance and make sure you aren't paying for anything you don't want. The cost of a basic funeral is set by the commune and is usually around €400 to €600, although the average funeral costs around €1,000 and top-of-the-range funerals €3,000 (undertakers can bury you only once and have to make the most of it!). Many people take out an insurance policy to pay for their funerals. Although banks will block the deceased's accounts (unless joint accounts), the next of kin may withdraw up to €5,300 to pay for a funeral, on production of the *acte de décès* and an undertaker's bill. The spouse or partner of a person who dies before retirement is also entitled to a death benefit (*capital décès*) to offset funeral costs, etc..

A 30-year burial plot can cost between €150 and €500 depending on the area, and a perpetual plot between €1,500 and €4,000. The cost of cremation is around half that of a burial, unless you want the ashes scattered from a helicopter on top of Mont Blanc!

Information

Further information about funerals can be obtained from the Association Française d'Information Funéraire (☎ 01 45 44 90 03 – 24 hours, 💻 http://www.afif.asso.fr). If you wish to be an organ donor or want information about donating organs, contact the Etablissement Français des Greffes (☎ 08 00 20 22 24, 💻 http://www.efg.sante.fr).

13.

Insurance

It's unnecessary to spend half your income insuring yourself against every eventuality from the common cold to being sued for your last *centime*, but it's important to insure against any event that could precipitate a major financial disaster, such as a serious illness or accident. Most residents in France are covered by French social security (see page 323) and are entitled to higher benefits than residents of most other European Union (EU) countries. Nevertheless, you'd be unwise to rely solely on social security to meet your insurance needs. **It's your responsibility to ensure that you and your family are legally insured, and French law is likely to differ from that in your home country or your previous country of residence, so never assume that it's the same.**

There are a few occasions where insurance (*assurance*) for individuals is compulsory, including third-party car insurance, third-party liability insurance for tenants and homeowners, and mortgage life insurance if you have a mortgage (depending on the amount borrowed). If you lease a car or buy one on credit, a lender will insist that you have comprehensive car insurance (see page 255). Voluntary insurance includes car breakdown insurance (see page 259), third-party liability insurance for schoolchildren (see page 179), supplementary pensions, disability, health, household, dental, travel and life insurance (all covered in this chapter). If you fancy hunting in France, you can even take out insurance, costing from around €20, against being shot or having a leg chewed off by a *sanglier*!

If you're planning to take up residence in France, you should ensure that you and your family have full health insurance during the interval between leaving your last country of residence and obtaining health insurance in France. You should bear in mind that in some countries, e.g. the UK, if you inform your insurance companies that you're moving abroad permanently, they may automatically cancel your insurance policies without notifying you! One way to cover yourself for this interim period is to take out a travel insurance policy (see page 346). However, it's better to extend your present health insurance policy than to take out a new policy (most policies can be extended to provide international cover). This is particularly important if you have an existing health problem that won't be covered by a new policy.

When buying insurance shop till you drop! Obtain recommendations from friends, colleagues and neighbours (but don't believe everything they tell you). Compare the costs, terms and benefits provided by a number of companies before making a decision. Simply collecting a few brochures from insurance agents or making a few telephone calls could save you a lot of money. Premiums are often negotiable.

Further information about insurance can be found on the Service Public website (🖥 http://www.service-public.fr) and from the Centre de Documentation et d'Information de l'Assurance (CDIA), Fédération Française des Sociétés d'Assurances (☎ 01 42 47 90 00, 🖥 http://www.ffsa.fr).

INSURANCE COMPANIES & AGENTS

Insurance is one of France's major business sectors. There are 550 French insurance companies and mutual benefit organisations to choose from, many providing a range of services, while others specialise in certain fields only. The major insurance companies have offices or agents throughout France, including most large towns. Most insurance companies provide a free appraisal of your family's insurance needs. Many of the largest companies, such as Groupement d'Assurances Nationales and Assurances Générales de France, which were previously nationalised, have now been largely privatised, although the government maintains considerable regulatory control over the insurance industry. The insurance business is governed by regulations set out in the 'insurance code' (*code des assurances*) and insurance companies are supervised by the Direction Générale des Assurances. If you find it difficult to obtain insurance cover, the Bureau Central de Tarification (☎ 01 53 21 50 40, 🖳 http://www.service-public.fr) can demand that the company of your choice provide you with cover, with the premium fixed by the Bureau.

It's possible to take out certain types of insurance in another country, e.g. property insurance, although the policy must usually be written under French law. The advantages are that you will have a policy you can understand (apart from all the legal jargon!) and can make claims in your own language. This is usually a good option for the owner of a holiday home in France. However, bear in mind that insuring with a foreign insurance company may be more expensive than insuring with a French company. Since 1993 EU residents have been entitled to obtain insurance from any EU country and the Service Public website (🖳 http://www.service-public.fr) has links to the latest Ministry of Finance list of foreign and domestic companies licensed to sell insurance in France. In practice, however, it may be difficult or impossible to obtain insurance with a foreign company.

Insurance companies and *mutuelles* (see below) sell their policies in a number of ways. There are 'general agents' (*agent général*), which is a misleading term for agents who represent a single company and sell the policies of that company only, and there are brokers (*courtier*), who sell policies from a number of insurance companies and *mutuelles*. Most *mutuelles* and some insurance companies also sell their policies direct to the public, transactions often taking place by telephone and post. Note that it's often difficult to obtain impartial insurance advice, where brokers may be 'influenced' by the high fees offered for selling a particular policy. (Regrettably, you cannot sue an insurance agent for giving you bad advice.) Insurance agents, brokers and companies are listed in the yellow pages under *Assurances*.

Mutual Benefit Organisations

A mutual benefit organisation (*mutuelle*) is an association made up of individuals who are grouped together, e.g. by profession or area, in order to insure themselves for a favourable premium. There are two kinds of *mutuelle*: one is a sort of provident society or sick fund, which is a non-profit organisation that ploughs its profits back into the fund, and the other an insurance company operating at a profit (or not). A provident *mutuelle* provides fixed tariffs irrespective of the number of claims and is **greatly preferable** to an insurance company.

Most trades and occupations have their own *mutuelle*, commonly providing supplementary health insurance and pensions (see page 339). There are around 400 *mutuelles*, and it pays to choose one that's widely recognised by medical practitioners (see page 339). Further information about *mutuelles* can be obtained from the Fédération Nationale de la Mutualité Française (☎ 01 40 43 30 30, 💻 http://www.mutualite.com).

INSURANCE CONTRACTS

Read insurance contracts carefully before signing them. If you don't understand a policy, get someone to check it and explain the terms and the cover provided. Policies often contain traps in the small print and, like insurance companies everywhere, some French insurance companies will do almost anything to avoid honouring claims. Therefore it pays to deal only with reputable companies (not that this provides a guarantee!).

Premiums

An insurance premium (*cotisation*) should be paid within ten days of the due date. If it isn't, you will be notified; if it's still unpaid after 30 days, your policy may be suspended. You will, however, still be liable to pay the premium. Bear in mind that insurance companies often take eons to bill new customers and in the meantime you should obtain documentary evidence that you're insured, e.g. from an agent. You will normally be issued with a provisional contract and, several weeks later, a definitive contract (the French **love** paperwork).

Claims

If you wish to make a claim, you must usually inform your insurance company in writing by registered letter within two to five days of the incident (e.g. for accidents) or 24 hours in the case of theft. Thefts should also be reported to the local police station within 24 hours, as you must provide proof that you've filed a police report (*récépissé du dépôt de plainte*) when making a claim. **In some cases, these are legal requirements.** An insurance company will normally send an adjuster to evaluate the extent of the damage, e.g. to your home or car. You should obtain legal advice for anything other than a minor claim. You can hire an insurance expert to negotiate with your insurance company on your behalf.

In certain cases, claims for damaged property (such as storm-damaged buildings or vehicles damaged by hailstones) aren't considered by insurance companies unless the government declares the situation a natural catastrophe or 'act of God'.

Cancellation

Always check the notice period required to cancel (*résilier*) a policy. Note that, insurance policies are usually automatically extended (*tacite reconduction*) for a further period (usually a year) if they aren't cancelled in writing by registered letter two or three months before the expiry date. **If you don't cancel a policy, you must pay the next year's premium, even if you no longer require the insurance.** If you don't pay, you will be sued for the whole premium plus the credit agency's fees and interest. Your name may also be added to a debtor's list, your bank account frozen and the bailiffs called, resulting in even more costs!

You may cancel an insurance policy before the term has expired without penalty if the premium is increased, the terms are altered (e.g. the risk is diminished), an insured object is lost or stolen or, in the case of home insurance, if you move; in certain circumstances you may cancel without penalty if your personal circumstances change, e.g. you change jobs, are made redundant or retire, get married or divorced, or a member of your family dies. A cancellation for any of the above reasons must still be done in writing and sent by registered post.

SOCIAL SECURITY

France has a comprehensive social security (*sécurité sociale*) system covering healthcare, injuries at work, family allowances, unemployment insurance, and old age (pensions), invalidity and death benefits. France spends more on 'welfare' than almost any other EU country: over 30 per cent of GDP. Total social security revenue is around €200 billion per year and the social security budget is higher than the gross national product (GNP), i.e. social security costs more than the value of what the country produces!

Not surprisingly, social security benefits are among the highest in the EU (the average household receives around a third of its income from social support payments such as family allowances and pensions), as are social security contributions. Total contributions per employee (to around 15 funds) average around 60 per cent of gross pay, some 60 per cent of which is paid by employers (an impediment to hiring staff). The self-employed must pay the full amount (an impediment to self-employment!). However, with the exception of sickness benefits, social security benefits aren't taxed; indeed they're deducted from your taxable income. Equally unsurprisingly, the public has been highly resistant to any change that might reduce benefits, while employers are pushing to have their contributions lowered.

Despite the high contributions, the French social security system is under severe financial strain due to an ageing population, which has contributed to a huge increase in spending on healthcare, pensions and unemployment benefits in recent years (France's health spending alone is around 10 per cent of its GNP – the highest in Europe), and the government has the unenviable task of erasing some €38 billion of social security debt by 31st January 2009. Measures introduced recently include an enforced employee contribution towards 'the reimbursement of the social debt' (*contribution au remboursement de la dette sociale/CRDS* or *remboursement de la dette sociale/RDS*) – known unofficially as 'the social hole' (*le trou social*) – in addition to the existing employee levy (*CSG*) of 5.1 per cent (both contributions are levied against 95 per cent of total salary up to certain limits, which can be found on 🖳 http://www.legislation.cnav.fr). The combined *CRDS/CSG* now amounts to 8 per cent, which is only partly deductible from income taxes.

The Caisse Nationale d'Assurance Maladie (CNAM), which is part of the Ministry of Health and Social Security, is the public authority responsible for ensuring that social security policy is carried out on a national level and for negotiating conventions and agreements with medical professions. Sixteen regional sickness insurance fund offices (Caisse Régionale d'Assurance Maladie/CRAM) deal with questions regarding accidents at work and retirement and coordinate the actions of local social security offices (Caisse Primaire d'Assurance Maladie/CPAM), of which there are around 130 throughout the country (at least one in each department) and which deal with everyday matters and reimbursements.

Information

Information about social security is available online, e.g. the Service Public site (🖥 http://www.service-public.fr) and the Assurance Maladie site (🖥 http://www.ameli. fr – it stands for *Assurance Maladie en ligne*), where some information is available in English. There are a number of books (in French) about social security, including *Tous les Droits de l'Assuré Social* (VO Editions), and consumer magazines regularly publish supplements on various aspects of social security, particularly pensions and health insurance. For information in English about the French social security system, you can call the French Health Insurance Advice Line, set up by the CPAM of Manche but available to all residents (☎ 08 20 90 42 12).

Eligibility & Exemptions

Your entitlement to health and other social security benefits depends on your nationality, your work status (e.g. whether you're employed, self-employed or retired) and your residence status.

Unless you're covered by a reciprocal social security agreement, you must normally contribute to French social security for a certain period before you're eligible for benefits. For example, you must contribute for three months before being entitled to family allowances, and you must contribute for at least a year before claiming maternity benefits. Different periods of salaried employment are required to qualify for 'cash' benefits (*prestations en espèces*), e.g. disability payments, and benefits 'in kind' (*prestations en nature*), e.g. free medicines. For example, for *prestations en espèces* you must have been in salaried employment for at least 120 hours in the last quarter, while for *prestations en nature* you must have been salaried for at least 200 hours. Full details can be obtained from your local social security office. If you no longer meet the qualifying conditions, your benefits are extended for a maximum of a year from that date. (Benefits are extended indefinitely for the long-term unemployed, provided they're actively seeking employment.)

If you don't qualify under any of the categories below, don't have private health insurance (see page 339) and your annual income is below €6,965, you may be entitled to the most basic of state healthcare, known as *Couverture Maladie Universelle* (*CMU*), a programme introduced in January 2000 and intended to ensure that all French residents have social security cover. Information is available from your local CPAM office and on a dedicated government website (🖥 http://www.cmu.fr).

UK citizens wishing to claim family allowances in France must obtain a 'signing off paper' from the Child Benefit Office (PO Box 1, Newcastle-upon-Tyne, NE88 l88,

☎ 0845-302 1444, 🖳 http://www.newcastle.gove.uk) and may also need proof of income and health insurance. For further information, contact the Longbenton Contact Centre for Non-Residents Helpline [*sic*], Department of Work and Pensions (formerly Department of Social Security), Benton Park View, Newcastle-upon-Tyne, NE98 1ZZ, UK (☎ 0191-203 7010), which can send you a useful booklet (no. SA29) entitled *Your social security insurance, benefits and healthcare rights in the European Economic Area*, or visit the websites of HM Revenue & Customs (🖳 http://www.hmrc.gov.uk) and the Department of Work and Pensions itself (🖳 http://www.dwp.gov.uk).

EU Nationals

If you're an EU resident visiting France, you can take advantage of reciprocal healthcare agreements. You should apply for a certificate of entitlement to treatment at your local social security office (or a post office in the UK). The paper form called an E111 has been superseded by a plastic card called a European Health Insurance Card (EHIC), and there have been a number of changes to procedures and conditions of use.

First, an EHIC must be applied for (by post, phone or internet) at least a month before travel and cannot simply be obtained the same day from a post office. An EHIC covers only one person and not a family, as did the E111. Its period of validity varies with the country of issue: in the UK, it's valid for three to five years (an E111 had to be renewed annually). However, you must continue to make social security contributions in the country where it was issued and, if you become a resident in another country (e.g. in France), it becomes invalid in that country. Although an EHIC entitles you to much better cover than an E111 (which covered only emergency hospital treatment, whereas the EHIC covers 'any necessary medical treatment arising during a temporary stay in another EU member state'), it still doesn't entitle you to 100 per cent reimbursement of all medical expenses in France. Rather, it gives you entitlement to the same cover as a French resident, i.e. normally around 70 per cent of routine healthcare and treatment costs. **You can still receive a large bill from a French hospital, as the National Health Service assumes only a percentage of the cost (see page 293)!** You're therefore recommended to enquire about the availability of 'top-up' insurance plans, covering the balance of costs.

If you do incur medical costs in France, you must obtain a treatment confirmation (*feuille de soins*) and go to the local CPAM, the authority which deals with health insurance, to apply for reimbursement, which will be sent to you or credited to your UK bank account. Details of the procedure are included in the booklet that comes with the EHIC form. Note that it can take months for medical expenses to be reimbursed.

As soon as you have a permanent address in France, even if this is within the six month period the EHIC covers you for, you must obtain an E106 (for people below retirement age) or an E121 (for retirees), which is available in the UK from the Inland Revenue's International Pension Service (☎ 0191-218 7777). This form entitles you to cover while you transfer out of your home country's system (you must inform the relevant authority, e.g. the Department of Work and Pensions in the UK) and into the French system.

British visitors or Britons planning to live in France can obtain further information about reciprocal health treatment in France from the Department of Work and Pensions' Medical Benefits department (☎ 0191-218 7747) or, if they're of pensionable age, from the Pension Service (☎ 0191-218 7777) and about the new EHIC from the post office (☎ 0845-606 2030) and via the internet (e.g. 🖳 http://www.dh.gov.uk/travellers).

Employees

France has social security agreements with over 40 countries (including all other EU countries and the US), whereby employees on a short-term assignment in France can continue to make contributions to social security in their home country and be eligible for social security benefits in France. An EHIC (see **EU Nationals** above) is required for the first year of employment and forms E102 and E106 for an extension. The maximum period to which this arrangement applies is usually five years, although you may be required to contribute to French social security if you work in France for more than two years. The exact terms of social security agreements vary from country to country and you should check before starting work in France. However, if you qualify to pay contributions abroad, it's usually worthwhile doing so, as contributions in most countries are much lower than those in France.

If you're from a country which doesn't have a social security agreement with France and are employed in France, your employer must declare you to the URSSAF (see page 328) and pay social security contributions on your behalf.

If you require just health insurance, it's **much** cheaper to take out private health insurance (see page 339) than pay high French social security payments. Private health policies also offer a greater choice of health facilities and may provide a wider range of benefits than social security.

Unemployed & Low Income

If you aren't employed, you may still be able to make contributions in your home country and claim benefits in France for a period. If you're unemployed and seeking work in France, you may be entitled to medical treatment for up to three months on presentation of form E119. Those on low incomes (e.g. under €6,965 for a single person and €13,930 for a couple) are exempt from social security contributions and also qualify for free complementary insurance (see page 339). When you no longer meet the qualifying conditions, benefits are extended for a maximum of a year from the applicable date. In the case of long-term unemployed people actively seeking employment, benefits are extended indefinitely. **Non-salaried Americans aren't covered by French social security and must have private health insurance** (see page 339). If you're receiving social security benefits in the US, you may be restricted as to the number of hours you can work in France (e.g. 45 per month).

Students

If you're a student following a standard course at a French state-suppported institution, you're normally covered by French social security. However, if you're attending a private institution, e.g. the American University of Paris, or are following a non-standard programme, e.g. French language and culture classes, you must have (and must produce evidence of) private health insurance (see page 339). Those coming to France under an exchange scheme must be covered for healthcare by the exchange authorities.

Retirees

Retirees receiving a state pension from another EU country are entitled to the same health benefits as French retirees. EU retirees over 60 going to live permanently in France aren't required to contribute to French social security, but must register with their local CPAM (and present forms E106 and E121). You're now required to have a form E121 for **each** member of your household. If you're receiving a state pension in another EU country, you may be subject to an annual check that you're still receiving it.

EU citizens who retire before qualifying for a state pension can receive French social security health cover for up to 30 months by obtaining a form E106 from their country's social security department; you must have made full contributions in your home country during the last two years. You need to register at your local CPAM, where you must present a copy of your *carte de séjour/résident* or your temporary authorisation (*récépissé de demande de carte de séjour*), proof of your relationship with any dependants who don't qualify in their own right (e.g. a marriage certificate), and your bank account details (*relevé d'identité bancaire*). If the temporary cover expires before you reach retirement age, you must take out private health insurance (see page 339) or make voluntary social security contributions in order to qualify for benefits, with contributions based on your income (which must be confirmed by your tax return). If you're of retirement age but are still working, you may qualify for an E106 and obtain health benefits for up to 30 months.

Registration

If you're working in France, your employer will usually complete the necessary formalities to ensure that you're covered by social security. If he doesn't, you must obtain confirmation that you're employed in France (*déclaration d'emploi*) and register at your local CPAM. Your town hall will give you the address or you can find it under *Sécurité Sociale* in your local yellow pages. In certain cases, you will need to visit the *Relations Internationales* department of social security, e.g. if you're retired with a pension in another EU country.

You must provide your personal details, including your full name, address, country of origin, and date and place of birth. You will also need to produce passports, *cartes de séjour* and certified birth certificates for your dependants, plus a marriage certificate (if applicable). You may need to provide copies with official translations, but check first, as translations may be unnecessary. You will also need proof of residence such as a rental contract or an electricity bill.

When you've registered, you will receive a registration card (*Carte Vitale*), which looks like a credit card and contains a smart chip (*puce*). The card has your name and your social security number (*No. d'Immatriculation de l'Assuré*) printed on the front. (Social security numbers are issued by l'Institut National de la Statistique et des Études Economiques/INSEE.) Additional information is coded into the chip, which is needed to process any claim for reimbursement or services. Contrary to some fears, there's no detailed information regarding your health or medical condition on the chip, although these may be included on the *Carte Vitale 2*, intended to supersede the *Carte Vitale* in 2006.

Along with a *Carte Vitale*, you will receive a certificate (*attestation*) containing a list of those entitled to benefits on your behalf (*bénéficiaires*), i.e. your dependants, and the address of the office where you must apply for reimbursement of your medical expenses. (This address is normally indicated in small type just above your name and address and is easy to miss.) Dependants include your spouse (if he isn't personally insured), dependent children under the age of 16 (or under the age of 20 if they're students or unable to work through illness or invalidity), and ascendants, descendants and relatives by marriage supported by you and living in the same household.

If you move home, acquire or need to change or transfer beneficiaries or find any errors in the information on your *attestation*, you must inform your CPAM. If a social security official makes a regular visit to your town hall, you may be able make changes to your records and ask questions during a scheduled visit.

The date when your entitlement to social security benefits expires is shown on the certificate (*droits jusqu'au…*). Just before the end of the year when your benefits expire, you should receive a new certificate, along with instructions as to how and where to update your card. There are machines in most public hospitals and in some town halls in which you can simply insert your *Carte Vitale* and update the chip. Alternatively, you can post the card to the office that sent it to you and ask for it to be updated. Make sure you keep your certificate in a safe place, as you may be required to show it if you require services from a medical practitioner chemist who isn't linked to the card system or whose computer is out of order.

Contributions

Social security contributions (*cotisations sociales* or *charges sociales*) are calculated as a percentage of your taxable income, although for certain contributions there's a maximum salary level. Contributions start as soon as you're employed or start work in France and not when you obtain your residence permit (*carte de séjour*). Contributions are paid directly to the Union de Recouvrement des Cotisations de Sécurité Sociale et d'Allocations Familiales (URSSAF), which has 105 offices throughout France. URSSAF offices collect contributions for their area and send them to the central social security agency (Agence Centrale des Organismes de Sécurité Sociale/ACOSS) that distributes funds to the various benefit agencies (e.g. CNAF, CNAV and CRAM). It's possible to pay contributions monthly (actually, you pay ten monthly instalments from January to October based on an estimated total contribution; any necessary adjustment is made in November or December); you must apply before 1st December for monthly payments from the following 1st January.

Employees

The total social security contributions for employees (*salarié*) are an average of around 60 per cent of gross pay, some 60 per cent of which (i.e. around 35 per cent of gross pay) is paid by employers. The employees' portion comes to around 25 per cent of gross pay. All contributions are withheld from pay cheques, so no action is required (except to mourn the loss of so much hard-earned money). Salaried employees come under the general regime for salaried workers (*régime général des travailleurs salariés*). There are special regimes for agricultural workers (*régime agricole*), called MSA or GAMEX, and for miners, seamen, railway workers and various other state employees. All these are termed obligatory regimes (*régimes obligatoires*). It's also possible to make voluntary contributions (if you can't think of anything better to do with your money).

Self-employed

Before you can be recognised as a self-employed person (*travailleur indépendant*) in France you must register with the appropriate organisation (see **Self-employed** on page 380). As a self-employed person you must deduct social security contributions from your own earnings and pay them directly to URSSAF. Once registered, you may choose from a selection of recognised organisations providing pensions and health insurance (see **Supplementary Pensions** on page 339).

Recent legislation has provided some more than welcome respite for the newly self-employed, who, instead of making crippling social security contributions from their start-up, now make contributions (as well as income tax) as their business generates income. For example, if you earn less than €27,000 from a non-salaried source, you can declare the income as *Micro-BIC* (for commercial earnings – *bénéfices commerciaux*) or *Micro-BNC* (non-commercial earnings – *bénéfices non commerciaux*) on your tax return (see page 381) and you may be entitled to exoneration from part or all of the social security contributions on this income, as well as to generous VAT (*TVA*) exclusions (see page 372). Contributions are payable in two lump sums on 1st April and 1st October each year.

The table below shows the percentage of gross income you must pay in social security contributions if you're self-employed, and the actual payments you will make if you earn €50,000. All percentages apply to full salary unless otherwise stated. Note that the figures below are for *artisans* in 2005; figures for traders and other types of self-employed person are currently slightly different, but within the next few years, it's intended that all self-employed people will make the same contributions.

Type of Contribution	Contribution	Contribution on €50,000
Health Insurance	7.5%	€3,750
Family Allowances	5.4%	€2,700
Pension*	25.05%	€12,525
CSG (income tax deductible)	5.1%	€2,550

CSG/CRDS (non-deductible)	2.9%	€1,450
Total		**€22,975**

* The pension contribution is in fact three separate contributions: 16.35 per cent for a basic state pension; 6.7 per cent for a supplementary pension; 2 per cent for death and invalidity insurance.

If you're continuing a business that you were conducting in your previous country of residence, where you were making social security contributions until the date of your move, you will be charged contributions in your first year of residence in France at a 'forfetary' level equivalent to 30 per cent of the minimum contributions (around €1,100). In your second year of operation, you will be charged contributions according to your declared income for Year 1 on a pro rata basis (e.g. 50 per cent if you moved to France on 1st July) plus an adjustment for Year 1. Your Year 3 contributions will be calculated on your full year's salary in Year 2, and so on in subsequent years.

Within a limited period of starting business activity, you must register with the Caisse d'Allocations Familiales (CAF) for family allowances, the Caisse Nationale de l'Assurance Maladie (CNAM) for sickness benefits, and the Caisse Nationale d'Assurance Vieillesse (CNAV) for an old-age pension. You may also be required to sign up with a special social security association if you receive payments from a hobby or other activity (e.g. writing) that exceed around €6,000 during any calendar year.

If you form a limited company, you can decide the salary you pay yourself and therefore limit your social security contributions. However, your total contributions are higher than for a sole trader, although you receive higher benefits. If you're the boss of a company employing members of your family and you own over 50 per cent of the shares, you're treated as self-employed and must pay social security contributions as a sole trader. For further details of this complex subject, refer to *Making a Living in France* (Survival Books – see page 587).

Employers

If you employ full-time staff, you must make social security contributions for your employees equivalent to over 35 per cent of their salary (see table below). If you employ someone to undertake work for you, you should ensure that he has adequate insurance (e.g. accident and third-party liability) or is registered as self-employed and therefore making social security contributions. If you pay someone to do a job on a casual basis (e.g. gardening) and he isn't registered as self-employed, you can make the necessary contributions on his behalf in order to ensure that both he and you are insured in the event of an accident. This can be done by using the *Chèque Emploi Service* system (see page 364). **If you agree to pay anyone in cash or by ordinary cheque and they have an accident on your premises, you can be sued for a very large sum of money.**

Calculation

The table below shows the percentage of gross income paid in social security contributions by employers and salaried employees, and the actual payments for an employee based on an annual gross salary of €20,000 – contributions apply to the whole salary unless otherwise stated. Figures in brackets refer to the notes below.

Type of Contribution	Contribution Employer	Employee	Contribution on €20,000
Health Insurance	12.80%	0.75%	€2,560
Widow's Insurance (*FNAL*)	0.10% (1)	-	€20
Family Allowances	5.40%	-	€1,080
Basic Pension			
(total salary)	1.60%	0.10%	€320
(first €30,192)	14.75%	8.20%	€2,950
Obligatory Complementary			
Pension – Managers (2)			
ARRCO (first €30,192)	4.50%	3.00%	€900
Death benefit (first €30,192)	1.50%	-	€300
AGFF (first €30,192)	1.20%	0.80%	€240
AGFF (above €30,192)	1.30%	0.90%	-
AGIRC (above €30,192)	12.50%	7.50%	-
APEC (above €30,192)	0.036%	0.024	-
CET	0.22%	0.13%	€44
CSA (3)	0.30%	-	€60
Unemployment Insurance	4%	2.00%	€800
Workers' Compensation	1%	-	€200
CSG – deductible (95% of salary)	-	5.10%	-
CSG/CRDS – non-deductible (95% of salary)	-	2.40%	-
AGS/FNGS	0.45%	-	€90
Total Employer Contributions for Employee Earning €20,000			**€9,564**

1. This rate applies only to employers with fewer than ten employees. For ten or more, the rate is 0.40 per cent.

2. Contributions for non-managers are lower. Note that for employees, the basic pension (*vieillesse*) contributions are paid to URSSAF and the complementary pension (*retraite complémentaire*) paid to a separate organisation (actually to two separate organisations!), whereas for the business owner both are paid to the same retirement fund.

3. The *contribution de solidarité pour l'autonomie* is a new charge introduced in July 2004 (supposedly to prevent a recurrence of the 'disaster' of summer 2003, when thousands of old people died during the heat wave), collected by URSSAF.

Benefits

Under French social security you're entitled to health, sickness and maternity, work injury and invalidity, family allowance, unemployment, and old age, widow(er)'s and death benefits, each of which is described below. With the exception of health benefits, these are known as 'cash' payments (*prestations en espèces*). Health benefits are known as payments 'in kind' (*prestations en nature*), e.g. free medicines. Most social security benefits (*allocations*) are paid as a percentage of your salary rather than at a flat rate, subject to minimum and maximum payments. You must have been employed for a minimum period and/or earn a minimum salary to qualify for certain benefits, as detailed below.

Health Benefits

To qualify for health benefits you must have been employed for 600 hours in the last six months (or for six months at the minimum wage), 200 hours in the last quarter or 120 hours in the last month. There's no minimum qualifying period during the first three months after registration. For details of health benefits, see **Chapter 12**.

Sickness Benefit

To qualify for sickness benefit you must have been employed for 200 hours in the last three months or six months at the minimum wage. To qualify for extended cash sickness benefit you must have been insured for 12 months before your incapacity and for 800 hours of employment in the last 12 months. This includes 200 hours in the first 3 of the last 12 months or 2,080 hours at the minimum wage, including 1,040 hours during the first 6 of the last 12 months. Employees who aren't automatically covered by sickness insurance can contribute voluntarily. As with unemployment benefit (see below), sickness benefit is paid as a percentage of your previous salary (e.g. 50 per cent) rather than at a flat rate. A leaflet explaining sickness benefit is available from CPAM offices (listed on 🖳 http://www.ameli.fr). Information is also available on the Service Public website (🖳 http://www.service-public.fr).

Maternity Benefit

To qualify for maternity benefit you must have been insured for at least ten months before your pregnancy began and have been employed for 200 hours in the first 3 of the last 12 months or have made six months' contributions. Benefits are payable for an extra two weeks before the birth if there are complications and for up to 12 weeks for multiple births. A monthly allowance or milk coupons are available for four months after the birth. Benefits are also paid for adoptions. Employees who aren't automatically covered by maternity insurance can contribute voluntarily.

Work Injury & Invalidity Benefits

Industrial accident insurance pays all medical and rehabilitation costs associated with work injuries (*accident de travail*) and provides a pension for you or your dependants in the case of injury or death. Insurance starts from your first day at work, with the variable contributions paid wholly by your employer. A benefit of 60 per cent of earnings is paid (up to a maximum amount) during the first 28 days of disability and thereafter 80 per cent of earnings. Self-employed workers are excluded and are covered under the state sickness insurance programme.

In the case of injury resulting in permanent total disability, a pension equal to 100 per cent of average earnings during the last 12 months is paid from the day following the accident. In the case of partial disability, average earnings are multiplied by between 0.5 and 1.5 depending on the degree of disability. A lump sum payment is made if a disability is below 10 per cent. All necessary associated medical treatment, surgery, hospitalisation, medicines, appliances, rehabilitation and transportation are paid 100 per cent by social security. Those over 60 with at least 80 per cent invalidity are also entitled to an *allocation compensatrice tierce personne* (*ACTP*).

Family Allowances

France is a great place for large families (*famille nombreuse*), as there are high family allowances and other benefits (including lower taxes) to encourage couples to have more children. To qualify for the basic family allowance (*prestation* or *allocation familiale*) you must have a *carte de séjour* and at least two children living at home with you, and your household income must be below a certain level (which depends on your circumstances). Your child(ren) must usually be under 16, but he can be 20 if unemployed or earning no more than 55 per cent of the legal minimum wage (*SMIC* – see page 24). The monthly basic family allowance in 2005 was €115.64 for two children and €148.16 for each subsequent child; these sums are increased by €32.52 for children between 11 and 16 and by €57.82 for children over 16. There's no allowance for the first child (to encourage you to have more!). A 'family supplement' (*complément familial*) of €150.51 is paid if you have children under six or have three or more children over the age of three and your household income is below a certain level. There are different schemes for agricultural, railway and public utility employees.

Other family allowances include a birth or 'adoption allowance' (*prime à la naissance ou à l'adoption*), which pays €830.25 per child expected in the seventh month of pregnancy, a 'starter allowance' (*allocation de base*) of €166.05 per month from birth until the child is three years old, plus additional amounts if one or both parents stops work or works part-time (these two allowances are part of the *prestation d'accueil du jeune enfant/PAJE*, which also includes an allowance for giving up work and for employing a child minder), a 'school start allowance' (*allocation de rentrée scolaire/ARS*), a 'single parent allowance' (*allocation de parent isolé/API*), a 'family support allowance' (*allocation de soutien familial*), a 'parental education allowance' (*allocation parentale d'éducation*), a 'special education allowance' (*allocation d'éducation spéciale*), a 'parental presence allowance' (*allocation de présence parentale*) for parents taking time off work to look after a sick or disabled child, an 'aid to resuming activity' (*aide à reprise d'activité des femmes/ARAF*) for women whose children are all at school, grants for employing a child-minder (*aide à la famille pour l'emploi d'une assistante maternelle agréée*), an allowance for moving house if you have (or are expecting) at least three children and need a larger home (*prime de déménagement*), and various rent allowances for the low-paid (e.g. *aide personnalisée au logement* and *allocation de logement familiale*). In 2006 the government announced a further incentive for couples to procreate: a grant roughly equivalent to the minimum wage (see page 24 on the birth of a third child. Most of these allowances, including the young child allowance, are also means tested.

In addition to the above, there are various holiday benefits (*aide aux vacances*) for low-income families, including vouchers for holiday camps (*coupon vacances en camps et colonies*) and activity centres (*coupon centres de loisirs sans hébergement*), cultural and sporting activity vouchers (*chèque loisirs*), and family holiday vouchers (*coupon vacances familiales*).

If you're entitled to family allowances in another EU country, you must provide a certificate of termination of payments in that country. Some family allowances are 'exportable' and paid to families with parents resident in France and children abroad, e.g. for education or health reasons. If one parent lives abroad with the children and is unemployed and the other lives and works in France, the parent in France is entitled to claim family allowances. If the parent abroad works and is paid family allowances by his country of residence, the difference is paid to the parent working in France (provided this is less than the French family allowance, which is likely). For further information enquire at your local CAF in France or at a social security office abroad or visit the CAF website (🖥 http://www.caf.fr).

Unemployment Benefit

In order to qualify for unemployment benefit (*allocation d'assurance chômage*) you must be under 60 and must have been employed for at least three months during the last year, and for two of the last three years. You must also be registered at your local unemployment office (Agence Nationale Pour l'Emploi/ANPE), be capable of work and be actively seeking employment. The ANPE sends your details to the Associations pour l'Emploi dans l'Industrie et le Commerce (ASSEDIC), which will send you the appropriate forms to complete. It's usually two to three months before you receive your first payment, made by direct transfer into a bank or post office account, although payments are back-dated. Unemployment benefit in France is paid as a percentage of your previous salary (e.g. 40 per cent) rather than at a flat rate. Once you're receiving unemployment benefit, you're sent a form each month on which you must declare that you're still unemployed.

In the last few years the government has had an unemployment payments crisis due to the high number of unemployed. Certain categories of self-employed and managing directors (*gérants*) of even the smallest companies aren't eligible for unemployment benefit at all (and they don't have to pay the contributions for unemployment), although they can voluntarily enrol in an insurance plan that combines limited unemployment cover with a supplementary pension. Domestic and seasonal workers aren't covered, and there are 'special' (i.e. restricted) schemes for building and dock workers, merchant seamen and pilots. If unemployment was due to voluntarily leaving a job without a legitimate reason, dismissal due to misconduct, or your refusal of a suitable job offer, unemployment benefit won't be paid or will be discontinued.

If you're entitled to unemployment benefit from another EU country and have been claiming unemployment for at least four weeks, you can continue to receive unemployment benefit (at your home country's rate) in France for up to three months while looking for work. However, you must inform the unemployment office in your own country that you intend to seek work in France well in advance of your departure (e.g. six weeks in the UK, where you should apply using the form contained in leaflet UBL22, *Unemployment Benefit for People Going Abroad or Coming From Abroad*). If you qualify for transfer of benefits to France, your home country's unemployment service will provide a certificate of authorisation, which is required to register in France. You must register for work at the nearest office of the ANPE (see page 31) in France within seven days of leaving your home country, so that your eligibility for benefits isn't interrupted. However, there may be a delay of up to three months before you actually start to receive benefits, so you must be able to finance yourself during your job search in France. During this period you're entitled to healthcare in France, for which you require a certificate of entitlement (form E119). **French bureaucrats aren't very co-operative with this scheme (i.e. even more obstructive than they are usually) and you must persevere to obtain your rights.**

Even if you **aren't** entitled to unemployment benefit, you may be eligible for other benefits aimed at unemployed people, e.g. a free transport pass. To qualify for these benefits, you must obtain a letter of 'rejection' (*rejet*) from the ANPE. (The ways of French bureaucracy are strange indeed!)

Old Age Pensions

The state pension scheme comprises both basic and supplementary schemes (see **Pensions** below).

Widow(er)'s & Death Benefits

Some 85 per cent of elderly people are cared for at home (around 4m people over 75 compared with only 450,000 in old people's homes) and the number is increasing annually. A new allowance, *allocation personnalisée à l'autonomie* (*APA*), was introduced in January 2001 to help those over 60 who are no longer able to look after themselves or who require regular home help. There's also a state widow(er)'s allowance in France (*allocation veuvage*), which is now available also to childless widow(er)s, and the spouse or partner of a person who dies before retirement. Divorced and widowed people continue to receive benefits for at least a year after the divorce or spouse's death, separated people for as long as their spouse is employed, provided they aren't eligible for benefits from any other sources. Widow(er)s are also entitled to a death benefit (*capital décès*) to offset funeral costs, etc., but this is limited to around three months' salary or a maximum of around €6,600. Indeed, social security isn't generous when it comes to death and pays only around three months' salary or a maximum of around €6,000 to a widow or dependants. If your employer doesn't provide life insurance (or if the cover provided is inadequate), you should consider taking out a private policy (see **Life Insurance** on page 348).

PENSIONS

There's a worsening crisis in state pension funding in France, which has the largest proportion of inactive people over 55 in the EU, high unemployment, one of Europe's highest life expectancies, and over 40 per cent of 18 to 25-year-olds in full-time education. The French pension system is largely unfunded, which means that the active population pays the pensions of those who are retired or otherwise inactive – known as a *régime de répartition*. As in many countries, there are plans to transfer the burden from the public to the private sector, although this is likely to create controversy and social unrest. The state pension scheme comprises both basic and supplementary schemes. The main scheme covers employees in business and industry and there are other schemes for various government employees, small businessmen, shopkeepers and farmers. Contributions are paid by both employers and employees and vary with income. Certain non-employed people can contribute voluntarily to the state pension scheme.

Basic Pension

The national retirement insurance fund, the Caisse Nationale d'Assurance Vieillesse (CNAV, 🖥 http://www.cnav.fr), for employees is the largest pension fund in France, and basic state pensions are paid at 60 for both men and women (among western European countries, only Italy pays state pensions at a lower age – 57 for women). Certain categories of civil servant receive full pension benefits after just two-thirds of the time required for those working in the private sector and the self-employed. For example primary school teachers, nurses and postal workers can retire on a full pension at 55, and police officers, prison warders and train drivers can retire at 50. A mother with three or more children has the right to retire on a full pension after just 15 years' public service.

When you register with social security, a record is opened in your name where your payments are recorded. Your insured period is determined from your record and periods of absence from work due to sickness, work accidents, childbirth, unemployment and military service are credited for pension purposes. To receive a full pension you must have contributed for at least 160 'terms' (meaning quarter-years), i.e. around 40 years, but there are plans to extend this to 42.5 or even 45 years. If you don't qualify for a full pension, your pension is proportional to the number of terms you've contributed for, i.e. 1/160 of the full pension multiplied by the number of terms' insurance. A full pension is equal to 50 per cent of your average earnings in your 19 highest paid years (earnings are re-valued in line with inflation), which is progressively being increased to 25 years. The maximum pension is currently €15,534. With at least 150 terms (37.5 years) of coverage, you're guaranteed a minimum annual pension of around €6,641.28 irrespective of your income level during your working life. Basic state pensions are automatically adjusted bi-annually in accordance with the national average wage.

Supplementary Pensions

Most employees contribute to a supplementary pension plan (*caisse complémentaire de retraite*), which may be state-funded or private, in addition to the obligatory state pension fund. In many industries, supplementary pension schemes are provided for employees earning above a certain salary, e.g. €2,000 per month; these are called *institutions de réparation*. Almost every trade or occupation has its own scheme and in many companies it's obligatory for employees to join. For example, executives and managerial staff must contribute to a supplementary pension scheme called a *caisse de retraite des cadres ou des cadres supérieurs*. These schemes generally offer little flexibility, and you may be committed to regular payments for a fixed number of years and no option to take a lump sum at the end. In addition to providing a supplementary pension, however, most schemes are allied to a complementary health insurance fund (*assurance complémentaire maladie*) that pays the portion of medical bills that isn't paid by social security (see **Private Health Insurance** below).

An employee is attributed a number of points each year and the pension rate is based on the number of points accumulated at the age of 60, although a lower pension may be taken at 55. A survivor is entitled to 60 per cent of a deceased employee's pension. In most cases your supplementary pension and your state pension provide a pension equal to around 80 per cent of your final salary at retirement, provided that you've contributed for the maximum 40 years. If you already contribute to a company scheme and are transferred to France, you should make sure that you can continue to contribute while employed there (see below). Many company pension schemes are 'portable' and can be transferred to another employer or converted to a private pension scheme. However, contributions to foreign pension schemes aren't usually tax deductible in France.

If your French employer doesn't provide a supplementary pension scheme or you're self-employed, you may wish to contribute to a personal scheme (*assurance retraite*), which operates in the same way as a life assurance policy (see page 348). This is usually more flexible than a company scheme: you can choose how much to pay in each year and may take a lump sum or an annuity when you retire. A new pension savings plan is the *plan d'épargne retraite populaire* (*PERP*), introduced by the government in 2003. It's similar to a British 'approved pension' scheme, whereby funds deposited are 'locked' until your retirement, when you must take an annuity, which will be liable for income tax. Ten per cent of your deposits can be deducted from your taxable income (up to a ceiling – initially €2,920). See also **Savings Accounts** on page 365. **A self-employed person must pay around €2,000 to €2,500 per year into a private pension fund for a pension of around €300 per month.**

If you already have a private pension scheme in your home country, it may be advantageous to transfer your savings to a French scheme (e.g. the Inland Revenue in the UK allows 10 per cent of foreign pensions to be taken tax-free). Your home country may impose certain transfer conditions, however; the Inland Revenue, for example, stipulates that you must be leaving the UK permanently and entering employment in France, and that your money is transferred into a bona fide pension plan. **Before transferring a private pension to France, you should consult an expert who is familiar with pension schemes in France and your home country.**

Retiring in France

If you intend to retire while in France, you should check regularly that your pension contributions are up to date. A state pension is paid only when you cease full-time employment and not until you make an application to your regional sickness insurance fund office (Caisse Régionale d'Assurance Maladie/CRAM). The procedure is as follows:

● When you reach the age of 58, go to a retirement information centre (*point d'accueil*) to obtain information about retiring (contact a CRAM or visit the CNAV website 🖳 http://www.retraite.cnav.fr to find your nearest centre).

● Four months before you reach 60, apply for a state pension (*demande de retraite personnelle* or *demande de retraite progressive* if you continue working part-time) as well as for any private pension you've been contributing to. You can check on the progress of your application by calling Allô Retraite (☎ 08 26 82 67 00). The CNAV website also contains helpful information about retirement. If you're self-employed, refer to 🖳 http://www.espaceretraite.tm.fr. In any correspondence with your local CRAM or CNAV office you should give your full name, address, social security number and the number of your local social security office.

If you move to France after working in another EU country (or move to another EU country after working in France), your state pension contributions can be exported to France (or from France to another country). French state pensions are payable abroad, and most countries pay state pensions directly to their nationals resident in France. But if you receive a 'tax-free' lump sum from a foreign pension fund, it will be regarded as taxable income in France. If you receive a British government service pension, however, this will be taxed in the UK and not in France. British pensioners should also note that, if they were receiving a winter fuel allowance before leaving the UK, they can continue to receive it in France; contact the Winter Fuel Payments Centre, Southgate House, Cardiff CF91 1ZH (☎ 029-2042 8635). Americans who retire in France can receive their pensions (and other benefits) via the Social Security department of the French Embassy in Paris.

If you plan to retire to France, you should ensure that your income is (and will remain) sufficient to live on, bearing in mind devaluations if your pension or income isn't paid in euros, rises in the cost of living (see page 396), and

unforeseen expenses such as medical bills or anything else that may reduce your income, e.g. stock market crashes.

Information about retirment homes in France can be found in *Buying a Home in France* (Survival Books – see page 587).

PRIVATE HEALTH INSURANCE

If your stay in France is short, you may be covered for emergency medical treatment by a reciprocal agreement between your home country and France (see **Eligibility & Exemptions** on page 324), but this may not cover you for routine treatment, for which you may need to take out private health insurance. This may take the form of a holiday and travel policy (see page 346) or a comprehensive international health policy (see below). **It's essential to make sure you're fully covered in France before you receive a large bill. If you or your family aren't adequately insured, you could be faced with some very high medical bills.**

When changing employers or leaving France, you should ensure that you have continuous health insurance and, if you're planning to change your health insurance company, you should ensure that important benefits aren't lost.

Once you become resident in France, you must register with social security (see **Registration** on page 327), which will cover you for most of your medical expenses, although you may wish to take out a complementary health insurance (or 'top-up') policy (*assurance complémentaire maladie*, commonly called a *mutuelle*, although strictly a *mutuelle* is a particular kind of benefit organisation – see page 321), which pays the portion of medical bills that isn't paid by social security (see 293). A complementary scheme may also provide a supplementary pension (see above), and the *Loi Madelin* allows you to deduct your contributions from taxable income provided you join the *mutuelle*, which costs around €15.

Almost every trade or occupation has its own complentary fund and in many cases it's obligatory for employees to join. If you're self-employed (*travailleur indépendant*), you must take out a health insurance policy (known in this case as an *assurance au premier franc*) through your social security office or through the relevant professional organisation. Information about insurance for the self-employed can be obtained from offices of the Caisse d'Assurance Maladie des Professions Libérales. If you aren't employed in France but have a social security card (*Carte Vitale*), you can join a complentary fund of your own choosing. **Premiums are normally quoted as a flat rate per person covered, so unlike social security health cover, insuring a large family will cost considerably more than insurance for just a single person.**

Many *mutuelles* base their reimbursements on those of social security (see page 293) and reimburse a patient only after social security has paid a proportion of the fee. Therefore, in a case where social security doesn't contribute, e.g. when a medical practitioner isn't part of the national health system (*non-conventionné, non-agréé*), a complentary fund may also pay nothing. However, some *mutuelles* pay the whole cost or part of the cost of treatment or items that aren't covered or are barely covered by social security, such as false teeth and spectacles. Most *mutuelles* will (from 1st January 2006) reimburse the statutory €1 charge on all consultations introduced in October 2004 (see **Reimbursement Procedure** on page 295) in the case of group policies (e.g. company schemes), but some may not do so on individual policies and you should check before taking out a policy.

Reimbursement applies only to the standard medical charges (*tarif de convention*). For example, if a blood test costs €50 and the *tarif de convention* is €40, your complentary fund will normally pay only the 30 per cent of the €40 that isn't refunded by social security. You must pay the €10 charged in excess of the *tarif de convention* yourself. However, for a higher premium you can insure yourself for the actual charge (*frais réels*). Most policies offer different levels of cover. It's sometimes necessary to have been a member of a complentary fund for a certain period before you're eligible to make a claim, e.g. three months for medical claims and six months for dental claims.

Different health practitioners 'recognise' different *mutuelles*. Reimbursement is triggered automatically in the case of those that are recognised, but must be applied for in the case of those that aren't, which will involve you not only in a certain amount of paperwork but also in delays before receiving reimbursement. Unfortunately, it's almost impossible to find out which *mutuelles* are most widely recognised. However, if you're likely to be using a particular practitioner (e.g. acupuncturist or physiotherapist) regularly, you should ask which *mutuelles* he recognises and consider joining one of those. Health insurers are listed on 🖳 http://www.canam.fr.

There are few foreign insurance companies which offer top-up policies for expatriates living in France. For UK nationals, only Goodhealth Worldwide (☎ 0800-6248 1000, 🖳 http://www.goodhealthworldwide.com) currently offers one, although a number of other international health policy providers (see page 340) are considering introducing such policies.

When choosing a complementary fund, ask your friends, colleagues and neighbours, or simply look under *Mutuelles d'Assurances* in the yellow pages. Compare the costs, terms and benefits provided by a number of funds before making a decision. It's wise to choose an insurer who's regulated by the *Loi Evan*, which means that after a certain period (e.g. two years) he isn't permitted to alter your terms and conditions, increase the premiums if your health deteriorates with advancing years or refuse to continue your insurance after an accident or illness.

International Health Insurance

Non-residents who spend time in different countries should take out an international health policy (sometimes referred to as private medical insurance or PMI), which should provide the following:

- Immediate emergency healthcare.

- Immediate access to a doctor.

- Referral to a specialist if required.

- Routine treatment, including dental treatment – if necessary in a hospital.

Cover for treatment of chronic conditions is rarely included in individual policies – Allianz Worldwide Care (see below) is one of the few major insurers to offer it, although several insurers include it in group policies. Most private health insurance policies don't pay standard doctors' consultation fees or pay for medicine that isn't provided in a hospital (or they charge a high 'excess', e.g. €100, which often exceeds the cost of treatment). Most will, however, pay for 100 per cent of specialist fees and hospital treatment in the best French hospitals. If pregnancy is a possibility, you should carefully check what's included and what isn't (e.g. regarding complications), as there may be a fixed monetary limit on claims; you may also have to wait ten months before becoming eligible for pregnancy benefits.

Before choosing a policy, compare not only costs but also benefits and conditions, or use an independent broker to do so for you, which shouldn't cost you any more. A broker can also help with claims or any difficulties you might encounter in dealing with an insurer. You should check, however, that a broker is reputable, e.g. by contacting the relevant regulatory body (the Financial Services Authority in the UK, ☎ 020-7066 1000, 💻 http://www.fsa.gov.uk) or a recognised brokers' association, e.g. in the UK the Association of Medical Insurance Intermediaries (☎ 0870-112 0431) or the British Insurance Brokers' Association (☎ 0870-950 1790, 💻 http://www.biba.org.uk). A policy should have a 'cooling-off' period of 14 to 30 days.

It's an advantage to be insured with a company that will pay large medical bills directly, because if you're required to pay bills and claim reimbursement from the insurance company, it can take you several months to receive your money. All French health insurance companies pay hospital bills directly, unlike some foreign companies. Some foreign companies limit your choice of hospitals to those with which they have a specific contract for rates and services. If you're planning to use the American Hospital of Paris, for example, make sure that your private insurer will cover the costs (and ideally, will make payment directly to the hospital), as treatment there isn't covered under all private insurance plans. If you already have private health insurance in another country, it may be possible to extend it to cover you in France.

Major international health insurers are listed in **Appendix A**. When choosing an insurer, ask the following questions:

● Who owns the company.

● Who underwrites its insurance.

● What its financial standing is (ask for a copy of its annual report and accounts).

● How long it has been operating (if it's a new company, ask whether the directors or managers have experience of international health insurance provision).

● Whether it's a member of the relevant governing body (e.g. the Financial Services Authority/FSA or the General Insurance Standards Council/GISC in the UK).

● Who administers claims (small companies may use a third-party administrator/TPA).

- Which international emergency assistance company it uses (the most widely used is International SOS).

- Whether cover is available only up to a certain age.

- Whether critical illness cover and/or income protection are provided and, if so, at what cost.

- Whether hospital treatment is available only in certain hospitals.

- Whether cover is still valid if you return to your home country.

You should also consider whether the insurer has a French office or offices, which at least demonstrates that it's committed to providing a high-quality service in France. **Take care over choosing an insurer, as it may be difficult (or expensive) to change.**

Dental Insurance

It's unusual to have full dental insurance (*assurance dentaire*) in France, as the cost is prohibitive. Basic dental insurance is provided under social security (see **Dentists** on page 310) and by *mutuelles* (see above). A *mutuelle* may offer additional cover for a higher premium. Most private health insurance companies offer dental cover (or extra dental cover) for an additional premium, although there are many restrictions and cosmetic treatment is excluded. Where applicable, the amount payable by a health insurance policy for a particular item of treatment is fixed and depends on your level of dental insurance. It's often necessary to request 'pre-approval' for certain dental treatment and services, particularly such things as crowns, caps or bridge work. A list of specific refunds is available from insurance companies.

Other Health Insurance

In France, children are obliged to care for their parents if they're unable to care for themselves, but it's possible to take out insurance against becoming a burden on your children in old age or following an illness or accident (*assurance dépendance*). This can cost at least €300 to €500 per month, however, and may be much more, depending on your age and health. Policies can normally be taken out between the ages of 45 and 75, and contributions are tax-free.

Another kind of insurance recently introduced in France is the *garantie des accidents de la vie* (*GAV*), which pays out in the event of death or disability to any member of a family as a result of an accident, whether domestic or medical, an attack, or a natural or other disaster (e.g. a plane crash, but not usually a road accident). *GAV* for an average family costs between €10 and €20 per month depending on the amounts paid, which vary with the severity of the accident (there may be a required minimum level of disability, e.g. 30 per cent).

HOUSEHOLD INSURANCE

Household insurance in France generally includes third-party liability (*responsabilité civile* – see also page 346), building and contents insurance, all of which are usually contained in a multi-risk household insurance policy (*assurance multirisques habitation*). Nine out of ten homeowners have a multi-risk policy, but not all policies cover the same risks: for example, while over 90 per cent of policies cover water damage, fewer than 90 per cent include third-party liability, only around 75 per cent include theft, and just over half cover you for glass breakage. For details contact the CDIA (see **Information** on page 320).

All buildings under construction and major renovation or repair work on existing buildings must be covered by damage insurance (*assurance dommages*) that guarantees the work for ten years after completion. It's the builder who is responsible for taking out this cover, but during the first ten years of the building's life it passes automatically to a new owner and will pay for damage caused by faults in the original construction.

Building

Although it isn't compulsory for owners, it's wise to take out building (*bâtiment*) insurance covering damage due to fire, water, explosion, storm, freezing, snow, theft, malicious acts, terrorism and natural catastrophes, all of which are usually covered by a multi-risk policy (see above).

In certain cases, claims for certain kinds of property damage aren't considered unless the government declares the situation a natural catastrophe or 'act of God'. For example, after the floods in southern France in recent years, many people discovered that their household insurance didn't cover them for water coming in from ground level, only for water seeping in through the roof! Read the small print and, if floods are one of your concerns, make sure that you're covered. It's particularly important to have insurance for storm damage in France, which can be severe in some areas. However, that if you live in an area that's hit by a succession of natural disasters (such as floods), your household insurance may be cancelled.

Property insurance is based on the cost of rebuilding your home and is increased each year in line with an industry-agreed inflation figure. **Make sure that you insure your property for the true cost of rebuilding.**

Apartments & Rented Accommodation

If you're a *copropriétaire*, building insurance is included in your service charges, although you should check exactly what's covered. You must, however, still be insured against third-party liability in the event that you cause damage to neighbouring apartments, e.g. through flooding or fire (see page 346).

If your accommodation is rented, your landlord will usually insist that you have third-party liability insurance (see page 346). A lease requires you to insure against 'tenant's risks' (*risques locatifs*), including damage you may make to a rental property and to other properties if you live in an apartment, e.g. due to floods, fire or explosion. You can choose your own insurance company and aren't required to use one recommended by your landlord but your landlord is entitled to void your lease if you don't provide him with proof of adequate cover within the time specified (usually a month or two after moving in).

Contents

Contents (*contenu*) are usually insured for the same risks as a building (see above) and are insured for their replacement value. Items of high value must usually be itemised and photographs and documentation (e.g. a valuation) provided. When claiming for contents, you should produce the original bills if possible (always keep receipts for expensive items) and bear in mind that replacing imported items may be much more expensive than buying them abroad. Contents policies usually contain security clauses; if you don't adhere to them, a claim won't be considered. Theft is covered only under certain conditions (e.g. that doors and windows were locked and that thieves had to break in to a property.)

Holiday Homes

Premiums are generally higher for holiday homes (*résidence secondaire*) than for main residences (*résidence principale*) because of their vulnerability, particularly to burglaries, and are usually based on the number of days per year a property is inhabited and the interval between periods of occupancy. Cover for theft, storm, flood and malicious damage may be suspended when a property is left empty for more than three weeks at a time (or if there's no visible forced entry). It's possible to negotiate cover for periods of absence for a hefty surcharge, although valuable items are usually excluded. If you're absent from your property for long periods, e.g. more than 60 days per year, you may also be required to pay an excess (e.g. €500) on a claim arising from an occurrence that takes place during your absence (and theft may be excluded). You should read all small print in policies. **It's important to ensure that a policy specifies a holiday home and not a principal home.**

In areas with a high risk of theft (e.g. some parts of Paris and the Côte d'Azur), you may be required to fit extra locks (e.g. two locks on external doors, one of a deadlock type) and internal-locking shutters or security bars on windows. A policy may specify that all forms of protection on doors must be employed whenever a property is unoccupied for two or more days and after 22.00. Some companies may not insure holiday homes in high risk areas. It's unwise to leave valuable or irreplaceable items in a holiday home or a home that will be vacant for long periods. **Some insurance companies will do their utmost to find a loophole which makes you 'negligent' and relieves them of their liability.** Always carefully check that the details (*conditions particulières*) listed on a policy are correct; otherwise your policy could be void.

Insuring Abroad

It's possible (and legal) to take out building and contents insurance in another country for a property in France, although the policy is usually written under French law. The advantage is that you will have a policy you can understand and you will be able to handle claims in your own language. This is usually a good option for the owner of a holiday home in France, although it can be much more expensive than insuring with a French company, so it pays to compare premiums. While it may be more convenient to take out contents insurance abroad, you should be aware that this can lead to conflicts when the building is insured with a French company, e.g. in France door locks count as contents and in the UK as part of the building.

Premiums

Premiums are usually based on the size of a property – either the habitable area in square metres or the number of rooms – rather than its value. Usually the sum insured (house and contents) is unlimited, provided the property doesn't exceed a certain size, e.g. 1,200m^2 (12,900ft^2), and is under a certain age, e.g. 200 years. However, some companies restrict home insurance to properties with a maximum number of rooms (e.g. seven) and/or a maximum value of contents. e.g. €50,000. The cost of multi-risk property insurance in a low risk area is around €120 to €150 per year for a property with one or two bedrooms, €180 to €240 for three or four bedrooms and €240 to €275 for five or six bedrooms. Premiums are much higher in high-risk areas. If you have an index-linked policy, your cover is increased each year in line with inflation. French insurance premiums include a tax of over 25 per cent.

Claims

If you wish to make a claim on a household insurance policy, you must usually inform your insurance company by registered letter (*lettre recommandée*) within two to five days of the incident or within 24 hours in the case of theft. Thefts should also be reported to the local police within 24 hours, as the police statement (*déclaration de vol/plainte*), of which you receive a copy, is required when submitting a claim to your insurance company. You should check whether you're covered for damage or thefts that occur while you're away from the property and are therefore unable to inform the insurance company immediately; if not, you may need to ask someone to check your home periodically while you're away. See also **Claims** on page 322.

Cancellation

Like other insurance policies, a household policy is automatically renewed annually unless you cancel (*résilier*) in writing, in which case you must normally cancel at least two months before the end of your annual insurance period, although the notice period is sometimes only a month, so you should check.

There are certain circumstances in which you're entitled to a refund for the unexpired period of the insurance contract, including the following:

- Moving home.
- Selling the property.
- Changing your marital status (e.g. becoming divorced).
- Changing your profession (if the change is relevant to your home ownership) or retiring.
- If the insurance company increases your premiums by more than the official index (*indice*), based on the Index of Construction Costs published by INSEE.

If you cancel a policy for any other reason, you won't get a refund. Standard cancellation letters (*lettre type de résiliation*) are usually provided by insurance companies and brokers.

THIRD-PARTY LIABILITY INSURANCE

It's customary to have third-party liability insurance (*assurance responsabilité civile*) for all members of your family. This covers you for damage done or caused by you, your children and even your pets, e.g. if your dog bites someone, although where damage is due to negligence, benefits may be reduced. Check whether insurance covers you against accidental damage to your home's fixtures and fittings. If you have children at school, they must also be covered by third-party liability insurance (*assurance scolaire* – see **Insurance** on page 179). Third-party liability insurance is usually combined with household insurance (see above). The cost of third-party liability insurance when not included in household insurance is around €160 per year and you may need to pay an excess, e.g. the first €75 to €150 of a claim.

If you're self-employed or run a business, you must also have third-party liability insurance for 'managers' (*assurance responsabilité civile chef d'entreprise*), the cost of which depends on your line of work.

If you're letting a property, make sure that you're covered for third-party liability in respect of your tenants, as most home insurance policies exclude such 'commercial' liability.

HOLIDAY & TRAVEL INSURANCE

Holiday and travel insurance (*assurance voyage*) is recommended for all who don't wish to risk having their holiday or travel spoilt by financial problems or to arrive home broke. As you're no doubt already aware, innumerable things can (and often do) go wrong with a holiday, sometimes before you even reach the airport or port, particularly when you **don't** have insurance.

Travel insurance is available from many sources, including travel agents, insurance agents, motoring organisations, transport companies and direct from insurance companies. Package holiday companies also offer insurance policies, **most of which don't provide adequate cover.** It isn't wise to depend on travel insurance provided by charge and credit card companies, household or car insurance policies or private medical insurance, none of which usually provide adequate cover (although you should take advantage of what they offer). For example, car insurance may include personal accident and health insurance (e.g. through Mondial Assistance) even if you don't take your car but won't cover you for belongings or cancellation of flights.

Before taking out holiday or travel insurance, carefully consider the level of cover you require and compare policies. Most policies include cover for loss of deposit or holiday cancellation, missed flights, departure delay at both the start and the end of a holiday (a common occurrence), delayed baggage, lost or stolen money, luggage and other belongings, medical expenses and accidents (including repatriation if necessary), personal liability, legal expenses and a tour operator or airline going bankrupt.

Medical expenses are an important aspect of travel insurance and you shouldn't rely on reciprocal health arrangements (see **Medical Treatment Abroad** on page 296). The minimum medical insurance recommended by experts is €500,000 in Europe and €1m to €2m in North America and some other destinations, e.g. Japan. If applicable, check whether pregnancy-related claims are covered and whether there are restrictions for those over 65 or 70. Third-party liability cover should be around €1.5m in Europe and €3m in North America. Always check any exclusion clauses in contracts by obtaining a copy of the full policy document (all relevant information isn't included in the insurance leaflet).

The cost of travel insurance varies considerably according to your destination and the duration of your trip. Usually the longer the period, the lower the daily or weekly cost. You should expect to pay around €25 for a week's insurance in Europe, €30 for two weeks and €50 for a month. Premiums are around double for travel to North America, where medical treatment costs an arm and a leg (although they also accept dollars!). Premiums may be higher for those over 65 or 70. Winter sports policies are available and are naturally more expensive than ordinary holiday insurance, or you can pay for a 'top-up' policy costing between €2 to €4 per day depending on the cover.

Annual travel policies, costing from around €150, are good value for frequent travellers, although you should check exactly what's covered (or omitted), as these policies may not provide adequate cover. However, it's almost impossible to obtain annual travel insurance in France, and you may need to take out a policy abroad, although most insurers won't insure foreign residents; exceptions in the UK include Expat Health Direct (🖳 http://www.expathealthdirect.co.uk) and Travel Protection Group (☎ 028-9032 0797).

Although travel insurance companies gladly take your money, they aren't usually so keen to honour claims and you may have to persevere before they pay up. Always be persistent and make a claim **irrespective** of any small print, as this may be unreasonable and therefore invalid in law. Insurance companies usually require you to report a loss (or any incident for which you intend to make a claim) to the local police (or carriers) within 24 hours and obtain a written report. Failure to do this usually means that a claim won't be considered.

LIFE INSURANCE

There are worse things in life than death (like spending an evening with a life insurance salesman) and your dependants may rate your death without life insurance high on their list. There are two types of 'life insurance' in France: life assurance (*assurance vie*) and death insurance (*assurance décès*). A life assurance policy is valid until you die and is essentially the same as a pension scheme, whereas a life insurance policy pays out only when you die. A life assurance policy benefits you, whereas a life insurance policy benefits your survivors. A life insurance policy can also be useful as security for a bank loan and can be limited to cover the period of the loan; a life assurance policy (sometimes known in the UK as a personal portfolio bond or PPB) can be a useful tax planning tool, reducing your tax rate on investment income (see below). The term 'life insurance' is used for both types of insurance in this section, but you should ensure that you know which type of insurance you're buying.

Social security pays only around three months' salary or a maximum of around €6,600 to a widow or dependants. Many companies provide free life insurance as an employment benefit, although it may be accident life insurance only (i.e. if you die as the result of an accident). If your employer doesn't provide life insurance (or if the cover provided is inadequate), you should consider taking out a private policy.

You can take out a life insurance or endowment policy with numerous French or foreign insurance companies, although a life insurance policy that complies with and is intended to take advantage of French law is best taken out in France. With all French life insurance policies you're entitled to a 30-day 'cooling off' period, during which you may cancel a policy without penalty.

New laws are removing many of the tax exemptions previously accorded to life assurance policies. In certain cases, however, premiums and dividends are tax-deductible and income from a life assurance policy is taxed at a low rate provided the policy is allowed to mature for at least four years and the fund is redeemed as a lump sum: if you redeem a policy within four years, you pay income tax on the gain at 35 per cent and social taxes at 10 per cent; if you redeem it between the fifth and eighth year, taxes are at 15 and 10 per cent; and after eight years you're taxed at just 7.5 and 10 per cent. Even if you make withdrawals during the investment period, only the growth element of the withdrawal is taxable. Because a life assurance policy reduces your income tax liability, it may also reduce your wealth tax liability (see page 387). If you take out a policy before moving to France, it will be exempt from French inheritance tax (unless you were over 70 when you set up the policy).

One possible catch with a life assurance policy is the *prélèvement libératoire*, which exempts you from paying tax at the highest level and which may automatically be deducted unless you specify otherwise. Unless you're in the top tax bracket (see page 373), you should benefit by not paying the optional *prélèvement libératoire*, but you must make it clear that you don't want to pay it. **Seek the advice of an accountant before committing yourself to a contract.**

You can choose the beneficiaries and the amount to be paid to them in the event of your death (e.g. €15,000 or €150,000), which will obviously affect the amount you pay, as will your age and state of health (e.g. non-smokers are usually offered a 20 per cent reduction on life policies). You may pay as little as €7 per month at the age of 30 for a benefit of €30,000, but premiums will increase with age and there's a maximum age for taking out most policies, e.g. 45, 55 or 60.

Instead of taking a lump sum on retirement, you can opt for life annuities (*rente viagère*), whereby you're 'paid' a fixed amount each year for the rest of your life, but payments are subject to income tax (on a sliding scale according to your age – e.g. you're taxed on 40 per cent of the annuity between 60 and 70 and on 30 per cent after 70). Note also that, when you die, payments stop and your spouse cannot continue to benefit from your pension, unless you make the annuity 'reversible' (*reversible*), in which case you receive a lower annuity but your spouse (if he or she survives you) continues to receive either all or part of the annuity for the rest of his or her life. You may have to pay a monthly minimum (e.g. €75) into a pension plan, although some plans allow you to make a minimum payment (e.g. €100) every three or six months.

Related beneficiaries (your spouse and children) aren't liable for French gift or inheritance tax, but unrelated beneficiaries are liable for inheritance tax at 60 per cent (see page 390), although they may be able to delay paying the tax until they're 70. However, the government is looking for new sources of tax revenue, and under new rules life insurance benefits may be taxed either as income or under wealth or inheritance tax laws, depending on how a policy is set up.

Finally, it's wise to leave copies of all insurance policies with your will (see page 394) and with your lawyer. If you don't have a lawyer, keep copies in a safe place (but make sure your dependants know where they are!). A life insurance policy must usually be sent to the insurance company upon the death of the insured, with a copy of the death certificate (see **Deaths** on page 306).

14.

FINANCE

Although the French aren't renowned for their proficiency in financial services, they've improved markedly in the last decade. Financial services are offered by numerous banks (commercial, co-operative, savings, investment, etc.), the post office, investment brokers and other financial institutions. Compared with many other Western countries, particularly the UK and the US, France isn't a credit economy and the French prefer to pay in cash or by cheque, debit card or charge card rather than by credit card. In fact, many French people don't understand the concept of credit cards. Nevertheless, the French are getting increasingly into debt (*surendettement*) as they spend beyond their means – so much so that the government recently changed the law to make personal bankruptcy possible (previously only businesses could go bust, except for some obscure reason in Alsace and Moselle). The amount of private debt increased by almost 10 per cent in 2004 and even faster in 2005, reaching over four times the level of private savings.

You should ensure that your income is (and will remain) sufficient to live on, bearing in mind possible devaluations, rises in the cost of living (see page 396), and unforeseen expenses such as medical bills or anything else that may reduce your income (e.g. stock market crashes and recessions!). France is one of the highest taxed countries in the European Union (EU) when both income tax and social security contributions are taken into consideration (see pages 373 and 323). **Foreigners, particularly retirees, often under-estimate the cost of living and many are forced to return to their home countries after a year or two.**

FRENCH CURRENCY

The euro became France's currency on 1st January 2002. The French franc, introduced by King Jean le Bon in 1360 to show that his part of France was free of the English (*franc des anglais*), has officially ceased to exist in France, although it continues to be the official currency of Monaco, French overseas territories, such as Guadeloupe and Martinique, and many former French colonies, and is still 'used' in conversation by the vast majority of French people.

As in other countries where there has recently been a change of currency, the French have yet to 'think' in euros and commonly talk in francs (which they often refer to as *balles*). In fact, when referring to large sums (e.g. the cost of a property), many French people – even young people – use old francs, which became obsolete in 1958! The term *brique* refers to am old francs. It's therefore worth remembering that one euro is equivalent to 6.55957 'new' francs (i.e. exactly two-thirds of ten francs) and one new franc was 100 old francs. For example, if you're told that a house is selling for *cinq cents briques*, it will cost you 500 million old francs or 5 million new francs or around €327,800.

The euro (€) is divided into 100 cents (nostalgically called *centimes* by the French) and coins are minted in values of 1, 2, 5, 10, 20, 50 cents, €1 and €2. The 1, 2 and 5 cent coins are brass-coloured (and virtually worthless!), the 10, 20 and 50 cents copper-coloured. The €1 coin is silver-coloured in the centre with a brass-coloured rim, and the €2 coin has a brass-coloured centre and silver-coloured rim. (Euro coins contain so much nickel that they can cause skin irritation.) The reverse ('tail' showing the value) of euro coins is the same in all euro-zone countries, but the obverse ('head') is different in each country. French coins carry traditional designs (e.g. Marianne), the letters RF (*République Française*) and the date of minting. All euro coins can, of course, be used in all euro-zone countries (although minute differences in weight occasionally cause problems in cash machines, e.g. at motorway tolls!). Some euro coins and banknotes have been found to contain faults, which has made them worth more than their face value!

Euro banknotes (*billets*) are identical on both sides throughout the euro-zone and depict a map of Europe and stylised designs of buildings (as the then 12 countries couldn't agree which actual buildings should be shown!). Notes are printed in denominations of €5, €10, €20, €50, €100, €200 and €500 (worth over GB£300 or US$600!). The size of notes increases with their value. Euro notes have been produced using all the latest anti-counterfeiting devices. Nevertheless, there are more counterfeit euro notes in circulation in France than in any other country and you should be wary of accepting €200 and €500 notes: even if they're genuine, you may be unable to spend them, as many businesses won't accept them!

Money is *argent* in French and *monnaie* means currency or change (*change* means exchange, as in *bureau de change*). To pay 'in cash' is either *en espèces* or *en liquide*, although the word *cash* is increasingly used. (According to French law, transactions in excess of €3,000 cannot be made in cash.)

The euro symbol may appear before the amount (as in this book), after it (commonly used by the French, who have been used to putting F after the amount) or even between the euros and cents, e.g. 16€50. Values below one euro are usually written using the euro symbol, e.g. €0,75, rather than with a US-style cent symbol, although small amounts (e.g. telephone call charges) are sometimes expressed as, for example, *3 ct €*. For information about writing figures in France see **Writing Cheques** on page 362.

It's wise to obtain some euro coins and banknotes before arriving in France and to familiarise yourself with them. You should take some euros in cash, e.g. €75 to €150 in small notes. This will save you having to change money on arrival, although you shouldn't carry a lot of cash and should avoid high value notes, which sometimes aren't accepted, particularly for small purchases or on public transport.

IMPORTING & EXPORTING MONEY

There are no limits on the import or export of funds, and a French resident is permitted to open a bank account in any country and to export an unlimited amount of money from France. However, if you're a French resident, you must inform the French tax authorities of any new foreign account in your annual tax return. Sums in excess of €7,500 deposited abroad, other than by regular bank transfers, must be reported to the Banque de France. If you send or receive any amount above €1,500 by post, it must be declared to customs. Similarly if you enter or leave France with €7,500 or more in French or foreign banknotes or securities (e.g. travellers' cheques, letters of credit, bills of exchange, bearer bonds, giro cheques, stock and share certificates, bullion, and gold or silver coins quoted on the official exchange), you must declare it to French customs. **If you exceed the €7,500 limit and are found out, you can be fined €1,500 or more.**

When you arrive in France to take up residence or employment, you should ensure that you have sufficient cash (preferably deposited in a French bank account), travellers' cheques or credit card limits to last at least until your first pay day, which may be some time after your arrival.

If you're planning to invest in property or a business that's financed with funds in a non-euro currency (e.g. GB£ or US$), it's important to consider both present and possible future exchange rates (don't be too optimistic!). On the other hand, if you will be earning your income in euros, this may affect your financial commitments abroad. **If you need to borrow money to buy property or for a business venture in France, you should carefully consider where and in what currency to raise finance.** Note that it's difficult for foreigners to obtain business loans in France, particularly for new ventures, and you shouldn't rely on doing so.

It's possible to 'fix' the exchange rate to guard against unexpected fluctuations by buying a 'forward time option' from your bank or through a specialised currency exchange firm; the further in advance you buy, the more you pay. Note, however, that you may regret doing so if there's a big swing in your favour!

When transferring or sending large amounts of money to (or from) France, you should be aware of the alternatives available, which include the following:

- **Bank Draft (*chèque de banque*)** – A bank draft should be sent by registered post. However, in the unlikely event that it's lost or stolen, it's impossible to stop payment and you must wait six months before a new draft can be issued. Bank drafts aren't treated as cash in France and must be cleared, like personal cheques. You should try to give a couple of days' notice if you require a bank draft.

- **Bank Transfer (*virement*)** – A 'normal' transfer should take three to seven days, but in reality it usually takes much longer and an international bank transfer between non-affiliated banks can take weeks! (It's usually quicker and cheaper to transfer funds between branches of the same bank than between non-affiliated banks.) In fact, the larger the amount the longer it often takes (I wonder why?), which can be particularly awkward when you're transferring money to buy a property. When making a bank transfer, make sure you have the full details of the recipient's bank account: if it's a foreign account, obtain the international bank account number (IBAN) and bank identifier code (BIC); if it's a French account, ensure that you give the name, account number, branch number (*code agence*) and the bank code (*clé*) or simply ask for a *RIB* (see page 361), which contains all this information. Otherwise, your money can be 'lost' while being transferred and it can take weeks to locate it.

- **SWIFT Transfer** – One of the safest and fastest methods of transferring money is via the Society of Worldwide Interbank Financial Telecommunications (SWIFT) system. A SWIFT transfer **should** be completed in a few hours, funds being available within 24 hours, although even SWIFT transfers can take five working days. Australian and UK members of the SWIFT system are listed on the Society's website (🖳 http://www.swift.com).

The cost of transfers varies considerably – not only commission and exchange rates, but also transfer charges.

If you plan to send a large amount of money to France or abroad for a business transaction such as buying property, you should ensure you receive the commercial rate of exchange rather than the tourist rate. Always check charges and rates in advance and agree them with your bank (you may be able to negotiate a lower charge or a better exchange rate).

Smaller amounts of money can be sent by international money order from a post office or by telegraphic transfer, e.g. via Western Union (the fastest and safest method, but also the most expensive). Money can be sent via American Express offices by Amex card holders. It's also possible to send cheques drawn on personal accounts, although these take a long time to clear (usually a number of weeks) and fees are high. Postcheques (see page 366) can be cashed at any post office in France, and most credit and charge cards can be used to obtain cash advances (see page 366). Don't rely entirely on a card to obtain cash, however, as they're sometimes 'swallowed' by cash machines and it can take a few weeks to retrieve them or obtain a replacement. Some machines refuse foreign cards for no apparent reason (if this happens, try another bank).

It isn't wise to close your bank accounts abroad, unless you're certain that you won't need them in the future. Even when resident in France, it's cheaper to keep money in local currency in an account in a country that you visit regularly than to pay commission to convert euros. Many foreigners living in France maintain at least two accounts, a foreign bank account for international transactions and a local account with a French bank for day-to-day business. If you open a euro account in another EU country, transfers to a French account are now subject to the same charges as domestic French transfers, although there's currently a limit of €50,000 per transfer.

One thing to bear in mind when travelling anywhere is not to rely on one source of funds only.

Changing Money

Most banks and main post offices in major cities have foreign exchange windows, and there are exchange bureaux (*bureaux de change*) in all major cities as well as at airports and major Paris railway stations. Here you can buy or sell foreign currencies, buy and cash travellers' cheques, and obtain a cash advance on credit and charge cards. At airports and in tourist areas in major cities, there are automatic change machines accepting major currencies, including US$ and GB£.

Bureaux de change often have longer business hours than banks, particularly at weekends. Most offer competitive exchange rates and low or no commission (but check). They're easier to deal with than banks and, if you're changing a lot of money, you can also usually negotiate a better rate, although generally banks offer better rates. Never use unofficial money changers, who are likely to short change you or give you a poor exchange rate. The euro exchange rate (*cours de change*) for most major international currencies is listed in banks and daily newspapers, and is also given online (e.g. 🖥 http://www.x-rates.com).

Prepaid Currency Cards

Prepaid currency cards are a new alternative to travellers' cheques and debit and credit cards, and can be used to withdraw cash from ATMs and to purchase goods in shops and restaurants, although few French businesses as yet accept this form of payment. The cards, known by different names, are offered by several finance companies including International Currency Exchange (which calls its card 'Cash2go'), Maestro ('I-Travel Prepaid'), Travelex ('Cash Passport') and Western Union ('Travel Cash Card'). Euros and US dollars are currently the only currencies available, and most companies allow 'loads' of between €150/$200 and €7,500/$10,000, the exchange rate being fixed when you 'load' the card. You're then given a PIN, which allows you to withdraw cash at ATMs.

Advantages of prepaid currency cards include greater security – if the card is lost or stolen there's no link between it and your bank account, unlike a credit card, for example – and the card has no name on it so there's no risk of identity fraud. Your cash withdrawals aren't subject to exchange rate fluctuations – which may be an advantage or a disadvantage depending on whether the rate goes up or down. On the other hand, there are charges for most transactions, e.g. £2 for a cash withdrawal and £3 for a top-up. Read the small print carefully and make sure you understand all the associated charges before you take out a prepaid currency card. It's also worth comparing the charges with those incurred on a credit or debit card, which may well be cheaper.

Travellers' Cheques

If you're visiting France, it's safer to carry travellers' cheques (*chèque de voyage*) than cash. It's best to buy euro travellers' cheques, although they aren't as easy to cash as in some other countries, e.g. the US. They aren't usually accepted as cash by businesses, except perhaps in Parisian hotels, restaurants and shops. You can buy travellers' cheques from any French bank, usually for a service charge of 1 per cent of the face value. There should be no commission charge when cashing euro travellers' cheques at any bank in France (you must show your passport). However, charges and rates can vary considerably on travellers' cheques in foreign currencies. Banks usually offer a better exchange rate for travellers' cheques than for banknotes, although they often levy a high commission, e.g. between €3 and €5 per cheque. Always keep a separate record of cheque numbers and note where and when they were cashed. American Express provides a free, 24-hour replacement service for lost or stolen travellers' cheques at any of their offices worldwide, provided you know the serial numbers of the lost cheques. Without the serial numbers, replacement can take three days or longer. All companies provide local telephone numbers for reporting lost or stolen travellers' cheques.

BANKS

There are two main types of bank in France: commercial and co-operative. The largest commercial banks have branches in most large towns and cities and include the Banque Nationale de Paris (BNP Paribas), Crédit Lyonnais and Société Générale. All three have now been privatised and, in order to compete with other larger European banks, are intent on merging, the latest proposal being a union between BNP and Société Générale. Village branches are rare, although in many villages there are bank offices (*permanence*), which usually open one morning a week only.

The largest co-operative banks are Crédit Agricole, Crédit Mutuel and BRED Banque Populaire. They began life as regional, community-based institutions working for the mutual benefit of their clients, but most are now represented nationally and offer a full range of banking services. Unlike commercial banks, each branch office of a co-operative bank is independent and issues its own shares. Anyone can become a member and invest in their shares, which is usually mandatory if you wish to take out a mortgage or loan but isn't necessary to open a current account.

Crédit Agricole is the largest co-operative bank – in fact it's the largest retail bank in Europe, with around 10,000 branches and some 17 million customers. (It's also the biggest landholder in France.) Crédit Agricole is the only French bank to offer an English-language service (see **Foreign Banks** below). The top four French banks (Crédit Agricole, Crédit Lyonnais, Société Générale and BNP Paribas) are among the world's top ten banks. (In March 2003, Crédit Agricole bought Crédit Lyonnais, which, however, continues to trade as Crédit Lyonnais, albeit with fewer branches.) The Banque de France is the authority which sets interest rates and regulates other banks; you cannot open an account with the Banque de France. All banks, including foreign banks, are listed in the yellow pages under *Banques*.

French banking has become highly automated in recent years, and all banks now offer an efficient and wide-ranging service, including online banking (for which there's usually a charge, e.g. €3 per month).

If you need or want to change banks, you should be aware of the restrictions and costs involved. You cannot transfer a mortgage or life insurance policy. In the former case, you can ask your new bank for a loan to pay off the mortgage with your old bank, although this is unlikely to be to your financial advantage. With some mortgages, you're liable for penalties if you redeem them before the agreed term. In the case of life insurance, you may be able to 'cash in' your policy, provided it has run for at least eight years (or you will be liable for income tax on the amount you receive), but again there may be penalty charges. There are also charges for transferring other 'products', such as certain savings plans, although your bank manager may waive these. Send a recorded letter to your bank manager informing him of the accounts you wish to transfer and giving him a *RIB* from your new bank.

Post Office Banking

As in many other countries, the most popular banking facility in France is operated by the post office (*La Poste*), which also offers some of the 'cheapest' banking. In terms of the amount of money handled, *La Poste* is the country's third-largest 'bank' (after Crédit Agricole and Caisse d'Epargne – see below). In rural areas, where the nearest bank is often many kilometres away, many people use the post office as their local bank. Another advantage of the post office is that many branches are open for longer hours than banks, although many aren't (see page 128). Post office accounts provide the same services as bank accounts, including international money transfers (by post and telegraph to many countries) and payment of bills. Post office account holders are issued with a (free) cash card for withdrawals from a cash machine located outside main post offices. Every transaction is confirmed with a receipt by post. The Post Office started offering mortgages in 2005.

Savings Banks

There are also savings banks, the largest of which is the Caisse d'Epargne (*caisse d'épargne* is also the French for savings bank), with over 400 branches. Savings banks are similar to British building societies and US savings and loan organisations and offer savings schemes and loans for property and other purchases, although general banking services are limited compared with commercial and co-operative banks.

Foreign Banks

There are some 175 foreign-owned banks in France – more than in any other European country except the UK, although they have a relatively small market share. However, competition from foreign banks is set to increase, as EU regulations allow any bank trading legitimately in one EU country to trade in another. Among foreigners in France, the British are best served by their national banks, both in Paris and in the provinces, particularly on the Côte d'Azur. The most prominent British bank is Barclays with around 100 branches, including at least one in all major cities. National Westminster has branches in most major cities, the Abbey National has around 12 branches, and Lloyds and HSBC one each (in Paris). If you do a lot of travelling abroad or carry out international business transactions, you may find that the services provided by a foreign bank are more suited to your needs. They're also more likely to have staff who speak English and other foreign languages. However, many foreign banks (and some French banks) handle mainly corporate clients and don't provide banking services for individuals; even those that do may not operate in the same way as branches in their 'home' country or even have foreign-language-speaking staff. One notable exception is Barclays' branch at 15 rue Jeanne d'Arc in Rouen (☎ 02 35 71 70 60, 🖳 http://www.barclays.fr), which has English-speaking account managers. Most major foreign banks are present in Paris, but branches are rare in the provinces.

The Crédit Agricole has an English-language service, known as 'Britline', based at its Caen branch (☎ 02 31 55 67 89, 🖳 http://www.britline.com).

Opening Hours

Normal bank opening hours are from 09.00 to 17.30 or 17.45, Mondays to Fridays, although banks may open any time between 08.30 and 09.30 and some close between 16.00 and 17.00. Larger branches may stay open until 18.30 or 19.00 on certain days or every day in cities. Banks at main railway stations in Paris are open from 09.00 until between 20.00 and 23.00, although they usually have long queues.

In small towns, banks close for lunch from 12.00 or 12.30 until 13.30 or 14.00. Many banks open on Saturdays (e.g. 09.00 to 16.00), although when a bank in a rural area opens on Saturdays it may close on Mondays. Banks are closed on public holidays; when a public holiday falls on a Tuesday or Thursday, banks usually also close on the preceding Monday or the following Friday respectively.

At major airports such as Paris' Charles de Gaulle and Orly airports, *bureaux de change* are open from 07.00 to 23.00 daily. In Paris and other cities, private *bureaux de change* are usually open from 09.00 to 18.00, Mondays to Saturdays.

Using Banks

The following general points are applicable to French banking:

- For security purposes, most banks have two entrance doors, the second of which is opened only after the first has closed (intended to trap robbers as they attempt to flee with their booty). In some cases, you must press a bell and wait for a staff member to press a button to open the outer door.

- Banks usually have a more casual air than banks in many other countries and most use open counters rather than protected teller windows, as most cash operations are automated.

- When making payments into an account, a distinction is made between cash deposits (*versement en espèces*) and cheque deposits (*versement de chèques*), which must be listed on the paying-in form. Cheques to be paid in must be signed on the back. When paying in a foreign cheque, even one in euros, you may incur a charge (e.g. 0.1 per cent or a minimum of €15 and a maximum of €60), although charges are supposed to be the same as those for domestic transactions.

- When making a deposit 'manually' (i.e. at a counter), you may not be given a receipt (*reçu* or *double*) and should request one if required.

- All regular bills, such as electricity, gas, telephone, mortgage and rent, can be paid by direct debit (*prélèvement automatique*) by your bank free of charge. A direct debit instruction form (*autorisation*) is provided by your bank. This method of payment has the advantage that payments are automatically recorded on your monthly statement. Bills can usually be paid onlin, although many banks charge for online services. If you need to pay an individual a regular sum, you can set up a standing order (*virement permanent*), which is also free. Note that if you don't pay a bill on time, interest (*majoration*) can be charged at 1.5 times the official rate.

- Many banks offer customers safe deposit boxes with annual rents ranging from around €75 to €300, depending on their size. However, most banks restrict compensation for losses to around €15,000.

- Buying stocks and shares is normally done through your bank, rather than a stockbroker (*agent de change/courtier*), although it's also possible to buy and sell directly (e.g. via the internet). Banks make a charge that's added to the broker's commission, plus VAT (*TVA*) at 19.6 per cent. New share issues can usually be bought through newspaper advertisements in newspapers such as *Le Monde*. French banks also sell shares in their own unit trusts.

● If you have a problem with a bank, write to the mediator (*médiateur*), which all banks are now obliged to have and whose name and address should be shown on your statements. Model letters in French, as well as the definitions of hundreds of banking and other financial terms, can be found on the website of the Fédération Bancaire Française (🖳 http://www.lesclesdelabanque.com – click on '*Documents téléchargeables – lettres type*').

Opening an Account

You can open a bank account whether you're resident or non-resident (see below). It's better to open a bank account in person than by correspondence from abroad. Ask friends, neighbours and colleagues for their recommendations and go to the bank of your choice and introduce yourself. You must be at least 18 and provide proof of identity, e.g. a passport (although you may need more than one form of identification), and of your address in France if applicable (e.g. a utility bill).

If you wish to open an account with a French bank while you're abroad, you must first obtain an application form, available from overseas branches of French banks (e.g. the Crédit Lyonnais in the UK, which calls itself Calyon, at 5 Broadwalk House, Appold Street, London EC2A 2DA, ☎ 020-7214 5000). If you open an account by correspondence, you must provide a reference from your current bank, including a certificate of signature or a signature witnessed by a solicitor. You also need a photocopy of the relevant pages of your passport and a euro draft to open the account.

Any account holder can create a joint account by giving his spouse (or anyone else) signatory authority. A joint account can be for two or more people. If applicable, you must state that cheques or withdrawal slips can be signed by any partner and don't require all signatures. However, in the event of the death of a partner, a joint account is blocked until the will has been proven.

Non-residents

If you're non-resident (i.e. spend at least six months per year outside France), you're only entitled to open a non-resident account (*compte non-résident*). There's little difference between non-resident and resident accounts and you can deposit and withdraw funds in any currency without limit, although there may be limits on the amount you can transfer between accounts (an anti-money-laundering measure). Non-resident accounts have a ban on ordinary overdrafts (*découverts*), although loans for a car or house purchase are possible. French banks are imposing increasing minimum deposits on non-resident accounts; these can be up to €3,000, although it isn't usually necessary to maintain this balance once an account is open. Shop around for the best deal.

To open a non-resident account, you must usually produce two pieces of identification, two proofs of address no more than three months old and a letter of recommendation from your existing bank. You can have documentation (e.g. cheque books, statements, etc.) sent to an address abroad.

If you're non-resident with a second home in France it's possible to survive without a French account by using travellers' cheques and credit cards, although this isn't wise and is an expensive option.

Residents

You're considered to be a resident of France if you have your main centre of interest there, i.e. you live or work there for at least half the year. To open a resident account you must usually have a residence permit (*carte de séjour*) or evidence that you have a job in France.

Current Accounts

The normal account for day-to-day transactions is a current or cheque account (*compte courant* or *compte de chèques*), which don't accrue interest. (It's illegal for banks in France to pay interest on current accounts.) Most people deposit their 'rainy day' money in a savings account (see page 365). However, most banks will automatically transfer funds above a specified sum from a cheque account into an interest-bearing savings account. Post office cheque accounts (*compte chèques postal*) are referred to by the initials *CCP*. Information about post office accounts is also available via a free telephone number (☎ 08 00 02 50 25) and online: there's a dedicated website (💻 http://www.labanquepostale.fr) as well as the main Post Office website (💻 http://www.laposte.fr).

When opening a cheque account, you should request a bank card, which can be used to pay bills throughout France (see page 366). **Bank cards aren't cheque guarantee cards, which don't exist in France** (see below). You will receive a cheque book (*chèquier/carnet de chèques*) and your bank card around two to three weeks after opening an account (although some banks don't issue a cheque book until an account has been operated for at least two months). You must usually collect your cheque book and bank card in person from your branch, although they can be sent to you abroad by registered post at your expense. New cheque books are sent to you automatically before your current one runs out.

Your bank will usually supply you with a number of slips showing your essential bank details (*relevé d'identité bancaire* or *RIB*, pronounced 'reeb'), which you can send to anyone who requires them. Many employers pay their employees' salaries into a bank or post office account by direct transfer (*virement*), so make sure that you give your employer your account details or you won't be paid!

You may withdraw any amount up to the balance (*solde*) of your account by cashing a cheque (*encaisser un chèque*) at the branch where you have your account. At any other branch of your bank, you can usually withdraw up to €500 per week but must provide identification and your cheque book. If the branch has a computer link to your branch, you may withdraw any amount up to the balance of your account. Most cash withdrawals are made by card (see page 366).

Cheque clearing (*encaissement*) is quicker in France than in some other countries, and cheques from other branches of your bank may be cleared on the day of deposit, while cheques from other banks usually take around two days to clear (see **Statements** below). **Always make sure that cheques, including bank drafts (which aren't treated as cash in France), have been cleared before making a withdrawal against them.**

Personal cheques are widely accepted throughout France and many people use them to buy everything from petrol to food, from restaurant meals to travel tickets. Many shops and businesses have cheque-writing machines so that all you have to do is check the details and sign. (There may be a sign such as *Les chèques sont rédigés automatiquement*.) As there are no cheque guarantee cards, you're usually asked to produce identification, e.g. a passport or *carte de séjour*, when paying large amounts (e.g. over €100) by cheque. A 'cash back' system (whereby you write a cheque for a larger amount than you're paying and receive the difference in cash) doesn't operate in France.

Usually cheques are crossed (*chèques barrés*) and personal cheques aren't negotiable, i.e. they cannot be signed and endorsed for payment to a third party. They can be paid into an account in the name of the payee only (who must sign the back). This means that you cannot cash a cheque unless you have your own bank account. It's possible to obtain 'open' uncrossed cheques (*chèques non-barrés*), although your bank is required to notify the tax authorities of all uncrossed cheques issued, as using uncrossed cheques is a good way of avoiding tax – a national sport in France. (For this reason, few people request uncrossed cheques!)

In theory, a trader can refuse to accept a cheque for goods or services costing less than €1,500 and can refuse cash for anything above €1,500 (although most people are usually happy to accept any amount of cash at any time). In fact, in order to prevent tax evasion, French law states that rent, office supply services and any work costing over €150 **must** be paid by cheque. Some businesses have signs stating that below a certain amount, e.g. €15, cheques aren't accepted.

It isn't possible to postdate a cheque, as cheques are payable on the date presented irrespective of the date written on them and are valid for one year and eight days after this date. It's difficult to stop the payment of a cheque (*faire opposition à un chèque*) and it's usually possible only if your cheque book is lost or stolen, or the payee loses a cheque or has it stolen. It isn't normal to stop a cheque when, for example, goods or services aren't as specified.

If your cheque book is lost or stolen, you must notify your bank by telephone immediately or call the national helpline (☎ 08 92 68 32 08) and confirm the loss in writing. Any cheques written after you've informed your bank aren't your responsibility.

Writing Cheques

The design of a French cheque may be different from what you're used to. On the right-hand side is a box or line where the value of the cheque is written in numerals. The line *payez contre ce chèque* is where the value of the cheque is written in words. Write the name of the payee (or *moi-même* when writing a cheque for cash) next to the line marked *à* or *à l'ordre de*. The date line is in the lower right-hand corner above the signature position and is preceded by the town where the cheque was written (*lieu de creation* or simply *à*). French cheques also show your name and address. When writing figures in France, or anywhere on the continent of Europe, the number seven should be crossed to avoid confusion with the number one, written with a tail and looking like a seven to many foreigners. Beware also of French fours, as they can look like nines (which are written with a curly tail) or twos! You should use a comma to separate whole numbers and decimals (e.g. 123 euros and 45 cents is written €123,45), whereas a full-stop (period) or a space is used to separatems and thousands (e.g. €1.234.567,89 or €1 234 567,89 is one million, 234 thousand, 567 euros and 89 cents – a nice healthy bank balance!).

The date is written in the standard European style; e.g. 10th March 2005 is written 10.3.05, not as in the US, 3.10.05. If there's a difference between the amount written in figures and the amount in words, the amount written in words is assumed to be correct. Most banks supply a specimen cheque showing how it should be written. If you make an error when writing a cheque, it isn't necessary to initial a correction.

Unless you have an overdraft facility (see page 369), you should **never** write a 'rubber' cheque (*chèque sans provision* or *'chèque en bois'*, literally a wooden cheque). **Writing cheques for more than you have in your account is a criminal offence.** If you accidentally overdraw (*mettre en découvert*) your account, your bank will send you a registered letter demanding that the necessary funds be paid into the account within 30 days. You will also incur a fine of between €30 and €130 depending on the amount (the maximum penalty for a cheque for less than €50 is €30) plus an unauthorised overdraft charge. (Persistent cheque bouncers can be fined from €400 to €35,000 and receive prison sentences of one to five years.) In the meantime, you mustn't write any more cheques. If the funds aren't deposited within 30 days or if you overdraw your account twice within a 12-month period, your account will be closed! If this happens, you must return your cheque book to your bank (and also cheque books for other bank accounts in France); your name will be entered on a blacklist (*interdit bancaire*) maintained by the Banque de France, and you will be unable to operate a cheque account at any bank in France for a year – your name will remain on the blacklist for five years. If you're blacklisted, you may be unable to obtain a French mortgage or loan for years afterwards. Some 750,000 people are forbidden to operate bank accounts in France each year. If you can prove that overdrawing your account was due to the fault of another party, you can avoid being blacklisted. It's usually possible (and **much** safer) to ask for an overdraft facility (see page 369).

Bank cheques are valid for six months, whereas post cheques (*chèques postaux*) must be cashed within two months.

Statements

Account statements (*relevé de compte*) are normally sent on a monthly basis, although you can usually choose to receive them weekly or quarterly. Your account details, such as your bank, branch and account number, are printed at the top of statements. It's also possible to obtain 'mini-statements' (showing your last few transactions) via cash machines (a facility known as *guichet automatique bancaire/GAB*). You can check the balance of your post office account via telephone

(*Audioposte*, which costs around €0.60 per call) 24 hours a day, including the last five transactions or all transactions during the last ten days. You're given a personal access code to access your account. If you have a post office account, you can also sign up for access via the internet (a service strangely called *Vidéoposte*), whereby you can check your balances and make most transactions, including buying and selling shares. Whereas most banks in France charge a monthly service fee for accessing your account online, *Vidéoposte* is (currently) free.

Two dates are usually shown on statements: the date a transaction was recorded by the bank (*date de traitement*) and the date the amount is credited or debited to your account (*date de valeur*). A cheque deposit, for example, may not be credited to the account until a few days afterwards, whereas a payment by card or cheque can be debited **before** the date it was handled! Bank statements may not show a cumulative balance, except at the end of the month, making it difficult to check that you haven't overdrawn your account at any point.

Charges

There are no monthly charges on a cheque account, unless you want an overdraft facility (see page 369), and no charges for transactions such as direct debits or (usually) standing orders, except when made overseas. However, banks normally charge around €30 per year for a bank card and may charge you if your account is left 'inactive' for a period. Some banks also charge for cash withdrawals (see **Cash & Debit Cards** on page 366). A leaflet (*Conditions et Tarifs des Principales Prestations Financières Applicables aux Particuliers*) is available from post offices listing the range of services and the costs associated with post office accounts, including savings account interest rates.

Chèque Emploi Service

Another kind of cheque account, now called *Chèque Emploi Service Universel* (formerly *Chèque Emploi Service*), is available for those wanting to pay casual workers who don't have accident or third-party liability insurance (see **Employers** on page 330). You must apply to your bank for a special cheque book, which usually takes two to three weeks to arrive and is accompanied by instructions for use. Before any work is done, complete the *volet social* corresponding to the cheque to be issued (it has the same number at the bottom) with the worker's details and details of the work to be done and the rate. Tick the box *base fortaitaire* for basic insurance, *salaire réel* for comprehensive insurance.

Preferably before the work is done, send the *volet social* to the Centre National de Traitement du Chèque Emploi Service Universel, 42961 Saint-Etienne Cedex 9 (addressed envelopes should be supplied) and the relevant social security contributions will be deducted automatically from your bank account. (You will receive notification of the amounts to be deducted at the beginning of the following month and the deduction will be made at the end of that month.) If you're over 70, you're exempt from making contributions on behalf of casual workers, but you must complete the form at the front of the cheque book as well as the *volet social*. There are even prewritten cheques for standard amounts (*chèques préfinancés*) for those who aren't up to writing French numbers!

A leaflet entitled *Chèque Emploi Service Universel* providing details of the system is available from your bank or from URSSAF offices. Information is also available on the URSSAF website (🖳 http://www.cesu.urssaf.fr). **If you pay casual workers in cash or by ordinary cheque and they have an accident on your premises, you can be sued for a very large sum of money.** A useful source of information (in French) for those contemplating taking on staff is the Fédération Nationale des Particuliers Employeurs (🖳 www.fepem.fr).

Savings Accounts

In addition to a current account (see above) you can open a savings account (*compte d'épargne* or *compte rémunéré*) or deposit account (*compte à terme*) with commercial, co-operative and savings banks, but these are strictly controlled and there isn't the vast choice of plans available in some countries. As well as earning interest on your money (albeit at no more than 3 per cent per year), you can save tax by opening a savings account, although there are usually maximum deposit limits. With some savings accounts you're given a savings book (*livret*), in which deposits and withdrawals are recorded (a savings account is often referred to as a *compte d'épargne sur livret*), although these are increaingly being superseded by ordinary printed statements.

The standard savings account is a *compte pour le développement industriel* (*CODEVI*), on which there's a deposit limit of €4,600, although a couple may have two accounts, effectively doubling the limit. The limit on a *livret d'épargne populaire* is currently €7,700, but this is restricted to those who pay less than €684 per year in income tax. La Poste offers a *livret A de la caisse national d'épargne* (*CNE*) with a limit of €15,300, on which interest isn't taxed; a *livret B* for larger amounts but whose interest is taxable. With deposit accounts, you must be prepared to invest for between 1 and 12 months, during which period your money is tied up. The longer the term, the higher the return.

A new savings plan is the *plan d'épargne retraite populaire* (*PERP*), introduced by the government in 2003 in an attempt to induce people to save for their retirement (in anticipation of the chronic underfunding of pensions caused by an ageing population!). A *PERP* is similar to a British approved pension scheme, whereby funds deposited are 'locked' until your retirement, when you must take an annuity, which will be liable for income tax. Ten per cent of your deposits can be deducted from your taxable income (up to a ceiling – initially €2,920). The *plan d'épargne populaire* (*PEP*) has been abolished.

Many people have a government-subsidised, guaranteed interest (currently 4.5 per cent) savings account called a *plan d'épargne logement* (*PEL*). This is designed to accrue credits towards a future low-interest loan for the purchase of a home or home improvements, although many people take out a *PEL* for other purposes (there's currently no penalty for doing this, although restrictions may be introduced). The maximum amount that can be put into a *PEL* is €61,200 but you can open one for each member of your family (including children!). The minimum initial deposit in a *PEL* is €225 and the minimum monthly deposit thereafter €45 and it must be maintained for at least four years for you to benefit (the maximum limit is ten years).

Another type of savings account is a *compte d'épargne logement* (*CEL*), in which you may put up to €15,300 with a minimum initial deposit of €300 and minimum monthly deposits thereafter of €75. The current interest rate on a *CEL* is 2 per cent. If you withdraw money from a *PEL* before the four-year limit, you can convert it into a *CEL* in order not to lose your right to a low-interest loan. There are still more savings plan options for businesses, e.g. a *plan d'épargne entreprise* (*PEE*), *plan d'épargne interentreprises* (*PEI*), *plan d'épargne retraite collectif* (*PERCO*) and *plan d'épargne retraite collectif interentreprises* (you've guessed it: *PERCOI*).

Another way to invest small or large sums is to buy units in a managed fund organisation called a *Société d'Investissement à Capital Variable* (*SICAV*) or a *Fonds Commun de Placement* (*FCP*). *SICAV*s and *FCP*s are offered by most banks and are similar to unit trusts, unit prices starting low and increasing to around €150. There's no limit to the amount you can invest, although *FCP*s are designed for larger amounts than *SICAV*s (e.g. over €10,000). You choose the level of risk you wish to take, and interest rates are linked to market rates; units can be cashed at any time.

The post office also offers a range of savings accounts. Post office savings accounts (*CCP Service Plus*) operate through the national savings bank (Caisse Nationale d'Epargne) and include tax-free savings accounts (*livret A*), house purchase savings plans (*plan d'épargne logement/PEL* – see below) and retirement plans.

CASH & DEBIT CARDS

Most banks offer customers a combined cash and debit card called a *carte bancaire* or *carte bleue* (both or which are abbreviated to *CB*), widely accepted throughout France. Confusingly, the term *carte bleue* is often also applied to credit and charge cards (see below). Banks normally charge around €30 per year for a *CB* (€15 for a second card on a joint account). Although it's integrated with both the Visa and MasterCard/Eurocard network, a *CB* isn't a credit card (see **Credit & Charge Cards** below). However, for an extra €5 or €6 you can have a *carte différée*, with which debits are made at the end of each month rather than immediately after each purchase (cash withdrawals are always debited immediately, even with a *carte différée*). The most common bank card is a Visa card (*carte bleue Visa*) card.

The key benefit of the *CB* is that it's accepted almost everywhere in France. It can therefore be used to pay for practically everything, including motorway tolls, parking and train and bus tickets, and most shops will accept payment by card for even small purchases, although a new system, called *Monéo* (see below) is designed to allow you to pay for items such as newspapers, bread and drinks with your *CB*. All bank cards have a microchip (*puce*) – a combination invented by a Frenchman, Roland Moreno, in 1974.

A standard *CB* allows you to withdraw up to around €900 per week from a cash machine (properly termed an automated teller machine or ATM – *distributeur automatique de billets/DAB*) operated by your own bank or €300 from a another bank's machine (displaying a *CB* sign) or €450 from a bank abroad, and to spend up to around €3,000 in France or €4,500 abroad without authorisation. 'Gold' and other privilege cards allow you higher limits. Some banks charge at least €1 each time you use one of their ATMs, and most charge for using other banks' ATMs. (BNP Paribas charges you €5 to withdraw less than €150 over the counter!) Note that an agreement between BNP Paribas, Barclays Bank (UK), Deutsche Bank (Germany), Scotiabank (Canada) and Westpac (Australia) allows card holders of any of these banks to use ATMs belonging to any of the others without charge. **Take care when withdrawing cash from a machine at night, as some machines are popular venues for muggers.**

You can also obtain account balances and mini-statements from a cash machine using your card. Some machines offer the option to display instructions in English and other languages. When using your *CB* in a cash machine or when making a purchase, simply enter your four-digit personal identification number/PIN (*code secret/confidentiel*) on the keypad provided. In an increasing number of shops, you must insert your card yourself into a slot in the keypad and wait for the message '*tapez votre code confidentiel*'; withdraw your card when you see '*retirez votre carte*'. There's no need to sign anything. (With most banks, it **isn't** possible to change your PIN, e.g. to a number you can easily remember!)

If you lose your *carte bleue*, report the loss to the central office (☎ 08 92 69 08 80) and inform your bank as soon as possible. Further information about French bank cards can be found on the website of the Groupement des Cartes Bancaires (🖳 http://www.cartes-bancaires.com – in English).

Moneo

Moneo (sometimes written *Mon€o*) is a new system, introduced in 2003, which works in a similar way to telephone cards. You 'charge' your card from your account (with between €20 and €100) using a special machine at your bank and use it like cash at retail outlets participating in the scheme (displaying a '*Mon€o*' sign). These include bakers', bars, take-aways, newsagents' and chemists'. (There has been some resistance from retailers, particularly bakers and tobacconists, to participation owing to commission charges of up to 3 per cent, but it's expected that an increasing number of outlets will accept payment by this method in the coming years.) As with a normal card payment, you must enter your PIN, but you don't receive a receipt; a display tells you how much has been debited from your card and the remaining credit balance. There are three types of *Mon€o* card: green (an independent card, like a telephone card); blue (linked to your current account); and your ordinary *CB* with a *Mon€o* chip – all new *CB*s have the *Mon€o* logo and can be used in this way. You must pay between €7 and €10, depending on the issuing bank, to use the system.

CREDIT & CHARGE CARDS

The concept of the credit card isn't recognised in France, where all bank cards are debit cards and are referred to collectively as 'blue cards' (*carte bleue*), although some operate as a charge card for a limited period – see **Cash & Debit Cards** above. The nearest thing to a credit card is a *carte privative*, which is usually issued by a shop or retail chain (e.g. But, Galeries Lafayette, Monoprix, Printemps and Uniprix) rather than a bank and provides you with a limited 'fund' (e.g. €3,000) from which you can borrow to make purchases at that shop or chain and 'top up' your credit allowance by monthly payments (known as *crédit revolving*). Mail-order companies (see page 503) offer similar facilities. However, interest rates with this type of card are high. If you want a 'normal' credit or charge card, you must therefore obtain one abroad.

Foreign credit cards, principally Visa and MasterCard, are accepted by most large businesses, although charge cards such as American Express and Diners Club aren't as common. Nevertheless, you should never assume that a business (such as a restaurant) accepts a particular credit or charge card, but check **before** running up a bill. Note also that some foreign cards without a microchip cannot be used in French cash machines, and some businesses refuse to accept British cards without a microchip, although they're valid in France, or staff may not know how to 'swipe' them (or the machine may not work); you may need to explain how this is done or, after a couple of failed attempts, you may be told '*ça passe pas*' ('it doesn't work')! Because of an increase in credit card fraud, many businesses require customers to present an identity card or passport when using a credit card, even though cashiers never check your signature against the card!

Most credit and charge cards allow you to withdraw cash from machines (e.g. with a Visa card you can usually withdraw up to €300 per week from banks and post offices displaying a *CB/Visa* sign). You will normally be charged a withdrawal fee, although a few foreign banks have arrangements with French banks to waive this charge (e.g. Barclays in the UK with BNP Paribas). Before obtaining a credit or charge card, compare the costs and benefits, particularly the interest rates charged.

If you maintain a bank account abroad, it's best to retain your foreign credit cards. An advantage of using a credit card issued abroad is that payment isn't required until up to eight weeks later, thus giving you interest-free credit (provided you pay the full amount by the due date). However, if your card is in a foreign currency, e.g. US$ or GB£, you're at the mercy of exchange rate fluctuations.

France is one of the worst countries in the world for credit card theft (Paris and Nice are the worst cities), but you can insure against losing credit cards or you may be able to pay a fee to the card company, relieving you of any liability. To report lost or stolen credit cards in France call the following numbers:

- **American Express** – ☎ 01 47 77 72 00.
- **Carte Bleue Visa** – ☎ 08 92 70 57 05 (24 hours).
- **Diners Club** – ☎ 08 10 31 41 59.
- **Eurocard/MasterCard** – ☎ 08 92 69 70 57 05 (24 hours).

Even if you don't like credit cards, they do have their uses; for example, you don't need to pay a deposit when hiring a car or to pre-pay hotel bills, you can make bookings via telephone and the internet, they're 'safer' than carrying cash, and above all, they're convenient, particularly when travelling abroad. **However, you should never rely solely on a credit card in France.**

LOANS & OVERDRAFTS

All French banks provide overdrafts (*découvert*) and loans (*emprunt/prêt*), although they aren't as free with their money as banks in many other European countries – particularly regarding business loans to foreigners. A few banks allow a cheque account holder whose salary is paid directly into his account to overdraw a specified sum without making special arrangements, when the current overdraft rate applies. Check with your bank. You must normally pay (e.g. €5 per month) for an overdraft facility (euphemistcally termed a *facilité de caisse*), you must pay interest on the overdraft (bizarrely termed *agios*), and you won't be allowed to remain overdrawn for long periods. Nevertheless, these strictures are preferable to the penalties you can incur for overdrawing an account without authorisation (see page 363).

Loans are subject to your credit rating, income and the amount of debt you already have. French law doesn't permit banks to offer loans where the repayments are more than 30 per cent of your net income (see **Mortgages** below). It pays to shop around for a loan, as interest rates vary considerably with the bank as well as with the amount and the period of the loan. Don't neglect smaller banks; it isn't always necessary to have an account with a bank to obtain a loan. Note, however, that decisions regarding loans and other transactions often aren't made by managers at local level and must be referred to a regional head office. Ask your friends and colleagues for recommendations. If you have collateral, e.g. French property or an insurance policy, or you can get someone to stand as a guarantor for a loan, you will be eligible for a secured loan at a lower interest rate than an unsecured loan. Some banks may insist that clients take out a life insurance policy for the term of a loan.

The interest rate is quoted as the *taux effectif global* (*TEG*), the French equivalent of the annual percentage rate (APR) used in the UK and the US. In September 2006, maximum interest rates on loans ranged from 8.48 per cent (on sums over €1,524) to 20.36 per cent (on sums under €1,524).

Borrowing from private loan companies, as advertised in newspapers and magazines, is expensive with **very** high interest rates and should be a **last resort**. Even then, as a foreigner, you may need to find a homeowner or French citizen to act as a guarantor, in which case you will be able to borrow from a bank. The more desperate your financial situation, the more suspicious you should be of anyone willing to lend you money (unless it's your mum!).

The local Direction Départementale de la Concurrence, de la Consommation et de la Répression des Fraudes ('agency for competition, consumption and fraud repression') for your department can provide information about loan contracts and agreements. For contact details look under *Les infos administratives: information des consommateurs* at the front of the yellow pages or go to ⌨ http://www.minefi.gouv.fr.

MORTGAGES

Mortgages or home loans (*hypothèque*) are available, to both residents and non-residents, from all major French banks and many foreign banks. It's possible to obtain a foreign currency mortgage, i.e. other than in euros. However, **you should** be extremely wary of taking out a foreign currency mortgage, as interest rate gains can be wiped out overnight by currency swings and devaluations. It's generally recognised that you should take out a loan in the currency in which you're paid or in the currency of the country where a property is situated. In this case, if the foreign currency is devalued you will have the consolation of knowing that the value of your French property will have increased by the same percentage when converted back into the foreign currency.

When choosing between a euro loan and a foreign currency loan, be sure to take into account all costs, fees, interest rates and possible currency fluctuations. **However you finance the purchase of a home in France, you should obtain independent professional advice.**

Most French banks offer euro mortgages on French property through foreign branches in the EU and other countries. Most financial advisers recommend borrowing from a large, reputable bank rather than a small one. Crédit Agricole is the largest French lender, with a 25 per cent share of the French mortgage market.

Both French and foreign lenders have tightened their lending criteria in the last few years as a result of the repayment problems experienced by many recession-hit borrowers in the early 1990s. Some foreign lenders apply stricter rules than French lenders regarding income, employment and the type of property on which they will lend, although some are willing to lend more than a French institution. It can be difficult to obtain a mortgage in France, particularly if you have neither a regular income nor assets there (or if you're a single woman!). If you have difficulty, you should try a bank that's experienced in dealing with foreigners, such as the Banque Transatlantique (💻 http://www.transat.tm.fr). More information about mortgages can be cound in *Buying a Home in France* (Survival Books – see page 587).

Types of Mortgage

All French mortgages are repaid using the capital and interest method (repayment); endowment and pension-linked mortgages aren't offered. Interest rates can be fixed or variable, the fixed rate being higher than the variable rate to reflect the increased risk to the lender. Variable rate loans may be fixed for the first two or more years, after which they're adjusted up or down on an annual basis in line with prevailing interest rates, but usually within preset limits, e.g. within 3 per cent of the original rate. You can usually convert a variable rate mortgage to a fixed rate mortgage at any time. There's normally a redemption penalty, e.g. 3 per cent of the outstanding capital, for early repayment of a fixed rate mortgage, although that isn't usual for variable rate mortgages. If you think you may want to repay early, you should try to have the redemption penalty waived or reduced before signing the agreement.

Terms & Conditions

It's customary for a property to be held as security for a loan taken out on it, i.e. the lender takes a charge on the property, and some foreign banks won't lend on the security of a French property.

French banks aren't permitted to offer mortgages where repayments are more than 30 per cent of your net income. Joint incomes and liabilities are included when assessing a couple's borrowing limit (usually a French bank will lend to up to three joint borrowers). Note that the 30 per cent limit includes existing mortgage or rental payments, both in France and abroad. If your total repayments exceed 30 per cent of your income, French banks aren't permitted to extend further credit. Earned income isn't included if you're aged over 65. In September 2006, the maximum interest rate a bank could charge on a fixed rate mortgage was 5.99 per cent and the maximum on a variable rate mortgage 5.57 per cent.

For a mortgage above a certain amount (e.g. €150,000), you must normally take out a life (usually plus health and disability) insurance policy equal to 120 per cent of the amount borrowed. An existing insurance policy may be accepted, although it must be assigned to the lender. A medical examination may be required, although this isn't usual if you're under 50. You're also responsible for obtaining building insurance (see page 343) on a property and must provide the lender with a certificate of insurance.

French mortgages are usually limited to 70 or 80 per cent of a property's value (although some lenders limit loans to just 50 per cent). A mortgage can include renovation work, when written quotations must be provided with a mortgage application. Note that you must add expenses and fees, totalling around 10 to 15 per cent of the purchase price on an 'old' property, i.e. one over five years old.

Mortgages can be obtained for any period from 2 to 20 years, although the usual term is 15 years (some banks won't lend for longer than this). In certain cases, mortgages can be arranged over terms of up to 25 years, although interest rates are higher. Generally the shorter the period of a loan, the lower the interest rate. All lenders set minimum loans, e.g. €15,000 to €30,000, and some set minimum purchase prices. Usually there's no maximum loan amount, which is subject to status and possibly valuation (usually required by non-French lenders).

In France, a mortgage cannot be transferred from one person to another, as is possible in some countries, but can usually be transferred to another property.

Fees

There are various fees associated with mortgages. All lenders charge an administration fee (*frais de dossier*) for setting up a loan, usually 1 per cent of the loan amount. There's usually a minimum fee, e.g. €350 (plus VAT) and there may also be a maximum. Although it's unusual to have a survey, foreign lenders usually insist on a valuation (costing around €250) before they grant a loan. If a loan is obtained using a French property as security, additional fees and registration costs are payable to the *notaire* for registering the charge against the property.

If you borrow from a co-operative bank (see **Banks** on page 356), you're obliged to subscribe to the capital of the local bank. The amount (number of shares) is decided by the board of directors and you will be sent share certificates (*certificat nominatif de parts sociales*) for that value. The payment (e.g. €75) is usually deducted from your account at the same time as the first mortgage repayment. When the loan has been repaid, the shares are reimbursed (if required).

If you have a foreign currency mortgage or are a non-resident with a euro mortgage, you must usually pay commission charges each time you make a mortgage payment or remit money to France. However, some lenders will transfer mortgage payments to France each month free of charge or for a nominal amount.

Remortgaging

Until recently, French lenders have generally been reluctant to remortgage and you couldn't mortgage a property you already owned outright, but new rules introduced in spring 2006 mean that 'equity release' mortgages should be available by 2007. There will be two types of 'product': a *crédit hypothécaire rechargeable*, which allows you to reborrow the amount you've already paid off on an existing mortgage, and a *prêt viager hypothécaire*, which enables you to release the 'capital' tied up in a property as a result of an increase in value. Before taking out either type of mortgage, you must visit a *notaire*, who will warn you of the risk you're undertaking!

VALUE ADDED TAX

Value added tax (VAT), called *taxe sur la valeur ajoutée* (*TVA*), accounts for around 45 per cent of government revenue (twice as much as income tax!). Most prices of goods and services are quoted inclusive of tax (*toutes taxes comprises/TTC*), although sometimes business supplies are quoted exclusive of tax (*hors taxes/HT*). France has the following rates of VAT:

Rate (%)	Applicability
0 (exempt)	Basic foodstuffs, children's clothes, medical and dental care, educational services, insurance, banking and financial services, and various transactions subject to other taxes
2.1 (super-reduced)	Medicines reimbursed by social security; newspapers and magazines
5.5 (reduced)	Certain foodstuffs (including most drinks and take-away food); agricultural products; non-reimbursed medicines; books; public transport; canteen food; cinema, theatre and concert tickets; travel agency fees
19.6 (standard)	All other services and goods

VAT is payable on goods purchased outside the EU, but not on goods purchased in an EU country where VAT has already been paid, although you may be asked to show a VAT receipt to prove this. VAT on imported second-hand goods, on which VAT hasn't previously been paid, is subject to a complex calculation based on their second-hand value.

Business activity may or may not be subject to (*assujetti à*) VAT, and you should check with your local Centre des Impôts. Generally, a business providing a service (*prestation de service*) with an annual turnover of more than €30,500 must register for VAT and charge VAT to its customers. If VAT relates to sales (*vente*), these must exceed €84,000 before registration is necessary. If you're self-employed (*travailleur indépendent*) or a sole-trader, you must register with the appropriate organisation (see **Self-employed** on page 380) and will automatically be given a VAT number. With the exception of very small businesses, VAT returns must be made monthly and not quarterly as in some other EU countries. VAT refunds aren't paid automatically and must be applied for on certain dates. **Make sure you obtain and keep VAT receipts for all business-related expenditure.** See also **Customs** on page 92 and **Shopping Abroad** on page 504.

INCOME TAX

Personal income tax (*impôt sur le revenu des personnes physiques/IRPP* – the information below applies only to personal income tax and not to company tax) in France is below average for EU countries, particularly for large families, and accounts for only 20 per cent of government revenue. The government has been reducing income tax levels for the past decade, although there was no reduction in 2006. (Corporation tax has also been reduced by 10 per cent to 33.3 per cent.) However, when income tax is added to social security contributions (see page 328), regarded as a form of tax, and other indirect taxes, French taxes are among the highest in the industrialised world (around 50 per cent).

Employees' income tax **isn't** deducted at source (i.e. 'pay-as-you-earn'), although the government has considered introducing such a system, and individuals are responsible for declaring and paying their own income tax. Tax is withheld at flat rates and at source only for non-residents who receive income from employment and professional activities in France, who must file a statement with the Centre des Impôts de Non-Résidents (9 rue d'Uzès, 75094 Paris Cedex 02, ☎ 01 53 00 14 50) each year. Most taxpayers pay their tax a year in arrears in three instalments, although it can be paid in ten monthly instalments (see **Tax Bills** on page 383).

The French have a pathological hatred of paying taxes, and tax evasion is a national sport (most French people consider cheating the *fisc* a challenge rather than a crime). It's estimated that around a third of non-salaried taxpayers don't declare a substantial part of their income. Consequently, if your tax affairs are investigated, the authorities often take a hard line when they find you've been 'cheating', even if you made an 'innocent' mistake. If your perceived standard of living is higher than would be expected on your declared income, the tax authorities may suspect you of fraud, so contrive to appear poor. In extreme circumstances, additional income tax or a higher rate of tax can be arbitrarily imposed by tax inspectors (*régime d'imposition forfaitaire*). **The French tax authorities maintain details of tax declarations, employers and bank accounts on computers to help them expose fraud and can use social security numbers and access all other government computer systems to identify residents and compare their declarations with their circumstances.** Indeed, individuals are encouraged – and even rewarded – to denounce tax dodgers! In any case, foreigners running a business in France are far more likely to be 'investigated' than natives: it's reckoned that foreign business accounts are checked every six years, whereas farming families may avoid inspection for six generations!

As you would expect in a country with a 'billion' bureaucrats, the French tax system is inordinately complicated and most people don't understand it – not even the tax authorities, from whom it's difficult to obtain accurate (or even consistent) information, and errors in tax assessments are commonplace. Unless your tax affairs are simple, it's prudent to employ an accountant (*expert comptable*) to complete your tax return and ensure that you're correctly assessed. In fact, a good accountant will help you (legally) to save more in taxes than you will pay him in fees. A list of registered tax consultants is available from the Conseil Supérieur de l'Ordre des Experts-Comptables (☎ 01 44 15 60 00, 💻 http://www.experts-comptables.fr). Details of Franco-British tax consultants are available from the French Chamber of Commerce in London (☎ 020-7304 4040).

Many books are available to help you understand and save taxes, and income tax guides are published each January, including the *Guide Pratique du Contribuable* (published by the Syndicat National Unifié des Impôts, 💻 http://www.snui.fr), available in book shops and newsagents' for around €7. The Service Public website (💻 http://www.service-public.fr) has extensive tax information under '*Impôts*'. If your French isn't up to deciphering tax terminology, refer to *Taxation in France* by Charles Parkinson (PKF Publications). It's possible to reduce your income tax bill by taking out a life assurance policy (see **Life Insurance** on page 348).

Liability

Your liability for French income tax depends on where you're domiciled. Your domicile is normally the country you regard as your permanent home and where you live most of the year. A foreigner working in France for a French company who has taken up residence in France and has no income tax liability abroad is considered to have his tax domicile (*domicile fiscal*) in France. A person can be resident in more than one country at any given time, but can be domiciled only in one country. The domicile of a married woman isn't necessarily the same as her husband's but is determined using the same criteria as for anyone capable of having an independent domicile. Your country of domicile is particularly important regarding inheritance tax (see page 390).

Under the French tax code, domicile is decided under the 'tax home test' (*foyer fiscal*) or the 183-day rule. You're considered to be a French resident and liable to French tax if **any** of the following applies:

- Your permanent home, i.e. family or principal residence, is in France.

- You spend over 183 days in France during any calendar year.

- You carry out paid professional activities or employment in France, except when secondary to business activities conducted in another country.

- Your centre of economic interest, e.g. investments or business, is in France.

If you intend to live permanently in France, you should notify the tax authorities in your present country (you will be asked to complete a form, e.g. a form P85 in the UK). You may be entitled to a tax refund if you depart during the tax year. The tax authorities may require evidence that you're leaving the country, e.g. evidence of a job in France or of having bought or rented a property there. If you move to France to take up a job or start a business, you must register with the local tax authorities (Centre des Impôts) soon after your arrival.

Double Taxation

French residents are taxed on their worldwide income, subject to certain treaty exceptions (non-residents are taxed only on income arising in France). Citizens of most countries are exempt from paying taxes in their home country when they spend a minimum period abroad, e.g. a year. According to the Convention for the Avoidance of Double Taxation and the Prevention of Fiscal Evasion, France has double-taxation treaties with over 70 countries, including all members of the EU, Australia, Canada, China, India, Israel, Japan, Malaysia, New Zealand, Pakistan, the Philippines, Singapore, Sri Lanka, Switzerland and the US.

Treaties are designed to ensure that income that has already been taxed in one treaty country isn't taxed again in another treaty country. The treaty establishes a tax credit or exemption on certain kinds of income, either in the country of residence or in the country where the income is earned. Where applicable, a double-taxation treaty prevails over domestic law. Many people living abroad switch their investments to offshore holdings to circumvent the often complicated double-taxation agreements. If you're in doubt about your tax liability in your home country, contact your nearest embassy or consulate in France. The US is the only country that taxes its non-resident citizens on income earned abroad, although there are exclusions on foreign-earned income (around US$76,000 per spouse).

Leaving France

Before leaving France, foreigners must pay any tax due for the previous year and the year of departure by applying for a tax clearance (*quitus fiscal*). A tax return must be filed prior to departure and should include your income and deductions from 1st January of the departure year to the date of departure. The tax office will calculate the tax due and provide a written statement. When departure is made before 31st December, the previous year's taxes are applied. If this results in overpayment, a claim must be made for a refund. A French removal company isn't supposed to export your household belongings without an official 'tax clearance statement' (*bordereau de situation*) confirming that all taxes have been paid.

Note that leaving (or moving to) France may offer an opportunity for 'favourable tax planning', i.e. tax avoidance, rather than tax evasion. To take the maximum advantage of your situation, you should obtain professional advice from a tax adviser who's familiar with both the French tax system and that of your present or future country of residence.

Taxable Income & Exemptions

Income tax is calculated upon both earned income (*impôt sur le revenu*) and unearned income (*impôt des revenus de capitaux*). Taxable income includes:

- Base pay.
- Overseas and cost of living allowances.
- Contributions to profit sharing plans.
- Bonuses (annual, performance, etc.).
- Storage and relocation allowances.
- Language lessons provided for a spouse.
- Personal company car.
- Payments in kind (such as free accommodation or meals).
- Stock options.
- Home leave or holidays (paid by your employer).
- Children's education allowances.
- Property and investment income (dividends and interest).

If you have an average income and receive interest on bank deposits only, tax on unearned income won't apply, as it's deducted from bank interest before you receive it.

Certain types of income are exempt from income tax, including payments from a complementary insurance policy or a temporary accident and illness insurance policy, life annuities (*rentes viagères*) paid to invalids, military pensions, payments by social services, severance pay (up to certain limits), certain payments into a company holiday savings plan (*compte épargne-temps*), certain contributions to a company holiday voucher scheme (*chèques-vacances* – see page 63), allowances for obligatory training courses, gifts of home computers from an employer, and maintenance payments from a parent or guardian.

Allowances

Although the tax percentage rates in France are high, your taxable income is considerably reduced by allowances. These include the following:

- Social security payments, which **aren't** taxed and are deducted from the gross income of salaried employees (see page 328).

- A 10 per cent allowance (*déduction forfaitaire*) for 'professional' or 'notional' expenses, to which all salaried taxpayers are entitled, unless such expenses are specified. (If your expenses exceed 10 per cent, you may itemise them and claim an additional allowance.) The standard allowance is a minimum of €389 and a maximum of €13,093 (the maximum is around a quarter of this amount in the case of pension income).

- A further general deduction (*abattement général*) of 20 per cent, which is then applied to certain categories of income, including salary, pensions and life annuities, up to a limit €120,100. This also applies only to salaried employees.

The self-employed don't qualify for the 10 per cent allowance or the 20 per cent general deduction. If you're self-employed, however, you can obtain a 20 per cent reduction on your taxable income by joining your regional Association Agréée des Professions Libérales (commonly known as a *centre de gestion*), a government-sponsored body that regulates the income tax declarations of self-employed people. You must join before the end of March in the year for which you want to claim the 20 per cent reduction, and the joining fee is around €110. You must then pay an annual subscription of around €150 (payable at the end of the year). This means that, provided your taxable income is above around €9,000, joining is to your financial advantage; it's to your advantage anyway, as your accounts are less likely to be queried by the authorities!

Certain losses are also allowable against income tax (e.g. from letting furnished accommodation, and from agricultural and certain other investments), as are certain expenses (e.g. support for a relative in need, taxes on historic or listed buildings, subscriptions to certain cultural organisations, improvements to a property you're letting or modifications to a property for an old or disabled person, the installation of a condensing gas boiler, and capital invested in a business). The *contribution sociale généralisée* (*CSG* – see page 323) is also allowable under certain circumstances.

Under certain circumstances, the parents of a married dependent child can claim an allowance against income tax. There are further allowances for those over 65 (on 31st December of the relevant tax year) who are still working and for those receiving an invalidity pension.

The figure you arrive at after deducting all allowances is your net taxable income (*revenu net imposable*).

Family Quotient

Families are taxed as a single entity, although you can elect for a dependent child's income to be taxed separately if this is advantageous (a dependant's income up to €7,640 is exempt from income tax). The French income tax system favours the family, as the amount of income tax paid is directly related to the number of dependent children. Tax rates are based on a system of 'parts' (*parts*), reflecting the marital status of the taxpayer and the number of dependent children, as shown below. The number of parts is known as the 'family quotient' (*quotient familial/QF*).

- A single, divorced or widowed person with no dependent children counts as 1 part.

- A single, divorced or widowed person with no dependent children but one adult child counts as 1.5 parts.

- A married couple with no dependent children counts as 2 parts. French law distinguishes between living with someone on an 'unofficial' basis (*en union libre*) and cohabiting with a spouse or 'official' partner (*en concubinage*). A partner can be made 'official' by entering into an agreement called a *pacte civil de solidarité* (*PACS* – see page 525). If you live *en union libre*, you're treated for tax purposes as two single people, whereas if you're '*pacsés*' you're treated as a couple and are entitled to a number of tax advantages; they must complete the relevant section of the tax return.

● People with dependent children are allocated parts as shown in the table below. The first two children count half a part each, each subsequent child a full part.

Dependent children are normally classified as those under 18 and unmarried, or disabled children of any age. However, if children aged 18 to 25 are divorced or widowed and without children of their own, they can be claimed as dependants; a form requesting dependent status must be signed by the child and must be sent with the parents' tax return.

Dependent Children	En Union Libre	Parts Single/Divorced	Married/En Concubinage/ Widowed
1	1.5	2	2.5
2	2	2.5	3
3	3	3.5	4
4	4	4.5	5
(and so on for each additional child)			

Calculation

The tax year runs for the calendar year (i.e. from 1st January to 31st December). The income tax rates for a single person (1 part) for 2006 income (2007 tax return) are shown in the table below. Note that taxable income is income after the deduction of social security contributions and various allowances (see above). Your tax 'base' (*assiette fiscale*) is calculated by multiplying the taxable income within a particular bracket by the tax rate.

Taxable Income	Tax Rate	Tax	Aggregate Tax
Up to €4,412	0%	€0	€0
€4,412 to €8,677	6.83%	€286.18	€291.30
€8,677 to €15,274	19.14%	€1,240.27	€1,553.97

€15,274 to €24,731	28.26%	€2,625.35	€4,226.52
€24,731 to €40,241	37.38%	€5,694.84	€10,024.16
€40,241 to €49,624	42.62%	€3,928.71	€14,023.19
Over €49,624	48.09%		

The tax rate for other taxpayers can be calculated (approximately) using the above table by multiplying the taxable income by the number of parts. For example, if you're a married couple with no children (2 parts) simply double the taxable income amounts shown (i.e. income up to €8,668 is exempt and income up to €17,048 is taxed at 6.83 per cent, etc.); if you're a married couple with two children (3 parts) treble the taxable income shown. Note, however, that above certain thresholds married couples pay less tax than widows or those living *en concubinage*, who pay less than single parents (see table below).

If your taxable income is below the following thresholds (*seuil de non-imposition*), you pay no income tax: €8,782 (1 part); €11,178 (1.5 parts); €13,384 (2 parts); €15,590 (2.5 parts); €17,796 (3 parts); €20,002 (3.5 parts); €22,208 (4 parts); €24,414 (4.5 parts); €26,620 (5 parts). If the tax due is less than €61 (known as the *seuil de non-recouvrement* or *franchise*), payment is waived (the generosity of the French government knows no bounds).

The following table shows the amount of tax payable for selected taxable incomes from €10,000 to €50,000 (2004 income) for various family quotients:

| Taxable Income | Parts | | | | | |
	1	1.5*	2**	2.5**	3	3.5*
€10,000	410	0	0	0	0	0
€20,000	2,890	1,774–2,061	1,089	512	3286	0
€30,000	6,196	4,334–5,367	3,003	2,318	1,634	994
€40,000	9,934	7,775–9,105	5,779–6,198	4,398	3,548	2,863
€50,000	14,204	12,045–13,375	8,654–10,468	7,224–8,309	5,843	4,777

* The tax due varies with the status of the child.

** Above certain thresholds married couples pay less tax than widows or those living *en concubinage*, who pay less than single parents.

Reductions & Credits

Once you've calculated your tax 'base', you may be eligible for reductions (*réductions*) or credits (*crédits*) to this amount. (The difference between a reduction and a credit is that a credit can result in a negative amount of tax due – i.e. a refund

– whereas a reduction cannot.) Tax reductions may apply to the following (there's no longer a reduction on life insurance premiums):

- Children at school or university (€61 per child at secondary school, €153 per child at a *lycée*, €183 per child in higher education).

- 10 per cent of contributions to a *plan d'épargne retraite populaire* (see page 365).

- Contributions to a complementary health insurance scheme in accordance with the *Loi Madelin* (see page 339).

- 50 per cent of the cost of home help up to €12,000 per year.

- Costs of long-term care for elderly relatives.

- Payments made to a former spouse.

- Dividends from a French company.

- Purchase of a car running on GPL (see page 247) or another low-pollution fuel: the credit is between €1,525 and €2,300 per vehicle.

- Purchase of forest or woodland.

- Investment in an overseas company, a 'rural regeneration area' (*zone de revitalisation rurale*), a small or medium-size enterprise (*PME*) or an innovative job-creation project (*fonds communs de placement dans l'innovation*).

- Management training expenses.

- Union subscription fees.

If you have a child or children under seven in registered day care and both parents work and earn less than a certain amount (or cannot work), you qualify for a tax credit (known as a *réduction d'impôt pour frais de garde*) of 25 per cent of annual expenses up to €2,300 per child. If you employ a child-minder at home, you can claim an allowance for a home help (see above).

Tax credits may also apply to the following: energy-saving home improvements; VAT on major items of domestic equipment purchased from and installed by a VAT-registered company; the purchase of a low-pollution car (see page 249) – a credit of €2,000 or €3,000 if you've taken a car more than ten years old off the road in exchange; those on low incomes (under certain circumstances) according to a scheme called *prime pour l'emploi*.

Self-employed

Those who qualify as self-employed in France include artisans or craftsmen (*professions artisanales*) such as builders, plumbers and electricians. Others include those involved in trading activities such as shopkeepers, anyone buying and selling goods, agents, brokers and property dealers. If you're a professional (*profession libérale*) such as an accountant, doctor or lawyer or a freelance worker (*travailleur indépendent*) such as an artist or writer, you may complete a *déclaration contrôlée* (form 2035) requiring you to keep accounts of income and expenses, including all related receipts and documents, or, if your earnings are below €27,000, a *micro-entreprise* or *micro-BNC*, on which you declare all earnings and qualify for a 50 per cent tax reduction. Those in commercial enterprises, e.g. shpkeepers, should complete a normal tax return, unless their earnings are below €76,300, in which case they may complete a *micro-BIC*. If your income is from letting a property privately, you can complete a *micro-foncier*, provided you've earned less than €15,000; otherwise, you need to complete form 2044.

The self-employed don't qualify for the 10 per cent allowance or the 20 per cent general deduction on taxable income, although they can obtain a 20 per cent reduction by joining their local Association Agréée des Professions Libérales (see page 377). The self-employed can also claim against tax any payments made to a *mutuelle* (see page 321), provided the contract is drawn up according to the *loi Madelin*. If you run a business from home, you must also pay *taxe professionelle*, although you can claim a reduction in property tax (see page 384).

UK Pensioners

If you're a UK national with a British state retirement or occupational pension and become a French resident, your pension will be taxed as income in France (see **Income Tax** on page 373). However, you will qualify for certain deductions, including the 10 per cent *déduction forfaitaire* and 20 per cent *abattement général* (see **Allowances** on page 376). You will also be exempt from social charges on your pension income provided you have a healthcare form E121 or E106 (see 325). All UK pensions are paid in sterling and will need converting to euros for declaration to the French tax authorities. You can normally have your pension paid directly into a French bank account, but some occupational pensions cannot be paid into a foreign account. Government service pensions are taxed in the UK, irrespective of your place of residence or domicile, unless you transfer them out of the UK before you start receiving payments. The taxation of personal pensions is a complicated subject and you should obtain expert advice before retiring to France. Similarly with regard to the taxation of 'tax-free' lump sums, which may be subject to French tax if received while resident in France.

If your UK pension is supposed to be taxed at source, you must advise the Inland Revenue that it will be taxed in France in order to avoid being taxed twice. You will need to request form *FRA/Indivduel* at your tax office in France, which will be stamped and sent to the IR. British pensioners should also be aware of changes to the rules governing pensions introduced in April 2005, including a lifetime allowance.

Income Tax Return

You're sent an annual tax return (*déclaration des revenus*) by the tax authorities in late February or early March of each year. From 2006 these have been pre-filled, so in theory all you have to do is check the figures, sign it and post it back, although the self-employed will inevitably have to enter new figures. If you aren't sent a form, you can obtain one from your town hall or tax office (look in the yellow pages under *Impôts, Trésor Public*). The standard return is the 2042; there are supplementary forms for non-commercial profits (forms 2035, 2037), property income (2044), foreign source income such as a pension or dividends (2047), capital gains on financial investments (2074), and other capital gains (2049).

There's no 'head of the household' in France (at least, not as far as the tax office is concerned), and either spouse or partner may complete and sign a tax return for a family, including all family members' income, although it's possible for children under 18 with their own income, e.g. income from an inheritance or their own earnings, to be independently assessed.

In the year of their marriage, a couple must provide three separate declarations: one for each partner for the period between 1st January and the date of the marriage, and a joint declaration for the period between the marriage and 31st December. An unmarried couple living together 'unofficially' (*en union libre*) is treated as two single people for tax purposes. If they enter into a *PACS* (see page 525), they're taxed as a couple from the year after making the agreement. A divorced couple continue to be taxed jointly at least until receipt of an *ordonnance de non-conciliation* (*ONC*).

French tax returns are complicated, despite attempts to simplify them in recent years. The language used is particularly difficult to understand for foreigners (and many French). Local tax offices (Centre des Impôts) will usually help you to complete your tax return, either in person or via the telephone (☎ 08 20 32 42 52 – between 08.00 and 22.00 Mondays to Fridays and from 09.00 to 19.00 on Saturdays) but, of course, mostly in French only. Dordogne residents can take advantage of an English service offered by Sykes Anderson Solicitors (🖳 http://www.sykesanderson.com), who aim to extend it to other parts of France. Tax declarations can be made online, but not the first time you make a declaration; once you've been issued with a taxpayer number, you can use the online facility, which is free and allows you an extension of one to three weeks on the filing deadline (for some reason, the date varies according to where you live). You can make an appointment for a free consultation with your local tax inspector at your town hall. However, if your French isn't excellent you will need to take someone with you who's fluent. Alternatively you can employ a tax accountant (*expert comptable/conseiller fiscal*).

If you pay income tax abroad, you must return the form uncompleted with evidence that you're domiciled abroad. Around a month later you should receive a statement from the French tax authorities stating that you have no tax to pay (*vous n'avez pas d'impôt à payer*). The French tax authorities may request copies of foreign tax returns. Americans who are going to be abroad on 15th April should ask for an *Extension Form*. **US income tax returns cannot be filed with the IRS office in Paris but must be sent to the IRS in the US.** IRS Publication 54, *Tax Guide for US Citizens and Resident Aliens Abroad*, can be downloaded from the IRS website (🖳 http://www.irs.gov/pub/irs-pdf/p54.pdf).

Although you're allowed to accidentally under-declare by up to 5 per cent, you will have to pay the difference, and penalties for grossly understated or deliberately undeclared income and unjustified deductions range from 40 to 80 per cent for fraud, plus interest on the amount owed. Note also that you may make yourself liable for penalties if you display 'exterior signs of wealth' (*signes extérieurs de richesse*), so don't drive to the Centre des Impôts in your new BMW to deposit your tax return!

Tax returns must be filed by late March (by employees) or late April (by the self-employed). Late filing, even by one day, attracts a penalty of 10 per cent of the amount due. Changes in your tax liability may be made by the tax authorities up to three years after the end of the tax year to which the liability relates. Therefore you should retain all records relating to the income and expenses reported in your tax returns for at least three years, even if you've left France.

Tax Bills

Some time between August and December, you will receive a tax bill (*avis d'imposition*). There are two methods of paying your tax bill: in three instalments (*tiers provisionnels*) or in ten equal monthly instalments (*mensualisation*).

Three Instalments

The more common method of payment is in three instalments. The first two payments, each comprising around a third (*tiers*) of the previous year's tax liability, are provisional (*acompte provisionnel*) and are payable by 15th February and 15th May each year. The third and final instalment, the balance of your tax bill (*solde*), is payable by 15th September. The tax authorities adjust your third payment to take into account your actual income for the previous year. Payment dates are officially 31st January, 30th April and 31st August, but the tax authorities allow you an extra two weeks (or 15 days) to pay bills. If you pay your tax bill late, you must pay a penalty equal to 10 per cent of your annual tax bill.

During your first year in France you won't have a previous year's tax liability (in France). Therefore the income tax computed with the information contained in the tax return filed at the end of March of the following year is payable in full by 15th September of the same year. In the following year, the normal procedure is applied. The following schedule applies to a new arrival in France:

Year	Date	Action
1 (arrival in France)		Tax payable in previous country of residence
2	End March	File tax return for first year's income
	15th September	Pay entire tax bill for first year
3, etc.	15th February	Pay first instalment of second year's tax
	End March	File tax return for second year's income
	15th May	Pay second instalment of second year's tax
	15th September	Pay final instalment of second year's income

Monthly Instalments

You can choose to pay your tax in monthly instalments (*mensualisation*) by direct debit, in which case you need to write to the collector of taxes in your tax region requesting this method of payment. If you make your request before 10th May, monthly payments will begin immediately (with an adjustment for any instalments already paid); if you apply after 10th May, they won't begin until the following January. Once started, monthly payments continue automatically each year unless you cancel them in writing.

Under this system, you pay one tenth of your previous year's tax bill on the 15th of each month from January to October. If your income is less in the current year than the previous year, the tax office will stop payments when it has received the full amount. On the other hand, if you earned more the previous year than the year before, the tax office will take a final balancing payment (*solde*), usually in December.

Monthly payments are a good budgeting aid, particularly if you're prone to rushing out and spending your salary as soon as you receive it. However, most French people prefer to pay in three instalments, with the advantage that you can invest the amount set aside for tax until each payment is due.

PROPERTY TAXES

There are four types of local property tax (*impôt local*): *taxe d'habitation* (referred to here as 'residential tax'), *taxe foncière* (or *taxes foncières*, referred to as 'property tax'), *taxe assimilée* ('sundry tax') and *taxe professionelle* ('professional tax'). Taxes pay for local services, including rubbish collection, street lighting and cleaning, local schools and other community services, and include a contribution to departmental and regional expenses. You may be billed separately for rubbish collection (see page 124).

Both residential and property taxes are payable whether a property is a principal residence (*maison principale*) or a second home (*résidence secondaire*) and whether the owner is a French or foreign resident. There's no reduction in either tax for a second home; in fact, your *taxe d'habitation* is likely to be higher, as there's a reduction for principal residences. Both taxes are calculated according to a property's notional 'cadastral' rental value (*valeur locative cadastrale*), which is reviewed every six years. If you think a valuation is too high, you can contest it.

Property and residential taxes vary from area to area and are generally higher in cities and towns than in rural areas and small villages, where few community services are provided, although this isn't necessarily the case (Paris has some of the lowest tax rates). They also vary with the type and size of property and will be significantly higher for a luxury villa than for a small apartment. If you're renting a property, check whether you're required to pay part of the *taxe foncière* as well as the *taxe d'habitation*.

Forms for the assessment of both residential and property tax are sent out by local councils and must be completed and returned to the regional tax office (Centre des Impôts) by a specified date, e.g. 15th November or 15th December for residential tax. They will calculate the tax due and send you a bill. You may be given up to two months to pay and a 10 per cent penalty is levied for late payment. It's possible to pay residential tax monthly (in ten equal instalments from January to October, sometimes with the addition of an 'adjustment' in November) by direct debit from a French bank account, which helps to soften the blow.

Property Tax

Property tax (*taxe foncière*) is paid by owners of property in France and is similar to the property tax (or rates) levied in most countries. It's payable even if a property isn't inhabited, provided it's furnished and habitable. Property tax is levied on all 'shelters' for people or goods, including warehouses and house boats (fixed mooring). The tax is split into two amounts: one for the building (*taxe foncière bâtie*) and a smaller one for the land (*taxe foncière non bâtie*). Tax is payable on most land whether or not it's built on. Property tax isn't applicable to buildings and land used exclusively for agricultural or religious purposes.

The amount of property tax payable varies by up to 500 per cent with the region, and even between towns or villages within the same region, and may be as little as €300 or as much as €1,500 per year, although there are plans to make the application of the tax 'fairer'. Strangely, the Paris area has some of the country's lowest rates.

Property tax is normally payable by mid-October. When you move to France, you should notify the local Service du Cadastre (part of the Tax Office) **and** the local Trésorerie; otherwise, you may find that your first property tax bill is sent to your previous address (even if this is abroad) and, when you fail to pay (because you haven't received it), you're charged for late payment!

Exemptions

New and restored buildings used as main or second homes are exempt from property tax for two years from 1st January following the completion date (new houses and apartments financed by certain types of government loan or purchased by an association for letting to people on low incomes may be exempt for 10 or 15 years). An application for a temporary exemption from property tax must be made to your local property tax office (Centre des Impôts Fonciers) or Bureau du Cadastre before 31st December for exemption the following year. Applications must be made within 90 days of the completion of a new or restored building.

Certain people (e.g. those over 75 and those receiving a disability pension below a certain level) are exempt from property tax, and others (e.g. those over 65 on low incomes) may qualify for a discount (*allégement*) of around €100. You may claim a reduction in your *taxe foncière* if you work from home (see **Professional Tax** below).

If you sell a property part of the way through a year, the purchaser isn't legally required to reimburse you for a proportion of the property tax due (or paid) for that year. However, it's customary for property tax to be apportioned by the *notaire* handling the sale between the seller and buyer from the date of the sale (a clause to that effect should be included in the *promesse de vente*). Therefore, if you purchase a property in July, you will normally be asked 'reimburse' the vendor for half the annual property tax. Because you aren't obliged to do so, you can negotiate the amount (or the purchase price of the property), although you may not make yourself popular with the vendor!

Residential Tax

Residential tax (*taxe d'habitation*) is payable by anyone who resides in a furnished property on 1st January, whether as an owner, as a tenant or rent-free. **Even if you vacate or sell a property on 2nd January, you must pay residential tax for the whole year and may not reclaim part of it from a new owner.** The amount payable is determined by the property (see below), irrespective of the number of occupants.

Residential tax is payable not only on residential properties (used as main or second homes) but also on outbuildings (e.g. accommodation for servants, garages) located less than a kilometre from a residential property, and on business premises that are an indistinguishable part of a residential property (e.g. bed and breakfast or *gîte* accommodation). It's calculated on the 'habitable' area of a property, including swimming pool, covered terrace and garage, and takes into account factors such as the quality of construction, location, services (e.g. mains water, electricity and gas) and facilities such as central heating. Properties are placed in eight categories ranging from 'very poor' to 'luxurious'. Changes made to a building, such as improvements or enlargements, must be notified to the land registry within 90 days.

Residential tax is levied by the town where the property is located and varies by as much as 400 per cent from town to town. As with property tax (see above), the Paris area has some of the country's lowest rates. Generally, you should expect to pay around half the amount paid in *taxe foncière*. Tax is usually payable in November or December (depending on the commune) of the year to which it applies. Residential tax includes the 'tax' on televisions (see **TV Licence** on page 172).

Exemptions

Premises used exclusively for business, farming and student lodging, and official government offices are exempt from residential tax. Residential tax isn't paid by residents whose income is below a certain level (around €16,300 for a single person), nor by certain retirees whose income in the preceding year was below around €7,200 (plus around €2,000 for each dependant). To qualify for exemption, it's sufficient for one person in the household to meet the criteria (e.g. if one spouse is retired but the other isn't).

Sundry Tax

In some areas, a regional or sundry tax (*taxe assimilée*) is also levied, particularly if a property is in a popular tourist area. This is because the local authorities must spend more than usual on amenities and the upkeep of towns (gardens, etc.).

Professional Tax

Professional tax (*taxe professionelle*) is payable on your business premises and is levied at between around 15 and 20 per cent (the exact percentage varies with the commune) of a 'base', which is currently 8 per cent of your annual income including VAT (*TVA*). For example, if you earn €30,000 per year, your tax base will be €2,400; if professional tax is levied at 20 per cent in your commune, you will pay €480.

If you work from home, you're liable for professional tax as well as residential and property taxes (and sundry tax, if applicable – see below), but you can claim a reduction on your property tax according to the proportion of your home that's used for business purposes. To calculate this, measure the total area of your living room, dining room, bedrooms and office (if separate). If your office occupies 10 per cent of the total area, for example, you may claim a 10 per cent reduction in *taxe foncière*. Certain types of worker are exempt from professional tax, including creative writers and artists and people letting holiday accommodation. You should check with an accountant.

Professional tax is assessed as follows: in your first year of French residence, you will pay nothing; in your second year, you will pay according to your earnings in Year 1 (pro rata if you moved to France part way through the year); in Year 3, your tax will again be based on your Year 1 earnings, in Year 4 on your Year 2 earnings, and so on. It's normally payable by 15th December.

WEALTH TAX

A wealth tax (*impôt sur la fortune/ISF*) is payable by each 'fiscal unit' (*foyer fiscal*), e.g. couple or family, when its annual income exceeds €732,000. The following rates apply to 2005 assets:

Assets (€'000)	Rate	Cumulative Liability
Up to 750	0%	€0
750 to 1,200	0.55%	€2,475
1,200 to 2,380	0.75%	€11,325
2,380 to 3,730	1.00%	€24,825
3,730 to 7,140	1.30%	€69,155
7,140 to 15,530	1.65%	€207,590
Over 15,530	1.80%	

If you're domiciled in France (see **Liability** on page 374), the value of your estate is based on your worldwide assets. If you're resident in France but not domiciled there, the value of your estate is based on your assets in France only. Wealth tax is assessed on the net value of your assets on 1st January each year and is payable by the following 15th June by French residents (15th July for other European residents and 15th August for all others). The amount payable is reduced by €150 for each dependant. The taxable estate **doesn't** include:

- 'Professional assets' (*biens professionnels*), which may include shares in a company in which you're active, if they total at least 25 per cent of the equity.

- Works of art and antiques.

- Artistic and literary rights and commercial copyrights.

- The value of forest and woodland property.

- Rural property let on a long-term basis.

- Pensions and life annuities.

CAPITAL GAINS TAX

Capital gains tax (*impôt sur les plus-values*) is payable on the profit from sales of certain assets in France, including antiques, art and jewellery, securities and property. Gains net of capital gains tax (CGT) are added to other income and are liable to income tax (see page 373). Capital gains are also subject to *CRDS* and *CSG* (see page 323).

Principal Residence

CGT isn't payable on profit made on the sale of your principal residence in France, provided that you've occupied it since its purchase (or for at least five years if you didn't occupy it immediately after purchase). You're also exempt from CGT if you're forced to sell for family or professional reasons, e.g. you're transferred abroad by your employer. Income tax treaties usually provide for capital gains on property to be taxable in the country where the property is located.

If you move to France permanently and retain a home abroad, this may affect your position regarding capital gains. If you sell your foreign home before moving to France, you will be exempt from CGT, as it's your principal residence. However, if you establish your principal residence in France, the foreign property becomes a second home and is thus liable to CGT when it's sold. **EU tax authorities co-operate in tracking down capital gains tax dodgers.**

Second Homes

Capital gains on second homes in France worth over €15,000 (i.e. anything other than a caravan!) are payable by both residents and non-residents up to 15 years after purchase (until 2004, the period was 22 years). The basic rates of CGT are 26 per cent for residents, 16 per cent for non-resident EU citizens, and 33.3 per cent for non-resident non-EU citizens. Any inheritance or gift tax paid at the time of purchase is taken into account when determining the purchase price, and there are certain exemptions to the above tax rates, as follows:

- If you've owned a property for more than five years but less than 15, you're entitled to a 10 per cent reduction in CGT for every year of ownership over five (i.e. 10 per cent for six years' ownership, 20 per cent for seven years', etc.).

- If you've owned a property for at least five years and can produce proof of substantial expenditure on improving it (e.g. receipts for work done by professionals), you can claim a further deduction of 15 per cent of the property's purchase price against CGT (irrespective of the actual cost of the work), but you're no longer entitled to claim for work you've done yourself, nor any materials purchased for DIY improvements.

The purchase price of a property is no longer 'indexed' to increases in the cost of living, so any increase in the value of a property since purchase is reckoned as a gain. If you make a loss on the sale of a second home, you cannot claim this against other CGT payments, nor against income tax! Payments of CGT can be spread over five years, but you must apply to pay by this method.

The CGT due is calculated and paid on your behalf by the *notaire* handling the sale (or an *agent fiscal accrédité*); you aren't required (or rather, you aren't trusted!) to make a CGT declaration yourself.

You should keep all bills for the fees associated with buying a property (*notaire's*, estate agent's, surveyor's, etc.), plus any bills for renovation, restoration, modernisation and improvements of a second home, as these can be offset against CGT and are index-linked. DIY improvements and painting and decorating costs (*embellissement*) cannot be claimed against CGT. Part of the interest paid on a loan taken out to purchase or restore a property can also be offset against any gain, as can costs relating to the sale of the property.

Other Assets

CGT at 16 per cent is payable on the sale of French or foreign quoted or unquoted securities (stock and rights to stock) if the total sale exceeds €76,250 in value or half this amount on certain mutual funds. CGT also applies to the sale of certain items (e.g. pleasure boats, race horses, carpets, tapestries, precious stones and metals, works of art, stamps and antiques over 100 years old) worth over around €3,050 (each). Furniture, household goods and cars are exempt.

Liable assets are taxed in the same way as second homes (see above). As with CGT on property, a general allowance of €915 is made, and assets worth less than €4,600 qualify for a discount equal to the difference between the selling price and €4,600 (e.g. an object sold for €3,600 is discounted to €2,600 for CGT purposes). Precious stones, works of art and antiques attract CGT at 4.5 per cent, and precious metals at 7.5 per cent, plus 0.5 per cent *CRDS* (see page 323).

INHERITANCE & GIFT TAX

Dying in France doesn't free your assets from the clutches of the taxman, as the government imposes both inheritance and gift taxes.

Inheritance Tax

Inheritance tax (*droits de succession*) – or estate tax or death duty – is levied on the estate of a deceased person. **Both residents and non-residents are subject to inheritance tax if they own property in France.** The country where you pay inheritance tax is decided by your domicile (see **Liability** on page 374). If you're living permanently in France at the time of your death, you will be deemed to be domiciled there by the tax authorities. If you're domiciled in France, inheritance tax applies to your worldwide estate (excluding property); otherwise it applies only to assets located in France. **It's important to make your domicile clear, so that there's no misunderstanding on your death.**

When a person dies, an estate tax return (*déclaration de succession*) must be filed within six months of the date of death (within 12 months if the death occurred outside France). The return is generally prepared by a *notaire*. Inheritance tax is paid by individual beneficiaries, irrespective of where they're domiciled, and not by the estate. Tax may be paid in instalments over five or, in certain cases, ten years or may be deferred.

The rate of tax and allowances varies according to the relationship between the beneficiary and the deceased. French succession laws are quite restrictive compared with the law in many other countries. The surviving spouse has an allowance (*abattement*) of €76,000 and the children and parents of the deceased an allowance of €200,000 each. There's an additional allowance of €50,000 (in total) when a spouse and children survive. After the allowance has been deducted, tax is applied on a sliding scale up to a maximum of 40 per cent on assets over €1.7m, as shown in the table below:

Value Above Allowance		Tax Rate
Spouse	**Children/Parents**	
Up to €7,600	Up to €7,600	5
€7,600 to €15,000	€7,600 to €11,400	10
€15,000 to €30,000	€11,400 to €15,000	15
€30,000 to €520,000	€15,000 to €520,000	20
€520,000 to €850,000	€520,000 to €850,000	30
€850,000 to €1.7m	€850,000 to €1.7m	35
Over €1.7m	Over €1.7m	40

An unmarried couple with a *PACS* agreement (see page 525) qualifies for an allowance of €57,000 from the third year after making the agreement. Inheritances from the other partner above that amount are taxed at 40 per cent up to €15,000 and at 50 per cent above €15,000.

There's an allowance of €15,000 for each brother and sister under certain circumstances, but the normal allowance is just €1,500, and the tax rate thereafter is 35 per cent up to €23,000 and 45 per cent above this amount. Mentally or physically disabled brothers and sisters who are unable to earn a living receive an allowance of €46,000 in addition to the usual €15,000 or €1,500.

Any heir who doesn't benefit from any of the above allowances is entitled to €1,500 tax free. Between relations up to the fourth degree, i.e. uncles/aunts, nephews/nieces, great uncles/aunts, great nephews/nieces and first cousins, there's a flat rate tax of 55 per cent. For relationships beyond the fourth degree or between unrelated persons, the tax rate is 60 per cent. (As you can see, it's best to leave property in France to your spouse, children or parents, in order to take advantage of the relatively low tax rates.)

Changes to inheritance tax rules due to come into force in January 2007 include the option for a child to renounce his inheritance in favour of his children (so that they can inherit tax-free from their grandparents), permission to include your grandchildren in a legacy, and permission for childless couples to leave property up to a certain value tax-free to siblings and nephews/nieces.

Exemptions

Exemptions from inheritance tax include:

- Payments from life insurance policies (many people take out a life insurance policy to reduce the impact of inheritance tax).

- Certain buildings constructed between 1st June 1993 and 31st December 1996 and inherited for the first time (on the first €46,000 of their value).

- Historic or listed buildings.

- Works of art donated to the state.

- Certain woodlands and rural properties.

- Legacies to charities and government bodies.

Certain expenses may also be deducted from inheritance tax, including costs associated with a final illness, funeral expenses up to around €900, taxes (including income, wealth, property, residential and value added tax) from 1st January of the year of death until the date of death, notary's fees (for proving the will) and certain debts incurred by the deceased.

If you're resident in France and receive an inheritance from abroad, you're subject to French inheritance tax. However, if you've been resident for less than six years in France, you're exempt (or, if you paid the bill in another country, the amount is deducted from your French tax bill).

Gift Tax

You may make tax-free gifts every ten years to a spouse (up to €76,000), child (up to €46,000) or grandchild (up to €30,000). (Each of these figures is increased by €46,000 if the recipient is disabled.) As gift tax is payable on gifts (above these limits) made between spouses, assets should be equally shared **before** you become domiciled in France. There are no allowances for gifts between brothers and sisters or between unrelated people.

Gift tax (*droits de donation*) is calculated in the same way as inheritance tax (see above), according to the relationship between the donor and the recipient and the size of the gift. Any gifts made within ten years of the death of the donor (*en avancement d'horie*) must be included in the inheritance tax return and are valued at the time of death rather than at the time of donation. Payment of gift tax can be spread over a number of years, except in the case of the donation of a business.

Avoiding Inheritance & Gift Tax

It's important to understand French inheritance laws, which apply to both residents and non-residents with property in France.

First, property is divided into 'movable' and 'immovable' property: *meubles*, including not only furniture but all belongings except land and buildings, and *immeubles*, including land and buildings. Immovable property must be disposed of in accordance with French law, irrespective of whether you're resident or non-resident in France, whereas movable property is subject to French law only if you're resident (or spend the majority of your time) in France.

Second, all property subject to French law is divided into a 'disposable part' (*quotité disponible*) and a 'heritary part' (*réserve héréditaire* or *réserve légale*). Irrespective of your will(s), the hereditary part **must** be disposed of according to French law. The size of the hereditary part depends on how many children you have. If you have one child, half of your affected property must be left to him; if you have two children, they must inherit two-thirds; three or more children three-quarters. If you have no children but a living parent or grandparent, a quarter of the property must be left to him.

A couple's marital status is also of relevance to inheritance. French couples normally enter into a marriage contract, whereby their assets are either shared (*communauté universelle*) or owned separately (*séparation de biens*). Foreign couples who don't have a marriage contract will normally be regarded as having separate ownership unless they state otherwise in a property purchase contract. This means that, if one spouse dies, the other retains ownership of his part of the property and only the deceased's part is disposed of as explained above. If, on the other hand, you've specified that your marital 'arrangement' is similar to the French *communauté universelle*, ownership of all property will pass to the surviving spouse on the death of the other.

In view of the above, **couples considering buying property in France should decide in advance how they wish to dispose of it**.

There are a number of ways of limiting or delaying the impact of French inheritance laws, including inserting a clause (such as a *clause tontine*) in a property purchase contract (*acte de vente*), officially changing your marital regime in France, e.g. to joint ownership or *communauté de biens*, and buying property through a company. The *clause tontine* (or *pacte tontinier*) – an obscure law hardly used by French people – allows a property to be left entirely to a surviving spouse or partner and not shared among the children until he dies. Because it places the entire inheritance tax burden on the surviving partner, rather than sharing it among the partner and children, it's particularly advantageous for inexpensive properties; with more expensive property, it may be advantageous only for married couples, who are entitled to higher inheritance tax allowances (see above). However, a *clause tontine* is likely to be valid only if both partners have a similar life expectancy (otherwise, it could be argued that it was used expressly as a way of disinheriting children). Another consideration to be made before using a *clause tontine* is that, if you want to sell the property but your spouse objects, there's nothing you can do to force a sale.

A surviving spouse can also be given a life interest (*usufruit*) in an estate in priority to children or parents through a gift between spouses (*donation entre époux*). This is also known as a 'cross-purchase' (*achat croisé*) and means that the spouse may occupy the property for life and take any income generated by it but may not sell or otherwise dispose of it; on the other hand, the property cannot be sold or disposed of without the spouse's consent. A gift between spouses therefore delays the inheritance of an estate by any surviving children, who will have a 'reversionary interest' (*nue-propriété*) in it, i.e. ownership reverts to them on the death of the spouse. A donation must be prepared by a notaire and signed in the presence of the donor and the beneficiary. You must take along your passports, marriage certificate, birth certificates, *carte de séjour* (if applicable) and evidence of your address and occupations; a *donation entre époux* costs around €160. Note, however, that it may not apply to non-residents, who will be governed by the law of their home country.

French law doesn't recognise the rights to inheritance of an unmarried partner, unless a *PACS* agreement has been signed (see page 525), although there are a number of solutions to this problem, e.g. a life insurance policy, which may be of benefit to anyone in reducing inheritance tax (see **Life Insurance** on page 348). Another way to reduce your inheritance liability is to make a *donation partage* to your children, although gift tax will be payable (see above). One of the best solutions for a non-resident who wishes to avoid French inheritance laws regarding immovable property located in France may be to buy it through a French holding company, in which case the shares of the company are 'movable' assets and are therefore governed by the succession laws of the owner's country of domicile.

Whatever your marital situation, it's important to make a French will (even if you already have a foreign will that's valid in France), which can help to reduce your French inheritance tax liability or delay its payment (see below).

French inheritance law is an extremely complicated subject, and professional advice should be sought from an experienced lawyer who understands both French law and that of any other country involved.

WILLS

It's an unfortunate fact of life that you're unable to take your hard-earned assets with you when you take your final bow (or come back and reclaim them in a later life!). All adults should make a will (*testament*) irrespective of how large or small their assets. The disposal of your estate depends on your country of domicile (see **Inheritance & Gift Tax** above). As a general rule, French law permits a foreigner who isn't domiciled in France to make a will in any language and under the law of any country, provided it's valid under the law of that country. If you're domiciled in France, you should make a French will. **Whatever type of will you wish to make, 'immovable' property (*immeubles*) in France, i.e. land and buildings, must be disposed of (on death) in accordance with French law.** All other property in France or elsewhere (defined as 'movables' – *meubles*) may be disposed of in accordance with the law of your country of domicile. Therefore, it's extremely important to establish where you're domiciled under French law.

French law is restrictive regarding the distribution of property and the identity of heirs and gives priority to children, including illegitimate and adopted children, and the living parents of a deceased person. Under French law, you cannot disinherit your children, who have first claim on your estate, even before a surviving spouse, although you can delay their inheritance (see **Avoiding Inheritance & Gift Tax** above). If you die leaving one child, he must inherit half of your French estate and two children must inherit at least two-thirds; if you have three or more children, they must inherit three-quarters of your estate. If a couple has no surviving children, the deceased's parents each inherit a quarter of the estate and the surviving spouse half (if only one parent is alive, the spouse inherits three-quarters). If there are neither children nor parents, the spouse inherits the whole estate apart from family possessions, half of which must go to any surviving brothers or sisters of the deceased.

The part of a property that must be inherited by certain heirs (*héritiers réservataires*) is called the legal reserve (*réserve légale* or *réserve*). Once the reserved portion of your estate has been determined, the remaining portion is freely disposable (*quotité disponible*). Only when there are no descendants or ascendants is the whole estate freely disposable.

If you take up residence in France and decide to have only a French will, check that it covers any assets you have in another country. It's possible to make two wills, one relating to French property and the other to foreign property. Opinion differs on whether you should have separate wills for French and foreign property, or a foreign will with a codicil (appendix) dealing with your French property (or vice versa). However, most experts believe it's better to have a French will for winding up your French estate and a will for any country where you own immovable property. **If you have French and foreign wills, make sure that they don't contradict one another (or worse still, cancel each other out, e.g. when a will contains a clause revoking all other wills).**

Note the following information regarding wills in France:

● Marriage doesn't automatically revoke a will as it does in some other countries, e.g. the UK.

- Wills aren't made public and aren't available for inspection.

- **Where applicable, the rules relating to witnesses are strict and, if they aren't followed precisely, a will may be rendered null and void.**

- The role of the executor is different from that in many other countries; his duties are supervisory only and last for a year and a day. He's responsible for paying debts and death duties and distributing the balance in accordance with the will. The executor who's dealing with your affairs must file a *déclaration de succession* within a year of your death. At your death your property passes directly to your heirs and it's their responsibility to pay any outstanding debts and their own inheritance tax.

- Winding up an estate takes much longer than in many other countries and usually isn't given priority by *notaires*.

You should keep a copy of your will(s) in a safe place and another copy with your solicitor or the executor of your estate. Don't leave them in a bank safe deposit box, which in the event of your death is sealed for a period of time under French law. You should keep information regarding bank accounts, pensions and benefits, investments and insurance policies with your will(s), but don't forget to tell someone where they are! You should also make a separate note of your last wishes (e.g. regarding funeral arrangements) where your next-of-kin can find it immediately after your death, along with your social security number, birth, marriage, divorce and spouse's death certificates (as applicable) and the names and whereabouts of any children.

French inheritance law is a complicated subject and it's important to obtain professional legal advice from someone familiar with the laws of all relevant countries when writing or altering your will(s).

Types of Will

There are three kinds of will in France: holographic (*olographe*), authentic (*authentique*) or notarial and secret (*mystique*), described below.

Holographic Will

This is the most common form of will used in France. It must be written by hand by the person making the will (i.e. it cannot be typewritten or printed) and be signed and dated by him. No witnesses or other formalities are required. In fact it shouldn't be witnessed at all, as this may complicate matters. It can be written in English or another language, although it's preferable if it's written in French (you can ask a *notaire* to prepare a draft and copy it in your own handwriting). A holographic will must be handed to a *notaire* for filing. He sends a copy to the local district court, where the estate is administered. A holographic will can be registered in the central wills registry (*fichier de dernières volontés*). For anyone with a modest French estate, e.g. a small second home in France, a holographic will is sufficient. It costs around €30.

Authentic or Notarial Will

This is used by 5 per cent of French people. It must be drawn up by a *notaire* in the form of a notarial document and can be handwritten or typed. It's dictated by the person making the will and must be witnessed by two *notaires* or a *notaire* and two other witnesses. Unlike a holographic will, an authentic will is automatically registered in the central wills registry. An authentic will costs around €45 plus a percentage of the value of your estate; for an average estate, the cost is around €80.

Secret Will

A secret will is rarely used and is a will written by or for the person making it and signed by him. It's sealed in an envelope in the presence of two witnesses. It's then given to a *notaire*, who records on the envelope that the envelope has been handed to him and that the testator has affirmed that the envelope contains his will. The *notaire* then files the will and sends a copy to the district court where the estate is administered. A secret will costs the same as an authentic will (see above).

End of Life Will

A new type of will, made possible by a law passed in April 2005, is an 'end of life will' (*testament de fin de vie*), which contains instructions as to medical treatment in the event of incapacitation, known as *directives anticipées*. The will, which is similar to a British 'living will', can either specify the type of treatment desired or appoint someone to decide on the appropriate treatment. An end of life will is valid only for three years and renewable for a further three years, yet must have been made at least three years before incapacitation (?).

COST OF LIVING

No doubt you would like to estimate how far your euros will stretch and how much money (if any) you will have left after paying your bills. Anyone planning to live in France, particularly retirees, should take care not to underestimate the cost of living, which isn't as low as is commonly supposed. France is a particularly expensive country by American standards, and in recent years many US visitors have found it difficult or impossible to remain within their budgets. (Americans will be particularly shocked by the price of gasoline, electricity, clothing, paper products and English-language books.) Social security costs are extremely high, particularly for the self-employed, and the combined burden of social security, income tax and indirect taxes make French taxes among the highest in the EU. Inflation in France in mid-2006 was around 2 per cent, having risen from an all-time low of 0.5 per cent in 1999 (largely as a result of the introduction of the euro, which provided retailers with a convenient smoke-screen for price increases!).

With the exception of Paris and other major cities, where the higher cost of living is offset by higher salaries, the cost of living in France is similar to that of Germany and the UK and around 25 per cent higher than the US. You should, however, be wary of published cost of living comparisons with other countries, which are often wildly inaccurate (and often include irrelevant items which distort the results).

In any case, the cost of living depends on each individual's circumstances and lifestyle. Your food bill, for example, will depend on what you eat and whether you adapt to French eating habits or insist on importing foods from your native country. Food in France costs around 50 per cent more than in the US but prices are similar overall to most other western European countries. From €300 to €500 should feed two adults for a month, excluding fillet steak, caviar and alcohol (other than a moderate amount of inexpensive beer or wine). Shopping abroad (e.g. via the internet) for selected 'luxury' items, such as stereo equipment, household apparatus, electrical and electronic goods, computers and photographic equipment, can result in significant savings (see page 504).

Approximate **minimum** monthly major expenses for an 'average' single person, couple and family with two children are shown in the table below. They include rent or mortgage payments for a modern or modernised property (a studio or one-bedroom apartment for a single person, a two-bedroom property for a couple, a three-bedroom property for a couple with two children) in an average town or village; electricity, gas, water, telephone, cable TV and heating; entertainment, restaurant meals, sports and holiday expenses, newspapers and magazines; unning costs for an average family car plus third-party insurance (but not depreciation and credit purchase costs); and important 'voluntary' insurance such as supplementary health, home contents, travel, car breakdown and life insurance. They don't include luxuries or expensive alcoholic drinks.

	Monthly Costs		
	Single	**Couple**	**Family of Four**
Housing	€425	€575	€750
Food	€200	€375	€475
Utilities	€50	€80	€110
Leisure	€100	€160	€200
Transport	€100	€100	€130
Insurance	€75	€110	€135
Clothing	€50	€100	€200
Total	**€1,000**	**€1,500**	**€2,000**

15.

<u>LEISURE</u>

When it comes to leisure, few countries can match France for the variety and excellence of its attractions – from its outstanding natural beauty to the sophistication and grandeur of its cities. France is the world's most popular tourist destination, and tourism is the country's most important industry and the third-largest tourist industry in the world (after those of the US and Spain), earning the 'country' €40m annually and employing almost a million people. Over 175m people visit France each year, of whom 75m spend at least one night in the country (figures which are expected to double in the next 20 years). Paris alone attracts over 25m visitors (the Eiffel Tower in Paris is the most visited admission-charging monument in the world, attracting 6m visitors annually). Visitor attractions are generally good value and many are free, and many places that aren't normally open to the public can be visited free on the 'heritage days', *journées de patrimoine*, usually the third weekend in September.

France is one of the most beautiful countries in Europe, if not **the** most beautiful, and has the most varied landscape, offering something for everyone: magnificent beaches, spectacular countryside, mountains and seas. France also boasts vibrant nightlife, particularly in Paris, some of the world's greatest wines, *haute cuisine*, an abundance of culture, and rural tranquillity. The pursuit of *la bonne vie* is a serious business (most French people rate the pursuit of pleasure and style way ahead of success and wealth) and even bons viveurs (*bons vivants* in French!) are spoilt for choice. Nowhere else in the world is there such an exhilarating mixture of beauty, culture, tradition, sophistication and style.

Paris is one of the world's great cities and a treasure house of national monuments. It's also one of the least expensive and cleanest major capitals in the world (on the negative side, watch out for pickpockets, bag snatchers and canine waste). There's much to be enjoyed that's inexpensive or even free, not least its beauty and the extravagant street entertainment, both cultural and sartorial. Paris dominates the cultural scene in France, even more so than capital cities in other European countries, such as London and Rome. France spends an enormous amount of public money promoting the arts, particularly in Paris, widely recognised as the art capital of Europe. Cultural policy is a political priority and the government even appoints a Minister of Culture.

Many provincial towns have a cultural centre (*maison de la culture*), where exhibitions, plays, music festivals, debates and art classes are held. There are many excellent provincial art galleries and museums, and art and music festivals are staged in all regions and major towns. Traditional folk festivals are held throughout the country, most notably in Brittany and the south; France boasts more festivals than any other European country – and some 700,000 clubs and associations catering for every conceivable hobby and leisure activity. Holders of a *carte famille nombreuse* (see page 224) can benefit from discounts at over 30 national museums and certain theme parks, including Parc Astérix and Futuroscope (see page 417).

Information

Information regarding local events and entertainment is available from tourist offices, and is published in local newspapers and magazines, as well as in many foreign publications (see **Appendix B**). In most cities there are magazines and newspapers devoted to entertainment, and free weekly or monthly programmes are published by tourist organisations in major cities and tourist centres. Many city newspapers publish weekly magazines or supplements containing a detailed programme of local events and entertainment. The Paris Tourist Office provides a 24-hour recorded information service in English for performances and shows in Paris (☎ 08 92 68 31 12) or you can refer to its website (🖳 http://www.parisinfo.com).

Guide Books

The aim of this chapter, and indeed the purpose of the book, is to provide information that isn't found in standard guide books. General tourist information is available in numerous French and foreign guide books, including a range of indispensable books produced by Michelin. The *Michelin Green Guides* encompass 25 books, around 15 published in English, each covering a different area in detail. They contain a wealth of information about local history, architecture and geology, and numerous maps and plans. The *Michelin Blue Guide to France* contains detailed itineraries and is oriented for the art lover.

The annual *Michelin Red Guide* (Editions des Voyages) is the most comprehensive hotel and restaurant guide available anywhere, and is priceless for both residents and visitors. It's an institution in France and many French people won't stay or eat anywhere that isn't recommended by the latest *Red Guide*. It contains all the necessary information about prices, opening times and facilities (including special facilities for children and the disabled), as well as town maps, and references to other Michelin guides. Although published in French only, the *Red Guide* contains an introduction and an explanation of symbols in English and other languages. It takes a while to decipher and recognise all the symbols, but it's well worth the effort. Michelin also produces many excellent maps (see page 284).

Although you may prefer to buy a foreign guide book written by a fellow countryman, guides such as the *Michelin Red Guide*, the *Gault-Millau Guide de la France* (see page 443) and the *Logis de France* guide (see page 404) are unrivalled for their breadth of up-to-date information. Good general English-language guide books include the *Baedeker Guide to France*, *Birnbaum's France*, the *Blue Guide France*, *Fodor's France*, *Let's Go France* and *France: The Rough Guide*.

Over 500 villages and towns meeting certain standards relating to natural attractions, accommodation, leisure facilities, shops and information facilities, plus general appearance and cleanliness, are listed in the *Guide des Stations Vertes* (guide to country resorts) obtainable from La Fédération Française des Stations Vertes (☎ 03 80 54 10 50, 🖳 http://www.stationsvertes.com).

Among the best Paris guides are the *Time Out Paris Guide*, the *Rough/Real Guide to Paris* and *Pauper's Paris* for those on a tight budget. The best map of Paris is the *Plan de Paris par Arrondissements*, containing detailed maps of each *arrondissement*, the *métro* network and bus routes and a comprehensive street index. A free Paris map is available from French Tourist Offices (see page 402), hotels and the Printemps and Galeries Lafayette department stores, and the Paris tourist office distributes a free monthly booklet, *Paris Sélection*, also available at some hotels. Many hotels offer their guests free copies of *Pariscope* (see below).

Among the plethora of information published by the French Tourist Office, one of the most useful booklets is *The Traveller in France and Reference Guide*. It contains a comprehensive list of hotels and self-catering accommodation, package and special interest holiday companies (including caravan and camping, touring and sporting holidays), helpful hints, maps, motoring tips and a list of local addresses. Other French Tourist Office publications include *The Short Break Traveller*, *The Touring Traveller*, *The Winter Traveller*, *France for Active Holidays*, *France Youth Travel*, and *Festive France*, an annual directory of festivals, light and sound shows, and other events throughout France. Publications can be ordered on or downloaded from the French Tourist Office website (🖳 http://www.franceguide.com).

There are many weekly entertainment guides to Paris, including *L'Officiel des Spectacles*, *Pariscope* (which has a section in English), *7 à Paris* – a pun on *sept* (*jours*) and *c'est* – and *Zurban*. There's also the English-language *Paris Voice/Paris Free Voice*, available free from bookshops, public offices and some restaurants (particularly Mexican restaurants) in Paris (see **Appendix B**).

Tourist Offices

Most towns have a tourist office: an *office de tourisme* in larger towns and a *syndicat d'initiative* in smaller towns. A directory listing 3,400 offices is published by the Fédération Nationale des Offices de Tourisme et Syndicats d'Initiative (☎ 01 44 11 10 30, 🖳 http://www.tourisme.fr). Around 45 major cities and tourist areas have an *Loisirs Accueil France* office open every day of the year, which makes hotel bookings for personal callers (for a small fee) anywhere in France, up to a week in advance. For information contact Loisirs Accueil France (☎ 01 44 11 10 44, 🖳 www.loisirs accueilfrance.com). A recent development is a computerised tourist information service available in motorway rest areas (*aires d'autoroute*).

Each department and region of France (see **Appendix E**) has a tourist authority, and many of the regions have tourist offices in Paris. The main tourist office in Paris is the Office de Tourisme de Paris, 127 avenue des Champs Elysées, 75008 Paris (☎ 08 92 68 31 12, 🖳 http://www.paris-touristoffice.com). There are also tourist offices at the Gare de Lyon and the Eiffel Tower, which can be contacted via the above telephone number. There are tourist offices at international airports in Paris and other cities, where you can make hotel bookings. The Maison de la France (☎ 01 42 96 70 00, 🖳 http://www.franceguide.com) provides tourist information about most regions and will send information. (Its office in avenue Opéra isn't open to the public.) Information can also be found on 🖳 http://www.paris.fr/en. Official interpreters are available on the streets during the main tourist season and wear armbands indicating the languages they speak.

Outside France, the French Tourist Office or Maison de la France is a mine of information and has offices in Austria, Belgium, Brazil, Canada, Denmark, Finland, Germany, Hungary, Ireland, Italy, Japan, Luxembourg, the Netherlands, Norway, Portugal, Spain, Sweden, Switzerland, the UK and the US. For details consult the Tourist Office website (🖳 http://www.franceguide.com).

Opening Hours

Tourist offices in the main cities are open daily, including Saturdays and Sundays. Telephone the tourist office or consult a guide book to check the exact opening hours. In major towns, reduced opening hours are in operation during winter, while in smaller towns and resorts tourist offices close for lunch (e.g. 12.00 to 14.00m) and may be open only during the summer or winter (e.g. in ski resorts). The main tourist office in Paris (see above) is open from 09.00 to 20.00. The office at the Gare de Lyon is open from 08.00 to 20.00 Mondays to Saturdays and the Eiffel Tower office from 11.00 to 18.00 from May to September only.

Services

Most tourist offices will find you a hotel or hostel room locally for a fee, e.g. €2 to €6.50, depending on the standard. Many departments provide official booking services under the name *Loisirs-Accueil*, through which you can book a hotel, *gîte*, campsite or a special activity or sports holiday. *Loisirs-Accueil* is operated by the Fédération Nationale des Offices de Tourisme et Syndicats d'Initiative (see **Information** above), but has its own website (🖥 http://www.loisirsaccueil france.com). Many tourist offices also change foreign currency, although they may not offer the best rates.

If you write to a local tourist office for information, you should include an international reply coupon and shouldn't expect a reply in English, although most offices have staff that can understand letters written in English.

HOTELS

There are thousands of hotels in France (including *hôtels de ville*, *hôtels dieu* and *hôtels de police*!), with some 1,500 in Paris alone, catering for all tastes and pockets – from sumptuous 'five-star palaces' and *châteaux* to a small family hotels, offering good food and accommodation, and good value (although they aren't as good value as they once were). Children and animals are usually welcome.

Classification

Hotels are classified from one to four star de luxe (five stars on the international star-rating system) by the French Ministry of Tourism, depending on their facilities and the type of hotel. This provides a guarantee of standards related to the price. Note, however, that stars are based on facilities, e.g. the ratio of bathrooms to guests, rather than quality, meaning you can often find excellent ungraded and one-star hotels. Two-star hotels are usually small family-run hotels.

Logis et Auberges de France

The backbone of the hotel network is the Logis et Auberges de France, the world's largest hotel consortium, whose trademark is a green and yellow sign of a fire burning in a hearth. Logis members include over 3,500 privately run hotel/restaurants in the countryside (none in Paris). Members must conform to strict standards of comfort, service, hygiene, safety, quality of food and price. Most are one- or two-star hotels in popular locations, with prices ranging from €25 to €65 per night for a double room. The Logis guide is available from French Tourist Offices (see page 402), many of which operate a video desk service where personal callers can select a hotel. A number of Logis hotels can also be booked through the 'Logis Stop' service offered by Gîtes de France (see page 412). Contact the Fédération Nationale des Logis et Auberges de France (☎ 01 45 84 83 84, ⌨ http://www.logis-de-france.fr) for further information. A Logis de France handbook is available from bookshops and French Tourist Offices as well as via the Logis website.

Chain Hotels

In addition to thousands of small family-run hotels, France has its share of soulless 'business' hotels, such as Ibis, Mercure, Novotel and Sofitel, although many have been refurbished and updated in recent years. International chains including Hilton, Holiday Inn, Intercontinental and Trust House Forte are represented in Paris and other major cities. One advantage of staying at chain hotels is that the standards and facilities are consistent and any hotel can book you a room at any other in the chain.

If you wish to indulge yourself, you need look no further than the Relais et Châteaux chain of over 250 independently-owned elegant three- and four-star hotels (many occupying châteaux and other former stately homes) and exquisite restaurants (relais). They produce a guide detailing their establishments throughout the world and it's available from French Tourist Offices (see page 402) or the Centre d'Information, Relais & Châteaux (☎ 01 44 56 07 57 or ☎ 08 25 32 32 32 for bookings, ⌨ http://www.relaischateaux.fr). They publish a free map showing their hotels. It's also possible to stay in many private châteaux, manors, abbeys and priories, 70 of which are listed in the Château Accueil directory available from French Tourist Offices or via the internet (⌨ http://www.chateau-accueil.com). A Bienvenue au Château guide, covering north-western France only, is also available from the French Tourist Office. An excellent association of privately-owned two- to four-star hotels where you're assured of peace and tranquillity is Les Relais du Silence (☎ 01 44 49 79 00 for information or 01 44 49 90 00 for bookings, ⌨ http://www.silencehotel.com).

At the other end of the scale are a number of budget hotel chains such as Formule 1, which are common on the outskirts of towns and cities (often close to motorways). From around €30 per night up to three people can share a room with a double and single bed and a TV. Shared toilets and showers are available in the corridors. Breakfast costs around €4 per person. You can arrive at any time of day or night and if there are no staff on duty you can pay for a room via a credit card machine at the entrance. If you arrive late, you can obtain the number of your room and the entry code by inserting the credit card used to book the room in the automatic reception machine (pressing the key indicated by a Union Jack displays the instructions in English). The machine will issue a receipt with a code number, allowing you to access both the hotel and your room. If you leave your room, e.g. to have dinner, don't forget to take your receipt with you! If the machine won't accept your card, press the *appel d'urgence* button near the entrance and a staff member will open the door for you. For a list of Formule 1 hotels, write to Chain Hôtels Formule 1, Le Grand Champs, boulevard Rû de Nesles, 93160 Noisy-le-Grand Cedex (☎ 08 92 68 56 85, 💻 http://www.hotelformule1.com). Other reasonably priced motorway hotel chains include Accor and Etap (both owned by Formule 1), Mister Bed (☎ 01 46 14 38 00, 💻 http://www.misterbed.fr), Première Classe (☎ 08 25 00 30 03 or ☎ 01 64 62 46 46) and Village Hotels (☎ 03 80 60 92 70).

Hotel Guides

Most guide books list a selection of hotels and there are many hotel guides. The most comprehensive hotel (and restaurant) guide is the *Michelin Red Guide*, which includes both the humblest and poshest of establishments (see page 401). Other good guides include *Les Routiers Guide to France* (Alan Sutton Publishing), *The Good Hotel Guide* by Hilary Rubinstein (Papermac) and the *Guide to Hotels and Country Inns of Character and Charm in France* (Rivages). A complete list of hotels and guest houses, the *Annuaire des Hôtels et Pensions de Famille de Tourisme à Prix Homologués*, is published annually by the French Tourist Office (see page 402). An online guide to hotels can be found at 💻 http://www.france-hotel-guide.com.

Prices

French hotels are among the cheapest in the Western world, including Parisian hotels, where you can still get an attractive double room for €60 to €75 per night (you can also rent some rooms by the hour!). The same standard room in the country costs as little as €40. However, you can easily pay €400 per night for a room in a 'palace' hotel on the French Riviera or in Paris, which has more luxury hotels than any other city in the world. A **rough** guide to room rates is shown below:

Star Rating	Price Range	Standard
L****	€160 to €250	*hôtel hors classe, palace* (luxury)
****	€100 to €200	*hôtel très grand confort* (top class)
***	€50 to €130	*hôtel de grand tourisme, grand confort* (very comfortable)
**	€30 to €60	*hôtel de tourisme, bon confort* (comfortable)
*	€25 to €40	*hôtel de moyen tourisme* (average comfort)
None	€20 to €35	*hôtel de tourisme/simple* (basic)

The prices quoted above are for a double room with bath for one night (prices are usually quoted per room and **not** per person). As in most countries, single rooms are only marginally cheaper (if at all) than doubles. Many hotels don't have single rooms and are reluctant to give a double room to one person.

Prices include service and VAT (*TVA*) but not *taxe de séjour*, which is added to the bill in some areas (e.g. €0.15 to €1 per day in Paris). Room prices don't usually include breakfast, which may cost an additional €6 to €10 (more in a four-star establishment). In some hotels, children under 16 sharing their parents' room receive a free breakfast. Rates must, by law, be prominently displayed where prospective guests can see them and must include seasonal rates and state whether the price includes tax and service. Room rates should also be displayed in rooms.

Many hotels in popular resorts have slightly higher room rates during July and August (the best time to visit Paris) and a minimum stay of three nights. Out of high season, hotels may offer a discount for stays of three nights or longer. Many hotels provide off-season discounts, particularly during the winter and early spring months, which may include three nights for the price of two or two nights for the price of one at weekends. You can book a room in around 50 (mainly three-star) Paris hotels through Abotel (☎ 01 47 27 15 15) and receive a discount of 20 to 40 per cent, depending on the season.

Room rates in Paris are up to 100 per cent higher than in the provinces, although still relatively inexpensive compared with some other European capitals (e.g. London). There are plenty of one- and two-star hotels in Paris, with prices starting at around €30, although you must be prepared to share bathroom facilities. In the cheapest establishments you may be charged extra to use a bath or shower. Inexpensive hotels are usually found close to main railway stations in major cities.

Many hotels have rooms for three or four guests at reduced rates or provide extra beds for children in a double room free or for a small charge. A double room may contain one or two 'double' beds, although they may not be full-size double beds; often a room will have a double bed and one or two single beds.

Meals

Breakfast times vary considerably, so check in advance. You can usually choose from coffee, tea or hot chocolate, accompanied by croissants and rolls, butter and jam, and perhaps orange juice. High-class hotels offer a choice of expensive cooked breakfasts. Many hotels don't provide a very appetising or good value breakfast, which may consist of half a *baguette* and weak coffee only. If you're staying in or near a small town, it's often better to have breakfast at a local café.

Many hotels insist that guests eat dinner in the hotel before they let a room. Although it's officially illegal for them to insist on half-board (*demi-pension*), i.e. breakfast and dinner, or full board (*pension complète*), which includes all meals, you may be obliged to accept if you want to obtain a hotel room in a popular resort during the high season. Usually with half or full board you must stay for a minimum of three days. You should ask to see the menu before signing up for half or full board, as the cost of meals (and particularly wine) may make a room prohibitively expensive. Generally, the smaller the establishment, the better the food.

*Kite Festival, Dieppe
Seine-Maritime
© Survival Books*

▲ *French Alps, Chamonix
© LJM (www.bigstockphoto.com)*

*Cafe, Senlis, Oise
© Joe Laredo*

▼ *Rocamadour, Lot
© Survival Books*

▲ *Centre de Pompidou, Paris
© Aleksejs Kostins (www.shutterstock.com)*

◀ Street cleaners,
Paris
© Joe Laredo

© Joe Laredo

◀ Monaco Harbour
© Andres
(www.bigstockphoto.com)

▼ Mairie, Herqueville,
Eure © Joe Laredo

▼ La Rochelle at night, Charente-Maritime
© Survival Books

◀ © Wizdata
(www.bigstockphoto.com)

▶ House, Provence
© tonidesign
(www.bigstockphoto.com)

▶ Chambord Chateau,
Loire Valley
© ItalianStyle
(www.bigstockphoto.com)

▼ Shop, Paris
© Joe Laredo

▼ Barges on River Seine, Eure
© Joe Laredo

© Survival Books

▲ *Benedictine Distillery, Fécamp, Seine-Maritime*
  © Survival Books

▲ *Biarritz, Landes*
  © Survival Books

▶ *Honfleur, Calvados*
   © Survival Books

▼ *© Fanelie Rosier*
  (www.bigstockphoto.com)

Note that many family hotels close for two to three weeks between May and September for their holidays (nothing interferes with the 'Great French Holiday' – even peak time business!). Some hotels in villages and small towns also close their restaurants for one or two days a week, e.g. Sunday and/or Monday. On closing days, no breakfast or other meals are served. Seasonal closing and weekly closing days are shown in the *Michelin Red Guide* (see page 401).

Facilities

You should be shown a room. (No French person would dream of accepting a room without inspecting it, and especially the bed.) Often beds have long, hard, sausage-shaped bolsters (*traversin*) that serve as pillows. Usually the bottom sheet runs round them and substitutes for a pillow-case. Most foreigners find bolsters uncomfortable, although they're quite happily used by most French guests. In the wardrobe there may be pillows (*oreiller*), which, like bolsters, usually have no slips and are placed under the bottom sheet. Duvets are common.

Rooms with a private bath or shower may not have a WC. Rooms without a shower or bath usually have a washbasin. Most French hotel rooms have a *bidet* (see page 541). Don't expect to find soap or a decent towel in a cheap hotel (or a bedtime mint on your pillow!).

Most hotels have central heating in winter and are, if anything, too warm. Air-conditioning is generally found only in luxury hotels and large modern hotels, particularly in the south. Although windows are usually double-glazed, if you're staying in a city it's wise to ask for a quiet room. Some rooms have no curtains and are fitted with shutters or blinds, possibly located outside the window. Modern hotels have electric roller shutters.

Hotel rooms aren't always equipped with a radio or TV, irrespective of the price, with the exception of modern and luxury hotels. Satellite TV is provided in top-class hotels. All top-class hotel rooms have tea and coffee-making facilities, a radio and colour TV, bathroom or shower, a telephone, room service, and a mini-bar or refrigerator. Drinks from a hotel mini-bar are expensive, but the fridge is handy for storing your own food and drinks!

In general, French hotels don't cater well for business travellers, and business centres with secretarial staff and translation services are usually confined to a few luxury hotels in Paris and the French Riviera. Few hotels have swimming pools, and sports facilities or private parking; if you're staying at a hotel without a car park, ask the hotel staff to recommend a safe place to park your car, i.e. safe from both thieves and traffic wardens! However, most hotels have photocopy, fax and email facilities; high class hotels may have a wireless connection system (known as 'wi-fi') in all rooms and sell pay-cards (e.g. Meteor), costing around €5 for 30 minutes' connection. Most top-class hotels have a restaurant, coffee shop and bar, and many of France's best restaurants are found in top-class hotels. On the other hand, staff in inexpensive hotels may not speak English.

Hotel bulbs are usually dim and it's often wise to take a 60 or 100 watt bulb or a clip-on reading lamp (and a long lead) if you like reading in bed. Power points above wash basins are usually suitable only for electric razors. If you want to use a non-

French hairdryer or travel iron, you must bring a French adapter and try to locate a suitable power point, which may be outside the room.

Booking

It's wise to book during the high season (July and August), on public holidays and adjoining weekends, and during international trade fairs, conventions and festivals. At most other times it's usually unnecessary, particularly in rural areas and small towns. It's advisable to make bookings at least two months in advance in summer in major cities (particularly Paris), and around two weeks in advance at other times.

When booking by post for a period of a week or longer, you're usually asked to send a deposit (*arrhes*), which is non-refundable unless the booking is cancelled due to the landlord's fault, when you will receive double your deposit in compensation. Don't book and pay for a long period in advance, as you won't receive a refund if you leave early. Hotels can also be booked via the internet and at many tourist offices (for a small fee). A hotel is required to keep a booked room until 18.00 or 19.00, after which time it can be let to someone else unless you've paid in advance. If you plan to arrive later than this, advise the hotel of your estimated arrival time. Some hotels close overnight. If you plan to arrive after 23.00, notify the hotel 24 hours in advance and they will arrange to have someone meet you.

When checking in, you're required by French law to show your passport or identity card and complete a registration form (*fiche policière*). Checkout time is usually noon at the latest; if you stay any later, you may be charged for an extra day. If you're staying in a small hotel and wish to leave early in the morning, it's best to pay your bill (*note*) the evening before and tell the proprietor when you plan to leave (check your bill carefully for errors).

BED & BREAKFAST

France has numerous bed and breakfast (*chambres d'hôtes*) establishments, particularly in villages and on farms, where French (and many foreign) families let their spare rooms to visitors as part of a move towards 'agritourism' necessitated by falling agricultural profits (look for signs such as *ferme auberge, ferme de découverte/pédagogique/équestre* and *goûter à la ferme*).

Many *chambres d'hôtes* operate under the sponsorship of Gîtes de France (see **Self-catering** below) and are classified according to their comfort and environment with one to three ears of corn (*épi*). The cost is usually around €50 per night for a room (possibly with a private bath or shower) for two people including breakfast. In addition to single and double rooms, many *chambres d'hôtes* have accommodation for families and most serve meals (*table d'hôtes*). The standard of *chambres d'hôtes* is usually high and the home-cooked food delicious, owners being required to use fresh local produce. When staying in bed and breakfast accommodation, it helps if you speak some French, as your hosts may not speak any English, although the Paris Tourist Board has introduced a scheme called *Hôtes Qualité Paris* whose participating B&B owners must have at least a smattering of English (for details go to http://www.parisinfo.com and click on 'Hotels & accommodation' and then 'hôtes qualité Paris').

Information

There are many guides to bed and breakfast, including the AA's *Guide to Bed & Breakfast in France*, Karen Brown's *French Country Bed & Breakfast* (Travel Press), Alistair Sawday's *Guide to French Bed & Breakfast* (Alistair Sawday Publishing), *Bed & Breakfast of Character and Charm in France* (Fodor's Rivages), *Charming Small Hotel Guides: France Bed & Breakfast* by Paul Wade & Kathy Arnold (Duncan Petersen Publishing), *French Country Welcome* (Gîtes de France) and *French Entrée Bed and Breakfast in France* by Patricia Fenn & Rosemary Gower-Jones (Quiller Press). All regional tourist offices produce annual listings of *chambres d'hôtes*.

SELF-CATERING

France has an abundance of self-catering accommodation. You can choose from literally thousands of cottages (*gîtes*), apartments, villas, bungalows, mobile homes, chalets, and even *châteaux* and manor houses. The most luxurious dwellings have private swimming pools, tennis courts and acres of private parkland, although you may need to take out a second mortgage to pay the bill! Self-catering serviced apartments are provided in Paris and other major cities. Rates vary considerably and may be per person per night, e.g. €20, or a fixed rate per night irrespective of the number of guests, e.g. €100 for a studio sleeping four. Rates usually decrease for longer stays, e.g. €400 per week for a studio. See also **Temporary Accommodation** on page 104.

Self-catering is particularly popular in ski resorts and along the Atlantic and Mediterranean coasts, where there's a wealth of purpose-built apartments. Standards vary considerably, from dilapidated, ill-equipped cottages to luxury villas with every modern convenience. You don't always get what you pay for and, unless a company or property has been highly recommended, it's best to book through a reputable organisation such as Gîtes de France (see **Information** on page 411).

Gîtes

The word *gîte* means simply 'home' or 'shelter' but is nowadays widely used to refer to any furnished self-catering holiday accommodation. A typical *gîte* is a small cottage or self-contained apartment with one or two bedrooms (sleeping four to eight and possibly including a sofa bed in the living-room), a large living-room/kitchen with an open fire or stove, and a toilet and shower room. There are usually shutters on the windows (possibly no curtains), stone or wooden floors with a few rugs and possibly bare stone walls (designed to facilitate cleaning). There's usually a garden with garden furniture and possibly a swimming pool (if it's a shared pool, ask how many people or *gîtes* will be sharing it). In certain parts of France, notably the overcrowded French Riviera, *gîtes* may be no more than purpose-built concrete rabbit hutches.

Equipment

Properties are generally well equipped with cooking utensils, crockery and cutlery, although you're usually required to provide your own bed linen and towels (they can be rented for an extra charge, but can be expensive). Equipment and facilities may include central heating, a washing machine, dishwasher, microwave, covered parking and a barbecue. Some owners provide bicycles and badminton and table tennis equipment. If you need a cot or a high chair, mention it when booking. Some basic food stuffs (e.g. sugar, salt and pepper) and essentials such as toilet paper and soap may be provided, but don't count on it. Most people take a few essential foods and supplies with them and buy fresh food on arrival. Some things that may come in handy are a sharp kitchen knife, a teapot (if you use one), and a few of your favourite foods such as tea (French tea is terrible), instant coffee (although most *gîtes* have filter coffee machines) and relishes you cannot live without.

Most *gîtes* in rural areas have a septic tank (*fosse septique*) and items such as sanitary towels, toilet paper (other than French toilet paper), disposable nappies, condoms, and anything made of plastic mustn't be flushed down the toilet.

Costs

The cost is normally calculated on a weekly basis (Saturday to Saturday) and depends on the standard, location, number of beds and the facilities provided. The rent is higher for a *gîte* with a pool. The rent for an average *gîte* sleeping six is typically from €200 to €320 per week in June and September, and €250 to €400 in July and August. Those for whom money is no object can rent a luxury villa. A villa in the Dordogne with swimming pool and sleeping eight rents for between €1,300 and €2,000 per week in July and August, and you can pay up to €8,000 per week in high season for a villa sleeping eight to ten people on the Côte d'Azur.

The rest of the year may be classified as the low season, when rents are slightly lower. Sometimes the year is divided into low, mid- and high seasons, although many owners offer accommodation from June to September only. If you're making a late booking, try to negotiate a lower price, as it's often possible to obtain a large reduction (if you're into brinkmanship and are flexible as to location, it may pay you to leave it until the last minute).

Electricity, gas and water charges aren't always included, particularly outside high season (June to August), and may be charged at high rates. There's usually a charge for cleaning, e.g. €35 to €65 per week, but this may be waived if you leave the place spotless (where applicable, the cost is usually deducted from your deposit). Heating (if necessary) is also usually extra and can be expensive. You may need to pay a small local tax (*taxe de séjour*).

Holiday Villages

Holiday villages and club resorts (such as Club Méditerranée) are increasingly popular among holidaymakers. They're usually self-contained with everything available on site, including shops, restaurants, swimming pools, and a wide range of sports and entertainment facilities. Children's clubs leave parents free.

Holiday parks are similar to club resorts, except that sports and leisure facilities may be housed in a temperature-controlled (e.g. 21°C) plastic dome, e.g. at Center Parcs' site at Les Bois-Francs near Verneuil-sur-Avre, around 120km (80mi) west of Paris (☎ 08 10 80 06 00, 💻 http://www.centerparcs.com). Guests stay in villas set in attractive country locations or by the sea.

Inexpensive holiday village accommodation is available through Villages-Vacances-Familles (☎ 08 25 80 88 08, 💻 http://www.vvf-vacances.fr), which is a non-profit organisation created in 1958 to provide holidays for low-income families. Villages-Vacances-Familles holiday villages provide child-minding and entertainment for children and are open to foreign visitors.

Another chain of holiday villages (around 500) is Loisirs de France, operated by UNAT (☎ 01 42 73 13 74, 💻 http://www.loisirsde france.com).

There are also many mobile home holiday centres in France, usually located on superb campsites with similar facilities to holiday villages. Camping in fully-equipped 'permanently' erected family tents is another self-catering option for those who don't need every mod con.

Booking & Deposits

It may be necessary to book six months in advance for popular areas in July or August, when there may be a minimum two-week rental period. Outside high season it's possible to find a *gîte* on the spot. When booking, you're usually required to pay a 'damage' deposit (*caution*), which cannot be more than 25 per cent of the rental charge and cannot be requested more than six months in advance. A deposit is termed either *arrhes* or *acompte*. When it's *arrhes*, you can back out of the agreement and forfeit your deposit; if the owner cancels he must pay you double the deposit. When a deposit is *acompte* it means that you have a binding contract: if you back out of the agreement, you must still pay the full rental fee, although you can claim damages if the landlord cancels your booking.

Information

Outside France, the best place to start looking for self-catering accommodation is your local travel agent or French Tourist Office (see page 402). *Gîtes* can be booked through French Tourist Offices in many countries, where Gîtes de France (see below) may also have an office. Many properties are let by holiday companies and associations, often as part of a holiday package, e.g. including the cost of a ferry from the UK. Properties are also let directly by owners through advertisements in French property magazines (see **Appendix B**) and newspapers. Many *gîtes* are second homes and are let when not in use through organisations such as Gîtes de France (see below), although many owners prefer to let them themselves. Note that, if you rent directly from the owner, you may find it difficult to receive satisfaction or redress if you have a complaint.

The biggest and most reputable self-catering organisation is Gîtes de France, handling over 45,000 properties. Properties are called *gîtes ruraux* and are classified and approved (standards are guaranteed by the local Relais Départemental des Gîtes de France). *Gîtes ruraux* are classified according to their comfort and environment, and are awarded one to four ears of corn (*épi*). For more information contact the Fédération Nationale des Gîtes Ruraux de France (☎ 01 49 70 75 75, 🖳 http://www.gites-de-france.fr), which publishes *Les Nouveaux Gîtes Ruraux*.

Another major national organisation, which handles around 24,000 *gîtes* registered in 80 departments. Unlike Gîtes de France, Clévacances handles urban as well as rural properties, including houses, flats and maisonettes. Properties are graded with one to five *clés* (keys), a similar system to GdF's *épis* or tourist board stars. Further information is available from the Fédération Nationale des Locations de France Clévacances (☎ 05 61 13 55 66, 🖳 http://www.clevacances.com).

A handbook listing over 2,500 *gîtes* is published by the French Tourist Office in the UK and is provided 'free' in return for a nominal annual membership fee that also entitles you to use a computerised booking system to reserve a *gîte*. Most French *départements* publish a list of local *gîtes* (write to the tourist office in the local departmental town). One of the most popular guides to self-catering accommodation in France is the *Guide des Locations Vacances Loisirs*, published quarterly. There are a number of books for self-caterers, including *Self-Catering France* by John P. Harris and William Hedley (Collins), *The Gîtes Guide* (FHG Publications) and *Guide Gîtes d'Etapes et Refuges France et Frontières* by Annick and Serge Mouraret (🖳 http://www.gites-refuges.com).

HOSTELS

There's a variety of inexpensive accommodation in France, although less than in many other European countries.

Youth Hostels

Youth hostels (*auberge de jeunesse*) – in fact, there are no age restrictions – are open to members of national hostelling associations affiliated to Hostelling International (HI, 🖳 http://www.hihostels.com) – formerly the International Youth Hostel Federation. HI membership must be taken out in your home country (the HI website includes a list of affilated organisations) and costs around €15 a year, or €10 if you're under 26. One-night membership of HI is available for around €3.

There are two French youth hostel associations: the Fédération Unie des Auberges de Jeunesse (FUAJ, ☎ 01 44 89 87 27, 🖳 http://www.fuaj.fr), operating over 200 youth hostels, and the Ligue Française pour les Auberges de Jeunesse (LFAJ, ☎ 01 44 16 78 78), both affiliated to HI. There are three youth hostels in Paris requiring HI membership.

French hostels are classified into three grades with accommodation usually in single-sex rooms and dormitories with two to eight beds. The cost is generally from €4 to €14 per night (there are usually cheaper rates for groups), plus an additional rental charge for a sheet sleeping bag if you don't provide your own. Some hostels allow you to use your own sleeping bag. Breakfast costs from around €3.

Although inexpensive, hostels aren't always cheaper than budget hotels for two or three people sharing a room, particularly in major cities. They may also be situated on the edge of town, thus necessitating an additional train or bus fare. The main advantage for budget travellers is that most hostels have cooking facilities or inexpensive cafeterias, allowing savings to be made on meals. Hostels fill early in July and August, when you should book in advance, although some hostels don't accept bookings and restrict stays to four nights or less.

All hostels have a curfew from 22.00 or 23.00 (from between 00.00 and 02.00 in Paris) and are usually closed between 10.00 and 17.00, although some are flexible. There are restrictions on smoking and alcohol consumption and guests may be required to help with chores.

Other Hostels

In major cities there are *hôtels de jeunesse*, which are a cross between a hotel and a youth hostel, and *Foyers des Jeunes Travailleurs/Travailleuses*, which are residential hostels for students and young workers. Ethic Etapes (formerly the Union des Centres de Rencontres Internationales de France, ☎ 01 40 26 57 64, 💻 http://www.ethic-etapes.fr) links *foyers* throughout France and publishes a list of members and services. Room rates are usually from around €12 to €20 per night for singles and €25 to €35 for doubles. *Foyers* usually have an inexpensive cafeteria or canteen. In many areas there are guesthouses providing dormitory accommodation from around €6 per night.

During July and August you can also stay in student accommodation at most French universities. Rates are from around €8 per night and you can book through the Centre Régional des Oeuvres Universitaires (CROUS, ☎ 01 40 51 36 05). Many monasteries and convents also accept paying guests and are listed in the *Guide des Monastères* available from book shops.

In rural areas there are unmanned hostels or shelters providing dormitory accommodation called *gîtes d'étapes*. They're listed in footpath guides and marked on IGN walkers' maps (see page 461), and are usually reserved for walkers, cyclists, horse riders and skiers. The most basic have bunks, showers and cooking facilities, although some are very comfortable. *Gîtes d'étapes* are often run by local communities and the key is kept by a caretaker (who may be the local mayor) at a nearby house or by the local tourist office (*syndicat d'initiative*). The rate per night is usually from €10 to €12. A list of *gîtes d'étapes* is included in *Accueil à la Campagne* (together with places offering bed and breakfast and farm campsites) available from the Fédération Nationale des Gîtes Ruraux de France (see page 412). An even more basic form of shelter, common in remote hill and mountain areas, is a mountain hut called an *abri*. Information about these can be obtained from local *Bureaux des Guides* or tourist offices.

A useful publication for young people seeking temporary accommodation is *Le Logement des Etudiants et des Jeunes* (Editions de Vecchi). The *Guide Gîtes d'Etapes et Refuges France et Frontières* by Annick and Serge Mouraret (💻 http://www.gites-refuges.com) lists over 1,600 places providing inexpensive accommodation.

CAMPING & CARAVANNING

Camping and caravanning are extremely popular, with both the French and the many thousands of tourists who flock to France each year to spend their holidays in the open air (*en plein air*). The French are the most camping-conscious nation in Europe and have elevated *le camping* to a high level of sophistication and chic. There are over 11,500 campsites, including over 2,000 rural and farm sites, and France is Europe's largest camper van (*camping-car*) market, with around 18,000 vehicles sold annually.

Permission is required to park or camp on private property or anywhere outside official campsites. It's strictly illegal in most regions to camp on private or public land (including beaches) without permission; farmers may shoot first and ask questions afterwards! Off-site camping (*camping sauvage*) is restricted in many areas, particularly in the south of France, due to the danger of fires. For example, you need permission from the local Office des Eaux et Forêts to camp in state forests (*forêts domaniales*). You can also camp on a farm (*camping à la ferme*) in rural areas, although there are generally no facilities. A maximum of six camping spaces are permitted on farm land or in a park near a *château*. Many campsites are open from June to September only and most have fewer than 150 pitches.

Classification

Campsites vary considerably from small municipal sites (*camping municipal*) with fairly basic facilities to luxury establishments with a wide range of facilities and amenities. Many sites are situated in popular hiking and climbing areas. Like hotels, campsites are classified from one to four stars, as shown below.

Star Rating	Standard
****	*très grand confort* (luxury)
***	*grand confort* (high)
**	*confort* (medium)
*	*confort moyen* (basic)

A four-star rating indicates a comfortable, low-density site with a range of amenities and electric hook-ups for one-third of spaces or even all spaces at a top site. There's a range of indoor recreation areas, showers, sauna, toilets, washing machines, shops, lock-up storage for valuables, and a wide choice of sports facilities. These usually include a swimming pool (outdoor and/or indoor) and tennis courts, and there may also be facilities for golf or crazy golf, volleyball, cycling, table tennis, trampolining, canoeing, fishing and boating. Large campsites usually have a restaurant and a bar (or a selection).

Three-star sites are roughly the same as four but with slightly fewer amenities, less camping space, and fewer electric hook-ups, e.g. just 10 per cent of spaces. Only basic amenities such as toilets, hot and cold water, public telephone and electric razor power points are provided at one and two-star sites, although some one-star sites may not have hot water.

There's a further classification scale, which denotes the length of time a site may stay open: a *camp de tourisme aire naturelle* may open six months in the year, whereas a *camp de tourisme saisonnier* may remain open for no more than two months. On a *camp de loisirs*, pitches are rented long term, i.e. for a month or more.

Many campsites have tents, caravans, mobile homes and bungalows for hire, and some provide (heated) winter accommodation. Some also provide fully-furnished luxury canvas 'houses' with all modern conveniences including fully-sprung mattresses, refrigerators, four-burner stoves and electric lighting. Some sites have facilities for the disabled, which is usually noted in guide books. French campsites are usually extremely clean.

Costs

Most sites have different rates for high season (*haute saison*) and low season (*basse saison*). Although reductions for low season are usually minimal, out of season package holidays often yield considerable savings. The following table shows approximate costs per person per night during high season, including camping or caravan space, car parking and use of facilities. Note that prices can vary considerably between campsites with the same star rating.

Star Rating	Price Range (€)
****	10 – 15
***	8 – 12
**	5 – 10
*	3 – 5

Some sites charge extra to use showers, sports facilities (e.g. tennis courts) and other amenities, such as ironing facilities or use of a freezer.

Booking

Booking is often possible at three and four-star sites and is essential during the summer, particularly for sites on the coast and near lakes and waterways or if you require an electric hook-up. In fact, high season is best avoided altogether, if possible, as sites can be overcrowded, particularly on the French Riviera. Outside peak periods, you can usually find a campsite without difficulty on the spot, but don't leave it too late in the day if you're in a popular area (after noon is too late at some sites).

Information

The Fédération Française de Camping et de Caravanning (FFCC) publishes a *Guide Officiel* describing in detail the facilities at around 11,500 sites, including naturist and farm sites. It's available direct from La Fédération Française de Camping et de Caravanning (FFCC, ☎ 01 42 72 84 08, 💻 http://www.ffcc.fr) and from book shops and camping, caravanning and motoring organisations. The FFCC also offers insurance for campers and caravanners and an international camping carnet. Many sites are members of other associations or groups, which include the following:

- Camping Qualité (☎ 02 40 82 57 63), with around 220 sites throughout France.

- Sites et Paysages de France (☎ 08 20 20 46 46, 💻 http://www.sites-et-paysages.com) with 52 members.

- Airotels (☎ 08 25 70 37 04, 💻 http://www.airotels.com) with 58 campsites in France.

To find the most lavish campsites contact Castels et Camping Caravaning (☎ 02 23 16 03 20, 💻 http://www.les-castels.com), which has around 50 sites in the grounds of beautiful châteaux or manors or in exceptional natural settings.

Camping and caravanning guides are published for all areas and are available from local regional tourist offices. There are also many national camping guides, including *Camping à la Ferme* published by Gîtes de France (see page 412), Alan Rogers' *Good Camps Guide, France* (Deneway Guides) and the *Michelin Green Guide – Camping and Caravanning, Caravan and Camping in France* by Frederick Tingey (Mirador). The French Tourist Office (see page 402) publishes an excellent free booklet, *The Camping Traveller in France*. If you wish to rent a mobile home, caravan or tent on site, Alan Rogers' *Rented Accommodation on Quality Sites in France* (Deneway Guides) provides a comprehensive list.

If you're a newcomer to camping and caravanning, it's wise to join a camping or caravan club, which usually provide useful information (e.g. guides to the best campsites), lists of approved sites, caravan and travel insurance and travel services, organise rallies and holidays and make bookings for members. Recognised clubs include the Camping & Caravanning Club in the UK (☎ 0845-130 7632, 💻 http://www.campingandcaravanningclub.co.uk) and the Camping Club de France (☎ 01 58 14 01 23, 💻 http://www.campingclub.asso.fr). Further information about camping and caravanning in France can be obtained via the internet (e.g. 💻 http://www.campingfrance.com/fr). When writing to sites from abroad, you should enclose an international reply coupon.

NATURISM

France is the naturist capital of Europe (having supplanted the former Yugoslavia), with numerous naturist beaches, villages and over 60 holiday centres, including a huge number of superbly equipped naturist camping centres (for those who don't want to bother with laundry while on holiday). Topless bathing is accepted almost everywhere, even in Paris along the banks of the Seine, but nude bathing should be confined to naturist beaches. The main naturist areas include Aquitaine, Brittany, Corsica, Languedoc, Provence and the Midi-Pyrénées. Cape d'Agde on the Languedoc coast is the largest naturist resort in the world, with a population of 40,000 from Easter to September. Naked day trippers are allowed in most resorts, although single male visitors aren't usually admitted.

Information about naturist holidays can be obtained from the French Tourist Office, which publishes *France, a Land for all Naturisms*. If you aren't a member of a naturist association in another country, you must join the Fédération Française de Naturisme (☎ 08 92 69 32 82, 🖳 http://www.ffn-naturisme.com), or pay a fee in proportion to duration of your stay. You must be 18 and need a colour (head and shoulders only) photograph for your naturist 'passport' or carnet. Membership includes third-party liability insurance for up to 12 people (depending on where you buy it) at all authorised sites in Europe. Campers usually also need an international camping carnet, which costs around €5 and is available from French and foreign camping and motoring associations (see **Information** on page 416).

THEME PARKS

France has over 300 theme parks and similar attractions of varying size and scale, and these are increasing in popularity at the expense of traditional attractions such as *châteaux* (even in the Loire valley!). Details of all the major theme parks and attractions in France are provided by the annual *Guide Officiel des Parcs d'Attractions* (Guides Larivière).

Disneyland Paris

The most famous French theme park is Disneyland Paris (formerly Eurodisney) at Marne-la-Vallée 32km (20mi) east of Paris, which opened in April 1992 and is the fourth most-visited attraction in the world. It was originally smaller than other Disney parks, but a number of expansions have taken place in recent years and more are planned. Its 23ha (56 acres) contain five themed 'lands', each with around 40 attractions as well as shops and restaurants. There are six hotels and an 18-hole golf course on site.

The best way to get to Disneyland from Paris is via the *RER* express suburban railway (see page 231) on Line A terminating at Marne-la-Vallée/Chessy (a station specially built for Disneyland).

Disneyland is open year round, from 09.00 until 23.00 daily in spring and summer, and from 10.00 to 18.00 daily in autumn and winter except Saturdays and Sundays, when it closes at 23.00. Check opening and closing times, as they're liable to change. It's best to arrive early and make for the most popular rides first (you will spend a lot of your time queuing). Avoid public holidays and weekends.

There's a picnic area outside and a left luggage area (for picnic hampers) at the entrance. Picnics are banned inside the park (to increase profits at the restaurants), and bags are sometimes searched for illicit drinks and sandwiches.

The entrance fee all year round for Disneyland only is €43 for adults and €35 for children aged 3 to 11 during the high season; a combined pass for Disneyland and Walt Disney Studios (see below) costs €53/€45. You can buy passes for two or three days or, if you're addicted, an annual pass.

When you visit Disneyland it's sometimes difficult to imagine that you're still in France. The squeaky-clean staff wear permanent smiles and endlessly parrot 'have a nice day', albeit in French. The main difference between Disneyland Paris and the American Disney parks is that in North America it's hot and sunny most of the time (pixie dust loses its magic sparkle in the rain and cold, although you can buy a Mickey Mouse plastic raincoat).

There's a surfeit of Disneyland Paris guides, including the Michelin *Plan-Guide Disneyland Paris* and *Green Guide Disneyland Paris*, Fodor's *Disneyland Paris*, *Disneyland Paris: The Guide* (Harmsworth) and *Disneyland Paris Berlitz* (Berlitz). Further information can be obtained direct from Disneyland Paris (☎ 08 25 30 02 22 or ☎ 08 25 30 60 30 or ☎ 08 25 80 24 02, 💻 http://www.disneylandparis.com).

Near Disneyland is another Disney theme park, called Walt Disney Studios, where you can take a studio tour and pretend you're in Los Angeles.

Futuroscope

One of the most unusual theme parks in France and its third-most popular (after Disneyland and Parc Astérix – see below) is Futuroscope (☎ 05 49 49 11 12, 💻 http://www.futuroscope.com) near Poitiers in Vienne, which is dubbed the 'European Park of the Moving Image'. Attractions include the Omnimax room, where a film is projected onto the inside of a domed ceiling 17m in diameter (800m^2/8,611ft^2); the Kinémax, housing a cinema with a 600m^2 (6,458ft^2) flat screen that's higher than a seven-storey building; the Dynamic Motion Theatre, where the seats move in tune with the action (e.g. motor racing and bobsleigh); the Magic Carpet, with a 700m^2 (7,534ft^2) screen in front and another beneath your feet; a 360° Cinema with wrap-around films; and a 3D cinema.

Admission all year round is €31 per day (€59 for two days) for adults and €24 (€44 for two days) for children under 16; out of season admission prices are €22/15 for one day and €38/27 for two days. You should allow two days to see everything (Futuroscope has its own hotels). Admission for the evening only costs €15 (€10 for a child). If your French isn't fluent, you can obtain free headphones that provide an English translation.

Other Attractions

France's other major theme parks, aquariums and water parks include the following:

● **Aventure Parcs** – Activity parks in Autrans (department 38), Biscarosse (40), Les Deux Alpes (38), Les Gets (74), Guyonvelle (52), Nançay (18), Quelneuc (56), Pays-des-Lacs (54), Serre-Chevalier (05), Trivisy (13) and Val Louron (65), where you can swing from the trees and bungee jump (💻http://www.aventure-parc.fr).

- **Bioscope** – A new theme part in Ungersheim in Alsace devoted to 'man and the environment', including a 550-seat theatre where shows on 'natural' themes are presented. Open June to November (☎ 03 44 62 30 77, 💻 http://www.le bioscope.com).

- **Cap Découverte** – A 650 ha (1,600-acre) activity park in a converted coalmine at Blaye-les-Mines in Tarn where you can ski, toboggan, cycle, go-kart, skateboard, rollerblade or 'zip-line' (slide along a rope on the end of a pulley, usually high off the ground) all year round. Open February to December (☎ 08 25 08 12 34, 💻 http://www.capdecouverte.com).

- **Cité de la Mer** – Includes Europe's deepest aquarium and the largest nuclear submarine ever opened to the public, in Cherbourg-Octeville. Open May to September (☎ 02 33 20 26 26, 💻 http://www.citedelamer.com).

- **France Miniature** – If you haven't much time and wish to see France in a day, all the major sites, in miniature, are at Elancourt, west of Paris. Open April to November (☎ 08 26 30 20 40, 💻 http://www.franceminiature.com).

- **Micropolis** – Not for arachnaphobes, the theme of this park, in Saint Léons in Aveyron, is insects and it features 15 areas devoted to different types of creepy-crawly, including a giant beehive complete with swarming bees! Open February to November (☎ 05 65 58 50 50, 💻 http://www.micropolis.biz).

- **Nausicaä** – One of the largest and most comprehensive aquariums in the world and one of France's most popular attractions, near Boulogne. Open all year (☎ 03 21 30 98 98, 💻 http://www.nausicaa.fr).

- **Parc Astérix** – A traditional French theme park based on the popular comic strip, in the Jean-Jacques Rousseau forest near Paris's Charles de Gaulle airport. Open from April to early October (☎ 08 26 30 10 40, 💻 http://www.parcasterix.fr).

- **Vulcania** – Experience volcanic eruptions and other seismic sensations near Clermont-Ferrand. Open every day all year (☎ 04 73 19 70 98 or ☎ 08 20 82 78 28, 💻 http://www.vulcania.com).

- **Walibi** – Watersport theme parks at Agen, Lyon, Metz and Roquefort. (💻 http://www.starparks.com).

Traditional travelling fun fairs are installed each year at the Bois de Vincennes in Paris. The French also love the circus, and travelling circuses are common in all areas. Sound and light (*son et lumière*) shows are held at historic sites during summer, including Les Invalides in Paris, the Palais des Papes in Avignon, and at many *châteaux* and stately homes, particularly in the Loire valley. The latest sound and light shows incorporate images projected onto the facades of buildings (e.g. Rouen and Amiens cathedrals). Reckoned to be the most spectacular show of its kind in Europe is the one performed at the ruined Château du Puy du Fou in Les Epesses between Nantes and La Roche in Vendée on Saturday evenings from June to August, which features 800 actors and 50 horsemen; at other times (June to

September), you can watch mock Viking invasions and Roman gladiatorial contests in a 6,000-seat amphitheatre (⌨ http://www.puydufou.com).

MUSEUMS & GALLERIES

France has around 7,000 museums and many important historical collections. There are over 100 museums and some 500 historic monuments in and around Paris alone, ranging from one of the largest museums and galleries in the world, the Musée National du Louvre, to some of the smallest and most specialised. The Louvre, which is over 200 years old, is the most important museum in France and houses, among many famous exhibits, the Mona Lisa and the Venus de Milo. It takes around a week to see everything in the Louvre (if you really want to), which is also the world's largest (ex-)royal palace and a national treasure in itself (⌨ http://www.louvre.fr).

One of Paris's most popular art venues is the the Centre National d'Art et de Culture Georges Pompidou (known as the Centre Pompidou), housing the Musée National d'Art Moderne, the Public Reference Library, with over a million French and foreign books, the Institute of Sound and Music and the Industrial Design Centre. Other important Paris museums and galleries include the Musée Rodin, Musée Picasso, Musée d'Orsay and the Cité des Sciences et de l'Industrie. Recent additions to the capital's museum and gallery collection include the Orangerie near the Place de la Concorde, closed since 2000 for renovation and housing Monet's grandest waterlily paintings, the Petit and Grand Palais just off the Champs-Elysées, closed since 2001, the Cité de la Mode et du Design, in a converted Seine-side warehouse, the Musée du Quai Branly near the Eiffel Tower (Jacques Chirac's cultural legacy to France and the largest museum to be built in the capital since the Pompidou Centre in 1977), dedicated to the art and culture of Africa, Asia, Oceania and the Americas, and the Musée de l'Erotisme in Pigalle – Paris's only museum open till 2 o'clock in the morning! In addition to its national galleries, Paris boasts around 300 commercial galleries displaying the most innovative contemporary art (admission is free).

France also has a wealth of provincial museums devoted to such varied subjects as farming, local history, industry, crafts, cultural heritage, transport, archaeology, art, textiles, folklore, war, technology, pottery and nature. You can also visit numerous manor houses (*manoir*) and *châteaux*. When visiting *châteaux* and other country houses, try to arrive early (before the coach parties). Visiting gardens isn't particularly popular in France, although there are a number of notable gardens well worth seeing.

It's also possible to visit numerous businesses in France, particularly those connected with the food and drink industry such as vineyards, distilleries, breweries, mineral water springs, farms and dairies, while technology enthusiasts may prefer to visit a hydroelectric dam or a nuclear power station.

Opening Hours

National museums usually open from 10.00 until 18.00 and close on Tuesdays with the exception of Versailles, Trianon Palace, the Musée d'Orsay and the Cité des Sciences et de l'Industrie/la Géode at La Villette, which close on Mondays. The Musée du Louvre is open from 09.00 to 18.00 (except Tuesdays) and on Wednesdays until 21.45. Other Parisian museums stay open until 20.00 on Thursdays, when they're practically deserted (lunchtimes, when the French are busy eating, are another good time to visit). Municipal museums have the same opening hours as national museums, but are closed on Mondays. Smaller collections may close during August. Most museums close on public holidays, an irritating continental habit. Commercial galleries are open from Tuesdays to Saturdays from 14.00 to 19.00.

Most *châteaux* and other stately homes are open during the high season only, from May or June to September. Many are closed one day a week and most close from 12.00 until 14.00. Always check opening times before visiting.

Costs

The entrance fee for those aged 26 to 59 is usually €2.50 to €7.50, with half price or free entry on Sundays and sometimes Wednesdays. For example, entrance to the Musée d'Orsay is free on Sundays and the Louvre is free on the first Sunday of the month. Most museums offer free entry to those under 18 and a 50 per cent reduction for those aged 18 to 25 and 60 or over. Entrance to provincial museums is free for those under 7 and over 60 at all times. Most Parisian museums offer free entrance or substantial reductions during late afternoon (e.g. the Louvre is cheaper after 15.00). Tickets at many museums and galleries must be purchased from a complex multi-lingual machine.

A museum and monument card (*Carte des Musées et Monuments*) allows entry to over 60 museums and monuments in the Paris area. It's valid for one (€18) or three (€36) consecutive days. You need to visit a few museums to get your money's worth, but it's good value for 'culture vultures'. It's obtainable from participating museums, the Paris tourist office, *métro* stations and French Tourist Offices abroad. The *carte* allows you to bypass queues and ticket offices (or machines) and enter via a 'group admission' door. Regional passes are sometimes available, and most museums and special exhibitions charge half-price to holders (aged 60 or over) of the *Carte Sénior* rail card (see page 223) or a *Carte Vermeil*.

Information

There are innumerable guides to museums, galleries and other places of interest in France. The French Tourist Office (see page 402) publishes a brochure, *Châteaux, Museums, Monuments*, listing 200 cultural attractions. A leaflet listing 128 gardens is available from French Tourist Offices, and keen gardeners may be interested in *Les Guides des Jardins de France* by Michael Racine (Guides Hachette). Current museum and gallery exhibitions in Paris are listed in weekly entertainment magazines such as *Pariscope* and *l'Officiel des Spectacles*. Useful websites for museum information include 🖳 http://www.museums-of-paris.com and 🖳 http://www.rmn.fr (site of the Réunion des Museés Nationaux, which operates 32 museums across France).

CINEMA

French cinema (known as the 'seventh art') has resisted the threat of television (which is generally dreadful in France – see **Chapter 8**) far better than the cinema in most other Western countries. The French are huge film fans, and Paris is the cinema capital of the world, with some 350 cinemas, most of which are packed every day (Parisians buy some 80 per cent of all cinema tickets sold in France). 2004 was the biggest year for French cinema in two decades, with almost 200m tickets sold. Some US-made films are even shown in Paris before they're screened in the US.

In Paris you can see a different film (in a different cinema) every day of the year, and every film you ever wanted to see (and lots more that you wouldn't watch if you were paid to) is usually showing somewhere. Many cinemas in Paris show old films or reruns (*reprises*) of classics and many hold seasons and festivals featuring a particular actor, director or theme. Film lovers shouldn't miss the 'cinema days' (*journée du cinéma*) in summer, when films are shown non-stop for 24 hours at low prices.

As in other Western countries, most old cinemas have been replaced by modern multiplexes, with ten or more screens and state-of-the-art technology. Cinemas listed as *grande salle* or *salle prestige* have a large screen (*grand écran*), comfortable seats and high projection and sound standards. Smoking isn't permitted in cinemas, some of which are air-conditioned (a relief in summer). There are also private *ciné-clubs* in most cities.

France has a dynamic and prosperous film industry, which receives the bulk of its funding from a tax levied on cinema tickets (which critics claim allows French film-makers to produce poor films that nobody wants to watch). Some 200 French films are made each year, and only India and South Korea have a better record in resisting the invasion of US-made films (40 per cent of French ticket sales are for home-made films, compared with around 15 per cent in Germany, Italy and the UK, despite the fact that many French films sell fewer than 10,000 seats compared with over 1m for blockbuster US movies). It's also common for a cinema to be showing a film from Eastern Europe or Asia alongside the staple French/US fare.

In Paris and other major cities, foreign films are shown in their original version (*version originale/VO*) with French subtitles (*sous-titres français*). Dubbed films are labelled *VF* (*version française*). You may also come across *VA* (*version anglaise*), denoting an English-language film made by a French-speaking director (beware!). Note that French translations of English film titles often bear little relationship to the original, although an increasing number of titles aren't translated.

Films are classified and entrance may be prohibited to children under 18, 16 or 12 – listed as *interdit aux moins de 18 (16, 12) ans*. Children who look younger than their years may be asked to prove their age and should carry some form of identification (with a photo) showing their age.

The time listed for each performance is usually ten minutes before the film starts, when there are trailers and advertising. The last performance usually starts around 22.00 from Sundays to Thursdays and at 00.00 on Fridays and Saturdays. In Paris, performances are usually continuous from 14.00 until around midnight or 01.00.

Costs & Booking

Ticket prices range from €7 to €10 in Paris and the same prices are usually charged for reruns of old classics as for the latest hits. Cinema chains such as Gaumont and UGC offer season tickets (*cartes privilèges*) for frequent customers. The *UGC carte privilège* costs around €28 for five entries from Sunday to Friday, and €38 for seven entries. Gaumont operates a 'membership' system costing €30 plus €19.50 per month – strictly for addicts! Some independent cinemas offer a free ticket after five or six visits, while others sell reduced price cards for a number of admissions. Cine-addicts should obtain a *carte cinéma*, entitling them to discounts at most cinemas.

Tickets are reduced by 20 to 30 per cent on Mondays and/or Wednesdays in many cinemas. Midday (or 11.00) screenings are also cheaper, usually costing around €5. Reduced price tickets (30 to 50 per cent off) are available for students, senior citizens, the unemployed, military personnel and families with three or more children. Children and students must produce a student card and senior citizens (over 60) a passport, identity card or *Carte Senior* rail card (see page 223).

You can buy tickets in advance, although this must often be done via a premium-rate automated telephone booking system, for which your French comprehension needs to be first rate. If you book by telephone and pay by credit card, you can often collect your ticket from a machine simply by swiping your card.

It's no longer usual to tip the usher in cinemas – a practice that is now restricted to theatres and concert halls. In fact, in many cinemas you may sit anywhere and there are no ushers to show you to your seat.

Film Festivals

Europe's largest and most important film festival is the Cannes Film Festival, although access to films is limited to those in the film industry (or with the right contacts). Other major film festivals include the American Film Festival (Deauville in Calvados), the Comedy Film Festival (Chamrousse in Isère) and the Sciene-Fiction Film Festival (Avoriaz in Haute-Savoie).

Information

There are many French magazines devoted to films, including *Studio*, *Première* and *Positif*. English-language film magazines are also available from international news kiosks. An excellent website for film information is 🖥 http://www.cinefil.com, where you can find details (in French) of films showing in every department in France, including whether they're in *VO* or *VF*.

THEATRE, OPERA & BALLET

High quality theatre, opera and ballet performances are staged in all major cities, many by resident companies.

Theatre

Parisian theatres include the famous Comédie Française (classics), founded by Louis XIV, and the Théâtre National Populaire (contemporary). Other than the classics (Molière, Racine, Corneille, Feydeau, etc.), most French-language shows are translated hits from London and New York. There are also many café-theatres, where performances may not always be memorable but are usually enjoyable. Children's theatres in Paris and other cities perform straight plays, pageants and magic shows. There are also a number of English-language theatre venues in Paris, including the Théâtre Marie Stuart, ACT, Theatre Essaion, Voices and the Sweeney Irish Pub.

In the provinces, performances are often held in theatres that are part of a cultural centre (*maison de la culture* or *centre d'animation culturelle*), and the only national theatre outside the capital is the Théâtre National de Strasbourg. In total over 400 theatre companies receive state subsidies, including 150 in Paris. In addition to the large and luxurious state-funded theatres, there are many good medium and small-size theatres where performance quality varies considerably. Performances aren't always top quality, but there's plenty of variety. Performances usually start at 20.30 or 21.00 and theatres close one day a week. As in cinemas, smoking isn't permitted.

Tickets usually cost between €5 and €45 for national theatres (although you can obtain half-price tickets if you subscribe to 🖥 http://www.theatreonline.com) and between €8 and €20 for private theatres. Midweek matinee subscriptions are available at reduced rates. The Kiosque Théâtre (place de la Madeleine, 75008 Paris) in Paris sells half-price tickets on Tuesdays to Saturdays from 12.30 to 20.00 for shows on performance days, and many theatres offer student discounts. Just before a show starts, seats are often available at huge discounts. Students can also obtain reduced price tickets from the Centre Régional des Oeuvres Universitaires et Scolaires/CROUS (see page 208). Ushers expect a small tip.

Obtaining theatre tickets in advance is difficult in Paris, where many theatres allow booking only one or two weeks in advance. Many theatres don't accept credit card bookings and don't use ticket agencies. Bookings can be made up to three weeks before a performance via the website 🖥 http://www.theatreonline.fr.

Drama festivals are also popular and include the world-renowned Festival d'Avignon in July/August, encompassing drama, dance, film, concerts, exhibitions and many other events.

Ballet

The Paris Opéra Ballet has a history going back three centuries and is one of the world's foremost ballet companies (it no longer stages opera). Although tickets are cheaper than in London and New York, they're hard to obtain, as most seats are sold by subscription months in advance. For information and booking details, see **Opera** below. Paris also boasts the Théâtre du Châtelet in the 1st *arrondissement*, where a variety of shows are staged, including ballet productions (🖥 http://www.chatelet-theatre.com). Modern and contemporary dance thrives and the Centre Pompidou stages some 'interesting' avant-garde programmes by French and international dance companies. Many small dance companies perform in small theatres and dance studios.

Opera

The new Opéra de la Bastille (☎ 08 92 89 90 90) is France's major opera venue, although it has been plagued by problems (e.g. lack of funding, sackings and strikes) since its opening. Paris also boasts the celebrated Opéra Garnier in the 9th *arrondissement* (details of both Paris operas can be found on 💻 http://www.opera-de-paris.fr; tickets can be booked online or via ☎ 08 92 89 90 90) and the Théâtre du Châtelet in the 1st, where a variety of shows are staged, including opera productions (💻 http://www.chatelet-theatre.com). France also has 12 regional opera companies, most notably Bordeaux, Lille, Lyon and Toulouse.

MUSIC

Although the French don't have a reputation as music lovers, France boasts some 5m amateur musicians and stages over 300 music festivals a year.

Classical Music

The French are rather parochial when it comes to classical music, preferring to hear French music performed by French musicians. France has no world-renowned orchestra and few internationally famous performers and, compared with many other capital cities, Paris has a dearth of classical music. The capital's only large, modern, purpose-built concert hall is in the Maison de Radio France, well away from the city centre; otherwise, concert venues tend to be unwelcoming, uncomfortable and acoustically-challenged.

Fortunately, international orchestras and soloists regularly tour France and there are frequent concerts in Paris and the provinces by the Orchestre de Paris, the Orchestre Philharmonique de Radio France, and various other national and provincial orchestras (among the best are Bordeaux, Lille, Lyon and Toulouse).

The Parisian concert season runs from October to June. Students at the Conservatoire National perform regularly in the Paris *métro* and on the city's streets as well as at the Cité de la Musique in north-east Paris, where there's a fascinating museum of musical instruments. Recitals of organ and sacred music are held in churches and cathedrals such as the Notre Dame, and many churches sponsor concerts with good soloists and excellent choirs. Paris also has a number of music halls where top international artists regularly perform. There's plenty of classical music outside the capital, although much of it is poorly advertised.

There are discounts at classical music concerts for senior citizens on production of identification or a *Carte Senior* (see page 223). The main agency for tickets to almost any concert or cultural event in Paris is FNAC at 136 rue de Rennes, 6e (☎ 08 92 68 36 22, 🖳 http://www.fnac.fr) and in the Forum des Halles Level 3, 1–5 rue Pierre-Lescot, 1er (☎ 08 92 68 36 22). You can also buy tickets from the Virgin Megastore, 52 avenue des Champs Elysées, 8e (☎ 01 49 53 50 00). Some hypermarkets (e.g. Carrefour) have ticket booking or *spectacles* counters.

Popular Music

French popular music is generally poor and unoriginal (even the imitators are bad) and the rock music scene is usually several decades behind that of London and New York. This is reflected in the fact that the 1960s rock star Johnny Hallyday, who's now over 60, and octogenarian crooner Charles Aznavour remain France's biggest box office draws. Foreign bands are much better known to French fans than any French group. Most rock venues can be divided into those where you sit and listen and dance clubs. The former (in Paris) include Bataclon, Bercy, Bobigno, Olympia, the Palais des Congrès and Zénith, although none of these is an 'automatic' stop on the world tour. Tickets for club performances cost around €15 and concerts €25 or more. Drinks are expensive in music clubs and may run to €15 for a beer.

Jazz

What Paris lacks in classical and popular music it makes up for with the superiority of its jazz clubs. It's easily Europe's leading jazz venue and attracts the world's best musicians. France is also the venue for many excellent jazz festivals, including the Festival de Jazz in Paris in autumn, the Antibes-Juan-les-Pins Festival and the Nice Jazz Festival in July, one of the most prestigious jazz and blues festivals in Europe. France even has a nationally-funded National Jazz Orchestra. Most jazz is performed in cellar clubs, where there's usually a cover charge and expensive drinks. Music starts at around 22.00 and lasts until around 04.00 at weekends and includes everything from trad to be-bop, free jazz to experimental.

Music Festivals

Open-air music festivals are common and popular in summer throughout the country, many of them staged in spectacular venues such as cathedrals and *châteaux*. Music festivals embrace all types of music, including classical, opera, chamber music, organ, early music, piano, popular, jazz and folk, many of which are listed in a booklet, *Festive France*, available from French Tourist Offices (see page 402). Every year, over a weekend in May, in around 40 towns the bandstand (*kiosque à musique*) is given over to the performance of music of the Belle Epoque.

Information

French music magazines include the *Guide des Concerts* and *Les Activités Musicales*. Two publications provide a guide to what's on in Paris: *L'Officiel des Spectacles* and *Pariscope*, the latter having an English supplement.

SOCIAL CLUBS

There are many social clubs and organisations catering for both foreigners and the French. These include Ambassador Clubs, American Women's and Men's Clubs, Anglo-French Clubs, Kiwani Clubs, Lion and Lioness Clubs and Rotary Clubs, along with clubs for business people and others.

Paris is home to number of clubs and societies founded and run by groups of expatriates, including national groups (e.g. American Citizens Abroad, the American Club of Paris and the Association of American Residents Overseas, the Association Franco-Écossaise, The Clan MacLeod Society of France, The Caledonian Society of France, The Paris Welsh Society and The Royal Society of Saint George), university-based groups (e.g. The Alumnae Club of Paris, the Alumni of the University of Edinburgh in France, The Cambridge Society of Paris and The Oxford University Club), professional associations (e.g. The Association of British Accountants in France, The Chartered Management Institute, The Institute of Directors, The Institution of Civil Engineers and The Institution of Electrical Engineers), women's clubs (e.g. American Women's Group of Paris, The British and Commonwealth Women's Association, the International Women's Club, WICE and MESSAGE – the Mother Support Group) and others (e.g. the Association France Grande-Bretagne, The British Freemasons in France, French branches of British Guides in Foreign Countries and of the Scouts, The English-speaking Union France, The Royal British Legion for ex-servicemen, The Salvation Army and the TOC H Association for elderly people). During October, many organisations hold 'open houses' or other events to welcome new expatriates, including the popular 'Bloom Where You Are Planted' programme, organised by and at the American Church in Paris (see **Finding Help** on page 95).

There's also a number of English-speaking sports clubs in the Paris region, including the British Rugby Club of Paris in Saint-Cyr-l'Ecole (78), the Standard Athletic Club in Meudon-la-Forêt (92) and the Thoiry Cricket Club in Château-de-Thoiry (78), and several arts groups, including The English Cathedral Choir of Paris, The International Players (an amateur drama group), the Paris Decorative and Fine Arts Society and The Royal Scottish Country Dance Society. There's also an English Language Library for the blind in the 17th *arrondissement*.

Outside the capital, there are Anglophone clubs and societies in certain areas only, such as Dordogne, Bordeaux and the Côte d'Azur, although most are in the Ile-de-France. The British Consulate publishes a free *Digest of British and Franco-British Clubs, Societies and Institutions* (published by the British Community Committee and available free from the British Embassy in Paris – see **Appendix A**).

Details of English-language clubs are also included in *The Best Places to Live in France* (Survival Books – see page 587). Other sources of information about English-speaking clubs are *The Connexion* and *The News* (see **Appendix B**) and the English-speaking church (see **Religion** on page 535).

Most private and international schools (see page 199) have an active parents' association and often need volunteers to help organise and run after-school activities for students.

For French speakers, the Accueil des Villes Françaises (AVF), a French organisation designed to welcome newcomers to an area, is an option (see page 97). And many local clubs organise activities and pastimes such as chess, bridge, art, music, sports activities and sports outings, theatre, cinema and local history. Joining a local club is one of the easiest ways to meet people and make friends. If you want to integrate into your local community or French society in general, one of the best ways is to join a local club. Ask your local town hall (*mairie*) for information.

NIGHTLIFE

French nightlife varies considerably with the town or region. In small towns, you may be fortunate to find a bar with music or a *discothèque*, while in Paris (which has the most varied nightlife of any city) and other major cities you will be spoilt for choice. Paris by night is usually as exciting and glamorous as its reputation and it offers a wide choice of entertainment, including jazz and other music clubs, cabarets, discos, theme bars, nightclubs and music halls. The liveliest places are the music clubs, which are infinitely variable and ever-changing with a wide choice of music, including reggae, jazz, funk, rock and techno. High-tech discos are popular, where lasers and high decibels (not to mention drugs) combine to destroy your brain. Note that drunkenness and rowdy behaviour are considered bad taste and bouncers are often over-eager to flex their muscles. The most popular clubs change continually and are listed in newspapers and entertainment magazines.

The action starts around 23.00 or midnight and goes on until dawn (05.00 or 06.00). The admission fee to Parisian clubs is usually high, e.g. from €15 to €30 (possibly less on certain days, when women may be offered free entry), and generally includes a 'free' drink. Some clubs offer free entry but drinks are expensive.

A traditional and entertaining night out in Paris is is to be had at one of the city's many cabaret venues, which include the Crazy Horse Saloon, the Folies Pigalle, the Lido and the Moulin Rouge (the celebrated Folies Bergère closed its doors in 1992 after 125 years). The entertainment, which features an endless stream of topless dancers (male and female), doesn't come cheap and runs to between €80 and €170 per head, depending on whether you just see the show or have champagne or dinner as well. Cabaret is unfortunately a dying art and nowadays caters mainly to foreign tourists.

For those who prefer more sober entertainment, 'tea dancing' halls (*guinguette*) can be found throughout France. Old-style dance halls (*bal musette*), where dancing is to a live orchestra, are making a comeback in Paris and are popular with both young and old. The French have even discovered the 'art' of making fools of themselves in public through karaoke (*karaoké*), which is becoming increasingly popular in Paris and other cities.

GAMBLING

French law forbids gambling for money . . . but exceptions are made for the national lottery, horse racing and casinos, all of which are state-controlled. The French spend over €15 billion on gambling every year, and its popularity is increasing. Over 20m people regularly play LOTO, France's national lottery (*loterie nationale*), on which millions of euros are wagered annually. The lottery draw is made live on TV and takes precedence over all other 'news'. The LOTO and a plethora of scratch card systems are run by a company called La Française des Jeux (🖳 http://www.fdjeux.com). Tickets and cards can be bought at tobacconists'.

Gambling on horse racing is also popular, with betting on the tote system controlled by the Pari Mutuel Urbain (PMU, 🖳 http://www.pmu.fr), which has branches (around 7,500) at cafés throughout France. The most popular bet is the *tiercé*, which entails forecasting the first three horses to finish in the correct order; you can also choose four (*quarté*) or five (*quinté*) horses. Sunday is the most popular day for race meetings and the major races are the Prix de l'Arc de Triomphe, the Prix du Président de la République and the Prix d'Amérique.

Until 1988, only spa and seaside resorts in France were allowed to have casinos, but there are now over 170 French casinos, the largest being at Aix-les-Bains, Biarritz, Cannes, Deauville (which offers the biggest gross in France thanks to its €1 one-armed bandits, seldom found elsewhere), Divonne and Evian. The most famous casino of all is that of Monaco (which is almost French). Not surprisingly, the greatest concentration of casinos is along the French Riviera; surprisingly, the second-greatest concentration is along the coast of Normandy. Gamblers must be over 18 and be smartly dressed. However, French casinos have recently been losing out to online gambling – some 4m French people are reckoned to use 'cybercasinos' – and it may not be long before they're calling '*Rien ne va plus!*' Blackjack and roulette are the most popular casino games. Details of all casinos can be found on 🖳 http://www.journaldescasinos.com, which is partly in English.

BARS & CAFES

There's at least one bar or café in virtually every town and village in France, although the number has fallen from over 500,000 at the turn of the 20th century to around 60,000 today. In major towns and cities, watering holes include wine bars, café-bars, brasseries, bar-brasseries and tea-rooms (*salon de thé*). Although they don't have a reputation as hard drinkers, the French spend a lot of time in bars and cafés, perhaps nursing a single drink (locals often use them as their sitting rooms) and playing games, such as *belote* (a mixture of bridge, rummy and solo, played with a standard card pack minus all cards below nine). Usually nobody will rush you to finish your drink, unless it's the height of the tourist season and people are waiting for tables.

Bars

A bar (*bar* or *bar-comptoir* – also known as a *zinc*, after the traditional zinc counters) sells alcoholic drinks and perhaps coffees and snacks but doesn't usually serve complete meals. Bars have been rapidly disappearing throughout France and especially in Paris, where over 30,000 have closed in the last decade and many more have been 'modernised' by the installation of TVs, video games, pinball machines (*flipper*) and piped music. There are also 'English' and 'Irish' pubs in Paris and other cities serving a range of British and other imported beers and 'authentic' pub food. The US chain Starbucks opened the first of a planned chain of Parisian cafés in early 2004. There are also wine bars in Paris and some other cities, where fine wines are served by the glass and snacks are available, although they're expensive and aren't common or popular.

A bar-brasserie or brasserie serves a wider selection of food than a café and is more like a restaurant (see page 435).

Cafés & Salons de Thé

Cafés (or café-bars) and bistros (see page 435) serve alcoholic drinks, soft drinks, and hot drinks such as tea and coffee. They usually serve snacks (e.g. sandwiches) and ice-cream all day and may serve meals at lunchtime. If you just want a drink, don't sit at a table with a tablecloth, which indicates that it's reserved for customers wishing to eat. Some cafés are best avoided at lunchtimes, e.g. between 12.00 and 14.00, when they're extremely busy (although it's usually an excellent sign). Most cafés have outside tables or terraces on the street, depending on the season and the weather.

Cafés are an institution and have been called the life support system of French culture (there are over 10,000 in Paris alone). They aren't simply places to grab a cup of coffee or a bite to eat, but are meeting places, shelters, sun lounges, somewhere to make friends, talk, write, do business, study, read a newspaper or just watch the world go by. Like restaurants, cafés are supposed to provide no-smoking areas, although the law is openly flouted.

As in other countries, there's a recent trend in theme cafés, such as *cafés sports* (where you can watch big matches on giant screens), and *cafés philos* (where you can indulge in a little philosophical debate over your absinthe).

A *salon de thé* is a tea-room serving tea and coffee, sandwiches, cakes and pastries, but no alcohol. Tea-rooms are fashionable in Paris (e.g. Angelina and Ladurée) and other major cities, but are more expensive than cafés or brasseries. Afternoon tea (*goûter* or *collation*) isn't usually served in France.

Drinks

A wide variety of drinks are served in bars, cafés, bistros and brasseries in France, including the following.

Coffee, Tea & Chocolate

If you ask for *un café* or *un express*, you will be served a small black coffee or espresso. A *café noir double* is a double espresso, for those with strong hearts. A *café allongé* (or *café long*) is an espresso with extra hot water and a *café serré* is an extra strong espresso with half the usual amount of water (guaranteed to keep you awake!). *Un crème* is an espresso with steamed milk and comes in small (*petit*) and large (*grand*) sizes. (The term *café au lait* is seldom used nowadays for white coffee.) If you don't specify a small coffee, many places will serve a large one. *Une noisette* is a black coffee with a dash of milk. Decaffeinated coffee (*déca*) is also widely available.

Tea is usually drunk black (*thé nature*), unless you specify tea with lemon (*thé au citron*) or milk (*thé au lait*). Note that French tea is extremely weak. Herbal teas (*tisane*) are popular and include camomile (*camomille*), mint (*menthe*), lime blossom (*tilleul*) and verbena (*verveine*). See also **Coffee & Tea** on page 496.

Hot chocolate (*chocolat chaud*) is a popular drink, and iced tea and coffee are often drunk in summer.

Soft Drinks

Popular soft drinks include flavoured syrups (*sirop*), such as *menthe* (bright green) and *grenadine* (bright red), cola (*coca*) and freshly-squeezed lemon or orange juice (*citron/orange pressé*), the former served with water and sugar and wonderfully refreshing. Sparkling (*gazeuse/pétillante*) and still (*non-gazeuse/plate*) mineral waters are popular, although mineral water and soft drinks are often more expensive than wine or beer.

Beer & Cider

Beer is popular in all areas, although most is consumed in the north and east. French beer is usually of the lager variety and among the most popular French brands are Fischer/Pêcheur, Kanterbräu, Kronenbourg, Météor, Millbrau, Mützig, Pelforth, Slavia, '33' Export and Valstar. Foreign beers such as Stella Artois (Belgium) are available in major towns but are more expensive than French beer. Beer is usually served draught (*pression*), and you can order a *bock* (half a 25cl glass), a *demi* (not a half litre as you may expect, but 25cl), a *sérieux* (50cl) or a *formidable* (a litre). Expect to pay three to five times the supermarket price for a 25cl beer in a bar. If straight beer isn't to your taste, you can try a shandy (*panaché* or *bière limonade*) or a *bière amère* – beer mixed with 'bitters' made with orange peel and quinine! See also **Beer** on page 495.

Apple cider (*cidre*) is a popular drink in Brittany and Normandy (especially with pancakes), although it isn't drunk much in other parts of the country and is often more expensive than wine. It comes dry (*brut*), sweet (*doux*) and 'golden' (*doré*). Pear cider (*poiré*) is also drunk in parts of Normandy and is a refreshing alternative to apple cider.

Wine

Wine is commonly drunk in cafés and bars, although it's rarely drunk in fashionable places. It's usually served in small (*petit*) and large (*ballon*) sizes for around €1 to €2, and can also be ordered in a quarter-litre (25cl) or half-litre pitcher (*pichet*) for around €3 and €5 respectively. You usually order simply red (*rouge*), pink (*rosé*) or white (*blanc*). Don't expect good quality wine, except in wine bars, where it's appropriately priced. Champagne is popular in fashionable places, but **very** expensive. See also **Wine** on pages 441 and 490.

Spirits & Other Drinks

Gin and tonic (*gin Schweppes*) and scotch whisky (*whisky*) – particularly malt whisky, which far outsells brandy in France – are popular. Favourite *apéritifs* (or *apéros*) include *kir*, a mix of white wine and *crème de cassis* (a blackcurrant liqueur), *kir clair*, white wine with just a drop of cassis, and *kir royal*, made with champagne instead of white wine. *Pastis*, an aniseed or liquorice-flavoured drink diluted with water and usually ice, is popular, particularly in the south, and *absinthe*, once banned, is making a comeback.

Other popular drinks include Cinzano, Dubonnet, Martini (out of a bottle, not dry with an olive), port (*porto*), cognac, armagnac, calvados (apple brandy) and a wide variety of liqueurs such as Bénédictine, Chartreuse, Cointreau and Grand Marnier. Alcohol flavoured with fruit and other things is common throughout France and every region has its own variations, such as *crème de cassis*, *crème de menthe* and *crème de cacao*. The French aren't renowned for their drink-mixing ability, with the exception of bartenders in expensive cocktail bars in top class hotels, where prices start at around €8 (some have a 'happy hour' when drinks are half price). See also **Spirits** on page 495.

Snacks

Bars and cafés usually serve a range of snacks, including a *croque monsieur* (toasted cheese and ham sandwich), *croque madame* (like a *croque monsieur* but with a fried egg on top), omelettes (plain, ham, mushroom), pancakes (the savoury buckwheat variety, *galettes*, are served as a main course, the sweet white flour type, *crêpes*, as a dessert), sandwiches (€3 to €5) usually consisting of half a baguette filled with ham, cheese or *pâté*, and filled croissants. Many cafés and fast food outlets accept coupons provided by employers, similar to luncheon vouchers and called *tickets restaurants*. Establishments accepting them have stickers on their windows (don't expect to find them on Michelin-starred restaurants!). Note that a snack in a bar can cost as much as a three-course lunch in a modest restaurant (see page 433).

Opening Hours & Licensing

There are no licensing hours in France, and alcohol can be sold at any time of the day or night, although an official permit is required. Generally a bar or restaurant closes when the *patron(ne)* decides it should. Most bars and establishments selling alcohol open some time between 06.00 and 11.00 and close between 00.00 and 02.00. Many Parisian cafés open at 07.00 or 08.00 and close at around 14.00. Most brasseries and cafés open at around 11.00 and remain open until 23.00 or later. Cafés and bars near markets often keep the same hours as the market. Like restaurants, most bars and cafés close on one day a week (*jour de repos*), usually shown on the door.

The legal age for drinking in public establishments in France is 16, although children aged 14 to 16 may drink beer or wine when accompanied by an adult. Officially, unaccompanied children under 16 aren't allowed into establishments serving alcohol. However, there's virtually no enforcement and children are readily served and sold alcohol everywhere.

Costs

The cost of all drinks varies considerably with the establishment and its location. A bar or café must display its prices (*tarif de consommations*). At café terraces on major boulevards such as the Champs Elysées or the rue de Rivoli in Paris, you're charged two or three times as much as in a less fashionable street. A bar or café may serve drinks at the counter (*au comptoir*), at a table inside (*en salle*) or an outside table (*en terrasse*). You pay more for sitting at a table than standing at the bar and there's usually an even higher charge for a table outside or in the window. If you order a drink at the bar and sit down to drink it, you must pay more! The cost of a coffee varies from around €1.20 standing at the bar to €5 or more when seated in a Parisian tourist spot. Beware of high prices at railway stations, airports and in tourist areas.

Paying

In a bar or café, each drink is usually presented with a cash register receipt and you pay for your drinks when you leave, although you may be asked to pay when you're served if it's very busy or you're in a tourist spot. If your waiter is going off duty, he will also ask you to pay. When you've paid, your receipts are torn or crumpled by the waiter. Service and tax is included in the price and it's unnecessary to tip, although French people often leave a few small coins. At the counter you usually receive your change in a little plastic dish that's upturned to signify that you've paid.

RESTAURANTS

One of the prerequisites for a happy and rewarding life in France is a love of good food and wine. No other country is so devoted to its cuisine and the French are among the world's most avid eaters (the French rarely snack but eat civilised meals). They like nothing more than to talk about food and wine (sex and politics lag way behind). Good French food is noted for its freshness, lack of artificial ingredients and preservatives (the French are fighting a rearguard action against the onslaught of GM food and crop spraying), and exquisite presentation. French cooking is an art form and master chefs are national heroes, although French food reflects not only the expertise of its chefs but also the attitude of the customers, who are the most discerning in the world.

Foreigners are often surprised at how restaurants can serve such excellent food at such modest prices (the French aren't telling). Almost everyone can afford to eat out and culinary treats await you around every corner. The average person spends around 20 per cent of his food budget in restaurants and eats out on average three times a week. However, not all restaurants offer good value (*rapport qualité-prix*) and it's possible to eat badly in France. One simple rule is to frequent establishments packed with local residents. If you want good French food without breaking the bank, look out for establishments awarded a single knife and fork and marked with a red 'R' (*repas*) in the *Michelin Red Guide* (see page 401 and **Information** on page 443).

Top-class restaurants are classified by Michelin (one to three stars/*étoiles*) and Gault-Millau (up to four chef's hats/*toques*). Ratings are reviewed annually, and there are usually fewer than 20 restaurants in the whole of France with three Michelin stars. Paris is widely recognised as the gastronomic capital of the world and has more restaurants than any other city, although Lyon has more Michelin-starred chefs and is rated by many as the centre of French cuisine. (Others claim that the south-west is France's culinary nirvana, particularly for healthy eating . . .) Every region of France has its specialities, which it proudly offers and jealously guards (see **French Cuisine** on page 436).

Surprisingly, many restaurants (including expensive ones) are lacking in what might be assumed to be a quintessentially French quality: ambience. In particular, it isn't unusual for restaurants to be brightly lit, so it pays to visit a restaurant before booking a 'candle-lit dinner' for two.

Given the quality and variety of French cooking, it's little surprise that most restaurants serve French food, and foreign restaurants are somewhat thin on the ground (except in Paris). In Paris, the abundance of African, Middle Eastern, Vietnamese and West Indian restaurants reflects the colonial history of France, although foreign restaurants rarely make the top grade. In the provinces, Italian restaurants are the most common (many of them serving mainly pizzas), followed by Chinese. Indian restaurants are scarce. If you're used to spicy foreign food, however, you may find familiar dishes disappointingly bland in France.

Types of Restaurant

Eating houses encompass a wide range of establishments; some of the most common are described below.

Auberge

An *auberge* (or *hostellerie* or *relais*) was originally a coaching-inn or hostelry. Today it's generally an alternative name for a restaurant and may no longer provide accommodation. An *auberge de jeunesse* is a youth hostel (see page 412).

Brasserie

A brasserie (or bar-brasserie) is a down-to-earth café-restaurant serving meals throughout the day (unlike a restaurant) and often remaining open until the early hours of the morning, particularly in Paris. See also **Bars & Cafés** on page 429.

Bistrot

A bistrot is generally a small, simple restaurant (or café-restaurant), although they can be trendy and expensive, particularly in Paris and other cities. The hallmark of a bistrot is basic French cuisine at reasonable prices. They also provide venues for artists, a place to meet and talk and a stage for musicians. Unfortunately, like cafés, bistrots have long been in decline and their numbers have fallen dramatically in the last few decades.

Buffet & Fast Food

A buffet is a self-service restaurant, usually found in railway stations and airports. A *libre-service* (or a *self*) establishment is a self-service cafeteria often found in department stores, hypermarkets and shopping centres, in motorway service stations and in city centres. There are many US-style fast food outlets in Paris and other French cities, including McDonald's (which has even invaded the Champs Elysées in Paris and the Promenade des Anglais in Nice and has around 1,000 outlets) and Quick (the Belgian competitor to McDonald's with around 325 outlets and entertaining 'Franglais' menus) as well as pizzerias and pancake stalls (*crêperies*).

Relais Routier

A relais routier is a transport café, although these are nothing like the 'greasy spoon' establishments found in other countries and are usually excellent, good value restaurants (mostly on trunk roads) patronised by all travellers, particularly truck drivers (a car park full of trucks outside any establishment is usually a good sign).

Restaurant

A restaurant is a serious eating place that serves meals at normal meal times and isn't somewhere for just a drink or snack, unless it's a café-restaurant. Note that you can expect to spend at least two hours and often four or five over a meal in a French restaurant.

Rôtisserie

A rôtisserie specialises in grills, although it may serve a wide range of other dishes.

Meals

Although the French eat much the same meals as people in most other countries, they may have a different emphasis. The following is a guide to French eating habits.

Breakfast

Breakfast isn't important to most French people and usually consists of just coffee, which is freshly brewed, strong and drunk out of bowl-sized cups with milk. Tea and hot chocolate are occasional alternatives. When eaten, breakfast is usually of the continental variety, consisting of croissants or rolls (or a *baguette*), butter and jam (often dunked in the coffee or chocolate!). French families are increasingly eating breakfast cereals, thus confirming that they don't always have good taste.

Lunch

Lunch is sacred and the most important meal of the day. However, contrary to popular belief, some 75 per cent of the workforce takes less than a hour for lunch, not two or three hours, although long lunch breaks are still common in the provinces, where life proceeds at a more leisurely pace. Lunch is generally served from 12.00 until 14.00, when nearly everything closes in rural areas, although most people lunch around 12.30 in the provinces and at 13.00 in Paris. You will find it difficult to get a hot meal almost anywhere in rural areas after 14.00 or 14.30.

Sunday lunch is the main gastronomic event of the week for French families and often lasts over three hours. Many restaurants put on a special Sunday menu for an extra charge, although inexpensive set meals are usually unavailable.

Dinner

Dinner is usually served from 19.00 until 21.30 or 22.00, although in the main cities many restaurants stay open until after midnight (in Paris, a few are even open 24 hours). In the provinces people usually eat between 19.00 and 20.00, or between 20.00 and 21.00 in the extreme south. You will be lucky to get dinner after 21.00 or 21.30 in most places or perhaps *à la carte* meals only will be served. Usually dinner is a lighter meal than lunch, particularly in the provinces. There's often little difference between lunch and dinner menus, except perhaps in small village restaurants, which may serve dinner by prior arrangement only. A meal eaten late in the evening, perhaps after a cinema or theatre visit, is called supper (*souper*) and may be eaten as late (or early) as 02.00.

French Cuisine

French cooking (*cuisine*, which also means 'kitchen') is divided into a range of categories or styles including the following:

Cuisine Bourgeoise

Cuisine bourgeoise (or *cuisine paysanne* or *cuisine traditionelle*) consists of excellent but plain fare such as meat or game stews and casseroles made with wine, mushrooms and onions, with a liberal dose of garlic and herbs. *Cuisine bourgeoise* is commonly found in *relais* (see above) and middle-class restaurants and, although sometimes lacking in imagination, is universally popular, particularly among those with hearty appetites.

Cuisine Minceur

Cuisine minceur is gourmet food for slimmers (invented by Michel Guérard) and is the most delicious slimming food in the world. It's similar to *nouvelle cuisine* (see below) but with the emphasis on the avoidance of fat, sugar and carbohydrates, and using substitute fat-free ingredients.

Cuisine Régionale

Cuisine régionale (or *cuisine des provinces* or *cuisine campagnarde*) is cooking that's particular to one of the 22 regions of France (see map on page 570), each of which has its own style of cooking and specialities, often influenced by the surrounding countries. *Cuisine régionale* was traditionally based on the availability of local produce, although many well-known regional dishes are becoming increasingly difficult to find in restaurants while others have become ubiquitous.

Haute Cuisine

The cream of French cooking and naturally the most expensive, although it isn't as popular as it once was. It comprises a vast repertoire of rich and elaborate sauces (originally added to disguise the poor quality of the main ingredients but now designed to complement them) made with butter, cream and wine, and a variety of exotic ingredients such as truffles, lobster and wild boar.

Nouvelle Cuisine

A healthier version of *haute cuisine* with the emphasis on freshness and lightness, i.e. pretty food in small portions artfully arranged on large plates. The accent is on minimum cooking to retain natural flavours, with sauces designed to enhance rather than hide the taste of the main ingredients. Chefs are encouraged to experiment and create new dishes; indeed, if master chefs wish to retain their ratings in the gastronomic bibles, it's mandatory. *Nouvelle cuisine* has become less fashionable in recent years as its popularity has spread and many top class restaurants have abandoned it.

Menus & Prices

Menus with prices must be displayed outside restaurants, with the exception of small village restaurants, where you're offered whatever is being served on a particular day (and you must be either adventurous or starving, especially if your French isn't fluent!). All restaurants must offer a fixed-price menu (*menu à prix fixe, menu conseillé, menu formule* or simply *menu* – the word for 'menu' is *carte*) with from three to seven courses (commonly four), and many offer a choice of fixed-price menus. A fixed-price menu may offer a choice between two or three dishes for each course, although in humble village restaurants there's usually no choice (but the price may include wine). The more expensive the menu, the wider the choice of dishes and the larger the number of courses (see below). You can also order separate dishes from the *carte* (the French don't use the term *à la carte*!), although this may not be an option in basic restaurants and it invariably works out much more expensive. Watch out also for the words *en supplément* (sometimes abbreviated to *en suppt*) after items on a menu, as you will be charged extra!

A *menu dégustation* or *menu gastronomique* is often served in a top-class restaurant. It consists of many small portions of the specialities of the house, designed to display the chef's expertise, each of which may be served with a complementary (but not complimentary!) wine.

The sign of good food in an unpretentious establishment is often a hand-written menu (possibly on a blackboard outside), which is an indication that the dishes change frequently. Generally the shorter the menu, the better the food and it's best to avoid tourist menus (*menus touristiques*) and places catering largely to tourists (check the cars in the car park).

Most restaurants are more than happy to cater for children. Some have a children's menu (*menu d'enfants*) and many local restaurants provide a free (or low-priced) place setting (*couvert*) for a young child eating from his parents' order. Most restaurants will happily accommodate a push-chair or baby seat.

Fixed menu prices range from as little as €8 per head in a village café/restaurant up to €150 or more at a two or three-star Michelin gastronomic shrine (excellent places to dine when someone else is paying!). Between these extremes are numerous restaurants with menus between €15 and €30. Note that, although a meal for around €8 can be excellent in some rural establishments, you shouldn't expect too much for this sum. Needless to say, a dish costing €7.50 in a rural restaurant may cost three times as much in Paris, on the French Riviera or in other fashionable areas.

Although menu prices are low compared with those in many other countries, the cost of wine, coffee and other drinks may be high (wine is often three or four times supermarket prices and not always served at an appropriate temperature). Those on a tight budget and with limited time may prefer to eat in a self-service restaurant (*self* – see page 435), where you can eat well for around €8 or less. Holders of a *carte famille nombreuse* (see page 224) can benefit from discounts at a number of restaurant chains, including Buffalo Grill.

Menu prices are legally required to include tax and service, although some restaurants still add 15 per cent for service (see **Tipping** on page 539). French restaurateurs are clamouring to have the rate of VAT they must charge reduced from 19.6 to 5.5 per cent (the rate that applies to take-away food) – so far without success.

Courses

The composition and number of courses of a meal can vary greatly, and there are often surprises. In higher-class establishments you may be offered canapés (*amuse-bouche*) before your first course and in others peanuts or something similar with aperitifs. These are 'free' (i.e. the cost is included in the price of other courses and drinks). All restaurants serve an unlimited amount of bread as part of a meal, which isn't cut with a knife but broken with your hands. Butter isn't normally served but can be requested (if you want everyone to know that you're a Philistine foreigner).

First Course

The first course (*entrée* or *hors d'oeuvre*) may vary from a hearty soup in a no-menu establishment to a range of exquisite, mouth-watering concoctions in a top-class restaurant. An intermediate course may be served in medium or top-class restaurants and usually consists of fish, although it can also be an omelette, chicken, rabbit, frogs' legs or snails. In some areas, you may be offered a 'refresher course' between the *entrée* and main course: apple sorbet and calvados in Normandy (known as a *trou normand*), for example. You can order an *entrée* as your main course (it's often difficult to distinguish between the two), although you may be charged more.

Main Course

The main course (*plat principal* or simply *plat*) is traditionally a meat course, although you can choose fish (vegetarian options are rare – see **Vegetarian Food** below). Meat is usually served rare, unless specified otherwise. The various degrees of cooking meat in France are very rare (*bleu*), rare (*saignant*), medium (*à point*) and well done (*bien cuit*). If you want your meat **really** well done, you must ask for it *très bien cuit* (or go to England). In most restaurants the main course is served with vegetables (*garni*), although they may be served separately, particularly in the south. In a village or country restaurant, the main course is usually automatically accompanied by chips (*frites*) and a seasonal vegetable (e.g. peas, green beans or carrots). In inexpensive restaurants it's common to use the same knives and forks throughout a meal. A green salad may be served as a separate course after the main course.

Cheese

The cheese course is served after the main course and precedes the dessert. A good cheese board contains local cheeses made from cow's, goat's and possibly even sheep's milk. In cheaper restaurants, you may have no choice of cheeses.

Dessert

The dessert course is usually fairly standard in humble establishments, consisting of a choice between ice-cream, sorbets, cream caramel, chocolate mousse and fruit. However, in first-class restaurants the offerings will be as elaborate and delicious as the rest of the meal.

Coffee

Finally you will be offered small cups of strong black coffee, possibly accompanied by a bowl of *petits-fours*. Coffee isn't usually included in a fixed-price menu. Brandy and liqueurs are often drunk with coffee.

Vegetarian Food

The French have a generally unsympathetic (or uncomprehending) attitude towards vegetarians (*végétarien*), who are thin on the ground, although gradually increasing in number. You need to be courageous to be a vegetarian in France, where the number of carnivores (per capita) is exceeded in Europe only in Belgium. You will constantly be asked why you're a vegetarian and have to explain that chicken, pork (including bacon pieces or *lardons*), sausage and fish are in fact types of meat (see **Vegetarian Food** on page 489). There are only a few vegetarian restaurants in the major cities, although crêperies and pizzerias usually serve vegetarian dishes and you can request vegetarian food (e.g. an omelette) as an alternative to the listed dish in most restaurants, as there's unlikely to be a vegetarian option. A useful book for vegetarians wanting to eat out is *Vegetarian France* (Vegetarian Guides/Editions La Plage), which lists over 150 vegetarian establishments, including some hotels. Vegans (*végétalien*) will find it almost impossible to eat out.

Food to Avoid?

The French have a recipe (or half a dozen) for everything that walks, crawls, slithers, jumps, swims or flies – no living thing is safe from the French cooking pot! If you're at all squeamish or fussy about what you will eat, it's wise to learn what to avoid. However, irrespective of how repulsive something may be in its natural state, the French usually contrive to make it taste (and possibly even look) delicious.

Things you may wish to avoid include frogs' legs (*cuisses de grenouilles*), snails (*escargots*), bird's wing (*aile*), little eels (*anguillette*), brain (*cervelle*), tripe (*tripes*), lung (*mou*), brawn or boar's head (*hure*), sweetbreads/pancreas (*ris* – rice is *riz*), calf's innards (*fraise de veau*), kidney (*rognon*), liver (*foie*), tongue (*langue*), pig's head/brawn (*fromage de porc/tête*), calf's head (*tête de veau*), testicles (*rognons blancs/animelles*), horsemeat (*cheval*: France is Europe's second-largest consumer of horse meat after Belgium), pig's trotters (*pieds de porc*), pig's ears (*oreilles de porc*), pig's tail (*queue de porc*), and a variety of songbirds, including blackbirds (*merles*), buntings (*ortolans*) and warblers (*beguinettes*). If you don't like garlic, avoid anything that's *à l'ail* (although it's good for you).

Wine

In France, wine is regarded as a necessary accompaniment to even the humblest of meals and in rural restaurants it's even included in fixed-price menus (most French believe that a meal without wine is like a day without sunshine, although a surprising number of French people drink no wine – or no alcohol at all). Nevertheless, the French value quality rather than quantity and will gladly stretch a good bottle between four people rather than guzzle a bottle of cheap wine each. Generally, the better the restaurant, the better the range and quality of the cellar, particularly in major wine-producing areas such as Bordeaux, Burgundy and the Rhône valley. Some restaurants offer up to 1,000 wines, while modest rural restaurants may offer just a small selection of local wines, although they usually complement the local food and are mostly good value and palatable.

If wine is included in a fixed-price menu, it's shown on the menu (*vin compris*) and includes, within reason, as much (table) wine as you want. You must pay for drinks other than wine (except tap water). When drinks are included (*boisson comprise*), you can usually choose between wine, beer or mineral water, but must usually pay for anything more than a quarter of a litre of wine or a small bottle of beer or water per head.

In restaurants serving good food, the cheapest house wine (*vin de la maison/vin du patron*) is often good. In cheaper eating-places, house wine can be ordered by the glass (*verre*) or carafe (*carafe*), which usually comes in litre, half-litre (50cl) and quarter-litre (25cl) sizes. Wine may also be served in a jug or pitcher (*pichet*). Quality wine is ordered by the half-bottle or bottle, although the cheapest bottles may be inferior to the house wine.

If there's no house wine or wine by the carafe, wine will be expensive, particularly when compared with the modest cost of the food. A bottle of wine usually costs from €12 for a quality that's probably no better than carafe wine. The cost of a good bottle of wine is generally around three times the supermarket price, although the mark-up can be even greater. This is because many restaurants make little profit on their food and must make up for it with the wine. Not surprisingly, there are no 'BYO' (bring your own wine or other drinks) restaurants. When staying in a hotel with a restaurant, it's common practice to have a bottle of wine re-corked and kept for your next meal.

Although you can drink any wine with any food (and the French, surprisingly, drink red wine with almost everything), particular wines complement certain food. The *patron(ne)* or, in a top-class restaurant, the wine waiter (*sommelier*) will be happy to suggest a wine to complement a particular dish.

Children under 14 aren't permitted to drink alcohol in a restaurant (see **Opening Hours & Licensing** on page 432).

Other Drinks

It isn't mandatory to drink wine with a meal and you can drink water (tap or mineral), beer, cider (excellent with pancakes) or nothing at all. If you want free tap water, ask for a *carafe d'eau fraîche* or *eau de robinet*, which must be provided by law, or you may be served mineral water, which you will have to pay for. (Waiters are often reluctant to bring water – particularly if it's free – and you may need to ask several times.) Drinks such as beer and mineral water have the same mark-up as wine (see above), prices depending on the brand, so beer isn't necessarily an inexpensive alternative to wine.

Opening Times

Most restaurants close one day a week, often on Sundays or Mondays, although many open every day, particularly those in tourist resorts and large cities. Always check in advance, as some restaurants close on unexpected days, e.g. Saturdays. Most restaurants also close for one or two months a year for a holiday (*fermeture annuelle*). Those in winter holiday resorts may close for part or the whole of the summer, while those in summer resorts generally close in winter. In Paris, restaurants close at various times of the year and many close for part of the annual summer evacuation in July and August (at the height of the tourist season!). Many top class Paris restaurants close for the whole of August to avoid lowering their standards for the hordes of foreign tourists.

Booking

Always book for popular restaurants, inexpensive restaurants offering exceptional value, and any restaurant in a holiday resort. Top-class restaurants (particularly those that are Michelin or Gault-Millau rated) are often booked up months ahead. If you're eating (or rather worshipping) at one of these gastronomic temples, you should reconfirm your booking the day before. It's particularly important to book or at least to arrive early, e.g. by noon, for Sunday lunch; any later and you will be lucky to find a seat at a popular restaurant.

Etiquette

Eating out in France isn't simply a matter of consuming food and wine. There are also certain niceties to be observed, including the following:

● Restaurants are generally wary of doing anything that may deter customers and, apart from a few pretentious places in Paris that insist on a jacket and tie, most don't impose dress restrictions. Most people don't dress up to eat, and smart casual dress is usually good enough for even for the best of restaurants. On the other hand, shorts and a T-shirt are not *de rigueur*.

● You should wait to be seated by a waiter or the proprietor in any establishment. Many people smoke throughout a meal (or between each course) and you should ask to be seated in a non-smoking area if you don't want to be bothered by cigarette smoke. If applicable, check in advance that a restaurant has a proper non-smoking area and not merely a corner of the main room.

- It's considered bad manners (particularly by waiters) to call a waiter *garçon*. They should be called *monsieur*, and waitresses *madame* or *mademoiselle* (if obviously young). Snapping your fingers to attract the waiter's attention is also frowned upon; you should merely raise a hand and say *s'il vous plaît*. When you wish to pay the bill, ask for *l'addition*.

- Not all restaurants accept credit cards, and you should check in advance if you intend to pay by credit card.

- Somewhat surprisingly, dogs are permitted in most restaurants, although you should check first.

Information

There are innumerable publications relating to French restaurants. Two invaluable books for gourmets (and gourmands) are the *Michelin Red Guide* (see page 401) and the *Gault-Millau Guide de la France*. The *Gault-Millau* (published only in French) is primarily a restaurant guide but includes a selection of hotels. It isn't as comprehensive as the *Michelin Red Guide* but makes up for it with its mouth-watering descriptions of gastronomic delights on offer. The annual *Guide des Relais Routiers* is a guide to the excellent *Relais Routiers* inexpensive roadside restaurants (or transport cafés) found throughout France. Guides to local restaurants are published in all areas and are available free from tourist offices.

A priceless little book packed with useful information and containing an excellent dictionary of menu terms is *The Pocket Guide to French Food and Wine* by Tessa Youell & George Kimball (Carbery). *Bon Appétit* by Judith White (Peppercorn) is a handy, pocket-size menu dictionary.

LIBRARIES

France isn't well provided with libraries (*bibliothèque – librairie* is a book shop) and has a poor library service compared, for example, with the UK and the US. Most French people don't do a lot of reading and most homes possess few books (a 2003 survey revealed that 44 per cent of French people didn't buy books and 39 per cent didn't even read them!). Consequently libraries aren't popular. However, libraries have improved in the last ten years, particularly the semi-private *bibliothèques pour tous*, and many have metamorphosed into *médiathèques*, offering audio-visual material as well as books. Most libraries have photocopy machines.

Paris is better served than most cities, with over 50 public libraries open from Tuesdays to Saturdays, many with a selection of English-language books. Paris also boasts the Bibliothèque d'Information Publique in the Centre Georges Pompidou and the Bibliothèque Nationale, both of which are free (although the latter is open only to graduate students and bona fide researchers), as well as the new Bibliothèque de France, which isn't free. The Bibliothèque Nationale (☎ 01 53 79 59 59, 🖳 http://www.bnf.fr) contains a copy of every book published in France. The Bibliothèque de

France is the world's largest library. It covers 365,000m^2 (almost 4m square feet) and houses some 12m volumes. A day pass costs €3 and the library is open Tuesdays to Saturdays from 10.00 to 19.00, and from 12.00 to 18.00 on Sundays.

In addition to public libraries there are private libraries in Paris and other major cities. The American Library in Paris (🖥 http://www.americanlibraryinparis.org) is open Tuesdays to Saturdays from 10.00 to 19.00 and houses the largest collection of English-language books in France. Annual membership costs €96 for individuals (there are reductions for children, teenagers, students and the unemployed) and €150 for families; day membership is available for €11 (€8 for students and the unemployed). The British Council in Paris (🖥 http://www.britishcouncil.org) closed its lending library in June 2002 but still operates a 'Knowledge and Learning Centre' (open Mondays to Fridays from 14.00 to 18.00). Other English-language libraries in Paris include the Benjamin Franklin Documentation Centre and the Canadian Embassy Special Library.

If you're lucky enough to find a library in a small town (some have a visiting 'bibliobus'), it will usually have limited opening hours (perhaps no more than ten hours per week), a poor selection of books and probably nothing in foreign languages.

Many libraries are reference (*consultation sur place*) rather than lending libraries and don't allow members to borrow books. Often you don't have direct access to books but must complete a form describing what you want. It can take as long as 20 minutes to obtain a book, which is collected from a distribution point. (As with most things that are publicly funded in France, the system is designed to keep the maximum number of civil servants in 'employment'.)

When you're allowed to borrow books, you need a library membership card (for which there may be an annual charge). An identity document and a photograph are required, as well as proof of your address, e.g. an electricity bill showing your current address. Under 18s require parental authorisation. Some reference libraries insist that you register and obtain a membership card just to enter and look at books.

DAY & EVENING CLASSES

Adult day and evening classes are run by various organisations in all cities and large towns and even in many small towns and villages. In addition to formal adult and further education (see page 208), day and evening classes offer courses and lectures in everything from astrology to zoology. The range and variety of subjects offered is endless and includes French and foreign languages, handicrafts, hobbies and sports, and business-related courses.

Many expatriate clubs and organisations organise day and evening classes in a variety of subjects. These include the Women's Institute for Continuing Education (☎ 01 45 66 75 50). Some expatriate organisations provide classes for children (e.g. English), particularly during school holidays. French universities run non-residential language and other courses during the summer holiday period.

Among the most popular classes with foreigners are those concerned with cooking (and eating), which have enjoyed increasing popularity in recent years. Most courses are taught by master chefs in their own kitchens and vary from a weekend to a week. Some courses take you through everything from buying food at markets to devising the menu, selecting the wine and cheese and, of course, preparing and cooking the food. Others teach students about good food and wine through savouring the results of someone else's labour, rather than slaving over a hot stove (much more enjoyable). A full list of companies offering cookery courses and gastronomic breaks is included in the *Reference Guide to Travellers in France* available from the French Tourist Office. The most famous French cookery school is the École Cordon Bleu (☎ 01 53 68 22 50, 🖥 http://www.cordonbleu.edu). Many famous French chefs have founded cookery schools, including Auguste Escoffier, Michel Guérard, Roger Vergé and Paul Bocuse, whose website (🖥 http://www.bocuse.fr) includes a history of French cuisine as well as a few of his recipes.

Adult further education programmes are published in many cities and regions, and include courses organised by local training and education centres. Local newspapers also contain details of evening and day courses. See also **Further Education** on page 208 and **Language Schools** on page 209.

16.

<u>Sports</u>

Sports facilities in France are generally good, although sometimes lacking in some rural areas. France isn't generally noted for its famous sportsmen and recreational sports don't play an important part in most French lives. School and university sports are low key compared with many other countries and schools aren't the breeding ground for professional sportspeople that they often are abroad. However, an increasing number of people have taken up sports and regular exercise in recent years, as the fashion for a healthy lifestyle has gathered momentum.

With a few exceptions, when participating in sports the French generally prefer solo sports to team sports. Among the most popular sports are *boules*, cycling, fishing, hiking, horse riding, hunting, swimming, tennis and skiing. France is a mecca for watersports enthusiasts and canoeing, sailing, waterskiing, surfing and windsurfing have a large following, as do aerial sports such as microlighting, hang-gliding, para-gliding and gliding. In fact, France recently topped a survey (conducted by American Express Travel) of countries boasting facilities for outdoor activities. Basketball, football (soccer) and rugby are popular, although most people prefer to watch rather than participate. The most popular spectator event is the annual *Tour de France* cycle race (see page 454).

When the French decide to take a sport seriously they do it with a vengeance, as is the case with skiing and tennis, where France has unrivalled facilities. The latest sport to get similar treatment is golf, which although still exclusive, is one of the fastest growing sports in France. Many less well-known sports are popular in the summer in the French Alps and the Pyrenees, including rock climbing, white water rafting, glacier skiing, mountain biking, grass skiing and off-road driving.

Participation in many sports is expensive, although costs can be reduced through season tickets or annual membership or by joining a club. Fashion is very important in France and whether you're skiing, playing tennis or sailing, it's more important to look the part than perform like a champion.

Gymnasiums & Health Clubs

Health clubs have mushroomed in recent years, and there are gymnasiums (*gymnase*) and health clubs (*club de forme*) in most towns. Most have swimming pools, saunas, Jacuzzis and steam baths as well as the usual expensive bone-jarring, muscle-wrenching apparatus. Fees are from around €80 per month or €250 to €750 per year, plus a registration fee. Most clubs permit visitors, although there's usually a high hourly or daily fee. Some clubs are small and extremely crowded, particularly during lunch hours and early evenings. Some first-class hotels have fitness rooms. Gym, training and exercise classes are provided by sports centres and clubs throughout France and these often charge reasonable fees (e.g. €3 per session).

Information

The French Government Tourist Office (FGTO – see page 402) and other tourist offices are an excellent source of sports information. The FGTO publishes a free brochure, *France for Active Holidays*, describing many of France's sporting attractions. Many specialist publications promoting sporting events and listing local sports venues are available from regional and local tourist offices. Sports fans may be interested in the all-sports daily newspaper *L'Équipe*, which publishes fixtures, results and details of all sporting events in France, plus major events abroad.

AERIAL SPORTS

France has a historical and abiding passion for aviation; from the Montgolfier brothers and Blériot to Concorde, the Arianne rockets and the Airbus, it has always been at the leading edge of aeronautics. The love affair extends to all aerial sports, including light-aircraft flying, gliding, hang-gliding, paragliding, parachuting, sky-diving and ballooning. The most important assets for aerial sports enthusiasts are madness and money, both required in abundance.

The Alps and Pyrenees are excellent venues for aerial sports, particularly hang-gliding (*delta plane*) and paragliding (*parapente*), due to the updrafts and the low density of air traffic. Paragliding, which entails jumping off a steep mountain slope with a parachute, is technically easier than hang-gliding. The Pyrenees are reckoned to be the best mountains in Europe for paragliding, with their warm summers and wide valleys. Participants must complete an approved course of instruction, after which they receive a proficiency certificate and are permitted to go solo.

There are flying clubs at most airfields, where light aircraft and gliders can be hired. Parachuting and freefall parachuting (sky-diving) flights can also be made from many private airfields. The south of France is an excellent place to learn to fly, as flying is rarely interrupted by bad weather. The latest American craze to have (literally) taken off in France is microlight (*ultra-léger motorisé/ULM*) flying. A microlight (or ultralight) is a low-flying go-cart consisting of a hang glider attached to a lawn-mower engine, and is one of the cheapest (and noisiest) ways to experience powered flight. For further information contact the Aéro-club de France (☎ 01 47 23 72 72, 🖳 http://www.aeroclub.com) or the Fédération Française de Vol à Voile (☎ 01 45 44 04 78, 🖳 http://www.ffvv.org).

The first manned flight was made in France in 1783 by Pilatre de Rozier and the Marquis d'Arlandes in a hot-air balloon designed by the brothers Montgolfier (hot-air balloons are still referred to as *montgolfières*), and ballooning remains popular. There are balloon meetings throughout France, particularly in summer. It's an expensive sport, however, and participation is generally limited to the wealthy, although you can enjoy a flight (in someone else's balloon) for around €150.

Those who prefer to keep their feet *sur le plancher des vaches* may like to try kite-flying, which has increased dramatically in popularity in recent years in Europe. A huge nylon kite can cost €4,000 or more, although more modest kites can be bought for a few euros. The biggest European kite-flying festival is held in Dieppe.

BOULES

Boules has been unkindly referred to as a 'glorified game of marbles', probably by some poor foreign loser. There are in fact three principal games of *boules* (which is also the word used for the balls themselves): *boules lyonnaise*, *pétanque* and *le jeu provençal* (or *La Longue*), from which *pétanque* derived. In *le jeu provençal*, which is still played in Provence, players take three running steps before 'shooting' and the game is played on a pitch (*piste* or *terrain*) measuring 21m by 15m (68ft by 49ft). *Boules lyonnaise* is also played on a large pitch and with larger *boules* than the more popular *pétanque*, which uses a pitch measuring 10m by 6m (33ft by 20ft) and requires the player to keep his feet together when throwing. (The word *pétanque* derives from *pieds tanqués*, southern dialect for 'feet together', and the game supposedly originated when one Jules Le Noir, a champion *jeu provençal* player from La Ciotat, a little port between Marseille and Toulon, was confined to a wheelchair as a result of an accident and was therefore unable to take a run-up.) It's generally recognised that *pétanque* is easier to play, as no special playing area is required and the rules are simpler.

There are also a number of regional variations of *boules* – there's even a game played in central France using square *boules* (*boules de fort*)! (The British claim that the *boules* derives from a game invented in the UK and played with cannon balls and that it was a game of *boules* and not bowls that Sir Francis Drake famously refused to interrupt when informed of the impending arrival of the Spanish Armada.)

For most people, *pétanque* is a pastime or social game rather than a serious sport. However, it managed to earn recognition as an Olympic demonstration 'sport' in the Barcelona Olympics in 1992 and even has World Championships, which are held in Marseille. It's played throughout France, but particularly in the south, where most village squares have a pitch (*piste*) and many towns have a special arena called a *boulodrome*. It isn't unusual, however, to find people playing on almost any patch of ground – even in the middle of the road! The more uneven the surface the better, although grass is totally unsuitable. The other essential requirement is an unlimited supply of *pastis*.

Boules is usually played by two teams of two (*doublettes*) or three (*triplettes*) players (a singles match is a *tête à tête* or head-to-head). A member of the starting team throws a small wooden marker ball or jack, called the *cochonnet* ('piglet' in French, although many other names are used in different areas), up the pitch, between 6m and 10m (20 to 33ft) from the throwing point. The object is for players to pitch their balls as close to the *cochonnet* as possible.

Players have a choice of two shots: *pointer*, to get as close to the *cochonnet* as possible; and *tirer*, to scatter their opponents' *boules* to all corners of the land (which is quite legitimate). The thrower stands in a circle 35 to 50cm (14 to 20in) in diameter – just large enough for both feet – and launches his *boule* from a standing or crouching position.

After one player from each team has thrown, the next thrower is decided by whose *boule* finished closer to the *cochonnet*. The team further from the *cochonnet* continues to throw until they get a closer *boule* than the other team or until they have no more *boules*, and so on until both teams have thrown all their *boules*. The team whose *boule* (or *boules*) lies closest to the *cochonnet* wins the 'end'. When *boules* are too close to call, their distances from the *cochonnet* are measured (roughly with the feet, twigs or bits of string, or accurately with measuring tapes or specially designed devices depending on the seriousness of the game). One point is earned for each *boule* lying closer to the *cochonnet* than the closest *boule* of the opposing team. For example, if the three closest *boules* belong to the same team, they earn three points. A player on the winning team then starts the next end (usually from the opposite end of the pitch) by throwing the *cochonnet*.

A match continues until a team scores 13 points (a *partie*). A second or return match in a series of three is called *la revanche* and, when each side has won one match, the deciding match is called *la belle*.

You can buy sets of (six) plastic *boules*, but they're just for children and tourists. Serious players play with stainless steel *boules*, which (for competition use) must have their weight (in grammes) and the manufacturer's registration number stamped on them. There are a variety of finishes, weights and even colours of *boules*, so take advice before buying a set. Those who find bending a problem can buy a magnetic device to pick up their *boules* while standing (although standing can also be a problem after a surfeit of *pastis*). In a singles or doubles game, each player has three *boules* (two each in triples).

In the last decade, the number of registered *boules* players has doubled and the Fédération Française de Pétanque (FFP, ☎ 04 91 14 05 80, 🖥 http://www.petanque.fr) now has over 500,000 members. Although traditionally a male dominated game, many young players now are female. Beware of hustlers and **never** play locals for money!

CLIMBING & CAVING

Those who find hiking a bit tame may like to try mountaineering (*alpinisme*), rock-climbing, caving or pot-holing, all of which are popular in France. France has the best rock-climbing and some of the best mountaineering 'facilities' in Europe. The French have always been avid climbers and France has some of the world's leading exponents. A new mountain sport is 'canyoning' (*canyoning*), which is rapidly gaining popularity. It combines abseiling down rock faces with sliding down gentler slopes and jumping into rock pools. A safety helmet and wetsuit are essential, a qualified instructor recommended and a love of getting cold and wet desirable.

If you're an inexperienced climber, it's advisable to join a club and 'learn the ropes' before heading for the mountains. You will also need a guide when climbing in an unfamiliar area, particularly when climbing glaciers (don't, however, follow your guide too closely – if he falls down a crevice, it isn't necessary to accompany him!). Mountain guides are available in the main climbing areas, including Briançon, La Chapelle, Embrun, La Grave and Pelvoux for the high Alps; Chamonix and St-Gervais for the Savoie-Dauphiné (Chamonix is the centre of French climbing and its Compagnie des Guides is renowned as the world's oldest – established 1821 – and best association of mountain guides); Gavarnie, Luchon and Saint-Lary for the mid-Pyrenees; and Bastia for Corsica. Guides are available at mountaineering schools and in many smaller resorts and should be members of the International Federation of Mountain Guides Associations (IFMGA, known in French as the UIAGM and in German as the IVBV, 🖥 http://www.ivbv.info), which has strict standards. If you find a guide other than through a recognised school or club, you should make sure that he's qualified.

Many climbers lose their lives each year in France, many of them inexperienced and reckless (or just plain stupid). Many more owe their survival to rescuers, who risk their own lives to save them. Mont Blanc, Western Europe's highest peak at 4,800m (15,780ft), has seen a record number of deaths in recent years and over 1,000 in the last 20 years. **Needless to say, it's highly dangerous to venture into the mountains without proper preparation, excellent physical condition, adequate training, the appropriate equipment *and* an experienced guide.**

Information

Information about climbing clubs is available from the Club Alpin Français, officially called the Fédération Française des Clubs Alpins et de Montagne (FFCAM, ☎ 01 53 72 87 00, 🖥 http://www.ffcam.fr).

CYCLING

France is one of Europe's foremost cycling countries, and cycling is both a serious sport and a relaxing pastime. French motorists usually give cyclists a wide berth when overtaking (apart from Parisians, who respect nobody else's right to use the road), although tourists aren't always so generous, particularly those towing caravans. Bicycles aren't expensive in France, where you can buy an 18-gear racing bike for around €250 and a 'shopping' bike for around €150. Mountain bikes (*vélo tout terrain/VTT*) with 21 or more gears cost as little as €100 (children's mountain bikes cost from around €80) and can be bought in supermarkets and hypermarkets. An 'all-purpose' bicycle, called a *vélo tout chemin/VTC*, can be bought for around €200. Serious bikers can pay up to €4,000 for a *VTT* and €6,000 for a racing machine. Mountain biking is a serious sport in France with sponsored events and even professional riders. There are *VTT* bike trails in many areas, although bikes aren't permitted on hiking tracks.

Safety & Security

Cycling in Paris and other cities can be dangerous and isn't recommended (except perhaps on Sunday mornings between 05.00 and 06.00). Cyclists must use cycle lanes (*piste cyclable*) where provided (there are few in France) and mustn't cycle in bus lanes or on footpaths. If you cycle in cities, you should wear reflective clothing, protective head gear, a smog mask and a crucifix. It isn't necessary to wear expensive sports clothing when cycling (although French cyclists invariably do), but a light crash helmet is advisable, particularly for children. Head injuries are the main cause of death in bicycle accidents, most of which don't involve accidents with automobiles but are a result of colliding with fixed objects, or falls. Always buy a quality helmet that has been approved and subjected to rigorous testing.

Cycles must be roadworthy and fitted with a horn or bell and front and rear lights. You should buy an anti-theft device such as a steel cable or chain with a lock. If your bicycle is stolen you should report it to the local police, but don't expect them to find it.

Take particular care on busy roads and don't allow your children onto public roads until they're experienced riders. A cyclists' safety manual, specifically aimed at children, is available from La Prévention Routière (☎ 01 44 15 27 00, 🖳 http://www. preventionroutiere.asso.fr).

Transporting & Renting Bikes

The government (which owns the national railway company) is keen to encourage cycling and many trains are equipped with bicycle areas. You can travel with your bicycle (as 'hand' baggage) on any day of the week on over 2,000 short-distance trains, marked with a bicycle symbol in timetables (subject to space). In many regions, e.g. the Ile-de-France, you can transport your bicycle free at any time on Saturdays, Sundays and public holidays, and during off-peak times on other days, i.e. between 09.30 and 16.30 and from 19.00 to 06.30; you're responsible for loading and unloading it from the luggage van. Bicycles must be sent separately on most long-distance trains and must usually be registered for each journey (delivery usually takes around five days). They can be insured during transportation and can also be delivered to your home. If your bicycle is demountable (to no more than 1.2m x 0.9m), you can transport it free on *Corail* trains and *TGV*s. If it isn't, transport is free on *Corail* and *TER* trains if there's a bicycle area but otherwise costs €45. To take your bicycle on Eurostar costs €24. As a provisional security measure (*vigi-pirate*), the SNCF no longer stores bicycles, but bars near a station may offer this facility for a small charge.

Bicycles can be rented from over 200 SNCF stations in the principal tourist regions, particularly on the coasts. The SNCF usually provides three types of bicycle: a traditional bicycle with a 'unisex' frame, adjustable seat and handlebars, with or without gears; a touring model with ten speeds, with either a unisex or a men's frame; and a mountain bike with 18 or 21 gears. The rates for one or two days are around €8 per day for a traditional bike and around €10 per day for a touring or mountain bike (there are reductions for longer periods). You must show a passport or driving licence and pay a deposit of around €150 for a traditional bike and €225 for touring or mountain bikes. Payment can be made in cash, by cheque or by credit card at certain stations, when no deposit is necessary. Payment is made when you return the bike, which can be to the station you rented it from or any other station renting bikes. Bikes can be booked. A list of stations where you can rent a bike is contained in a brochure, *Guide Train + Vélo*, available from SNCF stations. Some *métro* and RER stations in Paris also rent bikes.

Bicycles can also be rented from bicycle shops (*marchand de vélos*) in Paris and other cities and towns, but it's expensive, e.g. from €4 per hour in Paris or €15 per day (around double the rate charged by the SNCF).

Tour de France & Other Events

The *Tour de France* is the ultimate challenge on wheels and is probably the toughest sporting event in the world. It's also France's and the world's largest annual sporting event and is watched by some 20m people along the route. It has its own radio station, bank and telephone exchange, and is administered by a 3,000-strong organisation team. The *Tour de France* is held in July and consists of three weeks of cycling (around 100 hours), covering as much as 4,000km (2,175mi) on the toughest roads in France and its neighbouring countries (there have even been stages in England and Ireland). The route and length of the race changes each year, with towns paying handsomely to be a 'stage town', but it always finishes on the Champs-Elysées in Paris. The race leaders wear various distinctive jerseys, including a yellow jersey (*maillot jaune*) for the overall race leader, a green jersey (*maillot vert*) for the most consistent rider, and a white jersey with red polka dots (*maillot à pois*) for the 'King of the mountains'.

France has other important road races, including the Paris-Nice in March. Professional track racing is also popular and includes the *Six Jours Cycliste de Paris*.

Associations & Clubs

Keen cyclists may wish to join the Fédération Française de CycloTourisme (FFCT), 12 rue Louis Bertrand, 94207 Ivry-sur-Seine Cedex (💻 http://www.ffct.org) or the Fédération Française de Cyclisme (FFC, ☎ 01 49 35 69 00, 💻 http://www.ffc.fr). The FFCT sells a wide range of articles for cyclists, including maps, books, camping carnets and cycling accessories. There are cycling clubs in all medium to large towns. Cycling tours are arranged in most cities and many tourist areas. When going on a day tour or longer, take drinks, first-aid and tool kits, a puncture repair outfit and a good map. Among the best maps for cycling are the Michelin yellow maps (scale: 1cm = 2km).

Information

Many books are written for cyclists, including *Cycling France* by Jerry H. Simpson (Bicycle Books), *Cycle Touring in France* by Richard Neillands (Oxford Illustrated Press), *France by Bike* by Karen and Terry Whitehill (Cordee) and *Cycling in France* by Susi Madron (George Philip), who also operates the UK's largest French cycling holiday company, Cycling for Softies (☎ 0161-248 8282, 💻 http://www.cycling-for-softies.co.uk).

FISHING

Although not particularly well known internationally, France is a paradise for fishermen, with over 4,800km (3,000mi) of coastline, 240,000km (150,000mi) of rivers and streams, and 120,000ha (300,000 acres) of lakes and ponds. There's excellent fishing in rivers, lakes and ponds throughout France, many of which are stocked annually with trout, grayling and pike. Fishing (*pêche*) is enjoyed regularly by around 4m French people and irregularly by some 20 per cent of the population, and is claimed by many to be France's national sport (football fans would disagree).

Fishing is permitted on beaches and other public areas of seafront but not in ports, and there are restrictions on the type of equipment you may use and the kind of fish you may catch (e.g. you aren't allowed to catch young fish); the amount of shellfish (especially sea urchins and oysters) you may gather is strictly limited. For details, contact the regional Direction des Affaires Maritimes (a list of regulations can be found on 🖥 http://www.mer.equipement.gouv.fr/administration/02_serv_prox/ 01_dram_ddam/directions_regionales.htm).

Rivers are divided into two categories. The first category (*première catégorie* or *salmonidés dominants*) covers headwaters and rivers suitable for salmon, trout and grayling, where maggots are banned as bait. The second category (*deuxième catégorie* or *salmonidés non dominants*) usually includes the lower stretches of rivers populated mainly by coarse fish, where bait can include practically anything except fish-eggs.

Almost all inland waters, from the tiniest stream to the largest rivers and lakes, are protected fishing areas. Fishing rights may be owned by a private landowner, a fishing club or the state, as described below. Wherever you fish, however, you must pay a fishing tax (*taxe piscicole*) by means of a *timbre fiscal* (obtainable from tobacconists'), which varies between €10.50 and €41 depending on the type of water and the kind of fishing (e.g. you pay more to fish salmon, which are now rare in French rivers). You can pay a supplement of €15 to use your permit in another area (a scheme known as *réciprocité*). A permit known as a *vignette UPIF* is available for all fishing in the Ile-de-France region, costing €25. Permits are sold by fishing tackle shops, who can also advise you of the best local fishing spots, and in some cases by local cafés. Always carry your fishing permit with you, as wardens (who patrol most waters) may ask to see it.

To obtain a permit to fish state-controlled water, you must in effect join a recognised fishing association, which will issue your *carte de pêche* as part of an annual membership. For a list of associations, ask at a tackle shop or contact the Union Nationale pour la Pêche en France (☎ 01 48 24 96 00, 🖥 http://www.unpf.fr). There are various types of *carte de pêche*, including the following (valid for a year unless otherwise stated):

- *Carte complète* for fishing using all methods in category 1 and 2 waters.

- *Carte réduite* for fishing using certain methods only in category 2 waters only.

- *Carte exonéré* for fishing using only a hand-held rod in category 1 and 2 waters.

- *Carte vacances* for fishing using all methods in category 1 and 2 waters for 15 days.

- *Carte journalière* for fishing using all methods in category 2 and certain category 1 waters for one day.

Stretches of a river are often divided between local clubs, and anglers must join a local fishing club to fish there. In addition to club fees, you may have to pay an annual fee (e.g. €15 to €30) to the local federation of clubs. You need a passport-size photograph for your membership card.

Signs such as *pêche réservée/gardée* are common and denote private fishing. Many of the best fishing waters are in private hands, although it may be possible to obtain permission to fish from the owners.

The fishing season varies with the area and type of fish, but is typically from around 1st March to 15th September for category 1 waters and from 15th January to 15th April for category 2. Fishing regulations vary from department to department, but you're generally permitted to fish from half an hour before sunrise until half an hour after sunset; night fishing is forbidden on all rivers (although permitted in certain lakes and ponds). There are limits on catches in most areas. Boats can be hired on inland waters and from sea ports, where deep-sea fishing expeditions are organised. Sea fishing is better in the Atlantic than the Mediterranean.

Information

Further information can be obtained from the Conseil Supérieur de la Pêche (☎ 01 45 14 36 00, 🖳 http://www.csp.ecologie.gouv.fr) or the Union Nationale pour la Pêche en France (see above). Various websites offer information about fishing in France, including 🖳 http://www.peche-direct.com and (for trout fishers) 🖳 http://www.pechetruite.com). A brochure, *Angling in France*, is available from the FGTO (see page 402). Information about local fishing areas and fishing permits is available from local tourist offices and town halls. There are a number of books on fishing in France, including *Pêche Française* by Phil Pembroke.

FOOTBALL

Association football or soccer (*le foot*) is generally reckoned to be France's national sport (except by *boules* players and fishermen), with over 7m players, and the country has firmly established itself as a major force in recent years, winning the World Cup in 1998 and reaching the final in 2006.

At club level, France has had little European glory, however, the most successful 'French' team recently being Monaco. The French soccer league has four divisions, and teams also take part in a national cup competition (*coupe de France*). The first division has 18 teams and top clubs include Auxerre, Bordeaux, Marseille and Paris Saint-Germain (and Monaco). Football takes a break from Christmas Eve until the end of January, in common with many other European countries. French clubs import many foreign players, mostly from Africa, although it also loses its best players to foreign (particularly English) clubs. In recent years, a number of first division clubs have run up huge debts and some have even been relegated as a result. Amateur football is widely played and there are clubs and leagues in all departments.

Information

Further information is available from the Fédération Française de Football (☎ 01 44 31 73 00, 💻 http://www.fff.fr) and, at local level, from town halls and *mairies*.

GOLF

Golf is one of the fastest growing sports in France, where there are over 200,000 registered players and the second highest number of golf courses (over 500) in Europe after the UK, the majority of which were built in the last decade. The largest number of golf clubs are found in Normandy (especially the department of Calvados), Brittany (especially Ille-et-Vilaine), the south-west (especially Gironde), the Côte d'Azur (especially Alpes-Maritimes and Var) and the Paris region, where there are no fewer than 24 courses in the department of Yvelines. Many courses have magnificent settings (seaside, mountain and forest) and many are linked with property developments. Properties on or near golf clubs, which may include life membership, are becoming increasingly popular with foreigners seeking a permanent or second home.

According to the *Peugeot Guide to Europe's Top 1,000 Golf Courses*, the following are France's ten 'best' courses:

- **Les Bordes** (Loir-et-Cher, 💻 http://www.lesbordes.com);

- **Golf de Chantilly** (Oise, 💻 http://www.golfdechantilly.com);

- **Le Kempferhof** (Bas-Rhin, 💻 http://www.golf-kempferhof.com);

- **Golf du Médoc** (Gironde, 💻 http://www.golf-du-medoc.com);

- **L'Albatros** (Yvelines, 💻 http://www.golf-national.com);

- **Spérone Golf Club** (Corse-du-Sud, 💻 http://www.sperone.com);

- **Golf Club Barbaroux** (Var, 💻 http://www.barbaroux.com);

- **Golf International de Soufflenheim** (Bas-Rhin, 💻 http://www.golfclub-soufflenheim.com);

- **Four Seasons Golf Club Provence at Terre Blanche** (Var, 💻 http://www.fourseasons.com/provence);

- **Golf Hotel de Seignosse** (Landes, 💻 http://www.golfseignosse.com).

Due to the relatively small number of players, golf is a more relaxed game in France than in many other countries and queues are virtually unknown. Many players treat the game as a leisurely stroll after lunch. Dress regulations are almost non-existent.

There are courses to suit all standards and green fees are low in comparison with many other European countries (particularly the UK). In fact, most golfers prefer to pay and play than to pay an annual membership fee. Most courses require a minimum handicap (e.g. 24 for men and 28 for women, although some are as high as 35 for both sexes). Green fees may vary with the season, e.g. €30 to €40 (for 18 holes) during high season and as little as €15 in low season. Fees at clubs are higher at weekends and on public holidays than during the week.

Golf holidays are popular and are a major source of revenue for golf clubs. Most courses welcome visitors and some clubs have special rates for groups. A golf pass is available in some areas and allows visitors to play at a number of courses in a particular area.

Most clubs have driving ranges (known as *practices*!), practice greens, bunker practice areas, a clubhouse (possibly a *château*), restaurant and bar. Many clubs are combined with country or sporting clubs boasting a luxury hotel, restaurant, swimming pool, gymnasium, tennis courts, billiards, croquet and *boules*. You can hire golf clubs, a golf trolley (around €3 per round) at all clubs and possibly a golf buggy (€25 to €30 per round or €45 per day). In major cities, there are indoor driving ranges where membership costs from €70 to €100 per month or €300 to €500 per year.

France hosts a number of international golf tournaments as part of the European tour, including the French Open, the Mediterranean Open, the Cannes Open and the Lâncome Trophy.

Information

For more information about golf contact the Féderation Française de Golf (☎ 01 41 49 77 00, 🖳 http://www.ffgolf.org). A free magazine, *Golf in France*, is published by Regional Golf (☎ 01761-472468, 🖳 http://www.regionalgolf.net). Useful websites for golfers are 🖳 http://www.golf.com.fr and 🖳 http://www.backspin.com, the latter providing detailed information (in English as well as French) about every course in France. The Institut Géographique National (IGN) publishes a general golf map of France (ref. 910).

HIKING & RUNNING

France has some of the finest hiking (*tourisme pédestre*) areas in western Europe. Almost nowhere else offers the combination of good weather, variety of terrain and outstanding beauty that's commonplace in France. Spring and autumn are the best seasons for hiking, when the weather is cooler and the routes less crowded, although the best time for mountain flowers is between May and August. There are pleasant walks in all regions but most serious walkers head for the Alps, Pyrenees, Vosges, Auvergne and Jura mountains. France has six national parks, all with an inner zone where building, camping and hunting are prohibited, and 85 state-run natural reserves created to preserve the most-threatened areas of national heritage, which are ideal for hikers.

France has the finest network of walking trails in Europe, including some 30,000km (18,600mi) of footpaths known as *Grande Randonnée* (*GR*). The *GR* network was started in 1947 and has since been expanded into every corner of

France under the guidance of the Fédération Française de la Randonnée Pédestre (FFRP), Sentiers et Randonnée (☎ 01 44 89 93 93, 🖳 http://www.ffrp.asso.fr). The FFRP issues permits and provides insurance, although these aren't compulsory. A *GR de pays* is a country walk and a *Promenade Randonnée* (*PR*) a one-day or weekend excursion from a *GR*.

Routes are marked with white/red or yellow/red bars on trees, rocks, walls and posts. Trails are mostly public and are accessible to all over ten years old. Among the longest trails are the 605km (375mi) *GR1* (*Sentier Tour de l'Ile de France*), circling Paris, and the 800km (500mi) *GR65* (*Sentier St Jacques*) following the old pilgrim route to Santiago de Compostela from Le Puy. One of France's most famous long-distance walks is the *Tour de Mont Blanc*, a two-week ramble around the famous mountain. It begins in Chamonix and runs through France, Switzerland and Italy before returning to the Vallée Blanche.

In mountain areas there are refuge huts on the main *GR* routes, although these are usually open only in summer. They're basic but much better than being stranded in a storm. The cost is around €10 per night or less if you're a member of a climbing association or a club affiliated to the Club Alpin Français (☎ 01 53 72 87 13, 🖳 http://www.ffcam.fr). More comfortable accommodation is provided by France's 130 *RandoPlume* establishments – B&Bs conveniently located for hikers.

There are hiking clubs in most areas, all of which organise local walks, usually on Sundays. Local footpaths include forest paths (*routes forestières*) and 'little walks' (*petites randonnées*), usually between 2km and 11km.

Orienteering

Orienteering (a cross-country race where competitors use a map and a compass to navigate between control points, visited in sequence) is a popular sport in France. It can be enjoyed as a competitive sport or as a leisure activity for all ages. Ask the FGTO (see page 402) or a local hiking club for information. There are several variations, including cross-country skiing, mountain-biking and even snow-shoeing.

Hash House Harriers

Those who don't take their exercise too seriously may like to join the Hash House Harriers, which describes itself as 'the drinking club with a running problem' and aims to promote physical fitness (particularly among older people) in a relaxed atmosphere. The Hash House Harriers (which has nothing to do with drugs) originated in 1938 in Kuala Lumpur and now has over 2,350 groups in 200 countries. French clubs include those in Paris, Saint-Cloud, Grenoble and Toulouse, on the Côte d'Azur and at Canigou in Pyrénées-Orientales. 'Runs' (you don't have to!) are held once a week, at the weekend or in the evening, and last around an hour, culminating in strange rituals. Both sexes and all ages run together. There's a small fee for refreshments (usually beer).

Safety

When hiking in France (or anywhere else) you should observe the following guidelines, which may help you survive a walk on the wild side.

- Don't over-exert yourself, particularly at high altitudes, where the air is thinner; mountain sickness usually occurs only above 4,000m (13,000ft) but can happen at lower altitudes. It's easy to underestimate the duration or degree of difficulty of a hike. Start slowly and build up to those weekend marathons. If you're unfit, use chair-lifts and cable-cars to get to high altitudes.

- Never attempt a major hike alone, as it's too dangerous. Notify someone about your route and destination, and your estimated time of return. Check the conditions along your route and the times of any public transport connections, and take into account the time required for both ascents and descents. If you're unable to return by the time expected, let somebody know (if possible). If you realise you will be unable to reach your destination, e.g. due to tiredness or bad weather, turn back in good time or take a shorter route.

- Check the local weather forecast (see page 513). Generally, the higher the altitude, the more unpredictable the weather. If you're caught in a heavy storm, descend as quickly as possible or seek protection. Even if you're setting out in fine weather, it's wise to take a cagoule (K-way) with you.

- Hiking, even in lowland areas, can be dangerous, so don't take unnecessary risks. There are enough natural hazards, including bad weather, rockfalls, avalanches, rough terrain, snow and ice, and wet grass, without adding to them by carelessness. Don't walk on closed tracks at any time (they're signposted). This is particularly important in the spring, when there may be a danger of avalanches or rockfalls. If in doubt about whether a particular route is open, ask at the local tourist office.

- Take sun protection, for example a hat, sunglasses, and barrier cream. This is particularly important if you're hiking at high altitude, where you will burn more easily due to the thinner air. Use a total sunblock on your lips, nose and eyelids, and take a scarf or handkerchief to protect your neck. You will also need to protect yourself against ticks and mosquitos in some areas.

- Take a water bottle and, if possible, a mobile phone, in case you get into difficulties.

- Wherever you walk in France, be alert for savage dogs. In rural areas it seems that almost everyone keeps a fierce dog to deter unwelcome strangers (many are no doubt warm and cuddly when you get to know them, but it pays not to take chances). Carry a stick or walking cane to defend yourself (pointing it at a dog is usually enough to prevent it attacking you). Don't venture too far off the path during the hunting season, when you risk being shot.

- If you're gathering mushrooms, present them to your local chemist, who's also an official 'mushroom inspector'. Some species are deadly poisonous and people die each year from eating them.

Information

The basic source of information for the *GR* network is the Institut Géographique National (IGN) map number 903 (*Sentiers de Grandes Randonnée*), showing all *GR* trails. The FFRP (see above) publishes a series of topographic guides (*Topo-guides*) covering all of France's long-distance footpaths and an annual *Rando Guide*. Most *Topo-guides* are available in English and French and contain 1:50,000 scale maps, describe routes, explain how to get to the start, and include a wealth of information about accommodation, restaurants, shops and attractions along routes. The Michelin 1,100 orange series (scale 1:50,000 or 1cm = 500m) are good for walking, although for the ultimate in detail, you need the IGN *Rando* series of 2,000 maps. The scale is 1:25,000, which is detailed enough to show individual buildings. A route-planning CD ROM is available from retailers or the IGN website (🖳 http://www.ign.fr) for around €40.

Among the best English-language books for hikers in France are *Classic Walks in France* by Rob Hunter and David Wickers (Oxford Illustrated Press), *Walking in France* by Rob Hunter (Oxford Illustrated Press) and *Walking Through France* by Robin Neillands (Collins).

HUNTING

Hunting (*la chasse*) is viewed as a privilege hard won (during the Revolution) from the aristocracy and is indulged in by a large proportion of the rural population. France has 1.6m registered hunters (*chasseurs*), more than all other European countries combined. Hunting is a key part of the masculine culture (fewer than 2 per cent of hunters are women). It's even a way of doing business (*chasses d'affaires*) and companies often invite their most important clients to shoots. Hunting rights are jealously guarded and hunters pay €1,500 per year or more for rights in some areas.

French hunters are notoriously bad marksmen and around 50 people are killed by hunters each year (often other hunters). Many are inexperienced and some are downright dangerous, especially if they've been at the bottle before taking to the land. Although they won't deliberately shoot you (unless you're a conservationist or *garde-chasses*), it's advisable to steer clear of the countryside during the hunting season. The tendency in recent years has been towards stricter regulation of hunting, largely to prevent human accident and the following regulations must be observed:

- Hunters must have comprehensive accident insurance (costing from around €20).

- Hunting within 150m (500ft) of a house is forbidden.

- All hunters must be clearly visible against foliage, usually by wearing fluorescent bibs and caps. The rule extends to dogs, which are collared in similar fashion.

- Roaming is no longer permitted and stalking of prey discouraged. Muster points are easily recognisable by the roadside, usually signposted *'point de chasse'*.

- Guns must be carried in the 'broken' position to prevent accidental discharge.

Nevertheless, a licence isn't required for a shotgun, which can be bought by mail-order or in a shop. The minimum age for hunting is 15 (although those under 18 must have parental consent) and a permit (*permis de chasser*) is necessary. Hunters must pass a practical as well as a theoretical exam set by the Fédération Départementale des Chasseurs (FDC, ☎ 01 43 27 85 76). An application form can be obtained from your local *mairie* and the exams cost €15 (which is effectively a membership fee for the FDC). When you pass the exams, you receive a permit, which costs around €30 (plus a supplement for certain types of hunting) and is renewable annually.

Non-residents may obtain special permits (*licence de chasse*) from local *préfectures*, for which they require two passport-sized photographs, a passport and a shotgun licence (with a French translation). Permits are valid for nine consecutive days and you may obtain up to three per year. However, non-resident permits are severely restricted and are expensive (e.g. around €150) owing to the scarcity of game and the already fierce competition among local hunters. For further information about permits, contact the FDC (see above) or the Office National de la Chasse (see below).

Popular prey includes wild boar (*sanglier*), deer, partridge, pheasant, duck, snipe, pigeon, rabbit, hare and (for unfit hunters) snails. Hunting is legal from September to February, although the exact dates vary according to the department and the prey (e.g. the close season for snails is 1st April to 30th June). No hunting is permitted during the breeding and suckling periods, and the species and numbers of game that can be shot is (at least in theory) carefully controlled. The wildfowl hunting season was recently shortened to the end of January to protect migrating birds during their return to breeding grounds despite angry objections by hunters, who are notorious for their often violent attacks on anyone who threatens to restrict their 'right' to hunt. There isn't a tradition of conservation in France, although most hunters claim to be nature lovers, tending the land and conserving wildlife; in fact, they're inclined to shoot anything that moves (including each other). Many millions of birds are shot illegally each year, most for 'sport' rather than the table, and poachers do a thriving business providing songbirds for private 'gourmet' dining clubs and restaurants. Fortunately for France's hapless wildlife, many hunters spend more time trying to find their dogs than actually hunting.

Before buying a property, you should make yourself aware of any hunting rights on or adjacent to your land and check before planning any fencing or walling that this won't raise objections. Although hunters don't have the right to hunt on private land (*propriété privée*) without permission, when land has traditionally been used by hunters they won't bother to ask. Where hunting is forbidden it's usually shown by a sign (*'chasse interdite/gardée'*). Certain areas are denoted as *réservé pour repeuplement*, which means that hunting access is prohibited in order to allow wildlife to reproduce; red public notices are attached to the perimeter. It's possible to apply for your land to be designated a 'refuge' to the Association pour la Protection des Animaux Sauvages (☎ 04 75 25 10 00), although this may not do much for your local popularity!

Information

For further general information contact the Office Nationale de la Chasse (☎ 01 44 15 17 17, 🖳 http://www.oncfs.gouv.fr). Local information, including the dates of the hunting season, can be obtained from your Direction Départementale de l'Agriculture et de la Forêt or Fédération Départementale des Chasseurs. There are many magazines devoted to hunting in France.

RACKET SPORTS

Tennis is by far the most popular racket sport in France; squash and badminton are also practised, but facilities can sometimes be poor. There are two main kinds of racket club: sports centres open to all, and private clubs. Sports centres require no membership or membership fees and anyone can book a court. Clubs tend to have little or no social aspect, as for example in the UK, but are principally facilities for playing a sport; there may not even be club nights or tournaments. Costs are around €8 per hour for a squash or indoor tennis court, €4 per hour for an outdoor court or €6 if it's floodlit. Most towns and villages have municipal courts that can be rented for €3 to €5 per hour. Some hotels have their own tennis and squash courts, and organise coaching holidays throughout the year.

Tennis

The French invented tennis – or so they would have you believe – and the country has over 2.5m players and some 10,000 clubs. Tennis's popularity has grown tremendously in the last few decades and there are courts in most towns and villages, although in small villages there may be one court only and it may be in poor repair. Courts are usually hard (*court en dur*), although clay courts (*court en terre battue*) are also popular; many courts are floodlit. One of the reasons for the popularity and high standard of tennis in France is that there are hundreds of covered and indoor courts, enabling tennis to be played year round.

Tennis was long regarded as an elite sport in France and remains that way in many private clubs, which are usually expensive and exclusive and rarely accept unaccompanied visitors. Membership runs to several hundred euros per year and most clubs have long waiting lists. At an elite private club you can pay €30 per hour for a court. France has many tennis schools and resorts, and in Paris and other cities there are huge tennis complexes with as many as 24 courts, open from 07.00 to 22.00 daily. Many tennis clubs provide saunas, whirlpools, solariums and swimming pools, and most have a restaurant.

The French Open is one of the world's four 'grand slam' (*grand chelem*) events, along with the US and Australian Opens and Wimbledon. It's held during the last week of May and the first week of June at the Stade Roland Garros in Paris (the French refer to the tournament as the *Roland Garros*) and is the only grand slam event played on clay courts. The site incorporates the only French museum dedicated to tennis, Le Tenniseum.

France has a number of women players ranked in the world's top 20, but they're still seeking another male superstar since Yannick Noah (the last Frenchman to win the French Open) retired and became a pop star.

Squash & Badminton

There are squash clubs in most large towns, although many have only one or two courts. There are also many combined tennis and squash clubs. The general standard of squash is low due to the lack of experienced coaches and top competition, although it's continually improving. Frenchman Thierry Lincou is currently no.1 in the world and the French team came third behind England and Egypt in the 2005 World Men's Team Championship. Rackets and balls for racketball (a 'simplified' version of squash played with a larger, bouncier ball and shorter rackets) can also be hired from most squash clubs.

Some tennis centres also provide badminton courts and there are around 600 badminton clubs, although facilities tend to be poor.

Information

Further information about racket sports can be obtained from the Fédération Française de Tennis (☎ 01 47 43 48 00, 🖳 http://www.fft.fr), the Fédération Française de Squash (☎ 01 55 12 34 90, 🖳 http://www.ffsquash.com) and the Fédération Française de Badminton (☎ 01 49 45 07 07, 🖳 http://www.ffba.org). Local information is available from racket clubs, travel agents and tourist offices.

RUGBY

France is unusual among continental countries in that rugby is hugely popular and the national team is one of the best in the world (thanks to the British, who introduced rugby during World War I). France (*les tricolores*) plays in the annual 'European' championship along with England, Ireland, Italy, Scotland and Wales, home games being staged at the Parc des Princes or the Stade de France in Paris.

French rugby owes its popularity (and existence) to clubs rather than schools or universities, as, for example, in the UK. It has its stronghold in the south-west of the country (the *Midi*), where every town has a team. Among the most famous clubs are Agen, Bayonne, Béziers, Brive, Narbonne and Toulouse. French clubs compete in an annual European Cup competition with British clubs. There's even a British Rugby Club in Saint-Cyr-l'Ecole in Yvelines near Paris.

Most rugby in France follows the rugby union code (15 players a side), although rugby league (13 players a side) is also popular, particularly in Carcassonne and Perpignan.

Information

Further information is available from the Fédération Française de Rugby website (⌨ http://www.ffr.fr), where you can find a list of clubs in your region.

SKIING

Both downhill skiing (*ski alpin*) and cross-country skiing (*ski de fond/ski nordique*) are popular, although downhill skiing is greatly preferred. France is Europe's number one destination for serious downhill skiers and some 15 per cent of the French population ski regularly. The French mountain ranges have the largest number of resorts and the most extensive network of ski lifts in the world (over 4,000). France boasts over 3,000km^2 (over 1,150mi^2) of skiing areas spread over six mountain ranges. The ski season runs from December to April (or May in the higher resorts, which are the best choice for early or late season skiing).

The major skiing area is, of course, the French Alps, but there's cheaper skiing in some 35 resorts in the French Pyrenees, e.g. Barèges and Cauterets, nine resorts in the Massif Central (Auvergne) and a number of resorts in the Vosges and Jura mountain ranges along the German border, although these resorts cater mostly for beginners and intermediates rather than experts.

Alpine skiing areas include a number of vast inter-linked regions with over 300km (186 miles) of runs (*piste*) and some with over 600km (372mi), e.g. the Portes du Soleil, the Trois Vallées and the recently formed 'Paradiski' area (combining Les Arcs and La Plagne), providing the largest skiing area in the world. There are many long runs, including the *Vallée Blanche* at Chamonix (24km/15mi), the *Aiguille Rouge* at Les Arcs and the *Sarenne* at Alpe d'Huez (both 16km/10mi). A number of French resorts are linked with Italian and Swiss resorts (don't forget your passport).

The French invented the purpose-built ski resort, where you jump out of bed in the morning directly onto the slopes (but put your salopettes and skis on first!). However, purpose-built resorts are mostly lacking in character and charm (some are downright ugly), and the country also has many traditional village resorts rivalling the best in Austria and Switzerland. The main advantages of purpose-built resorts are that they're situated at high altitude where there's reliable snow and are designed so you can ski from door-to-door (in some resorts almost all runs start and finish in the village). The trend nowadays is away from monolithic concrete blocks and back to traditional wooden chalets.

The largest and most famous Alpine French ski resorts include Alpe d'Huez, Les Arcs, Argentières, Avoriaz, Chamonix, Courchevel, Les Deux Alpes, Flaine, Les

Menuires, Megève, Méribel, Morzine, La Plagne, Tignes, Val d'Isère, Valmorel and Val Thorens (the highest resort in Europe). Chamonix, Courchevel and Megève are France's most fashionable ski resorts. Many French resorts are situated at high altitude and have excellent snow records, even when most of the rest of the Alps is without snow. Many resorts also boast snow cannons, enabling them to guarantee skiing throughout most of the season.

It's also possible to ski on artificial slopes and even indoors: Amnéville in Moselle boasts Europe's first indoor artificial ski slope, built on a the waste tip of a disused steel works and measuring 500m by 35m.

Facilities

Most resorts have a range of ski lifts, including cable cars, gondolas, chairlifts and drag lifts. Drag lifts are usually 'Pomas' for single riders, rather than two-person T-bars. Lifts are marked on *piste* plans, as are all runs, which are graded green (for beginners), blue (easy), red (intermediate) and black (difficult).

Ski resorts provide a variety of accommodation, including hotels, self-catering apartments and chalets. Accommodation is more expensive during holiday periods (Christmas, New Year and Easter), when lift queues are interminable and runs are overcrowded. During public and school holidays (see page 63) the crowds of school children may drive you crazy, both on and off-piste. These periods are best avoided, particularly as crowding on the runs greatly increases the risk of collisions.

Costs

Alpine or downhill skiing is an expensive sport, particularly for families. The cost of equipping a family of four can easily reach €1,500. If you're a beginner, it's better to hire ski equipment (skis, poles and boots) or buy second-hand equipment until you're addicted, which can happen on your first day on the slopes (most people are either hooked or scared stiff). Most sports shops have pre-season and end of season sales of ski equipment. Ski passes cost between around €100 and €200 (depending on the extent of the lift system) for six days. Ski hire costs €15 to €25 and boot hire €5 to €15 per day. Some resorts have low and high season rates for passes and equipment hire.

Other Activities

If you find black runs child's play, you may like to try something more exciting such as freestyle, off-piste, speed, heli- or 'extreme' skiing or snow-boarding (*surfing*). Snow-boarding is particularly popular and is taught in most resorts. The French invented 'extreme' skiing, which involves negotiating slopes steeper than 60 degrees (and is only for the seriously foolhardy). Heli-skiing, where helicopters drop skiers off at the top of inaccessible mountains, is illegal in France. However, 'powder hounds' can ski into un-navigable areas and be picked up by helicopter (if they're lucky) or can be dropped by helicopter in Italy or Switzerland (where heli-skiing is legal) and ski back to France. It costs around €160 per drop. Other activities may include paragliding, parasailing, hang-gliding, snow-shoe walking, dog-sledding, tobogganing, snow-mobiling and, for the seriously suicidal, snow-joering (being towed on skis by a horse!), bob-sleighing and ice-diving.

Most winter resorts also provide heated indoor swimming pools, gymnasiums, fitness centres, saunas and solariums along with a variety of mostly indoor activities, including tennis, squash, ice-skating, curling, indoor golf and tenpin bowling. There's an excellent choice of restaurants and bars in most resorts, although they can be expensive. Other entertainment includes discos, cinemas, nightclubs and casinos.

Summer skiing is available in Alpe d'Huez, Les Deux Alpes, La Plagne, Tignes, Val d'Isère, Val Thorens and can be combined with other sports such as tennis, swimming, golf, horse riding, grass skiing, fishing, watersports, hiking, climbing and a range of other activities.

Safety

Safety is of paramount importance in any sport but it's particularly important when skiing, where the possibility of injury is ever-present. In recent years, skiing-related deaths and serious injuries have increased considerably as slopes have become more crowded. Around 200 skiers die each year in Europe and thousands more are injured, many seriously. Unless you're an expert skier, it's best to avoid skiing in bad weather and poor snow conditions, e.g. ice, when the danger of injury increases considerably, particularly for beginners and intermediates. Young children should wear safety helmets in all conditions as soon as they're able to use normal runs and lifts.

If you have your own skis, it's important to have them serviced each season by a qualified ski mechanic. If you're using hired skis, double check that the bindings are set correctly and that they release freely in all directions. Look for ski hire shops complying with standard (norme) NF X50-007. If you aren't entirely happy with hired equipment, never hesitate to request adjustments or an exchange.

Try to ski with people of the same standard as yourself or with an experienced skier who is willing to ski at your pace and don't be in too much of a hurry to tackle those black runs. Stop skiing and rest when you feel tired, a sure sign of which is when you keep falling over for no apparent reason (unless you've had a large liquid lunch). **It's better to ride down in a cable car than on a stretcher.** Most ski accidents happen when skiers are tired. If you injure yourself, particularly a knee, stop skiing and seek medical advice as soon as possible. If you attempt to ski with an injury or before an injury has had time to heal, you risk aggravating it and doing permanent damage.

Don't ski off-piste unless you're an experienced skier and never on your own. In an unfamiliar area it's important to hire an experienced local ski guide. **Never** ignore avalanche warning signs – denoted by black and yellow flags, signs reading 'Danger d'Avalanches' or flashing lights – or attempt to ski on closed (barré) runs.

Always abide by the International Ski Federation's (FIS) Safe Skiing Code, which can be found on, for example, 💻 http://www.clubdirect.com/safe-skiing.cfm. If you're hit by a reckless skier, you can sue for damages under France's civil negligence laws. Conversely, you can be sued if you're the guilty party. Make sure that you're well insured for both accidents and public liability (for a minimum of €1.5m). Further safety guidelines are contained in the booklet *Pour Que la Montagne Reste un Plaisir*, available from tourist offices and ski hire shops in resorts. See also **Holiday & Travel Insurance** on page 346.

Learning to Ski

If you're a newcomer to downhill skiing, it's worthwhile enrolling in a ski school to learn the basics; it's much safer (particularly for other skiers) than simply launching yourself off the nearest mountain. Good skiing is all about technique and the value of good coaching cannot be over-emphasised. France has 11,000 instructors and all French resorts have ski schools (École de Ski Français) where classes are organised at all levels, from beginner to competition. Ski school costs from around €75 to €125 for six half days, usually three hours in the morning or afternoon, or from around €100 to €160 for six full days, usually six hours per day. Individual lessons are available for around €50 for an hour and a half or €65 for two hours. In some resorts, many instructors don't speak English. English-speaking instructors are more common in the most popular resorts such as Chamonix, Méribel, Tignes and Val d'Isère. It's worth noting that ski instructors have priority at lifts, so hiring an instructor can save you a lot of time queueing.

If you plan to take young children on a skiing holiday, you should choose a resort with a *crèche* or *garderie* and good non-skiing facilities. A *garderie* for infants of between six months and three years costs around €20 per half-day (mornings or afternoons) or €30 per full day, excluding meals. Children aged three to four can attend a special ski school at reduced rates (see above for full rates). Tourist offices organise baby-sitters in many resorts.

Cross-country Skiing

Cross-country skiing (*ski de fond/ski nordique*) doesn't have the glamorous and exciting image of downhill skiing, but it's nevertheless a popular sport in France. It appeals to both young and old, particularly those whose idea of fun is a million miles away from careering down a hill at 100kph, with a thousand metre drop on one side and avalanche warning signs on the other. Cross-country skiing can be enjoyed at any pace and over any distance and a variety of terrains and therefore has great appeal to both the unfit and the keen athlete. Not everyone finds it easy, however, as cross-country skis are narrow and good balance is essential.

Cross-country skiing has the advantages over downhill skiing of cheaper equipment, no expensive lift passes, no queues **and** fewer broken bones! Essential equipment (i.e. skis, bindings, poles, boots and gloves) can cost as little as €250. No other special clothing is necessary, although you should wear something warm and preferably waterproof. Trails, usually consisting of two sets of specially prepared tracks (*pistes de ski de fond*), are well signposted. Some resorts have floodlit trails for night skiing. You can enjoy cross-country skiing anywhere there's sufficient snow, although using prepared trails is easier than making your own.

Information

For further information about skiing and other winter sports contact the Club Alpin Français (☎ 01 53 72 87 13 or ☎ 01 53 72 88 00), the Fédération Française de Ski (☎ 04 50 51 40 34, 🖳 http://www.ffs.fr) or the Association des Maires des Stations Française de Sports d'Hiver (also known simply as SkiFrance, ☎ 01 47 42 23 32, 🖳 http://www.skifrance.fr). The latest weather and snow conditions are available via telephone (☎ 08 92 68 08 08), internet (e.g. the France Météo website, 🖳 http://www.meteofrance.com), teletext, daily newspapers and direct from resorts. The FGTO (see page 402) publishes a *Winter Holiday Guide*. General information on health and safety for skiing can be obtained from the Médecins de Montagne website (🖳 http://www.mdem.org). It may pay you to invest in a good skiing book, such as the *Sunday Times We Learned to Ski* (Collins), which is an excellent choice, not only for beginners but for any skier.

SWIMMING

Not surprisingly, given France's generally hot summer weather and miles of beautiful sandy beaches (*plage*) as well as numerous public swimming pools (*piscine*), swimming (*natation*) is one of the country's favourite sports and pastimes. Beaches vary considerably in size, surface (sand, pebbles, etc.) and amenities, and most are notable for their cleanliness. Most resorts provide beach clubs for the young (*club des jeunes*) and all but the smallest beaches have supervised play areas where you can leave young children for a fee. Deckchairs and umbrellas can be hired on most beaches. Most beaches are free, although there are private beaches in some areas, particularly along the Mediterranean coast.

In a few areas, public beaches are dirty and overcrowded, although this is very much the exception. Officially, 96 per cent of French beaches are 'clean' and over a third have been awarded an EU 'blue flag' (*pavillon bleu*) for the quality of their water (97 out of 271 beaches), although many that fail the tests are dangerously polluted. The dirtiest beaches are on the northern coast between Calais and Cherbourg, the cleanest around Nice (although not all). The pollution count must be displayed at the local town hall: blue = good quality water, green = average, yellow = likely to be temporarily polluted, and red = badly polluted. A list of blue flag beaches can be found on the Blue Flag website (🖳 http://www.blueflag.org) and a list of 'black flag' beaches on that of the Surfrider Foundation Europe (🖳 http://www.surfrider-europe.org), which draws attention to what it considers to be unacceptably high levels of pollution.

Swimming can be dangerous at times, particularly on the Atlantic coast, where some beaches have very strong currents. Most beaches are supervised by lifeguards who operate a flag system to indicate when swimming is safe. You should always observe flags and other beach warning signs. When a beach is closed or swimming is prohibited, it's shown by a sign (*'baignade interdite'*). There are stinging jellyfish in parts of the Mediterranean and along the Atlantic coast but no sharks.

Swimming Pools

Most French towns have a public swimming pool (*piscine municipale*), including heated indoor pools (*piscine chauffée couverte*) and outdoor pools (*piscine en plein air*). Paris now boasts 35 public pools, a floating pool on the river Seine having been opened in mid-2006 to complement the annual 'Paris-Plage' initiative, which transforms 3.5km of river bank into a sandy beach for five weeks of the summer.

Opening hours may vary from day to day (and are usually different during school holidays) and most municipal pools aren't open after 20.00. Heated indoor pools are open year round and outdoor pools are open during the summer only, e.g. from 15th June to 31st August. Many hotel and public pools may be open in July and August only. Admission to municipal pools is usually around €3.50 for adults and €2 for children. Since 2003, all French children have been required to follow a 'learn to swim' programme and take swimming tests at regular intervals.

Public pools in cities are usually overheated and overcrowded, particularly when children aren't at school, e.g. Wednesdays, weekends and school holidays. Pools in hotels and health clubs are less crowded, although expensive. It's sometimes compulsory to wear a swimming cap in a public pool. In country areas, lakes, rivers and canals are employed as swimming pools (*piscine naturelle*), although you should avoid those flowing through urban areas which are often polluted. Most swimming pools and clubs provide swimming lessons (all levels from beginner to advanced) and run life-saving courses.

France also has a number of huge watersports centres with indoor and outdoor pools, slides, flumes, wave machines, whirlpools and waterfalls, plus sun-beds, saunas, solariums, Jacuzzis and hot baths.

WATERSPORTS

France is a paradise for watersports enthusiasts, which is hardly surprising considering its immense coastline, numerous lakes, and thousands of kilometres of rivers and canals. Popular watersports include sailing, windsurfing, waterskiing, jet-skiing, rowing, canoeing, kayaking, surfing, barging, rafting and subaquatic sports. Wetsuits are recommended for windsurfing, waterskiing and subaquatic sports, even in summer. Rowing and canoeing are possible on most lakes and rivers, where canoes and kayaks can usually be rented. France has Europe's best surfing beaches, on the extreme south-west Atlantic coast, including Biarritz (the capital of European surfing), Capbreton, Hossegor and Lacanau. Scuba diving and snorkelling are popular, particularly around the coasts of Brittany, the French Riviera and Corsica. There are clubs for most watersports in all major resorts and towns throughout France, where instruction is usually available.

Offshore windsurfers, jet-bikers and motorboaters must use marked channels, on beaches as well as in the sea and give priority to swimmers, even in channels. There's a speed limit of 10kph (6mph) within 300m of a coast and a distance limit of 1.8km (3mi). If you need rescuing, you must pay between around €90 and €125 per hour (swimmers are rescued free – if they're lucky!).

France has 8,500km (5,300mi) of inland waterways, controlled by Voies Navigables de France (VNF, 🖳 http://www.vnf.fr), and it's possible to navigate from the north coast to the Mediterranean along rivers and canals. Canals aren't just for pleasure craft, and millions of tonnes of freight are transported on them annually. Life on France's waterways continues at a leisurely pace, not least due to maximum speed limits of as little as 5kph (3mph). The principal inland boating areas are Alsace, Brittany, Burgundy, Champagne and Picardy-Flanders. The most popular waterway is the Canal du Midi in the south of France. Except for parts of the Moselle river, all French waterways provide free access, although you must have a navigation licence to drive a boat with a motor larger than 9hp.

Be sure to observe all warning signs on lakes and rivers. Take particular care when canoeing, as even the most benign of rivers have 'white water' patches that can be dangerous for the inexperienced. Some rivers have strong currents and require considerable skill and experience to navigate. It's sensible to wear a life-jacket, whether you're a strong swimmer or a non-swimmer. On some rivers there are quicksand-like banks of silt and shingle where people have been sucked under.

Boating holidays are popular in France. Boats vary from motorboats for two to four people to barges or houseboats (*pénichette*) with accommodation for 10 to 12 people. A boat with four to seven berths costs from around €850 per week in low season and from around €1,500 per week in high season depending on the specification. You must have an International Certificate of Competence (ICC), which is valid for five years, to hire a boat over 15m (50ft) long. If you prefer to let someone else do the work, there are hotel barges, some with heated swimming pools, air-conditioning, and suites with four-poster beds!

France has hundreds of harbours, and sailing has always been a popular sport with the French and there are 750,000 yacht owners in France. The French have a long tradition of seafaring and are prominent in international yachting, particularly long-distance races, which are avidly followed by the general public. Boats of all shapes and sizes can be hired in most resorts and ports, where there are also sailing clubs and schools. If you have a few (thousand) euros to spare and wish to impress your friends, you can even rent a luxury yacht with crew for a modest €100,000 to €200,000 per week (plus tips!).

If you wish to berth a boat in France, you need to find a caretaker (*gardien/ne*) to look after it. The cost of keeping a yacht on the Atlantic coast is much lower than on the Mediterranean, although even there it needn't be too expensive providing you steer clear of the most fashionable ports. Mooring fees vary considerably, e.g. from around €15 per day in Normandy to €150 per day in Saint-Tropez; permanent moorings can cost €3,000 per metre per year or more. Wherever you berth your boat, it should be fully insured. A growing number of luxury yachts disappear each year, particularly on the French Riviera, although the police believe this is due more to insurance fraud than theft.

French residents must obtain a certificate of competence to pilot power boats of 9 to 50hp; separate certificates are required for inland waters (*permis fluvial*) and coastal waters, including rivers within five nautical miles of a harbour (*permis mer*). If you're inexperienced, you should steer well clear of jet-skis, which can be deadly in the wrong hands.

Information

Further information about inland waterways can be obtained from Voies Navigables de France (VNF, ⌨ http://www.vnf.fr). The FGTO (see page 402) publishes a free booklet, *Boating on the Waterways*. A book which may be of interest to boat owners is *The French Alternative: The Pleasure and Cost-Effect of Keeping your Boat in France* by David Jefferson (Waterline).

FOREIGN SPORTS

Many other indigenous and foreign sports are practised in France, where groups of expatriate fanatics play American football, baseball, boccia, cricket, croquet, pelote (pelota/jai-alai), polo and softball. There are over 35 cricket clubs – mostly in the south-west – participating in an annual cup competition, and the French national cricket team recently won its first ever match: in the ICC Trophy for 'second division' cricketing nations! Only around 25 per cent of players are French, and there's even an English-speaking cricket club in Château-de-Thoiry in Yvelines near Paris. The Fédération Française de Baseball et de Softball (⌨ http://www.ffbsc.org) provides information (in French) about those sports and cricket. For information about other local expatriate sports facilities and clubs enquire at tourist offices, town halls, embassies and consulates (see **Appendix A**).

OTHER SPORTS

The following is a selection of other popular sports and activities in France, where traditional games such as *longue paume* (a relative of tennis) and *ballon au poing* (resembling handball and reputedly the most-played sport in Picardy) are still thriving:

Athletics

Most towns have athletics clubs organising local competitions and sports days. Paris hosts an annual marathon attracting over 15,000 runners. Jogging (*footing*) isn't as popular in France as it is in many other countries; cycling is preferred.

Basketball

Basketball is surprisingly popular in France, where CSP Limoges became the first French team to win the European Clubs Championship, Europe's top basketball title, in 1993. There are amateur clubs in large towns and cities.

Billiards, Pool & Snooker

Many hotels, bars and sports clubs have billiards, pool and/or snooker tables, and there are billiards clubs in the larger towns where facilities may include French billiards, British snooker and American pool. French billiards is played with just three balls on a table with no pockets. In Paris, some billiards halls are as elegant as art galleries, e.g. the Clichy Montmartre billiards club.

Bungee Jumping

If your idea of fun is jumping off a high bridge or platform with an elastic rope attached to your ankles to prevent you merging with the landscape, bungee jumping (*saut à l'élastique*) may be just what you're looking for. Although late starters, the French have taken to bungee jumping with a vengeance. Most venues use purpose-built platforms and cranes, rather than natural locations (among the most spectacular of the latter is the bridge over the Gorges du Verdon, Europe's deepest canyon, in the south-east). If you're paying on a one-jump basis, e.g. at a fair, check what you're agreeing to (as well as the *élastique* if possible), and make sure you've turned out your pockets (including a copy of your will) to a trusted companion.

Handball

There are over 300,000 handball players in France and dozens of local leagues. Handball is also played professionally and the top French teams compete (with some success) in European championships.

Horse Racing

France has 265 racecourses headed by Longchamps (the world's longest track), Chantilly and St Cloud near Paris, and Deauville on the Normandy coast. There are large provincial courses in Bordeaux and Marseille, but the majority of courses are small. The popularity of horse racing has declined considerably in recent years. Nevertheless, the annual prize money of €1.2m is the highest in Europe and turnover from race betting is greater than from the national lottery. All legal betting is via the Pari Mutuel Urbain (PMU) monopoly totaliser system (there are no bookies in France). Chantilly is the centre of French horse racing and stages the French Derby in June. The top flat race in Europe (if not the world) is the *Prix de l'Arc de Triomphe*, held the first weekend in October at Longchamps. Trotting is also popular in France, where the top race is the *Prix d'Amérique*, held at Vincennes in Paris and attracting a greater following even than the *Prix de l'Arc de Triomphe*.

Horse Riding

Horse riding is widely practised in France, which has thousands of kilometres of groomed bridlepaths (*randonnées équestres*). The French are passionate about horses (they also like to eat them) and there's a large horse population in France, where horses are cheaper to buy and keep than in most other European countries. There are thousands of riding schools, equestrian centres and pony clubs, and hundreds of horse shows are staged throughout the year. In addition to cross-country riding, you can take try dressage and show jumping. Cross-country riding holidays and trekking are popular, riders staying overnight in *gîtes*. One of the most beautiful areas to enjoy a riding holiday is the Camargue, riding the famous Camargue white horses. For more information contact the Fédération Française d'Équitation (☎ 01 58 17 58 17, 🖳 http://www.ffe.com) or the Ligue de Paris de la Fédération Française d'Equitation (☎ 01 42 12 03 43).

Motor Racing

Motor racing is very popular (particularly on public roads!) in France, which is famous for the Le Mans 24-hour sports car race (founded in 1923) held in June and the Monte Carlo rally in January (founded in 1913), the most famous of all road rallies (although upstaged by the arduous Granada-Dakar race in recent years). France stages many other international motor races, including the famous Monaco Formula 1 Grand Prix in May, which is the most popular on the circuit – so popular in fact that owners of apartments overlooking the course are able to charge up to €40,000 rent for the two days of the meeting. Racing on two or three wheels also has a strong following, including motorcycling, motocross, side-car racing and scrambling. The latest craze is quad biking.

Shooting

As well as animal shooting (see page 461), skeet (*skeet*), clay pigeon (*ball-trap*) and range (*stand*) shooting are popular.

Ten-pin Bowling

There are ten-pin bowling (*bowling*) centres in all major cities, usually open from around 15.00 until 03.00 or 04.00. Ten-pin bowling and skittles (*jeu de quilles*) can also be played in many hotels and restaurants.

Volleyball

In recent years, volleyball (played indoors and outdoors) has become almost as popular as basketball, particularly beach volleyball (*beach volley*), which is played just two-a-side on a smaller (sand) court than traditional six-a-side volleyball. Marseille hosts international beach volleyball tournaments.

17.

<u>Shopping</u>

France is one of Europe's great shopping countries, and shops are designed to seduce you with their artful displays of beautiful and exotic merchandise. Paris is a shoppers' paradise, where even the shop windows are a delight, although it isn't the place for budget shoppers. Nevertheless, Paris attracts an army of foreign shoppers keen to pay for top quality labels such as Chanel, Dior, Hermès and Louis Vuitton. French products are distinguished by their attention to detail, elegance, flair and quality (as well as high prices).

Most towns have a supermarket or two and, on the outskirts of large towns, there are usually huge shopping centres with hypermarkets, do-it-yourself (DIY) stores and furniture warehouses. In many city centres there are pedestrian streets (*rue piétonne*), where you can walk and shop without fear of being mown down.

The French don't usually make good servants, and shop staff are often surly and unhelpful, particularly in department stores, where you can wait ages to be served while staff chat among themselves (in France the customer often comes last). Nevertheless, shopkeepers are usually honest and won't try to rob you, although you should always check your change. In some stores you don't pay the person serving you but a cashier, who may be the owner.

In Paris and other cities and tourist resorts, you **must** be wary of pickpockets and bag-snatchers. **Never** tempt fate with an exposed wallet or purse or by flashing your money around.

For those who aren't used to buying articles with metric measures and continental sizes, a list of comparative weights and measures is included in **Appendix D**.

PRICES

French retailers are among the world's most competitive and have smaller profit margins than those in many other countries. Price fixing isn't permitted, except on books, although the *Loi Lang* (named after Culture Minister Jack Lang) allows up to a 5 per cent discount off the 'recommended retail' price. Prices of bread and pharmaceuticals are government controlled. Otherwise, as in most countries, it's important to shop around and compare prices, which can vary considerably (not only between small shops and hypermarkets, but also between different supermarkets and hypermarkets in the same town). However, price differences usually reflect different quality, so make sure that you're comparing similar products.

Some products are particularly expensive in France and are worth importing. These include electronic and audio equipment, cosmetics, furniture, books and almost anything that's manufactured outside the EU. Among the best buys in France are pottery, decorative glass, kitchenware, quality clothes (including children's), fashion accessories, toys, domestic electrical equipment, wines, spirits (but not imported ones), luxury foods and perfumes.

Sales & Bargain Shopping

There are relatively few bargain shops in France (certainly compared with the UK or US), although there's usually at least one cheap 'bazaar' in each town. The French generally don't go in for buying second-hand goods, and charity shops are virtually non-existent, apart from the those of Emmaüs (🖥 http://www.emmaus.asso.fr), an international charitable organisation with around 140 shops in France, and a few *dépôts-vente*, where you can leave unwanted clothes (or other articles) and claim 50 per cent of the selling price if they're sold. On the other hand 'boot sales' (*foire à tout*) and 'garage sales' (*vide grenier*) are becoming increasingly common (see **Markets** on page 486). There are second-hand book shops in most large towns and cities. If you're into buying (or selling) second-hand items online, you might like to investigate France's answer to Ebay, 'Flog It!' (🖥 http://www.flogit.ws). See also **Clothing** on page 497 and **Furniture & Furnishings** on page 500.

Traditionally, all shops have been limited to just two sales (*solde*) a year, each for a maximum of two months: one in summer (usually July) and one after Christmas (around the second week in January until mid-February), although from January 2007 all sales are due to start on the same day. Items sold in sales must show the lowest price offered during the previous month and the sale price, stock must not be changed during a sale, and the same consumer rights apply to sale items as to non-sale items. Note, however, that these rules are set to change in a government drive to increase consumer spending. A *liquidation totale* (which requires official authorisation) isn't a closing down sale but a clearance sale. Holders of a *carte famille nombreuse* (see page 224) can benefit from discounts at a number of shops, including Auchan and Printemps.

It's possible to buy goods direct from factories, with discounts of between 30 and 70 per cent, although factory shops aren't nearly as common as in the US. Most of them are to be found in the north and east of France, although the factory-shopper's Mecca is Troyes in Aube, where there are around 250 'factory' outlets. Keen bargain hunters may want to track down *The Factory Shop Guide for Northern France* by Gillian Cutress & Rolf Stricker, which is now out of print, *Le Guide France-Europe des Magasins d'Usine* (Editions du Seuil) and *Paris Pas Cher* (Flammarion).

You should also be on the lookout for fake goods, as some 70 per cent of all fake products are copies of French brands, reckoned to cost the country 30,000 jobs and €6bn in lost sales annually. Perfumes are a favourite target, but counterfeit goods include leather products, CDs and DVDs, household goods and food. Even French truffles, which can cost as much as €650 per kilo, have been replaced by inferior Chinese truffles in recent years! Bringing counterfeit goods into France is a criminal offence and, in theory, owning a pirated Cartier watch or fake Louis Vuitton handbag can result in a jail sentence and/or a fine of up to €20,000, although in practice it will usually just be confiscated. The number of articles confiscated soared from 3.5m in 2004 to over 5.5m in 2005. Having more than one item, however, implies commercial activity and you can be fined up to €75,000 and sentenced to two years in prison!

SHOPPING HOURS

Shopping hours vary considerably according to the city or town and the type of shop. Food shops cannot legally open for more than 13 hours per day, and other shops are limited to 11 hours per day. Food shops in the provinces (such as bakeries) are open from as early as 06.30 or 07.00 until 12.00 or 12.30, and again from between 15.00

and 16.00 until 19.00 or 20.00. Non-food shops usually open from 09.00 or 10.00 to 12.00 and from 14.00 until 18.30 or 19.30. Small shops tend to tailor their opening hours to suit their customers rather than their staff. Large shops and super/hypermarkets remain open at lunchtime, although smaller stores usually close, except perhaps on Fridays and Saturdays. Most hypermarkets are open from 09.00 until between 20.00 and 22.00 Mondays to Saturdays.

France is generally closed on Sunday, although some village shops, particularly *boulangeries*, *charcuteries* and *pâtisseries*, open on Sunday mornings. There's widespread opposition to Sunday trading from the unions and small shopkeepers, although French shops are permitted to open on five Sundays a year and those in designated 'tourist' areas (e.g. coastal and ski resorts) can open on any Sunday.

Many shops are closed on Monday mornings or all day Mondays, particularly those that open on Sundays. In many cities and towns, shops have a late-opening day (*nocturne*) once a week, e.g. Wednesdays in Paris, until between 20.00 and 22.00. It's generally best to avoid shopping on Wednesdays if possible, as many children are off school and either go or are taken shopping on that day. Paris has food shops that stay open until 22.00 or 00.00 and a few that open 24 hours. Many small Parisian boutiques open at around 10.00 or 10.30 until 19.00 or 19.30. Some shops close for the whole of August or for another month in the year.

Shops and restaurants often indicate the days they're open or closed, e.g. every day (*tous les jours* or *TLJ*), every day except Monday (*sauf lundi*), and Saturdays, Sundays and holidays (*samedis, dimanches et fêtes* or *S, D & F*). Most shops close on public holidays (see page 63) and virtually all (except some newsagents') shut on 1st January, 1st May, 14th July and 25th December.

SPECIALIST FOOD SHOPS

Buying food is a serious business in France, where the range and quality of fresh food is without parallel. The French have a passion for eating, and shopping for food is a labour of love and not to be rushed. When they have time, people usually shop in small specialist food shops and markets rather than in large, soulless supermarkets and hypermarkets. Consequently, the average French person spends more time shopping than his counterpart in other Western countries, although less than previously. This also means that, despite intense competition from supermarkets and hypermarkets, traditional, small, family-run shops still thrive in villages and towns and enjoy some 60 per cent of the general retail trade and around 50 per cent of the food trade. Although their numbers are decreasing – more as a result of the depopulation of rural areas than because of competition from supermarkets – they survive by offering friendly and personal service (advice, tastings, etc.) and high quality, as well as providing a meeting place for locals.

When living in France, one of the best ways to integrate with the local community is to support local businesses. The quality and range of food provided by small shops varies considerably, so shop around to find those you like best and become a regular customer. In many rural villages, there are mobile shops (*marchands ambulants*) selling bread, meat, fish, dairy products, fruit and vegetables. They usually visit once or twice a week. Ask your neighbours what days they call and listen for their horns.

Despite the availability of almost any fruit and vegetable at almost any time of year (from somewhere in the world), the French tend to eat only what's in season locally (i.e. in France) and generally avoid imported produce. You may find this limiting if you're used to eating melons in March or strawberries in September but it's all part of the great French culinary tradition – and means you aren't tempted to spend a fortune on produce that has been flown half way round the world.

Similarly, many French people shop for basics such as bread daily – even twice a day! – and are reluctant to freeze food, preferring to eat fresh produce. They also value quality, and there are a number of quality designations. An *appellation d'origine contrôlée* (*AOC* or *AC*) can apply to food as well as to wine (see page 492), protecting them from 'inferior' imitations both nationally and internationally. An *AC* specifies not only the area of production but also the ingredients or feed, variety or breed (in the case of meat or poultry), and methods of production and manufacture. Foods covered by an *AC* include cheese, butter, poultry, fruit and vegetables. Another recognised quality mark is *Label Rouge* for meat and fish, but you should ignore meaningless 'accolades' such as *Grand Cru* (except on wine) and anything including the word *qualité*.

Food is sold by the kilo or by the 'piece' (*pièce*). *Une livre* (not to be confused with *un livre*, meaning 'book') means 'pound' (either in weight or in money) and is equivalent to half a kilo or 500g.

Farmers and producers sell their produce direct to the public and you will often see signs, e.g. '*produits de la ferme – vente directe*', in country areas for fruit, vegetables, wine (and other drinks), cheese, pâté, honey, eggs and other foods. There's also a growing trend to 'pick your own' fruit and vegetables. (If you're tempted to pick mushrooms in the forest, take them to a chemist and check that they're safe to eat.)

Boucherie

Most villages and all towns have a butcher's shop (*boucherie*) selling all kinds of meat, including pork, although generally speaking pork is the preserve of the *charcuterie* (see below). A *boucherie* doesn't sell horse meat (*cheval*), which is sold by a specialist horse butcher (*boucherie chevaline*), denoted by a sign with a horse's head (it's also sold in some supermarkets and hypermarkets) and is similarly priced to beef (many people believe it's the best of all meats). A butcher may also sell poultry, although this is sold exclusively by specialist poultry shops (*volailler*) in some towns. Butchers will often cook meat purchased from them at little extra cost and many also sell spit-roasted chickens and other cooked meats.

The French are voracious carnivores and are second in Europe only to the Belgians in the quantity of meat they consume per capita. When the French kill an animal for food, nothing is wasted, not even the ears and tail, not to mention its innards and private parts (offal), which is highly prized. The French are puzzled by many foreigners' aversion to eating certain parts of an animal (see page 440). However, since the 'mad cow disease' (*maladie de la vache folle*) epidemic, butchers must display details of the life and manner of slaughter of all bovines, including the country or area of origin, on a *ticket de pesée* attached to the joint or carcass.

Unless your French is particularly good, you're better off buying your meat pre-packed from a supermarket. However, if your French is up to the task, your local butcher is a better choice and is usually an excellent source of cooking tips.

Butchers often open on Sundays but close all day on Mondays or just in the morning, whereas supermarkets have a meat counter and are open on Mondays.

Boulangerie

Thanks to a 19th century law, all towns and villages above a certain size must have a baker's (*boulangerie*), or an outlet selling bread (*dépôt de pain*), e.g. a café, newsagent's, supermarket or petrol station. The French love their daily bread (many old country homes have a bread oven) and won't keep bread for more than a few hours (let alone freeze it – heaven forbid!), although consumption has fallen from some 84kg per head per year in 1965 to around 40kg today (or from 230g to around 110g – half a *baguette* – per day).

The weight and price of bread are government regulated and are uniform throughout the country (e.g. a *pain* must weigh 400g and a *baguette* 200g). French bread **must** be freshly made (and is best when still warm), as it goes stale quickly, so bakers bake twice or even three times a day (although bread in inferior bakers' has been frozen at the dough stage or after being three-quarters baked). The types of bread offered by bakers often vary considerably and many bake special loaves to their own recipes. You should try a few bakers until you find one that's to your taste. In cities and large towns, a *boulangerie* is sometimes combined with a *pâtisserie* and/or *confiserie*, although this is rare in country areas.

When foreigners refer to French bread, they usually mean a *baguette*, although there are many other varieties of loaf. *Pain* (or *pain parisien/gros pain*) is the thickest and longest, while the narrowest and shortest is the *ficelle* (literally a 'piece of string'). Other common types of loaf are *flûte* and *bâtard*. Note also that otherwise identical loaves are often cooked in different ways, e.g. in a mould (*moulé*) or on a flat baking tray or tiles (*pavé*) and you should specify which you prefer.

Wholemeal bread is called *pain complet/intégral*. Village bakers don't sell a lot of different types of 'wholemeal' bread, although you can usually find *pain de campagne* (country bread, made with a blend of white, wholemeal and rye flour), *pain de seigle* (rye and wheat bread) and *pain au son* (with added bran). Unlike a *baguette* or *pain*, these can be kept for a few days. Wholemeal or mixed grain *baguettes* are sometimes available. *Pain de mie* is a tasteless sandwich loaf used for toast.

You can ask for almost any bread to be sliced (which is usually done free), although it's impossible to slice fresh bread while it's still warm. Some bakers sell bags of dry slices of left-over bread, which make excellent croutons.

A *boulangerie* also sells *croissants*, chocolate *croissants* (*pains au chocolat*), *brioches* (a type of bun), special breads made with raisins, nuts (e.g. almonds, hazelnuts or walnuts) and a limited range of cakes and biscuits, although for fancy cakes you must go to a *pâtisserie* (see below), sometimes as well as sandwiches and other snacks, such as quiches and mini-pizzas. Like bread, *croissants* vary considerably in quality and taste and it's well worth shopping around for the best. Always avoid packet *croissants*.

Bakeries usually close one day a week, although in a town with more than one they won't all close on the same day. When the only baker in a village closes, bread (usually *baguettes* and *pains* only) is usually available from another outlet, such as the village café.

Charcuterie

A *charcuterie* (literally pork butcher's) is a delicatessen selling mostly cooked meats, including ham, bacon, roast beef, sausages, salami and black pudding, plus pâtés, pies, quiches, omelettes, pizzas, salads and prepared dishes. Each region has its own pork specialities, as does each *charcutier*. A *charcuterie* may also have a *rôtisserie*, where meat and poultry is spit-roasted. A *charcutier* may also be a caterer (*traiteur*), who can create delicious dishes for two or a banquet for 100. (This is the crafty way to impress your guests without so much as cracking an egg.)

Confiserie

A *confiserie* is a high-class confectioner's, not to be confused with a common sweet shop (which don't exist in France!). Every town has a *confiserie*, where you can buy hand-made chocolates and confectionery made with every fattening (and expensive) ingredient under the sun. They may also make excellent home-made ice-cream. A *confiserie* isn't the place to buy children's mass-produced sweets, bought in bulk at the supermarket, but confectionery to win somebody's heart (or placate your mother-in-law when you've forgotten her birthday!). A *confiserie* may be part of a cake shop (*pâtisserie* – see below).

Crémerie

A *crémerie* ('dairy shop') sells butter, cream, cheese, eggs, yoghurt, ice-cream, and a variety of other foods, many having nothing to do with milk. Surprisingly, *crémeries* don't usually sell fresh milk. They're mainly found in rural areas where there are lots of cows, such as Normandy and the Jura. Both salted (*demi-sel*) and unsalted (*doux*) butter (*beurre*) is available, made from both pasteurised and unpasteurised (*cru*) milk. (Low-fat, margarine-like spreads are available in supermarkets, although they aren't usually used as a substitute for butter.) A *crémerie* usually sells dozens of different cheeses, many of which cannot be found elsewhere. If it doesn't, there's probably a cheese shop (*fromagerie*) nearby (see below).

Épicerie/Alimentation Générale

A grocer's or general store (*épicerie/alimentation générale* – *épicerie* is literally a 'spice shop') sells most everyday foods, including butter, cheese, coffee, fruit, vegetables, wine and beer, plus a range of preserved and pre-packaged foods. Many general stores are now self-service (*libre-service*). Prices are usually considerably higher than in supermarkets; you pay for convenience and personal service. With the exception of market stalls, there are few specialist greengrocers or fruit and vegetable shops in France. In Paris and other cities, many grocers stay open late.

Fromagerie

France produces around 400 varieties of cheese, including many made with unpasteurised milk (*lait cru*). This practice is under threat from Brussels' eurocrats, although under the French *AC* system it's illegal to make cheeses from pasteurised milk! Many thousands of cases of food poisoning are attributed to cheese each year, although nobody knows for sure whether the cheese is infected before, during or after it's made. Imported cheeses are rare, although the French make their own 'foreign' cheeses, particularly Emmenthal. Goat's milk cheese (*fromage de chèvre*) is popular and comes in numerous varieties (and prices). It's also possible to buy ewe's milk cheese (*fromage de brebis*). When buying a soft cheese such as brie or camembert, you should state whether you want it ripe (*fait*) or unripe (*pas fait*).

Pâtisserie

A *pâtisserie* is a cake shop selling wonderful (but expensive) home-made pastries, fruit tarts and chocolate éclairs, and perhaps home-made ice-cream. It's possible to buy just one or two slices of a fruit tart or flan or a whole one. Every town and region tends to have its own specialities. Cakes are made to order for special occasions. All creations are beautifully wrapped, even when you buy only a single small *tarte*. Like a *confiserie*, which may be part of a *pâtisserie*, it isn't a safe place for dieters or anyone with a sweet tooth.

Poissonnerie

Fishmongers' (*poissonnerie*) are rare in inland France compared with other food shops, although fish stalls are common in markets. France has unrivalled seafood (*fruits de mer*) and in Europe only the Portuguese eat more fish. Fish isn't, however, an inexpensive alternative to meat and is often expensive, although it's reasonably priced in fishing ports and mussels (*moules*) can be bought for less than €2 per kilo.

Most foreigners find it difficult to identify the myriad types of fish sold in France (French fishermen don't throw **anything** back, except foreign fishermen), which vary from region to region. The most common species include anchovy (*anchois*), bass (*basse*), bream (*acarne*), eel (*anguille*), haddock (*aiglefin* – *haddock* is smoked haddock), mackerel (*maquereau*), monkfish (*baudroie/lot*), mullet (*barbeau*), octopus (*pieuvre*), plaice (*carrelet*), salmon (*saumon*), sardine (*sardine*), sea bass (*bar/loup*), skate (*raie*), sole (*sole*), squid (*calmar*), trout (*truite*), tuna (*thon*), turbot (*turbot*), whitefish (*blanc*) and whiting (*merlan*). Fish are cleaned, scaled and 'topped and tailed' free on request.

Common shellfish (*coquillage*) include clams (*clovisse/flie/palourde/vernis* according to size), cockles (*coque*), crab (*crabe*), crayfish (*langoustine*), lobster (*langouste* or *homard*), mussels (*moules*), oysters (*huîtres* – see below), prawns (*crevette rose*), scallops (*coquille Saint-Jacques*) and shrimps (*crevette*). The 'queen' of mussels, *moules de bouchot* from Normandy's Mont St Michel bay, have recently become the first seafood to be awarded an *AOC*.

France is by far Europe's largest producer of oysters (150,000 tonnes annually compared with Ireland, the second-largest, with a mere 4,000), which aren't just for millionaires and cost as little as €2.50 to €3 per dozen in fishing ports, depending on the size (they're graded into six sizes, including the monster *pied du cheval*, which can weigh up to 2kg!) and variety (the queen of oysters is the *huître de claire*), although they can cost up to three as much in markets and supermarkets. Oysters are 'properly' eaten raw (despite periodical 'scares'), although they're equally tasty cooked.

All fish must be labelled with its source (e.g. wild or farmed), the location of the catch (if wild), and its commercial and scientific names. There are three quality grades: *Label Rouge* (top quality, like meat), *Certification de Conformité Produit/CCP* (medium quality) and *Qualité Aquaculture de France* (basic quality).

Health Food Shops

There are few 'health food' shops in comparison with many other Western countries (e.g. the UK) – the French believe **all** food is healthy! – and they sell meat products as well as vegetarian and vegan food (see **Vegetarian & Vegan Food** on page 489). The best known chain is Naturalia France.

Foreign Food Shops

As Europe's largest agricultural nation, France promotes and sells its own produce in preference to importing food. In fact, there's almost a national conspiracy to keep foreign (especially British!) produce out. French supermarkets sell few foreign foods, with the exception of biscuits, coffee and tea, confectionery, preserves, Italian pasta, Chinese foods, delicatessen foods (e.g. *charcuterie*) and perhaps a few cheeses, particularly Dutch (many French people are unaware that there are any British cheeses!). You may also find American hamburger buns, and British-style (sliced) bread, marmalades and sauces (e.g. HP).

Foreign food shops are common in Paris and some other cities (notably Toulouse), including shops selling American, Arabic, British, Chinese, Greek, Hebrew, Indian, Italian and Japanese specialities. In Paris, Galeries Lafayette features a British Food Hall and the Grande Épicerie de Paris is an international grocery store offering foods from the UK, the US and other countries. Other American food shops in the capital include Thanksgiving (4th *arrondissement*) and The Real McCoy (7th).

The CityVox website (⌨ http://www.cityvox.com) provides details of shops selling foreign food and other products in selected cities. Foreign food can be ordered from abroad via the internet, although prices are inevitably high. Delivery usually takes around a week and the carriage charge for a 20kg (45lb) parcel is around €15.

MARKETS

Markets are a common sight in towns and villages and are an essential part of French life, largely unaffected by competition from supermarkets and hypermarkets. They're colourful, entertaining and an experience not to be missed, even if you don't plan to buy anything. There are generally three kinds of market in France: indoor markets, permanent street markets and travelling open-air street markets that move from neighbourhood to neighbourhood on different days of the week or month. Many small towns hold a market or fair once a month, usually on the same date each month.

The *raison d'être* of the French market is its fresh meat, fruit, vegetables, fish, cheese, bread and other foods, most of which is produced locally, although it's generally more expensive than in supermarkets. In many markets a wide range of live 'food' is available, including snails, lobsters, crabs, ducks, chickens, guinea fowl, pigeons and rabbits. Most rural food markets have a selection of stalls run by organic farmers. A variety of other goods are commonly sold in markets, including flowers, plants, clothes and shoes, ironmongery, crockery and hardware.

Specialist markets (particularly in Paris) include antiques, books, clothes, stamps/postcards, flowers, birds and pets. Antique and flea markets (*marché aux puces*) are common, the largest being held at Saint-Ouen in Paris, with 7km (4mi) of shops selling second-hand goods, antiques and curios (*brocante*). It's open every Saturday, Sunday and Monday from 07.30 until 19.00. Paris also has a number of smaller flea markets. Don't expect to find many bargains in Paris, where anything worth buying is snapped up by dealers. However, in provincial *foire à tout* (a cross between a flea market and a car boot sale) you can turn up some real bargains, particularly fine china (e.g. Limoges). For further money-saving tips, see **Sales & Bargain Shopping** on page 478.

All produce is clearly marked with its price per piece (*pièce*) or per kilo (*kilo*). When shopping for food in markets, most vendors object to customers handling the fruit and vegetables, as their job is to serve you the best available items, although you needn't be shy about asking to taste a piece of cheese or fruit (markets are the best place to taste the flavour of the real France). Best buys are often found when stallholders are closing, particularly at the weekend. It's wise to take a bag when buying fresh produce, as they aren't always provided.

The most popular days for markets are Wednesdays and Saturdays, although they can be found somewhere every day of the week except Mondays. In the provinces, markets are often held in the mornings only, from around 06.00 until 12.00 or 13.00 (shrewd shoppers get there before 09.00). You need to get up with the birds to shop at some wholesale markets (e.g. in Paris), open from around 04.00 to 08.00.

Every district (*arrondissement*) in Paris has at least two or three weekly street markets, some of which close for lunch, e.g. from 13.00 to 16.00, and continue until 19.00 or 20.00. There are Sunday morning markets in many towns.

To find out when local markets are held, ask at your local tourist office or town hall. Market days may be listed on a sign when entering a town (which will also indicate related parking restrictions). A useful guide to French markets is Anne Gregg's *Tarragon & Truffles* (Bantam Books), according to which the following are France's 'best' markets: L'Aigle (Normandy, Tuesdays), Arcachon (Aquitaine, daily), Bordeaux (Aquitaine, especially Sundays), Cahors (Midi-Pyrénées, Saturdays), Clamecy (Burgundy, Saturdays), Fère-en-Tardenois (Picardy, Wednesdays), Forcalquier (Provence, Mondays), La Mouff' (Paris, daily), Strasbourg (Alsace, Tuesdays, Wednesdays, Fridays and Saturdays and the Christmas market throughout December) and Uzès (Languedoc-Roussillon, Saturdays and Sundays).

DEPARTMENT & CHAIN STORES

France invented the department store (*grand magasin*) and it has many excellent ones, although they've suffered falling sales in recent years and a number have failed. Among the most famous department stores are Au Bon Marché (the first department store in France, founded in 1852), Printemps (best for perfumes), Galeries Lafayette (famous for high fashion) and La Samaritaine, the largest department store in Paris.

Fashion is the forte of most Parisian department stores, many of which stage regular fashion shows. Most also specialise in cosmetics and provide money-changing services, export discounts (i.e. VAT refunds), a travel agency, and theatre and concert ticket sales. Some department stores, such as Printemps, give foreign visitors a 10 per cent discount on all purchases. Many department stores also have a food (*alimentation*) department.

Department stores don't close for lunch and usually open from 09.30 to about 19.00 Mondays to Saturdays, with late-night shopping on one day until around 21.30. Most deliver goods within a certain radius and also send goods overseas (for a fee). If you're making a number of purchases from different departments, you can often obtain a *carnet d'achats* and pay for everything at the same time.

Chain stores are rarer than in most other European countries. French chain stores include Bally and Eram (shoes), and FNAC (audio, books and video). Department stores such as Printemps, Au Bon Marché, Trois Quartiers, La Samaritaine and Nouvelles Galeries are also chain stores, with branches in several towns. Chain stores such as Monoprix and Prisunic (subsidiaries of Galeries Lafayette and Printemps respectively) and Uniprix, which are like budget department stores and known as *magasins populaires*, have outlets throughout France.

There are also a number of British and other foreign chain stores operating in France, including The Body Shop, Brentanos, Burton, C & A, Espirit, Gap, Habitat, Ikea, Jaeger, Toys 'R' Us, Virgin Megastore, WH Smith and Zara.

SUPERMARKETS & HYPERMARKETS

There are supermarkets (*supermarchés*) and hypermarkets (*hypermarchés*) – both often referred to as 'large areas' (*grandes surfaces*) – in or just outside most towns. Among the leading supermarket and hypermarket chains are Auchan/ATAC,

Carrefour, Casino, Champion, Intermarché, E. Leclerc, Prisunic and Super U/Hyper U. A hypermarket is officially defined as a supermarket with over 2,500m^2 (27,000ft^2) of floor space. Hypermarkets are often located in a shopping or commercial centre (*centre commercial*) with many smaller shops, cafés and restaurants (often including a self-service restaurant), toilets, telephone booths, a huge free car park, and a petrol station (usually the cheapest source).

Hypermarkets are generally open all day from 08.00 until 21.00 or 22.00 from Mondays to Saturdays and don't close for lunch. Supermarkets usually open at 08.00 or 09.00 and close earlier than hypermarkets, e.g. 19.00 or 19.30, or perhaps later on Fridays. Some small supermarkets close for lunch, e.g. 12.30 to 15.00, although not usually on Saturdays, and some supermarkets are open on Sunday mornings. Many supermarkets and hypermarkets have petrol stations which are open 24 hours a day for credit or debit card users.

Hypermarkets sell everything you would expect to find in a supermarket plus books, CDs, DVDs and cassettes (and players), TVs, stereo equipment, computers and accessories, cameras, furniture, textiles, household goods, gardening equipment and garden furniture, domestic electrical equipment, DIY goods, 'white' and 'brown' goods (refrigerators, freezers, washing machines, cookers, etc.), sports equipment, jewellery, bicycles, tools, car accessories, kitchenware, clothes and shoes, toys, and magazines and newspapers (including foreign newspapers). Many supermarkets and hypermarkets have heel (and key) bars, cash machines, photocopiers, instant photo booths and other ancillary facilities. All supermarket and hypermarket chains publish regular brochures and leaflets containing special offers.

One thing you won't find in supermarkets or hypermarkets is much in the way of medicines, which can be bought only at a chemist's (see **Medicines** on page 299), or any tobacco products, for which you must go to a *tabac* (see **Tobacconists'** on page 497).

The French are keen on DIY (*bricolage*) and there are numerous DIY superstores, some of which (e.g. Castorama) offer free telephone advice and DIY courses. There are also supermarkets for furniture (e.g. But) and electrical goods (e.g. Darty). France even has funeral supermarkets (Roc-Eclerc), where you can choose your coffin and headstone at your leisure.

The French are fanatical gardeners (a fairly recent phenomenon), and many hypermarkets have extensive garden departments, often selling plants as well as gardening equipment. There are also dedicated garden centres (*jardinerie*) and nurseries (*pépinerie*) in or on the outskirts of most towns.

When you enter a supermarket or hypermarket, there's often a counter, called a *consigne*, where you must leave bags and goods purchased elsewhere. You should provide your own shopping bags, as apart from flimsy plastic bags (*poches/sacs*), of which you may be allowed only a few (e.g. for fruit and vegetables), supermarkets don't provide free bags, although bags can usually be purchased for a few centimes (and are replaced free when they wear out). You may also be able to buy insulated bags for preventing frozen food from thawing in your car. Note, however, that plastic bags are due to be banned altogether from 2010. Checkout staff don't bag your purchases or take them to your car for you.

It's essential to have a €1 coin (or similar size token/*jeton*) to use a trolley. You insert the coin in a slot to release the trolley and, when you return it to the trolley park and lock it into another trolley, your coin is returned. This isn't to prevent trolley theft but so that trolleys aren't left all over the car park (although this deprives many people of jobs as trolley-collectors).

Food

Most supermarkets and hypermarkets that sell food have separate counters for meat, fish, bread and cheese. The French generally don't like to buy pre-packaged meat, fish, fruit or vegetables. Supermarkets sell excellent fresh fruit and vegetables, the best and cheapest usually being local produce (French farmers do their utmost to ensure that inexpensive foreign produce never reaches the shops), although the choice may be limited to what's in season and there may be little in the way of 'exotic' (i.e. imported) produce at any price. Supermarkets sell few foreign foods, although some have sections (usually hidden) where imported products can be found (see **Foreign Food** on page 485). Some supermarkets also have a salad bar. Fruit and vegetables may be sold individually (*la pièce*) or by kilo (*le kg*). In the latter case, they may be weighed by an assistant or you weigh them yourself on scales with buttons depicting the various produce. **They aren't weighed at checkouts** (If you forget to weigh something, you will be instructed by the checkout assistant to go and do so, while frustrated shoppers in the queue behind tut!).

There's a huge choice of tinned vegetables (and tinned meats) in French supermarkets, most superior to foreign varieties, but few frozen vegetables (except diced vegetables in various regional 'recipes'). There may be a limited choice of frozen and convenience foods, although what's available is reasonably priced and of good quality, and microwave meals are rare. However, the French are consuming more fast foods than ever (to the detriment of traditional foodstuffs).

As in other countries, perishable items have a sell-by date (*date limite de vente*) or use-by date (*date limite d'utilisation optimale/DLUO*), which may also be described as a 'consume-by-date' (*date limite de consommation/DLC*) or 'expiry date' (*date de péremption*). Eggs are sold in two 'grades': *frais* (with a sell-by date 28 days after laying) and *extra frais* (sold within nine days of laying); some producers put the laying date on the box. Only *extra frais* eggs should be eaten raw (e.g. in mayonnaise). Most items are bar-coded; if there's a bar code but no price (e.g. on frozen items), you can usually check the price at a bar code reading machine nearby.

Vegetarian & Vegan Food

France is a nation of carnivores, and vegetarian food (other than fruit and vegetables) is in short supply, although supermarkets are beginning to stock vegetarian prepared meals, and other products. Vegans will have a difficult time living in France, where veganism isn't even widely understood. Information about vegetarianism in France can be found on the website of the French vegetarian association, the Alliance Végétarienne (🖥 http://www.vegetarisme.fr). Vegetarians looking for recipe ideas should consult 🖥 http://www.cuisine-vegetarienne.com.

Diet Food

There's less 'diet' (*diététique*, *minceur* or *lite*) food than in some other Western countries (e.g. the UK and US), although the French buy around four times more diet food than a decade ago. Low-fat yoghurts in particular have proliferated and other low-fat foods (e.g. cheeses, milk and cream) are widely available.

Organic, GM & 'Fair Trade' Food

As in other Western countries, there's an increasing amount of organic agriculture (*agriculture biologique*) in France, where there are now some 10,000 organic farms. Organic products, which are widely available in supermarkets and hypermarkets, are labelled '*bio*'. However, organic food tends to be 30 to 100 per cent more expensive than 'ordinary' food, and a new type of food called *agriculture raisonnée* is now available offering a compromise (in both price and production methods).

France imposes strict regulations regarding the production and sale of genetically modified (GM) food (*organismes génétiquement modifies/OGM*). Although GM tests are now being carried out at around 40 sites, only two GM plants have so far been authorised: a herbicide-resistant soya and an insecticide-producing corn, both of which are used mainly in animal feed. However, they can also be used as additives in food such as biscuits, desserts and 'ready meals' without any indication on the label, unless they constitute more than 0.5 per cent of the total content. On the other hand, food containing no GM plants may be labelled '*sans OGM*' and certain French food manufacturers, including Danone, Knorr, Marie Surgelé and Nestlé claim not to use any GM products.

'Fair trade' food (*commerce équitable*) recently made an appearance in French supermarkets, although it hasn't yet caught on.

DRINK

Drinking is an integral part of everyday life in France, where most people have a daily tipple. (Even children can purchase alcohol, although they aren't allowed to drink it until they're 16.) The days of cheap French booze, however, may be numbered, as the government is raising taxes on alcoholic drinks (which currently account for 16.6 per cent of a bottle of wine, 22.6 per cent of a bottle of beer and around 38 per cent of a bottle of spirits) ostensibly to reduce the incidence of alcoholism and its cost to the state, although even a 1 per cent increase will conveniently raise an extra €30m in revenue. There's also plenty of choice among non-alcoholic drinks.

Wine

France is, of course, world-famous for its wines, and one of the essential features of a civilised home is a large cellar (*cave*), where wines are left to mature for years. Despite its renown, the French wine industry is in crisis as more and more foreigners switch to 'new world' wines (see **Vin à Appellation d'Origine Contrôlée** below) and the French themselves, though inseparably wedded to their own wines, drink less and less. Indeed, the popular view of the French as great drinkers could hardly be further from the truth: their alcohol consumption per head is relatively low (wine consumption has reduced by a third in the last 25 years) and there's a growing anti-alcohol lobby.

The laws governing the production of wine in France are the strictest in the world but have recently been revised in order to give wine makers greater scope for experimentation and 'characterisation' of their products. French wine is classified under four categories, officially recognised and enforced by the French government and EU wine legislation, as detailed below. Early or new (*primeur* or *nouveau*) 'first pressing' wines are produced in most areas and include the famous (and over-priced) Beaujolais *nouveau* (more correctly termed Beaujolais *primeur*), although other *primeurs*, which include white wines, are as good or better. See also **Wine** on page 431.

Vin de Table

Vin de table is the lowest wine classification in France. Produced from any number of different varieties of grape, it may also be a blend of wines from different regions or even countries. The designation *vin de table* isn't necessarily an indication of inferior quality, however, as some *vins de table* are better quality than *AOC* wines (see below). Producers of *VDQS* and *AOC* wines may be limited in the amount they can sell under that classification and the rest becomes *vin de table* or *vin de pays* (you need to be 'in the know' to snap up a good wine masquerading as ordinary plonk). On the other hand, some *vins de table* are virtually undrinkable. Bottles with screw tops are usually a sign of poor quality, but the very worst wines are sold in returnable litre bottles with plastic caps, the only good thing about which is that you're refunded a deposit (*consigne*) when you take them back. Table wine is widely referred to as *vin ordinaire*, although this isn't an official classification but a generic term used to refer to inexpensive wine.

Vin de Pays

Vin de pays (literally 'country wine') is produced from specified types of grape and grown in a particular area (indicated on the label) and isn't a blend. As with *vin de table* wines, quality varies considerably; unlike *vin de table*, *vin de pays* can be expensive. Both *vin de pays* and *VDQS* wines (see below) must undergo official annual independent tastings to be awarded or retain their classifications.

Vin Délimité de Qualité Supérieure

Introduced in 1945, a *VDQS* classification originally served as a proving ground for quality wines before they were awarded full *AOC* status (see below), but the classification became rare as an increasing number of *VDQS* wines attained *AOC* status and it has recently been abolished, although you may still come across some *VDQS* wines made before 2006.

Vin à Appellation d'Origine Contrôlée

Appellation d'origine contrôlée (*AOC*) wines comprise some 40 per cent of total output and are subject to stringent regulations established by the Institut National des Appellations d'Origine des Vins et Eaux-de-Vie (INAO). There are 466 *appelations*, each produced in a strictly defined area under exacting regulations including the types of grape used, the quantity of vines planted per hectare, vine pruning and fertilising methods, the quantity of wine produced per hectare, the method of harvesting and bottling, the minimum alcohol content of the wine . . . even the size of the label! In areas such as Bordeaux and Burgundy, where there's a concentration of quality wine growers, wines from top-ranking vineyards are further categorised into growths (*cru*) such as *grand cru* and *premier cru*, denoting the highest quality (and most expensive) wines. Those with deep pockets may like to invest in some 2005 wines, as this is generally regarded to have been a 'vintage' year.

All fine wines have an *AOC* classification, but it isn't a guarantee of quality, and a good *vin de pays* is often better than a second-rate *AOC* wine. It's reckoned that almost 10 per cent of *AOC* wines are 'undrinkable' and up to a third unsuitable for serving to a discerning drinker.

Falling sales of fine French wines (up to 5 per cent per year for the last three decades in the domestic market and almost 10 per cent annually for the past few years in the export market), particularly in the Bordeaux region, where it's estimated that up to 1,000 small producers are on the verge of bankruptcy, have recently prompted the INAO to revise the 70-year-old *AOC* system, although the changes don't go nearly far enough. 'Elite' wines – i.e. those that conform to even more stringent production and quality controls – will (ungrammatically) be labelled *'appellation d'origine contrôlée excellence'* (*AOCE*), while producers of lesser *AOC*s are now allowed to 'tinker' with them, for example by adding wood chips and even water. It's doubtful, however, that this reactionary policy will do much to make French wines more competitive with those produced under more liberal conditions in the 'new world' and in 2006 Bordeaux winegrowers agreed to turn 5 per cent of their production into spirits (known as 'crisis distillation'), while in other areas surplus production has ended up as vinegar and even 'biofuel', although typically the French have managed to optain a government subsidy to offset their losses.

Champagne

Champagne is produced in the area of the same name centred around the towns of Reims and Epernay. Champagne drinking has less snob appeal in France than in many other countries, and most French families will crack open a bottle of 'champers' to toast a success or for a family celebration (in fact, they rarely bother with anything less). Champagne costs around €12 per bottle from an 'anonymous' producer or from around €20 from a well-known house. You pay a premium for the famous names (*grandes marques*), and champagne from smaller producers (*petits champagnes*) is usually excellent.

Many other sparkling wines are made by the champagne method (*méthode champenoise*) and sold in champagne bottles, including Blanquette de Limoux (Roussillon), Crémant (from Alsace, Burgundy, Loire and other regions), Saumur and Vouvray (from the Loire), all excellent and costing less than half the price of inexpensive champagne (around €5 per bottle).

Other Wines

There are various sweet wines (*vin doux naturel/VDN*) and wine-based aperitifs (*vin de liqueur/VDL*), many of which are available only in the region where they're produced, e.g. Muscat and Banyuls (naturally sweet), sparkling Brut de Pêche and Brut de Mure (made with peach and blackberry juice respectively), Byrr (wine mixed with alcohol and quinine) and Lillet (wine and fruit liqueur). These are not to be confused with 'proper' dessert wines, made from grapes that have begun to rot, of which the most famous (and, needless to say, expensive) is Sauternes (from the Bordeaux wine region).

Merchants

There are few specialist wine merchants (*marchand de vins/caviste/négociant*) in France, although there's usually at least one in most large towns. There are, however, a few chains of wine shops (such as Nicolas), where prices are fixed throughout the chain, and independent wine shops and local chains in Paris, such as Le Repaire de Bacchus. Most wine shops will deliver if you buy more than a few bottles. A good *épicerie* or *charcuterie* usually also sells wines, although they're generally considerably more expensive than in supermarkets.

Most people buy their wine from supermarkets and hypermarkets, although the quality and range isn't usually outstanding. Some stores have a poor choice and stock few inexpensive or top-of-the-range wines and hardly any more than five years old. In any case, you should avoid buying expensive wines from a supermarket, as they're generally badly stored (e.g. upright and at the wrong temperature). Different branches of the same store often stock completely different wines, even when located in the same region. Some supermarkets sell good wines under their own label and most have special offers.

Nowhere are the French more parochial and nationalistic than when it comes to selling wine. Most supermarkets and hypermarkets stock a wide selection of local wines, but may stock little from other regions of France apart from Bordeaux and, to a lesser extent, Burgundy. You're likely to find few (if any) non-French wines in your local supermarket, where they're normally segregated from French wines (e.g. hidden behind a pillar) and are overpriced.

Buying Direct

Buying direct is the best way to buy wine in France, where many wine lovers buy the bulk of their wine direct from growers, either by making an annual visit to vineyards or by mail-order. Vineyards selling wine direct usually have signs inviting you to free tastings (*dégustation gratuite* or *dégustation et vente*), with the hope of selling you a few bottles or cases. Most vineyards and distillers are geared to receive visitors, particularly the great champagne and cognac houses, which often make a small charge for a conducted tour and tasting. Appointments must be made to visit some smaller vineyards and most are closed during lunchtimes.

The quality of wines you're invited to taste often depends on your ability to make the right comments (and whether you appear to be rich!). Wine tasting has its own unique vocabulary and if you aren't an expert it's best to stick to *bon*, *très bon* and perhaps *très très bon* if you're really impressed!

When free tastings are offered, you can leave without buying, although there's an unwritten rule that you should buy something. Some producers operate a better system, whereby you pay a nominal tasting fee that's returned if you buy six bottles or more. Some producers sell only half-dozens or dozens (cases). Bottles of wine purchased from a grower may be no cheaper than from a supermarket, although you have the advantage of tasting it and an assurance of quality, usually as well as the cachet of having a wine that isn't available in the shops.

If you're serious about buying wine for your cellar, you should go to a recommended producer rather than take pot luck. One way is to consult *Le Guide Hachette des Vins*, an authoritative 950-page annual wine directory that lists producers in all regions with their addresses, telephone numbers and opening hours. Most importantly, it also lists the wines for sale and provides a quality rating. Another way is to obtain recommendations from local experts such as wine waiters or the regional *maison du vin*.

Buying in Bulk

Those who are in the know often buy their wine in bulk (*en vrac*) direct from producers such as wine co-operatives (*cave coopérative*) and wine-growing unions (*unions des viticulteurs*). If you buy in bulk, you may pay as little as €1 per litre for a good *vin de pays*, costing around €2 in a labelled bottle (i.e. 0.75l) in a supermarket. However, *AOC* wines are rarely sold in bulk.

When buying in bulk, you will usually need large white plastic jerricans with a spout, available from *drogueries* (hardware stores) and supermarkets. The best sizes are five or ten litres. You can also buy a collapsible plastic cube (*cubitainer*) with a tap (like a wine box) holding 10 to 20 litres. Some co-operatives sell wine in 5 or even 12-litre bottles.

Wine bought in bulk should be bottled or drunk within a few months, or immediately if you extract some from the container. You will need a good supply of bottles, corks, a corking machine, labels and storage racks (corks and labels are provided free by some co-operatives). Wine can also be stored in demijohns that hold around 4.5 litres.

The grower must fill in a VAT form (*acquit*), obtainable from local tax offices. This form states the type of wine, the quantity, the date it left the producer, the registration number of the vehicle, its destination and even its planned arrival date. It must accompany all shipments of wine no matter how small.

Information

As even teetotallers are no doubt aware, there's more to wine than its colour, which may be red, white, pink or even yellow (e.g. *vin jaune* from the Jura and most dessert wines). It's a well known fact that the more you know about wine, the more you will enjoy it. There are numerous excellent books about wine, including Hugh Johnson's *Pocket Wine Book*, *World Atlas of Wine* and *The Story of Wine* (all published by Mitchell Beazley), *Oz Clarke's Wine Guide* (Webster's), *The Sunday Telegraph Good Wine Guide* (Pan), the *Which? Wine Guide* (Hodder & Stoughton) and, for those who don't know when they've had enough, *Floyd on Hangovers* (Michael Joseph). Information about wine-related tours and holidays can be found on 🖳 http://www.winetourisminfrance.com.

Beer

French beer (*bière*) is usually of the 'lager' variety and comes mainly from the north-east (e.g. Alsace, Lorraine, Picardie and Nord-Pas-de-Calais). As well as the well-known brands, there are many excellent and strong beers (e.g. top-fermented *bières de garde*) brewed by farmhouse breweries. The French also drink Belgian beer but rarely beer from any other country.

Beer is usually sold in packs of 6 to 24 x 25cl or 33cl bottles and is much cheaper than in most other European countries, an average pack of two-dozen 25cl bottles costing around €4 in a supermarket, or just €0.15 per bottle. Supermarkets have frequent special offers on beer, although the practice of selling beer in returnable bottles (*bouteilles consignées/verres consignés*), which works out even cheaper than small bottles, has practically died out. See also **Beer & Cider** on page 431.

Spirits & Other Alcoholic Drinks

Spirits are cheaper in France than in many other European countries, although more expensive than in Italy and Spain. Among the many popular spirits in France are cognac, armagnac, marc (a grape brandy from Burgundy), calvados (apple brandy from Normandy), kirsch (cherry brandy from Alsace) and a wide variety of liqueurs, such as Bénédictine, Chartreuse, Cointreau and Grand Marnier. Imported gin and, especially, scotch whisky are also popular. France is the world's largest whisky market after Spain, and the French buy 12 times as much whisky as brandy, which is suffering as a result. Brandy is classified by age, i.e. *vieux* or *réserve* (three years old), *vieille réserve* (four years old), *VSOP* (an abbreviation of the English 'very special old pale', indicating five years' ageing), and *hors d'âge* (literally 'ageless' but meaning over six years old). France also produces its own gin and whisky, although they're usually terrible (and conspicuous by their silly names).

Aniseed liqueurs (*pastis*) such as Pernod and Ricard are brewed in the south, and Alsace is home to Fleur de Bière – distilled malt beer. If your taste is for the really exotic, try Soho or Yachting Cocktail Litchi (made with lychees), Passoã (alcoholic passion fruit juice), Ortilette or Fleur de Pissenlit (the former made from nettle leaves, the latter from fermented dandelion flowers, whose reputed effect is indicated by the French name!).

Among the many other other popular alcoholic drinks in France are apple and pear cider (brewed in Brittany and Normandy), Dubonnet and fortified wines, drunk as aperitifs. Alcohol flavoured with fruit and other things is common throughout France, every region having its own variations such as *crème de cassis* (which is added to wine to make *kir*), *crème de menthe* and *crème de cacao*, Pineau des Charentes (grape juice and cognac), Floc de Gascogne (grape juice and armagnac) and pommeau (apple juice and calvados). See also **Spirits & Other Drinks** on page 432.

Coffee & Tea

Coffee is cheaper and better in France than in most countries, and decaffeinated coffee (*café décaféiné* or simply *déca*) is widely available. Almost unbelievably, tea-drinking is on the increase in France, where almost a quarter of the population start the day with a cup of tea rather than coffee. Don't even **think** about buying 'French' tea bags, which are expensive and taste of nothing, no matter how familiar-sounding the brand. See also **Coffee, Tea & Chocolate** on page 431.

Milk & Cream

Milk is expensive in France, and many supermarkets sell little or no fresh milk, as most French people buy long-life (*UHT*) milk; this initially tastes awful in tea but most foreigners get used to it. It usually comes in skimmed (*écrémé*) and semi-skimmed (*demi-écrémé*) versions and is sold in litre cartons or (plastic) bottles. 'Fresh' milk may be days old when purchased and consequently goes sour quickly. Similarly, you may have difficulty finding the type of cream you're used to: *crème fraîche* isn't 'fresh cream' but slightly soured cream, and the nearest you will get to British 'single' and 'double' cream are *crème entière* and *crème entière épaisse*, which, like milk, are usually sold in 'long-life' cartons (it may keep for only a few weeks). Sweetened 'whipped' cream (*crème Chantilly*) in an aerosol can (*bombe*) is also available.

Water

Although French tap water is safe to drink and often tastes rather good, most French people prefer to buy bottled water (the average French person drinks 100 litres every year!), of which there's a bewildering variety in most supermarkets (France has over

100 spas). Most mineral water is still (*plate* or *sans gaz*), although sparkling water (*eau gazeuse/pétillante*) is also available, the most famous brand being Perrier. If you drink only bottled water, you're advised to change brands regularly, as each contains a proponderance of certain minerals rather than a healthy mixture.

TOBACCONISTS'

The tobacconist's (*bureau de tabac*, commonly called simply *tabac*) is a unique French institution. They're identified by a vertical orange sign representing a carrot (which dates back to when slices of raw carrot were put in tobacco to keep it moist). Not only are *tabacs* the sole authorised vendors of cigarettes and other tobacco products (see **Smoking** on page 315), but they're also mini-stationers. A *tabac* sells postage stamps, postcards, single envelopes and writing paper, as well as gifts and souvenirs, cigarette lighters, photographic film, and other odds and ends. They also sell lottery tickets and may be agents for PMU off-track betting (see page 429).

Bizarrely, a *tabac* is also the source of government forms and the official outlet for fiscal stamps (*timbre fiscal*) used to pay fines (e.g. parking tickets), government taxes and official fees such as those required for a residence permit (*carte de séjour*). Stamps are sold in denominations of €0.50, €1, €2, €5, €8, €10, €20, €30 and €90, although few *tabacs* stock the whole range of fiscal stamps and you may need to try a few to get the stamp you need.

A *tabac* is usually combined with a bar or newsagent's, and there's often a post box (*boîte aux lettres*) outside. They're usually open late, and some Parisian *tabacs* are open 24 hours.

CLOTHING

Clothing outlets range from street bazaars selling cut-price clothes to elegant boutiques offering the ultimate in chic. The fashion industry is France's second-largest employer, accounting for some 375,000 jobs and worth around €25 billion a year. French men and (particularly) women have a formidable sense of style and are the best dressed in the world (when they choose to be). Even children's fashion is big business, and there are fashion shops in the major cities devoted exclusively to children. Paradoxically, however, the French spend a smaller proportion of their income on clothes than many other Europeans. On the other hand, French women are Europe's biggest shoe buyers, buying an average of over five pairs a year. As with quality clothes, good shoes are expensive (and difficult to find in wide fittings).

The flagship of the French fashion industry is *haute couture*: made-to-order clothes employing the best designers (many are British!), craftsmanship and materials. Garments are outrageously expensive (costing from €3,000 to €8,000 or more). Not surprisingly, the world-wide clientele for *haute couture* clothing is estimated to be no more than a few thousand people, with just a few hundred regular customers.

Everyday clothes are expensive compared with those in other Western countries, mainly because of a lack of imports. As with other things in life, the French generally prefer quality to quantity, and 'classic' clothes are made to last and never go out of fashion. One of the best value ready-to-wear labels is Tati, who have their flagship store at boulevard Rochechouart in Paris and branches in a number of other cities.

Bargains can be found in cities if you're willing to hunt around or wait for the sales (see page 478). Last season's designer labels are usually sold at half-price (i.e. ridiculously instead of outrageously expensive). Most shops hold sales in January and at the end of June, and bargains can be found year round in Alésia, the major discount shopping district in Paris' 14th *arrondissement*. The Forum des Halles in Paris is a giant subterranean shopping centre where you can find every kind of clothing at bargain prices. There are also 'label villages' (*ville de marques*), where designer clothes and other luxury goods can be bought at up to 30 per cent less than in 'ordinary' shops: one has been set up by the English company GVA Collyer-Coxhead near Dijon and another is planned for Damazan in Lot-et-Garonne. Popular women's ready-to-wear shops include Benetton, Cacharel, Caroll, Franck et Fils and Infinitif. Top men's shops include 100,000 Chemises, Alain Figaret, Cacherel, Cerrutti 1881, Charles Le Golf, Kenzo and New Man.

There are also many second-hand shops selling clothes, euphemistically referred to as 'twice twice' (*bis bis*), especially in Paris – e.g. the Magasin du Troc, which sells slightly used *haute couture* clothes and accessories, perhaps worn only by models. Here you can pick up a Chanel suit for as little as a third of the new price (merely excessively expensive). Second-hand clothing stores for men are also becoming increasingly popular among Parisians.

Costume and formal wear hire is possible from many shops in Paris and other cities. There are many excellent women's fashion magazines in France, including *Modes et Travaux* and *Vogue*.

For those unfamiliar with European sizing, a size-conversion table is included in **Appendix D**.

NEWSPAPERS, MAGAZINES & BOOKS

The French aren't great newspaper readers, and only one household in four buys a newspaper. French newspapers are more expensive and smaller than many foreign newspapers, although, like most things in France, they receive a multi-billion euro annual subsidy from the government in the form of tax breaks, reduced distribution costs via the state-owned postal service, subsidised newsprint and direct payments.

There are over 200 daily, weekly and monthly newspapers and magazines in France, not including trade magazines and reviews. However, there are few, if any, national newspapers, as French people generally prefer to read local news. Most daily newspapers are published for a region, such as *Le Progrès de Lyon*, *La Voix du Nord* (Lille), *Sud-Ouest* (Bordeaux) and *Ouest-France* (published in Rennes and France's biggest-selling daily paper, with a circulation of over 1m). *Le Parisian* is the capital's daily newspaper (and the nearest France comes to a 'tabloid'), with regional editions named *Aujourd'hui*.

There are three papers that can claim to be national. The two best-known are *Le Monde* (independent, liberal/centrist), published in Paris in the afternoon and given the following day's date (which can be confusing!), and *Le Figaro* (moderate right, conservative – similar to the UK's *Daily Telegraph*). *Le Monde* is the most intellectual and respected of all newspapers (centre-left – similar to *The Times*) as well as the best-selling 'national' daily. Until recently, it was also the most drab with few photographs and advertisements and little colour, although it has recently had something of a facelift. The third, *Libération* (known colloquially as *Libé*) is an intellectual and one-time fashionable tabloid of the centre-left (it was co-founded by Jean-Paul Sartre).

Other popular newspapers include *l'Humanité* (known as *l'Huma* – the French will abbreviate anything), the recently revamped, official organ of the French Communist Party, *L'Equipe*, a daily newspaper devoted entirely to sport, and *La Croix*, a right-wing Catholic newspaper. There are also a number of financial newspapers, including *Les Echos* and *La Tribune* (France's answer to the *Financial Times* or *Wall Street Journal*), and *Le Monde* has a number of offshoots, such as *Le Monde d'Education* and *Le Monde Diplomatique*, the latter a monthly international newspaper. *France Soir*, a 'popular' and once popular broadsheet, recently ceased trading.

Surprisingly, Sunday newspapers are almost unknown apart from the undistinguished *Le Journal de Dimanche* and *L'Humanité Dimanche*. Many newspapers provide excellent weekly magazines (see below) and reviews, and free local weekly newspapers are delivered to homes in many areas.

A 'tabloid press' is also virtually non-existent, as scandal-mongering is largely the preserve of magazines. France has strict laws regarding personal privacy, although this hasn't prevented the publication of a number of scandal sheets in recent years, including *Minute* and *Voici*, and there are two weekly satirical papers, *Le Canard Enchaîné* (similar to the UK's *Private Eye*) and *Charlie Hebdo* (more juvenile), both published on a Wednesday.

French newspapers are expensive in comparison with, for example, British papers, the 'nationals' costing over €1. On the other hand, they contain 'real' news as opposed to magazine-style articles and the standard of journalism is high.

Where the French excel is in the field of magazines and they produce a larger number than any other European country (around 1,200 monthly, 900 weekly and 700 quarterly titles). *Le Figaro* and *Le Monde* come with Saturday magazines (*Fig Mag* and *Le Monde2*). Popular weekly current affairs magazines include the best-selling *Paris Match* (largely 'celebrity' news), *Le Nouvel Observateur* (left), *L'Express* (right of centre), *Le Point* and *L'Express* (middle-of-the-road conservative), *Marianne* (left, tabloid-like) and *VSD* (semi-serious). Business and financial titles include *Enjeux les Echos*, *L'Expansion* and *Le Nouvel Economiste*. Among the many women's magazines are *Biba*, *Elle*, *Femme Actuelle*, *Marie Claire* and *Marie France* and there are French versions of men's magazines such as *FHM* and *Men's Health*. Other popular magazines include *Figaro Magazine* and *Madame Figaro*, and *Jours de France*.

Newspapers and magazines are sold at tobacconists' (*tabac*), newsagents' (e.g. the Maison de la Presse chain) and railway station kiosks, and in supermarkets. Some are available online, e.g. ⌨ http://www.lecanardenchaine.fr, ⌨ http://www.figaro.fr, ⌨ http://www.liberation.fr, ⌨ http://www.lemonde.fr, ⌨ http://www.marianne-en-ligne.fr and ⌨ http://www.monde-diplomatique.fr (or ⌨ http://www.mondediplo.com for the English version).

Books are expensive in France, where there are no discount book shops, although paperbacks in the *Livres de Poche* series are good value (if your French is up to it). It used to be cheaper to buy best-selling books, such as Michelin guides, from hypermarkets. However, the French government introduced fixed prices to protect small book shops from going out of business, thus restricting the availability of most books. In small towns there are usually a few small shops selling a limited selection of books, rather than one large book shop. There are second-hand book shops in larger towns and cities. Second-hand and rare book shops and markets are especially common in Paris, notably the *bouquinistes* along the banks of the river Seine. Note that the French for book shop is *librairie*; a library is a *bibliothèque*.

English-language Publications

Major foreign European newspapers are available on the day of issue in Paris and a day or two later in the provinces. Some English-language daily newspapers are widely available on the day of publication, including *USA Today*, *International Herald Tribune* (edited in Paris), *Wall Street Journal Europe*, the *Guardian* and the *European Financial Times*, printed in Frankfurt.

Many British and foreign newspapers produce weekly editions, including the *Guardian Weekly*, *International Express* and the *Weekly Telegraph*, which are available on subscription. The price of foreign newspapers sold in France is stated in the newspaper, usually on the front or back page. *Le Monde* publishes a supplement in English on Saturdays. A number of other English-language publications are available in Maisons de la Presse and major supermarkets and on subscription (see **Appendix B**).

Most French book shops don't stock English-language books. There are, however, English-language book shops in most large towns and cities. English-language book shops in Paris include the Abbey Bookshop (5th *arrondissement*), Librairie Albion (4th), Brentano's (2nd), Galignani (1st), San Francisco Book Co. (6th), Shakespeare & Company (5th), WH Smith & Son (1st), Tea and Tattered Pages (6th), and the Village Voice (6th). English-language books are also sold at the Virgin Megastore on the Champs-Elysées. However, imported English-language books are expensive (except for this one, which is an absolute bargain!), usually costing around double their 'recommended' home country price. Americans in particular will be appalled.

Many expatriate organisations and clubs run their own libraries or book exchange schemes, and some French public libraries keep a small selection of English-language books (see **Libraries** on page 443).

FURNITURE & FURNISHINGS

Furniture (*meubles*) is generally quite expensive in France compared with many other European countries and the choice is usually between basic functional furniture and high-quality designer furniture, with little between. Exclusive (i.e. expensive) modern and traditional furniture is available everywhere, including bizarre pieces from designers such as Gaultier for those with money to burn and a need to impress. Many regions have a reputation for high-quality hand-made furniture.

If you're looking for antique furniture at affordable prices, the best bargains are to be found at flea markets (*foire à tout*) in rural areas. However, you must arrive early and drive a hard bargain, as the asking prices are often a joke. You can often buy good second-hand and antique furniture at bargain prices from a *dépôt-vente*, where people sell their old furniture and courts sell repossessed household goods. Look under *Dépôts-vente Ameublement et Divers* in your local yellow pages. There are also companies selling furniture repossessed from bankrupt businesses at bargain prices. A useful guide to antique buying is *Antiques en France: an English [sic] Buyer's Guide.*

Modern furniture is popular and is often sold in huge stores in commercial centres (inexpensive chain stores include But, Conforama and Fly) and hypermarkets, some of which provide the free loan of a van. Pine furniture is inexpensive. Beware of buying complicated home-assembled furniture with indecipherable French instructions (translated from Korean) and too few screws. If you want reasonably priced, good quality, modern furniture, you need look no further than Ikea, a Swedish company manufacturing furniture for home assembly with a 14-day money-back guarantee. (Note that the price of Ikea furniture varies with the country and most items are much cheaper in France than, for example, in the UK.) If you're buying a large quantity of furniture, don't be reluctant to ask for a reduction, as many stores will give you a discount.

When buying furniture for a home in France, don't forget to take the climate into consideration. The kind of furniture you buy may also depend on whether it's a permanent or holiday home. Note also that, if you intend to furnish a holiday home with antiques or expensive furniture, you will need adequate security and insurance.

HOUSEHOLD GOODS

Household goods are generally of good quality and the choice, although not as wide as in some other European countries, has improved considerably in the last decade. Not surprisingly for a nation that spends much of its time in the kitchen (the rest is spent in the dining room!), French kitchenware in particular is among the best in the world. Prices are also competitive, with bargains to be found at supermarkets and hypermarkets. Apart from hypermarkets, one of the best stores for household appliances is Darty, which has outlets in most towns.

Interest-free credit or deferred payment is common and goods can usually be paid for in ten monthly instalments. (If you choose to buy outright a product advertised with an interest-free credit period, you're entitled to a discount in proportion to the length of the credit period, e.g. around 2 per cent for a six-month period, 3.5 per cent for 12 months and 6.5 per cent for two years.) You can also obtain an extended guarantee (for an extra charge), which enables you effectively to 'trade in' nearly new articles for a state-of-the-art model.

Bear in mind when importing household appliances which aren't sold in France that it may be difficult or impossible to get them repaired or serviced locally. If you bring appliances with you, don't forget to bring a supply of spares and refills, such as bulbs for a refrigerator or sewing machine, and bags for a vacuum cleaner.

Similarly, the standard size of kitchen appliances and cupboard units in France isn't the same as in other countries, and it may be difficult to fit an imported dishwasher or washing machine into a French kitchen. **Check the size and the latest French safety regulations before shipping these items to France or buying them abroad, as they may need expensive modifications.**

If you already own small household appliances, it's worthwhile bringing them to France, as all that's usually required is a change of plug. However, if you're coming from a country with a 110/115V electricity supply, such as the US, you will need a lot of expensive converters or transformers (see **Power Supply** on page 118) and it's better to buy new appliances in France. Small appliances such as vacuum cleaners, grills, toasters and electric irons aren't expensive and are of good quality (the label 'NF' indicates compatibility with appropriate safety standards). Don't bring your TV without checking its compatibility first, as TVs from many countries won't work (see page 164).

Subject to electricity supply compatibility, foreign computers will work. Those who don't know the difference between a *fiche* and a *fichier* may be interested in an English-language computer service called Computers4brits (UK ☎ 01273-602623 in or France ☎ 02 33 90 42 64, 🖳 http://www.4brits.net), which will (hopefully) solve your computer problems for £35 per hour and even supply you with British plugs! If you need to buy a computer while in France but don't want it to have a French operating system or an AZERTY keyboard, you can order one from an international supplier or buy one in the UK or Ireland. It's possible, however, to 'convert' a French computer to work with a QWERTY keyboard.

If you need kitchen measuring equipment and cannot cope with decimal measures, you will need to bring your own measuring scales, jugs, cups and thermometers (see also **Appendix D**). Pillows and pillowcases aren't the same size in France as, for example, in the UK or US, and the French use duvets and not blankets to keep warm in winter (besides more 'natural' methods!).

LAUNDRY & DRY CLEANING

Thanks to the French obsession with their appearance, all large towns have laundries (*blanchisserie*) and dry cleaners' (*nettoyage à sec/pressing*), most of which also do minor repairs, invisible mending, alterations and dyeing. (There are more dry cleaners and laundries in Paris than in the whole of many other European countries!) Dry cleaning is expensive, however, and you must usually pay in advance. Cleaning by the kilo with no pressing is possible in some places, and you can also save money by having your clothes brushed and pressed, rather than cleaned. Note also that 'express' cleaning may mean a few days rather than hours, even at a dry cleaner's where cleaning is done on the premises (nothing is rushed in France). Some shops will collect and deliver items for a small fee.

With the exception of Paris, there are few self-service launderettes (*laveries automatiques*), as the French prefer not to wash their dirty linen in public.

Launderette machines are usually operated by tokens (*jetons*) marked with the price and purchased from an attendant. Machines usually take around 7kg (15lb) of washing, although there are often machines of different sizes. Washing powder and softeners are available from vending machines, although it's much cheaper to provide your own. Launderettes have heavy-duty spin dryers (*super-essorage*) that reduce the time required to dry clothes but may make them impossible to iron! Dryers can be very hot, so take care with delicate items requiring little drying.

In some villages, there are still communal *lavoirs*, usually located by a river or near a spring, although these aren't recommended for everyday use.

MAIL-ORDER SHOPPING

Shopping by mail-order (*vente par correspondance* or *vente à domicile*) and by telephone has long been popular, but shopping online has yet to take off, as the French are still wedded to traditional buying methods (although a number of large retailers, e.g. Conforama and Darty, have online catalogues). TV shopping (*téléachat*, 'abbreviated' to *TVHA*) is becoming increasingly popular and is worth around €200m a year.

Mail-order shopping is regulated in France by the Fédération des Entreprises de Vente à Distance, 60 rue de la Boétie, 75008 Paris (💻 http://www.fevad.com). You must be allowed at least seven days to cancel an order (door-to-door sales people aren't allowed to take money).

When ordering goods outside France, ensure that you're dealing with a bona fide company and that the goods will work in France (if applicable). If possible, **always** pay by credit card when buying by mail-order or over the internet, as the credit card issuer may be jointly liable with the supplier if there's a problem. Also take into account shipping costs, duty and VAT. If you purchase a small item by post from outside the EU, you may need to pay French VAT (*TVA*) on delivery or at the post office on collection.

Catalogues

The French mail-order catalogue business is the third-largest in Europe after Germany and the UK, and most French catalogue companies have an up-market, modern image, particularly when compared with the rather old-fashioned image of mail-order in some countries. The leading companies include Camif (💻 http://www. camif.fr); Neckermann (💻 http://www.neckermann.fr), cheap but reasonably quality; Quelle (💻 http://www.quelle.fr), mid-price, medium quality and aimed mainly at women and children; La Redoute (💻 http://www.laredoute.fr), with around 9m customers and specialising in fashion; 3Suisses (💻 http://www.3suisses.fr), with an extensive clothing range; and Vert Baudet (💻 http://www.vertbaudet.fr). Most of these also have stores in major cities and collection points throughout the country.

Goods can be ordered directly from home via catalogue databases and paid for with credit cards (most companies issue their own credit cards). All the major companies offer a money-back guarantee, although the procedure can be complicated, and expensive for heavy items.

Many foreign mail-order companies will send goods anywhere in the world, e.g. Fortnum & Mason, Habitat and Harrods in the UK. Most provide account facilities, or payment can be made by international credit cards. Even if a foreign company won't send goods abroad, there's nothing to stop you obtaining a catalogue from a friend or relative and ordering through them.

Internet Shopping

With internet shopping the world is your oyster and savings can be made on a wide range of goods, including CDs, clothes, sports equipment, electronic gadgets, jewellery, books, CDs, wine and computer software, and services such as insurance, pensions and mortgages. Huge savings can also be made on holidays and travel. Small, high-price, high-tech items (e.g. cameras, watches and portable and hand-held computers) can usually be purchased cheaper somewhere in Europe or (particularly) in the US (for cameras try 🖥 http://www.normancamera.com) than in France, with delivery by courier within as little as three days.

There are literally thousands of shopping sites on the internet; portals include 🖥 http://www.iwanttoshop.com and 🖥 http://www.virgin.com, which contains a directory of British shopping sites. French sites include 🖥 http://www.fnac.com (books, records and audio) and 🖥 http://www.darty.com (household goods).

Internet shopping is generally secure (servers with addresses beginning https:// rather than http:// are almost impossible to crack) and in most cases safer than shopping by phone or mail-order. Nevertheless, internet fraud is on the increase and you should use only sites with secure transaction systems (indicated by a padlock symbol at the bottom of the screen) and, preferably, with the logo of the Fédération des Entreprises de Vente à Distance (FEVAD – see above).

If you buy something via the internet, you have up to seven days in which to return it without penalty and the vendor must reimburse you within a further 30 days. (If the goods aren't as described or cost more than advertised or took too long to reach you, you may return them up to three months after receipt.)

SHOPPING ABROAD

The information in this section applies both to French residents shopping outside France and to foreign residents shopping in France. Shopping abroad can save you money and make a nice day out for the family. Many families, especially those living in border areas, take advantage of lower prices outside France, particularly when it comes to buying alcohol (e.g. in Andorra, Belgium and Italy). Whatever you're looking for, compare prices and quality before buying and bear in mind that, if you buy goods that are faulty or need repair, you may need to return them to the place of purchase. When you buy expensive goods abroad, have them insured for their full value.

Since 1993, there have been no cross-border shopping restrictions within the EU for goods purchased duty and tax paid, provided goods are for personal consumption or use and not for resale. Nevertheless, there are 'indicative levels' for certain items, above which goods may be classified as commercial quantities and therefore subject to scrutiny. For example, people aged 17 or over may import the following amounts of alcohol and tobacco into France (or the UK) without question:

- 10 litres of spirits (over 22° proof).

- 20 litres of sherry or fortified wine (under 22° proof).

- 90 litres of wine (or 120 x 0.75 litre bottles) of which a maximum of 60 litres may be sparkling wine.

- 110 litres of beer.

- 3,200 cigarettes and 400 cigarillos and 200 cigars and 3kg of smoking tobacco.

There's no limit on perfume or toilet water. Don't forget your passports or identity cards, car papers, dog's vaccination papers and foreign currency, if applicable (e.g. if shopping in the UK or Switzerland) – Schengen agreements notwithstanding!

Thousands of Britons have got into the habit of popping across the Channel to do some shopping in the last few years, particularly for alcohol and tobacco. The vast complex Cité Europe, situated just two minutes from Eurotunnel's terminal, is one of Europe's biggest shopping centres, with more than 150 shops and restaurants (attracting over 17m visitors a year). A number of books have been published on the subject, including *The Cross-Channel Drinks Guide* by Tom Stevenson (Absolute Press), *A Bootful of Wine* by Alec King (Mandarin), and *The Calais Beer, Wine & Tobacco Directory* by Alan Kelly and Kim Whitaker (Euro Publishing). The huge difference in the price of alcohol and tobacco between the UK and France has been called 'a bootleggers' charter', although there are large fines for anyone caught selling duty-paid alcohol and tobacco in the UK, which is classed as smuggling.

Never attempt to import illegal goods and don't agree to take a parcel into or out of France without knowing exactly what it contains. A popular confidence trick is to ask someone to post a parcel in France (usually to a *poste restante* address) or to leave a parcel at a railway station or restaurant. **The parcel usually contains drugs!**

Duty-free Allowances

Duty-free (*hors-taxe*) shopping within the EU ended in 1999, although it's still available when travelling further afield. According to guidelines introduced in 2003, travellers aged 17 or over (unless otherwise stated) are entitled to import into an EU country from a non-EU country the following goods purchased duty-free:

- One litre of spirits (over 22° proof) or two litres of fortified wine (under 22° proof) or two litres of sparkling wine.

- Two litres of still table wine.

- 200 cigarettes or 100 cigarillos or 50 cigars or 250g of tobacco.

- 50g of perfume.

- 250ml of toilet water.

- 500g of coffee (or 200g of coffee extract) and 100g of tea (or 40g of tea extract) for people aged 15 or over.

- Other goods, including gifts and souvenirs, to the value of €182.94 (€91.47 for those aged under 15).

Duty-free allowances apply to both outward and return journeys, even if both are made on the same day, and the combined total (i.e. double the above limits) can be imported into your 'home' country. Residents in towns bordering non-EU countries (e.g. Switzerland) and international lorry drivers are subject to reduced allowances. Duty-free sales are 'vendor-controlled', meaning that vendors are responsible for ensuring that the amount of duty-free goods sold to individuals doesn't exceed their entitlement.

If you're entitled to export goods duty-free, you can obtain a VAT (*TVA*) refund on purchases made in France if the total value (excluding books, food, services and some other items) is above a certain amount (around €300; check the exact figure at the time of purchase). Large department stores, particularly in Paris, often have a special counter where non-EU shoppers can arrange for the shipment of duty-free goods. An export sales invoice (*bordereau pour détaxe*) is provided by retailers, listing all purchases and comprising three pages (each of which must be signed), two pink and one green. When you leave France, your purchases must be validated by a customs officer, who will retain the two pink pages. The third (green page) is stamped and returned to you and is your receipt. At major airports (e.g. in Paris) there are *douane de détaxe* offices, where you can obtain a VAT refund on the spot, but you must present your purchases, so don't pack them in your checked baggage. French bureaucracy ensures that the process takes at least an hour to complete. If the refund is made by the vendor, it can take up to six months!

DEPOSITS, RECEIPTS & CONSUMER RIGHTS

Under the French Civil Code, all products sold must be suitable for the use for which they're intended. If they aren't, you're entitled to exchange them or obtain a refund and it's illegal for traders to use 'small print' (*clauses abusives*) to try to avoid liability, although they will often examine products to check that they haven't been misused. You have the same legal rights whether goods are bought at the recommended retail price or at a discount during a sale. Despite all this, obtaining an exchange, let alone a refund, in France can be a difficult, long-winded and frstrating experience, although some hypermarkets now have an automatic refund policy within a limited period (e.g. two weeks), provided you produce your receipt, and will even (if you're very lucky or charming) exchange goods or provide a voucher (*bon*) if you don't have a receipt.

You should always insist on a receipt (*quittance/ticket/reçu*) and keep it until you've left the shop or reached home. This isn't just in case you need to return or exchange goods, but also to verify that you've paid if an automatic alarm sounds as you're leaving a shop or any other questions arise. It's wise to keep receipts and records of all major purchases made while you're resident in France, particularly if your stay is for a short period. This may save you both time and money when you leave France and are required to declare your belongings in your new country of residence.

If you're asked to pay a deposit for an item, check whether this is an *acompte* or *arrhes*. With *arrhes* you have the right to cancel your order, although you will lose your deposit (if the vendor cancels the agreement, he must return twice the amount of the deposit), whereas an *acompte* constitutes the first instalment payment for the item as part of a binding contract to pay the full amount.

If you break something in a shop, you're legally liable to pay for it, although the shopkeeper may not wish to enforce the law.

Consumer Protection

There are strict consumer protection laws (*code de la consommation*, which can be consulted on 🖳 http://www.legifrance.gouv.fr/WAspad/UnCode?code=CCONSOML.rcv) in France, where the price of goods and services must be clearly displayed and indicate whether tax and service is included (as applicable) and refunds must be made for faulty or inadequate goods returned within seven days (or if a refund is requested within ten days in the case of goods installed in the home); after that period, a credit note, replacement or alternative product can be offered.

Every department has a Direction Départementale de la Concurrence, de la Consommation et de la Répression des Fraudes (departmental agency for competition, consumption and fraud repression), whose job is to prevent dishonest vendors from cheating consumers, although it deals only with 'minor' complaints. The national body, the Direction Générale de la Concurrence, de la Consommation et de la Répression des Fraudes (DGCCRF), can be contacted by telephone (☎ 01 40 27 16 00); if you write (in French) with details of your complaint and supporting paperwork (e.g. receipts) to the DGCCRF, BP 5000, 75153 Paris Cedex 03, it will be forwarded to the relevant organisation; sample letters can be obtained from the DGCCRF or its departmental offices and are downloadable from its website (🖳 http://www.minefi.gouv.fr/dgccrf – click on '*Fiches pratiques à la consommation*'). However, the mere threat of an official complaint will often have the desired result. For other contact details look under *Les infos administratives: information des consommateurs* at the front of the yellow pages or go to 🖳 http://www.minefi.gouv.fr.

The Institut National de la Consommation (INC, ☎ 08 92 70 75 92, 🖳 http://www.inc60.fr) is the umbrella organisation for all French national consumer associations. Its website (🖳 http://www.conso.net) provides links to regional consumer organisations, government agencies and other consumer sites, and around 100 model letters. It can provide you with the name of an appropriate consumer association if you require information or have a particular complaint or problem. The INC publishes a monthly magazine, *60 Millions de Consommateurs*, containing comparative product tests, practical and legal information, loan calculations and insurance surcharges. It's available on subscription and from newsagents or via a dedicated website (🖳 http://www.60millions.net).

Other consumer associations include the Union Fédérale des Consommateurs Que Choisir (☎ 01 43 48 55 48, 🖳 http://www.quechoisir.org).

18.

<u>O</u>DDS & <u>E</u>NDS

This chapter covers miscellaneous information. Although not of vital importance, most of the topics covered are of general interest to anyone living or working in France, including everything you ever wanted to know about *toilettes* and *tutoiement* (but were afraid to ask).

CITIZENSHIP

There are three ways you can acquire French citizenship: by being born in France, through marriage or through naturalisation:

- **Birth** – France operates the *droit du sol*, whereby anyone born on French soil automatically becomes a French citizen at the age of 18 (unless he wishes not to), provided that he has lived in France for at least five years between the ages of 11 and 18, but children born of foreign parents acquire their nationality until the age of 13, when they can choose to become dual nationality (French and their parents' nationality) provided they've lived in France for a total of at least five years since the age of eight (i.e. continuously if 13). To register a child as a national of a foreign country, you will need to send certain documents to your embassy or consulate, which may include the following:

  - A *copie intégrale de l'acte de naissance* (see **Childbirth** on page 306).

  - The mother's and the father's birth certificates (originals).

  - Their marriage certificate (original) if applicable.

  - Two colour photographs (of the appropriate size) of the child's face on a white background.

  - The fee.

- **Marriage** – The marriage of a non-French citizen to a French citizen entitles him to French citizenship after three years of marriage, unless they have a child in France, in which case naturalisation is immediate. If you divorce soon after obtainig citizenship, you may be suspected of fraud!

- **Naturalisation** – To obtain French citizenship through naturalisation, as opposed to acquisition through marriage, you must have lived in France for at least five years, be at least 18 and satisfy the authorities that you're of good character and have an adequate knowledge of the French language. The period of residence may be reduced (e.g. to two years) if you've attended certain French institutions of higher education or have rendered special services to the country. An application for naturalisation takes between around 12 months and two years to be processed and must be made to the *préfet* of your local *département*. He will pass your file to your local mayor for investigation and, if you haven't committed mass murder and have paid your taxes, your application will be sent to the Ministry of Foreign Affairs with the *préfet*'s recommendation. The minister's decision is final and there's no appeal against a refusal to grant naturalisation.

Around 20 per cent of applications are rejected or postponed (usually because of inadequate language skills). Since April 2006, citizenship has been conferred upon successful applicants at a solemn ceremony, along with information about citizens' rights and duties and, if appropriate, suggestions for the 'Frenchification' of your surname! Naturalisation confers French nationality upon the applicant, his spouse and his children aged under 18.

While awaiting naturalisation – and indeed to be entitled to remain in France – non-EU immigrants must meet certain 'citizenship' criteria, including the ability to speak French, and earn a minimum amount (which is now higher than the normal minimum wage – see page 24) and must wait 18 months before being allowed to bring family members to France.

Whether or not you must renounce your existing citizenship or can become a citizen of France as well as your home country depends on your nationality. For example, citizens of Norway and Spain must give up their original nationality. Both France and the UK allow dual (and even multi-nationality), but British subjects resident in France should note that they may retain a UK passport only for 15 years, although the period can be 'renewed' if they spend at least six months in the UK.

A passport isn't obligatory for French citizens, although it's required for anyone travelling abroad. A passport can be obtained, within two to six weeks, from a *Commissariat de Police* and costs around €60. French passports are valid for ten years (with a possible extension for a further five years) at a time and can be renewed free of charge. *Cartes d'identité*, which are obligatory but free, are also valid for ten years and obtainable from a *Commissariat de Police*. You must obtain a new one if you change your marital status.

CLIMATE

France is the only country in Europe that experiences three distinct climates: continental, maritime and Mediterranean. It isn't easy to generalise about the weather (*temps*), as many regions and areas are influenced by two of these as well as my micro-climates created by mountains, forests and other geographical features. Generally the Loire river is considered to be the point where the cooler northern European climate gradually begins to change to the warmer southern climate. If you're planning to live in France and don't know whether the climate in a particular region will suit you, it's advisable to rent accommodation until you're absolutely sure, as some people find the extremes of hot and cold in some areas unbearable. If you're seeking 'guaranteed' sun you need to head south. Spring and autumn are usually fine throughout France, although the length of the seasons varies with the region and altitude.

The west and north-west (principally Brittany and Normandy but also parts of Poitou-Charentes) have a maritime climate tempered by the Atlantic and the Gulf Stream, with mild winters and warm summers, and most rainfall in spring and autumn. The area around La Rochelle in the west enjoys a pleasant micro-climate and is the second sunniest area of France after the Côte d'Azur. Many people consider the western Atlantic coast to have the best summer climate in France, with the heat tempered by cool sea breezes. The Massif Central (which acts as a weather barrier between north and south) and eastern France have a moderate continental climate with cold winters and hot, stormy summers. However, the centre and eastern upland areas have an extreme continental climate with freezing winters and sweltering summers. The northern Massif is prone to huge variations in temperature and it was here that a record 41°C (106°F) minimum/maximum temperature difference occurred **in one day** (on 10th August 1885). In Paris, it's rare for the temperature to fall below minus 5°C (41°F) in winter or to rise above 30°C (86°F) in summer.

The Midi, stretching from the Pyrenees to the Alps, is hot and dry except for early spring, when there's usually heavy rainfall; the Cévennes region is the wettest in France with some 200cm (79in) of rain a year. Languedoc has hot dry summers and much colder winters than the French Riviera, with snow often remaining until May in the mountainous inland areas. The Riviera enjoys mild winters, daytime temperatures rarely dropping below 10°C (50°F), and humid and very hot summers, with the temperature often rising above 30°C (86°F). The average daily sunshine on the French Riviera is five hours in January and 12 hours in July. Note, however, that it isn't always warm and sunny on the Riviera and it can get quite cold and wet in winter.

The higher you go, the colder it gets, so if you don't like cold and snow, don't live up a mountain. The Alps and Pyrenees experience extremes of weather with heavy snow in winter and hot summers, although the western Pyrenees have surprisingly mild winters. The Alpine range disrupts normal weather patterns and there are often significant local climatic variations. Central and eastern France have the coldest winters. One of the most unpleasant aspects of very cold winters is motoring. If you need to commute in winter, bear in mind that roads are treacherous at times and can be frightening if you aren't used to driving on ice and snow (fog is also a hazard).

Average annual sunshine hours and days' rainfall in selected towns and cities are shown below:

Town/City	Region	Sunshine Hours	Days' Rainfall
Bordeaux	Aquitaine	2,084	125
Carcassonne	Languedoc-Roussillon	2,506	94
Clermont-Ferrand	Auvergne	1,907	90
Limoges	Limousin	1,974	135
Nantes	Pays-de-la-Loire	1,956	118
Nice	Provence-Alpes-Côte-d'Azur	2,694	64
Paris	Ile-de-France	1,800	112
Poitiers	Poitou-Charentes	1,930	113
Quimper	Brittany	1,749	146
Rouen	Upper Normandy	1,687	131
Toulouse	Midi-Pyrénées	2,047	101
Vannes	Brittany	2,024	131

France experiences many strong, cold and dry winds (*vent violent*) including the *Mistral* and the *Tramontane*. The *Mistral* is a bitterly cold wind that blows down the southern end of the Rhône valley into the Camargue and Marseille. The *Tramontane* affects the coastal region from Perpignan, near the Pyrenees, to Narbonne. Corsica is buffeted by many winds, including the two aforementioned plus the *Mezzogiorno* and *Scirocco*. There are over 800 other named winds in France – from the *A de Pargues*, a cold easterly wind felt in the north-east of France, to the *Zéphyr*, a warm westerly wind felt in the west – listed and described in the *Petite Encyclopédie des Vents de France* (J C Lattès). France occasionally experiences extreme and unpredictable weather, particularly in the south, where flash floods can be devastating. Wherever you live, if you're anywhere near a waterway you should ensure that you have insurance against floods.

Average daily maximum/minimum temperatures for selected cities in Centigrade and Fahrenheit (in brackets) are:

Location	Spring	Summer	Autumn	Winter
Bordeaux	17/6 (63/43)	25/14 (77/57)	18/8 (64/46)	9/2 (48/36)
Boulogne	12/6 (54/43)	20/14 (68/57)	14/10 (57/50)	6/2 (43/36)
Lyon	16/6 (61/43)	27/15 (81/59)	16/7 (61/45)	5/-1 (41/30)
Nantes	15/6 (59/43)	24/14 (75/57)	16/8 (61/46)	8/2 (46/36)
Nice	17/9 (63/48)	27/18 (81/64)	21/12 (70/54)	13/4 (55/39)
Paris	16/6 (61/43)	25/15 (77/59)	16/6 (57/43)	6/1 (43/34)
Strasbourg	16/5 (61/41)	25/13 (77/55)	14/6 (57/43)	1/-2 (34/28)

A quick way to make a *rough* conversion from Centigrade to Fahrenheit is to multiply by two and add 30 (see also **Appendix D**). Weather forecasts (*météo*) are broadcast on TV and radio stations and published in daily newspapers. You can obtain weather forecasts by telephone, e.g. ☎ 3201, ☎ 3250 or ☎ 08 92 68 08 08 (or ☎ 08 92 68 02 followed by a two-digit department code for a local forecast), ☎ 08 99 70 08 08, ☎ 08 99 70 11 00 or ☎ 08 99 70 12 34 (the French are as obsessed with the weather as the British!) or via the internet (e.g. 🖳 http://www.meteo.fr or 🖳 http://www.meteoconsult.fr). French weather forecasts now include an index for afternoon ultraviolet light levels: 1 is the lowest, 10 the highest.

CRIME

France has a similar crime rate to most other European countries and in common with them crime has increased considerably in recent years; the number of reported crimes has almost doubled in a decade: an estimated 18m offences are reported to the police each year (over half of which are for noise nuisance!), 5m of which result in an official crime report (*procès verbal/PV*) and 1.3m in legal procedings, 650,000 in court, although more than half of these cases are dropped. Such figures have been compiled only since 2003, when the government set up the Observatoire National de la Délinquance, and available to the public only since February 2006 (go to 🖥 http://www.inhes.interieur.gouv.fr and click on 'OND' and then 'Bulletins mensuels').

Stiffer sentences have failed to stem the spiralling crime rate, and prisons are bursting at the seams with almost 60,000 inmates (around 95 per cent of them men) – nearly 12,000 more than their official capacity, some housing almost twice as many prisoners as they were designed for, although 28 new prisons are due to open by 2007 and the 'occupancy rate' is much lower than the UK's: 88 prisoners per thousand population compared with 143 (and 724 in the US!). More than 35 per cent of those sentenced to prison terms manage to avoid them, and 1,160 convicted offenders are on parole, wearing an electronic bracelet. There's no death penalty in France, where the maximum prison sentence is 30 years.

Although most crimes are against property, violent crime is increasing, particularly in the Ile-de-France. Mugging is on the increase throughout France, although it's still relatively rare in most cities. In some towns in southern France pensioners have been the target of muggers and even truffle hunters have been robbed of their harvest at gunpoint. Since 2001, a security system called *vigi-pirate* has been in operation near schools and at the entrances to public and official buildings. Sexual harassment (or worse) is common in France, where women should take particular care late at night and never hitchhike alone.

The worst area for crime is the Mediterranean coast (one of the most corrupt and crime-ridden regions in Europe), particularly around Marseille and Nice, where most crime is attributable to a vicious underworld of racketeers and drug dealers. Marseille is notorious as the centre of organised crime such as drug-trafficking, money-laundering, robbery and prostitution. There's a growing use of guns in urban crime, and gang killings are fairly frequent in Marseille and Corsica, where separatist groups such as the *Front Libéral National Corse* (*FLNC*), *Cuncolta Naziunalist* and the *Mouvement pour l'Autodétermination* (*MPA*) have become increasingly violent in recent years.

Thefts are soaring (around half of crimes involve theft) and burglary has reached epidemic proportions in some areas (holiday or second homes are a popular target). Many people keep dogs as a protection or deterrent against burglars and fit triple-locked and steel-reinforced doors. However, crime in rural areas remains relatively low and it's still common for people in villages and small towns not to lock their homes or cars. Car theft and theft from cars is rife in Paris and other cities. Foreign-registered cars are a popular target, particularly expensive models, which are often stolen to order and spirited abroad. Car burning has become a popular 'sport' among urban youth gangs. An average of 200 cars are set alight in various cities (especially Mulhouse and Strasbourg) every weekend. Other 'games' include driving without lights at night and shooting at the first car to flash its headlights!

Pickpockets and bag-snatchers have long been a plague in Paris, where the 'charming' street urchins (often gypsies) are a highly organised and trained bunch of pickpockets. They try to surround and distract you, and when your attention is diverted pick you clean without your noticing. Keep them at arm's length, if necessary by force, and keep a firm grip on your valuables. Always remain vigilant in tourist haunts, queues and on the *métro*. **Never** tempt fate with an exposed wallet or purse or by flashing your money around and hang on tight to your bags. One of the most effective methods of protecting your passport, money, travellers' cheques and credit cards, is with a money belt. Tourists and travellers are the targets of some of France's most enterprising criminals, including highwaymen (see page 280) and train robbers.

Although the increase in crime isn't encouraging, the crime rate in France – especially in rural areas – is relatively low, particularly violent crime. This means that you can usually safely walk almost anywhere at any time of day or night and there's usually no need for anxiety or paranoia about crime. However, you should be 'street-wise' and take certain elementary precautions. These include avoiding high-risk areas at night, such as tower block suburbs, which are inhabited or frequented by the unemployed, drug addicts, prostitutes and pickpockets. Street people (*clochards*) in Paris and other cities may occasionally harass you, but they're generally harmless. You can safely travel on the Paris *métro* (and other *métros* in France) at any time, although some stations are best avoided late at night and you should **always** beware of pickpockets, who tend to snatch bags and jump off trains just as the doors are closing.

When you're in an unfamiliar city, ask a policeman, taxi driver or other local person whether there are any unsafe neighbourhoods – and avoid them! **Note that it's a criminal offence not to attempt to help someone who has been a victim of crime, at least by summoning assistance.** See also **Car Theft** on page 279, **Security** on page 113, **Household Insurance** on page 343, **Legal System** on page 520 and **Police** on page 531.

DISABLED PEOPLE

Since 11th February 2005, when the *Loi pour l'Egalité des Droits et des Chances des Personnes Handicapées* was passed, disabled people (unfortunately still known as *handicapés*) have – at least in the eyes of the law – had equal rights with the able-bodied regarding employment, education, leisure activities and physical access. Specifically, the law provides for the creation of a *Maison des Personnes Handicapées* in each department, where information can be obtained, a nationwide assessment of facilities for the disabled (particularly those relating to public transport) and improvements where necessary, the creation of financial allowances for disabled people to cover the cost of, for example, special equipment in the home or car (in 2006), the enrolment of disabled children at their local school (rather than in 'special' schools), and a campaign against discrimination by employers when engaging staff. Information relevant to disabled people is contained throughout this book.

GEOGRAPHY

France, often referred to as *l'hexagone* on account of its hexagonal shape (the French are also known as *les hexagonaux*), is the largest country in western Europe. Mainland France (*la métropole*) covers an area of almost 550,000km² (212,300mi²), stretching 1,050km (650mi) from north to south and almost the same distance from west to east (from the tip of Brittany to Strasbourg). Its land and sea border extends for 4,800km (around 3,000mi) and includes some 3,200km (2,000mi) of coast. France is bordered by Andorra, Belgium, Germany, Italy, Luxembourg, Spain and Switzerland. Its borders are largely determined by geographical barriers, including the English Channel (*la Manche*) in the north, the Atlantic Ocean in the west, the Pyrenees and the Mediterranean in the south, and the Alps and the Rhine in the east. Mainland France is divided into 22 regions and 94 departments, the Mediterranean island of Corsica (*Corse*) comprising a further two departments (see **Appendix E**). Corsica is situated 160km (99mi) from France and 80km (50mi) from Italy, covering 8,721km² (3,367mi²) and with a coastline of 1,000km (620mi). There are also six overseas departments (*département d'outre-mer/DOM*) – French Guyana (*Guyane*), Guadeloupe, Martinique, Mayotte, Réunion and Saint-Pierre-et-Miquelon – and three overseas territories (*territoires d'outre-mer/TOM*) – French Polynesia (*Polynésie-française*), New Caledonia (*Nouvelle Calédonie*) and the Wallis and Futuna islands. (Although situated within France, Monaco is an independent principality and isn't governed by France.)

The north and west of France is mostly low-lying. The basin in the middle of the country, with Paris at its centre, occupies a third of France's land area and is one of Europe's most fertile agricultural regions. The Massif Central to the south is noted for its extinct volcanoes, hot springs and many rivers. In general, the south and south-east of France are mountainous, although despite its many mountain ranges (Alps, Auvergne, Jura, Massif Central, Pyrenees and Vosges), France is largely a lowland country with most of its area less than 200m (650ft) above sea level. The Massif Central has many peaks rising above 1,500m (5,000ft) and Mont Blanc – at 4,810m (15,781ft) western Europe's highest mountain – is situated in the French Alps.

Almost 90 per cent of the land is productive, with around one third cultivated, one quarter pasture and almost a third forest. While other countries suffer deforestation, France has enjoyed a doubling of its forested area in the past two centuries and an increase of 35 per cent (to 16m hectares/40m acres) since 1945 – a growth of 30,000ha (75,000 acres) per year – so that forest now covers almost a third of the country. France has a comprehensive network of rivers and canals comprising some 40 per cent of European waterways, including the Garonne, Loire, Rhine, Rhône and Seine. The Loire, 1,020km (634mi) in length, is France's longest river. In recent decades, however, France has lost half its wetlands (*zones humides*), which now account for a mere 2.5 per cent of the country's area.

GOVERNMENT

France has a republican form of government dating from 1792, three years after the Revolution, although it has been much modified and refined over the years. Since 1792 there have been five Republics (new constitutions) lasting from 3 to 70 years: the First from 1792 to 1795; the Second, after a revival of the monarchy, from 1848 to 1851; the Third from 1870 to 1940; the Fourth from 1946 to 1958; and the Fifth from 1958 to the present. Since 1870, the government has been headed by a president with a prime minister and two houses of parliament. France's rulers are bound by a written constitution detailing the duties and powers of the president, government and parliament, and the conditions of election. Central government is divided into three branches: executive, legislature and judiciary. The executive is headed by the president, who's the head of state. The legislative branch is represented by parliament, comprising the national assembly and the senate. The constitution is protected by a nine-member constitutional council.

French government has traditionally been highly centralised, edicts regularly issuing from Paris and filtering down to local administrators. However, in accordance with a Decentralisation Law passed in August 2004, a number of responsibilities have been delegated to regional and departmental administrations. *Routes nationales* and minor airports, for example, are now under the control of each department, as are social housing, professional training and certain other educational, cultural and healthcare functions.

The President

The French president – currently Jacques Chirac, who was re-elected in May 2002 – wields more power than his US counterpart and can assume dictatorial powers in a national emergency. He 'leads and determines the policy of France' and appoints the prime minister and government. He can dissolve the house (once a year) should it pass a vote of no confidence against his prime minister and he has considerable powers in the fields of foreign affairs and defence. The French president lives, appropriately, like a king in the Elysée Palace in Paris.

The president is directly elected by the people and must have an absolute majority. Should a candidate not achieve an absolute majority on the first ballot, which is unusual, a second ballot is held two weeks later between the two candidates with the highest number of votes after the first ballot. Just two weeks' campaigning is allowed for the first ballot and one week for the second and there's also a strict limit on election expenses.

Although the president can dissolve parliament and call new elections, he cannot block legislation passed by parliament, but can appeal directly to the people by calling a referendum. This is rarely done (there have been only nine referenda since 1789), the last two being in October 2000, when the presidential mandate was reduced from seven to five years, in line with that of the National Assembly (see below), and in May 2005, when the people rejected the EU constitution.

Parliament

Parliament plays a secondary role in France compared with many other democracies, and it meets in two sessions for a total of just 120 days a year. It has two houses, the National Assembly (*Assemblée Nationale*) and the Senate (*Sénat*). The National Assembly is the 'lower' house, to which its 577 deputies (*députés*) are directly elected by the people every five years. Although well paid, many deputies have other jobs as well. The Senate ('upper' house) is indirectly by a college of some 130,000 local councillors. It consists of 318 senators (mostly local politicians), one third of whom are elected every three years. The Senate has limited powers to amend or reject legislation passed by the National Assembly; when an impasse is reached, the National Assembly has the final decision.

The French use a modified 'first-past-the-post' voting system for deputies. As with presidential elections, unless a candidate receives over 50 per cent of the votes on the first ballot, there's a second ballot a week later. Only candidates who received at least 12.5 per cent in the first round are eligible, although usually only the top two candidates contest the second round, while first round losers encourage their supporters to back their preferred candidate. Most French citizens are apathetic towards politics and abstentionists are the biggest electoral group.

Political Parties

The main political parties are as follows: the now dominant, right-wing *Union pour la Majorité Populaire* (*UMP*), which subsumed the *Rassemblement pour la République* (*RPR*), the conservative Gaullist party founded by de Gaulle, the *Démocratie Libérale* party and the *Parti Radical*; the moderate right-wing *Union pour la Démocratie Française* (*UDF*), incorporating the *Parti Républicain*, founded by former president Giscard d'Estaing; the left-wing *Parti Socialiste*, *Parti Communiste Français* and *Parti Radical de Gauche*; and the extreme right-wing parties *Front National*, led by the notorious racist Jean-Marie Le Pen, and the slightly more 'respectable' *Mouvement Pour la France*. (The concept of 'left' and 'right' in politics originated in France where, after the 1789 Revolution, monarchists sat to the right and republicans to the left of the president of the Assemblée Constituante.) Fringe parties include *Les Verts* (Green Party) and *Génération Ecologie*.

Local Government

For political and administrative purposes, France is divided into 22 regions (*région*), 96 departments (*département*), 3,509 cantons (*canton*) and 36,851 communes (*commune* or *municipalité*). The regions were created in 1972, each consisting of a number of *départements* (see map on page 570). Many correspond (more or less) to the old provinces of France such as Burgundy, Normandy and Provence. Each region has an elected council (*conseil régional*) and executive (*conseillers*), its seat being the region's designated 'capital' town (*chef-lieu*). Each *commune* or *municipalité* (see below) contributes a number of *conseillers* according to its size (from a minimum of nine for a commune with under 100 inhabitants to a maximum of 69 for a town of over 300,000). Regional elections take place in March and the term of office is six years. Regions are responsible for adult education and certain aspects of culture, tourism and industrial development. The state retains control of general education, justice and health services. Expatriates are entitled to vote in certain local elections and should register on the electoral roll at their *mairie*.

Departments

Each *département* has an elected council whose seat is the prefecture (*préfecture*) run by a prefect (*préfet*). *Départements* are responsible for welfare, social services and law enforcement. They're numbered roughly in alphabetical order with a two-digit number, from Ain (01) to Val d'Oise (95). There are also four overseas departments (*départements d'outre-mer/DOM*) – Guadaloupe (951), Martinique (972), French Guyana (973) and Réunion (974). The *département* number comprises the first two digits of post codes and the last two digits of vehicle registration numbers. Departmental elections are held every six years.

Communes

Communes vary in size from large cities to tiny villages with a handful of inhabitants and are governed by a municipal council headed by a mayor (*maire*), who is the most important person in the commune and definitely not someone you want to fall out with! Communes control their own town planning, including granting building permits, buildings and environment. The town hall (*hôtel de ville* in towns, *mairie* in villages) also functions as a registry of births, marriages and deaths, passport office, citizens' advice bureau, land registry, council headquarters, and general information office.

Mayors

Mayors are both the elected head of the municipal council and representatives of the state and have wide powers, including acting as chief of the local police, issuing building permits and performing marriages as well as presiding over local social services, schools and cultural and sports facilities. Municipal elections are held to elect the local mayor, whose term of office is six years. Mayors are frequently re-elected and often serve a number of terms of office. The mayor works in conjunction with the municipal council (*conseil municipal*). Almost all prime ministers and presidents of France have been mayors of their home towns, as are most central government ministers: 80 per cent of deputies and 90 per cent of senators. (A controversial aspect of the French political system is the *cumul des mandats*, whereby individuals are allowed to hold more than one post, e.g. at local and national level.)

France has three times as many mayors as any other EU country, and fraud, corruption and sleaze are even more widespread in local municipal politics than at national level; in recent years there has been an increasing number of scandals involving mayors, a number of whom have absconded with public funds. In addition, many towns and cities have been forced to increase taxes to pay for grandiose schemes embarked upon by megalomaniac mayors, costing local taxpayers millions of euros. Unlike members of parliament, however, mayors don't enjoy *immunité parlementaire*, whereby they cannot be prosecuted!

Paris

Paris is unique in that it has 20 mayors, one for each *arrondissement*. Since 1977, Paris has also had a 'overall' mayor, chosen by the 163 councillors of the municipal council. Paris is both a *département* and a commune, and therefore its council sits as both a departmental council and a municipal authority. *Arrondissements* are shown on post codes (e.g. 75001 signifies the 1st *arrondissement*) and are also written as *1e, 2e, 3e* (1st, 2nd, 3rd) or *Xe, XVe* and *XXe* (10th, 15th, 20th).

Voting & Elections

Only French citizens aged 18 or older are permitted to vote in French elections, sensibly always held on a Sunday. (In fact, they aren't eligible to vote until March of the year after they turn 18.) To register to vote you must have been resident for at least six months in a community. Foreign EU citizens resident in France are eligible to vote in elections to the European Parliament and local municipal elections, provided they've registered at the town hall (first time registrations must be made between 1st September and 31st December), and they may also stand as candidates for councillors in municipal elections, but not as mayors or deputy mayors. To retain your right to vote in your native country, you may need to register as an 'overseas elector'. British subjects should note that they may continue to vote in UK elections for only 15 years after moving abroad.

LEGAL SYSTEM

The French legal system is based entirely on written civil law. The system of administrative law was laid down by Napoleon and is appropriately called the *code Napoléon* (Napoleonic code). The code governs all branches of French law and includes the *code civil*, the *code fiscal* and the *code pénal*. It's regularly updated (e.g. in 1994 a new criminal code was introduced, including clauses on sexual harassment, ecological terrorism, crimes against humanity and maximum jail sentences, which are 30 years). France has two judicial systems: administrative and judiciary. The administrative system deals with disputes between the government and individuals, while the judiciary handles civil and criminal cases. France doesn't have a jury system (abolished in 1941) but a mixed tribunal made up of six lay judges and three professional judges, with convictions decided by a two-thirds majority. However, in the *cour d'assises* (see below), nine ordinary citizens make up a *jury populaire*.

Under the French criminal law system, cases are heard by a variety of courts, depending on the severity of the alleged offence. Civil courts include a *tribunal d'instance* (for small claims, up to around €5,000), a *tribunal de commerce* (for commercial disputes), a *tribunal de sécurité sociale* (for disputes over social security payments), a *tribunal de grande instance* (for cases relating to divorce and adoption, etc. as well as some criminal cases) and a *conseil de prud'hommes* (an arbitration service for labour disputes). Criminal courts include a *tribunal de police* (for minor contraventions such as parking fines), a *tribunal correctionnel* (for more serious offences), a *cour d'assises* (for major cases) and a *cours d'appel* (for appeals; the supreme appeal court is the *Cour de Cassation*). A new kind of judge called a *juge de proximité*, created in September 2002, can deal with claims worth up to €1,500.

It's unnecessary to employ a lawyer or barrister (*avocat* – also the word for avocado pear) in a civil case heard in a *tribunal d'instance*, where you can conduct your own case (if your French is up to the task). If you use a lawyer, not surprisingly, you must pay his fee. In a *tribunal de grande instance* you must employ a lawyer. An *avocat* can act for you in almost any court of law. A legal and fiscal adviser (*conseil juridique et fiscal*) is similar to a British solicitor and can provide legal advice and assistance on commercial, civil and criminal matters, as well as on tax, social security, labour law and similar matters. He can also represent you before certain administrative agencies and in some courts. A bailiff (*huissier*) deals with summonses, statements, writs and lawsuits, in addition to the lawful seizure of property ordered by a court. He's also employed to officially notify documents and produce certified reports (*constats*) for possible subsequent use in legal proceedings, e.g. statements from motorists after a road accident.

A public notary (*notaire*, addressed as *Maître*) is a public official authorised by the Ministry of Justice and controlled by the Chambre des Notaires. Like a *conseil juridique* he's also similar to a British solicitor, although he doesn't deal with criminal cases or offer advice concerning criminal law. *Notaires* have a monopoly in the areas of transferring property, testamentary and matrimonial acts, which by law must be in the form of an authentic document (*acte authentique*), verified and stamped by a *notaire*. In France, property conveyance is strictly governed by French law and can be performed only by a *notaire*. A *notaire* also informs and advises about questions relating to administrative, business, company, credit, family, fiscal and private law. In respect to private law, a *notaire* is responsible for administering and preparing documents relating to leases, property sales and purchases, divorce, inheritance, wills, loans, setting up companies, and buying and selling businesses. He guarantees the validity and safety of contracts and deeds, and is responsible for holding deposits on behalf of clients, collecting taxes and paying them to the relevant authorities. *Notaires'* fees are fixed by the government and therefore don't vary from one *notaire* to another (i.e. they're invariably astronomical!).

Never assume that the law in France is the same as in any other country, as this often isn't the case. If you need an English-speaking lawyer, you can usually obtain a list of names from your country's embassy or a local consulate in France (see **Appendix A**). Certain legal advice and services may also be provided by embassies and consulates in France, including an official witness of signatures (Commissioner for Oaths). French residents have the right to a free consultation with a lawyer; ask at your local Tribunal de Grande Instance for times. Legal aid (*aide juridictionnelle*) is available to EU citizens and regular visitors to France on low incomes.

Anyone charged with a crime is presumed innocent until proven guilty, and the accused has the right to silence. All suspects are entitled to see a lawyer within three hours of their arrest, a person under judicial investigation must be notified in writing, and an examining magistrate may not remand suspects in custody in a case he's investigating. Under France's inquisitorial system of justice, suspects are questioned by an independent examining magistrate (*juge d'instruction*). Other types of judge include *juges du siège* (arbitration judges) and *juges d'instance* (presiding judges).

Under French law, you're required to retain certain documents for a minimum period, which varies from six months to life. For example:

- **Six Months** – Hotel and restaurant bills.

- **One Year** – Receipts for chimney sweeping; telephone bills; *huissier*'s fees; removal bills; children's school attendance records (*certificats de scolarité*); proof of payment of fines.

- **Two Years** – Insurance receipts and cancellation letters; receipts for professional fees; standing order instructions and bank deposit slips; employment contracts; credit notes; water bills; bills for electric appliances and clothing; social security and complementary insurance refunds; property tax demands; receipts for family allowance payments.

- **Three Years** – TV licence demands; currency exchange receipts.

- **Four Years** – Income and wealth tax bills and proofs of payment.

- **Five Years** – Life insurance receipts; pay slips other than salary statements; unemployment payment slips; divorce settlements; electricity and gas bills; rental charges and payment receipts; proof of payments to *notaires*; social security contribution records; receipts for non-salary income.

- **Six Years** – Letters of dismissal; income tax demands and returns plus supporting paperwork.

- **Ten Years** – House and car insurance contracts; mortgage contracts; business account cheque stubs and bank statements; self-employment records; receipts for co-ownership charges; credit notes relating to property ownership or rental; receipts for repairs by a shop or for building work; invoices from private clinics; documents relating to a community property; estate agent's bills.

- **Eighteen Years** – School reports; children's health records (for their first 18 years).

- **Thirty Years** – Building permits; architects' and builders' contracts; bills for building work; personal bank statements; loan and debt records; official papers relating to self-employment.

- **Life** – Identity cards and residence permits; marriage and divorce certificates; education certificates; life insurance contracts; receipts for legal fees; salary statements; building and other work guarantees; unemployment registration; marriage contracts and divorce papers; co-ownership agreements; bills for valuables; records relating to gifts; education certificates; medical records and certificates; hospital bills; local tax bills; savings account books; *livret de famille*; pension payment receipts and other documents.

Product guarantees and receipts should be kept for as long as you have the products, and rental agreements until the end of the rental period.

There are many books explaining the intricacies of French law, including *Un An de Chronique Juridique* and *Le Guide Juridique*, both published by VO Editions and *Principles of French Law* (OUP).

MARRIAGE & DIVORCE

The legal age of consent in France is 18; girls aged between 15 and 18 can be married with the consent of at least one parent, but the government is planning to abolish this concession. Non-French citizens are entitled to be married in France, but divorcees and widows must wait 300 days after their divorce or the death of their spouse before being allowed to remarry (in case of pregnancy).

Only some 50 marriages are performed each year for every 10,000 citizens – the lowest per capita number in Europe. As in many other Western countries, the average age for marriage is increasing and is almost 30 for men and 28 for women, who on average give birth for the first time at just under 30. Almost 7.5m French citizens live without a partner, around 1m of whom are divorcees, and the number is growing each year.

The number of unmarried couples in France has quadrupled to around 2m in the last two decades (among Europeans only the Swedes are less keen on marriage). It's estimated that 40 to 50 per cent of couples who get married have already cohabited for up to two years. Many couples don't bother to get married and simply live together, but French law distinguishes between partners living together 'unofficially' (*en union libre*) and 'officially' (*en concubinage*). Those living together *en concubinage* have some of the same privileges in law as married couples, including social security. To qualify for these, you may need to obtain a (free) certificate from your town hall testifying that you're living together 'as man and wife' (take identification, proof of address and two witnesses), although town halls aren't obliged to issue them, in which case you can both sign a 'sworn declaration' (*attestation sur l'honneur*) that you live together. The major disadvantage of *concubinage* is that it isn't recognised under French inheritance laws, so partners can inherit only the amount allowed to non-relatives (see **Wills** on page 394) and they receive no state pension when their partner dies. A *pacte civile de solidarité*, which is signed at a court, confers some but not all of the legal benefits of marriage (see **PACS** below). In certain parts of Paris, it's possible for couples to have an unofficial 'marriage' ceremony, although gay marriages aren't legal in France (a recent 'union' in Bordeaux was declared unlawful).

It's reckoned that over 40 per cent of French children are born out of wedlock and a fifth are raised by a single parent (85 per cent women). Illegitimacy no longer carries the stigma it once did, and all children have the same rights; an unmarried mother (*mère célibataire*) is even paid a generous allowance by the state.

Procedure

To arrange a marriage in France, either partner must apply at least a month in advance to the town hall where they normally live (they must have lived there for at least 40 days – 30 days' residence plus ten days for publication of the banns). The bride and groom must each provide at least one witness and may provide two, whose names must be given to the town hall when the wedding is arranged. Both partners must also provide passports, residence permits (if applicable), birth certificates (stamped by their country's local consulate not more than six months previously), proof of residence in France, and a medical certificate issued within the previous two months (see below). A divorced or widowed person must provide a divorce or death certificate. You may also be required to produce a *certificat de célibat* (which doesn't mean that you promise to be celibate but that you aren't already married!) no more than three months old, provided by your embassy and a notarised 'affidavit of law' (*certificat de coutume*), drawn up by a lawyer in your home country, to confirm that you're free to marry. For a church ceremony, you may be asked to produce other documents, such as a baptism certificate. All documents must be 'legalised' in your home country and translated into French by an approved translator.

No more than two months before marrying, a couple must undergo a medical examination (*certificat d'examen médical prénuptial*), including a blood test and chest X-ray. The cost is reimbursed by social security. The medical was originally intended to check compatibility between the blood groups of a couple, although with the advent of AIDS it has taken on a new significance. The results are confidential and cannot prevent a wedding from taking place. If a divorced or widowed woman wishes to remarry within 300 days of the divorce or death, she must provide a medical certificate verifying that she isn't pregnant. For a church wedding, you may be required to attend a day's *préparation de mariage* course.

You will then be issued with a pre-marital certificate. Notification of an impending wedding (*bans*) must be published ten days before the ceremony at the town hall where the wedding is to take place.

A civil ceremony, presided over by the mayor or one of his deputies, must be performed in France to legalise a wedding. Although around 50 per cent of couples choose to undergo a church 'blessing' ceremony, it has no legal significance and must take place after the civil ceremony. There's no fee for a marriage in France, although most town halls make a collection in aid of local charities.

Copies of the marriage certificate can be obtained at the *mairie*. Married couples are given a 'family book' (*livret de famille*) in which all official family events such as the birth of children, divorce or deaths are recorded.

Further information about getting married in France (and other countries) can be found on the website of the Confetti Network (⌨ http://www.confetti.co.uk), which publishes *Getting Married Abroad: A Practical Guide to Overseas Weddings*.

Matrimonial Regimes

Marriages are performed under a marital regime (*régime matrimonial*) that defines how a couple's property is owned during marriage or after divorce or death. If you're married in France, the rules of the marriage *régime* apply to all your land or land rights in France, irrespective of where you're domiciled, and your total assets if you're domiciled in France (see **Liability** on page 374). There are four matrimonial 'regimes' (*régime matrimonial*): two communal regimes (*régime communautaire*) and two 'separatist' regimes (*régime séparatiste*). Under a *communauté universelle*, all assets and all debts are jointly owned; under a *communauté réduite aux acquêts*, each spouse retains ownership of assets acquired before marriage (and assets acquired after marriage in the form of inheritances and gifts), while all assets acquired jointly after marriage are jointly owned. Under a *séparation de biens*, nothing is jointly owned; and under a *participation aux acquêts*, nothing is jointly owned but if the marriage is dissolved, assets acquired during the marriage are divided equally.

A marriage contract isn't obligatory but is strongly recommended. A *notaire* will charge at least €300 to draw one up. If you're married in France and you don't specify otherwise, you will normally be subject to a communal regime. If you choose a separatist regime, it's usual to detail in a notarised contract how your assets are to be disposed of. If you were married abroad and are buying a house in France, your *notaire* will ask you which matrimonial regime you were married under and whether there was a marriage contract. If there was no contract, you will usually be deemed to be married under a communal regime. You can change your marital regime, but not within two years of drawing up a marriage contract. However, changing your marital regime is expensive (up to €3,000) so it's best to make sure you set up the regime you want when you get married. If you're unsure about the implications of French marital regimes, you should seek advice from a *notaire* (see page 521).

Divorce

As in most other Western countries, the divorce rate has risen alarmingly (by around 40 per cent) in the last decade in France, where more than a third of marriages end in divorce (there was even a best-selling *Divorce* magazine!), although it's still lower than in some other European countries, e.g. the UK. You can be divorced under French law only when either spouse is a French citizen or when two non-French spouses are resident in France. To be divorced 'by mutual consent' (*divorce par consentement mutuel* or *divorce sur demande conjointe*), you must have been married for at least six months. Other types of divorce are 'consent to divorce but not to consequences' (*divorce sur demande acceptée*), divorce based on fault (*divorce pour faute*) such as adultery, and divorce based on termination of married life (*divorce pour rupture de la vie commune*). The grounds for a divorce needn't be disclosed, provided both parties agree on the repercussions such as the division of property, custody of children, alimony and maintenance. A divorce is usually granted automatically by a judge, although he may order a delay of three months for reflection. A divorce becomes final one month after judgement or two months if it has gone to appeal. A contested divorce must be decided by a court of law.

PACS

Cohabiting partners (even those of the same sex) may sign a *pacte civile de solidarité* (*PACS*), which protects the individual rights of each party and entitles partners to share property rights and enjoy income tax benefits (see page 377). To make a *PACS*, you must go to the local *tribunal d'instance* (listed in the phone book) and submit a written statement that you wish to draw up a *PACS* under law no.99-944 of 15th November 1999, including details of the division of possessions between you. There's no standard form for this. You must also provide identification, birth certificates, a certificate from the relevant *tribunal d'instance* confirming your place of birth, and 'sworn statements' (*attestation sur l'honneur*) that you live in the area and that there are no legal impediments to your making a *PACS* (e.g. one of you being married). Inheritance rights are the same as for married couples (see **Inheritance Tax** on page 390).

MILITARY SERVICE

France is one of the leading military powers (*force de frappe*) in western Europe and a member of NATO. Defence spending accounts for 15 per cent of the state budget and around 3.5 per cent of GDP. Compulsory military service is in the process of being phased out, and French males born after 1st January 1979 are no longer required to serve as conscripts. Instead, both males and females must attend a one-day training course, *Rendezvous Citoyen* or *Appel de Préparation à la Défense*. The course consists of lectures on the army and the country's defence systems and literacy and numeracy tests. If proof of attending the course cannot be provided, you face a variety of sanctions ranging from being excluded from public examinations at school or university to being unable to obtain a driving licence, or a fishing or hunting licence. If you're aged 18 to 26, you can become a part-time soldier (*volontaire militaire*) for a year, and 18 to 28-year-olds can become 'civil volunteers' (*volontaire civil*) and undertake various 'missions', e.g. protecting the environment, for between 6 and 24 months.

PETS

The French are generally unsentimental about pets (and animals in general) and keep them as much for practical purposes (e.g. to guard premises or catch vermin) or as fashion accessories as for companionship. Nevertheless, pets are more widely tolerated than in many other countries. French hotels usually quote a rate for pets (e.g. €8 per night), and most restaurants allow dogs and many provide food and water (some even allow owners to seat their pets at the table!). There are even exclusive dog restaurants. Although food shops make an effort to bar pets, it isn't unusual to see a supermarket trolley containing a dog or two (the French don't take much notice of 'no dogs' signs). There's usually no discrimination against dogs when renting accommodation, although they may be prohibited in furnished apartments. Paris has a pet cemetery (*cimetière des chiens*) at Asnières and there are others in Nice, Toulouse and Villepinte.

Exporting & Importing Pets

If you plan to take a pet (*animal domestique* or *animal de compagnie*) to France, it's important to check the latest regulations. **Make sure that you have the correct papers, not only for France but for all the countries you will pass through to reach France. Particular consideration must be given before exporting a pet from a country with strict quarantine regulations in case you wish to re-import it later.** For example, if you're exporting a cat or a dog or certain other animals from the UK, you should obtain a 'passport' for them confirming that they've been microchipped and that their vaccinations are up to date. You must then continue to have them vaccinated regularly while in France. **If you fail to do this and want to bring your pets back to the UK at any time, they will need to be quarantined for six months.** The cost of a pet passport (i.e. the tests and vaccinations required to obtain one) is around GB£165, plus GB£60 per year for follow-up vaccinations and around GB£20 for a border check on re-entry to the UK. Note that you may have to make arrangements well in advance; for example, a pet must be blood tested at least six months before it can be taken to the UK. Details of the scheme, known as PETS, can be obtained from the Department for Environment, Food and Rural Affairs (see **Information** below). An EU pet passport is due to be introduced soon.

You can take up to three animals into France at any time, one of which may be a puppy (three to six months old), although no dogs or cats under three months may be imported. Two psittacidae (parrot-like birds) can be imported into France and up to ten smaller species; all require health certificates issued within five days of departure. Other animals require import permits from the French Ministry of Agriculture.

If you're transporting a pet to France by ship or ferry, you should notify the ferry company. Some companies insist that pets are left in vehicles (if applicable), while others allow pets to be kept in cabins. If your pet is of nervous disposition or unused to travelling, it's best to tranquillise it on a long sea crossing. Pets can also be transported by air and certain pets can be carried with you (in an approved container), for which there's a charge (e.g. around €100 one-way from the US).

There are companies which will accommodate your pets while you move, take care of all export requirements and ship them to you when you've settled in, e.g. Pinehawk Kennels & Livestock Shippers (☎ 01223-290249) in the UK.

Vaccinations

France has almost eradicated rabies by vaccinating foxes, although there have recently been a number of reported cases in dogs (one in 2001, one in 2002 and three in the first half of 2004). Although there's generally no quarantine period for animals imported into France, there are strict vaccination requirements for dogs in certain departments, where they must be vaccinated against rabies and have a *certificat contre la rage* or have a health certificate (*certificat de bonne santé*), signed by an approved veterinary surgeon and issued no more than five days before their arrival. Resident dogs need an annual rabies booster and it's recommended that they're also vaccinated (*vacciné*) against the following diseases:

- **Babesia canis**, also known as *Piroplasma canis* or Canine piroplasmosis (*piroplasmose*), a parasitic disease carried by ticks (*tiques**) that also affects horses and cattle.

- **Distemper** or Carré's disease (*la maladie de Carré*, also known as *la maladie des jeunes chiens* and *la maladie du jeune âge*, as it mainly affects young animals), a potentially fatal viral infection.

- **Hepatitis contagiosa canis** or Rubarth's disease (*hépatite de Rubarth*), an acute viral disease which attacks the liver.

- **Leptosporosis** (*leptospirose*), a bacterial disease which can be transmitted to humans and can be fatal.

- **Parvovirus** or Parvo (*parvovirose*), an intestinal virus.

- **Tracheobronchitis**, known as kennel cough (*toux de chenil*), which is one of the most common canine diseases and can lead to fatal complications.

* Ticks are a problem in many parts of France and can be lethal. You should invest in a tick-remover (around €3.50 from vets) and treat your pets regularly with a preventive such as Frontline.

Vaccinations (*vaccin*) are initially in two stages, a 'booster' (*rappel*) being administered three or four weeks after the initial injection (*piqure*); a single annual renewal is required. Each injection costs between around €35 and €60, depending on the vet. Serums must be administered separately.

Cats aren't required to have regular rabies vaccinations, although if you let your cat roam free outside your home it's advisable to have it vaccinated annually and a rabies vaccination is compulsory for cats entering Corsica or being taken to campsites or holiday parks. All cats must, however, be vaccinated against feline gastro-enteritis and typhus.

All vaccinations must be registered with your veterinary surgeon (*vétérinaire*) and be listed on your pet's vaccination card or (preferably) in a *livret international de santé*, which, if you plan to take your pets abroad, must also certify that the animal has been confined to countries that have been rabies-free for at least three years.

Sterilisation

Sterlisation of pets isn't common practice in France, where stray dogs and cats are a problem in many areas. Nevertheless, vets are familiar with the procedures, which are usually straightforward. Sterilisation of bitches and female cats not only prevents them from becoming pregnant but can also protect them against the canine equivalent of breast cancer (*cancer des mamelles*), provided the operation is carried out before the animal's first heat. Sterilising a bitch costs between around €130 and €300 depending on the size of the animal, and the vet; sterilisation of female cats costs around €120. Castration of male dogs and cats costs approximately half as much and can be beneficial if an animal is aggressive or prone to running away.

Dogs

There are around 17 dogs to every 100 people in France, one of the highest ratios in the world, and an unofficial dog population of some 10m (over 500,000 in Paris alone). Around 40 per cent of French people list their dogs as the most important thing in their lives (even more important than their lovers!) and the French spend some €3 billion on them annually; there's at least one 'poodle-parlour' (*salon de toilettage*) in every town and there's even a canine *pâtisserie* in Paris, called unimaginatively 'Mon Bon Chien', where pampered pooches can be kitted out with *haute couture* clothing as well as treated to *haute cuisine* 'cakes'. On the other hand, many dogs are kept outdoors and some are almost permanently penned. It's rare to see French people walking their dogs (except for 'show').

Dogs don't wear identification discs and there's no system of licensing. However, all dogs born after 6th January 1999 must be given an official identifying number, either in the form of a tattoo or contained in a microchip inserted under their skin. This rule is designed to make it easier to find the owners of stray dogs and to reduce the incidence of 'dog trafficking'. Around 100,000 dogs are abandoned by their owners every year, many at the start of the long summer holiday or after the hunting season is over, and stray dogs are regularly rounded up and taken to the local pound (*fourrière*) to be destroyed. A further 60,000 dogs are stolen each year and certain breeds are highly prized. It's therefore recommended to have your dog tattooed or chipped even if it was born before this date. Some vets favour tattooing (*tatouage*) because the number is visible, whereas reading a microchip (*puce*) requires a special machine. Others recommend microchipping because a tattoo can be removed or wear off. Identity numbers are kept in a central computer controlled by the French Society for the Protection of Animals (Société Protectrice des Animaux/SPA), which is organised on a departmental basis. Contact your nearest SPA office if you lose your pet.

Dogs must be kept on leads in most public parks and gardens and there are large fines for dog owners who don't comply. Dogs are forbidden in some parks, even when on leads, and on most beaches in summer. On public transport, pets weighing less than 6kg (13lb) must usually be carried in a basket or cage; larger dogs must wear a muzzle and be kept on a lead (see **Pets** on page 225). Some 500,000 people are bitten by dogs each year, 60,000 of whom are hospitalised, and certain breeds of dog (e.g. pit-bull terriers) must be muzzled in public places.

The unpleasant aspect of France's vast dog population is abundantly evident on the pavements of towns and cities, where dogs routinely leave their 'calling cards' (officially known as *déjections canines*). You must **always** watch where you walk: many pavements aren't *trottoirs* but '*crottoirs*'. Over 600 Parisians are hospitalised every year after slipping on dog dirt, and there's a national association of mothers called Inter-Mamans, who have threatened to 'donate' their children's soiled nappies to mayors throughout France unless they take action to clear the streets of dog mess! In Paris and some other cities, there are dog toilet areas. However, most dog owners take their pets to a local park or car park or simply let them loose in the streets to do their business, although allowing your pooch to poop on the pavement is illegal and you can be fined up to €450 if you don't 'scoop' up after it. At the very least, owners are required to take their pets to the kerb to relieve themselves; you're reminded by dog silhouettes on the footpath in Paris and other cities, where signs encourage owners to teach their dogs to use gutters ('*Apprenez-lui le caniveau*'), which are regularly cleaned and disinfected. The capital's patrols of motorised pooper-scoopers (*moto-crottes*), which once picked up four tonnes of doggy-do daily, are being phased out in favour of 'hygiene inspectors' dishing out on-the-spot fines. (Although it's little consolation, it's supposedly good luck to tread in something unpleasant.)

Kennels & Catteries

There are many kennels and catteries (*refuge pour animaux* or *pension canine/féline*), where fees are around €6 per day for cats and €9 for dogs. A free list of over 300 kennels and catteries, *Le Guide des Voyages et des Pensions*, is available from Royal Canin, a pet food company (☎ 08 00 41 51 61), or you can search for a suitable kennel/cattery on the Royal Canin website (🖳 http://www. royalcanin.fr – click on '*Bien le soigner*' and then on '*Le faire garder*'). If you plan to leave your pet at a kennel or cattery, book well in advance, particularly for school holiday periods.

Health & Insurance

Veterinary surgeons (*vétérinaire*) are well trained in France, where it's a highly popular and well-paid profession. Emergency veterinary care is available in major cities, where there are also animal hospitals (*hôpital pour animaux*) and vets on 24-hour call for emergencies. A visit to a vet usually costs €23 to €30. Some vets also make house calls, for which there's a minimum charge of around €60 to €80. Taxi and ambulance services are also provided for pets.

Medical treatment for dogs can be just as expensive as human treatment (e.g. €200 for a scan and over €500 for a major operation) – and it isn't reimbursed by social security. Health insurance for pets is available from a number of insurance companies but in most cases provides only partial cover. There are essentially two types of pet insurance: insurance against accidents and insurance against illness and accidents. The former costs around €70 or €80 per year and covers only medical and surgical costs resulting from accidental injury, e.g. a broken bone, poisoning or a bite by another dog. The latter, which costs at least twice as much, also covers the treatment of certain illnesses and diseases.

As with human health insurance, you should check exactly what is and isn't covered and what conditions apply. Certain treatment may be excluded, e.g. vaccinations, sterilisation or castration, dental treatment and cancer screening, as may certain hereditary diseases. Conditions may include an upper age limit (usually nine or ten years for dogs), a waiting period (of up to four months) before insurance becomes effective, an annual claim limit (generally between €800 and €1,600) and an excess or deductible (*franchise*), which often applies to every claim and can be as much as 30 per cent.

Pet insurance doesn't cover you for third-party liability, e.g. if your pet bites someone or causes an accident, which should be included in your household insurance (see page 346); check with your insurer.

If you wish to have your pet cremated, you must now pay €150 (the service was previously free), although you may bury an animal weighing up to 35kg in your garden.

Information

For the latest regulations regarding the importation and keeping of pets in France contact the Sous-Direction de la Santé et de la Protection Animales, Ministère de l'Agriculture, de la Pêche et de l'Alimentation (☎ 01 56 79 21 21, 🖳 http://www. agriculture.gouv.fr – click on '*Ressources*'). If you wish to import an exotic pet or more pets than the standard quota, contact the Direction Générale des Douanes (☎ 01 40 04 04 04, 🖳 http://www.douane.gouv.fr – the website has information in English under 'Introduction of pets into France').

Further details of the British pet passport scheme can be obtained from the Department for Environment, Food and Rural Affairs (DEFRA, ☎ 020-7238 6951 or ☎ 0845-933 5577, 🖳 http://www.defra.gov.uk). A useful book is *Travel Tips for Cats and Dogs* by David Prydie (Ringpress Books).

POLICE

There are three main police forces in France: the *police nationale*, the *gendarmerie nationale* and the *Compagnie Républicaine de la Sécurité* (*CRS*). French policemen are addressed formally as *monsieur/madame l'agent* and colloquially called *flics* (cops), although there are many less polite names. The *police nationale* are under the control of the Interior Ministry and are called *agents de police*. They deal with all crime within the jurisdiction of their police station (*commissariat de police*) and are most commonly seen in towns, distinguished by the silver buttons on their uniforms. At night and in rain and fog, they often wear white caps and capes.

The *gendarmerie nationale/gardes-mobiles* is part of the army and under the control of the Ministry of Defence, although it's at the service of the Interior Ministry. *Gendarmes* wear blue uniforms and traditional *képis*, and are distinguished by the gold buttons on their uniforms. They deal with serious crime on a national scale and general law and order in rural areas and are responsible for motorway patrols, air safety, mountain rescue, and air and coastal patrols. *Gendarmes* include police motorcyclists (*motards*), who patrol in pairs. The 3,600 brigades of *gendarmes* are to be linked into groups of three or four to improve law enforcement in rural areas.

The *CRS* is often referred to as the riot police, as it's responsible for crowd control and public disturbances, although it also has other duties, including life-saving on beaches in summer. Over the years the *CRS* has acquired a notorious reputation for its violent response to demonstrations (*manifestations*) and public disturbances, although often under extreme provocation. The mere appearance of the *CRS* at a demonstration is enough to raise the temperature, although it has been trying to improve its public image.

In addition to the three kinds of police mentioned above, most cities and medium-size towns have a municipal police (*police municipale/corps urbain*), which deals mainly with petty crime, traffic offences and road accidents, and there's a general movement in favour of 'neighbourhood policing' (*îlotage*) throughout France. Municipal policemen traditionally wore a *képi* (like *gendarmes*), although this has been replaced by a flat, peaked cap. While officers of the *gendarmerie nationale*, the *police nationale* and the *CRS* are armed, *police municipale* aren't, unless the local *préfet* and *maire* decide that they should be.

There are also various special police forces, including the *Groupement d'Intervention de la Gendarmerie Nationale* (*GIGN*), a sort of SAS unit; the *Police de l'Air et des Frontières* (*PAF*), border guards; the *Direction Centrale des Renseignements Généraux* (*DCRG* or *RG*), the 'intelligence' squad; the *Police Judiciaire* (*PJ*), the criminal investigation department; *Surveillance du Territoire* (*SDT*), a counter-espionage division; an anti-terrorist unit called *Recherche, Assistance, Intervention et Discussion* (*RAID*); and the *CSP*, anti-terrorist police who guard embassies and government buildings in Paris, who wear blue windcheaters, carry machine guns and **aren't** the best people to ask directions to the Eiffel Tower.

In general, French police (of any type) aren't popular with the public and have an unenviable reputation, particularly among ethnic groups. Police 'brutality', usually directed towards racial minorities, has resulted in riots in some areas; in autumn 2005, the worst disturbances in Paris since 1968 were allegedly the outcome of police harassment. On the other hand, an increase in attacks on police in recent years prompted the government in 2001 to pledge over €300m for the recruitment of some 2,700 police to patrol the streets and, following the 2002 election, the new Prime Minister announced measures to recruit an additional 13,500 officers within the police and *gendarmerie* over the next five years. It's also planned to 'encourage' the police and *gendarmes* to work together, which they've traditionally been loath to do.

The police can stop you and demand identification at any time (*contrôle de papiers*), so it's advisable to carry your passport or residence permit (*carte de séjour*). If you don't have any identification, you can be arrested (the requirement to have at least 'ten francs', i.e. €1.67, to avoid a charge of vagrancy has recently been abolished!). If your identification documents are stolen or lost, you must report immediately to the nearest police station, where you must make a *déclaration de perte ou de vol*. You will be given a receipt, which will be accepted by the authorities until new documents are issued. It's wise to keep copies of all important documents (e.g. passport, visa and *carte de séjour*) in a safe place so that replacements are easier to obtain.

If you're arrested, you're required to state your name, age and permanent address only. **Never** make or sign a statement without legal advice and the presence of a lawyer. Unless your French is fluent, you should make it clear that you don't understand French and, in any case, ask permission to call your lawyer or embassy. Someone from your embassy should be able to provide a list of English-speaking lawyers.

The police can hold you in custody for 24 hours, although you're entitled to see a lawyer within three hours of arrest. After 24 hours they need the authority of a magistrate. If the offence under investigation involves state security, two further 48-hour extensions can be granted, making a total of five days. If you're accused of a serious offence, such as possession of, or trafficking drugs, it may be difficult to obtain bail. A Council of Europe commission recently stated that suspects in France ran a 'not inconsiderable risk' of being mistreated while in police detention.

The police don't prosecute criminal cases in France, which is done by a public prosecutor. Police can fine offenders (and do so, particularly if they're non-residents) on the spot for motoring offences such as speeding and drunken driving, and fines must be paid in cash (see **Traffic Police** on page 267). You're entitled to ask the name and particulars of any policeman who stops you, although it may be better to do this **after** you've found out what you've been stopped for!

All French residents have a police record (even if it's blank!) and you may be asked to produce it (e.g. if you need to travel to or work in certain countries). To obtain a copy of your record (*extrait de casier judiciaire*), you should send details of your date and place of birth and a copy of your passport and *carte de séjour* to the Service du Casier Judiciaire, 107 rue du Landreau, 44079 Nantes Cedex.

If you need to contact the police in an emergency, dialling 17 will put you in touch with your local *gendarmerie* or *commissariat de police*, listed at the front of your local telephone directory. If you lose anything or are the victim of a theft, you must report it in person at a police station and complete a report (*déclaration de vol/plainte*), of which you will receive a copy. This must usually be done within 24 hours if you plan to make a claim on an insurance policy. Don't, however, expect the police to be the slightest bit interested in your loss.

POPULATION

The last nationwide census (*recensement*) in France took place in 1999, when the population was 60,185,831, an increase of 3.6 per cent over the previous census figure (1990). The census system was changed in 2004 to an annual survey of approximately one-fifth of the population (communes of fewer than 10,000 inhabitants to be surveyed every five years, those over 10,000 to be surveyed annually, but only around 8 per cent of the population each time). The 2005 figures suggest that the population has risen to almost 63m, which indicates that government incentives to encourage families to have more children in order to reverse a declining birth rate, including generous family allowances (even for unmarried mothers) and tax breaks, are taking effect. In fact, it's estimated that the birth rate has risen from 1.71 (1999) to 1.94 (2005) – the second-highest rate in Europe after Ireland. On the other hand, according to the national statistics office, INSEE, which is responsible for the censuses, France's population is set to reach its peak in 2015, after which it will decline.

According to the 1999 census figures, just over 58.5m people live in metropolitan France (i.e. the 'Hexagon' and surrounding islands, including Corsica), the remainder inhabiting the four overseas departments and overseas territories (see **Geography** on page 515). The average density of the population of mainland France is around 100 people per km² (260 per mi²), one of the lowest in Europe. However, the density varies enormously from region to region. Paris is one of the most densely populated cities in the world, with over 20,000 inhabitants to the km² (over 52,000 per mi²), while in many rural areas there are just a handful. When Paris is excluded, the population density for the rest of the country drops to around 50 people per km² (130 per mi²).

Over 70 per cent of the French population lives in the urban areas of the north, east and Rhône valley, although the population of industrial cities such as Le Havre, Saint-Etienne and Toulon is in decline. France's urban population doubled between 1936 and 1999, since when the decline in rural population has been reversed: 72 of the 96 departments now boast a 'positive migratory balance'. Steps have been taken in some areas to revive dying villages, e.g. by linking them to nearby large towns and industrial zones to provide villagers with access to a wider range of facilities and services.

France has few large cities compared with other European countries with comparable populations, and Paris (2.5m) is the only city with over 1m inhabitants, excluding its suburban areas. If these are included, Paris has a population of almost 11m, Lyon 1.6m, Marseille 1.4m and Lille 1.1m. Only five other cities (Toulouse, Bordeaux, Nantes, Strasbourg and Nice) have more than half a million inhabitants, while there are over 32,500 villages with fewer than 2,000 inhabitants.

In the last 20 years there has been a shift away from the industrial regions of the north to the sunny south. There's also a drift away from the mountainous areas of central France and for the first time in history there's a shift away from Paris, as young executives and technocrats head for Avignon, Grenoble, Lyon, Montpellier, Nice, Toulouse and, more recently, the area around Aix-en-Provence and Marseille.

The average age of the population is around 37 years, with some 15 per cent over 65. France is becoming increasingly popular with retirees, particularly those from the

UK, Germany, the Netherlands and Scandinavian countries, which is putting further strain on its state healthcare and pension systems (see **Chapters 13** and **14**).

France has around 4.9m immigrants, i.e. people not born in France (around 7.4 per cent of the population and a net increase of over half a million since 1999, since when almost a million people have settled in the country). Some 1.6m of these are from EU countries, the vast majority Portuguese (the most numerous immigrants), Spanish and Italians, and around 2m have become naturalised. From the early 19th century until the late '50s/early '60s, Algeria was a French colony and Morocco and Tunisia protectorates, and there are around 1.3m North African immigrants in France (although perversely official census figures don't include a breakdown of the population by race, ethnic origin or colour), as well as around 400,000 people from sub-Saharan Africa and 700,000 people from other parts of Africa and the Caribbean. France also has a long tradition of welcoming immigrants, particularly political refugees, who number over 200,000 (most of them from Eastern Europe, Indo-China, the Middle East and Latin America). It's estimated that there are a further 400,000 illegal immigrants, most of them from Africa. The majority of immigrants (around 60 per cent) settle in Ile-de-France, Provence-Alpes-Côte d'Azur and Rhône-Alpes.

Immigration is a controversial and emotive subject in France, where there's a degree of 'racial tension' in some areas and overt racism is common – some 20 per cent of the population voted for the racist *Front National* party, led by Jean-Marie Le Pen, in 2002. EU immigrants are tolerated by most French people, although the same cannot be said of African and Arab immigrants. The majority of North Africans, for example, exist in 'ghettos' in run-down suburbs, particularly north of Paris, with large families, on incomes well below the official poverty line and in a vicious circle of deprivation and lack of opportunity.

RELIGION

France has officially been a secular state since the Revolution and therefore has a long tradition of religious tolerance; every resident has total freedom of religion without hindrance from the state or community, and the majority of the world's religious and philosophical movements have religious centres or meeting places in Paris and other major cities. The majority of the population is Christian, by far the largest number belonging to the Catholic faith (around 62 per cent of the population) and a mere 2 per cent Protestants. The second-largest religious group is Muslims (6 per cent), mostly immigrants from North Africa, and France is home to some 700,000 Jews – both groups being the targets of bigotry and racism. Details of mosques in France can be found on 🖳 http://mosquee.free.fr and a list of synagogues on 🖳 http://www.pages jaunes.fr (enter *Synagogues* in the first box and then the name of the town where you're looking for a synagogue).

Religious observance is declining and attendance at mass has dropped to around 15 per cent (attendance is lowest in Paris and among those aged 18 to 35). Only some 50 per cent of marriages are consecrated in a church and 60 per cent of babies baptised. Parish priests have lost much of their traditional influence and there's a serious shortage of recruits for the priesthood. Few French people are atheists, although many are agnostics. The most important religious shrine in France is that of

Our Lady at Lourdes, which receives hundreds of thousands of visitors every year in search of a miracle cure.

Church and state were officially divorced in 1905 and direct funding of the church by the state is illegal, which means that many churches are in poor repair. The Catholic church is prominent in education, where it maintains many private schools separate from the state education system, although largely funded by the state (see **Private Schools** on page 198). An attempt to abolish state funding for religious schools by the Socialists in the '80s generated fierce opposition and was quickly abandoned.

For information about local places of worship and service times, contact your local town hall or tourist information office. Churches and religious centres are listed in the yellow pages under *Eglises* and *Cultes*, and include American and English churches in Paris and other major cities. There are over 50 Anglican churches in France, and details of English-language services throughout France (and indeed the world) are contained in the *Directory of English-Speaking Churches Abroad*, published by the Intercontinental Church Society (☎ 01926-430347, 💻 http://www. ics-uk.org).

SOCIAL CUSTOMS

All countries have peculiar social customs (sometimes in both senses of the word!) and France is no exception. As a foreigner you will probably be excused if you accidentally insult your hosts, but it's better to be aware of accepted taboos and courtesies, especially as the French are much more formal than most foreigners (especially Americans and Britons) imagine.

Greeting

When you're introduced to a French person, you should say 'good day, Sir/Madam' (*bonjour madame/monsieur*) and shake hands (a single pump is enough – neither limp nor knuckle-crushing). *Salut* (hi or hello) is used only among close friends and young people. When saying goodbye, it's a formal custom to shake hands again. In an office, everyone shakes hands with everyone else on arrival at work **and** when they depart. It's also customary to say good day or good evening (*bonsoir*) on entering a small shop and goodbye (*au revoir madame/monsieur*) on leaving. *Bonjour* becomes *bonsoir* around 18.00 or after dark, although if you choose *bonsoir* (or *bonjour*), don't be surprised if the response isn't the same. *Bonne nuit* (good night) is used when going to bed or leaving a house in the evening. On leaving a shop you may be wished *bonne journée* (have a nice day) or variations such as *bon après-midi, bonne fin d'après-midi, bon dimanche* or *bon week-end*, to which you may reply *vous aussi, vous de même* or *et vous*. The standard and automatic reply to *merci* is *je vous en prie* ('you're welcome').

Titles should generally be used when addressing or writing to people, particularly when the holder is elderly. The president of a company or institution should be addressed as *monsieur* (*madame*) *le président* (*la présidente*), a courtesy title usually retained in retirement. The mayor must be addressed as *Monsieur/Madame le Maire* (even female mayors are *le Maire*!).

Kissing

To kiss or not to kiss, that is the question. It's best to take it slowly when negotiating this social minefield and to take your cue from the French. You shouldn't kiss (*faire la bise*) when first introduced to an adult, although young children will expect to be kissed. If a woman expects you to kiss her, she will offer her cheek. (Note that men kiss women and women kiss women but men don't kiss men, unless they're relatives or very close friends.) The 'kiss' is deposited high up on the cheek; it isn't usually a proper kiss, more a delicate brushing of the cheeks accompanied by kissing noises, although some extroverts will plant a great wet smacker on each side of your face.

The next question is which cheek to kiss first. Again, take your cue from the natives, as the custom varies from region to region (and even the natives aren't always sure where to start).

Finally, you must decide how many kisses to give. Two is the standard number, although many people kiss three or four or even six times. It depends partly on where you are in France. The British travel agent Thomas Cook recently published a *French Kissing Guide*, according to which four kisses are the norm in northern France, three in the mid-west and southern central areas and two in the west, east and extreme south, a single kiss being acceptable only in the department of Charente-Maritime! However, much also depends on how well you know the person concerned: acquaintances might kiss twice, friends four times and old friends six!

Kissing usually takes place when you take your leave, as well as when you greet someone. (It's also customary to kiss everyone in sight – including the men if you're a man – at midnight on New Year's Eve!)

Vous & Tu

When talking to a stranger, use the formal form of address (*vous*). Don't use the familiar form (*tu/toi*) or call someone by his Christian name until you're invited to do so. Generally the older, more important or simply local person will invite the other to use the familiar *tu* form of address (called *tutoiement*) and first names; in fact, the switch will suddenly happen and you should pick up on it immediately or you will forever be stuck with the *vous* form. The familiar form is used with children, animals and God, but almost never with your elders or work superiors. However, the French are becoming less formal and the under 50s often use *tu* and first names with work colleagues (unless they're of the opposite sex, when *tu* may imply a special intimacy!), and will quickly switch from *vous* to *tu* with new social acquaintances, although older people may be reluctant to make the change. Some people always remain *vous*, such as figures of authority (the local mayor) or those with whom you have a business relationship, e.g. your bank manager, tax officials and policemen.

Gifts

If you're invited to dinner by a French person (which is a sign that you've been accepted into the community), take along a small present of flowers, a plant or chocolates. Gifts of foreign food or drink aren't generally well received unless they're highly prized in France such as scotch whisky; foreign wine, however good the quality, isn't recommended! Some people say you must never take wine, as this implies that your hosts don't know what wine to buy, although this obviously depends on your hosts and how well you know them. If you do take wine, however, don't be surprised if your hosts put it to one side for a future occasion; they will already have planned the wine for the meal and know that a wine needs to settle before it can be drunk. Flowers can be tricky, as to some people carnations mean bad luck, chrysanthemums are for cemeteries (they're placed on graves on All Saints' Day), red roses signify love and are associated with the Socialists and yellow roses have something to do with adultery, and marigolds (*soucis*) simply aren't *de rigueur*. If in doubt, ask a florist for advice.

Eating & Drinking

You shouldn't serve any drinks (or expect to be served one) before all guests have arrived – even if some are an hour or more late! If you're offered a drink, wait until your host has toasted everyone's health (*santé*) before taking a drink. **Never** pour your own drinks (except water) when invited to dinner. If you aren't offered a(nother) drink, it's time to go home. Always go easy on the wine and other alcohol; if you drink to excess you're unlikely to be invited back! The French say *bon appétit* before starting a meal and you shouldn't start eating until your hosts do. It's polite to eat everything that's put on your plate. Cheese is served before dessert.

Conversation

The French love detailed and often heated discussions, but there are certain topics of conversation that need handling with care. These include money, which is generally avoided by the French; it's a major *faux pas* to ask a new acquaintance what he does for a living, as his job title will often give an indication of his salary. Far safer to stick to discussions of food and drink. When conversing, even in the midst of a heated debate, avoid raising your voice, which is considered vulgar. Note also that the French often stand close when engaging in conversation, which you may find uncomfortable or even threatening at first.

Gesticulating

Like the Italians, the French talk with their hands – often more than with their tongues – but the art of gesticulation can be as difficult to master (and as full of pitfalls for the unwary) as the spoken language. Here are a few tips that could help you avoid a faux pas: never point with your index finger, which is considered rude, but use an open hand (which should also be used when 'thumbing' a lift); similarly, beckon with your four fingers, palm down; the thumb is used to mean 'one' when counting, not the index finger; to indicate boredom, rub your knuckles against your cheek, to show surprise, shake your hand up and down, and to convey disbelief pull down your lower eyelid; tapping your fingers on the opposite forearm while raising the forearm slightly indicates an impending or actual departure – usually as a result of boredom! The classic French shrug is perhaps best left to the natives!

Cards

The sending of cards, other than birthday cards, isn't as common in France as in some other countries. It isn't, for example, usual to send someone a card following a bereavement or after passing a driving test. Instead of Christmas cards, the French send New Year cards, but only to people they don't normally see during the year.

Dress

Although the French are often formal in their relationships, their dress habits, even in the office, are often extremely casual. Note, however, that the French tend to judge people by their dress, the style and quality being as important as the correctness for the occasion (people often wear 'designer' jeans to dinner). You aren't usually expected to dress for dinner, depending of course on the sort of circles you move in. On invitations, formal dress (black tie) is *smoking exigé/tenue de soirée* and informal dress is *tenue de ville*.

Phone Calls

Always introduce yourself before asking to speak to someone on the telephone. Surprisingly it's common to telephone at meal times, e.g. 12.00 to 14.00 and around 20.00, when you can usually be assured of finding someone at home. If you call at these times, you should apologise for disturbing the household. It isn't always advisable to make calls after 14.00 in the provinces, when many people have a siesta.

Noise

It's common for there to be noise restrictions in French towns and villages, particularly with regard to the use of lawnmowers and other mechanical tools. Restrictions are imposed locally and therefore vary, but in general, noisy activities are prohibited before around 08.00 or 09.00 every day, after 19.00 on weekdays and Saturdays and after 12.00 on Sundays, and additionally at lunchtime on Saturdays.

TIME DIFFERENCE

Like most of the continent of Europe, France is on Central European Time (CET), which is Greenwich Mean Time (GMT) plus one hour. The French change to summer time (*l'heure d'été*) on the last Sunday in March, when they put their clocks forward one hour. On the last Sunday in October, clocks are put back one hour for winter time (*l'heure d'hiver*). Time changes are announced in local newspapers and on radio and TV, and take place at 02.00 or 03.00. (In 1997, the French tried to abolish the change of time, but were overruled by Brussels!)

Times in France, for example in timetables, are usually written using the 24-hour clock, when 10am is written as 10h or 10.00 and 10pm as 22h or 22.00. Midday (*midi*) is 12.00 and midnight (*minuit*) is 24.00 or 00.00; 7.30am is written as 7h30 or 07.30. However, the French use the 12- and 24-hour clocks interchangeably in conversation and it's wise to make sure you've understood. In some French towns, clocks strike twice, with a minute's pause in between, just in case you missed it the first time. The time (in winter) in selected major foreign cities when it's midday in Paris is shown in the table below:

LONDON	JO'BURG	SYDNEY	AUCKLAND	NEW YORK
1100	1300	2200	2400	0600

TIPPING

Tips (*pourboire*, literally 'in order to drink') aren't as freely offered as in the US or even the UK, and have become less common since the introduction of the euro. In some places you may even come across signs forbidding tipping (*pourboire interdit*)! Whether or not you should tip depends largely on whether a service charge has already been included in the price. If service is included, this should be indicated by the words *service compris* (*SC*), *service et taxe compris* (*STC*) or *prix nets/toutes taxes comprises* (*TTC*), which means that prices are inclusive of service and value added tax (*TVA*). If service is extra, *service non compris* (*SNC*) or *service en sus* may be indicated.

Service is now automatically included in all restaurant bills, although you may still leave a tip if you've had exceptional service. In hotels a 15 per cent service charge is usually included in the bill. In bars and cafés, prices usually include service when you sit at a table, but not when you stand at the bar (it should be shown on the menu or bill or the *tarif des consommations*). It's normal to leave your small change on the bar or in the dish provided.

Those who are usually tipped include porters (€0.80 to €1.60 per bag, which may be a fixed fee), tour guides (€0.80 to €1.60), taxi drivers (10 to 15 per cent) and hairdressers (10 per cent). In top-class hotels it's normal to tip a bellboy, porter, chambermaid or other staff members if you ask them to perform extra services. In public toilets where there's an attendant, there's usually a fixed charge and you aren't required to tip, although when no charge is displayed, it's usual to leave €0.15 to €0.30. It's usual to tip ushers (*ouvreuse*) in theatres and concert halls and sports stadiums (€0.30 to €0.80), as they may rely on tips for a good part of their income. However, this custom is dying out, and ushers at many cinema chains (e.g. Gaumont, Pathé and UCG) no longer expect tips. In fact, at many modern cinemas, seats aren't numbered and there are no ushers. It's unnecessary to tip a petrol station attendant (*pompiste*) for cleaning your windscreen or checking your oil, although they're poorly paid and are pleased to receive a small gratuity.

Christmas is generally a time of giving tips to all and sundry, including the postman, rubbish collectors (*éboueurs*) and firemen (*sapeurs-pompiers*), who will often call in early December or November (sometimes as early as October!) 'offering' you a calendar, for which you're nevertheless expected to pay – unless you don't want your post delivered, your rubbish collected or any house-fires extinguished for the following 12 months!

The size of a tip depends on how often someone has served you, the quality and friendliness of the service, your financial status and, of course, your generosity. Generally tips range from €5 to €15, although you may wish to give more to the *gardienne* of your apartment block (it pays to be nice to them). Large tips are, however, considered ostentatious and in bad taste (except by the recipient, who will be your friend for life). If you're unsure who or how much to tip, ask your neighbours, friends or colleagues for advice.

TOILETS

French public toilets vary considerably in their modernity (or antiquity!), and in addition to some of the world's worst, France – always a country of stark contradictions – also has some of the best. The French use a variety of names to refer to a toilet including *toilettes*, *WC* (bizarrely pronounced '*VC*'), *waters*, *lavabos*, *cabinets* (all in the plural, even if there's only one – as there often is) and colloquially *petit coin* (the little corner) and other less polite terms. Public toilets are labelled *messieurs/hommes* and *dames/femmes*.

'Turkish' loos (*cabinets à la turque/siège turc*) – i.e. those consisting simply of a hole in the floor – are still found on basic campsites, at motorway rest areas, and in many cheap bars and restaurants. Care must be taken when flushing, as it tends to soak the floor, and it's often difficult to keep your clothes and feet dry. Urinals (properly termed *Vespasiens*, after the Emperor Vespasian, who introduced them to ancient Rome, but more commonly referred to as *pissoirs* or *pissotières*) are thankfully no more but have been replaced by unisex, 24-hour *sanisettes* or 'superloos': cylindrical metal booths topped with a '*Toilettes*' sign. In some towns and cities, these cost €0.40 but all 420 *sanisettes* in Paris have recently been made free. You're forbidden to allow small children (e.g. under ten) to use them on their own, as they may be unable to open the door (a small child was once swept into a sewer by the cleaning process and drowned!), and relieving yourself in public can earn you a €183 fine. Plans are in hand to introduce a new type of automatic toilet, accessible by the disabled and incorporating a drinking water tap.

Some cafés and bars don't like non-customers using their toilets as a public convenience, although you're entitled to use them free of charge by law (but it's polite to buy a drink). In cities and towns, public toilets are also found at railway and bus stations, parking garages and in the street. In towns, there are often public toilets with attendants (commonly known as *'Dame Pipi'*), where there's a fixed charge of €0.15 to €0.30. If no charge is displayed, it's normal to leave €0.30. Toilet paper may be dispensed (piece by piece) by the attendant. In some rural areas you're given a key or even a detachable door handle to an outside toilet.

In many restaurants and bars, men and women share a common WC and there may be a urinal next to the wash basin. In cheap bars and restaurants there may be no toilet paper. Some toilets have no light switch and the light is operated automatically when you lock the door (to prevent people leaving the light on when they leave).

In private residences, Americans should ask for the toilet and not the bathroom (*salle de bains*), as the toilet is often separate from the bathroom. Most French bathrooms have a *bidet* in addition to a toilet bowl; these are for 'intimate ablutions' and aren't footbaths, drinking fountains or toilets! They're also common in hotels, where rooms may have a wash basin and a *bidet* but no toilet bowl, although they're going out of fashion.

French toilets employ a variety of flushing devices including a knob on top of the cistern which is pulled upwards, a push button on the cistern behind the bowl (often with two 'settings': short and long flush), a chain, or even a foot-operated button on the floor (in public toilets).

If a building has a septic tank (*fosse septique*), certain items must **never** be flushed down the toilet, including sanitary items, paper other than French toilet paper (which is designed to disintegrate and therefore anything but 'luxury'), disposable nappies (diapers), condoms or anything made of plastic. **You should also never use standard bleaches, disinfectants and chemical cleaners in systems with septic tanks (special products are available), as they can have a disastrous effect on their operation and create nasty smells!**

In Paris, it's common to see young children (assisted by their parents) relieving themselves in the gutter (*caniveau*), which is where dogs are also supposed to do their business (the gutters are swept and washed daily). In rural areas, the lack of public toilets is no obstacle to many Frenchmen, who are happy to relieve themselves by the side of the road (and even in your garden!) whenever the urge strikes them and generally make little attempt to conceal themselves behind a tree or other object, often not even bothering to turn their backs to passing women or children. Those of a delicate disposition beware!

19.

THE FRENCH

Who are the French? What are they like? Let's take a candid and totally prejudiced look at them, tongue firmly in cheek, and hope they forgive my flippancy – or that they don't read this bit, which is why it's at the back of the book. (French readers please note: This chapter isn't supposed to be taken too seriously!)

The typical French person is artificial, elitist, hedonistic, enigmatic, idle, civilised, insular, a hypochondriac, bloody-minded, spineless, a suicidal driver, misunderstood, inflexible, pseudo-intellectual, modern, lazy, disagreeable, seductive, complaining, a philosopher, authoritarian, cultured, gallant, provincial, educated, sophisticated, aggressive, flirtatious, unsporting, egocentric, unbearable, paternalistic, insecure, racist, an individual, ill-disciplined, formal, cynical, unfriendly, emotional, irritating, narrow-minded, charming, unhygienic, obstinate, vain, laid-back, a socialist **and** a conservative, serious, long-winded, indecisive, convivial, unloved, callous, bad-tempered, garrulous, inscrutable, ambivalent, infuriating, anti-American, incomprehensible, superior (inferior), ignorant, impetuous, a gastromaniac, blinkered, decadent, truculent, romantic, extravagant, reckless, sensuous, pragmatic, aloof, chauvinistic, capitalistic, courteous, chic, patriotic, xenophobic, proud, passionate, fashionable, nationalistic, bureaucratic, conceited, arrogant, dishonest, surly, rude, impatient, articulate, chivalrous, brave, selfish, imaginative, amiable, debauched, boastful, argumentative, elegant, a lousy lover, egotistical, cold, a good cook, sexy, private, promiscuous, contradictory, political, intolerant, inhospitable, brusque, handsome, an Astérix fan, and above all – insufferably French!

You may have noticed that the above list contains 'a few' contradictions (as does life in France), which is hardly surprising as there's no such thing as a typical French person. Apart from the numerous differences in character between the inhabitants of different regions of France, the population encompasses a potpourri of foreigners from all corners of the globe. However, while it's true that not all French people are stereotypes (some are almost indistinguishable from 'normal' people), I refuse to allow a few eccentrics to spoil my argument . . .

Living among the French can be a traumatic experience, and foreigners are often shocked by French attitudes. One of the first things a newcomer needs to do is discover where he fits in, particularly regarding class and status. In many ways the French are even more class and status conscious than the British (it was the Normans who introduced class into the UK), with classes ranging from the aristocracy (*les grandes familles*, otherwise known as the guillotined or shortened classes) and upper bourgeoisie, through the middle and lower bourgeoisie to the workers and peasantry. The French class system is based on birthright rather than wealth and money doesn't determine or buy status (so *ploucs nouveaux riches* needn't apply). As in most Western countries, there's a huge and widening gap between the rich and the poor, e.g. business tycoons and the lowest-paid workers, particularly those living in rural areas. The best way to become (and remain) rich in France is to be born with a platinum spoon in your mouth. However, the French don't generally flaunt their wealth, and many find the subject of money distasteful (especially the seriously rich).

The French are renowned for their insularity (worse than the Japanese!) and cannot stand foreigners. The butt of their jokes (not that there are many) are the Belgians and Swiss, whom they poke fun at out of jealousy for their linguistic versatility and superior cultural heritage. However, if it's any consolation, the French reserve their greatest enmity for their fellow countrymen (everybody hates Parisians – even other Parisians). The French are Alsatians, Basques, Burgundians, Bretons, Corsicans, Normans, Parisians, Provençals, etc. first and French second. Parisians believe that anybody who doesn't live in Paris is a peasant and beneath contempt. Paradoxically, most Parisians (half are interlopers) have a yearning to live in the country (*la France profonde*) and escape to it at every opportunity. Fortunately the French don't travel well, for which the rest of the world can be truly thankful.

There's a love-hate relationship between the French and Germans (the French love to hate the Germans), although they reserve their greatest animosity for *les Anglo-Saxons*, i.e. the very same foreigners who rescued them (twice) from the dreaded Hun. France owes its liberty, independence and status as a great (small 'g') power to American and British intervention in two World Wars, a humiliating fact they would prefer to forget (although it doesn't hurt to remind them now and again!). Although it's understandable when you've had your butt kicked by the Krauts three times in succession that you prefer not to dwell on it, they're still an ungrateful shower (next time the Germans can keep the damned place!).

Every setback is seen as part of an international conspiracy (naturally concocted by *les Anglo-Saxons*) to rob France of its farms, jobs, culture and very identity. The French bemoan the American influences seeping into their lives, such as *le fast food* (known as *le néfaste food* – 'unhealthy food'), American English, and worst of all, US 'culture', symbolised by Disneyland Paris (which patriotic French people are praying will go broke – again) and McDonald's 'restaurants' (known as *'macdos'*), which have become a target for self-styled cultural 'guardian angels', battling to prevent the Americanisation of France. However, French youth devours everything American including its clothes, films, music, food, drinks, toys, technology and culture.

Which brings us to a subject dear to every French person's heart – food. As everyone knows, food was a French invention (along with sex, the guillotine and VAT) and eating is the national pastime (more important than sex, religion and politics combined). The French are voracious carnivores and eat anything that walks, runs, crawls, swims or flies. They're particularly fond of all the nasty bits that civilised people reject including hoofs, ears, tails, brains, entrails and reproductive organs (the French are anything but squeamish). They also eat repulsive things such as snails and frogs' legs. The French are also partial to barbecued British lamb, which they prefer cooked alive over the embers of a burning truck. A nation of animal lovers, the French are particularly fond of the tastier species such as horses and songbirds, which are usually eaten raw with garlic (it's essential to develop a tolerance to garlic if you're to live in France). The French have an ambivalent attitude towards animals and those they don't pamper as pets are often treated abominably.

The French also know a thing or two about drinking and are among the world's most prolific consumers of alcohol (only the Luxembourgeois drink more), although you rarely see a legless French person. As every French person knows, intelligence, sexual prowess and driving skills are all greatly enhanced by a few stiff drinks. Not surprisingly, they are obsessed with their livers (when not eating those of ducks) and bowel movements, both of which have an intimate relationship with food and drink. The customary treatment for a liver crisis (*crise de foie*) and most other ailments is the suppository, used to treat everything from the common cold to a heart attack (the French are a nation of hypochondriacs and, when not eating, they're popping pills).

French people are never happier than when they're complaining about something, and protests (*manifestations*) are commonplace and an excuse for a good riot. Civil disobedience is the national sport and the French take to the barricades at the drop of a beret. France has numerous self-help groups (called anarchists in other countries) and many French people, e.g. fishermen, hunters, farmers and truck drivers, are a law unto themselves. Observing senseless edicts such as motoring laws, prohibitive signs (e.g. no parking, no smoking, no dogs, no riots, etc.) and other trivial rules is a matter of personal choice in France. Although France is ostensibly a country of written rules, regulations and laws, they exist solely to be waived, bent or adapted (*système débrouillard* or *système D*) to your own advantage.

Kind-hearted French farmers are famous for their love of animals and they often take their cows and sheep for a day out to Paris and other cities (they also regularly distribute free produce on the city streets for the poor town folk). The French, who are difficult to govern at the best of times, are impossible to rule in bad times. France always seems to be teetering on the edge of anarchy and revolution, and mass demonstrations have a special place in French political culture. The *CRS* (riot police) are the only people capable of communicating with rioting people, which they do by whacking them on the head with a large baton (while looking the other way). Not surprisingly, the French are the world's leading consumers of tranquillisers, not to mention aspirins to counter the effects of being frequently bashed on the head.

The French complain loud and long about their leaders and the merest mention of politics is a cue for a vociferous argument. They're contemptuous of their politicians, which isn't surprising considering they're an incompetent, licentious and corrupt bunch of buffoons who couldn't organise a *soûlerie* in a vineyard. They rate lower than prostitutes in the social order and the service they provide (prostitutes have morals and principles and do a sterling job – ask any politician!). French politics are a bizarre mixture of extreme left and extreme right, although paradoxically most French people are extremely conservative. The French (through Jean Monnet) invented the European Union (EU), a fact which should be patently obvious to anyone, considering it's one of the most bureaucratic and dictatorial organisations in the world. The French believe that the EU was a splendid institution while it pursued French ambitions and was led by France, but are ambivalent about it since all the Eastern European rabble were admitted and are positively hostile to Turkey's accession. General de Gaulle was adamant that the intractable British should never be allowed to join and the French have since been doing their utmost to keep them at arm's length (the French call the Channel 'the Sleeve').

France is the most bureaucratic country in the world, with almost twice as many civil servants as Germany and three times as many as Japan. In order to accomplish anything remotely official in France, 98 forms must be completed in quintuplicate, each of which must be signed by 47 officials in 31 different government departments. Only then do you get your bus pass! When dealing with civil servants you must **never** show your impatience, which is like a red rag to a bull. It's the fault of all those French cheeses; as de Gaulle so succinctly put it: "It's difficult to rule a nation with 265 cheeses" (or possibly 365, 400 or even 750). It's even harder to govern a country that has no idea how many cheeses it has!

The French aren't exactly noted for their humility and variously describe France (*la Grande Nation*) as the most cultured of countries, the light of the world, and a nation destined by God (who's naturally French) to dominate the continent. Not surprisingly, Paris is the capital of civilisation and the city of light. France lives on its past glories (*la gloire*) and clings tenaciously to its colonies (which it uses as a testing ground for its nuclear weapons) long after other colonists have seen the light. French history is littered with French delusions of grandeur (*la grandeur française*), which spawned such infamous megalomaniacs as Charlemagne, Napoleon, de Gaulle, and the most famous Frenchman of all, Astérix. France yearns for foreign adulation, the predominance of the French language and culture (Johnny Hallyday aside), and to be hailed as the undisputed leader of Europe. The French person's favourite word is appropriately *supérieur* (nobody **ever** accused the French of being modest).

The French language has divine status in France and is the language of love, food and the Gods. The French cling to it as their last vestige of individuality and its propagation by the foreign service is sacrosanct (mock it at your peril!). The French love their language and habitually use it as a blunt instrument to intimidate uneducated foreigners, i.e. anyone who doesn't speak it (only in France are tourists treated with contempt for not speaking the language). To fully understand the French you need an intimate knowledge of their beautiful and romantic language, which is the key to their spirit and character. In practice this consists of learning just two words, *merde!* and *NON!*, which can be used effectively to deal with every situation, as was aptly demonstrated by General de Gaulle (see also *le bras d'honneur* below). The French say no to every question and only afterwards (may) consider possible alternatives.

Most French people pretend not to speak English, usually because they speak it excruciatingly badly and have a gigantic inferiority complex about the English language, which they blame for the decline of the French language and empire (the ability to speak French is no longer the sign of a civilised person) while eagerly adopting English words, especially those ending in -ing (in fact, often inventing words ending in -ing that don't exist in English) in order to demonstrate their *sex-appeal*.

If you're unable to make yourself understood in English, you should resort to sign language, a scientific and highly developed art form in France. The supreme gesture is *le bras d'honneur*, meaning 'up yours' (or something less printable!): hold your right arm outstretched and smack your left hand against your right bicep, simultaneously bringing your right forearm smartly upwards. It isn't advisable, however, to make this gesture in the general direction of a *gendarme* or anyone with a gun.

When not eating, the French are allegedly making love. They're obsessed with sex and have a long tradition of debauchery. French men think they're God's gift to women and are in a permanent state of unbridled eroticism. Every attractive woman is a potential conquest, especially foreign ones, some of whom have a reputation for being 'easy' (if you want to know how good your wife is in bed, ask your French friends!). The French use sex to sell everything from cars to mineral water (what others find sexist, the French find sexy) and lack modesty in all things, discarding their clothes at every opportunity. French women enjoy being objects of desire and most care little for women's liberation and indulge their 'macho' (i.e. selfish) men, most of whom couldn't change a nappy if their lives depended on it. Flirting is an art form, where sexual overtones are part and parcel of everyday life.

The French are renowned for their sexual peccadilloes and are credited with inventing sadism (the Marquis de Sade), brothels (*bordellos*), French letters (Condom is a French town), masturbation and adultery. In France, *c'est normal* for a woman to seek lovers and for a man to have mistresses. If a married man is a philanderer it's a source of pride, a mark of respect and nothing to be ashamed of (a real vote-catcher for politicians!). A mistress is a status symbol, the absence of which casts grave doubts on a man's virility and sexual predilections. As a by-product of this rampant free love, the French have record numbers of illegitimate children, whom they have been forced to legalise (along with their concubines). They even have the gall to call homosexuality 'the English vice' (*le vice anglais*), although everyone knows why Paris, which is famous for its transvestites, is called gay Paris (France is the only country where the men wear more perfume than the women!).

Despite not washing, living on garlic and wearing their socks for weeks on end, Frenchmen have amazingly established a reputation for suave, seductive charm (surely women aren't still attracted to Alain Delon and Gérard Depardieu). However, despite his formidable reputation, the Frenchman's performance in bed is similar to his performance in the battlefield: lots of pomp and ceremony, but when the pantaloons are down he empties his cannon out of range and rolls over. Fittingly, the national symbol is the resplendent cockerel, which seduces and impregnates the submissive hens and then crows (*cocorico!*) triumphantly, even when it has nothing to boast about (after which it's cooked in wine and eaten). However, despite the fact that the rooster services many hens, the evidence is that he doesn't satisfy them (around half of French women declare their sex lives to be unsatisfactory).

The French are formidable sportsmen and have produced a long line of sporting heroes (although their names are difficult to recall). Among the most popular French sports are sex; beating the system (e.g. fare evasion, cheating the tax man, claiming unlawful social security and defrauding the EU); stock-car racing on public roads; corruption, fraud and sleaze; falling off skis; running (away from the Germans); falling off bicycles while following Americans, Belgians, Spaniards and assorted other foreigners around France; losing at football (1998 was a temporary aberration); *boules* (a form of marbles played by southerners plastered on *pastis*); rioting; horse riding (to escape from rampaging Germans); shooting themselves in the feet; tennis and sex. It's widely acknowledged that the French are cheats, poor losers and have absolutely no notion of *le fair-play*. After all, how can a nation which doesn't play cricket or baseball possibly be trusted to play by the rules?

Enough frivolity, let's get down to serious business. Like most capitalist countries, France is a sorely divided nation. While the elite and privileged bourgeoisie luxuriate in the sun, the inhabitants of the poor suburbs and immigrant ghettos remain permanently in the gloom, plagued by poor transport, soaring crime, extremist politics, and an acute sense of dereliction and hopelessness. There's a festering racial problem with suppressed and disadvantaged Africans and Arabs (enticed to France as cheap labour in the '50s to '70s) locked in a vicious circle of poverty and deprivation.

The increasingly destitute farming communities and thousands of rural villages are also firmly anchored in second-class France. The human fallout from *la bonne vie* and high unemployment occupy the streets and *métro* tunnels of French cities. France also suffers from increasing drug abuse, alcoholism, racism and violence. However, by far the biggest challenge facing France's leaders is how to reform the economy (e.g. debt-ridden public companies, a burgeoning social security deficit and soaring taxation) without provoking a(nother) revolution.

To be fair (who the hell's trying to be fair?), the French do have a few good points. They've managed (largely) to preserve the splendour of their countryside (when not inviting British architects to build giant bridges across it) and the charm and splendour of their villages, towns and cities. The French enjoy the best cuisine in the world and many of the world's great wines (although their failure to admit that anyone else can make decent wine is costing them dear). They have good public services, fine schools, exceptional social security benefits (although the country cannot afford them), superb hospitals (with virtually no waiting lists), excellent working conditions and employee benefits, and a first-class transportation system with magnificent *autoroutes* and among the world's fastest trains. The country enjoys a generally high standard of living, low inflation and a relatively healthy economy (despite the gloom). The French (unlike many other nations) haven't turned their backs on their roots and strong family and community ties and loyalties are a prominent feature of French life.

France is one of the most cultured countries in the world and the French are renowned for their insatiable appetite for gastronomy, art, literature, philosophy and music. Paris houses some of the world's greatest museums, monuments and architectural treasures, and is one of the world's most attractive and romantic cities, and its cleanest major capital (London and New York please note) – apart from the canine deposits on pavements. France is highly competitive on the world stage, notably in foreign affairs, business, technology, sport and culture, and is one of the few Western countries with the vision and boldness to conceive and execute grandiose schemes. The French are justifiably proud of their achievements (critical foreigners are simply jealous) and France is no longer an island unto itself, its traditional insularity having been replaced by a highly developed sense of international responsibility. It remains one of the most influential nations in the world and a positive power for good, particularly in the field of medicine, where *Médecins sans Frontière* and *Médecins du Monde* do exemplary work.

While doing battle with French bureaucracy is enough to discourage anybody, ordinary French people usually couldn't be more welcoming (apart from Parisians). If you're willing to meet them halfway and learn their language, you will invariably be warmly received by the French, who will go out of their way to help you – and 'educate' you in the finer points of civilised living. Contrary to popular belief, they aren't baby-eating ogres and, provided you make an effort to be friendly, they're likely to overwhelm you with kindness. Anyone planning to make their permanent home in France should bear in mind that assimilation is all-important. If you don't want to live **with** the French and share their way of life, language, culture and traditions, you're probably better off going somewhere else (or staying at home). Although it's difficult to get to know the French, when you do you invariably make friends for life.

The mark of a great nation is that it **never** breeds indifference in foreigners – admiration, envy, hostility or even blind hatred, but never indifference! Love it or hate it, France is a unique, vital, civilised, bold, sophisticated and challenging country. In the final analysis the French enjoy one of the world's best lifestyles and what many believe is the finest overall quality of life (French civilisation has been described as an exercise in enlightened self-indulgence). Few other countries offer such a wealth of intoxicating experiences for the mind, body and spirit – and not all out of a bottle! – or provide a more stimulating environment in which to live and work.

Vive la différence! Vive la République! Vive la France! Vive les Français!

20.

MOVING HOUSE
OR LEAVING FRANCE

When moving house or leaving France, there are numerous things to be considered and a 'million' people to inform. The checklists contained in this chapter will make the task easier and may even help prevent an ulcer or nervous breakdown – provided you don't leave everything to the last minute.

MOVING HOUSE

When moving house **within** France, don't forget the following:

- If you're renting accommodation, you must usually give your landlord at least three months' notice (refer to your contract). Your resignation letter must be sent by registered post (*lettre recommandée avec avis de réception*).

- Inform the following, as applicable:

  - Your employer.

  - Your present town hall and the town hall in your new community within a month of taking up residence. They will change the address on your *carte de séjour* if applicable.

  - Your local social security (Caisse Primaire d'Assurance Maladie/CPAM) and family allowance (Caisse d'Allocations Familiales) offices.

  - Your local income tax office (Centre des Impôts) and *trésorerie*.

  - Your local electricity/gas and water companies (at least two days in advance).

  - France Télécom (and other phone companies) if you have a telephone. You can have your new number announced to callers for six months.

  - Your regional TV licence centre (Centre Régional de la Redevance Audiovisuelle) if you have a TV.

  - Your insurance companies, e.g. health, car, house contents and public liability; hire purchase companies; lawyer; accountant; and local businesses where you have accounts. Obtain new insurance, if applicable.

  - Your banks and other financial institutions, such as stockbrokers and credit card companies. Make arrangements for the transfer of funds and the cancellation or alteration of standing orders.

  - Your family doctor, dentist and other health practitioners. Health records should be transferred to your new practitioners.

  - Your children's schools. If applicable, arrange for schooling in your new community (see **Chapter 9**). Try to give a term's notice and obtain copies of any relevant school reports and records from current schools as well as a *certificat de radiation*.

- All regular correspondents, publications to which you subscribe, including professional and trade journals, social and sports clubs, and friends and relatives. Arrange to have your post redirected by the post office by completing a permanent change of address card (*ordre de réexpédition définitif*), available from post offices, at least four days in advance.

- Your local consulate or embassy if you're registered with them (see page 95).

● If you have a French driving licence or a French-registered car and are remaining in the same department, you must return your licence and car registration document (*carte grise*) and have the address changed (see page 250). If you're moving to a new department, you must inform both your current and new *préfectures*. You must re-register your car (see page 249) and obtain a new licence (see page 252) from your new *préfecture* within three months of taking up residence.

● Return any library books or anything borrowed.

● Arrange removal of your furniture and belongings (or rent a vehicle, if you're doing your own removal).

● If you live in rented accommodation, obtain a refund of your deposit from your landlord.

● **Ask yourself (again): 'Is it really worth all this trouble?'**

LEAVING FRANCE

Before leaving France for an indefinite period, you should do the following **in addition** to the things listed above under **Moving House**:

● Check that your own and your family's passports are valid.

● Give notice to your employer, if applicable.

● Check whether any special entry requirements are necessary for your country of destination, e.g. visas, permits or inoculations, by contacting the local embassy or consulate in France. An exit permit or visa isn't required to leave France.

● Check whether you qualify for a rebate on income tax (see page 375) and social security payments (see page 323). Tax rebates are normally paid automatically. If you've contributed to a supplementary pension scheme, a percentage of your contributions will be repaid (see page 336), although your pension company will require proof that you're leaving France permanently.

● Arrange to sell anything you aren't taking with you (car, furniture, etc.) and to ship your belongings. Find out the procedure for shipping your belongings to your country of destination (see page 114). American removal companies with offices in France include Biard International (⌨ http://www.biard.fr), Team Relocations (⌨ http://www.teamrelocations.com) and Grospiron International (⌨ http://www. grospiron.com). Check with the local embassy or consulate in France of the country to which you're moving. Special forms may need to be completed before arrival. If you've been living in France for less than a year, you're required to re-export all imported personal effects, including furniture and vehicles (if you sell them, you may be required to pay tax or duty).

- Obtain a copy of your health and dental records and a statement from your health insurance company stating your present level of cover. You may wish to arrange health and dental check-ups before leaving France.

- Make arrangements to sell or let your house or apartment and other property in France.

- If you have a French-registered car that you intend to take with you, you can drive on your French registration plates for a maximum of three months.

- Pets may require special inoculations or may need to go into quarantine for a period (see page 526), depending on your destination.

- Contact France Télécom (see page 140) and anyone else well in advance if you need to recover a deposit.

- Arrange health, travel and other insurance (see **Chapter 13**).

- Terminate any French loans, lease or hire purchase contracts, and pay all outstanding bills (allow plenty of time, as some companies are slow to respond).

- Check whether you're entitled to a rebate on your car and other insurance. Obtain a letter from your French motor insurance company stating your no-claims bonus.

- Check whether you need an international driving licence or a translation of your French or foreign driving licence for your country of destination.

- Give friends and business associates in France a temporary address and telephone number where you can be contacted abroad.

- If you will be travelling or living abroad for an extended period, you may wish to give someone 'power of attorney' over your financial affairs in France so that they can act on your behalf in your absence. This can be for a fixed period or open-ended and can be limited to a specific purpose only. **You should, however, obtain expert legal advice before doing this.**

- Buy a copy of the relevant book in Survival Books' *Living and Working* series (see page 587) before leaving France. If we haven't published it yet, drop us a line and we'll get started on it right away!

Bon voyage!

APPENDICES

Appendix A: FURTHER INFORMATION

Embassies & Consulates

Foreign embassies are located in the capital Paris (those for selected English-speaking countries are listed below), and many countries also have consulates in other cities (all British consulates are listed below). Embassies and consulates are listed in the yellow pages under *Ambassades, Consulats et Autres Représentations Diplomatiques*.

Australia: 4 rue Jean Rey, 15e (☎ 01 40 59 33 00).

Ireland: 4 rue Rude, 16e (☎ 01 44 17 67 00).

Jamaica: 60 avenue Foch, 16e (☎ 01 45 00 62 25).

Malta: 92 avenue Champs Elysées, 8e (☎ 01 56 59 75 90).

New Zealand: 7ter rue Léonard de Vinci, 16e (☎ 01 45 01 43 43).

South Africa: 59 quai Orsay, 7e (☎ 01 53 59 23 23).

United Kingdom: 35 rue Faubourg St Honoré, 8e (see below) and 18 bis rue Anjou, 8e (☎ 01 44 51 31 02).

United States of America: 2 rue St Florentin, 1e (☎ 08 10 26 46 26) and 2 avenue Gabriel, 1e (☎ 01 43 12 22 22).

British Consulates-General

Consulates-General are permanently staffed during normal office hours.

Bordeaux: 353 boulevard du Président Wilson, BP 91, 33073 Bordeaux (☎ 05 57 22 21 10). Covers the departments of Ariège, Aveyron, Charente, Charente-Maritime, Corrèze, Creuse, Dordogne, Haute-Garonne, Gers, Gironde, Landes, Lot, Lot-et-Garonne, Pyrénées-Atlantiques, Hautes-Pyrénées, Deux-Sèvres, Tarn, Tarn-et-Garonne, Vienne and Haute-Vienne.

Lille: 11 square Dutilleul, 59800 Lille (☎ 03 20 12 82 72). Covers the departments of Aisne, Ardennes, Nord, Pas-de-Calais and Somme.

Lyon: 24 rue Childebert, 69288 Lyon Cedex 1 (☎ 04 72 77 81 70). Covers the departments of Ain, Allier, Ardèche, Cantal, Côte d'Or, Doubs, Drôme, Isère, Jura, Loire, Haute-Loire, Puy-de-Dôme, Rhône, Haute-Saône, Saône-et-Loire, Savoie, Haute-Savoie and the Territoire de Belfort.

Marseille: 24 avenue du Prado, 13006 Marseille (☎ 04 91 15 72 10). Covers the departments of Alpes-de-Haute-Provence, Hautes-Alpes, Alpes-Maritimes, Aude, Bouches-du-Rhône, Gard, Hérault, Lozère, Pyrénées-Orientales, Var and Vaucluse, as well as Corsica.

Paris: 35 rue du Faubourg Saint Honoré, 75008 Paris (☎ 01 44 51 31 02). Covers the departments of Aube, Calvados, Cher, Côtes d'Armor, Eure, Eure-et-Loir, Finstère, Ille-et-Vilaine, Indre, Indre-et-Loire, Loir-et-Cher, Loire, Loire-Atlantique, Loiret, Maine-et-Loire, Manche, Marne, Haute-Marne, Mayenne, Meurthe-et-Moselle, Meuse, Morbihan, Moselle, Nièvre, Oise, Bas-Rhin, Sarthe and Vosges, as well as the whole of the Ile-de-France and the overseas departments and territories.

British Honorary Consulates

Honorary consulates aren't permanently staffed and should be contacted **in emergencies only** (e.g. for urgent passport renewals or replacements).

Boulogne-sur-Mer: c/o Cabinet Barron et Brun, 28 rue Saint Jean, 62200 Boulogne-sur-Mer (☎ 03 21 87 16 80).

Cherbourg-Octeville: c/o P&O Ferries, Gare Maritime, BP46, 50652 Cherbourg-Octeville (☎ 02 33 88 65 60).

Dunkerque: c/o Lemaire Frères & Fils, 30 rue de l'Hermitte, BP 2/100, 59376 Dunkerque (☎ 03 28 58 77 00).

Le Havre: c/o LD Lines, 124 boulevard de Strasbourg, 76600 Le Havre (☎ 02 35 19 78 88).

Montpellier: 271 Le Capitole, Bâtiment A, 64 rue Alcyone, 34000 Montpellier (☎ 04 67 15 52 07).

Nantes: 16 boulevard Gabriel Giust'hau, BP 22026, 44020 Nantes Cedex 1 (☎ 02 51 72 72 60).

Toulouse: c/o English Enterprises, 8 allée du Commingues, 317700 Colomiers, 31300 Toulouse (☎ 05 61 30 37 91).

Tours: 7, rue des Rosiers, 37510 Savonnières (☎ 02 47 43 57 97).

Private Health Insurers

Major international private health insurers include the following (all telephone numbers are UK numbers unless otherwise stated).

A La Carte Healthcare – ☎ 01903-266516, 💻 http://www.alchealth.com.

Allianz Worldwide Care – Irish ☎ 01-630 1301, 💻 http://www.allianz-worldwidecare.com.

Axa PPP Healthcare International – ☎ 01892-612080, 💻 http://www.axappphealthcare.com.

BUPA International – ☎ 01273-208181, 💻 http://www.bupainternational.com.

Cigna International – ☎ 01475-492222, 💻 http://www.cigna.co.uk.

Exeter Friendly – ☎ 01392-353535, 💻 http://www.exeterfriendly.co.uk.

Expacare – ☎ 01344-381650, 💻 http://www.jltgroup.com/psexpacare.shtml.

Goodhealth Worldwide (☎ 0800-6248 2000, 💻 http://www.goodhealthworldwide.com.

HealthCare International – ☎ 020-7665 1727, 💻 http://www.health-careinternational.com.

Integra Global – US ☎ 1888-753 1377 or Germany ☎ 062-21 825650, 💻 http://www.integraglobal.com.

InterGlobal – ☎ 01252-745910, 💻 http://www.interglobalpmi.com.

International Health Insurance – Danish ☎ 033-153099, 💻 http://www.ihi.com.

International Medical Group – ☎ 01444-465577, 💻 http://www.imglobal.com.

International Private Healthcare – ☎ 020-8905 2888, 💻 http://www.iph.uk.net.

MediCare International – ☎ 020-7816 2033, 💻 http://www.medicare.co.uk.

Morgan Price International Healthcare – ☎ 01379-646730, 💻 http://www.morgan-price.com.

Appendix B: FURTHER READING

This appendix lists the major English-language publications about France and books on France published by Survival Books, which can be ordered using the forms at the back of the book. Other books and magazines are mentioned in the relevant chapters.

English-language Newspapers & Magazines

The Connexion (☎ 04 93 32 16 59, 🖥 http://www.connexionfrance.com). Monthly newspaper.

Everything France Magazine, Brooklands Magazines (UK ☎ 01342-828700, 🖥 http://www.everythingfrancemag.co.uk). Bi-monthly lifestyle magazine.

Focus on France, Outbound Publishing (UK ☎ 01323-726040, 🖥 http://www.outboundpublishing.com). Quarterly property magazine.

France Magazine, Archant Life (UK ☎ 01242-216050, 🖥 http://www.francemag.co.uk). Monthly lifestyle magazine.

France Review (☎ 05 53 91 65 44, 🖥 http://www. france review.com). Bi-monthly magazine in French and English.

France-USA Contacts (☎ 01 56 53 54 54, 🖥 http://www.fusac.fr). Free bi-weekly magazine.

French News, SARL Brussac (☎ 05 53 06 84 40, 🖥 http://www.french-news.com). Monthly newspaper.

French Property News, Archant Life (UK ☎ 020-8543 3113, 🖥 http://www.french-property-news.com). Monthly property magazine.

The Irish Eyes Magazine (☎ 01 41 74 93 03, 🖥 http://www.irisheyes.fr). Monthly Paris cultural magazine.

Living France, Archant Life (UK ☎ 01858-438832, 🖥 http://www.livingfrance.com). Monthly lifestyle/property magazine.

Normandie & South of England Magazine (☎ 02 33 77 32 70, 🖥 http://www.normandie-magazine.fr). News and current affairs about Normandy and parts of southern England, published eight times a year in English and French.

Paris Voice/Paris Free Voice (☎ 01 47 70 45 05, 🖥 http://www.parisvoice.com). Free weekly newspaper.

The Riviera Reporter (☎ 04 93 45 77 19, 🖳 http://www.riviera-reporter.com). Bi-monthly free magazine covering the Côte d'Azur.

The Riviera Times (☎ 04 93 27 60 00, 🖳 http://www.rivieratimes.com). Monthly free newspaper covering the Côte d'Azur and Italian Riviera.

Books

The following books about France and the French are published by Survival Books and can be ordered using the forms on pages 587 and 588.

The Alien's Guide To France, Jim Watson. A light-hearted look at life in France.

Brittany Lifeline, Val Gascoyne. A directory of services, amenities and facilities in Brittany for visitors and residents.

Dordogne/Lot Lifeline, Val Gascoyne. A directory of services, amenities and facilities in Dordogne, Lot and Lot-et-Garonne for visitors and residents.

Earning Money from Your French Home, Jo Taylor. How to make money from your home, including offering bed & breakfast and *gîte* accommodation.

Foreigners in France: Triumphs & Disasters, Joe & Kerry Laredo (eds). Real-life stories of people from all over the world who have moved to France.

Living & Working in France, David Hampshire. Everything you need to know about life and employment in France.

Making a Living in France, Joe Laredo. The ins and outs of self-employment and starting a business in France.

Normandy Lifeline, Val Gascoyne. A directory of services, amenities and facilities in Upper and Lower Normandy for visitors and residents.

Poitou-Charentes Lifeline, Val Gascoyne. A directory of services, amenities and facilities in Poitou-Charentes for visitors and residents.

Provence-Côte d'Azur Lifeline, Val Gascoyne. A directory of services, amenities and facilities in Provence-Alpes-Côte d'Azur for visitors and residents.

Renovating & Maintaining Your French Home, Joe Laredo. How to realise the renovation dream and avoid nightmares.

Rural Living in France, Jeremy Hobson. Enjoy the pleasures and avoid the pitfalls of life in the French countryside.

Appendix C: USEFUL WEBSITES

There are hundreds of general information websites and dozens of expatriate sites on the internet. Most information is useful, and websites generally offer free access, although some require a subscription or payment for services. Relocation and other companies specialising in expatriate services often have sites, although these may provide rather biased information. However, there are plenty of volunteer sites run by expatriates providing practical information and tips. A particularly useful section found on most expatriate websites is the 'message board' or 'forum', where expatriates answer questions based on their experience and knowledge and offer an insight into what living and working in is **really** like. Below is a selection of useful websites not otherwise mentioned in the text, listed under headings in alphabetical order.

General Information

All About France (🖳 http://www.all-about-france.com).

Alliance Française (🖳 http://www.alliancefr.org). The famous French language school.

Anglo Info (🖳 http://www.angloinfo.com). Information and forums specific to Aquitaine, Brittany, Normandy, Poitou-Charentes and Provence.

Australian Embassy in France (🖳 http://www.ambafrance-au.org). Plenty of useful information and fact sheets, not only relevant to Australia.

Electricité de France (🖳 http://www.edf.fr).

French Embassy in London (🖳 http://www.ambafrance-uk.org).

French Entrée (🖳 http://www.frenchentree.com). Information on every aspect of living in France and a useful forum.

French Tourist Board (🖳 http://www.franceguide.com).

Gaz de France (🖳 http://www.gdf.fr).

Invest in France Agency (🖳 http://www.afii.fr). Useful information on living and working in France.

Legifrance (🖳 http://www.legifrance.gouv.fr). Official legal information.

Living France (🖳 http://www.livingfrance.com). Uuseful information about all aspects of living in France and a lively discussion forum with over 6,000 members.

Ministry of Culture & Communications (🖳 http://www.culture.fr).

Ministry of the Economy, Finance and Industry (🖳 http://www.finances.gouv.fr). Economic and tax information.

Moving to France Made Easy (🖳 http://www.moving-to-france-made-easy.com). Plenty of information about life in France.

Paris Info (🖳 http://www.parisinfo.com). The site of the Paris Convention & Visitors' Bureau.

Paris Notes (🖳 http://www.parisnotes.com). A subscription newsletter about Paris, published ten times a year.

Pratique (🖳 http://www.pratique.fr). Practical information about life in France (in French).

SeniorPlanet (🖳 http://www.seniorplanet.com). Information for older people.

Service Public (🖳 http://www.service-public.fr). Official French government portal, with links to all ministry and other sites.

This French Life (🖳 http://www.thisfrenchlife.com). Articles about setting up a variety of necessary services, from bank accounts to internet connection, as well as some of the more enjoyable things about life.

Webvivant (🖳 http://www.webvivant.com). Online community for English-speakers in France and Francophiles everywhere.

World Health Organization (🖳 http://www.who.int).

Expatriate Sites

Americans Abroad (🖳 http://www.aca.ch). Advice, information and services to Americans abroad.

Australians Abroad (🖳 http://www.australiansabroad.com). Information for Australians about relocating and a forum.

British Expatriates (🖳 http://www.britishexpat.com). This website keeps British expatriates in touch with events and information about the UK.

Contact Expats (🖳 http://www.contactexpats.com). A new 'forum' for expatriates worldwide.

ExpatBoards (🖳 http://www.expatboards.com). A comprehensive site with discussion boards and areas dedicated to Americans and Britons.

Escape Artist (🖥 http://www.escapeartist.com). A comprehensive site with resources, links and directories covering most expatriate destinations, as well as a free monthly online expatriate magazine, *Escape from America*.

Expat Exchange (🖥 http://www.expatexchange.com). Articles on relocation and a question and answer facility.

Expat World (🖥 http://www.expatworld.net). Information for American and British expatriates, including a subscription newsletter.

Expatriate Experts (🖥 http://www.expatexpert.com). A website run by expatriate expert Robin Pascoe, providing invaluable advice and support.

Family Life Abroad (🖥 http://www.familylifeabroad.com). A wealth of information and articles on coping with family life abroad.

Foreign Wives Club (🖥 http://www.foreignwivesclub.com). An online community for women in bicultural marriages.

Francopats (🖥 http://www.francopats.com). Online expatriate community.

Real Post Reports (🖥 http://www.realpostreports.com). Provides relocation services, recommended reading lists and 'real-life' stories.

Southern Cross Group (🖥 http://www.southern-cross-group.org). A website for Australians and New Zealanders providing information and the exchange of tips.

Suzy Lamplugh Trust (🖥 http://www.suzylamplugh.org). Information about personal safety, particularly for women, including a country directory.

Third Culture Kids (🖥 http://www.tckworld.com). A website designed for expatriate children living abroad.

Travel Documents (🖥 http://www.traveldocs.com). Useful information about travel, specific countries and documents needed to travel.

Travel for Kids (🖥 http://www.travelforkids.com). Advice on travelling with children around the world.

Women of the World (🖥 http://www.wow-net.org). A website designed for female expatriates.

World Travel Guide (🖥 http://www.wtgonline.com). A general website for world travellers and expatriates.

APPENDIX D: WEIGHTS & MEASURES

France uses the metric system of measurement – in fact the French invented it! Those who are more familiar with the imperial system of measurement will find the tables on the following pages useful. Some comparisons shown are only approximate but close enough for most everyday uses. In addition to the variety of measurement systems used, clothes sizes often vary considerably with the manufacturer (as we all know only too well). Try all clothes on before buying and don't be afraid to return something if, when you try it on at home, you decide it doesn't fit (most shops will exchange goods or give a refund – eventually!).

Women's Clothes

Continental	34	36	38	40	42	44	46	48	50	52
UK	8	10	12	14	16	18	20	22	24	26
US	6	8	10	12	14	16	18	20	22	24

Pullovers

	Women's						Men's					
Continental	40	42	44	46	48	50	44	46	48	50	52	54
UK	34	36	38	40	42	44	34	36	38	40	42	44
US	34	36	38	40	42	44	sm	med	lar	xl		

Men's Shirts

Continental	36	37	38	39	40	41	42	43	44	46
UK/US	14	14	15	15	16	16	17	17	18	-

Men's Underwear

Continental	5	6	7	8	9	10
UK	34	36	38	40	42	44
US	sm		med		lar	xl

Note: sm = small, med = medium, lar = large, xl = extra large

Children's Clothes

Continental	92	104	116	128	140	152
UK	16/18	20/22	24/26	28/30	32/34	36/38
US	2	4	6	8	10	12

Children's Shoes

Continental	18	19	20	21	22	23	24	25	26	27	28	29	30	31	32
UK/US	2	3	4	4	5	6	7	7	8	9	10	11	11	12	13

Continental	33	34	35	36	37	38
UK/US	1	2	2	3	4	5

Shoes (Women's and Men's)

Continental	35	36	37	37	38	39	40	41	42	42	43	44
UK	2	3	3	4	4	5	6	7	7	8	9	9
US	4	5	5	6	6	7	8	9	9	10	10	11

Weight

Imperial	Metric	Metric	Imperial
1oz	28.35g	1g	0.035oz
1lb*	454g	100g	3.5oz
1cwt	50.8kg	250g	9oz
1 ton	1,016kg	500g	18oz
2,205lb	1 tonne	1kg	2.2lb

Length

Imperial	Metric	Metric	Imperial
1in	2.54cm	1cm	0.39in
1ft	30.48cm	1m	3ft 3.25in
1yd	91.44cm	1km	0.62mi
1mi	1.6km	8km	5mi

Capacity

Imperial	Metric	Metric	Imperial
1 UK pint	0.57 litre	1 litre	1.75 UK pints
1 US pint	0.47 litre	1 litre	2.13 US pints
1 UK gallon	4.54 litres	1 litre	0.22 UK gallon
1 US gallon	3.78 litres	1 litre	0.26 US gallon

Note: An American 'cup' = around 250ml or 0.25 litre.

Area

Imperial	Metric	Metric	Imperial
1 sq. in	0.45 sq. cm	1 sq. cm	0.15 sq. in
1 sq. ft	0.09 sq. m	1 sq. m	10.76 sq. ft
1 sq. yd	0.84 sq. m	1 sq. m	1.2 sq. yds
1 acre	0.4 hectares	1 hectare	2.47 acres
1 sq. mile	2.56 sq. km	1 sq. km	0.39 sq. mile

Note: An *are* is one-hundredth of a hectare or 100m^2.

Temperature

°Celsius	°Fahrenheit	
0	32	(freezing point of water)
5	41	
10	50	
15	59	
20	68	
25	77	
30	86	
35	95	
40	104	
50	122	

Notes: The boiling point of water is 100°C / 212°F.

Normal body temperature (if you're alive and well) is 37°C / 98.4°F.

Temperature Conversion

Celsius to Fahrenheit: multiply by 9, divide by 5 and add 32. (For a quick and approximate conversion, double the Celsius temperature and add 30.)

Fahrenheit to Celsius: subtract 32, multiply by 5 and divide by 9. (For a quick and approximate conversion, subtract 30 from the Fahrenheit temperature and divide by 2.)

Oven Temperatures

Gas	Electric	
	°F	°C
-	225–250	110–120
1	275	140
2	300	150
3	325	160
4	350	180
5	375	190
6	400	200
7	425	220
8	450	230
9	475	240

Air Pressure

PSI	Bar
10	0.5
20	1.4
30	2
40	2.8

Appendix E: Map

The map opposite shows the 22 regions and 96 departments of France (excluding overseas territories), which are listed below. The departments are (mostly) numbered alphabetically from 01 to 89. Departments 91 to 95 come under the Ile-de-France region, which also includes Ville de Paris (75), Seine-et-Marne (77) and Yvelines (78), shown in detail opposite. The island of Corsica consists of two departments, 2A and 2B.

01 Ain	32 Gers	64 Pyrénées-Atlantiques
02 Aisne	33 Gironde	65 Hautes-Pyrénées
2A Corse-du-Sud	34 Hérault	66 Pyrénées-Orientales
2B Haute Corse	35 Ille-et-Vilaine	67 Bas-Rhin
03 Allier	36 Indre	68 Haut-Rhin
04 Alpes-de-Hte-Provence	37 Indre-et-Loire	69 Rhône
05 Hautes-Alpes	38 Isère	70 Haute-Saône
06 Alpes-Maritimes	39 Jura	71 Saône-et-Loire
07 Ardèche	40 Landes	72 Sarthe
08 Ardennes	41 Loir-et-Cher	73 Savoie
09 Ariège	42 Loire	74 Haute-Savoie
10 Aube	43 Haute-Loire	75 Paris
11 Aude	44 Loire-Atlantique	76 Seine-Maritime
12 Aveyron	45 Loiret	77 Seine-et-Marne
13 Bouches-du-Rhône	46 Lot	78 Yvelines
14 Calvados	47 Lot-et-Garonne	79 Deux-Sèvres
15 Cantal	48 Lozère	80 Somme
16 Charente	49 Maine-et-Loire	81 Tarn
17 Charente-Maritime	50 Manche	82 Tarn-et-Garonne
18 Cher	51 Marne	83 Var
19 Corrèze	52 Haute-Marne	84 Vaucluse
21 Côte-d'Or	53 Mayenne	85 Vendée
22 Côte-d'Armor	54 Meurthe-et-Moselle	86 Vienne
23 Creuse	55 Meuse	87 Haute-Vienne
24 Dordogne	56 Morbihan	88 Vosges
25 Doubs	57 Moselle	89 Yonne
26 Drôme	58 Nièvre	90 Territoire de Belfort
27 Eure	59 Nord	91 Essonne
28 Eure-et-Loir	60 Oise	92 Hauts-de-Seine
29 Finistère	61 Orne	93 Seine-Saint-Denis
30 Gard	62 Pas-de-Calais	94 Val-de-Marne
31 Haute-Garonne	63 Puy-de-Dôme	95 Val-d'Oise

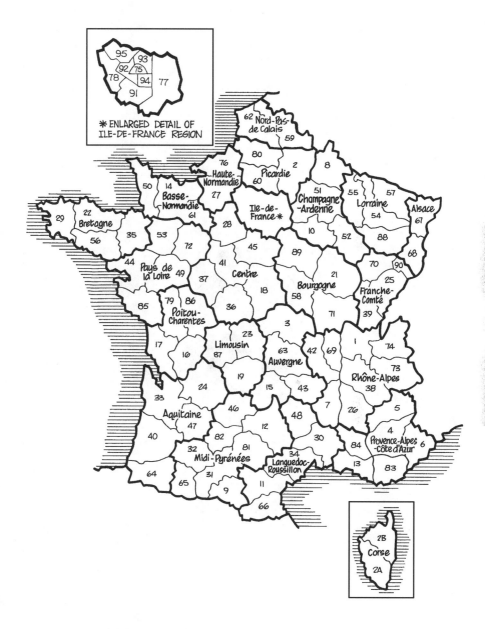

* ENLARGED DETAIL OF
ILE-DE-FRANCE REGION

INDEX

A

Abortion 305
Accidents 277
Accommodation 101
  Buying Property 104
  French Homes 102
  Moving House 114
  Relocation Consultants 104
  Rented 108
  Security 113
  Temporary 104
  Utilities 116
Addresses 558
Aerial Sports 449
AIDS 314
Airline Services 214
  Airports 216
  Domestic Flights 215
  International Flights 214
  Tickets 215
Airports 216
Alcohol
  Beer 495
  Champagne 492
  Wine 490
Annual Holidays 62
Appendices 557
  Further Information 558
  Further Reading 561
  Map 570
  Useful Websites 563
  Weights & Measures 566
Apprenticeships 202
Arrival 91
  Checklist After 99
  Checklist Before 98
  Customs 92
  Finding Help 95
  Immigration 92
  Registration 94
Au Pairs 42

B

Ballet 423
Banks 356
  Cash & Debit Cards 366
  Cheque Accounts 361
  Chèque Emploi Service 364
  General Points 359
  Opening an Account 360
  Opening Hours 358
  Savings Accounts 365
Bars 429
  Costs 433
  Drinks 430
  Licensing 432
  Opening Hours 432
  Paying 433
  Snacks 432
Bed & Breakfast 408
Benefits 57
Bilingual Schools 199
Bonuses 57
Books 498, 562
Boucheries 481
Boulangeries 482
Boules 449
Broadband 143
Building Insurance 343
Buses & Trams 233
Buying a Business 49
Buying a Car 245
  New 246
  Used 247
Buying Property 104

C

Cable TV 168
Cafes 429. See also Bars
Camping 414
Capital Gains Tax 388
  Other Assets 389

Principal Residence 388
Second Homes 388
Caravanning 414
Carnet de Santé 309
Cars. See Motoring
Carte Grise 250
Cash Cards 366
Casual Work 37
Catalogues 503
Catteries 529
Caving 451
Chain Stores 487
Champagne 492
Changing Money 355
Charcuteries 483
Charge Cards 367
Chemists' 300
    Prescriptions 301
Chèque Emploi Service 364
Childbirth 306
Children's Health 309
    Carnet de Santé 309
    Vaccinations 310
Cinema 422
Citizenship 510
Climate 511
Climbing 451
Clinics 301
Clothing 497
Consumer Rights 506
    Protection 507
Contents Insurance 344
Contraception 305
Cost of Living 396
Counselling 313
    AIDS 314
    Alcoholism 313
    Drugs 313
    Other STDs 314
Credit Cards 367
Crime 279, 513
Currency
    French 352
Customs 92
    Non-EU Nationals 93
    Prohibited & Restricted Goods 94
    Visitors 93
Cycling 452

D

Day Classes 444
Death 316
    Wills 394
Debit Cards 366
    Moneo 367
Dentists 310
Department Stores 487
Deposits 506
Directory Enquiries 146
Disabled People 515
Dismissal & Redundancy 71
Disneyland Paris 417
Divorce 522
Doctors 296
    Hours 297
    Medical Examinations 298
    Treatment 298
Dogs 528
Drink 490
    Beer 495
    Coffee & Tea 496
    Milk & Cream 496
    Spirits 495
    Water 496
    Wine 490
Drinking & Driving 278
Drivers 275
Driving. See Motoring
Drugs 313
Dry Cleaning 502
Duty-free Allowances 505

E

Economy 21
Education 68, 177
    Adapting 180
    Apprenticeships 202
    Further Education 208
    Higher Education 203
    Home Education 182
    Insurance 179
    Language 181

Language Courses 209
Private Schools 198
State Schools 184
Electricity 116
  Billing 120
  Connection 117
  Meters 120
  Power Supply 118
  Tariffs 119
Embassies & Consulates 558
Emergencies 292
Emergency Numbers 140
Employment
  Agencies 31
  Contracts 54
  Prospects 26
Employment Conditions 53
  13th Month's Salary 57
  Acceptance of Gifts 71
  Bonuses 57
  Changing Jobs & Confidentiality 71
  Compassionate Leave 65
  Contracts 54
  Dismissal & Redundancy 71
  Education 68
  Expenses 58
  Flexi-time 61
  Holidays & Leave 62
  Insurance 66
  Maternity & Paternity Leave 64
  Overtime 62
  Part-time Job Restrictions 71
  Pensions 67
  Retirement 67
  Salary & Benefits 57
  Sick Leave 65
  Special Leave 65
  Training 68
  Trial & Notice Periods 70
  Union Membership 69
  Working Hours 60
English-language Publications 500, 561
English-language Radio 174
Epiceries 483
Eurostar 220
Eurotunnel 237
Evening Classes 444
Exporting Money 353

F

Fax 159
Ferries 235
  Cross-Channel Services 235
  Domestic Services 237
Finance 351
  Banks 356
  Capital Gains Tax 388
  Changing Money 355
  Charge Cards 367
  Cost of Living 396
  Credit Cards 367
  Exporting Money 353
  French Currency 352
  Gift Tax 390
  Importing Money 353
  Income Tax 373
  Inheritance Tax 390
  Loans 369
  Mortgages 369
  Overdrafts 369
  Prepaid Currency Cards 355
  Property Taxes 384
  Travellers' Cheques 356
  Valued Added Tax 372
  Wealth Tax 387
Finding a Job 19
  Au Pairs 42
  Casual Work 37
  Economy 21
  Employment Prospects 26
  Government Employment Service 31
  Illegal Working 51
  Industrial Relations 25
  International Organisations 35
  Internet 34
  Job Hunting 30
  Language 29
  Language Teachers 41
  Medical Examination 29
  Newspapers & Publications 33
  Qualifications 28
  Salary 23
  Seasonal Jobs 38
  Self-Employment 44

Starting a Business 46
Summer Jobs 39
Temporary Work 37
Unemployment 25
Voluntary Work 43
Winter Jobs 41
Women 22
Work Attitudes 22
Workforce 21
Finding Help 95
    AVF 97
    CIRA 97
    Colleagues & Friends 95
    Company 95
    Disabled Services 98
    Embassy Or Consulate 96
    Expatriate Organisations 96
    Hand-holding Services 96
    Local Community 95
    Publications 98
Fishing 454
Food. See Specialist Food Shops
    Vegetarian & Vegan 489
Football 456
Foreign
    Food 485
    Schools 199
French 209
    Citizenship 510
    Currency 352
    Homes 102
    Language 29, 181, 209
    Roads 270
Fuel 282
Furniture & Furnishings 500
Further Education 208
Further Reading 561

G

Galleries 420. See also Museums
Gambling 429
Garages & Servicing 284
Gas 121
    Billing 121
    Bottled 122
    Mains 121
    Tanks 122
    Tariffs 121
Geography 515
Gift Tax 390
Gîtes 409
Giving Blood 315
Golf 457
Government 516
    Communes 519
    Departments 518
    Local 518
    Mayors 519
    Paris 519
    Parliament 517
    Political Parties 518
    President 517
    Voting & Elections 520
Green Cards 256
Guide Books 401
Gymnasiums 448

H

Health 289
    Abortion 305
    AIDS 314
    Benefits 332
    Chemists' 300
    Childbirth 306
    Children 309
    Clubs 448
    Contraception 305
    Counselling 313
    Death 316
    Dentists 310
    Doctors 296
    Emergencies 292
    Giving Blood 315
    Hospitals & Clinics 301
    Insurance 339
    Medicines 299
    National Health System 293
    Opticians 312
    Prescriptions 301
    Risks 291

Smoking 315
STDs 314
Help. See Finding Help
Higher Education 203
    Ecoles Supérieures 206
    Grandes Ecoles 206
    Information 208
    Universities 203
Hiking 458
Holidays 62
    Annual 62
    Insurance 346
    Public 63
    School 187
Home Education 182
Hospitals & Clinics 301
    Accommodation 303
    Children 304
    Costs 305
    Long-Term Care 303
    Private 302
    Procedure 304
    Public 302
Hostels 412
Hotels 403
    Bed & Breakfast 408
    Booking 408
    Classification 403
    Facilities 407
    Meals 406
    Prices 405
    Restaurants 433
Household Goods 501
Household Insurance 343
    Buildings 343
    Claims 345
    Contents 344
    Holiday Homes 344
    Insuring Abroad 345
    Premiums 345
Hunting 461
Hypermarkets 487

I

Illegal Working 51

Immigration 92
Importing Money 353
Income Tax 373
    Allowances 376
    Bills 383
    Calculation 378
    Double Taxation 375
    Exemptions 376
    Family Quotient 377
    Liability 374
    Reductions & Credits 379
    Return 381
    Self-employed 380
    UK Pensioners 381
Industrial Relations 25
Inheritance Tax 390
Insurance 66, 319
    Abroad 345
    Breakdown 259
    Cancellation 322
    Car 255
    Claims 322, 345
    Companies & Agents 320
    Contracts 322
    Dental 342
    Health 66, 342
    Holiday 346
    Holiday Homes 344
    Household 343
    Life 348
    Pensions 336
    Pets 530
    Premiums 322, 345
    Private Health 339
    Salary 67
    Schools 179
    Social Security 323
    Third-party Liability 346
    Travel 346
    Unemployment 67
International Calls 147
International Schools 199
Internet 159
    Email 160
    Modems 160
    Shopping 504
    Telephony 161

J

Job Hunting 30. See also Finding a Job

K

Kennels 529
Kissing 536

L

Language 29, 181
    Courses 209
    Schools 210
Language Teachers 41
Laundry 502
Leaving France 553
Legal System 520
Leisure 399
    Ballet 423
    Bars 429
    Bed & Breakfast 408
    Cafes 429
    Camping 414
    Caravanning 414
    Cinema 422
    Day & Evening Classes 444
    Galleries 420
    Gambling 429
    Guide Books 401
    Hostels 412
    Hotels 403
    Information 400
    Libraries 443
    Museums 420
    Music 425
    Naturism 416
    Nightlife 428
    Opera 423
    Self-catering Accommodation 409
    Social Clubs 427
    Theatre 423
    Theme Parks 417
    Tourist Offices 402

Letters 129
    Addresses 131
    Collection 133
    Deliveries 133
    Post & Letter Boxes 132
    Stamps 130
    Tariffs 129
Libraries 443
Life Insurance 348
Loans 369

M

Magazines 498. See also Newspapers
Mail-order Shopping 503
    Catalogues 503
    Internet 504
Maps
    France 570
    Hiking 461
    Road 284
Markets 486
Marriage 522
    PACS 525
Maternity & Paternity Leave 64
Medical Examination 29
Medicines 299
Métro 230
Military Service 525
Milk & Cream 496
Mobile Telephones 155
Money. See Finance
Mortgages 369
    Fees 371
    Remortgaging 372
    Terms & Conditions 370
    Types 370
Motorcycles 276
Motoring 241
    Accidents 277
    Breakdown Insurance 259
    Buying a Car 245
    Car Insurance 255
    Car Rental 286
    Car Theft 279
    Claims 258

Driving Licence 252
French Drivers 275
French Roads 270
Fuel 282
Garages & Servicing 284
Green Card 256
Importing a Vehicle 243
Maps 284
Motorcycles 276
Motoring Organisations 287
No-claims Bonus 258
Parking 280
Pedestrian Road Rules 287
Road Maps 284
Road Signs 264
Road Tax 252
Rules of the Road 260
Selling a Car 249
Speed Limits 266
Technical Inspection 251
Traffic Police 267
Vehicle Registration 249
Motorways 270
Moving House 114, 552
Museums 420
Music 425
Mutual Benefit Organisations 321
Mutuelles 321

N

National Health System 293
Reimbursement Procedure 295
Naturism 416
Newspapers 498
English-language 500
Nightlife 428
No-claims Bonus 258

O

Oil & Wood 122
Opera 423
Opticians 312
Overdrafts 369

P

PACS 525
Parcels 134
Express 135
Standard 135
Parking 280
Pedestrians 287
Pensions 67, 336
Basic 336
Retiring in France 338
Supplementary 337
Permits & Visas 75
Applications 80
Fiancé(e)s & Spouses 79
Long-stay Visa 78
Residence 84
Short-stay Visas 77
Student Visas 79
Visitors 76
Working 82
Petrol & Diesel 282
Pets 225, 526
Catteries 529
Dogs 528
Health 530
Insurance 530
Kennels 529
Vaccinations 527
Police 267, 531
Drinking & Driving 278
Fines & Penalties 268
Traffic 267
Population 533
Post Office Services
Banking 357
Postal Services 127
Business Hours 128
Letters 129
Parcels 134
Registered & Recorded Post 136
Pregnancy & Confinement 306
Prescriptions 301
Private Health Insurance 339
Private Schools 198
Curriculum 199
Fees & Enrolment 200

Property
    Buying 104
    French Homes 102
    Moving House 114
    Relocation Consultants 104
    Renting 108
    Security 113
    Temporary 104
Property Taxes 384
Public Holidays 63
Public Telephones 157
Public Transport 213
    Airline Services 214
    Buses & Trams 233
    Eurostar 220
    Eurotunnel 237
    Ferries 235
    Métro 229
    Paris 234
    Taxis 238
    Trains 217

Q

Qualifications 28

R

Racket Sports 463
Radio 173
    Cable, Digital & Satellite 175
    English-language 174
    French 173
Receipts 506
Registration 94
Religion 534
Relocation Consultants 104
Rental
    Bikes 453
    Cars 286
Rented Accommodation 108
    Contracts 112
    Costs 111
    Finding a Property 109
    Inventory 113

Residence Permits 84
    Applications 86
    Changes 88
    Permanent 86
    Renewals 88
    Temporary 84
Residential Tax 386
Restaurants 433
    Booking 442
    Courses 439
    Etiquette 442
    Food to Avoid? 440
    French Cuisine 436
    Information 443
    Meals 436
    Menus 438
    Opening Times 442
    Other Drinks 441
    Prices 438
    Types 434
    Vegetarian 440
    Wine 441
Retirement 67, 338
Reverse Charge Calls 148
Roads 284
    Accidents 277
    Drivers 275
    Information 274
    Motorways 270
    Paris 274
    Pedestrian Rules 287
    Rules 260
    Signs 264
    Tax 252
Rugby 464
Running 458

S

Salary 23, 57
    13th Month's 57
    Insurance 67
    Minimum Wage 24
Schools. See also Education
    Bilingual 199
    Foreign 199
    International 199

Language 210
Nursery 190
Preparatory 198
Primary 191
Private 198
Secondary 193
State 184
State or Private? 183
Seasonal Jobs 38
Holiday Villages 39
Security 113
Self-catering 409
Booking & Deposits 411
Costs 410
Equipment 410
Gîtes 409
Holiday Villages 410
Self-Employment 44, 380
Selling a Car 249
Service Numbers 140
Shopping 477
Abroad 504
Alcohol 490
Bargains 478
Books 498
Chain Stores 487
Clothing 497
Consumer Rights 506
Department Stores 487
Deposits 506
Drink 490
Dry Cleaning 502
Duty-free Allowances 505
Furniture & Furnishings 500
Hours 479
Household Goods 501
Hypermarkets 487
Laundry 502
Mail-order 503
Markets 486
Newspapers & Magazines 498
Prices 478
Receipts 506
Sales 478
Specialist Food Shops 480
Supermarkets 487
Tobacconists' 497

Skiing 465
Costs 466
Cross-country 468
Facilities 466
Information 469
Learning to Ski 468
Safety 467
Smoking 315
Social Clubs 427
Social Customs 535
Kissing 536
Vous & Tu 536
Social Security 323
Benefits 332
Calculation 331
Contributions 328
Eligibility & Exemptions 324
Information 324
Registration 327
Reimbursement Procedure 295
Solar Power 122
Specialist Food Shops 480
Alimentation Générale 483
Boucheries 481
Boulangeries 482
Charcuteries 483
Confiseries 483
Crémeries 483
Epiceries 483
Foreign Food 485
Fromageries 484
Health Food 485
Pâtisseries 484
Poissonneries 484
Speed Limits 266
Sports 447
Aerial 449
Boules 449
Caving 451
Climbing 451
Cycling 452
Fishing 454
Football 456
Golf 457
Gymnasiums 448
Health Clubs 448
Hiking 458
Hunting 461

Other 472
Racket 463
Rugby 464
Running 458
Skiing 465
Swimming 469
Watersports 470
Stamps 130
Starting a Business 46
Buying a Business 49
Finance 47
State Schools 184
Baccalauréat 196
College 193
Enrolment 186
Holidays 187
Hours 186
Lycée 194
Nursery School 190
Preparatory School 198
Primary & Nursery Cycles 189
Primary School 191
Provisions 188
School Hours 186
Secondary School 193
STDs 314
Summer Jobs 39
Supermarkets 487
Food 489
Swimming 469

T

Tax
Allowances 376
Bills 383
Calculations 378
Capital Gains 388
Exemptions 376
Gift 390
Income 373
Inheritance 390
Liability 374
Professional 387
Property 385
Residential 386
Return 381

Sundry 386
Tables 378
Value Added 372
Wealth 387
Taxis 238
Technical Inspection 251
Telephone Services 139
Alternative Providers 147
Bills 153
Cards 157
Charges 149
Custom Services 152
Directories 145
Directory Enquiries 146
Emergency Numbers 140
Fax 159
Greetings 149
Installation 142
International Calls 147
Internet 159
Mobile 155
Numbers 149
Optional Services 152
Person-to-Person Calls 148
Public 157
Registration 142
Reverse Charge Calls 148
Service Numbers 140
Usage 147
Television 163
Cable 168
Licence 172
Satellite 168
Standards 164
Terrestrial 165
Video & DVD 173
Temporary Accommodation 104
Temporary Work 37
Hotels & Catering 39
TGV 218
The French 543
Theatre 423
Theme Parks 417
Third-party Liability Insurance 346
Time Difference 539
Tipping 539
Tobacconists' 497
Toilets 540

Tour de France 454
Tourist Offices 402
Trains 217
    Booking 225
    Discounts 223
    Eurostar 220
    Facilities 221
    Finding Your Seat 227
    Information & Timetables 229
    Main Lines 217
    Métro 230
    Motorail 228
    Night 227
    Other 220
    Pets 225
    RER 231
    Scenic Trains 220
    Stations 221
    Tariffs 223
    TGV 218
    Tickets 222
    Underground 229
Travel Insurance 346
Travellers' Cheques 356
Trial & Notice Periods 70

U

Underground Railways 229
Unemployment 25
Union Membership 69
Universities 203
    Accommodation 206
    Curriculum 204
    Enrolment 205
    Exams 204
    Fees 206
    Grants 206
    Qualifications 204
Utilities 116
    Electricity 116
    Gas 121
    Oil & Wood 122
    Solar Power 122
    Waste Disposal 124
    Water 123
    Wind Power 122

V

Valued Added Tax 372
Vegan Food 489
Vegetarian
    Food 489
    Restaurants 440
Vehicles. See also Motoring
    Import 243
    Registration 249
    Rental 286
Visas. See Permits & Visas
Visitors 76
Voluntary Work 43
Vous & Tu 536

W

Waste Disposal 124
Water 123, 496
Watersports 470
Wealth Tax 387
Websites 563
Weights & Measures 566
Wills 394
    Types 395
Wine 432, 490
Winter Jobs 41
Winter Sports. See Skiing
Work Attitudes 22
Work Permits 82
    EU Nationals 82
    Non-EU Nationals 83
    Students 83
Workforce 21
Working. See Finding A Job and
        Employment Conditions
Working Hours 60
Working Women 22

Y

Youth Hostels 412

LIVING AND WORKING SERIES

Living and Working books are essential reading for anyone planning to spend time abroad, including holiday-home owners, retirees, visitors, business people, migrants, students and even extra-terrestrials! They're packed with important and useful information designed to help you **avoid costly mistakes and save both time and money.** Topics covered include how to:

- Find a job with a good salary & conditions
- Obtain a residence permit
- Avoid and overcome problems
- Find your dream home
- Get the best education for your family
- Make the best use of public transport
- Endure local motoring habits
- Obtain the best health treatment
- Stretch your money further
- Make the most of your leisure time
- Enjoy the local sporting life
- Find the best shopping bargains
- Insure yourself against most eventualities
- Use post office and telephone services
- Do numerous other things not listed above

Living and Working books are the most comprehensive and up-to-date source of practical information available about everyday life abroad. They aren't, however, boring text books, but interesting and entertaining guides written in a highly readable style.

Discover what it's *really* like to live and work abroad!

Order your copies today by phone, fax, post or email from: Survival Books, PO Box 3780, YEOVIL, BA21 5WX, United Kingdom (☎/▤ +44 (0)1935-700060, ✉ sales@survivalbooks.net, ⌨ www.survivalbooks.net).

Buying a Home Series

Buying a Home books, including **Buying, Selling & Letting Property**, are essential reading for anyone planning to purchase property abroad. They're packed with vital information to guide you through the property purchase jungle and help you **avoid the sort of disasters that can turn your dream home into a nightmare!** Topics covered include:

- Avoiding problems
- Choosing the region
- Finding the right home and location
- Estate agents
- Finance, mortgages and taxes
- Home security
- Utilities, heating and air-conditioning
- Moving house and settling in
- Renting and letting
- Permits and visas
- Travelling and communications
- Health and insurance
- Renting a car and driving
- Retirement and starting a business
- And much, much more!

Buying a Home books are the most comprehensive and up-to-date source of information available about buying property abroad. Whether you want a detached house, townhouse or apartment, a holiday or a permanent home, these books will help make your dreams come true.

Save yourself time, trouble and money!

Order your copies today by phone, fax, post or email from: Survival Books, PO Box 3780, YEOVIL, BA21 5WX, United Kingdom (☎/▤ +44 (0)1935-700060, ✉ sales@survivalbooks.net, 🖳 www.survivalbooks.net).

OTHER SURVIVAL BOOKS

The Alien's Guides: *The Alien's Guides to Britain and France* will help you to appreciate the peculiarities (in both senses) of the British and French.

The Best Places to Buy a Home in France/Spain: The most comprehensive homebuying guides to France and Spain, containing detailed regional profiles.

Buying, Selling and Letting Property: The most comprehensive and up-to-date source of information on buying, selling and letting property in the UK.

Earning Money From Your Home: Essential guides to earning income from property in France and Spain, including short- and long-term letting.

Foreigners in France/Spain: Triumphs & Disasters: Real-life experiences of people who have emigrated to France and Spain, recounted in their own words.

Lifelines: Essential guides to life in specific regions of France and Spain. See order form for a list of current titles in the series.

Making a Living: Essential guides to self-employment and starting a business in France and Spain.

Renovating & Maintaining Your French Home: The ultimate guide to renovating and maintaining your dream home in France.

Retiring: *Retiring Abroad* is the most comprehensive source of practical information available about retiring to a foreign country. *Retiring Abroad in Spain* and *Retiring Abroad in France* provide up-to-date information on the two most popular retirement destinations.

Rural Living in France: The most comprehensive source of practical information available about life in rural France.

Shooting Caterpillars in Spain: The hilarious but compelling story of two innocents abroad in the depths of Andalusia in the late '80s.

Surprised by France: Even after living there for ten years, Donald Carroll finds plenty of surprises in the Hexagon.

Broaden your horizons with Survival Books!

Order your copies today by phone, fax, post or email from: Survival Books, PO Box 3780, YEOVIL, BA21 5WX, United Kingdom (☎/▤ +44 (0)1935-700060, ✉ sales@survivalbooks.net, ▣ www.survivalbooks.net).

Qty.	Title	Price (incl. p&p)			Total
		UK	Europe	World	
	The Alien's Guide to Britain	£7.45	£9.45	£12.95	
	The Alien's Guide to France	£7.45	£9.45	£12.95	
	The Best Places to Buy a Home in France	£14.45	£16.45	£19.95	
	The Best Places to Buy a Home in Spain	£14.45	£16.45	£19.95	
	Buying a Home Abroad	£14.45	£16.45	£19.95	
	Buying a Home in Australia & NZ	£14.45	£16.45	£19.95	
	Buying a Home in Cyprus	£14.45	£16.45	£19.95	
	Buying a Home in Florida	£14.45	£16.45	£19.95	
	Buying a Home in France	£14.45	£16.45	£19.95	
	Buying a Home in Greece	£14.45	£16.45	£19.95	
	Buying a Home in Ireland	£12.45	£14.45	£17.95	
	Buying a Home in Italy	£14.45	£16.45	£19.95	
	Buying a Home in Portugal	£14.45	£16.45	£19.95	
	Buying a Home in South Africa	£14.45	£16.45	£19.95	
	Buying a Home in Spain	£14.45	£16.45	£19.95	
	Buying, Letting & Selling Property	£12.45	£14.45	£17.95	
	Buying or Renting a Home in London	£14.45	£16.45	£19.95	
	Buying or Renting a Home in New York	£14.45	£16.45	£19.95	
	Earning Money From Your French Home	£14.45	£16.45	£19.95	
	Earning Money From Your Spanish Home	£14.45	£16.45	£19.95	
	Foreigners in France: Triumphs & Disasters	£12.45	£14.45	£17.95	
	Foreigners in Spain: Triumphs & Disasters	£12.45	£14.45	£17.95	
	Costa Blanca Lifeline	£12.45	£14.45	£17.95	
	Costa del Sol Lifeline	£12.45	£14.45	£17.95	
	Dordogne/Lot Lifeline	£12.45	£14.45	£17.95	
	Normandy Lifeline	£12.45	£14.45	£17.95	
	Poitou-Charentes Lifeline	£11.95	£14.45	£17.95	
	Provence-Côte d'Azur Lifeline	£12.45	£14.45	£17.95	
	Living & Working Abroad	£15.45	£17.45	£20.95	
	Living & Working in America	£17.45	£19.45	£22.95	
	Living & Working in Australia	£17.45	£19.45	£22.95	
	Living & Working in Britain	£17.45	£19.45	£22.95	
	Living & Working in Canada	£17.45	£19.45	£22.95	
	Living & Working in the European Union	£17.45	£19.45	£22.95	
Total carried forward (see over)					

ORDER FORM

Qty.	Title	UK	Europe	World	Total
		Total brought forward			
	Living & Working in the Far East	£17.45	£19.45	£22.95	
	Living & Working in France	£17.45	£19.45	£22.95	
	Living & Working in Germany	£17.45	£19.45	£22.95	
	L&W in the Gulf States & Saudi Arabia	£17.45	£19.45	£22.95	
	L&W in Holland, Belgium & Luxembourg	£15.45	£17.45	£20.95	
	Living & Working in Ireland	£15.45	£17.45	£20.95	
	Living & Working in Italy	£17.45	£19.45	£22.95	
	Living & Working in London	£14.45	£16.45	£19.95	
	Living & Working in New Zealand	£17.45	£19.45	£22.95	
	Living & Working in Spain	£17.45	£19.45	£22.95	
	Living & Working in Switzerland	£17.45	£19.45	£22.95	
	Making a Living in France	£14.45	£16.45	£19.95	
	Making a Living in Spain	£14.45	£16.45	£19.95	
	Renovating Your French Home	£17.45	£19.45	£22.95	
	Retiring Abroad	£15.45	£17.45	£20.95	
	Retiring in France	£14.45	£16.45	£19.95	
	Retiring in Spain	£14.45	£16.45	£19.95	
	Rural Living in France	£14.45	£16.45	£19.95	
	Shooting Caterpillars in Spain	£10.45	£12.45	£15.95	
	Surprised by France	£12.45	£14.45	£17.95	
	Grand Total				

Order your copies today by phone, fax, post or email from: Survival Books, PO Box 3780, YEOVIL, BA21 5WX, United Kingdom (☎/▤ +44 (0)1935-700060, ✉ sales@ survivalbooks.net, 🖥 www.survivalbooks.net). If you aren't entirely satisfied, simply return them to us within 14 days for a full and unconditional refund.

I enclose a cheque for the grand total/Please charge my Amex/Delta/Maestro (Switch)/MasterCard/Visa card as follows. (delete as applicable)

Card No. _ _ _ _   _ _ _ _   _ _ _ _   _ _ _ _   Security Code* _ _ _

Expiry date _____   Issue number (Maestro/Switch only) _____

Signature _____   Tel. No. _____

NAME _____

ADDRESS _____

_____

* The security code is the last three digits on the signature strip.